ALSO BY BETTY MEDSGER

Winds of Change:
Challenges Confronting Journalism Education

Framed: The New Right Attack on
Chief Justice Rose Bird and the Courts

Women at Work

The Burglary

The Burglary

The Discovery of J. Edgar Hoover's Secret FBI

BETTY MEDSGER

ALFRED A. KNOPF NEW YORK

2014

THIS IS A BORZOI BOOK
PUBLISHED BY ALFRED A. KNOPF

www.aaknopf.com

Knopf, Borzoi Books, and the colophon are registered trademarks
of Random House LLC.

Library of Congress Cataloging-in-Publication Data
Medsger, Betty.
    The burglary : the discovery of J. Edgar Hoover's secret FBI / by Betty
Medsger.—First edition.
        pages cm
ISBN 978-0-307-96295-9 (hardcover) ISBN 978-0-307-96296-6 (eBook)
1. United States. Federal Bureau of Investigation—Corrupt practices—
History. 2. Hoover, J. Edgar (John Edgar), 1895–1972. 3. Intelligence
service—Moral and ethical aspects—United States. 4. Leaks (Disclosure
of information)—United States—Case studies. 5. Whistle blowing—
United States—Case studies. 6. Burglary—United States—Case studies.
I. Title.
HV8144.F43M43 2014
363.250973'0904—dc23   2013024540

Jacket image: J. Edgar Hoover, February 1, 1950 (detail). Bettmann / Corbis
Jacket design by Joan Wong

Book design by Cassandra J. Pappas

Manufactured in the United States of America
First Edition

For John
With love and gratitude

Never once did I hear anybody, including myself, raise the question: "Is this course of action which we have agreed upon lawful, is it legal, is it ethical or moral?" We never gave any thought to this line of reasoning because we were just naturally pragmatic. The one thing we were concerned about, will this course of action work, will it get us what we want, the objective we desire to reach.

—WILLIAM SULLIVAN, *head of the FBI's Domestic Intelligence Division under FBI director J. Edgar Hoover*

It was a matter of keeping alive a sense of purpose and accomplishment when the forces seemed so overwhelming. . . . Sometimes we accomplished more than we had reason to expect, as in Media. It was a long shot. We didn't know if we would find anything important. Other times, we never knew if we accomplished anything. . . . But it gave voice and a sense of purpose and built little pockets of life that made sense at a terrible time.

—WILLIAM DAVIDON, *leader of the Citizens' Commission to Investigate the FBI*

During most of my tenure as director of the FBI, I have been compelled to devote much of my time attempting to reconstruct and then to explain activities that occurred years ago. Some of those activities were clearly wrong and quite indefensible. We most certainly must never allow them to be repeated.

—CLARENCE M. KELLEY, *FBI director, apologizing to the American people in 1976 for the actions of his predecessor, J. Edgar Hoover*

Never doubt that a small group of thoughtful, committed citizens can change the world.

—MARGARET MEAD, *anthropologist*

Contents

The Burglary

1

In the Absence of Oversight

I N LATE 1970, William Davidon, a mild-mannered physics professor at Haverford College, privately asked a few people this question:
"What do you think of burglarizing an FBI office?"

Even in that time of passionate resistance against the war in Vietnam that included break-ins at draft boards, his question was startling. What, besides arrests and lengthy prison sentences, could result from breaking into an FBI office? The bureau and its legendary director, J. Edgar Hoover, had been revered by Americans and considered paragons of integrity for the nearly half century he had been director.

Who would dare to think they *could* break into an FBI office? Surely the offices of the most powerful law enforcement agency in the country would be as secure as Fort Knox. Just talking about the possibility seemed dangerous.

But Davidon, with great reluctance, had decided that burglarizing an FBI office might be the only way to confront what he considered an emergency: the likelihood that the government, through the FBI, was spying on Americans and suppressing their cherished constitutional right to dissent. If that was true, he thought, it was a crime against democracy—a crime that must be stopped.

The odds were very low that such an act of resistance could possibly succeed against the law enforcement agency headed by this man who held so much power. Nicholas Katzenbach, who as attorney general was Hoover's boss, had resigned in 1966 because of Hoover's resentment over being told by Katzenbach to manage the bureau within the law. The director's power was unique among all national officials, said Katzenbach. He "ruled the FBI with a combination of discipline and fear and was capable of acting in an excessively arbitrary way. No one dared object. . . . The FBI was a principality with absolutely secure borders, in Hoover's view." At the same time, he said, "There was no man better known or more admired by the general public than J. Edgar Hoover."

Such was the power and reputation of the official whose borders and files Davidon was considering invading. He knew Hoover was very powerful, but he didn't know—nor could anyone outside the bureau have known—how harshly he ruled it and how he protected the bureau from having its illegal practices exposed. Katzenbach believed that Hoover or one of the director's top aides had even forged Katzenbach's signature in order to make it appear that the attorney general had given permission for the FBI to plant an electronic surveillance device, a bug, in civil rights leader Martin Luther King Jr.'s New York hotel room. Despite what appeared to be his signature on the memorandum, Katzenbach was certain he never approved such a procedure, which he considered the "worst possible invasion of privacy."

Hoover's sensitivity to criticism, Katzenbach said when he testified in December 1975 before the committee then conducting the first congressional investigation of the FBI, "is almost impossible to overestimate. . . . It went far beyond the bounds of natural resentment. . . . The most casual statement, the most strained implication, was sufficient cause for Mr. Hoover to write a memorandum to the attorney general complaining about the criticism, explaining why it was unjustified, and impugning the integrity of its author.

"In a very real sense," Katzenbach testified, "there was no greater crime in Mr. Hoover's eyes than public criticism of the bureau."

A congressional investigation of the FBI during Mr. Hoover's lifetime, Katzenbach said, would have been utterly impossible. "Mr. Hoover would have vigorously resisted. . . . He would have asserted that the investigation was unnecessary, unwise and politically motivated. At worst, he would have denounced the investigation as undermining law and order and inspired by Communist ideology. No one [in Congress] risked that confrontation during his lifetime."

Said Katzenbach, "Absent strong and unequivocal proof of the greatest impropriety on the part of the director, no attorney general could have conceived that he could possibly win a fight with Mr. Hoover in the eyes of the public, the Congress or the President. Moreover, to the extent proof of any such impropriety existed, it would almost by definition have been in the Bureau's possession and control, unreachable except with Bureau cooperation."

Five years before Katzenbach made that public assertion, Davidon was planning to do something that had never been done—obtain official FBI information that was otherwise unreachable. Davidon had given a lot of thought to the question before he asked it—"What do you think of burglarizing an FBI office?"

If anyone else had asked that question of the nine people he approached, probably each of them would have swiftly ended the conversation. Because it was Davidon, they took it seriously and kept listening despite being shocked. They trusted him. They knew he wasn't reckless, and they knew he believed in protest that was effective, that could lead to results. Each of them respected him so much they thought that if they ever engaged in high-risk resistance, he was one of the few people they would want as partner and leader when the stakes were high. So they listened carefully.

Some of them wrestled with the implications of his question for several days. Two said yes immediately. Only one of them, a philosophy professor, turned him down. Eight agreed with him that, repugnant as burglary was as a method of resistance, it might be the only way to find documentary evidence that would answer important questions about the FBI that no journalist or government official responsible for the FBI had dared to ask in the past or, they concluded, was likely to ask now or in the future. All of them were passionate opponents of the Vietnam War and passionate opponents of the suppression of dissent.

Davidon and the eight people who said yes in response to his question met as a group for the first time shortly before Christmas 1970 and chose their name, the Citizens' Commission to Investigate the FBI. The name summed up their goal: In the absence of official oversight of this powerful law enforcement and intelligence agency, they, acting voluntarily on behalf of American citizens, would attempt to steal and make public FBI files in an effort to determine if the FBI was destroying dissent. They thought the name sounded dignified, like that of an official commission that should have been appointed years earlier by a president, an attorney general, or Congress.

Agreeing to break in only if it could be done without violating their deep commitment to nonviolent resistance, they concentrated on developing the skills necessary to conduct an unarmed burglary of the office. Beginning in January 1971, most weekday evenings, after they meticulously cased the area near the targeted FBI office for at least three hours, they drove to the Germantown neighborhood in northwest Philadelphia to the home of John and Bonnie Raines, a young couple who had agreed to participate. There, late at night in a room in the back of the Raines' third-floor attic, they trained themselves as amateur burglars and planned the break-in. They discussed the discoveries they had made during casing and how to work around serious obstacles they had determined could not be eliminated, such as the fact that security guards stood twenty-four hours a day behind the glass front door of the Delaware County Courthouse constantly monitoring an area that included the nearby entrance to the building the burglars would enter, as well as the windows of the FBI office. Just a few days before the burglary, another critical problem developed over which they had no control: One of the burglars abandoned the group, with full knowledge of what they were going to do. He later threatened to turn them in.

ON THE NIGHT of March 8, 1971, the eight burglars carried out their plan. Under the cover of darkness and the crackling sounds in nearly every home and bar of continuous news about the Muhammad Ali–Joe Frazier world heavyweight championship boxing match taking place that evening at New York's Madison Square Garden and being watched on television throughout the world, the burglars broke into the FBI office in Media, Pennsylvania, a sleepy town southwest of Philadelphia. At first, their break-in plan failed. The locks were much more difficult to pick than expected. Frustrated, the newly minted locksmith in the group found a pay phone, called the other burglars as they waited at the nearby motel room that served as the group's staging area, and told them the burglary might have to be called off.

Michael German, a former FBI agent who conducted undercover FBI operations for sixteen years before joining the staff of the American Civil Liberties Union in 2006, said he has often wondered how the Media burglars knew which files to take. "How did they know," for instance, he asked, "where the political spying files would be?" German said he has always assumed—and has talked to other agents who made the same assumption—that because it would have been impossible for an outsider to know where particular files were, the Media burglary must have been an inside job carried out by disgruntled FBI agents familiar with the files. But the burglars had found a foolproof solution to the problem of which files to take: They removed *every* file in the office. That's why, as they drove away from Media in their getaway cars late that night, they had no idea what they had stolen. For all they knew, they might have just risked spending many years in prison for a trove of blank bureaucratic forms.

Within an hour of opening the suitcases they had stuffed with FBI files, they knew their risk was not in vain. They found a document that would shock even hardened Washington observers when it became public two weeks later.

The files stolen by the burglars that night in Media revealed the truth and destroyed the myths about Hoover and the institution he had built since he became its director in 1924. Contrary to the official propaganda that had been released continuously for decades by the FBI's Crime Records Division—the bureau's purposely misnamed public relations operation—Hoover had distorted the mission of one of the most powerful and most venerated institutions in the country.

The Media files revealed that there were two FBIs—the public FBI Americans revered as their protector from crime, arbiter of values, and defender of citizens' liberties, and the secret FBI. This FBI, known until the Media burglary only to people inside the bureau, usurped citizens' liberties, treated black citizens as if they were a danger to society, and used deception, disinformation, and violence as tools to harass, damage, and—most important—silence people whose political opinions the director opposed.

Instead of being a paragon of law and order and integrity, Hoover's secret FBI was a lawless and unprincipled arm of the bureau that, as Davidon had feared, suppressed the dissent of Americans. To the embarrassment and frustration of agents who privately opposed this interpretation of the bureau's mission, agents and informers were required to be outlaws. Blackmail and burglary were favorite tools in the secret FBI. Agents and informers were ordered to spy on—and create ongoing files on—the private lives, including the sexual activities, of the nation's highest officials and other powerful people.

Electoral politics were manipulated to defeat candidates the director did not like. Even mild dissent, in the eyes of the FBI, could make an American worthy of being spied on and placed in an ongoing FBI file, sometimes for decades. As the authors of *The Lawless State* wrote in 1976, the FBI "has operated on a theory of subversion that assumes that people cannot be trusted to choose among political ideas. The FBI has assumed the duty to protect the public by placing it under surveillance."

Until the Media burglary, this extraordinary situation—a secret FBI operating under principles that were the antithesis of both democracy and good law enforcement—thrived near the top of the federal government for nearly half a century, affecting the lives of hundreds of thousands of Americans. The few officials who were aware of some aspects of the secret FBI silently tolerated the situation for various reasons, including fear of the director's power to destroy the reputation of anyone who raised questions about his operations.

When these operations became known as a result of the burglary, the foundations of the FBI were shaken. The significant impact of the burglary was both long-term and immediate. As soon as the files became public, Americans' views of the FBI started to change. Mark Felt—the future Deep Throat of Watergate fame, who at the time of the burglary was chief of bureau inspections and very close to Hoover—wrote in 1979 that the Media burglars' disclosures "damaged the FBI's image, possibly forever, in the minds of many Americans." Ironically, the burglary would not have been possible if Felt had not refused in the fall of 1970 a request to increase security at the Media office.

This historic act of resistance—perhaps *the* most powerful single act of nonviolent resistance in American history—ignited the first public debate on the proper role of intelligence agencies in a democratic society. Perceptions of the bureau evolved from adulation to criticism and then to a consensus that the FBI and other intelligence agencies must never again be permitted to be lawless and unaccountable. By 1975, the revelations led to the first congressional investigations of the FBI and other intelligence agencies and then to the establishment of congressional oversight of those agencies.

The writers of every history of Hoover or the bureau since the burglary have noted its significant impact. Sanford J. Ungar, author in 1976 of the first history of the bureau published after the burglary, *FBI: An Uncensored Look Behind the Walls*, wrote, "The Media documents . . . gave an extraordinary picture of some of the Bureau's domestic intelligence activities. . . . Judged by any standard, the documents . . . show an almost incredible preoccupation with the activities of black organizations and leaders, both on campuses and in the cities. . . . The overall impact of the documents could not be denied or explained away. They seemed to show a government agency, once the object of almost universal respect and awe, reaching out with tentacles to get a grasp on, or lead into, virtually every part of American society."

"In one fell swoop FBI surveillance of dissidents was exposed and the Bureau's carefully nurtured mystique destroyed," wrote Max Holland about the Media burglary in his 2012 book *Leak: Why Mark Felt Became Deep*

Throat. "Far from being invincible, the FBI appeared merely petty, obsessed with monitoring what seemed to be, in many cases, lawful dissent."

Historian Richard Gid Powers, in his 2004 book *Broken: The Troubled Past and Uncertain Future of the FBI,* described the burglary's impact:

> Hoover's power to conduct secret operations . . . depended on the absolute freedom he had won from any inquiry into the internal operations of the Bureau. . . . Except for a remarkably few breaches of security . . . Hoover had been able to pick and choose what the public would learn about the Bureau. He had never suffered the indignity of having an outside, unsympathetic investigator look into what he had been doing, what the Bureau had become, and what it looked like from the inside. And it had been that luxury of freedom that let him indulge himself with such abuses of power as his persecution of King, the . . . COINTELPROs, and his harassment of Bureau critics.

On the night of March 8, 1971, that changed forever. A group calling itself the Citizens' Commission to Investigate the FBI broke into the FBI resident agency in Media, Pennsylvania. The burglars were never caught.

As two hundred FBI agents searched for the burglars throughout the country in 1971, most intensively in Philadelphia, even people in the large peace movement there, where all of the burglars were activists, could not imagine that any of their fellow activists had had the courage or audacity to burglarize an FBI office. Many people feared then that the FBI might be stifling dissent, but most people found it difficult to imagine that anyone would risk their freedom—risk sacrificing years away from their children and other loved ones—to break into an FBI office to get evidence of whether that was true. People wondered:

Who would go to prison to save dissent?

That question will now be answered. For more than forty years, the Media burglars have been silent about what they did on the night of March 8, 1971. Seven of the eight burglars have been found by this writer, the first journalist to anonymously receive and then write about the files two weeks after the burglary. In the more than forty years since they were among the most hunted people in the country as they eluded FBI agents during the intensive investigation ordered by Hoover, they have lived rather quiet lives as law-abiding, good citizens who moved from youth to middle age and, for some, now to their senior years. They kept the promise they made to one another as they met for the last time immediately before they released copies of the stolen files to the public—that they would take their secret, the Media burglary, to their graves.

The seven burglars who have been found have agreed to break their silence so that the story of their act of resistance that uncovered the secret FBI can be told. Their inside account, as well as the FBI's account of its search for the burglars—as told by agents in interviews and as drawn from the 33,698-page official record of the FBI's investigation of the burglary obtained under the Freedom of Information Act—and the powerful impact of this historic act of resistance are all told here for the first time. It is a story about the destructive power of excessive government secrecy. It is a story about the potential power of nonviolent resistance, even when used against the most powerful law enforcement agency in the nation. It also is a story about courage and patriotism.

2

Choosing Burglary

T HE STORY OF the Media burglary begins with William Davidon.
It was his idea. He recruited people to consider the merit and feasibility of the idea. And then he led the planning and execution of
the burglary. He was also responsible for developing and carrying out the
plan to distribute copies of the stolen files to journalists and members of
Congress so the public would have access to them.

All this from a person so unassuming that the act of protesting—let
alone leading a group in planning and carrying out a burglary of an office of
the country's most powerful law enforcement agency—seemed to be almost
antithetical to his personality.

How was it possible for Davidon, who hated burglary, to think of becoming a burglar? And how was it possible for seven other people to agree to
participate in this radical action?

The answer to those questions is found, in part, in the evolution of Davidon's protest of the war and of the use of nuclear weapons. The answer also
is found in the very unusual moral and political dynamics that played out in
the United States the year before the burglary—a period of extreme actions
by the government and by diverse segments of the public. The accumulated
impact of those actions, some of them profoundly violent, upped the ante,
even for people who normally would never have considered doing anything
as extreme as burglarizing an FBI office.

It was natural for Davidon to care strongly about protecting dissent. By
1970, dissent had been part of the essential fabric of his life for more than two
decades. He had spoken out against the use and continued development of

ever more powerful nuclear weapons. He thought he had a responsibility to speak out forcefully against the world's most powerful armaments. He had opposed the war in Vietnam from the beginning on multiple grounds, but his deepest concern was that the United States might use nuclear weapons in Vietnam. Throughout the war, the administrations of both Lyndon Johnson and Richard Nixon refused to remove the nuclear option from the table.

In pursuit of his goals, Davidon moved during the 1960s from simple dissent to active protest to civil disobedience to nonviolent resistance. Many people moved through some or all of those phases in those years as their assumptions about the wisdom of their government's decisions and actions were shaken, but few did so with the mix of qualities that marked Davidon's activism—a combination of clear goals, the ability to solve problems, fortitude in the face of the peace movement's repeated failure to stop the war, a deep and enduring commitment to nonviolence, a modest ego, and a fierce reliance on evidence and refusal to accept speculation or conspiracy theories. He had the capacity to convince not only himself but also other people to consider stepping outside their secure lives to risk their freedom when normal means of petitioning the government were ignored or, even worse—as he feared in late 1970—were being suppressed.

As Davidon's concerns about the use of nuclear warfare in Vietnam deepened, he studied the war and kept track of its daily developments. He traveled to Vietnam in April 1966 with five other American peace activists, including the Reverend A. J. Muste, a New York pacifist who had been a leading antiwar and civil rights activist since World War I. As planned, they met with people whose positions were little known in the United States— Vietnamese people who opposed any outside interference in the country, whether by the Soviet Union, China, or the United States. Many of them were serving prison terms by that time. Davidon remembers acquiring a sad and ironic insight about dissent while he was in Vietnam: the leaders of all of the countries involved in the conflict—South Vietnam, North Vietnam, and the United States—had a profound dislike of dissent being expressed against the war by their own citizens, the people whose blood and money they were expending in the war. On this one matter, they were in agreement.

The Americans had congenial visits with Buddhists, Catholics, and other Vietnamese people who opposed the war, but their trip had a complex ending. Police and students broke up a press conference they held in their Saigon hotel the day before they left the country. As Davidon and the other Americans commented on the mutual interest of Americans and the Viet-

William Davidon (far left) with five other American pacifists, (left to right)
Bradford Lyttle, Voluntown, CT; the Rev. A. J. Mustic, New York; Karl Meyer,
Chicago; Charlotte Thurber, Greenwich, CT; and Barbara Deming Willflut,
MA; Vietnam, 1966. They met with Buddhists, Catholics, and other Vietnamese
who opposed the war; two weeks later they were expelled by South Vietnamese
officials. *(AP Photo)*

namese in ending the war, students in the audience shouted and threw eggs
at them and police banged their fists on tables and then rushed the stage,
shouting, "Either you are our friends or our enemies!" After the journalists
left, the scene changed dramatically as the students and police approached
the Americans and calmly apologized, telling them they had been ordered
by the South Vietnamese military police to disrupt the conference.

Like other reports on the press conference debacle, the *New York Times*
story by R. W. Apple Jr. missed that part of the story. But the *Times* headline two days later accurately captured what happened the day after the
press conference: "Vietnamese Seize Six U.S. Pacifists and Expel Them."
The group's morning meeting with the American ambassador was canceled.
Instead, they were grabbed by waiting Vietnamese police officers as they left
their hotel, thrown into a patrol wagon, and driven to Tan Son Nhat Airport, where they were forced to wait inside the locked and sweltering patrol
wagon for four hours.

After Davidon returned from Vietnam in 1966, he was determined to
work against the war as much as possible. He carefully organized his life so
he could increase the amount of time he gave to the effort. He never missed
a class or office hours. And he continued to share with his wife the work
involved in raising two small daughters. Beyond those key obligations, he
filled nearly all his other waking hours with antiwar activities.

There were countless opportunities to be a peace activist in Philadelphia. The peace movement there was one of the largest—if not the largest—most active, and most diverse peace movements in the nation during the Vietnam War. In all, it included about fifty organizations. Active in several of the organizations, Davidon worked, beginning in 1968, primarily with the Resistance, a new organization that offered support to men who refused to be drafted into the military. Its members also counseled active-duty soldiers who had turned against the war and wanted to leave the military. The Resistance, wrote historian Paul Lyons in his history of the Philadelphia peace movement during that era, was "the most significant antiwar organization in the city." Its members, he wrote, often pointed out "the contradiction between American ideals and American practice and demanded that those contradictions be resolved." Davidon, he wrote, was an "inspirational leader," one of the most effective in the organization.

Often, after Davidon taught his last class of the day, he drove to a GI coffeehouse the Resistance operated near Fort Dix in nearby central New Jersey. Resistance members hung out there with GIs, talking with them about the war, conscientious objection, and life in general. Davidon recalls that these exchanges were one of the most gratifying aspects of his antiwar activism. In contrast to the widespread assumption then and now that there was a hostile relationship between the antiwar movement and the troops during the Vietnam War, members of the Philadelphia Resistance, like many antiwar activ-

William Davidon being arrested at a peace demonstration, 1965
(Photo from Theodore Brinton Hetzel Collection, Swarthmore College Peace Collection)

ists elsewhere, regarded active-duty troops with respect, showed empathy for their plight, and offered moral and legal support to those who decided to resist military service. Davidon and his wife, Ann Morrissett, also aided troops by making their home on the Haverford campus available to service members who went AWOL and needed a place to stay while they considered their next steps: turn themselves in and face arrest and imprisonment or flee to Canada, Sweden, or France, three countries that welcomed many Americans who refused to serve in the military during the Vietnam War. Davidon and Morrissett did this as part of the vast national underground railroad that was organized to support soldiers who decided to become conscientious objectors after they entered the military.

In addition to its serious efforts, the Resistance also had a sense of humor, something Davidon appreciated. This was evident one autumn day when Resistance members attended one of the biggest annual events enjoyed by the Philadelphia establishment, the Army-Navy football game. From seats high in the stadium, Resistance members raised a large banner: "Beat Army, Beat Navy, Resist the Draft." Not all the fans were amused, but many were.

The group tried to maintain a sense of humor and stay on the high moral ground, even when tensions were high, as they often were then in Philadelphia in regard to the war and racial issues. They were able to do so, for instance, when Mayor Frank Rizzo dropped by the induction center near the University of Pennsylvania campus and, for no apparent reason other than that he supported the war and did not like people who opposed it, punched Resistance leader Tony Avirgan in the face as Avirgan distributed leaflets about the draft.

IN THE LATE 1960S and early 1970s, the Vietnam War touched the lives of more and more Americans in profound ways. Nearly everyone had family members, neighbors, or friends who had been called—or expected to be called—to serve in the military and be sent to Vietnam ready to kill or be killed. Many Americans' lives were shaped by the war in fundamental ways—those who died there, those who lost loved ones there, those who thought the United States must be victorious in Vietnam, those who refused to be drafted, and others who opposed the war, including people in military service who wanted to abandon their duty.

A sense of urgency about the war permeated the society. The country felt electric. It was a time when everything seemed to intensify—in the war, in the peace movement, among those who supported the war, among those who opposed it, and in actions against people who opposed it. The war seemed to be on everybody's mind. It was in new music. It was in daily conversations, sometimes even in conversations with strangers. In public places, while waiting in lines or flying on planes, it was not unusual for a stranger to turn to the person beside them and ask what they thought of the war. The war was part of daily discourse on campuses, in the streets of major cities, and in village squares. A person's opinion about the war often was seen as a test of how to judge that person. The war became our national personal litmus test of one another.

As the war continued relentlessly, by late 1969 Davidon was asking himself and others, as he had throughout the Vietnam War: What else can be done? He asked the question now with a deeper sense of urgency. After nearly a decade of failing to stop the war, people in the peace movement felt more hopeless than at any previous time. They searched for more effective nonviolent ways to make the case that the United States should withdraw from Vietnam. Davidon was generally an optimistic person, but even he found it difficult to remain so. He had to reach deeper now to retrieve his optimism.

He felt driven to find hope and to help others find it—especially people who by late 1969 had a sense of futility about whether any form of protest could be effective. In the early days of the war it was easier to feel hopeful. It seemed reasonable then to think the government would listen seriously to diverse opinions about the war. Given widespread analysis that indicated many mistakes had driven both the start and the continuation of the war, it was hoped the war policy would be reevaluated. When this did not happen, year after year in both the Johnson and Nixon administrations, hope became more scarce. There was a growing sense that young Americans' lives were being wasted both in Vietnam and on the streets of the country's increasingly violent poor neighborhoods, where hope of a better life was so absent that serving in Vietnam seemed like the best option for many poor young men.

Davidon realized futility could be disastrous. He was concerned about the people who were discouraged to the point of wondering if protest would ever be effective. He was also concerned about the small number of people who had turned to violent protest. Sometimes it felt as though the officials who were escalating the war and the few antiwar activists who had turned to violence as a strategy were engaged in a parallel group psychosis. He worried about how to keep hope alive—how to stop the spiral downward to hopelessness, to anger, and, for some, to rage. He pushed himself to find new ways to protest the war effectively and to keep hope alive. He wanted to find more aggressive ways to protest nonviolently. The methods of protest used by Quaker, academic, antidraft, and other antiwar networks no longer seemed to be enough at a time when the stakes were getting higher in both the war and the peace movement.

In his search for hope, Davidon found it where he had never expected—among Catholics. If he and the people who worked with him on the Media burglary had not become involved in 1970 with the Catholic peace movement, there would have been no burglary. People in that movement had invented the concept of burglary as a resistance method.

As a boy growing up in Newark, Davidon had never known a Catholic well, and did not until he worked with the activists in the Catholic peace movement. He never would have predicted that some of his closest allies—even his teachers—in finding and creating new ways to oppose the war would be Catholics. His surprise at finding Catholics who actively opposed the war was understandable. The leaders of the Catholic Church in the United States—especially key leaders Francis Cardinal Spellman of New York and John Cardinal Krol of Philadelphia—strongly supported the war. But at the Vatican in the 1960s, new ideas that opened the minds of Catholics on both religious and secular matters were propagated, thanks to a much-liked pope, John XXIII, and the international enclave of bishops, the Second Vatican Council, that he convened each year from 1962 through 1965. The transformative Catholic thinking that emerged from the council included condemnation of anti-Semitism and a mandate for Catholics to join in the search for world peace. In 1963, Pope John emphasized the mandate to work for peace by issuing an encyclical, *Pacem in Terris,* that called on Catholics to work actively with one another and with non-Catholics to create world peace. He advocated pacifism as an acceptable stance for Catholics, a concept relatively radical among American Catholics, for whom patriotism and religion were so intertwined that refusing to serve in the military was regarded as nearly heretical.

Pope Paul VI, successor to Pope John XXIII, pushed the Catholic peace mandate further. As the first pope to visit the United States, in October 1965, at a mass he celebrated before a large audience at Yankee Stadium he called for the United States to end the war in Vietnam. He issued the call again in a major speech at the United Nations at its twentieth anniversary ceremony and when he met privately with President Johnson at the Waldorf Astoria Hotel. At the United Nations, Pope Paul invoked remarks from John

F. Kennedy: "'Mankind must put an end to war or war will put an end to mankind.' It suffices to remember," the pope told the international gathering, "that the blood of millions of men, that the numberless and unheard-of sufferings, useless slaughter and frightful ruin, are the sanction of the pact which unites you with an oath which must change the future of the world." The pope raised his fist high and in a passionate voice said, "No more war, war never again! Peace, it is peace which must guide the destinies of people and of all mankind."

Spellman had always given the remarks of popes the highest respect, but now he made an exception. Shortly after Pope Paul's forceful antiwar speeches in New York, Spellman publicly stated an opinion that was diametrically opposed to what the pope had said: "Less than victory is inconceivable." Standing before troops in Vietnam two months later, Spellman said, "This war in Vietnam . . . is, I believe, a war for civilization." He had been blessing the war for years, and had even urged its start many years earlier with President Eisenhower and members of his cabinet. Spellman's role in promoting the war was so important, wrote James Carroll, that "the Vietnam war began as Spellman's war before it was Lyndon Johnson's war, or even Robert McNamara's war." Carroll, a *Boston Globe* columnist and author, is the son of the late General Joseph F. Carroll, confidant of Hoover and director of the Defense Intelligence Agency during the Vietnam War.

Despite the fiercely pro-war pronouncements of Spellman, many American Catholics enthusiastically embraced the new ideas from Rome. In addition to responding to the push for peace from Rome, they were encouraged by the teachings on peace of Dorothy Day, founder of the Catholic Worker movement, who served poor people in soup kitchens in New York and other cities, and by the teachings of Thomas Merton, a Trappist monk based at Our Lady of Gethsemane Abbey on a mountaintop in Kentucky. Formed primarily by young Catholics, the Catholic peace movement was based on a deep commitment to nonviolent protest. Often missing in histories of that era's antiwar movement, it was one of the most effective parts of the peace movement during the Vietnam War.

As the Catholic peace movement grew in influence in the mid-1960s, Spellman was infuriated. Jesuit authorities in New York and Rome were appalled when he demanded that they silence and banish to another country the Reverend Daniel Berrigan, a Jesuit priest and the best-known leader in the Catholic peace movement, but they complied. He was exiled to South America and, on Spellman's orders, his whereabouts were kept secret from his family and friends and he was prohibited from communicating with them before he left. As he waited to leave, no Jesuit community would let him live at their residence. Finally, Jesuits at Georgetown University let him stay in a Quonset hut on the edge of the campus.

Spellman's authoritarian treatment of Berrigan, especially his demands that he be banished and forbidden from doing peace work, was a turning point for many in the American church and in the Catholic peace movement. Even some Catholics who didn't agree with Berrigan's views on the war were upset by how Spellman had treated him. Protests against the cardinal for his action against Berrigan were one of the first signs that American Catholics were taking seriously the teachings of the Second Vatican Council, including those that called for Catholics to be active rather than passive in regard to church teachings and authority.

After repeated protests in support of Berrigan throughout the country, but especially in New York, his supporters placed a full-page ad in the *New York Times* on December 12, 1965, that was headlined "Open Letter to the Authorities of the Archdiocese of New York and the Jesuit Community in New York City." Stated his supporters in the ad, "The issue here is simply freedom of conscience." They asked the cardinal a crucial question: Could a priest "speak out on Vietnam only if he supports the American action there?"

Spellman eventually relented and let Berrigan return the next year. He returned to New York on March 8, 1966, and three weeks later he led a peace march of interfaith clergy, people who had opposed his exile and warmly welcomed him back to help lead the peace movement. As Murray Polner and Jim O'Grady wrote in their book on the Berrigan brothers, *Disarmed and Dangerous,* the large group walked by numerous churches and synagogues and then stopped to pray on Fifth Avenue in front of St. Patrick's Cathedral, where, as the archbishop of New York, Cardinal Spellman presided.

Davidon was attracted to the Catholic peace activists because of their search, by late 1969, for more aggressive forms of nonviolent resistance. He first met people in the Catholic peace movement a few months after some of its members, including Daniel Berrigan, were convicted for the resistance act for which the Catholic movement is probably best known—the public raid in May 1968 of the draft board in Catonsville, Maryland. Nine of them—including Daniel Berrigan and his brother Philip—burned draft files with homemade napalm in the draft board parking lot while they waited for police to arrive and arrest them. Because Davidon had recently been impressed by the writings of the Berrigan brothers, he said yes when a woman who was part of the Catholic peace movement invited him to have

dinner with about a dozen members of the movement. He had been especially impressed by the play Daniel Berrigan wrote, *The Trial of the Catonsville Nine*. It drew directly from the transcript of the group's 1969 trial,
including this statement made by him to journalists as the nine watched the
records burn and waited for the police to arrive:

"Our apologies, good friends, for the fracture of good order, the burning
of paper instead of children, the angering of the orderlies in the front parlor
of the charnel house. We could not, so help us God, do otherwise."

Davidon found the resistance ideas and methods of the Catonsville Nine
compelling. Berrigan's poetic writing and the stark trial testimony resonated
deeply with Davidon's values. Years later, he recalls that the play made him
"take seriously these kinds of things as a possibility" for himself. "I don't
think I would have even considered such steps had it not been for Dan
Berrigan."

Davidon shared Berrigan's deep concern for the people in the peace
movement who had despaired and turned to violent protest. Berrigan spoke
of his respect for them and also of his concern about their violence in a letter
he wrote to people in the Weather Underground and released for publication
while he himself was underground as he briefly avoided beginning his sentence for his Catonsville conviction. He sent the letter a couple months after
the March 1970 explosion at the Greenwich house where three members
of the Weather Underground were killed when a bomb they were building
accidentally exploded. He was critical of violence in both government and
the peace movement.

"Dear Brothers and Sisters, Let me express deep gratitude that the chance
has come to speak to you across the underground, . . ." he wrote. There was
a need, he continued, for "a new kind of anger which is both useful in communicating and imaginative and slow-burning, to fuel the long haul of our
lives":

> I hope your lives are about something more than sabotage. I'm certain
> it is. . . . I hope, indeed, that you are as uneasy about its meaning and
> usefulness. . . .
>
> How shall we speak . . . to the people? We must never refuse, in
> spite of their refusal of us, to call them our brothers. I must say to you as
> simply as I know how: if the people are not the main issue, there simply
> is no main issue and you and I are fooling ourselves. . . .
>
> No principle is worth the sacrifice of a single human being. That's a

very hard statement. At various stages of the movement some have acted as if almost the opposite were true, as people got purer and purer. . . .

When madness is the acceptable public state of mind, we're all in danger, all in danger; for madness is an infection in the air. And I submit that we all breathe the infection and that the movement has at times been sickened by it too. . . . In or out of the military, in or out of the movement, it seems to me that we had best call things by their name, and the name of this thing, it seems to me, is the death game, no matter where it appears. And as for myself, I would as soon be under the heel of former masters as under the heel of new ones. . . .

The question now is: what can we create? I feel at your side across the miles, and I hope that sometime, sometime in this mad world, in this mad time, it will be possible for us to sit down face to face . . . and find that our hopes and our sweat, and the hopes and sweat and death and tears and blood of our brothers and sisters throughout the world, have brought to birth that for which we began. Shalom to you.

Those ideas meshed completely with Davidon's as he searched for new, stronger ways to protest and hoped violence would be stemmed in both the government and on the fringes of the peace movement.

WHEN DAVIDON FIRST MET people in the Catholic group, he was impressed by their commitment to nonviolent resistance. He was startled, though, when he discovered that recently they had used a new method: burglary. Their goal with this approach was to slow down the operation of the draft system by breaking into draft boards at night while they were closed and stealing as many Selective Service records as possible. Unlike the symbolic acts they had carried out earlier, including Catonsville, in this new phase of the Catholic resistance they hoped to flee, never be arrested, and continue to steal more records in order to make the conscription of young men more difficult.

At first, Davidon thought the group was what he was looking for: people engaged in aggressive nonviolence. But burglary? That was not something he ever wanted to do. It was not what his and their heroes, Martin Luther King and Mahatma Gandhi, had done. Nor was it what either Daniel or Philip Berrigan had done. The brothers had engaged in public resistance and then waited to be arrested. But as Davidon examined what the Catholic group had accomplished, he had to admit that they had used burglary very effectively. More than five hundred people in this loosely structured movement, located primarily in the Northeast and upper Midwest, had burglarized dozens of draft boards and removed thousands of Selective Service records. Despite FBI investigations, very few of them had been arrested.

As burglars, they used some unusual techniques, ones Davidon enjoyed recalling years later, such as what some of them did in 1970 at a draft board office in Delaware. During their casing, they had noticed that the interior door that opened to the draft board office was always locked. There was no padlock to replace, as they had done at a draft board raid in Philadelphia a few months earlier, and no one in the group was able to pick the lock. The break-in technique they settled on at that office must be unique in the annals of burglary. Several hours before the burglary was to take place, one of them wrote a note and tacked it to the door they wanted to enter: "Please don't lock this door tonight." Sure enough, when the burglars arrived that night, someone had obediently left the door unlocked. The burglars entered the office with ease, stole the Selective Service records, and left. They were so pleased with themselves that one of them proposed leaving a thank-you note on the door. More cautious minds prevailed. Miss Manners be damned, they did not leave a note.

Sometimes they destroyed the files they stole. Other times they sent them to the young men whose records they had stolen. Each file was sent with an anonymous letter that explained to the young man that his file had been removed from official files by antiwar activists, and they hoped he would take advantage of this disruption of the system to think carefully about the war and whether he wanted to serve in the military. Each recipient was given contact information for the draft counseling offices closest to his home. Davidon appreciated the irony years later that his last duty in the Navy during World War II was typing separation papers for people leaving military service, and now during the Vietnam War he typed letters trying to discourage people from entering the military.

As Davidon thought about whether he should be willing to raid draft boards with the Catholic activists, he worried that what he once would have opposed doing he now thought might be acceptable. He probed his motivation. Given the madness of those days, he asked himself: Am I moving toward more effective protest, or am I moving down a slippery slope toward violence? The question was chilling. As he contemplated the challenge the question posed, he reminded himself that the war was escalating in new and terrible ways, and national leaders still didn't seem to be listening. He

Davidon with daughters Ruth and Sarah (in stroller) near his home on the Haverford College campus around the time of the Media burglary.

became convinced that neither he nor his new colleagues, the Catholic peace movement draft board raiders, would let themselves go down that slippery slope. He had come to regard them as so grounded and disciplined in their commitment to nonviolence as both a humane way to live and as a strategy against war and for peace that he did not think it was possible for them to move into violence.

Despite Davidon's initial reluctance to embrace the methods of the Catholic activists, by the time he decided to work with them, he had concluded that no other part of the peace movement was as effective or inspired as much hope during that hopeless time as they did. He regarded them as the most radical and courageous people he had met in the peace movement. He continued to work with the Resistance and other groups, but now he found a new home with these activists—priests and nuns, ex-priests and ex-nuns, the young sons and daughters of working-class Catholics, and other people who embraced their commitment to nonviolent protest. They reenergized Davidon's activism and gave him the hope he was searching for. Reluctantly, he became a burglar.

As he became more involved with the Catholics, Davidon's identity among his colleagues in the Philadelphia peace movement became even more confusing. For years, some people had assumed he was a Quaker

because of his involvement with Quaker peace organizations. Or was he
an Episcopalian? He occasionally worked with members of the Episcopal
Peace Fellowship, especially enjoying working with a peace activist Episcopal priest, the late Reverend David Gracie. But now some people assumed
Davidon was a Catholic. He became used to, and somewhat amused by,
having a mistaken identity. Actually, he was a secular Jewish humanist who
was willing to work with anyone, as were these Catholics, who shared his
passion for nonviolent protest in an effort to stop the war and the use of
nuclear weapons. Probably no one from the scientific, academic, or Quaker
organizations with which he had long been affiliated guessed he had added
another identity: burglar.

THE DESIRE OF DAVIDON and many other peace activists, including
the people in the Catholic peace movement, to find stronger forms of resistance came in part from a powerful cascade of extreme developments from
late 1969 through 1970, the year before the Media burglary. These developments greatly intensified reaction to the war. So extreme was that period
that it was hard to keep track of what was normal in the military, in the
White House, or in resistance to the war. People often thought nothing
more shocking could happen. And then it would. This remarkable cascade
of events started in a small hamlet in Vietnam, moved to a small campus
in Ohio, to a Mississippi campus, to the financial district of New York, and
then to the White House, where President Nixon dismissed most of the
events as inconsequential:

- In November 1969, the world was horrified to learn that American
  soldiers had massacred 504 unarmed Vietnamese children, women, and
  elderly people in March 1968 in My Lai, a small hamlet in Vietnam.
  Several old men were bayoneted, women and children were shot in
  the backs of their heads while cowering in ditches, and some young
  girls were raped and then killed. Though the evidence of the massacre
  was well established when it was first reported by journalist Seymour
  Hersh, President Nixon accused the press of inflating the case in order
  to "chip away" at support for the war. When Lieutenant William
  Calley, the commander of the group, was convicted of premeditated
  murder in My Lai of twenty-two people (he was charged with
  killing 150) and sentenced to life imprisonment at hard labor, Nixon

intervened and reduced his sentence to three months and ordered that he serve his time under house arrest instead of in prison.

- American officials lashed out at antiwar activists with extreme rhetoric in 1970. One of the most egregious attacks came from California governor Ronald Reagan, who in March 1970 declared that "if it takes a bloodbath to silence the demonstrators, let's get it over with."

- Three members of the Weathermen (later called the Weather Underground)—Theodore Gold, Diana Oughton, and Terry Robbins—were killed in an explosion they accidentally set off while making a bomb in a town house in New York's Greenwich Village on March 6, 1970.

- President Nixon announced in a televised address on April 30, 1970, that the United States was invading Cambodia after months of secretly bombing it. In immediate response, more antiwar protests took place the next day than ever before, including in towns and on campuses where antiwar protests had never taken place. This expansion of the ground war into Cambodia, along with the impact of the secret bombing the United States had been carrying out there for several months, killed many thousands of people, ravaged the countryside, and weakened the country in ways that set the stage for the takeover of Cambodia by the Khmer Rouge and the genocide that resulted in the deaths of 1.7 million Cambodians between 1975 and 1978. By the end of the war, the United States had dropped more bombs on Cambodia than it dropped in all of World War II in Europe and Asia.

- Two days after Nixon's Cambodia speech, Ohio governor James Rhodes declared martial law at Kent State University and ordered the Ohio National Guard to patrol the campus. Rhodes called the students "worse than the brown shirt and the communist element and also the night riders and the vigilantes. They're the worst kind of people we harbor in America."

- A day later, four students were killed and nine were injured, some of them permanently disabled, on the Kent State campus by National Guard gunfire as students assembled peacefully that Monday for a demonstration at noon. It was the first time Americans were killed while protesting the war. A few days later, according to White House presidential counsel John Dean, behind closed doors at a Department of Justice meeting, FBI director J. Edgar Hoover called one of the slain students a "slut" and seemed to have little interest in how they had been killed. No one was ever convicted of the killings.

- Shortly after the shootings at Kent State, Representative Tip O'Neill, Democrat from Massachusetts, said this on the House floor: "Look at the situation. No nation can destroy us militarily, but what can destroy us from within is happening now."
- Nixon, at the urging of his staff, formed a Commission on Campus Unrest to examine the causes of unrest, including the killings at Kent State. He rejected his commission's conclusions that White House policies and current social conditions in the United States were the cause of most student protest.
- Two students were killed several days after the Kent State shootings by local and state police one night at Jackson State University, a black campus in Jackson, Mississippi. Despite the fact that no students shot at police, and there was no evidence any students possessed guns, city and state police armed with carbines, submachine guns, shotguns, and service revolvers shot more than 460 rounds of ammunition at the windows of the dormitory where one of the killings took place. (The second student was shot dead on a nearby street as he carried milk home from a grocery store.) The shots by law enforcement officers shattered *every* window on one side of the dormitory. As at Kent State, no one was ever convicted for the killings.
- The Friday after the killings at Kent State, scores of students were bludgeoned in New York's financial district by hundreds of construction workers who rampaged through the streets attacking students with crowbars and other heavy tools wrapped in American flags. They did so as the students sang at a peaceful noon vigil at a day of mourning called for by New York mayor John Lindsay to honor the slain Kent State students. To prevent the people they injured from receiving medical care, the construction workers—most of them were from the building site of the Twin Towers—yanked down a Red Cross banner outside an emergency clinic that had been hastily set up at Trinity Church by New York University doctors. When Michael Belknap, a lawyer with the Sullivan & Cromwell law firm, tried to help a bleeding student, he was knocked down and stomped on his back by construction workers. "Someone yelled, 'He's a commie bastard. We ought to kill him,'" Belknap told a reporter. The *Wall Street Journal* reported that financial district workers threw streams of ticker tape and

data processing punch cards from their windows in celebration of the violence taking place in the streets below.

- Twenty-two of those New York construction workers were honored at the White House a few weeks later by President Nixon. He thanked them for showing their patriotism the day they beat students. He gave them flag lapel pins, and they gave him a yellow hard hat like the ones they wore the day they assaulted students, seventy of whom were seriously injured.

- Vice President Spiro Agnew wrote a letter of thanks to the union official who organized the attacks on the students, Peter Brennan, head of the New York City Building Trades Council. He congratulated him for his "impressive display of patriotism" the day of the attacks. When Nixon was reelected in 1972, the president rewarded Brennan, who was a leader of the movement to increase the number of labor Democrats who voted for Nixon in 1972, by appointing him secretary of labor.

- On August 24, 1970, a bomb exploded in front of Sterling Hall, a building that housed the Army Mathematics Research Center at the University of Wisconsin at Madison. A thirty-three-year-old physics researcher and father of three young children was killed and four people were injured. Three people were convicted for the crime and a fourth suspect is still being sought by the FBI.

That was America in 1970.

It was an extraordinary time in the life of the country. Not since the Civil War had Americans been so divided. Nearly all of the divisions were related to the war. It became clear that year that the war that had been tearing Vietnam apart for many years was now also tearing apart the soul of America—in the heartland and in the cities, from coast to coast. Frustrations were higher and hopes lower in the peace movement than they had been at any time. Many people wondered if this war, which by now in reports from Vietnam was often called a bloodbath, would end.

People had been asking: Can there be peace in Vietnam? Now people also asked: Can there be peace at home?

IT WAS IN 1970, that mad time, to use Daniel Berrigan's words, that Davidon became aware of another war: the war against dissent. As he moved from peace group to peace group that year, searching for more effective ways to escalate opposition to war, he repeatedly heard a very troubling rumor. He heard it from people in various types of peace organizations— academic, scientific, religious, antidraft. They told him there were growing fears that there were FBI spies in their midst. Fear of informers was having a poisonous impact, he was told. People worried about whether the person who stood beside them at a demonstration was an informer. Some wondered about their neighbor, their colleague at work, or the new volunteer in the peace organization office—were they informers? Trust was fraying. Some people considered colleagues with such concerns to be paranoid and dismissed them.

Davidon listened carefully, but he was cautious. At first, he did not take the concerns very seriously. True to his reluctance to accept either speculation or conspiracy theories, he thought people might be exaggerating, or that their frustrations about the war, after so many years of failing to stop it, might be fueling irrational fears. But the concerns were repeated to him again and again. Very reasonable people from a diverse range of peace organizations expressed them.

By the fall of 1970, Davidon no longer doubted what people were telling him. He concluded that the rumor probably was true: Peace organizations had been infiltrated by informers. One of the nation's most powerful leaders, J. Edgar Hoover, he now feared, might have turned the power of the FBI against people who opposed the war. Davidon thought about it constantly. If it turned out that the U.S. government was suppressing Americans' right to express dissent—including and especially dissent about the most crucial issues: the war, the use of apocalyptic weapons in the war, and racial equality—then much was at stake. Without the freedom to dissent without being spied on, Davidon thought, dissent was empty, erased, useless. Such spying, he thought, was gravely hypocritical in a nation that expressed great pride in being the land of the free. How could a government that claimed to be fighting a war for people's freedom in another country at the same time suppress its own people's right to dissent?

Finally, Davidon decided that it was as important to answer this question—was the FBI suppressing dissent?—as it was to oppose the war. Most people would have recognized the enormous inherent impediments to answering the question and concluded it would be impossible to do so, but Davidon decided the implications were simply too big, too important—too damaging to the heart of democracy—to let it go unanswered. As he had done when he became deeply concerned about the development and use of nuclear weapons in the Vietnam War, he now quietly did what he thought was a citizen's obligation: He took responsibility for finding the answer to the question.

Davidon focused his scientifically trained mind on how to prove or disprove the persistent rumor that the government was spying on Americans for reasons unrelated to suspicion of crime. He analyzed what was known about how J. Edgar Hoover operated. Little had been written about the FBI or the director, except for what had been ghostwritten by FBI staff and by the people the director referred to inside the bureau as "friendly" journalists. Prior to 1971, there had been very little public criticism of the director or the bureau except for occasional commentary by Alan Barth in the *Washington Post* and Tom Wicker in the *New York Times*. The only reporting that raised questions about the FBI had been done by Jack Nelson in the *Los Angeles Times*, a book by Nelson and Jack Bass, and Fred Cook's book and articles in the *Nation* magazine. As FBI policy dictated, journalists had been hampered by never having access to FBI records or officials, even after the Freedom of Information Act became law in 1966. From what he had absorbed about the director, Davidon had the impression that he was an extremely bureaucratic manager and an extremely conservative ideologue. That combination, he thought, could be a potentially potent and dangerous pair of defining characteristics when embodied in an extraordinarily popular and powerful person at the pinnacle of American law enforcement. He thought that if Hoover was a consummate bureaucrat, perhaps he kept and distributed within the bureau detailed records of his opinions and his operations. And, he thought, perhaps he also required those who carried out his orders to file detailed reports.

It was just a hunch.

As Davidon framed the problem to himself, he concluded that the question could be answered only by presenting hard evidence to the public. Neither rhetorical condemnation nor unproved assumptions would do. Rhetoric without supporting evidence of actual suppression of dissent could be dismissed easily and likely would lead to deeper cynicism than already existed. A great believer in the potential of average people to make wise decisions if they are armed with information, he was confident that if evidence of official suppression of dissent could be found and be presented to the public, people would demand that such suppression be stopped.

But how could evidence be found? In a life spent as a problem solver, in physics and in activism, this was the most difficult problem Davidon had ever faced. He could not shake the thought that evidence might exist, and if it existed, it should be possible to find it and prove conclusively whether the destructive rumors were true. But he could think of no lawful way to find evidence.

This perplexing dilemma led Davidon, in late 1970, to think again of burglary. He disliked the idea of using burglary as a resistance tool, just as he had when he reluctantly joined Catholic activists in raiding draft board offices in early 1970. But when he considered the options, there seemed to be no other way to get documentary evidence of FBI operations except by breaking into an FBI office and taking files.

Just as Davidon was ready to ask a few people he deeply trusted what they thought of his idea, two events in late 1970 focused national attention on Hoover and the FBI.

The first event took place November 27, 1970, the day after Thanksgiving, when the director made a rare appearance before the Supplemental and Deficiencies Subcommittee of the Senate Appropriations Committee. He went to Capitol Hill that day to make the case he made to Congress every year, usually before a House Committe: that a crisis atmosphere made it essential that Congress increase the bureau's budget. But today he had an additional reason for testifying: to disclose highly charged secrets his top aides had urged him not to reveal.

Hoover had little to worry about regarding budget increases. He had long had extraordinary success in getting the increases he wanted. As *Los Angeles Times* reporters Jack Nelson and Ronald J. Ostrow wrote in their 1972 book *The FBI and the Berrigans*, "Only twice since 1950 had the FBI not received the exact amount of its budget requests. On those two occasions, the FBI received *more* than he requested." With few exceptions in his nearly half century as director, his sessions before Congress were lovefests, not inquiries. Members of Congress would rise, one by one, to praise and thank him. They treated him as though they were there to serve him, not to question him. Years later, the public would learn that Hoover carefully cultivated this sense of intimidation, but at the time only the intimidated had a clue.

By then Hoover had been director of the bureau for forty-six years, since Calvin Coolidge was president. That made him the longest-serving appointed public official in U.S. history, a record that still stands. Though the attorney general was technically his supervisor—at this time it was John Mitchell, the future head of President Nixon's reelection campaign, who would later go to prison for his crimes in the Watergate scandal—Hoover acted as though he was his own boss. With very few exceptions, most attorneys general and presidents treated Hoover as though his perception of his power was correct.

Like most senators and members of Congress, Democratic senator Robert C. Byrd of West Virginia and Republican senator Roman L. Hruska of Nebraska—the only two senators present for his November 1970 presentation—had good working relationships with Hoover. They put this session together hastily. The long mahogany table in the chandeliered room would have accommodated at least two dozen senators, but because it was the day after Thanksgiving most were not available. Senators Byrd and Hruska sat beside each other on a long side of the table facing Hoover. Opposite them, the director's longtime colleague and companion Clyde Tolson sat on one side of Hoover, and John P. Mohr, an assistant to the director, sat on his other side as he read aloud to the two senators all of his twenty-seven pages of prepared testimony. He decried the amount of overtime agents had to work because of the "growing menace"—four million hours during fiscal year 1970, he said. That was one of his secret annual budget tricks. Hoover required agents to submit phony overtime records so he could use the contrived data when he made his annual case before Congress for a budget increase. In his testimony this day, he asked for an extra $14.5 million above the annual increase. This extra allocation, he said, was needed because of "terrorist tactics" that made it necessary to hire a thousand additional agents. These hires would bring the total number of agents to 8,350, an unprecedented 14 percent increase in one year.

Hoover always had a story line to justify his request for a budget increase. It usually was about frightening threats. Since the beginning of the Cold War, he had based his annual pitch on the need to strengthen the bureau's ability to fight the growth of communism in the United States. He stuck with this story long after communism had nearly disappeared in the country, even long after there were more FBI agents posing as party members than there were genuine party members at Communist Party meetings. Hoover's story line this day in late 1970 was different. The small number of senators present to hear him—two—was no indication of the profound implications of what he would say behind closed doors and then immediately release to journalists. The senators were willing props on a stage Hoover had designed in order to make secrets public.

He had given this same testimony before the House Subcommittee on Appropriations just two weeks earlier. It was not released to the press then. He had made sure it would be released today.

He told the senators about the bureau's increased responsibilities in the investigation of organized crime, an area he had long avoided. He talked about the growing dangers imposed by the New Left, especially the Weathermen, noting that one member of that radical group, Bernardine Dohrn, had recently been placed on the FBI's list of the "Ten Most Wanted Fugitives."

Then he came to the heart of what he said that day, what dominated national news that evening and the next day. He told his audience of two:

> Willingness to employ any type of terrorist tactics is becoming increasingly apparent among extremist elements. One example has recently come to light involving an incipient plot on the part of an anarchist group on the east coast, the so-called "East Coast Conspiracy to Save Lives."
>
> This is a militant group self-described as being composed of Catholic priests and nuns, teachers, students, and former students who have manifested opposition to the war in Vietnam by acts of violence against Government agencies and private corporations engaged in work relating to U.S. participation in the Vietnam conflict.
>
> The principal leaders of this group are Philip and Daniel Berrigan, Catholic priests who are currently incarcerated in the Federal Correctional Institution at Danbury, Connecticut, for their participation in the destruction of Selective Service Records in Catonsville, Maryland, in 1968.
>
> This group plans to blow up underground electrical conduits and steam pipes serving the Washington, D.C., area in order to disrupt federal government operations. The plotters are also concocting a scheme to kidnap a highly placed Government official. The name of a White House staff member has been mentioned as a possible victim. If successful, the plotters would demand an end to United States bombing operations in Southeast Asia and the release of all political prisoners as ransom. Intensive investigation is being conducted concerning this matter.

It was a bombshell.

Hoover had arranged to have a member of his staff call selected journalists and tell them that the director's testimony from the closed hearing would be available when the hearing ended. The FBI staffer assured reporters they were going to get a big story. As Hoover concluded his remarks, Mohr gave copies of Hoover's twenty-seven-page prepared statement to the clerk of the Senate committee and asked him to distribute them to the reporters who were waiting outside the closed hearing room door.

The director was so eager for the claims he made to have the widest possible public exposure that two weeks later, on December 11, he published a booklet containing his by then well-known "secret" testimony and had it mailed to journalists, public officials, business leaders, and other influential people throughout the country. In a cover letter sent with the booklet, Hoover wrote, "It is my hope that through this document a better understanding will result of the work and problems facing the FBI." The distribution of his testimony—first to journalists that day and later in the widely mailed booklet—marked the first time in the bureau's history that the director had made public unproven allegations about criminal acts by specific people who had not been charged.

It was not known at the time that Hoover's plan to make these accusations public had alarmed his top aides so much that they had tried to convince him not to include the accusations against the Berrigans in his testimony. By taking this step, his aides risked the possibility of being transferred to unacceptable posts or, worse, being fired and blackballed from future work in any law enforcement agency. That had recently happened to one agent in retaliation for rather gentle criticism. But because his top aides thought that what Hoover was about to do was a serious mistake, they took the extraordinary step of violating his complete lack of tolerance of criticism.

They knew Hoover had been told a few weeks earlier that the FBI and the Internal Security Division of the Department of Justice had investigated these allegations against the Berrigans and others and had decided that there was insufficient evidence to support them. Charles D. Brennan, assistant to the director, was so upset when he saw the accusations in an advance copy of the director's testimony that he wrote a memo to Hoover urging that his remarks about the Berrigans be deleted. In his memo, Brennan told Hoover that his plea that the accusations not be made public had been endorsed by all agents in the Domestic Intelligence Division, the largest division in the bureau and the division that had investigated the allegations. William C. Sullivan, assistant director, third in command at the bureau, and in the bureau for thirty years by this time, also sent Hoover a memo advising him not to make the accusations against the Berrigans.

It was an unprecedented instance of FBI officials banding together to oppose an action by Hoover. Instead of following their advice, he violated basic principles of due process and made sweeping public charges about accusations he knew had been determined to be without merit. In addition to whatever concerns his aides had about the unfairness of the accusations becoming public, they were concerned that by making these allegations the director would be violating the rule he considered most important and that he always had required adherence to by all FBI employees: Don't embarrass the bureau.

To many Americans, Hoover's testimony probably seemed like just one more ominous indication that the antiwar movement was becoming more violent, a claim frequently made by the Nixon White House, even in the aftermath of the killing of students on the Kent State campus the previous May. That, plus the fact that the public did not know the unusual circumstances under which Hoover's testimony was given, made it possible for Hoover to effectively recast the image of the Catholic peace movement that day from the nonviolent, pacifist organization it had claimed to be to a group of violent extremists who planned to kidnap and bomb. The very unusual image of priests and nuns engaged in bombing and kidnapping was the kind of sensational image that latched on to psyches.

Hoover's efforts that day were successful. In addition to creating a new public image of Catholic antiwar activists, he also received the money he wanted, $14.5 million, and a congressional authorization to hire a thousand extra agents to meet the new crisis caused by antiwar activists. Hoover probably never knew that among some people in the bureau these new agents quickly became known as "the Berrigan 1,000" in honor of the false story about the Berrigans the director had used to scare Congress into approving the special funding to hire them. Ironically, as a group they were resistant to spying on political dissidents and made it known that they were more interested in working on organized crime and other criminal cases.

That Hoover's testimony that day suddenly placed the FBI in a bright spotlight did not stop Davidon or even cause him to pause. In a strange twist of fate, the actions Hoover set in motion that day eventually threatened Davidon but later led to him being protected from the reach of the FBI.

The second event that drew attention to the FBI at that time took place in reaction to Hoover's congressional testimony. On December 9, 1970, less than two weeks after Hoover made his remarks to the two senators, he was criticized on the floor of the House of Representatives by Representative William R. Anderson, a World War II hero who had been much honored for his participation in eleven submarine combat patrol missions. Anderson was also celebrated for his role in 1958 as commander of the first underwater voyage under the North Pole, 8,000 nautical miles from the Pacific Ocean to the Atlantic. In that pre–space travel era, Anderson and his crew on the USS *Nautilus,* the first atomic-powered submarine, were regarded as heroes throughout the world. Their accomplishment seemed like the stuff of science fiction. Grand parades were held in their honor in London and in New York, and Anderson was honored at a special ceremony at the White House by President Dwight D. Eisenhower, who had chosen him to make the historic voyage.

In November 1970, just a month before he rose in the House chamber to speak about Hoover, Anderson had been elected to his fourth term in the House from his Tennessee district west of Nashville. He had received 82 percent of the vote, one of the highest margins of victory in Congress. Also notable was this World War II hero's move from hawk to dove in the last two years, a change in which the Berrigans had unintentionally played a supporting role.

A trip Anderson made to Vietnam in the summer of 1970 greatly increased his doubts about the war. He went there with Representative August F. Hawkins, Democrat from Southern California, and a congressional aide, Tom Harkin, who has been a Democratic senator from Iowa since 1985. Military officials tried to keep them from achieving the goal of their trip—touring what had become known as the "tiger cages" at the large South Vietnamese prison on Con Son Island, fifty miles off the coast of South Vietnam. Built by the French in 1862 as a penal colony, during the U.S. war in Vietnam the prison was managed by South Vietnam and supported and condoned by the United States.

Anderson and Hawkins managed to force their way into the buildings that contained the tiger cages, five-by-nine-foot cells beneath a floor, each containing three to five prisoners, about four hundred prisoners in all, men and women. The only openings on the cages were the spaces between bars on their tops. Many of the prisoners were political prisoners, students who were imprisoned after being arrested during antiwar demonstrations in South Vietnam because they were suspected of being communists. Anderson and his companions observed firsthand that the prisoners were treated cruelly. The catwalks above the cages were lined with buckets of lime, which the guards periodically dumped through the bars onto the prisoners. They were frequently beaten severely, fed rotten food and rice mixed with sand, urinated on from the catwalk, and shackled for days at a time.

Anderson, a graduate of the U.S. Naval Academy, was appalled that his country condoned such treatment of prisoners by its allies. He also was appalled by his House colleagues' reaction to the detailed report he and Hawkins submitted to them. Instead of acting on the report, many condemned them for conducting the inspection and refused to include more than a few lines of their report in a congressional committee document.

As Anderson increasingly questioned the conduct of the war, he had read exhaustively about it from a wide array of writers. Among the books that impressed him most were ones written by Daniel and Philip Berrigan. Through them, he came to understand why some people who were strongly opposed to the war had resorted to resistance, such as the resistance the brothers had engaged in at the Catonsville draft board and for which they were serving time.

Hoover's accusations about the Berrigan brothers in testimony the day after Thanksgiving deeply disturbed Anderson. He found it difficult to believe that Philip or Daniel Berrigan could have contemplated, let alone planned, violent acts of protest, such as bombing and kidnapping. Three days after Hoover made his claims, Anderson drove from Washington to the federal prison in Danbury, Connecticut, to question the brothers about Hoover's accusations. He believed their face-to-face claim to him that they were not involved in any such conspiracy and that they remained deeply committed to nonviolence. Reassured, in a letter to Hoover he expressed confidence in the Berrigans' continuing commitment to nonviolence and questioned the fairness and veracity of Hoover's accusations against them.

"If there is any substance to your allegations," Anderson wrote, "I respectfully submit that it is your duty to arraign them before a federal grand jury to seek an indictment. If on the other hand, there is no substance . . . then certainly we should expect an explanation, if not an outright retraction." The matter at hand, Anderson wrote, transcended the Berrigans and added to "a growing tendency on the part of our executive branch to employ the tactics of fear and to be less than candid in dealing with the public."

A stranger to criticism, let alone such strong criticism, from a member of Congress, Hoover was angry. He was especially angry that Anderson had made his letter public. After chiding him for that in a December 2 letter, Hoover insisted that "you may be assured my testimony was predicated on the results of careful investigation. All information developed regarding this matter is being furnished to the Department of Justice which has the responsibility for initiating prosecutive action."

After this exchange of letters, Anderson, still convinced that the director's accusations against the Berrigans were false, rose to speak on the floor of the House on December 9. He identified himself as a longtime admirer of Hoover and the FBI as he told the assembled members of Congress:

"We have suffered many casualties in the Vietnamese war. Most of our domestic and international problems are either caused by this unwanted, undeclared war or are intensified by it. It is now distressingly evident that one of the most ardent, devoted and presumably unassailable public servants in the lifetime of our Republic is, in a sense, a casualty of that same war." Anderson said he was speaking of J. Edgar Hoover. The director, in his recent testimony before the Senate committee, Anderson told his colleagues, had ignored the due process clauses of the Constitution; he had made his charges in public, through the Senate, rather than in the courts, where they belonged; and in doing so he had resorted to "tactics reminiscent of McCarthyism."

Some members of the House tried to force Anderson to stop speaking. Refusing to be intimidated, Anderson continued. His remarks were unprecedented public criticism of Hoover, especially in these chambers where Hoover always had been treated royally. In the heated discussion that followed on the House floor, ardent Hoover supporters rose to defend him. One of the staunchest defenders was Brooklyn Democrat John J. Rooney, the very powerful chair of the House Appropriations Committee, who had been hosting Hoover's successful appearances before that committee and shepherding his budget increases for decades.

A short time later, Hoover secretly began retaliating against Anderson in the way he had forcefully, and always secretly, done for years against the few people who dared to criticize him. Curt Gentry described Hoover's smear campaign against Anderson in his 1990 biography *J. Edgar Hoover: The Man and the Secrets*. Call girls in Washington were shown a photograph of Anderson and asked if he had been one of their clients. None of them said they recognized him, but FBI agents in Nashville found a madam who, when she saw the photograph, said Anderson "might" have visited her place of business several years earlier. That was good enough for Hoover. With that "evidence," he scribbled "whoremonger" on a memorandum about Anderson, put it in his secret files on members of Congress, and informed the Nixon White House that Anderson patronized prostitutes.

It was a brutal attack. A former aide to Hoover years later told Gentry, "Anderson's scalp was hung out to dry as a warning to others who might entertain the same notion." Hoover succeeded. Not only did his attack discourage other members of Congress from questioning his accusations about the kidnap-bomb plot, but in 1972 the FBI's smear campaign contributed significantly to Anderson, previously one of the highest vote getters in Congress, being defeated in his bid for reelection.

After these two events—Hoover's accusations against the Berrigans and Congress's circling the wagons to protect the director when Anderson raised questions about those accusations—it was evident to Davidon that Congress could not be expected to investigate whether the FBI was suppressing dissent. It seemed even more likely now that the documentary evidence needed in order to investigate the FBI could be gotten only by people willing to risk their freedom by burglarizing an FBI office.

3

The Team Is Formed

DAVIDON MADE a list of people he thought would be willing to consider his question. He focused on those he had worked with on a draft board raid. He liked many of them. He especially liked John Peter Grady, the leader of several of the raids and the person most responsible for the move by some Catholic peace activists from symbolic actions to clandestine draft board raids.

Grady stood out as a leader and as a personality. As Father Michael Doyle, a priest from Camden, New Jersey, who knew Grady well, said of him, "John's personality was like a big fish in the pond. He created a lot of circles, a lot of energy, a lot of excitement, a lot of laughter, a lot of celebration." Davidon enjoyed those qualities in Grady, but because security would need to be very strict for Media—more strict than it had been for any of the clandestine actions previously done by Catholic activists—he felt that quieter "fish," ones that would not generate circles of excitement, were essential for the FBI project. For that reason, he decided Grady should not be asked to be part of the Media group. After the group was formed, the others agreed with Davidon's assessment: Grady was a great guy and a person they respected, but not the right person for this project. This turned out to be an even wiser decision than they could have imagined. After the burglary, the FBI immediately targeted Grady as not only a participant in the Media burglary but as the leader of the group.

The people who said yes to Davidon's invitation to consider burglarizing an FBI office were diverse in various ways. They ranged in age from twenty to forty-four. They included three women and five men—a religion professor, a daycare center worker, a graduate student in a health profession, another professor, a social worker, and two people who had dropped out of college to work nearly full-time on building opposition to the war. Though all of them owed their awareness of burglary as an act of resistance to the Catholic peace movement, only one of them was a Catholic. Four were Jews and three were Protestants. They knew one another, but they were not close friends. Bonds developed among them as they tackled Davidon's idea. Four of them were parents of young children. None of them had ever thought of doing anything as extreme as burglarizing an FBI office.

DAVIDON FIRST POSED his question to John and Bonnie Raines. John was a veteran of resistance. He went south nearly every summer during the civil rights movement, beginning in 1961 when he was a Freedom Rider testing racial integration on interstate transportation from St. Louis to Little Rock and through Louisiana. His experience in the South and Bonnie's experience as a teacher in East Harlem had transformed their lives.

By the time Davidon asked them his unusual question, John Raines was a professor of religion at Temple University in Philadelphia, and Bonnie was the director of a daycare center and was studying for a graduate degree in child development at Temple University.

They were stunned by Davidon's question as they met with him one evening at his home. At first, they thought his question was strange and forbidding. So did Davidon's wife, Ann Morrissett. She recalled years later that she thought Davidon was proposing another draft board raid. Then she heard him ask, "What do you think of burglarizing an FBI office?" She remembered being repulsed by the idea. "I couldn't believe my ears." She said, "Leave me out," and quickly exited from the conversation in the living room and went to the kitchen. Morrissett regarded such a burglary with disdain, if not contempt. She thought the draft board raids were largely a macho exercise and that a raid on an FBI office was even more macho. She recalled years later that when she first heard the FBI mentioned, it occurred to her that "if they thought they could get away with burglarizing an FBI office, perhaps they are out of control."

As Davidon explained his rationale to the Raineses that evening, John and Bonnie found themselves agreeing with him. They too had begun to think the FBI might be infiltrating the peace movement. But breaking into an FBI office? They thought it was impractical, could not be done. Besides, it was unlikely that significant records would be found there. Surely, they

Bonnie and John Raines decided shortly after they were married in 1962 that they would risk their freedom in order to oppose injustice.

They made that decision at the same time they created a close-knit family, three children by the time of the burglary.

thought, important and sensitive FBI records, including ones that dealt with suppressing dissent, would be kept only in the FBI's Philadelphia office or at bureau headquarters in Washington.

For a week they discussed Davidon's question with each other every evening after dinner as their three children—Lindsley, seven; Mark, six; and Nathan, one—slept upstairs. They thought about the commitments they had made to each other and to their ideals, and about their love for and commitment to their children. With deep anguish, they questioned how much they were willing to let their family's future be threatened. Resistance, along with love, had been at the heart of their relationship from the beginning. Finally, they both agreed with Davidon's conviction that a crisis existed if dissent was being killed. They decided they were willing to join him in searching for evidence of whether that was true. They called him one evening and told him he could count on them to help solve this problem. They still thought an FBI office probably could not be burglarized.

A short time later, the Raineses met with John Raines's brother Bob and his wife and asked them, in strict confidence, one of the most important and painful questions they had ever asked anyone: Would they raise Lindsley, Mark, and Nathan if the Raineses went to prison? They were immensely grateful for the promise that they would.

KEITH FORSYTH WAS PLEASED to get a call from Davidon in late 1970. He knew it would have something to do with protesting the war. Davidon was always looking for ways to oppose the war, and so was Forsyth. Since moving to Philadelphia a year earlier, he had come to respect Davidon a great deal.

Their phone conversation went like this:

DAVIDON: We're thinking about having a party. Can you come?
FORSYTH: Sure, I love parties. What time?

Given the secrecy, Forsyth thought Davidon must have a very interesting idea to discuss. Little did he know.

When they met at the appointed time, Davidon wasted no time in telling Forsyth the reason for the "party." He laid out his concerns and asked Forsyth, "What do you think of burglarizing an FBI office?"

Forsyth remembers being somewhat nonplussed by Davidon's proposal. "You know, somebody says to you, 'Let's go break into the FBI office.' So you look at them and say, 'Yeah, okay, let's go break in. Then, after we finish that, let's go down to Fort Knox and steal a few million.' At first I thought, 'Who are you kidding?'"

That's what he thought, but he didn't say it. Instead of saying that, Forsyth thinks he probably nervously cleared his throat and stalled for time until he, somewhat falteringly, said something like, "Aren't these places, FBI offices, pretty tough to get access to?"

He wondered how Davidon could think this would be possible. But he knew Davidon didn't use dope and wasn't careless. Forsyth was even more surprised when Davidon told him he had already checked out an FBI office, the one in Media, and he thought it looked like it might be possible to break into it. Davidon also said he had first checked out the large FBI office in downtown Philadelphia and decided it definitely would not be possible to break into. Too tall, too secure. At that point, Forsyth realized, "This guy is serious."

Forsyth thought it would be impossible to burglarize an FBI office. He told Davidon he wanted to check out the office himself. After getting more proper—read: less hippie—clothes at a local thrift shop, he walked by the Media FBI office. He couldn't believe it. There was a simple lock on the door. It looked like security might be minimal. He remembers thinking, "'Man, these guys have lost their minds.' The only thing you could think was that they didn't think at all about security. They must have thought it

Keith Forsyth was a part-time cabdriver when Davidon asked him to consider participating in the Media break-in. He had dropped out of college to devote more time to stopping the war.

was just too crazy, that no one would ever break into an FBI office, so they didn't have to worry about it."

As he left the FBI office that day, he thought maybe Davidon was right. Maybe that office could be burglarized. Still, despite what appeared to be very weak security at the Media FBI office, Forsyth had lots of doubts. He recognized such a burglary would require a lot of meticulous testing and planning. Finally, he concluded that the potential value of what the burglary might accomplish was substantial. "I felt as though my enemy had expanded. It was no longer just the military machine that was waging a war in Vietnam. It was the United States government . . . and what it was doing, not just in Vietnam, but also to its own citizens. I wanted people to know that."

He decided the burglary might well be worth the risk. He called Davidon and—unaware, as all the other burglars were, that he was talking to him on a phone that was being tapped by the FBI—he told Davidon he could count on him to participate. While preparing for a draft board raid, Forsyth had enrolled in a lock-picking course. Now he thought those skills might be useful again.

LIKE FORSYTH, Bob Williamson, a state social worker, had dropped out of college to work against the war. Like many other young people in the antiwar movement, he had put his education and career goals on hold to focus, like a soldier, on what had become his self-imposed patriotic duty.

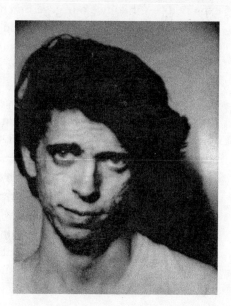

Bob Williamson was a social worker for the state of Pennsylvania. Like Forsyth, he had dropped out of college to spend more time as an antiwar activist.

He found it easy to answer Davidon immediately. He didn't need time to consider it. "I think it's a great idea," he remembers telling him. It simply seemed like an important job that needed to be done.

WHEN DAVIDON ASKED Susan Smith to meet to discuss an idea, she expected a challenge. Less than a year earlier, he had introduced her to the concept of raiding draft boards, something she had never imagined doing. By late 1970, she realized that if she wanted to engage in resistance against the war, Davidon was one of the best people to know. She was grateful for his leadership, but she did not expect it to lead to the question he posed to her now: "What do you think of burglarizing an FBI office?"

Smith eventually said yes to Davidon's question, but she did so with considerable reluctance and fear. She didn't like this sort of thing. It went against the core of her philosophy about political life. Engaging in clandestine acts, not taking public responsibility for them, was in opposition to her deepest ethical sense.

But as she thought about Davidon's question, she too regarded the official suppression of dissent as so important that she decided it was worth risking her freedom to search for the truth about such suppression. She had grown increasingly concerned about the destructive accusations that people were mentally ill if they expressed concern that the FBI was spying inside the peace movement. She thought the assumption that some people blithely expressed—"Of course our government would not do that"—was dangerous and should be challenged with evidence. Like Davidon, she thought this problem should not be ignored or left to fester.

She told Davidon she would participate.

RON DURST WAS a graduate student at the time, preparing for a career in a health profession. Recently divorced, he was willing to take risks he would not have been willing to shoulder just a couple years earlier.

Durst's first reaction to Davidon's question was "Brilliant idea." He respected Davidon as leader and as friend. He still marvels at the simplicity of the idea: get files that document what the FBI is doing, give those files to the public. Only an impressive mind, braced with great courage, could envision carrying out that obvious but frightening and challenging plan to get evidence. Durst thought the idea should be tested as soon as possible. He told Davidon he wanted to be part of the group.

Smith and Durst agreed to be interviewed for this book but not to be named. They and Janet Fessenden, the only member of the group who has not been found, will be referred to by fictitious names. The other five burglars have agreed to be identified.

DAVIDON FINISHED his recruitment shortly before the December holidays. He rarely shows pride, but he did years later when he thought about the people who had said yes to his invitation. He smiled as he remembered their good qualities. From the beginning, he was sure he had assembled a fine team. Together they deepened their skills as amateur burglars and after research decided the break-in should be attempted.

They were in many ways ordinary but at the same time extraordinary. They were part of that group of acutely aware people who during the Vietnam War took to heart and mind their belief that war was the most powerful act their government carried out on behalf of the public using citizens' money and lives. Therefore, they thought they had a responsibility to study and understand the war and to engage with fellow citizens and government officials regarding this monumentally important thing, war. In recent years, after many years of participating in rallies, demonstrations, and letter writing, they had engaged in acts of resistance, not with enthusiasm, but because to them doing so was a necessity in the face of government officials' continued refusal to consider arguments that the war was an unjust one and should stop.

The war was on their minds daily. They did not know how to be indifferent. They had a keen sense of empathy that led them to identify with the agony of American troops and the agony of the Vietnamese people. The numbers alone were enough to propel such people to think, in frustration, "How long can this go on? What else can we do?" For nearly a decade, Americans woke up hearing daily news reports about "yesterday in Vietnam," followed by the number of American troops, the number of South Vietnamese, and the number of North Vietnamese and Viet Cong who had been killed. This regular roll call of the dead was an ongoing marker of the dimensions of the war and, in the minds of many activists, a depressing reminder of their failure to stop it.

The downward spiral toward hopelessness in 1970 that Davidon wanted to stem was a reflection, in part, of those growing numbers. In some months, more than five hundred American soldiers were killed. In the end, the totals were: 58,152 Americans killed; 2 million Vietnamese civilians and 1.1 million Vietnamese military killed. For Americans, the losses were enormous. For the Vietnamese, they were simply staggering. Vietnam lost 12 to 13 percent of its population in the war. To put that loss in perspective, if the United States had lost the same portion of its 1970 population, 28 million people would have died—a number that would have represented the killing of every man, woman, and child who lived in California, Arizona, and Michigan at the time.

Other statistics reflect the amount of dissent that took place. Between 1965 and 1970, more than 170,000 young men were officially recognized as conscientious objectors who refused to fight for religious or moral reasons. Later in the war, others refused to serve because of their opposition to this particular war and sought recognition as selective conscientious objectors, a category of refusal to serve that was recognized as valid late in the war by the U.S. Supreme Court. Formal charges were brought against 209,517 young men for violating draft laws. An additional 360,000 were investigated but not charged. Opposition to the war among active-duty troops was unprecedented, but it was not widely reported. Americans were aware of veterans who opposed the war, such as Secretary of State John Kerry of Massachusetts, who with others formed Vietnam Veterans Against the War. But few Americans were aware that the antiwar movement was active in barracks, on aircraft carriers, and on the battlefields of Vietnam. According to Pentagon records, 503,926 troops deserted between 1966 and 1971. By 1972, there were reports of entire units refusing to go into battle. One group of soldiers, based at Fort Hood in Texas, refused to report for riot-control duty at the 1968 Democratic convention in Chicago. They knew their assignment would be to control antiwar activists. Because they agreed with those activists, they refused the duty and served time in a military prison.

THE MEDIA BURGLARS HOPED that if they were successful their effort would demonstrate that it was possible not to be powerless in the face of massive power. They hoped their aggressive nonviolent resistance would make it clear that to fight injustice it wasn't necessary to match the government's violence with violence. They also hoped their action would help defeat what they believed were the rampant enemies of dissent at that time—fear, apathy, hopelessness, and now the FBI.

They found the courage needed for this high-risk venture from diverse sources. Their consciences had been set on fire—by the Holocaust in Europe, by racial injustice in America, by the use of atomic bombs against

Japan in 1945, and, for all of them, especially the youngest members of the group, by the Vietnam War. They were determined—as was German theologian Dietrich Bonhoeffer, who heroically resisted the Nazis during the Holocaust, was—not to be silent, not to be passive. They rejected silence in the face of injustice. They regarded silence as collaboration with injustice.

They realized people would be shocked if they knew what they were about to do. Though the country was born as an act of resistance, many Americans had long ago become timid citizens, ready to accept whatever government officials told them, especially about war. Until the war in Vietnam, few Americans had raised questions about an American war, let alone engaged in acts of resistance against one. In recent years, though, more and more people had raised questions about the war in Vietnam. Consequently, as the burglars prepared to test the possibility of breaking into the FBI office in Media, resistance was not the totally strange and forbidding concept it had been just fifteen years earlier.

Resistance had not been embraced by the masses, but it had been seeping into the American conscience during the last decade. Courage had been made visible repeatedly by civil rights activists in the South. They had set examples. After hundreds of lynchings, and after being excluded from equality for nearly a century after the Civil War, more and more African Americans found the courage to say no to the suppression of their rights. In the late 1950s and early 1960s, as they stepped forward to claim their right to vote and other basic rights they had been guaranteed but denied, they faced arrest, imprisonment, even death. As they did so, Americans saw a new vision of courage on the evening news.

The faces of courage were no longer only faces from the past etched in history books. Courage was not just brave soldiers going ashore at Normandy. It was not just Harriet Tubman leading hundreds of slaves in the dark of night, helping them flee from slavery in the South to freedom in the North as she passed through the Underground Railroad station in the town the burglars soon would make famous again—Media, Pennsylvania. Courage was not just Mahatma Gandhi fasting as he led a massive movement of people in India seeking independence from the British.

Courage, as people had often seen since 1955 on the evening news on the televisions in their living rooms, was alive today. Courage was Rosa Parks refusing to go to the back of the bus. It was hundreds of black students quietly refusing to obey orders to leave segregated lunch counters in Nashville. It was black children walking through club-wielding mobs of spitting, screaming, face-scratching white people in Little Rock who didn't want black children to go to school with white children. Courage was Martin Luther King writing a "Letter from Birmingham Jail" urging people to engage in nonviolent civil disobedience against unjust laws, and then insisting, despite scars from being beaten, that "one who breaks an unjust law must do it openly, lovingly." Courage was Michael Schwerner, James Chaney, and Michael Goodman, three young civil rights workers, two of them white and one of them black, who were savagely lynched, murdered, and buried in a dam in Mississippi in the summer of 1964—Freedom Summer it was called, but it was not freedom for them.

Because courage had become more visible, more people found it. If it hadn't, thousands of young men probably would not have refused to serve in the Vietnam War. If courage had not become more visible, the Berrigan brothers and others in the Catholic peace movement probably never would have raided draft boards. If courage had not become more visible, Davidon and the other burglars probably never would have even thought of doing what they were about to do in Media.

Still, even in the context of the courage that had become visible in that era, an act of resistance as extreme as burglarizing an FBI office was something very few people would have been willing to do. Resistance this extreme was so rare that it seemed like something only fools or saints would attempt. However laudable the goals might have been, normal people did not train themselves to become amateur burglars in order to break into an FBI office. But these people, who were neither saints nor fools, agreed to do just that.

In the end, their decision to engage in this extraordinary act of resistance came down—as such decisions had for historic leaders of nonviolent resistance, including Gandhi and King—to this:

Fully aware that what they planned to do could, whether or not they achieved their goal, take away their freedom, perhaps even endanger their lives, they decided that their desire to stop injustice—the destruction of dissent by the FBI—was more important to them than their desire to lead a normal, uninterrupted life.

They moved forward.

4

The Burglars in the Attic

FROM THE BEGINNING, the Media burglars worked in total secrecy. "We pulled the curtains around us," Bonnie Raines recalls. As they closed the curtains, they recognized that the break-in they were about to plan might be more dangerous than anything any of them, or anybody they knew, had ever done. They intended to keep the curtains drawn before, during, and after the burglary.

Closely maintained security was new to all of them. Security had been loose, almost casual, in the draft board break-ins. Unlike the draft board raiders, the Media burglars would be silent and the group would be small. At their first meeting as a group in late December 1970, when they chose their name—the Citizens' Commission to Investigate the FBI—they all agreed that no one else would be invited to be part of the group. It would be only as large as necessary to accomplish their goals: get inside the Media FBI office, take as many files as possible, review the files, and, assuming they contained information the public needed, distribute them to the public.

The strict secrecy rules were not easy to maintain, especially about something they knew their friends in the antiwar movement would find riveting. Secrecy was against their nature. They enjoyed talking with friends about politics and about what they were doing as activists. Suddenly, such conversations had to stop. They realized that given what they planned to raid, an FBI office, they were likely to fail if any information about their plan leaked. If they were going to be arrested, they wanted it to be for something they actually did, not something they planned to do. There was no room for casual talk now.

With those conditions agreed to, the Citizens' Commission to Investigate the FBI started to plan. The first item on their agenda: pick a night for the burglary. In the annals of burglary, this surely was the only time a group of burglars purposely chose the night of a boxing match for their break-in.

They had to establish the day and time of the burglary at the outset so they could case the area during that time. As they discussed possible dates, it did not seem any one night would be any better or any worse than any other. But one of the burglars—none of them remembers who it was—made the case for scheduling the burglary on the night of the Muhammad Ali–Joe Frazier fight, March 8. For the first time, two undefeated heavyweight champions were going to compete against each other for the title. Ali would return to the ring that night for the first time since he was convicted in 1967 for refusing to be inducted into the U.S. Army. Frazier, a Philadelphia fighter who supported the war, had won the heavyweight title while Ali was kept out of the ring.

The burglars were not boxing fans, but they became fans of this match. All of them eventually grasped the idea that the match was going to be so special that it was possible nearly every sports-loving person in the country—maybe, they dared to think, even the people who lived in the apartments on the two floors above the FBI office—would be riveted to their televisions and radios that night.

Their discussion of which night to break in became very exciting. The buzz of a neighborhood full of televisions and radios tuned to the fight might provide white noise sufficient to muffle the noise of footsteps and other burglary-in-progress sounds. People might be totally absorbed and not easily distracted by random noise. And if there was any chance that a Media FBI agent would be inspired to work overtime at night—during casing, not once did the burglars observe an FBI agent working at the office after 5 p.m.—the night of the Ali-Frazier fight surely would be the least likely one for such inspiration to strike.

The possibility that noise generated by the fight could serve as a distraction struck the burglars as a great stroke of luck. Even the local police, they thought, might be so glued to their televisions and radios that evening that they would make few, if any, street patrols. That did it. They chose the night of the Ali-Frazier fight—Monday, March 8, 1971.

Actually, the fight was projected to be a much bigger phenomenon than the burglars realized. During his exile, Ali had become a hero throughout the world because he placed his opposition to the war above his boxing career, because he was brash and bold in his defense of the rights of black people not only in the United States but also in the emerging independent countries of Africa. Even Nelson Mandela, the great South African anti-apartheid leader, regarded Ali as a hero. In the middle of his long imprisonment on Robben Island in South Africa, Mandela later said, when Ali became a conscientious objector, he embraced Ali and saw him as a symbol of hope and courage. On a shelf behind Mandela's desk in his home are framed photographs of two Americans—Barack Obama and Muhammad Ali.

In December 1970, when the prohibition was lifted on Ali boxing, he immediately agreed to fight Frazier. Ali had defended the world heavyweight title nine times before he was shut out of the ring. Because he had not lost the title in a match, he and his supporters insisted he still held it. Frazier won the title in February 1970, but he knew he would not really be regarded as the heavyweight champion until he beat Ali. Frazier desperately wanted to fight Ali. He even enlisted President Richard Nixon in the effort, meeting with the president at the White House to get his assistance in helping Ali return to the ring. Frazier later described his conversation with Nixon: "I went down to DC to help Ali get his license back. President Nixon invited me up for tea: 'Joe, if I do that, can you take him?' I said, 'You dust him off, I'll beat him up.' Nixon kept his word. So did I."

It was the most anticipated heavyweight title fight since Joe Louis defeated Max Schmeling in their 1938 fight at Yankee Stadium when the world was on the brink of World War II. Schmeling was not a Nazi, but Hitler used his previous victory over Louis to promote the Nazi belief in Aryan superiority. The win by Louis against Schmeling in 1938 in that perilous time was considered a great triumph by Americans, especially African Americans.

Now another war hovered over the Ali-Frazier fight and also over the Media burglary. The strong cultural and political forces spawned by stances for and against the Vietnam War fueled both the burglary and the fight. Without the war, and the burglars' fear that the government was suppressing dissent against it, they would not have been planning to break into an FBI office. Without the Vietnam War, Ali and Frazier would not have faced each other in 1971 under such extraordinary conditions. Ali, the most famous conscientious objector to the Vietnam War, was embraced internationally by people who opposed the war. Frazier, who supported the war, was embraced by people who supported it, including the president. Ali was reviled by politicians throughout the country—first for choosing to be a Muslim and then for refusing to serve in Vietnam. Frazier, the son of a

South Carolina sharecropper who had fought his way to the championship, increasingly had become a symbol of conservative working-class Americans.

Anticipation for the fight intensified as Ali, in interview after interview in early 1971, promised he would make a comeback the night of the fight. "On that night," he playfully predicted, "they'll be waiting everywhere— England, France, Italy. Egypt and Israel will declare a forty-five minute truce. Saudi Arabia, Iraq, Iran; even Red China and Formosa. Not since time began has there been a night like this. People will be singing and dancing in the aisles. And when it's all over, Muhammad Ali will take his rightful place as champion of the world."

Ali's playful exaggerations aside, he was at that time, according to journalist and book editor Peter Osnos, "arguably the most charismatic popular figure around the world." In 2002, journalist Jack Newfield wrote that Ali achieved the distinction of being "the most famous face on the planet, and probably the most loved person, if a democratic election were held that included Africa, the Islamic world, America and Vietnam."

THE BURGLARS' DEFAULT HEADQUARTERS was the Raineses' home, a large gray stone house surrounded by tall, wide trees on Walnut Lane in the racially integrated Germantown neighborhood of northwest Philadelphia. Inside and outside, it looked solidly normal, old-fashioned, welcoming, and innocent. It did not look like a place where people perfected burglary skills and plans. Evenings often started with dinner at the Raineses' house. Bonnie Raines seemed to be able to expand spaghetti magically to serve everyone as many helpings as they wanted. The dinners were pleasant occasions, especially for the Raineses' three children. As far as the children were concerned, these new friends of their parents were part of their family during the three months burglary preparations were under way. They enjoyed the silly games and stories some of the burglars invented for them during those dinners. They especially enjoyed playing with Bob Williamson, who was warm and friendly with them. Most evenings, as dinner ended, a babysitter would arrive, and John and Bonnie and the other burglars would say goodbye to the children, drive to Media, usually two people per car, with each twosome armed with specific casing assignments for the evening.

After a few hours of casing, the burglars usually returned to the Raineses' house and went upstairs to the attic on the third floor, their well-concealed training ground. As they climbed the stairs, they passed the three Raines children asleep in their bedrooms. The children were a vivid reminder of the serious implications to be faced if the burglary failed.

The Media burglars had no idea, of course, that FBI agents conducted a lot of burglaries and that they too trained to be burglars in an attic. Classes for agents in how to break into homes and offices and conduct what the director called "black bag" jobs were taught regularly in the attic of the building where bureau headquarters were then located, in the Department of Justice Building.

Anyone visiting the Raineses' comfortable first-floor living room, as two FBI agents did several weeks after the burglary, would have found it difficult to imagine what took place in that attic late most evenings during that period. The conspirators tacked notes on the wall about observations made during casing. A large map of Media was placed on one wall. So were to-do lists. The attic was the only place where any of the burglars kept tangible information about their plans. Eventually, a diagram of the inside of the FBI office was added to a wall. They studied it very carefully, plotting how to move from room to room, file cabinet to file cabinet.

The Raineses' attic also was a place where some of the burglars crashed for the night when they worked very late, as they often did. John and Bonnie Raines dragged a few mattresses up to the attic, plus an old sofa and a couple of chairs, all bought at the secondhand furniture store a few blocks away on Germantown Avenue.

SHORTLY AFTER intensive planning started, the group was briefly interrupted by a startling development. On January 12, the leader of the group, Davidon, was named an unindicted coconspirator in an indictment that resurrected the accusations J. Edgar Hoover had made in November that the Berrigan brothers, Philip and Daniel, and others were plotting to kidnap a high national official and blow up tunnels under federal buildings in Washington. Despite the fact that FBI investigators and Department of Justice prosecutors had decided not to pursue the case, the department reopened it in December after Hoover's testimony and hastily presented it to a grand jury in Harrisburg, Pennsylvania. Six people, including Philip Berrigan, were charged as conspirators, and six other people, including Daniel Berrigan and Davidon, were named as unindicted coconspirators. The same officials who had considered the case baseless in the fall now, apparently in order to save Hoover's face, had produced an indictment in which the defendants, if convicted of the kidnap conspiracy charge, could be sentenced to life in prison. At the time of the indictment, FBI officials were told by prosecutors—as revealed in the official files of the Media burglary—that Davidon might be indicted in the case at a later date, a possibility that he of course did not know.

Davidon's circumstances made the burglars' situation somewhat surreal at this very early stage of the planning for Media. As they plotted in deep secrecy to burglarize an FBI office, the name of the leader of the group was reported prominently in national news stories for his alleged involvement in one of the most controversial criminal cases brought against antiwar activists during the Vietnam War.

The Department of Justice went out of its way to draw attention to the indictment. Not that it needed to. Any indictment of priests, nuns, and others who were well known for being nonviolent antiwar activists and were being charged with conspiracy to commit violent crimes, kidnapping and bombing, was guaranteed to attract significant attention, with or without a push from the Department of Justice. Nevertheless, the day the indictment was announced, Robert L. Stevenson, on the staff of the department's public information office, called reporters who covered the FBI and told them there would be a press conference very soon to announce a significant development. If measured "on a news scale of one to ten"—with ten the most sensational news—this story "would be twelve," he told them. Stevenson was known to reporters for calmness, so they took his sensational alert very seriously. The atmosphere at the press room was so hyperactive as reporters waited for the press conference to begin that they agreed among themselves that only two announcements would cause that much excitement at the department: the arrest of leading Black Panthers or the retirement of Hoover, then seventy-six, as director.

The indictment was a leading news story that evening and the next morning throughout the country and also abroad. It was reframed and reported again and again over the next few weeks. The rumor quickly spread that the high official the group allegedly was considering kidnapping was Henry Kissinger, then President Nixon's national security adviser, one of the most prominent and powerful people in the Nixon administration and a key architect of Vietnam War policy.

Davidon flew home from Puerto Rico the day after the indictment was announced. When the news broke, he was on the island of Culebra, with other pacifists, protesting the U.S. Navy's use of that inhabited island for bombing practice. He left as quickly as possible because he was afraid the presence of someone just named in a controversial antiwar case might taint the efforts of local residents to convince the Navy to stop bombing their island. Immediately upon his arrival in Philadelphia, he met with reporters and, in his typical way, was direct and forthright about a conversation that he assumed was the basis for the charges in the indictment. He said he had participated in that conversation the previous August at the Connecticut home of the in-laws of one of the now indicted parties, Pakistani scholar Eqbal Ahmad.

The conversation, Davidon told reporters, occurred at a time of great hopelessness in the peace movement, including for the few activists from the Catholic peace movement who had gathered there that Sunday afternoon for dinner. One of them suggested they should brainstorm about stronger nonviolent ways to protest the war. Several ideas, he said, were expressed in a conversation that lasted less than thirty minutes. Davidon recalled that someone suggested a small number of people could make a citizens' arrest of an official closely associated with decisions about the conduct of the war, someone like Henry Kissinger. It was suggested he could be taken to a meeting of antiwar intellectuals who would confront him with his "war crimes" and then release him unharmed. Two of the women present, he said, immediately pronounced the idea preposterous. Even Ahmad, who had originally spun the possibility, rejected it a few minutes after he suggested it. All of them readily agreed that the possibility of violence accidentally occurring during such an action was too great. The idea was rejected by all, Davidon said, nearly as quickly as it was suggested.

That Davidon was named in the indictment did not seem to make the burglars even pause. Their understated response to Davidon's situation was the first of several instances in which they faced circumstances that could have been regarded as serious impediments to moving ahead. Now, as later, they acknowledged the situation but were neither consumed nor deterred by it. Neither Davidon nor other members of the group seemed to be very concerned that the leader of the group was an unindicted coconspirator who should be assumed to be under close surveillance by their target, the FBI.

Perhaps it was fitting that at this stage of their planning Davidon taught the burglars telephone techniques to use while planning the burglary. His basic advice was simple: be natural but careful. He remembers that during the early days of planning one of the burglars said something like this to him during a phone conversation: "I really shouldn't tell you this on the phone . . ." As the conversation continued, Davidon remembers searching for his most relaxed voice and then casually saying, "Look, tell me anything you want to on the phone." At the next meeting of the group, he turned the incident into a lesson and strongly advised them not to show any suspicious behavior on the phone, never to reveal important information, and never to sound fearful or conspiratorial. "Sound perfectly normal" was his mantra for phone manners for burglars. They used phones as little as possible to communicate with one another about important matters during the weeks they were planning the burglary. They usually made their plans for next steps at meetings. Inevitably, though, they had to be in touch with one another by phone about changes in plans.

Davidon's approach to talking on the phone while planning a burglary was similar to his approach to all other aspects of the burglary: "I was careful in ways that were inconspicuous." For instance, "I didn't know I was being tapped, but I was suspicious about it and acted accordingly and advised others to do the same. . . . We were very careful." When years later he requested and received files the FBI had kept on him, he learned what he had suspected—that during the months when the Media burglary was being planned he "had *only* tapped phone conversations."

Despite the constant surveillance Davidon was under before and during that time, he was not arrested in connection with any of the draft board raids in which he had participated. He, his wife, Ann, and numerous AWOL soldiers had talked on the Davidons' tapped home phone while making clandestine arrangements for these soldiers to stay with them while they considered their next steps as conscientious objectors. All of those conversations were recorded and transcribed, word by word, by the FBI, including conversations of Media burglars about meetings and other matters related to the burglary. Apparently the meaning of the carefully transcribed conversations had eluded the FBI. During that time, Davidon used his phone to arrange to rent a car and a motel room for the night of the burglary. At least three of the burglars were recorded talking with Davidon and his wife. Even the conversations of his young daughters, Sarah, then age five, and Ruth, age seven, with their little friends were transcribed. Davidon received the lengthy transcripts years later in response to his Freedom of Information Act request.

WITH THE DATE of the burglary set, the burglars focused in early January on developing a comprehensive plan for casing. They approached casing with what they considered simple common sense. They were not frequent readers of mystery novels, with clever burglars' tricks stored in their memories. But they were smart. For them, the burglary was a problem-solving exercise. They relied primarily on simple logic: They figured out what they needed to do to accomplish their goal. There were, of course, no manuals on the thinking person's approach to successful burglary. This was a make-it-up-as-you-go project.

The overall strategy of casing was to become thoroughly knowledgeable about what normally happened near and inside the place to be burglarized. Casing was deadly dull, tedious and boring, the burglars all agree. But it was the most important part of preparing for the burglary. Discoveries made while casing revealed actions the burglars should take and actions they should avoid. From the outset, they realized discoveries made then would determine whether the burglary would take place.

The burglars started with the premise that they could not protect themselves against all irregularities—say, the rare instance when a Media FBI agent returned to the office to work after standard working hours—but they should be able to case so well that they could protect themselves against predictable events. For example, they should not plan to leave the FBI office, suitcases in hand, around the time when they knew from observation that a particular resident of the building usually arrived home after working an evening shift. The irregularities were numerous and troubling. Because of the open hallway and stairwell inside the building, for example, the burglars could not protect themselves against being seen by residents who lived in one of the apartments on the two floors above the FBI office. One of the residents might at any time leave their apartment in the middle of the burglary to go out to buy a quart of milk. They tried to be thorough, leaving as little as possible to chance, but they knew surprises could happen. Later that realization became more than an intellectual exercise.

Because the burglary was scheduled for a Monday evening, they cased the neighborhood on weekday evenings, between 7 and 11 p.m., from mid-January through the week before the burglary. The most difficult aspect of casing was sitting in cars for several hours on evenings during the coldest months of the year. The burglars watched the blocks near the building from inside parked cars and Williamson's van for three to four hours evening after evening. They prepared a to-do list of what they needed to monitor:

- The movement of vehicles on the two streets, Front Street and Veterans Square, that intersected at the corner where County Court Apartments, the building that housed the FBI office, was located;
- How parking patterns changed on those two streets and other nearby streets in the course of an evening;

- The movements of residents in and out of the building on the two floors above the FBI's second-story office;
- The movements of the building manager who lived directly below the FBI office;
- The movements of the people who worked in the offices in the basement and on the first and second floors of the building, including in the draft board office on the second floor;
- The movements of people who lived in nearby houses and apartment buildings;
- The schedules and routes of local police who patrolled the neighborhood;
- The lighting patterns in the FBI office and other nearby offices, apartment buildings, and houses;
- The schedules and routes of trains, buses, and taxicabs that served the area and how they affected the arrival and departure of people in the area;
- The closing times of nearby bars and restaurants;
- The movements of people who worked at night across the street from the FBI office at the county courthouse, especially the schedule and movements of the courthouse guards.

This information was vitally important. Knowledge about traffic patterns, for instance, determined where Forsyth would park when he arrived first to pick the lock. It also helped determine where and when the inside crew—the people who would enter the office and remove the files—should be dropped off and the routes the getaway car drivers should take after they picked up the inside crew.

Each burglar developed a practical approach to the project. Susan Smith had once built a cabin in the mountains by teaching herself basic carpentry skills. That same approach—anybody could learn to do this—helped her develop skills as a burglar. She was proud of her street casing skills. She often cased very late, gathering information that would be useful if the burglars needed to enter the building late, something they hoped they would not have to do. She had a casing problem no one else had—a car so beautiful it was likely to be remembered later. Because it was important not to be noticed, she had to leave her beautiful car at home. She borrowed a colleague's sedate Volvo that blended in nicely late at night on the quiet Media streets. The streets of Media, especially near the courthouse and the building where the FBI office was located, came alive during the day, with people continuously entering and leaving those buildings. After school, neighbor-hood children rode bikes in the streets. At night, by contrast, the streets were nearly dead. Any unusual-looking person or vehicle, such as Smith's flashy car, might have been conspicuous in that quiet environment.

Williamson, like Smith, was proud of his casing skills. He also likes to think that his ability to tell very long shaggy-dog stories was helpful as ten-sion relief during casing and while raiding draft board offices, but some of his fellow burglars disagree with him on that point. Casing was his real area of expertise, they say, rolling their eyes at the memory of his jokes. During one draft board raid, fellow burglars involuntarily risked arrest while hid-ing with Williamson in a closet, so loud were their groans when he finally finished one of his yarns. They affectionately advised him to stick with cas-ing and drop the jokes. The night of this burglary he expected to be totally preoccupied.

The burglars assumed that sitting for hours in parked cars in that quiet residential neighborhood might arouse suspicion. They decided that casing as male-female couples made them less suspicious. Couple cover stories were prepared in case someone asked them why they were lingering in a car on cold winter evenings. If a police car approached, the couple embraced and gave the impression they had been necking. In fact, those weeks before the burglary may be the only time when Media's Veterans Square, the street in front of the building where the FBI was located, might have appeared to the casual observer to be a lovers' lane. Another ruse called for a couple to start arguing if a police officer approached. They would tell him they were having a spat. In still another ruse, a couple would puzzle with the officer over the failure of their car to start. They would then say they were about to search for a pay phone so they could call for a tow truck.

Williamson remembers his adrenaline pumping one evening when someone parked a car next to his van and sat beside him and his companion for a few minutes. "We became very quiet and still, and afraid." On another occasion, "a police car drove down the street and shined a spotlight against the buildings on our side of the street." Calmness returned as the officer drove away. The evening continued, as usual, with what burglars hope for: "nothing remarkable happening."

Ultimately, the burglary schedule was shaped around the predictable uneventful hours the team had mapped after two months of observation. As planned, they became very familiar with the neighborhood. They learned the habits of people and the changing patterns of building lights and traffic so well that they even knew when dog owners in the neighborhood walked

their dogs, and when one resident of the FBI building often left and returned
from having a drink at a bar a block away on West State Street. One of the
most important things they learned from casing was the schedule of police
patrols. That information was essential to the timing of each phase of the
burglary. They hoped the police would be preoccupied with watching the
Ali-Frazier fight that night, but they were not going to take any chances.
They watched the police very carefully, and they hoped the police were not
watching them.

DURING AN EARLY PLANNING SESSION in the attic, one of the
burglars suggested they should use a crowbar to break into the office. Others agreed, but Forsyth said no. That would be much too noisy and take
much too long. Instead, he told them, he would learn to pick the lock. They
thought that was funny, but he was serious.

Earlier he had gone to a public library and discovered there were several
locksmith associations. He joined one of them. That made him eligible to
buy books from the Locksmith Library. As with his research on the Vietnam War two years earlier, he now thoroughly researched locksmithing. He
bought several books. "They were like training books you see advertised
on the back of matchbook covers—'How to be a locksmith in 10 easy lessons.' That kind of stuff. I got it all from the Locksmith Library." He took
a correspondence course and soon was on his way to becoming the group's
in-house locksmith.

He remembered what the lock on the FBI office main entrance looked
like when he walked by it after Davidon first told him about his interest in
burglarizing it. He recalls being amazed when he saw the lock on the door.
"That's really bizarre," he thought. He knew there were several types of
high-security locks available. The one on the FBI office door was not one of
those. It was a simple five-tumbler lock, easy to pick. Easy, that is, if you are
a bonded locksmith and therefore eligible to buy the tools needed to pick
locks. "I said, 'Screw that.'" Instead, he made his own tools so he would
leave no traceable evidence. There would be no receipts traceable to a store
that sold lock-picking tools, and there would be no salesperson to tell an FBI
agent that, yes, a tall skinny guy came in one day and bought lock-picking
tools.

With a precise image of the lock on the FBI door in mind, he went to a
hardware store and bought two locks that looked just like it—one to take

apart so he could figure out how to make picking tools to open it, and the other to pick again and again as he perfected his picking skills. Perhaps there were signs then of Forsyth's future as an engineer. He took the lock apart, studied how it was constructed, studied the diagrams and instructions in the books from the Locksmith Library, and figured out how to build the lock-picking tools he needed. Then he went to a machine supplies store and bought the materials he needed to make the tools. To his delight, they worked.

The burglars installed new sheetrock walls in the Raineses' attic and hung a door on one wall so Forsyth could install and practice picking a lock he was sure was exactly like the one on the FBI entrance. Night after night up there in the attic, while the other burglars discussed discoveries made during casing and added details to the map of Media and the to-do lists, Forsyth contributed to those conversations occasionally, but most of the time he focused on improving his timing. He stood in front of the door and picked the lock—again and again and again and again. Like a runner, he was improving his speed. His dedication was impressive. It was as though he were preparing for the lock-picking Olympics. "It's just like surgery or carpentry or any other manual skill," he said years later. "It's practice and touch. First time you try it, it takes ten minutes, next time five, next time three. Finally, you get it down to thirty seconds."

Given the interruptions he had to assume might happen—such as the possibility that a resident from one of the two floors above the FBI office might walk by him in the open hallway at any time while he was picking the lock on the FBI office door—he needed to be able to pick that lock as fast as possible the night of the burglary. He kept practicing. He was proud when he got it down to thirty seconds. He thought it would be a piece of cake that night. A few days before the burglary, he walked by the FBI office a second time so he could glance quickly and carefully again at the lock on the main entrance. He remembers feeling assured as he left the building.

The burglars decided that on the night of the burglary they would wear "proper" clothing and carry suitcases instead of the large canvas mail bags that had been used during most of the draft board raids. Unlike the draft board raiders, these burglars would not wear jeans and sweats. They would dress up for the occasion. They did that because of the odd circumstance of burglarizing an office upstairs in a residential building. They thought they needed to look like they might be residents of the building, or friends of a resident, returning from or leaving for a trip, carrying large suitcases. Their classy clothes, they hoped, would make their presence not seem too strange if, as they walked out of the FBI office with suitcases, they happened all of a sudden to come upon, say, Mrs. Smith leaving her apartment to take her garbage to the garbage can behind the building.

After casing the immediate area, they homed in on the building where the FBI office was located. On brief casing visits inside the building during workdays, the burglars had learned there was only one way they could enter and leave the building: the front door, which was always unlocked and always well lit, inside and outside, at night. That was bad news. Late afternoon and evening observation of light patterns revealed good news: It was extremely rare for anyone to work after five o'clock in any of the commercial or government offices in the building.

One enormous challenge remained. About two weeks before the burglary, the burglars prepared for the most important casing they would do: firsthand inspection inside the FBI office. So far they had felt encouraged, but this casing could lead to discoveries that would force them to abandon the burglary.

Casing inside an FBI office was much more difficult than casing inside a draft board office. Draft board offices were open to the public. It was easy to walk in and look around, because people routinely went to them to ask questions about the draft and about their own records. Those offices were busy places. By contrast, not many people visited FBI offices, especially a small one like the Media office. The burglars had to assume that anyone visiting any office in the building might be noticed by the people in the other offices, especially the ones on the same floor. But they could not learn what they needed to know about the office from just dropping in briefly or by observing the office from outside the entrance, as Davidon, Smith, and Forsyth had done. Someone would have to go inside and get answers to very important questions:

Were the cabinets and desks locked? Was there carpeting? What was immediately inside the other door that opened into the office from the outside hall but always was closed when they observed it? And the biggest question: Was there an alarm system in the office?

The burglars agreed that Bonnie Raines would be the best person for this important job. She was twenty-nine, but with her long dark hair and bright smile, she easily looked the part of the college coed the other burglars suggested she pose as. Not only did the other burglars think that Bonnie looked very young, but they thought she was the member of the group most capable of looking totally innocent. When she called the office to ask for an

This police artist's sketch of Bonnie Raines is based on Media agents' recall of "the woman" who visited the office and interviewed the agent in charge two weeks before the burglary. *(From FBI's MEDBURG investigation file)*

The Raineses with their children on their way to their annual summer vacation in Glen Lake, Michigan. The family station wagon served as a getaway car the night of the burglary.

appointment, she told Tom Lewis, the agent in charge there, that she was a student at a nearby college who was doing research for a class assignment and wanted to schedule an interview with someone at the Media FBI office about FBI hiring practices. She told him she already had talked with other employers in the Media area and she hoped an FBI agent would be able to give her about half an hour of his time. "He was extremely accommodating," she recalls. He agreed to see her at two o'clock a few days later.

The group enjoyed planning her pending visit to the FBI office—what her appearance should be, what her tone should be, and what she needed to look for. The burglars thought she should seem a little naïve and not supersmart. They spent a lot of time one evening developing questions she would ask.

It was an intimidating assignment, but Bonnie took it on with enthusiasm. She was grateful to be given this important responsibility. In the past, in nearly everything she did she felt she had been supplemental to other people. She felt she had been treated with respect but had not been given much responsibility. The heavier responsibility she carried as part of the Media group gave her confidence that she was, as she put it years later, finally "making progress" in that new life she had started to create nearly a decade earlier in New York when she and John Raines moved there in 1962 right after they were married. In addition to being an earth mother preparing those big spaghetti dinners for the group each evening before they cased Media, she remembers having a feeling of great contentment, a sense that "I was as much a part of that team as everyone else was."

As the burglars prepared Bonnie Raines for her walk-on, as it were, at the FBI office, they carefully considered how she should wear her long black hair. She often wore it in long pigtails that nearly reached her waist, making her look even younger than the college freshman she would pose as. It was decided that for her visit to the FBI office she would wear her hair pulled back in a barrette and tucked under an old wool stocking hat. She was sure she had never concealed her hair that way at any of the antiwar demonstrations, where, the burglars assumed, she and the rest of them had been photographed many times by FBI and other law enforcement officers. She decided to wear her horn-rimmed glasses because she didn't think she had ever worn them to a demonstration. The glasses would provide a good disguise, but they also posed a problem. They improved her distance vision but hampered her near vision while she took notes. Adding to the awkwardness, to avoid leaving fingerprints behind she would wear gloves throughout the time she wrote the notes that she would not be able to see as she wrote them.

All of the burglars thoroughly trained themselves in the habit of not leaving fingerprints behind at any point during planning, during the actual burglary, or when working with files. This was crucial to their success, including Bonnie Raines's casing visit in the office.

Following the group's advice, Bonnie dressed for the interview as a nerdish coed in a skirt, sweater, and long dark heavy winter coat. As planned, she arrived about fifteen minutes early. She apologized for that, telling the man seated at the reception desk right inside the open door that she had come on public transportation and that the bus had arrived earlier than she expected. Actually, John Raines had driven her to Media. She was invited to sit and wait until two o'clock, when Tom Lewis would be available to talk with her. That was just what she wanted. It meant she had time to sit quietly and survey the office slowly and carefully.

As her eyes scanned the rooms, she tried to mentally photograph as much detail as possible. After several minutes, she asked the man she thought was a receptionist, but who was actually one of the agents based at the office, if she could see an employment application form. That request was consistent with her request to interview an agent about hiring practices. The real purpose of her question about forms, though, was to observe whether he would have to unlock the file cabinet to retrieve a form for her. She was pleased that he obliged, and even more pleased that the file cabinet was not locked.

During the fifteen minutes she waited, seated across from an agent the entire time, she glanced around the room, trying to do so intensively while appearing to be casual and unengaged. She noted that in the office where she waited there were two desks, several file cabinets, one very tall cabinet with double doors, and a typical government-issue light khaki-green cabinet. From where she sat, she could see two other rooms in the office. She noticed that there were open venetian blinds on the windows. That meant the burglars would have to use flashlights very cautiously, if at all, during the burglary so no streams of light could be seen between the slats. By the time she left, she felt she would be able to draw a detailed sketch of the office.

When she was invited into the room where Lewis was waiting to talk with her, she had a choice of two chairs. She picked the one that provided the widest view of the room as well as a view through a window. She could see John and Nathan in the family's station wagon parked across the street. She could see that Nathan, small and rambunctious, wasn't very patient about waiting for his mother. Partway through her interview with the agent, she noticed that Nathan had calmed down and he and John were walking leisurely on the courthouse grounds.

As she talked with Lewis, she remembered the burglars' suggestion that she should seem a little naïve. She told him she was writing the paper for a class, but she hoped the local newspaper might publish it. "The guy acted as though he was flattered. I think he wanted to look like a newer breed of FBI agent, and I was able to play into that." She asked him if, in the event that they started hiring women as agents (which they first did in 1972, just two months after Hoover died), if agents' work time could be flexible. He said agents worked nine to five, and there really wasn't much need for flexibility. "There was none of this romantic stuff that these guys are out there working day and night," she recalled.

In response to several questions, she remembers that he repeated that "bureau guidelines" would have to be followed. She wondered at one point if the conversation had gone on too long and if he might be suspicious of her. She quickly dismissed that concern, confident that "he didn't have any antennae out for anything unusual." She took notes throughout the conversation but made sure she established eye contact with him often. If the agent thought she looked a little odd—as she sat there writing with gloved hands—he gave no clue. "He was a nice guy. The kind of guy you might like having as a neighbor." They chitchatted about college sports teams. He asked her where she had grown up. She lied and said she was from Hartford, Connecticut.

The office was very quiet, not a place where there were any signs of urgency or excitement. "I felt like I was in a CPA's office. I remember being struck by that. I felt as though they were drones. It was a rather nice office. It had wall-to-wall carpet." That was a welcome discovery. Carpet would help muffle burglary noises. The desks were made of wood. There was no art on the wall, unless the framed photographs of J. Edgar Hoover and President Nixon hanging in the entry room counted as art. In Lewis's office there was a framed photograph of Hoover standing beside the agent. It had been autographed by Hoover. There also were framed commendations from the director on the wall and photographs of Lewis's family on his desk.

When Bonnie Raines stood to leave, she thanked Lewis and walked toward the room where she had waited. But then she changed course and entered another room, one she had not been in before. An agent apparently thought she was confused and told her she could not leave from that room. She paused, looked around just long enough to take in as much as she could in that third room, and then returned to the first room, apologizing for getting lost and saying she had thought there might be a restroom off that room. No, the agent said, the restrooms were outside the bureau office. He gave her a key to the restroom and pointed to it down the hall. This was important information. The burglars wanted to know if there was an unlocked restroom where they could hide, if necessary, on the night of the burglary. Now that she knew a key was necessary to enter the restroom, she realized that was not going to be possible.

By the time she left, she had been in the office about an hour, longer than she had expected and much, much longer than any of the agents in the office would admit to bureau investigators shortly after the burglary. She thought she had accomplished her mission. Her biggest assignment was to determine if there was an alarm system in the office. She observed that some electrical cords were covered with old cracked paint. She had tracked the cords by eye and concluded they were phone lines and the cords of the old window air conditioners. She was confident she had traced and figured out the function of every cord. By the process of elimination, she concluded there was no alarm system. She knew the group would be excited to hear that.

As she left after returning the restroom key, the last thing she did was check again the lock on the front door, as Forsyth had prepared her to. She thought his description was correct: one simple lock that could be picked easily.

Almost as important as establishing that there was no alarm system was Bonnie's next discovery that the second door that opened from the FBI office to the external hall was blocked by a large cabinet. The inside crew, she told the burglars that night, would have to enter through the door she had entered—the main entrance, the door that opened into the reception room. She was insistent that the second external door, which she observed from the room she pretended to wander into to find a restroom, should not be broken into the night of the burglary. She remembers feeling relief that she had made that discovery. She assumed—correctly, it turned out—that this tall cabinet that barricaded that door was filled, like all the other cabinets in the office, with paper and therefore was very heavy. If Forsyth broke in through that door and in the process of pushing it open toppled the tall, heavy cabinet, the thud it would make as it hit the floor would be so loud that it could not be concealed, even if the broadcast of the Ali-Frazier fight was turned to the highest volume in every apartment in the building.

To her surprise, she felt at ease in the FBI office. Except for a few moments of doubt about whether Lewis was suspicious, she thought the interview went very well. She had collected important information the burglars needed. When she left, she felt sure she had not been regarded with suspicion.

The Raineses had agreed that about an hour after she arrived at the office, John would drive to a prearranged point a few blocks away so she would not be seen leaving in a car. She didn't want agents to wonder about her claim that she had come by public transportation.

When she opened the station wagon door, her calm veneer disappeared and she was visibly shaking as she sat in the passenger seat. John had been quite nervous about her visit to the office, so he was somewhat alarmed when he saw her. But her shaking stopped as quickly as it had started. She felt great relief. In fact, she was ecstatic. Now, she said, she was sure the burglary could be done. Until now, she had had many doubts. She couldn't stop telling John, as they drove toward home, how easy—how *very* easy—it was going to be to burglarize that office. John remembers that her certainty and her enthusiasm were infectious. Despite the deep foreboding he felt about the burglary, he couldn't help sharing her enthusiasm that afternoon. He remembers her excitement as she listed the reasons why the burglary was going to be easy. There was no alarm system. There were no surveillance cameras. The lock looked like it could be picked. There was carpet on the floor. As far as she could tell, there were no locks on the file cabinets. How lucky could they be, she asked, with the delightful certainty of the schoolgirl she had just posed as. "There was no sign of security. Nope, nothing."

She abruptly halted her hyper-elated recall and removed her gloves. She felt an urgency to write notes about what she had seen while her memory was fresh. She wrote during the ride home to Germantown and continued after they arrived there. She could hardly wait to tell the other burglars what she learned that day inside the FBI office. Thinking like a smart burglar, later that night she destroyed the notes she had written during and after the interview.

That night was a turning point.

After Bonnie Raines reported on what she had observed at the office, the other burglars felt relieved. They shared her optimism. For the first time, Davidon remembers, "We knew we could do it." As the person who had proposed the burglary, he was delighted to hear her positive assessment. It was very good news. Doubts about whether the break-in could be done faded away that night for all of the burglars.

Even John Raines regarded Bonnie's discoveries as good news, but, beginning that day, his concerns grew much deeper. "Until then, we didn't know we could do it. Then Bonnie got in there and discovered there was no alarm system. After that, we knew we had a going project. At that point I, more than Bonnie, began to have real worries about what might happen. . . . Once it became clear that this was in fact something we were going to do, it became clear to me that the FBI was going to be very, very angry about this. They were really going to come after us."

From then on, he found himself thinking—almost constantly—about the fact that he and Bonnie were moving into "very deep waters of jeopardy that we had not faced in the draft boards. . . . We were putting our families in jeopardy. I was aware that this was a much more dangerous undertaking, in terms of our parenting responsibilities, than anything we had undertaken before." No one else in the group, including Bonnie, seems to have focused as much as John did on the possible danger ahead. "We had faced danger and responsibility earlier, when I went south, but never as powerfully as we faced it in that last month before the action at Media."

When he was gripped by worry in those days leading up to the burglary, he'd think again about the children and how much he longed to be a part of their daily lives as they grew up. Sometimes the thought of the future they might be about to sacrifice was almost too painful to contemplate. His fear had not been great when they raided a draft board. Then they had had a community they were with before and after the raid. Whether they failed or succeeded, they had that solidarity with one another. They met afterwards and talked with the large community of resisters about what they had done. It was not going to be that way if they burglarized the FBI office. They were going to try to be completely silent about what they had done. He feared that might mean having a "sense of nothingness after the Media break-in and its aftermath were over. No community would be there for us. I remember thinking that we would have a great deal to worry about afterward— about whether they were going to find us and, also, whether we would have any community of solidarity. I didn't think we would. We would be alone." He found that a painful thing to contemplate. Smith felt the same concern. She realized that the aftermath of this burglary would be so much lonelier than working in Mississippi in 1964 was. There, even under the most dangerous conditions, you knew supporters would be waiting for you. By plan, that could not happen after Media.

Bonnie Raines had a chilling thought late the night after she visited the FBI office. She kept it to herself. That night, she understood deep in her bones for the first time what one of the other burglars had said the night she agreed to case inside. At the time, she had not fully absorbed the meaning of the comment. Now she did: As of her visit to the office today, FBI agents had a specific person to whom they later would tie the burglary—her.

Despite now thinking she was indeed a marked woman, she recalls that her strongest feeling that night was excitement about the possibility that the break-in could be accomplished. Originally doubtful that an FBI office could be burglarized, now she thought the action "was almost inviting. I almost felt, 'What is there to lose?' There was so little security. It was in this sleepy little town. We were going to do it the night of the boxing match. It just seemed there were a lot of things working in our favor." Given all the casing that had been done, including her time in the office that day, "We felt we had cased so completely that there could not be any surprises," she recalls thinking that night. "I was very up for it."

She was wrong about no surprises. There would be a big one.

But the night after she visited the office, she couldn't help smiling to herself as she thought about the deception she had pulled off. She enjoyed the irony then and years later. Her Michigan cheerleader good looks and earth mother qualities had turned out to be useful to the group. She had been able to use her all-American girl-next-door looks, still intact at twenty-nine, to move the burglary forward. Though there still was much work and possible danger ahead, she felt satisfied with her role and grateful that her fellow burglars had had enough confidence in her to ask her to case the office.

EXACTLY ONE MONTH BEFORE the day the burglary was scheduled to take place, an unprecedented public plea was made for an investigation of the FBI. How timely. The burglars were so busy, with their double schedules of day jobs and burglary preparation at night, that they were unaware that a prominent academic, H. H. Wilson, a professor of political science at Princeton University, issued a call for such an investigation in the *Nation* magazine on February 8, 1971. It was titled "The FBI Today: The Case for Effective Control." At that time, the *Nation* was the only publication where such a call would have been published. For years, it was nearly the only publication that published either reporting or analysis of the FBI. It would later be learned that the *Nation* articles about the FBI led to investigations not only of Fred Cook, the person who wrote most of the articles, but also of those who wrote letters to the magazine about the articles, as well as the neighbors of those letter writers. When Cook got his FBI file in 1986, he learned that his book and the *Nation* series that was the basis of the book had set off multipronged bureau investigations of him and the magazine.

Hoover ordered the Internal Revenue Service to check Cook's sources of income. The bureau's Liaison Section proposed that agents should try to prove that Cyrus Eaton, a Cleveland industrialist who had criticized the bureau, had "bought" the *Nation*. Evidence of this sort "could completely destroy *The Nation* as an allegedly independent, impartial publication." Hoover approved the proposal: "We should try to find out who is behind it. Yes." Cook's FBI file also contained documentation that "week after week, the Bureau's New York office sent the Seat of Government [FBI headquarters] a synopsis of what the *Nation* was running."

Hoover did not like Wilson's article any more than he had liked Cook's earlier ones.

Venturing where no analyst had gone before, in his February 1971 article Professor Wilson called for an independent investigation of the FBI that would lead to oversight and controls over the bureau. "If these controls are to be implemented," he wrote, "the public must be alert, informed and genuinely concerned. Instead, Mr. Hoover has cultivated over the last 46 years an uncritical, mindless adulation. The Director and the Bureau have become folk heroes, an atmosphere has been created wherein even to suggest that the Bureau is a legitimate subject for analysis and political discussion is enough to bring charges that one is subversive, un-American and probably godless."

The FBI's "strong ideological bias," Wilson wrote, "and lack of sophistication render it eminently unfit for the delicate task of conducting anti-subversion inquiries in a democracy." A "concerned public must demand change. This is no partisan political issue, but one that ought to arouse the most dedicated, tough-minded conservatives as much as convinced liberals or radicals. At stake is the preservation of personal liberty in any present or future conflict with the bureaucratic state.

"It is of tremendous importance," Wilson concluded, "that some independent organization takes the lead in stimulating a public discussion of the issues at stake."

There was no groundswell of response to Professor Wilson's article. He could not have imagined that, as he wrote his call for an independent investigation of the FBI, a very independent organization, a small dedicated group of amateur burglars who called themselves the Citizens' Commission to Investigate the FBI, was working feverishly on plans to find the evidence that would make his claims believable and his call compelling far beyond the small readership of the *Nation*. As the burglars sat in cars late at night on dark Media streets, they too thought "the public must be alert, informed and genuinely concerned" about the FBI.

Even before Professor Wilson's call for an investigation, Hoover's 1971 had started off badly. On January 3, Jack Nelson of the *Los Angeles Times* reported that each year the government spent $30,000 to purchase a new limousine for Hoover, in contrast to the $5,000 spent annually to lease a limousine for the president. On January 17, Nelson reported the case of Jack Shaw, an agent in the bureau's New York office who had mildly criticized the bureau in a letter to a professor in a course in which he was enrolled at John Jay College of Criminal Justice. Shaw's letter had been typed by someone in the typing pool at the FBI office in New York. Scraps of a copy of it were found during a wastebasket inspection and pieced together. Within hours, Hoover was informed about the letter. He expressed outrage at what Shaw had written and at his failure to report that his professor had criticized the bureau in class. The director fired Shaw "with prejudice" and ordered him and the other fifteen FBI agents enrolled at John Jay to withdraw from their classes. A short time later, FBI clerical employees enrolled at American University were required to drop out of classes there when the director learned that one of their professors had criticized the action he had taken against Shaw.

On February 1, Senator George McGovern spoke of the Shaw case on the floor of the U.S. Senate, calling it "an injustice that cries out for remedy." A few days later, McGovern announced that he had received an anonymous letter, claimed to have been written by ten current FBI agents, stating that morale was at an all-time low at the bureau and asking for a congressional investigation of the bureau's "cult of personality."

Hoover's response was swift and extreme, not to mention irrational. He said the letter was written by the Soviet Union's KGB and that McGovern had been duped by Soviet agents. Associate Director Tolson asked each of the twenty top executives at bureau headquarters to write letters to McGovern attacking him for making the ten agents' letter public. In various indignant ways, each of them accused McGovern of using the anonymous letter to buoy his political career. One of the executives was criticized for writing a letter that was not sufficiently indignant.

AS THE DAY the burglary was to take place grew close, there were logistical challenges the burglars could not remove. First, residents of the building, all of whom used the same door and open interior stairwell the burglars would have to use, might come and go at any time during the evening. These spontaneous actions could not be avoided; they could only be endured, and the burglars could not be sure they could be endured securely. The burglars' greatest protection against this problem would be Forsyth breaking in so quickly the night of the burglary that any burglar, including him, would be seen in the hallway only fleetingly. That's why they cheered him on each night in the attic as he repeatedly picked the lock, continuing to reduce the time it would take to break in.

Another unsolvable challenge was huge: County courthouse guards stood twenty-four hours a day across the street from the FBI office at a guard station immediately inside the clear glass front door of the Delaware County Courthouse. The burglars carefully observed the movements of the courthouse guards for weeks. Finally, they reached a certain and unwelcome conclusion: It would be possible for the courthouse guard to see the burglars when they arrived and when they left. Not only was the front door of the FBI building visible to these officers, but at least one of the rooms in the FBI office, the corner room, also was visible from the courthouse guard's observation station.

They could do nothing to avoid being within the line of sight of the courthouse guard who would be on duty that night. There was no time when they could be certain they could rush in or out of the building when the guard would not be watching them. They realized they should expect him to be watching them, from just yards away—as they entered the building, as they left the building with overhead lights shining on them both inside and outside the door, as they loaded the getaway cars, and as they drove away.

The best the burglars could hope for was that the guard on duty the night of the burglary would look at them in a mindless, distracted way and would not think about whether it was odd that four people were walking out of this small apartment/office building late at night, each of them carrying suitcases so heavy they strained to carry them and lift them into the trunks of waiting cars. Surely average burglars would have refused to bet their success on whether a guard would be mindless as he watched them. Not these people. The certainty of having their crime observed by a trained government county guard did not prompt them to question moving ahead.

MEANWHILE, the burglars' plans progressed. Then, just a few days before the burglary was to take place, they were confronted with what could have been a fatal threat to their plans. A person who had been part of the group from the beginning arrived at a regular working session one evening and announced that he no longer would be part of the group. This was stunning information. He was a man of few words, and if the burglars' memories are accurate, he offered few, if any, words of explanation that night as he told them he was quitting and then left. Perhaps even more remarkable is that none of the burglars expressed their shock to him that evening. None of them remembers asking him why he was leaving. Nor do they remember asking him to agree not to reveal the group's secret plans. He had been with them since that first meeting in December. He knew every detail of what they were about to do. And now he was gone. Only two of them, the Raineses, saw him again.

As with the other threats the burglars faced—Davidon being named recently in an indictment in a sensational antiwar case; the likelihood of a courthouse guard watching them as they arrived and left the FBI building; the possibility that people who lived in the building could see them at any time that night in the hallway outside the FBI office—they seemed to absorb this news and convince themselves that his leaving the group was just another problem to endure. Though they realized that he now had the power to destroy the burglary—not to mention their lives—the burglars don't remember discussing his departure with one another after he left. That puzzles some of them now. By leaving, he ripped open that curtain they had intended to keep securely closed forever to protect them and their secrets. He now stood outside their curtain with full knowledge of what they were planning to do. They had no idea what he might do with that knowledge.

IT WAS ALMOST March 8. Most of the burglars remember feeling confident the week before the burglary. Perhaps the source of their confidence was simply strong determination braced by courage. Perhaps they also were a little reckless. Some combination of unusual qualities made it possible for them to view the unavoidable threats they would face as worth the risk.

Any one of the threats that were beyond the burglars' control could easily have defeated them. But none of the burglars ever asked the group to consider whether any of those threats posed too great a risk. Failure seemed to be beyond their imagination.

5

Time Out for White House Meeting

B Y THE WEEKEND before the Media burglary, William Davidon had few worries about how the break-in would go. Without that confidence, he probably would not have been willing to travel to Washington that Saturday morning for a meeting at the White House. The circumstances were unusual. Here was the mastermind of the burglary of the Media FBI office, just two days before the burglary was to take place, on his way to meet with President Nixon's national security adviser, Henry Kissinger. Even more improbable, Davidon and the other two people who would meet with Kissinger that morning were all unindicted coconspirators in the recent indictment that charged Catholic peace movement activists with conspiring to bomb tunnels under federal buildings and kidnap Kissinger. These three people were supposed to have been part of the alleged plot.

Was this a bad joke or a stroke of clever diplomacy between a key architect of the Vietnam War and some of the strongest opponents of the war?

Davidon had a lot on his mind as he boarded an Amtrak train at Philadelphia's 30th Street Station that Saturday morning. He was ambivalent about this meeting. He was very busy. He still had burglary duties to perform that weekend. The meeting with Kissinger, he assumed, might be only a media stunt, one of those staged events that take place not because something important happened but, instead, to give the impression later that something important happened. He didn't think the three of them would influence Kissinger, but he welcomed the chance to try, as he welcomed any chance to make the case against the war. So he said yes to the invitation. Besides, as a chief architect of the escalation of the war since Nixon became president, Kissinger had indirectly played a major role in Davidon's increasingly narrowing the focus of his life to efforts to stop the Vietnam War. How could he say no to a meeting with Kissinger? Frankly, given the indictment, Davidon was a little surprised that Kissinger had agreed to it. That he did suggested that, in addition to his war strategy talents, Kissinger might have a sense of humor.

There already were signs of wit on Kissinger's part about the indictment. Shortly after it was announced, he feigned seriousness when he told reporters he understood that the plot to kidnap him had been created by "three sex-starved nuns." When that remark was criticized, he wrote a letter to Terence Cardinal Cooke, the archbishop of New York City, apologizing for it. Some nuns wondered why he apologized to Cooke instead of to them. He found another way to joke about his possible kidnapping. He told reporters that following the announcement of the indictment, his staff had written to President Nixon "stating that under no conditions am I to be ransomed." The target of the alleged plot didn't seem to be taking it very seriously.

Davidon and the two other activists, Tom Davidson and Sister Beverly Bell, met outside a side entrance to the White House that morning and told guards they had an appointment with Kissinger. When they passed through the first door, a metal detector set off an alarm. The problem was easily detected. Davidson had brought a bag of blue-and-white metal buttons that were boldly emblazoned with the question "Kidnap Kissinger?" The guards laughed when he opened the bag and revealed the buttons. They all wanted one. Davidson obliged, and for at least a few hours that Saturday uniformed White House guards wore the buttons as they monitored security.

The three were cleared by Secret Service agents before they were escorted to the room where they waited for Kissinger. Apparently security at the White House was a bit lax on Saturdays. When Department of Justice officials learned a few days later that White House guards had worn "Kidnap Kissinger?" buttons, they were not amused. They probably also were not amused that Kissinger had met with people the department had officially said were part of a plot to kidnap him.

This rather unusual meeting was arranged by Brian McDonnell, a twenty-seven-year-old pacifist from Philadelphia, who had fasted in the spring of 1970 for thirty-seven days in Lafayette Park, across the street from the White House, in protest of the U.S. invasion of Cambodia. He had sat on the ground day after day encouraging people to discuss the war.

During that time, he and Kissinger were introduced to each other by a mutual acquaintance, actress Shirley MacLaine. Kissinger occasionally spent evenings with McDonnell at his Quaker meetinghouse living quarters in Georgetown. McDonnell said he despaired about not being able to get Kissinger into the "nonviolence bag," and Kissinger said he despaired at not being able to "build a bridge between those who care and those who do," a dichotomy McDonnell rejected. Despite their philosophical differences, a warm friendship developed between them. Just a few months after they met, McDonnell's wife, Alice, was brutally murdered in Philadelphia. Kissinger quietly went to the memorial service without drawing public attention to his presence. He continued to be in touch occasionally with McDonnell until McDonnell died in Los Angeles in 2003.

It probably was because of Kissinger's affection for McDonnell that he agreed to meet with these three people who allegedly had conspired to kidnap him. It's also a safe bet he would not have met with them if he had believed there was a real plot to kidnap him. For his part, McDonnell, like Davidon, always was looking for ways to keep the conversation going between people who opposed the war and those who conducted it. It was in that spirit that he arranged for this unusual group of four to meet.

After setting off the metal detector, the three activists were escorted to the Situation Room in the basement of the White House, a room with a very large map of the world on one wall, and where many Vietnam War strategies had been discussed and crucial decisions made. As they waited for Kissinger, they were served tea in fine china teacups that bore the seal of the U.S. Navy, a fitting touch for Davidon, a Navy veteran. When Kissinger entered the room, the three activists stood and each of them shook his hand. He took a seat at the head of the table, in front of the map of the world, with Davidon seated beside him. Kissinger immediately turned to Sister Beverly, sitting on his other side, and apologized to her for his flippant "sex-starved nuns" comment. He then set the parameters for their conversation. He would not talk about any aspect of the kidnap/bombing conspiracy case with them. Other than that, he said, anything could be discussed. Kissinger said they could make the conversation public, but he would not initiate doing so. For the next seventy-five minutes they talked about the war.

Davidon remembers being impressed at first with the fact that Kissinger seemed to be "genuinely listening to us." He thinks it was very early in the meeting that he tried to discuss nuclear warfare, the issue that was Davidon's deepest concern. Kissinger, he recalls, refused to dismiss the possibility of the United States using nuclear warfare in the continuing war in Vietnam. Everything, he said, was being considered, and he wasn't willing to discuss reasons for removing nuclear options.

On the surface, the conversation seemed casual. "My guess is that he was pleased it was not a shouting match, that we were having a thoughtful discussion," Davidon said years later. "But as I looked around the room, I wondered what other kinds of discussions went on in that room. I felt Kissinger was one of the brighter people in the Nixon administration, brighter and more skillful at doing terrible things."

The next week, in an interview with Mary McGrory, then a *Washington Star* columnist, Davidon described the White House meeting as "bitter-sweet" and Kissinger as "an excellent listener. . . . He is part of a decision-making system which is grossly brutal. There we were, accused of wanting to bomb, sitting with a man whose policies had brought about a bombing that was actually going on as we talked. I was talking to a man who considers mass murder in certain circumstances justified. I told him I thought the war had no legitimacy." (McGrory had wanted to talk with Davidon the following Monday, but he told her he would be too busy—at a burglary, but he didn't say that—to talk with her then, so he made an appointment to call her the night after the burglary. The call to her was noted by the FBI in its records of his phone calls.)

Tom Davidson, then twenty-five, thought the conversation with Kissinger was surreal. Years later, he described it as "nice and sort of fun. It was polite discourse, but then he mines Haiphong after the nice discourse." He felt that in the end "we had a polite conversation with an engaging enemy."

What Davidson recalls most vividly about the session was Davidon's attempts to get Kissinger to discuss the United States' use of napalm in Vietnam. During that part of their meeting, Davidson was surprised by Davidon and appalled by Kissinger. When they worked together as activists, he had always seen Davidon as a "straightforward, easygoing guy." Now, in the presence of Kissinger, he saw an unexpected intensity in Davidon's usually relaxed face. "He came on pretty strong, in ways I hadn't seen. All of a sudden his face changes, and he's hammering Kissinger about the use of napalm in Vietnam."

Napalm was a very controversial aspect of the war. Now, in the Situation Room in the White House, Davidon and his two fellow activists faced a top official who had the power to stop the use of the syrupy jellied gasoline that was manufactured for the government by Dow Chemical Company and dropped from planes to burn forests, villages, and people. Davidon described the terrible damage caused by napalm. "It was a little scary watching it," said Davidson of Kissinger's reaction to Davidon's well-documented comments about the inhumane use of the weapon. "Kissinger just absorbed it and went on. He kept deflecting the facts. . . . To be four feet across a table from him. I was afraid I would scream."

The exchange about napalm was especially meaningful for Davidson because it was when he had learned about his government's use of napalm in Vietnam that he abandoned his life plans and rushed into the peace movement, and eventually into acts of resistance against the war. A few years before that White House meeting, when he was a college student in North Dakota, Davidson had listened one day as a speaker on his campus described how the United States used napalm in Vietnam. He said it was routinely dropped from planes and that it seriously damaged the landscape but, more important, seriously burned and often killed Vietnamese children. The speaker's comments angered Davidson. He remembers passionately confronting the speaker: "Our government would never do that!"

"The person insisted it was true," he recalls. "I went to the library and found photographs and articles that said it was true." He was astonished. Like many Americans who became opponents of the war, Davidson had a gut reaction to learning that such brutality was being carried out by his government. Like Forsyth, he decided he had to leave college and work against the war. He remembers thinking, "If my government is doing that, I have to stop it." That realization changed the direction of his life for the next fifteen years, if not forever. He refused to fight in the war and became a conscientious objector, the first in North Dakota since World War II. The son of an Episcopal bishop, he worked full-time for ten years trying to stop the war, participating in various acts of civil disobedience and resistance, including raiding draft boards in 1970. Davidson, like some of the FBI burglars, increasingly had found the locus of his activism in the Catholic peace movement. After the war ended, he delivered medical supplies to Vietnam, helping to meet a critical need in the war-devastated country.

Kissinger later wrote that he met with the three activists as an attempt "to transcend the bitterness of the public dialogue" about the war. In his 1979 memoir *White House Years,* he wrote of the meeting:

Gently, they expressed their deep and passionate opposition to the war; but they had no idea how to end it. The problem for me, on the other hand, was to translate inchoate ideas—however deeply felt—into concrete policy. Ours was the perpetually inconclusive dialogue between statesmen and prophets, between those who operate in time and through attainable stages and those who are concerned with truth and the eternal.

Kissinger's guests that day were, indeed, concerned about truth. In fact, they yearned for truth in the conduct of the war and in the administration's dealings with Congress, with the public, and in war negotiations. Their concerns about the role of truth were heightened three months after the White House meeting when the lies that were so much a part of government communication about the Vietnam War from its beginning were revealed when Daniel Ellsberg released the Pentagon Papers, the secret history of the war. It was then that Kissinger referred to Ellsberg as "the most dangerous man in America," a comment that became the title of the 2009 documentary about Ellsberg's act of resistance in releasing the secret history.

Thoughts about "the eternal," which Kissinger strangely seemed to think were a part of the antiwar activists' motivation, were irrelevant to his three visitors that Saturday, as he must have known. That interpretation by him, one often made by secular people about people they think are motivated primarily by religious views, allows the listener to dismiss the speaker as preoccupied with heaven and hell and therefore irrelevant to and not interested in the world as it is and as it could be. It was, however, the present, not eternity, that consumed and motivated these three people, just as the present consumed Kissinger. They were interested in the world as it is—as it was then—and how Kissinger was affecting the world by escalating the war. They did not see themselves as prophets. They too were interested in the attainable, but they saw peace as attainable through negotiations that included a willingness to reverse policy, admit error, tell the truth about the past and present of the war. Most important, they wanted the Nixon administration to be willing to stop the bombing, stop the fighting. They thought that what the United States had started it could and should end.

After the White House meeting, Davidon reluctantly turned down an invitation from Davidson and Bell to have lunch. Wanting to get back to Philadelphia as soon as possible, he took a cab to Washington's Union Station and boarded the first train to Philadelphia. As he did, he remembers, he had a mixture of reactions to what he had just experienced. He was glad the three of them had talked with Kissinger, but he also felt they probably had wasted their time. He hoped Kissinger would think about what they had said, but he was not very optimistic about that possibility.

Settling his small frame into his Amtrak seat, he turned his attention to the next matter on his agenda: the FBI burglary. As the train whizzed through Baltimore and the late-winter brown-and-gray countryside of Maryland and Delaware that afternoon, he went through the list of burglary-related tasks that should have been done by then, plus a couple essential ones he would do the next day. He thought nearly everything was in place, but he didn't want to take anything for granted. He made a to-do list. True to his by then well-trained burglar's caution, he left no paper trail. The only physical "trail" left by the burglars was on the walls of the Raineses' attic. By now, the weekend before the burglary, they had been to the attic for the last time. On the train, he "wrote" his to-do list in his mind, not on paper or sheetrock. Nothing would be traceable.

To do:

1. Call Sunday to reserve a room at the motel the group had chosen along U.S. Route 1, about two miles from downtown Media. That room would be the burglars' staging area. All of them would gather there at about seven o'clock on Monday evening. Some members of the group would wait in the motel room and be available by phone to those inside the FBI office in case they needed help and to respond when they called to say it was time to pick them up after the shelves and drawers had been emptied.

2. Call a rental car agency on Sunday and reserve the car he would use the night of the burglary. This was necessary because his wife needed the family's car that evening.

3. Call each burglar on Sunday and, in a cautious but natural way, ask if they were ready. Tell them what room he had reserved at the motel.

4. Make sure all that was needed was in place—suitcases, cars, maps, tools, escape plans, waiting farmhouse, good minds, and brave souls.

He followed up the next day. He reserved the room for Monday evening and then reserved a car. He made both reservations with his credit card, another sign of his belief that it was important to minimize cloak-and-dagger methods as much as possible, even in this burglary where he had insisted on tight security. "Simplicity makes it more possible to get things done," he said years later, relishing the fact that simplicity had worked all those years ago.

By Sunday evening, Davidon believed everything was in place and the burglars were ready.

6

With Thanks to Muhammad Ali and Joe Frazier

BEGINNING AT DAWN, the weather was good on the day the Media burglary was scheduled to take place. There were traces of snow and ice that morning, but the temperature in the Philadelphia area rose from 28 degrees in the morning to a sunny 54 degrees in the afternoon. That was good news for the people who were assigned to drive the getaway cars. It meant they would not have to worry about icy roads that night as they left Media and traveled narrow country roads late that evening, their trunks full of FBI files.

The eight burglars worked their day jobs that day. If all went as planned, beginning tonight they would be working two jobs for a while—their usual ones plus a night job as members of the Citizens' Commission to Investigate the FBI sorting and analyzing FBI files. Each of them felt a mix of fear and confidence as day turned to evening and it was almost time to leave their homes in various parts of the Philadelphia area and drive to the motel room Davidon had rented.

As John and Bonnie Raines ate dinner with their children that evening, there was continuous upbeat conversation. Just three days earlier, they had all celebrated Nathan's second birthday. Tonight he was still in a bubbly happy-birthday mood while Lindsley, eight, and Mark, seven, talked about what had happened in school that day.

To the children, this was just an ordinary evening. They knew the plan—dinner together, followed by Dad and Mom going to a meeting after a babysitter arrived. To Mom and Dad, the evening was of course anything but ordinary.

The Raineses' children were used to their parents going to meetings. In fact, they had the impression that their parents had done so just about every evening. The only thing different tonight was that only the family gathered for dinner. The other people who often had dined with them recently weren't here tonight. The children liked their parents' new friends. Of course, they had no idea that these people had gone to the Raineses' attic nearly every night in recent months to prepare themselves to pull off a burglary.

Now the Raineses and the other burglars were about to execute the burglary they had planned in the attic. Tonight was the night.

As the Raineses talked with the children over dinner that evening, John felt sick at times. The days leading up to tonight had been wrenching for him. He kept asking himself how he and Bonnie could possibly take the risks they were about to take. He never told her he thought they should drop out of the group; he didn't think they should. What they wanted to accomplish was very important and might only be possible by burglary. But he remembers thinking during the weeks leading up to this night that if Bonnie suggested they should drop out, he would agree immediately. Instead, as he became more frightened about the burglary, she became more and more confident. By dinner this evening, he had long realized that she was not going to suggest they back out. He watched her now as she talked with the children. In her smiling, responsive face, he saw a wonderful mother. He also saw determination and courage. He knew she was ready for tonight. He wasn't, but he knew they were going to move forward. He told himself that he too would find courage.

Normal moments can seem so wonderful. It is very painful, though, to think that normal moments may be about to end, especially when you know that you yourself may be about to cause them to end. That's how John Raines felt as he looked at the children at dinner on the night of the burglary. They were beautiful. Their chatter was cute. It was more than cute; it was downright precious. Such a wonderful normal thing it was to be sitting there at the dinner table with Bonnie and their three children. It was the kind of experience he took for granted every day. Over the nine years of their marriage, they had created a wonderful life together. They felt deep love and respect for each other. Their life seemed ideal, especially now. It was rich with shared passions, shared values, and shared daily joys. He found it impossible to imagine a better family life. Never again, he thought, would he take it for granted. He couldn't stop thinking about how what he and Bonnie were about to do could rob them and their children of such lovely normal moments, could rob them of years of normal, not to mention very special, moments. He had to fight hard to prevent these thoughts from consuming him.

The babysitter arrived. That meant it was time to go. They were going to be a little late. They were supposed to meet the other burglars at about seven o'clock. It was nearly 6:30 now, and the drive would take about forty-five minutes. As planned, they told the children they wouldn't be home until after the children were asleep. Actually, if all went according to plan, and they were not arrested tonight, they would not come home until shortly before the children woke up the next morning. They didn't want them to know they would be gone all night, or possibly much longer.

The children ran to hug their parents as they put on their heavy winter coats. They both remember kneeling and holding each child in a long, strong embrace, probably stronger than they had ever held them. They tried to act as though nothing unusual was happening. Each of them remembers that as they hugged the children, they hoped, with a nearly desperate feeling, that they would see them in the morning, that they would walk in the door, perhaps by 6 a.m., as quietly as possible, take a shower, get dressed for work, and then, as though they had been there all night, wake the children. They hoped that all would go as planned and that they would be back in the company of Lindsley, Mark, and Nathan, seated together again around the big kitchen table for breakfast the next morning as though nothing unusual—nothing that could take normal away—had just happened.

In those brief farewell moments, they knew with a painful sting that this—their family together—was the sacrifice they had very reluctantly agreed to make. They had agreed that this was a time of extraordinary injustice and that there was a need for nonviolent resistance by some people, including them, that might involve extreme sacrifice. Committed as they were now, as they hugged their children, more than ever they knew how much they longed for the sacrifice not to become a reality. They kissed them and said goodbye. As they were about to close the door, their eyes lingered briefly on the faces of the three children waving and gleefully shouting goodbye.

The Raineses got into their old maroon Ford station wagon, John at the wheel. Like the other burglars, they were going to participate in a burglary that late-winter evening because they felt a direct and personal responsibility for what their country did. They had come of age at a time when two opposite trends dominated American life. There was a strong desire in the 1950s to conform in nearly every way and create a happy family life in the new expanding suburbs that ringed American cities, and in the process become disengaged from the pressing issues of the day. By the late 1960s, though, another trend had grasped the minds and hearts of some Americans: disenchantment with disengagement. The Raineses were among the people who had embraced engagement as a necessity of citizenship, of life itself. Every one of the burglars felt a strong personal responsibility to correct injustices, even if doing so involved personal risks.

As they drove to the motel, not talking much, John Raines's stomach was churning. He silently and urgently asked himself, "Why are we doing this?" He knew the answer, and it was one he completely embraced. Still, as the time of the burglary grew closer, it was painful for him to live out the commitment he had made to Bonnie and the other burglars. He was sure, no matter how tonight turned out, that people would think it was an utterly wild idea. They would wonder how these burglars ever were able to think they could possibly get away with it. Right now, on the road to the burglary, he wondered the same thing.

He had taken serious risks before, even life-threatening ones. He remembered the night he spent alone in a cell in a dark jail in a small town in southwestern Georgia during one of the summers when he went to the South to join black people in the struggle for their basic rights. Black leaders had discovered that John was in danger. In an act of great generosity and solidarity, a local black farmer had put up his small farm as bail to get him out of jail, perhaps saving his life. Tonight was far more difficult for John to face than even that night he spent alone in jail. He didn't think their lives would be threatened tonight, but he did think their entire future would be. He had never felt as frightened as he did tonight on the way to Media.

THE OTHER BURGLARS WERE at the motel room by 7 p.m. John and Bonnie Raines were the last to arrive. Keith Forsyth and the four members of the inside team—the people who would enter the office and steal the files—were dressed, according to plan, in "uptown clothes," as Forsyth liked to call their special burglary clothes. Susan Smith remembers wearing a skirt for the occasion. By then she seldom wore skirts, and she thinks this may have been the last time she did, an accommodation to the burglary. Forsyth and Bob Williamson bought their secondhand but very sophisticated burglary clothes at a Main Line charity clothing store, the one where Forsyth had bought his used Brooks Brothers suit—"Best five-dollar Brooks

Brothers suit I've ever bought," he enjoyed saying years later—before he walked by the FBI office the first time to circumspectly inspect the lock on the entrance. By now he also had a fine secondhand Brooks Brothers topcoat, for warmth and to conceal burglary tools, purchased at the same charity store. Forsyth still enjoys thinking that their burglary clothes might have been previously owned and worn by some of the highest-ranking members of Philadelphia's old Main Line establishment. Williamson, the only somewhat hippie-looking member of the group, traded his dashiki, his frequent garb at that time, for more typical clothes. He had even trimmed his long hair a bit for this special occasion.

Davidon remembers feeling calmness mixed with both fear and the pumping drive of adrenaline as the burglars gathered in the motel room. Others described the atmosphere similarly—a combination of controlled excitement and fear. All agree that everyone was sober and serious. After weeks of planning together, they had confidence in one another. Each of them was aware that he or she held the future of everyone in the group in their hands. A mistake made by one could be disastrous to all. Bonds of trust seemed to be strong. Despite the pressure, no one in the group remembers hearing any expressions of concern from anyone about any other member's behavior that night, or, for that matter, at any time while they worked together.

They had no idea that night what, if anything, the person who had abandoned the group just a few days earlier, would do—or, for all they knew, already had done—with the comprehensive and potentially devastating information he possessed. The burglars moved into the first stage of the burglary as though no one except the eight of them knew anything about their plans.

Sometime between 7:30 and 8 p.m., Forsyth and John Raines got ready to leave the motel room—Forsyth to drive to Media to break into the FBI office, John to drive to a parking lot at Swarthmore College, where he would wait for Bonnie to arrive after the burglary along with suitcases to be transferred from Smith's car to the Raineses' station wagon. Words of reassurance were exchanged. There was a strong but quiet shared recognition among all of them that this moment was what they had been preparing for.

The burglary was beginning now.

IN NEW YORK, where prefight events were warming up, the scene was wild. The city was snowbound, but that didn't prevent thousands of people who could not get tickets to the Ali-Frazier fight from ringing the outside perimeter of Madison Square Garden. So great was the anticipation that thousands of people were arriving early—inside and outside the arena. About the time Forsyth and John Raines left the motel, a parade of celebrities was arriving at the Garden. So many were in the audience that when it was time to invite them into the boxing ring to be introduced, a common practice at boxing matches at the Garden, ring announcer Johnny Addie said he would not introduce the celebrities tonight because *everybody* was there.

That seemed to be true. A star-studded audience the likes of which had never been seen before at the Garden was there to watch these two undefeated heavyweight champions, Muhammad Ali and Joe Frazier, face off—Gene Kelly, Woody Allen, Ed Sullivan, Joey Bishop, Peter Falk, Robert Goulet, Carol Lawrence, Dick Cavett, Lorne Greene, Diana Ross, Michael Caine, Bill Cosby, James Taylor, David Frost, Diahann Carroll, Barbra Streisand, Buddy Rich, Andy Williams, former vice president Hubert Humphrey—who couldn't get a ringside seat and was in the balcony—Senator Edward Kennedy, Ethel Kennedy, Senator John Tunney—son of heavyweight champion Gene Tunney—Joe Namath, Sargent Shriver, and New York City mayor John Lindsay. Some new heroes were there—the three Apollo 14 astronauts who had returned from the moon just a month earlier—Alan Shepard, Stuart Roosa, and Edgar Mitchell. Shepard had charmed residents of planet earth less than a month earlier when he hit two golf balls on the surface of the moon. Now back on earth, these space heroes came to see the fight that preoccupied millions on planet earth the night of March 8.

The 20,455 seats in the Garden were sold out within hours when they went on sale. An overflow venue was set up for 6,000 people, including Bing Crosby, twenty blocks north of the Garden at Radio City Music Hall. The fight was broadcast live there on a large screen with commentary provided from the stage by actor Burt Lancaster, sports announcer Don Dunphy, and retired boxer Archie Moore.

At the Garden, Norman Mailer sat near the ring. He wrote *Life* magazine's main article on the fight. Ringside tickets were sold out by the time Frank Sinatra tried to buy one. Desperate, he asked the *Life* editors to give him one of the magazine's highly coveted press tickets. They struck a deal: He could have a pass if he shot photographs for them. Not many days before the fight, Sinatra had appeared in the office of the Garden's staff photographer, George Kalinsky, and said, "I hear you're the greatest photographer. I want you to teach me all you know about photography in five minutes."

Over a three-hour lunch, Kalinksy taught him some basics and advised him to "make sure you feel the atmosphere." Sinatra was at ringside early the night of the fight, ready with a wide-angle lens on his camera. The credits on the cover of *Life* the next week were unmatched, before or since: Norman Mailer and Frank Sinatra.

Fashions in the Garden that night matched the exciting mood. Diana Ross wore black velvet hot pants. Hugh Hefner's companion, Barbi Benton, wore black silk hot pants, a see-through chiffon blouse, and a monkey-fur coat. Someone wore a wolf coat with a matching hat that was rimmed with wolf tails. As Michael Arkush, writer of a 2007 book about the fight, wrote, "By comparison, Colonel Harland Sanders, of Kentucky Fried Chicken, was almost drab in his traditional white suit."

"I don't think there's ever been a night like it," John Condon, director of publicity at Madison Square Garden at the time, recalled years later. Everyone was standing or sitting on the edge of their seats from the time they arrived and throughout the fight. They screamed, they yelled, they gasped.

That was exactly what the Media burglars hoped for: an event so engrossing, a crowd so loud and excited that the steady static from the fight would help them go about their work inside the FBI office without being noticed. They hoped fans—especially fight fans in Media, including police and FBI agents—would be glued to their radios and televisions. They didn't know it, but that was happening all over the world. As the first stage of the burglary was taking place, in Buenos Aires the streets were deserted because so many people were watching the prefight events on television at home and in bars. In Europe and Africa, where it was several hours later, people were getting ready to waken their children so they could watch this historic fight. Fifty foreign governments, including that of Romania, purchased rights to broadcast the fight free to the general public in all of those countries. Translations were provided in twelve languages from ringside for the more than 300 million people who watched the fight around the world—still the largest number of people to watch a single sporting event as it took place.

In the rice fields of South Vietnam, American troops gathered around radios, getting ready to listen to this fight between Ali, who refused to serve in Vietnam, and Frazier, who supported the war but who also had not served in the military. The promoters of the fight, who controlled all broadcast access to it, tried at first to extract a heavy price from the Pentagon for the right to broadcast it to troops. After a furious reaction from the Pentagon, the promoters relented and provided free radio access to the approximately

326,200 Americans then stationed in South Vietnam and on some U.S. Navy ships at sea. As the *New York Times* noted at the time, the Pentagon was particularly eager to broadcast the fight because it was having "global difficulties with respect to racial tensions" in the military.

Remarkably, the televised fight was blacked out where the largest number of people wanted to see it—in the United States. The promoters, Jack Kent Cooke and Jerry Perenchio, had sold governments in those fifty countries the rights to broadcast the fight live, but to maximize their profits, the promoters prevented television networks in the United States from broadcasting either the fight or descriptions of it live as it happened on either television or radio. It was viewed live in the United States only by people who purchased tickets to watch the closed-circuit broadcasts shown by the promoters at three hundred theaters in various parts of the country. Those venues accommodated only a tiny fraction of the millions of Americans who wanted to see the fight.

The promoters even went to court the day before the fight in an attempt to end the agreement that gave Mutual Broadcasting System access to broadcast summaries after each round. The promoters failed in that effort. Because the fight was blacked out in the United States, many millions of Americans prepared early that evening to huddle around their radios and televisions to listen and watch announcers give brief summaries of the fight between rounds. They listened to commentary and color stories about the scene inside and outside Madison Square Garden. It was a less than satisfying way to watch the fight, especially in light of the live access in much of the rest of the world. But Americans were so passionate about the Ali-Frazier fight that they were eager to tune in to it whatever way it was available. Even with windows closed against the cold in much of the country, streets were filled that night with the sounds of sports announcers breathlessly talking about the fight.

IN MEDIA, 114 miles south of New York City, the contrast with the wild scene in New York—what the burglars hoped would be their decoy—could not have been greater. The initial steps of the burglary were sounds of silence. John Raines arrived at the dark parking lot at Swarthmore College. He continued to feel terrible. Afraid they would all be arrested that night, he tried to convince himself that because the burglary was very well organized, it should unfold smoothly and swiftly. It should, he told himself, all be over soon. It should take only a few seconds for Forsyth to break in. The burglary itself probably would take less than an hour. In less than two hours, Bonnie should show up, along with a portion of the files removed from the FBI office. He repeatedly convinced himself to be patient.

Forsyth arrived in Media in just a few minutes and parked a short distance from the building where the FBI office was located. This was a big moment for him. He had been preparing for it with a great deal of dedication and intense work from the time the burglars first met in December. He still felt sure he would pick that lock and be inside the office in thirty seconds flat, his best speed during lock-picking practice.

As he left the car, he carried a briefcase. In it were his homemade lock-picking tools. The smaller tools were in a pencil case tucked in a small inside pocket of his coat. His larger tools were covered by a few layers of paper so the paper, not the tools, would be seen first if the briefcase was opened in front of anyone. He had been meticulous in his preparations. Each of the metal lock-picking tools he had made was wrapped in foam rubber so they wouldn't clank against each other as he walked. The briefcase looked appropriate for someone wearing a Brooks Brothers suit. "That was so important," he says. "You can do anything you want in the United States if you wear a suit and tie . . . especially if you are white. That also helps." And the briefcase added, of course, to his all-American busy-businessman-coming-

The Media FBI office was located on the second floor, near corner, of the County Court Apartments Building, across the street from the Delaware County Courthouse. *(Photo by Betty Medsger)*

home-late-from-the-office look. He wore leather gloves appropriate for a businessman. Underneath them, he wore tight-fitting rubber gloves. The leather gloves would hamper his dexterity, so essential to his task tonight, so he planned to remove them and put them in his coat pockets and wear only the rubber gloves so he could pick the lock with the dexterity of a surgeon.

Acting as though he lived in the building, Forsyth opened the always unlocked front door, walked upstairs to the second floor, and went directly to the FBI office door. He felt slightly nervous but very confident.

His confidence quickly evaporated.

He could not pick the lock in thirty seconds. He could not pick the lock at all.

As he faced the object of his many rounds of picking practice, Forsyth was startled. There were two locks, not one, on the main entrance of the FBI office. One was the simple five-pin tumbler lock that he remembered seeing and was prepared to pick, the same one Bonnie Raines remembered. But now there was a second lock, a much more complex one—a high-security lock that was extremely difficult to pick. Forsyth's homemade tools were useless on this lock.

"I freaked out. First of all, I can't get in. Second of all, what does this mean? What's the probability of this lock appearing by purely random chance just at the moment when I'm about to break through the door? It's astronomically small. I was worried about the noise, because the caretaker of the building lived right underneath the FBI office.

"So I'm standing over the guy's ceiling. I'm thinking, 'Wait a minute. They put this other lock on there. What does that mean? They know? How the hell do they know? We've been pretty goddamn careful. We haven't said anything over the phone. We don't even talk in the same room where there's a phone because there are ways to listen to people's conversations even when the phone is hung up. We've been really careful. I felt really sure about all of these individuals. There are no informers in the group. What the hell is going on?'" He doesn't remember wondering then if the man who abandoned the group the previous week, might have alerted the FBI to the burglary. Forsyth thought there was a possibility that he had been so nervous both times he walked by the FBI office door, including just the previous week, that he didn't see the second lock. Could that be? He could not answer the question. He could not believe that he and Bonnie Raines both would have imagined there was only one lock. Finally, as he stood outside the door, he did not trust his memory.

He asked himself, "If I pop this door open, am I going to get a welcoming party of ten FBI agents with guns pointed at me?" Perhaps, he thought, the whole thing needed to be canceled. He hated that thought.

"So, I was not too happy. I had to collect my thoughts, so I left the building and went to the car." No solution came to mind as he sat in his car thinking about this potentially disastrous situation. So much was at stake, and it all hinged on whether he could open that door. From the beginning, he had thought he could. He thought it was a matter of how fast he could, not whether it was possible. He walked to a phone booth about a block away, called the motel, and asked for Davidon's room. When the phone rang, it resonated in everyone's gut. The people in the hotel room had been wondering why Forsyth had not returned yet. Davidon answered. The others could tell from the look on Davidon's face as he listened to Forsyth that the news was not good. Forsyth was telling Davidon what he had discovered. He suggested that maybe the burglary should be called off. He admitted he could not eliminate the possibility that maybe fear was playing tricks with his memory. He said that suddenly he couldn't be absolutely certain about what he had seen before. But he was certain of what he had just seen: two locks, not one—one he could pick, one he could not pick.

Even under these pressured circumstances, Davidon was calm. He listened to Forsyth and told him to come back to the motel. They would all consider the problem together, he said.

As Davidon recounted what Forsyth had said, the burglars were astonished. They couldn't imagine how things had gone so terribly wrong. When Forsyth arrived at the motel room, his fellow burglars looked confused and dejected. Some looked a little alarmed. That's how he felt as he told them the details of his failed attempt to break into the main door, the one they had agreed after Bonnie Raines's visit must be their way in. Anxiety took different forms among the burglars. Some of them were silent, almost frozen. Some were agitated. Whatever level of fear was in the room before was considerably higher now. Questions that could not be answered hung in the air. Did the FBI add another lock? If they did, why and when did they add it? Why would one have been added in the last two weeks? Did Bonnie Raines's visit prompt them to add a more secure second lock? What reason could there be for another lock other than the possibility that the FBI knew about plans for the burglary? If that was the case, were the burglars fools not to abort the burglary now?

There might have been a leak. What about the man who dropped out? He was the only person who might have informed on them. If he did, the burglary should be called off. But they could not know. They believed he would not turn them in, but now, faced with these unexpected circumstances, some of them thought of him. They were sure he was the only person other than the people gathered in that room—plus John Raines, who was still waiting in the Swarthmore parking lot with no idea what was happening—who knew about their plans. If the FBI knew the burglary was supposed to take place tonight, the burglars agreed with Forsyth that there might be armed agents waiting inside the office.

All of the possibilities that came to mind were terrible.

When he felt somewhat calmer, Forsyth closely questioned Bonnie Raines again about the details of everything she remembered about the second external door—the one she had strongly recommended they not enter, but that now seemed like the only way they could. She told them what she had seen: that it was barricaded on the inside by a tall double-door metal cabinet that she assumed was filled with paper. If that door had to be pushed open, she said now, it would have to be done extremely slowly and carefully in order not to topple it to the floor and cause a loud crash. But given the new situation, she reversed herself and said she thought they should enter through that door. She realized it would be difficult but necessary to do so.

From the time Forsyth returned to the motel until a decision was made, the intense discussion of alternatives lasted not more than fifteen minutes. Bonnie Raines recalls that it "was an extremely tense moment." After Forsyth described his failure to pick the lock and worried aloud about the long time, plus noise, it probably would take to pry the other door open, the burglars responded with a few questions and much empathy. Bonnie Raines answered his questions about the second door. When there seemed to be no more questions, Davidon summed up what they did and did not know. Then he said something like, "We've gone this far. There is no evidence we have aroused any suspicion. Everything else seems to be okay." He didn't think the doubt about whether the lock had been added should stop them. There were no other signs, he said, that they were being watched. Very calmly, but also urgently, he said they needed to make a decision quickly.

When he stopped speaking, the burglars searched one another's faces. There was total silence. Bonnie Raines remembers realizing that a consensus had been reached. "Suddenly," she said, heads began nodding affirmatively. "Everyone agreed to go ahead. I don't know what would have happened if one or two people had just said, 'Forget it, I'm outta here.'" But that didn't happen. Instead, everyone agreed to begin again. Whatever their risk originally, they realized the decision they had just made might have exponentially increased it.

Davidon's effective leadership was keenly evident during the anxious minutes in the motel room after the burglars absorbed the bad news from Forsyth. Recalling years later how Davidon imparted calmness and courage in those crucial minutes, Bonnie Raines is moved, as she was then, by the quality of his leadership. "We needed his great spirit. Without his spirit, we wouldn't have done it." The others agree. Every burglar who has been interviewed expressed that same view: Davidon's courage and his confidence in the plan they developed and in their being able to carry it out, despite what had just happened, made it possible for them to agree again to move forward. His calm words and clear thinking during those crucial minutes, they say, made it possible for them to find confidence despite their increased fear.

Forsyth drove to the FBI office. Again.

As his accomplices waited at the motel, they were, to put it mildly, very worried about what they had just agreed he should do. Small talk did not come easily among them after he left. There was a lot of pacing. The Ali-Frazier fight in New York may have been distracting the world at that hour, but it was not distracting them. They were preoccupied by fear that their elaborate plans might be spinning out of control—the opposite of the smooth operation they hoped all their weeks of planning would make possible.

The burglars didn't know it, but thanks to Forsyth's delay in breaking in, the timing of the burglary now aligned almost precisely with that of the Ali-Frazier fight. The burglars had assumed the fight would start about 8 p.m. and therefore so should the burglary. Actually, the Ali-Frazier fight did not start until 10:40. Consequently, in New York the noisiest part of the pre-event ceremony was just getting under way about the time Forsyth returned to the FBI office to start his second round, as it were. Whatever helpful sound the fight could provide this evening, the loudest noise would happen at just the right time.

AT 10:30 in New York, the ring announcer calmed the crowd enough to introduce great boxers from the past, all of whom came into the ring: James J. Braddock, Rocky Graziano, Willie Pep, Jack Dempsey, Archie Moore, Jack Sharkey, Sugar Ray Raineson, Billy Conn, and Joe Louis. There was a huge ovation as Louis climbed into the ring.

By that time, the excitement in New York was extreme. As it built, the sportswriter Dave Kindred wrote nearly thirty years later, "Such a night had never been seen in the history of sports. For here came two of the greatest fighters ever, both young and strong and nearly as good as they'd ever be, both to be paid $2.5 million . . . both certain they would leave the ring as he entered it, champion now and forever. . . .

"I don't remember breathing all night long," Kindred recalled.

What international tennis champion Arthur Ashe later described as "the biggest event in the history of boxing" was about to begin. "No fight ever transcended boxing," he later wrote, as that one did "throughout the world."

The excitement had been building to a high crescendo since eight o'clock. After the past greats were introduced and left the ring, the excitement was palpable. It was time. "The eyes of the world were focused on a small square of illuminated canvas, which had become one of the great stages of modern times," Thomas Hauser wrote of the extraordinary atmosphere as the fight was about to begin. The stars of the evening—in whom millions all over the world saw the reflection of their own values, hopes, and dreams—were at last coming down the aisle. Ali came first, followed by Frazier. Ali wore a white satin robe, red trunks, and white shoes laced with red tassels a fan had sent from Germany. On the back of Frazier's robe, the names of his five children were embroidered in gold between his first and last names. He was wearing green satin trunks.

In the seconds before the fight started at 10:40, the roar from the crowd was unlike anything Larry Merchant, longtime boxing reporter and analyst, says he ever heard before or since that night:

"There was this guttural roar. It came straight up from the stomach, from a place that went beyond the heart, that the heart could not control, much less the mind. People could hardly believe the fight was going to happen."

At 10:40 the bell rang. The fight started.

FORSYTH ARRIVED at the FBI office about that time. The thirty-second break-in plan now long gone, breaking in now seemed like it would be more like a small demolition job than a swift lock-picking exercise. Of course, he had no idea that the fight schedule and his revised break-in schedule might mesh, let alone whether it would matter. The fight was not on his mind.

Again he entered the building, briefcase in hand, trying again to look as though he either lived there or was on his way to see a client, though it was a little late for that. Given the crude and slow way the break-in would now have to be done, the odds of residents walking by or hearing the sound of wood breaking had increased.

This time, in addition to the set of homemade tools in his briefcase, Forsyth carried a crowbar. It fit fairly well in the deep inside pocket of his used Brooks Brothers overcoat. A long time later, he marveled in amusement at how well the overcoat's pockets, with their unusual depth, could be adapted to the special storage needs of a burglar. He easily picked the lock on the second door, the one that was not used as an entrance, in thirty seconds. But that was just the beginning. There was a deadbolt near the top of the door. He pulled out his crowbar and, with a quick maneuver, popped it. "I had to do it fast. Otherwise, there would have been a long creaking sound. I figured if you cause a quick bang, if someone hears it, they will think a cat knocked over the trash can in the alley, and it's all done with." He wasn't sure that rationale made sense, but he found it comforting at the time.

Then he pushed on the door. It wouldn't move. Yes, Bonnie Raines was right. He didn't remember exactly what she had said blocked the door; he just realized now that something "very big and very heavy" was on the other side. To move it even a tiny fraction of an inch, he had to lean on it with all his might. An agent who worked at the Media office said years later that, given the weight of the large cabinet leaning against that door, all of the burglars must have pushed the door open together. In fact, Forsyth alone did it, but with a great deal of worry. "It was obvious," he recalled, "that if that sucker hit the floor it was going to wake up the whole neighborhood, not just the caretaker who lived directly below the office.

"The only thing to do then . . . I got down on the floor, put the crowbar up against the door and tried to push against it. . . . I couldn't apply nearly enough force. Whatever was behind it, it was heavy as hell. I'm trying to slide it across a carpeted floor without tipping it and without being able to use the things you normally use when you move furniture. I thought that if I had a lot longer lever, a wrecking bar, it would be better. But it wasn't exactly the time to get that. There were no construction supply houses open where I could get a six-foot or a ten-foot bar. So I went out to the car and got one of those old trapezoidal bars you use on jack stands. I held it in place inside my overcoat. The bottom of it was about half an inch above the bottom of the coat, and the other part stuck up above one shoulder." He likes to think that he looked like a guy in an overcoat walking down the street with an unfortunate growth on one shoulder.

There in the well-lit second-floor hall, where residents might pass by at any time, Forsyth stretched his more than six-foot frame out on the floor and proceeded to use his leg muscles to push and pull the bar. As he rocked the bar, he feared a resident from an upstairs apartment might at any moment decide to go for a walk or a drink and come down the stairs, nearly stepping on his face as he lay stretched out on the floor near the stairs, huffing and puffing as he pushed on the FBI door. There he was—a man on the floor in a topcoat making a fulcrum of himself. "Hello . . . Good evening," he imagined himself wryly and politely saying as he looked up from the floor into the face of a very puzzled resident and did his best to act as though their bizarre encounter was natural and should not be reported to the police.

While Forsyth was working hard on the floor, he "heard this clank noise from inside the office. My heart dropped to my heels. Have you ever had that sinking feeling—like you're just about to get struck from behind by a speeding semitrailer or something like that? I thought, 'Here I go down the tubes and there's nothing I can do about it.' I'm thinking to myself, 'Was that a clumsy FBI agent, or was that the heating system?' And I'm thinking, 'What did it really sound like? It sounded metallic. Sounded like the sound of two pieces of metal hitting each other.'"

Still pushing and pulling, he was thinking, as he was earlier, "Well, if the lock was changed because the FBI knows about the burglary, agents might be standing in the darkened office with guns drawn waiting for me to step inside." Unlike his humorous musings about what he would say if a resident walked by, he had no musings about what he would say if he encountered agents with drawn guns on the other side of the door. "Hello . . . Good evening" seemed unlikely. "Finally, I said to myself, 'There's only one way to find out. I'm paranoid at this moment. I probably exaggerated the sound.' So I say to myself, 'Let's just go for it. Let's open the door and say, "Surprise!"'" His sense of humor may not have been quite that brash at that moment, but he did force himself to push through his fear. "There was a little moment of panic there," he recalls.

Forsyth has one very pleasant memory from the minutes when he was stretched out on the floor. While he was on his back pushing and shoving the door ever so carefully and repeatedly, he heard the crackling noise of the Ali-Frazier fight broadcast in apartments. At a time when a smile didn't seem possible, he smiled. Ali and Frazier were helping, as the burglars had hoped they would.

Then, finally, success.

The door creaked—the sound he hated to cause but had to—as pressure on the bar pushed the inside cabinet forward ever so slightly while simultaneously causing the wooden door to crack. No resident had come down the stairs to go on an errand and stepped on his face while he was stretched out on the floor. Now he stood and, for several more minutes, very slowly and cautiously pushed the door until it was open just far enough for him to squeeze inside. In the dark, he determined that no agents, with or without guns, were waiting for him inside the office. After he got in, and felt sure he was alone, he gently closed the now fragile door and slowly inched the tall double-door cabinet far enough away from the door that the inside team would be able to squeeze into the room with their big suitcases. He wore gloves, of course, throughout all these maneuvers.

Inside the dark office, he packed his supplies, hiding the big ones again inside his coat. He carefully eased the damaged door into its frame so that it appeared from the outside, if one did not examine it too carefully, to be closed and locked as usual. He walked to his car, took a few deep breaths, and drove to the motel.

He remembers that from the moment he arrived at the FBI office door the first time until he finished the job and returned to the motel the second time, the time that elapsed was "oh, a lifetime." What was supposed to take thirty seconds had taken hours. "I screwed up the schedule, I know that. I'll bet they [the burglars waiting at the hotel] were sweating blood. I know I was."

It would be an understatement to say that everyone was glad to see Forsyth when he arrived at the motel with good news this time—the door was unlocked, the office was ready to be entered. They had feared he would call again and say it was impossible to get in. When they saw his sweating but beaming face, it was clear he had been successful. This time he was greeted like a conquering hero. Forsyth told the inside crew of four—Williamson, Susan Smith, Ron Durst, and Janet Fessenden—that when they arrived at the office they would find an unlocked door that needed to be handled very gingerly. He answered their questions and then, drained from excessive relief, collapsed on one of the twin beds in the room. "It wasn't over, but the worst part was over for me. The chances of me getting busted had just dropped about seven million percent. Sure, I was worried about the other people, but, honestly, it's not as scary as when you're worried about yourself." He realized there was danger ahead, including when he would be driving a car with suitcases full of stolen FBI files, but he "thought the probabilities of arrest then would be much less. I was a little bit nervous about driving down the road, but I knew I wouldn't speed, and we didn't have drugs in the car or any of that kind of stuff. I knew I looked like a respectable citizen. That was no big deal as far as I was concerned." His big deal had just ended.

The next big deal was about to begin.

The inside crew members were driven to Media and dropped off near the front of the building. The drivers returned to the motel. During the draft board raids, drivers of getaway cars sometimes sat in their vehicles near the site of each raid and waited for the raiders to complete the job. The Media group decided they should not risk doing that. They could not be sure how long the inside crew would be in the office. In such a small town, they assumed, people hanging around in cars for a long time late at night might arouse suspicion. They had done enough of that during casing. The cars they were using tonight, as per a plan developed by Davidon, had not been seen in the neighborhood before. Knowing no one was waiting for them outside increased the pressure on the inside crew—what if they needed to escape quickly?—but they all agreed that being dropped off probably was a safer way.

Each of the four members of the inside crew carried two large "trip size" suitcases as they walked down the sidewalk and up the three stairs to the front door of the County Court Apartments building and then up the well-lit central stairwell. In stone silence, they awkwardly squeezed themselves and their suitcases through the FBI office door Forsyth had forced open. One fo them shut it after all of them were inside. After their eyes adjusted to the darkness, they explored the rooms. Some cabinets and drawers were locked, others were not. They used screwdrivers to force open the ones that were locked.

Seldom even whispering, they opened every drawer and every cabinet door. They broke locks on some of them. Operating mostly in the dark, they did what they had planned to do: They reached inside the drawers and cabinet shelves and removed every piece of paper, except for a stack of blank personnel forms they left behind in a cabinet. Williamson shined a flashlight on their work as they requested from time to time. He had covered the flashlight with tape so it produced only a narrow, sharply focused beam. He concealed the beam completely with his hands as he moved from one person to another, offering light as needed. It was important that the flashlight beam not be seen from outside the building, especially from the windows that were visible to the courthouse guard across the street. Williamson occasionally turned off the flashlight and walked to the office windows to check whether anything unwanted—such as a police car—was on the streets below.

He remembers the time inside the FBI office as "very scary." He had said yes immediately to Davidon when he proposed burglarizing an FBI office. But that did not mean Williamson had a casual attitude about the burglary. Far from it. "I was terrified before, during, and after. . . . Honestly, I think everyone was. We each had our own way of dealing with the fear. Mine was trying to distract myself and others with humor." But, given the weight of what they were doing in the FBI office, he gave no thought to telling one of his favorite shaggy-dog stories during the burglary, as he had during some draft board raids. Instead, like the others, he remembers being stoic and determined inside the FBI office, and utterly silent.

The burglars tried to unlock a small safe they found, but they gave up, realizing that a code was needed to open it. When every drawer and shelf was empty, except for a stack of personnel forms, and the suitcases were bulging, one of the burglars used a phone on an agent's desk to call the motel room. Forsyth recalls that the caller "made some cryptic spy remark like, 'Okay,' and hung up."

That's what the people at the motel were waiting for: the signal that the job was done, the inside crew was ready to be picked up. It was time to vacate the room at the motel and drive the getaway cars to Media to pick up the inside crew and the stolen files. Everyone in the motel room put on their coats, searched the room for any telltale belongings, and looked at one another knowingly. As the four inside crew members and Forsyth had done at the office, everyone had worn gloves while they were in the motel room. They felt confident there was no sign they had been there—unless, of course, someone checked the name of the person who had rented the room.

When the right number of minutes had elapsed—they had carefully timed how long the drive from the motel to the FBI building would take— the inside crew looked around the dark rooms they had just relieved of files. They left the office as quietly as they could. The suitcases were now quite heavy, and it took more effort to squeeze out through the narrow doorway than it had to squeeze in. The last burglar out set down his suitcases and eased the damaged door against the damaged frame so it looked as normal as possible under the circumstances.

The most important stage of the burglary had just been completed. The four members of the inside crew had in their possession what they had come for—all the files in the Media FBI office. Now they would place the stolen files safely into car trunks and take them to the remote farmhouse that had been loaned to Davidon by a friend who didn't ask and wasn't told why Davidon wanted access to the house for a couple weeks.

Feeling some trepidation, the inside team slowly carried the heavy suitcases down the stairs. They waited briefly in the well-lit space inside the front door. Right on time, the getaway cars arrived. Two of the drivers arrived and parked, as planned, on Veterans Square, just a few yards from the entrance of the FBI building. The inside crew members walked to the cars, opened the trunks, lifted the heavy suitcases, placed them inside, and then got in the cars themselves.

In another car, Bonnie Raines was about to become a decoy. She parked in the center of the street, a few car lengths behind the waiting parked cars and served as a distraction. She got out and lifted the hood, fiddled with the engine, and was prepared to tell any police officer who might stop and question her that her car wouldn't start. She would say she was trying to figure out what was wrong. If necessary, she was prepared to try to engage police officers in conversation about her "problem" long enough to distract them from noticing the people who were placing large suitcases in the trunks of parked cars.

She closed the hood on her "disabled" car. The ruse was not needed. No police car drove up, nor did any other car except the burglars'. That part of their plan had worked perfectly. Smith and she drove to the Swarthmore parking lot.

Forsyth, seated in one of the getaway cars as it was being loaded, remembers watching the courthouse guard as he stood inside the glass front door of the courthouse and looked directly at what was taking place: four people struggling with two suitcases each as they placed them in waiting cars. "He was standing right there," Forsyth recalls, still amazed years later at the circumstance. "I remember him in his uniform. At the moment these guys were coming out of the building and putting the suitcases in the cars, he was standing there looking out the window, watching it all happen. . . . We had tried to figure out how we could avoid being seen by him, but there was nothing we could do about it. We decided there was no way to avoid him seeing us. And there he was, seeing it all."

During questioning by FBI agents the next day and at least two more times over the next two months, the courthouse guard on duty that night told agents he saw nothing unusual take place late the evening of March 8 in front of the building that housed the FBI office. Perhaps he was watching mindlessly, as the burglars had hoped. Or perhaps he had a radio tuned to the Ali-Frazier fight and was distracted. Whatever the case, he claimed he saw nothing.

The burglars drove the loaded getaway cars to waiting parked cars a few miles away in various directions from Media. The suitcases were transferred to those cars. Davidon had added this extra layer of caution. As per his plan, this transfer meant the stolen files would travel to the farmhouse in cars that had never been seen near the FBI office.

Bonnie Raines and Smith arrived at the empty—except for John Raines in the maroon Raines family station wagon—parking lot at Swarthmore College and parked alongside him. During the hours he spent alone in the dark station wagon waiting for them, the intense, stomach-knotting fear John had felt for several weeks seemed to be more than justified. He imagined terrible scenarios for why Smith and Bonnie had been delayed more than three hours. He was enormously relieved when they arrived. The suitcases were transferred from Smith's car to the Raineses' station wagon.

They set out for the farm.

IN MEDIA, the verdict was not clear. Having taken enormous risks and pulled off the burglary, the burglars left town with no idea whether their suitcases were stuffed with anything other than heavy piles of uninteresting, unimportant bureaucratic files.

In New York, the verdict was very clear: Frazier won, Ali lost.

As the world watched, Ali did not "float like a butterfly, sting like a bee," as he had in the past and had predicted he would that night. Frazier's victory happened about the time the burglars were placing FBI files into the getaway cars. After forty-three minutes in the ring, in the fifteenth round, Ali, exhausted, took a hammerlike left hook to his jaw that lifted him off his feet. He crashed to the metal floor, causing a thunderclap that made fans cringe. He was on his feet in three seconds. But the fight was over. He had taken the worst beating of his career. It was a "savage attack," *New York Times* sports reporter Dave Anderson wrote. "It lifted Ali off his feet and dumped him on his back, his legs straight up," wrote Dave Kindred.

The atmosphere was wild and crazy throughout the fight, Anderson wrote the next day. A man in the audience died of a heart attack in the midst of the excitement.

The hearts of millions of people were broken when Ali lost. His defeat symbolized the defeat many feared for themselves in struggles then taking place for justice, basic rights, and the fight to end the war in Vietnam. Antiwar activists throughout the world felt dejected when they saw their hero lose. But probably no one felt the loss more acutely than young African Americans. Bryant Gumbel, then a recent college graduate living in a third-floor walk-up in New York and not yet a television journalist, described the impact: "I nearly died that night. I just died because this was a night when it all came together. If Ali lost, it was as though everything I believed in was wrong. . . . I was devastated. It was awful. I felt as though everything

I stood for had been beaten down and trampled. . . . It was a terrible night. I'll never forget it as long as I live."

In Washington, FBI director J. Edgar Hoover, a man who followed strict routines, probably dined out, as usual, at a favorite restaurant that evening with Clyde Tolson, his longtime close companion and the second highest official in the bureau. After dinner, the director probably was driven home as he routinely was to his redbrick northwest Washington home on 30th Place NW, where, until just a decade earlier, Lyndon and Lady Bird Johnson had been his neighbors. Tonight, after opening the back door so his two beloved dogs, the Cairn terriers G-Boy and Cindy, could return to the house, he probably locked the door and set the alarm system FBI workers had installed years earlier. As Hoover retired to his bedroom, passing a large bronze bust of himself at the top of the stairs, he could go to bed that evening warmed by the thought that in the public's mind he was still the hero he had set out to become many years ago. He could fall asleep feeling protected from vandals and by politicians in Washington, unaware that elsewhere, in a sleepy Pennsylvania town, burglars had just intruded in his world in ways he never would have thought possible.

7

Escape to the Farm

O N   T H E I R   W A Y to the farm, the burglars were relieved that the burglary was over. But they were worried about what could still happen that night. It was difficult to believe that at some point at least one of them had not inadvertently made a mistake that would lead to the discovery of one or more of them a few hours later, or perhaps now as they drove away from Media. Did people see them leave, burdened with heavy suitcases? Did anyone see suitcases being transferred from one car to another? Did someone follow one or more of the cars?

From Media, they drove northwest, each car taking a different route. Davidon thought it was important for them not to follow one another along the same route so that the arrest of burglars in one car would be less likely to lead to the arrest of those in other cars. He gave each driver a map and marked detailed directions for each one on how to get to the farmhouse from wherever they transferred files from one car to another.

Beginning now, Davidon advised, it should become standard procedure for the burglars to protect one another by not doing anything together— except hiding at the farm to read and analyze stolen files. He told them the trip to the farm would take about an hour. They drove along narrow, twisting suburban streets and then lonely dark country roads to get to their destination, a small farmhouse on the well-concealed grounds of Fellowship Farm. It was not far from Pottstown, Pennsylvania, a once thriving old mill town that provided steel for, among other massive projects, the building of the Golden Gate Bridge. Davidon thought this small house at Fellowship Farm, a Quaker conference center somewhat remote from Philadelphia and surrounded by woods, would be an ideal place to hide with stolen FBI files. Quakers from the Philadelphia area often held retreats on these grounds, and for many years the farm had spawned a commitment to social activism and to nonviolent resistance among thousands of people who attended retreats there. A very young Martin Luther King had once visited during a crucial time in his life to deepen his study of nonviolence. Tonight and for the next ten days, the burglars' presence there would give new meaning to the word "retreat" in relation to Fellowship Farm.

The drivers remember looking in their rearview mirrors more than usual that night. Each time headlights appeared in the rear distance, some of them remember, their stomachs tightened. Then they would feel relief as a car passed and sped ahead, with no apparent interest in stopping them and no sign it was a police car.

When John and Bonnie Raines arrived at the farmhouse, two other burglars had not yet arrived. After more than an hour of waiting, the six burglars at the house grew concerned about the missing burglars. They had felt somewhat elated when they first arrived at the house. But they put that feeling on hold when it seemed possible that two members of the group might be missing. Maybe their initial sense that at last they could be reasonably sure they had not been seen and had not been followed had been premature.

Every headlight they saw far away through leafless winter trees held their attention. Every car they saw in the distance that didn't turn down the road that led to the house produced a letdown. By an hour after the Raineses arrived, the six burglars felt certain that the missing burglars must have been arrested. If so, this could mean that all of them would be arrested soon. Or it might mean they would have to wait until the next day to find out what had happened. As time passed, they became convinced—as they had been just hours earlier when they heard Forsyth's dilemma—that all the likely possibilities were bad.

Finally, a car turned down the road and drove toward the house. By that time, they were so on edge that they assumed the approaching car might be police officers or FBI agents. To their great relief, it was the missing burglars. They had made a wrong turn and gotten lost. In the dark countryside, in those pre-GPS and pre–cell phone days, it was difficult to find their way back to the route Davidon had marked on their map.

At last, all of the burglars and all of the stolen documents were together. With everyone now present and safe, tensions finally melted. "There was a sense of excitement and accomplishment that the burglary was over, and that no one had been arrested," Davidon remembers. Faces that had been taut and tense just minutes earlier were now relaxed. Cool and somewhat emotionally detached from each other during their months of planning, now they hugged one another. Someone opened bags of sandwiches and bottles of beer. One of them opened a thermos of hot coffee, another a bag of apples. Someone had brought milk. It was a burglars' feast. With drinks of choice in hand, they stood around the table in the modest house and toasted one another and a job that seemed to have been done well.

They had come this far. They felt uncertain about the future, even about the next day, but they were happy to celebrate what had happened so far. There were smiles all around and then some more hugs. They felt secure and protected inside the little house. They had no idea whether they were actually safe, but they felt safe, and they cherished that feeling. "I remember that feeling of being safe," says Bonnie Raines. "We were a little giddy. We felt happy, very happy that we had done it. It looked like we had gotten away with it."

Their celebration was brief. Adrenaline was flowing. They could hardly wait to open the suitcases and see what they had stolen. They yearned to find out if they now had in their possession any significant files. Forsyth remembers being especially eager to read the files. For him, this was the most compelling aspect of the entire operation—discovering whether they had found anything important that would put the FBI on notice—not only that the bureau had been burglarized but that the American people could not be fooled forever. He desperately hoped there was valuable evidence in those suitcases.

All of the burglars stayed at the farm that first night. None of them slept. There was more than enough adrenaline to fuel them through the night. They opened the suitcases, removed the stolen files, and placed them in stacks on the dining table, coffee table, kitchen counters, chairs, and the floor—any flat surface available.

With the burglary behind them, in the wee hours of the morning they embraced the next—and what they hoped would be the most substantive—phase of their project. They embarked on the work that would determine the meaning of what had been done in the name of the Citizens' Commission to Investigate the FBI. Each of them took a portion of the files and settled into work at the table, counter, living room chair, or on the floor. They were very quiet, totally absorbed, as they started this phase of their work, the post-burglary analysis. They welcomed this task with a deep sense of responsibility and dedication. Now that the essential but dirty work of

The house on the grounds of Fellowship Farm, a small Quaker conference center about forty miles northwest of Philadelphia, where for ten days after the burglary the group analyzed the stolen files and prepared them for distribution. *(Photo by Betty Medsger)*

burglary was over, it was as though they were indeed the Citizens' Commission to Investigate the FBI, appointed not, as they were, by themselves, but by the president of the United States and tasked by him to do the work they had assigned themselves:

> Research and analyze, to the fullest extent possible through these documents, whether there is evidence that J. Edgar Hoover and his FBI are destroying dissent.

They had anticipated this moment and developed a plan. Confident they would find files of serious interest, Davidon guided them now. As they read the documents, they would sort them in categories—organized crime, other crime, political spying, draft board resistance. Depending on what they would find, new categories could be added. All files would initially be read by at least two burglars, who together would decide the importance of each document and how to categorize it.

The files, they agreed, would stay at the farm. Davidon and John Raines had been the key planners of this phase. They intended, after all documents had been read, to count the documents in each category and write an overall analysis to be released to the public, in addition to releasing copies of files. They would destroy some types of documents, such as criminal cases unrelated to politics or the military draft. They did not want to hinder the FBI's investigations of crimes it should be investigating. They agreed to be especially cautious about not revealing information about organized crime cases. They accidentally threw away a couple documents they later wished they had kept. For instance, they regretted that they destroyed a document from FBI headquarters that outlined detailed instructions on how agents should celebrate J. Edgar Hoover's birthday each year. Though it was not meant to be humorous, it was. They realized later that the document provided a glimpse of the needy ego of the director that led him, supported by those closest to him, to create the cult of personality that, it was learned later, permeated the bureau.

They didn't have to wait long to learn whether they had found anything of value. Within the first hour, one of them broke the silence with a sudden shout: "Look at this!" They all gathered around and together read the document that prompted the shout. It was advice to FBI agents, the outcome of a meeting at FBI headquarters a few months earlier of agents who specialized in investigating activists. Agents were advised, in a newsletter prepared for such agents, to "enhance the paranoia . . . and . . . get the point across there is an FBI agent behind every mailbox."

It took their breath away.

After the burglars' initial reaction, they read the document again to make sure they had read it right the first time: "enhance the paranoia . . . an FBI agent behind every mailbox." They were as stunned as millions of Americans would be two weeks later.

Despite having spent so much effort planning and executing the burglary in order to search for evidence of whether the FBI was suppressing dissent, when the burglars read that document they found it difficult to believe they had discovered a file so raw, cruel, and clear. Ron Durst remembers being surprised that official statements about the goals of spying—rather than only reports on specific spying—were in the files. Susan Smith said years later that when they read that document she realized that when it became public countless people who had been ridiculed for believing the FBI was spying on activists would read it and want to say, "Hey, Mom, everybody, I'm not mentally ill! They really are after me, you, lots of people." Two weeks later, people read that document on front pages and expressed shock and anger that the FBI was, by plan and assignment, creating paranoia.

In that first hour, they had found this powerful evidence that the bureau suppressed dissent—not an isolated specific example of suppression, many of which would be found later, but a statement of an overall philosophy about the atmosphere of suppression the bureau wanted to create.

In that moment, when the burglars discovered that damning evidence that the FBI was not what Hoover had long claimed it was—that creating paranoia among Americans was part of this law enforcement agency's mission—they knew that whatever would happen to them as a result of what they had done this night—arrest, trial, time in prison—the risk had been worthwhile. They were amazed that from the piles of files that surrounded them in the house they had found such a document, little more than an hour after arriving at the farm and opening their suitcases. It rewarded and motivated them through the long days and nights of little sleep ahead. They knew they had in their possession very important information Americans needed to know. They would find many important documents as they read the files, but this document would become emblematic of the burglary. People would remember the "paranoia" file years later when the Media burglary was mentioned.

That brief document spelled out the essence of what Davidon had feared was at the core of FBI practice—a policy about political spying that was the antithesis of what a law enforcement agency should be in a democratic society. The need for evidence had motivated him to propose this extreme means of citizen investigation: the burglary of an FBI office in the absence of oversight of the FBI by any government official or agency. Now it was clear he had been right. In that little house in the woods, in the middle of a Quaker retreat that had nurtured nonviolent political action, the eight burglars now held in their hands the first evidence that, except for fear, cowardice, and apathy, could have been unearthed by federal officials or journalists many years earlier.

THE BURGLARS READ FBI files all night that first night at the farmhouse. They were consumed by what they read. Every once in a while, one of them would gasp in surprise and yell, "Listen to this." They would gather around that person and read the newest discovery. They despaired about much of what they found. They felt like someone who has been suffering from a disease doctors have been unable to diagnose for years. Then one day a doctor accurately identifies the disease. The diagnosis is terrible, but the patient needs to know it in order to try to find a cure. They hoped a cure would be found for the serious problems the files revealed. It was unclear if oversight of the FBI, always dormant, if not dead, could come alive. Assuming they were not arrested and the files were not confiscated, they hoped they were now on their way to making public evidence that would cause the nation's leaders to recognize the need to establish oversight.

As they read, at times they were sad. At other times they were angry or amazed. They also were occasionally amused, even when they read the "mailbox" document, which included this statement:

"Some will be overcome by the overwhelming personalities of the contacting agent and volunteer to tell all—perhaps on a continuing basis." The burglars had attended many antiwar rallies and demonstrations and often observed FBI agents and informers writing notes and taking photographs. Some, if not all, of the group knew people who had been interviewed by FBI agents. Not once had any of them heard any of those people say they were "overcome by the overwhelming personalities" of the agents.

As of this point, these amateur burglars had succeeded in ways the most famous burglars of the century—the men who a little more than a year later would botch the break-in at Democratic National Committee headquarters at the Watergate in Washington in June 1972—would have envied. Each of those five burglars and their two leaders were well trained in the skills of burglary by their former employers, the FBI and the CIA. As former CIA agent Howard Hunt helped plan the Watergate burglary from his White House office, he called the CIA and, according to a CIA file on the conversation, asked a contact at the agency "if he had a retiree or resignee who was accomplished at picking locks." The agency recommended someone and sent his résumé, with lock-picking expertise cited. Even with training by lock pickers from the CIA, none of the Watergate burglars turned out to be as skilled as Forsyth.

BY THE TIME the Media burglars forced themselves to stop reading the morning after the burglary, at about 5 a.m., they felt a deep satisfaction from knowing already that their act of resistance should have a significant impact. Most of them drove home and then to their jobs in the city. Davidon had advised everyone to act as normal as possible, especially now during the immediate aftermath. For instance, he planned to be at his campus office, as he always was on Tuesday mornings, so no one, if interviewed later by an investigator or reporter, would be able to say, "Come to think of it, he wasn't there that Tuesday, like he usually is."

Durst stayed at the farmhouse with the documents. As a graduate student who worked part-time, he had a flexible schedule. Because of that, he volunteered to stay at the farm and protect the documents twenty-four hours a day until they had been analyzed, copied, and prepared for public distribution. The other burglars lived and worked in the city every day and then drove to the farm after work to carry out their file review duties for several hours each evening.

As they prepared to leave the house that first morning, some of them wanted to take care of what they considered unfinished business. At about five o'clock, between two pages of files, Davidon noticed a very small piece of paper with a series of handwritten numbers on it. He asked inside crew members if they had seen a safe in the office. They confirmed there was a safe with a combination lock. They had tried to open it but failed. Davidon felt sure the number he found must be the combination code. It tempted him. He remembers thinking that it "seemed such a shame to have this information and not use it."

He decided he would go to the FBI office on his way home and open the safe. He and Durst became preoccupied with what might be in it. They thought it was probably where agents put their most important, most explosive documents. It would be so easy to get inside, he thought. Thanks to Forsyth, of course, the door was unlocked.

At first, the brash idea seemed irresistible, but as he reconsidered it, he thought some of the residents in the building might leave early for work about the time he would arrive. His wiser self prevailed. He was tired and realized he could not trust his reflexes after a sleepless night and the pressures of the last twenty-four hours. He decided not to go to the office. Whatever was in the safe would have to remain undiscovered. Given what was in it, that was a fortunate decision.

Forsyth decided that on his drive back to Philadelphia he would get rid of some things he thought the burglars should not have—bullets. The inside crew had grabbed a large brown leather briefcase from the FBI office closet and scooped into it assorted small items from the agents' desk drawers, mostly paper clips and bullets. They packed the briefcase into one of the suitcases. Forsyth was perturbed when he discovered the bullets. A bunch of nonviolent antiwar activists, he thought, should not be caught with them. He also was mildly amused that agents kept bullets and paper clips side by side in their desk drawers, as if both were basic office supplies. Everyone agreed with Forsyth that they should get rid of the bullets immediately.

As the sun was starting to rise, Forsyth parked at the end of a bridge in a small village between the farm and the city. Once again making a proper appearance in his Brooks Brothers topcoat, but this time carrying an FBI agent's briefcase instead of his own, he walked to the center of the bridge and deep-sixed the briefcase, unwanted bullets included, into a turbulent spot in the Schuylkill River. He watched the briefcase sink and then he drove home confident that the only dangerous items the burglars now possessed were J. Edgar Hoover's secret files. Soon they would find out how dangerous they were.

IT WAS TIME to let the world know the burglary had taken place. The burglars hoped they would be ready to distribute copies of stolen files in about two weeks. Early this morning, though, they were ready to release a statement announcing what they had done and why they had done it. Everyone in the group had agreed to the statement, written a little more than a week earlier by Davidon and John Raines. It had been decided that John would call a reporter and read the release on the way home from the farmhouse the morning after the burglary.

The Raineses left for home and their special assignment at about six o'clock. They were eager to return before the children woke up. Bonnie was driving, and John was nervously reading the statement aloud, rehearsing the call he would make momentarily to the reporter. The reporter had been carefully chosen—Bill Wingell, a freelance reporter based in Philadelphia who wrote for the Reuters news service. Davidon had met Wingell at several antiwar events he covered, but John Raines had never met or talked with him, so his voice could not be recognized by Wingell.

As they got close to Chestnut Hill, a residential area in the far northwest corner of Philadelphia, they knew they couldn't put off the call any longer. In an area where there were no homes or offices, they saw a phone booth outside a closed gas station. Bonnie parked a few feet from the booth. John fumbled for coins as he entered the booth, closed it, and then dialed Wingell's number. It was a little before 6:30 a.m. The ringing phone wakened Wingell. John told him he wanted to read a statement to him and launched right into the rather lengthy statement. But Wingell stopped him. He needed a few moments to put paper in his typewriter and otherwise get prepared to take dictation, including clearing his mind of sleep and becoming fully alert. It was an awkward moment for both of them. Finally, Wingell said he was ready to take the statement. John started to read again, but now more slowly. This time his words jolted Wingell to full alertness:

On the night of March 8, 1971, the Citizens' Commission to Investigate the FBI removed files from the Media, PA, office of the FBI. These files will now be studied to determine:

- The nature and extent of surveillance and intimidation carried on by this office of the FBI, particularly against groups and individuals working for a more just, humane and peaceful society;
- How much of the FBI's efforts are spent on relatively minor crimes by the poor and powerless against whom they can get a more glamorous conviction rate, instead of investigating truly serious crimes by those with money and influence which cause great damage to the lives of many people; crimes such as war profiteering, monopolistic practices, institutional racism, organized crime, and the mass distribution of lethal drugs;
- The extent of illegal practices by the FBI, such as eavesdropping, entrapment, and the use of provocateurs and informers.

At this point in his slow reading, John noticed out of the corner of his eye that a police car was slowly driving by. Bonnie and John laugh as they recall the scene many years later. It was far from funny at the time. "John is sitting in the phone booth with his paper, reading away," Bonnie recalls. The police officer slowed down and peered in a very obvious way at John. He kept reading, but he was very aware that he was being observed. The police officer circled and came around again, driving even more slowly this time. Again he stared directly at John as he read.

Bonnie may have been more frightened at this moment than she was at any point before or during the burglary. She leaned over the passenger seat and knocked nervously and as loudly as she could on the front passenger window of the car, motioning for John to stop reading and return to the car. She wanted to drive away before the police car returned again. "This is the closest we came to blowing the whole thing," says John. "We didn't know what to think. It was clear the cop was trying to figure out what we were doing." It wasn't normal to see a middle-aged couple at a phone booth at 6:30 a.m., with one of them reading a document into the phone. They had contingency plans for how to deal with police while casing, and for how to block the street in front of the burglarized building with a fake breakdown, but they had no contingency plan for this situation. Here was a police officer looking into John's face from just a few yards away. In John's hands was what amounted to an elaborately detailed confession of the burglary—a bonanza for an arresting officer. What would he say if the police officer got out of his car and asked, "What are you doing?" John had no idea what he would say.

But in this critical moment, John changed.

He lost the fear that had nearly paralyzed him in recent weeks, especially the previous evening. He, who had been so frightened before the burglary, now, in a moment of potential crisis, summoned more courage than he knew he had and, in a split second, decided not to abort the call He continued reading:

> As this study proceeds, the results obtained, along with the FBI documents pertaining to them, will be sent to people in public life who have demonstrated the integrity, courage and commitment to democratic values which are necessary to effectively challenge the repressive policies of the FBI.
>
> As long as the United States government wages war against Indochina in defiance of the vast majority who want all troops and weapons withdrawn this year, and extends that war and suffering under the guise of reducing it, as long as great economic and political power remains concentrated in the hands of small cliques not subject to democratic scrutiny and control, then repression, intimidation and entrapment are to be expected. We do not believe that this destruction of democratic society results simply from the evilness, egotism or senility of some leaders. Rather, this destruction is the result of certain undemocratic social, economic and political institutions.

The police car did not return a third time. As he read, John comforted himself with the possibility that the police officer may have thought he was reading numbers to his bookie in the aftermath of the great fight the night before. He kept dictating the statement to Wingell:

> We have carried out this action in a way which does not physically threaten anyone. We intend no personal harassment of the people who work in the office from which files were taken. Indeed, we invite them and others to join with us in building a peaceful, just and open society; one which does not wage nor threaten war, which distributes human and material resources fairly, and which operates on the basis of justice rather than fear.
>
> We have taken this action because:
>
> - We believe that a law and order which depends on intimidation and repression to secure obedience can have but one name, and that name is tyranny;

- We believe that democracy can survive only in an order of justice, of an open society and public trust;
- We believe that citizens have the right to scrutinize and control their own government and its agencies;
- And because we believe that the FBI has betrayed its democratic trust and we wish to present evidence for this claim to the open and public judgment of our fellow citizens.

John thinks the timbre of his voice may have changed slightly at this point. Originally, the statement was to have ended here. A couple days before the burglary, John, feeling more and more concern about how heavy the impact of the burglary could be on the burglars' families, especially their children, asked the other burglars to consider adding a paragraph that would acknowledge the risk to their families. Though none of them seemed to feel the need for the additional words as urgently as he did, they all readily agreed to such an addition. With the sweet faces and hoped-for happy futures of Lindsley, Mark, and Nathan much on his mind, he wrote the new last paragraph. This paragraph meant a great deal to John Raines. In addition to reflecting his growing fears, it also was a public acknowledgment that the decision to conduct the burglary was made with full awareness of the potentially enormous danger to their families, but that they believed the danger to society posed by a secret police state was so great that this extreme step—the burglary of an FBI office—justified the high price they and their families might pay. Now, through Wingell, he was telling that to the world on behalf of all the burglars:

In doing this, we know full well the legal jeopardy in which we place ourselves. We feel most keenly our responsibilities to those who daily depend upon us, and whom we put in jeopardy by our own jeopardy. But under present circumstances, this seems to us our best way of loving and serving them, and, in fact, all the people of this land.

Finally, he read, with pride and a powerful emphasis, as though signing off:

The Citizens' Commission to Investigate the FBI.

When John Raines returned to the car, mission accomplished, he and Bonnie remember, they saw both relief and concern in each other's faces.

They wondered if the police officer was watching them from a location they couldn't see. Would he follow them as they pulled away? Bonnie drove home on a route that took them down Lincoln Drive, a graceful, undulating parkway that winds through a beautiful wooded part of Philadelphia. John remembers suddenly feeling great relief—that the burglary was done, that they already knew they had valuable FBI files in their possession, that the police officer had not stopped to question them, that the announcement of their deed was now in the hands of a reporter who would see that the world soon learned that an FBI office had been burglarized by unknown people. John let himself laugh and shout. He tore the long typed news release into small pieces, threw them out the window, and watched the wind carry them into the trees of Fairmount Park.

They laughed and laughed. It started as nervous laughter and became bold and happy laughter. It probably came from the enormous relief of not being arrested, from lack of sleep, and from the great sense of accomplishment they had started to feel a few hours earlier when they read some of the stolen files. Some of the files were important and might have an impact. All of it made them giddy the morning after the burglary on their way home to the children.

At their house, they unlocked the front door very quietly. Though they had not slept for twenty-four hours, they were not tired. The adrenaline produced by a burglary was a powerful stimulant. They showered, dressed for work, and—as though they had been there all night—woke the children and chatted with them over breakfast around the table where they had had such a good but also poignant time with them the previous evening.

Despite everything, life was still normal.

They were unbelievably happy to be there with the children. But they had no idea how long normal life would last. Over the next few intense months, the fear that they would lose their normal life ebbed and flowed, at times very forcefully. Each time a crisis threatened and then dissipated, the realization that their normal lives had not been disrupted was very precious. It was especially precious now, the morning after the burglary.

Bonnie Raines took Lindsley and Mark to school and Nathan to daycare that morning. As they would later say about themselves, Ozzie and Harriet, the quintessential American television sitcom couple of that era, were back to normal life—as much as they could be the morning after they had burglarized an FBI office. They had dinner that evening with the children and then left for the farm. That would be their pattern every day for a little more than a week: eat dinner with the children, welcome the babysitter, head to the farm, read and analyze FBI files, come home late, get a few hours of sleep, go to work.

In New York early that morning, Muhammad Ali, his face distorted dramatically and full of pain from Joe Frazier's hammerlike left hook to his jaw the night before, held a press conference in his room at the New Yorker Hotel, a short distance from Madison Square Garden. Dave Kindred wrote that "the good grace of commonsense fell into his oratory" that morning as he told reporters, "I've never thought about losing. . . . We all have to take defeats in life. . . . We lose loved ones. . . . All kinds of things set us back, but life goes on. You don't shoot yourself. Soon this will be old news. People got lives to live, bills to pay, mouths to feed. Maybe a plane will go down with ninety people on it. Or a great man will be assassinated. That will be more important than Ali losing. I never wanted to lose, never thought I would, but the thing that matters is how you lose. I'm not crying. My friends should not cry."

Someone interrupted, and said, "Champ . . ."

"Don't call me champ," Ali said. "Joe's the champ now."

In Washington early that morning, J. Edgar Hoover did not yet know that he had been hit. When he found out, unlike Ali, he was not philosophical.

8

J. Edgar Hoover's Worst Nightmare

IT WAS 7:40 A.M. Tuesday, March 9, at the Media FBI office. As usual, Frank McLaughlin was the first agent to arrive. There had been a burglary the night before—at a bank in nearby Glenolden. It was a failed burglary. Nevertheless, he had worked on it until 2 a.m. He went home after he was done rather than return to the office to file a report, and slept very little before he left for work.

McLaughlin was tired, but he was not too tired to notice, as he approached the office entrance, that something looked different. "It looked to me like somebody had tried to force something in the lock." He tried to open the door. As he wrote later in an official report, when he inserted his key, "it turned completely around as though it was in putty."

He "automatically looked at the second door, and I could see that it was ajar. I suspected that there was a burglary. I mean I've been in this business a lot of years. . . . About this time, another agent came up, and I said, 'I think we've got a burglary.'"

One of them very cautiously pushed the door open as far as it would go. The two agents squeezed through the narrow opening. McLaughlin remembers scanning the scene:

"The place was ransacked. The doors of cabinets were open and files were gone. I walked into my office, and the desk drawers were rifled."

Soon all five agents who worked in the office had arrived and were taking in the unprecedented scene: an FBI office emptied of its files, apparently by burglars. One of the agents "immediately and quickly searched the Resident Agency [what small regional FBI offices like this one in Media were called] to determine that no one was in the RA." They moved from room to room and soon discovered that all drawers and file cabinets had been emptied. Locked desk drawers had been pried open. The extension cord to a radio transmitter was cut.

At 7:50 a.m., McLaughlin called supervisor J. Clifford Ousley at the Philadelphia office and told him the Media office "has been broken into and all the files are gone. Nobody's hurt. Nobody's injured." At this time, he told Ousley, the resident agency "was secured and a neighborhood investigation was instituted." According to the investigative record, he gave Ousley these details:

> Immediate exhaustive search of the Resident Agency and surrounding area for evidence of burglary tools pertinent to this case . . . included a complete search of the trash cans located in the rear of the Resident Agency building and the recesses and culverts at the base of the surrounding buildings and at the curb line in front of the building. . . . No physical evidence of burglary tools were found.

McLaughlin's call to Ousley set in motion one of the most intensive investigations in the history of the FBI, one that would consume the director, beginning the moment he arrived at his office in Washington about an hour later.

Ousley, the supervisor in Philadelphia, immediately alerted Joe D. Jamieson, the special agent in charge (SAC) in Philadelphia. It fell to Jamieson to notify the director's office that the Media office had been burglarized. When Jamieson had been transferred from the Savannah, Georgia, office to Philadelphia as SAC in March 1964, he had told a reporter that FBI work, including his job as SAC in Philadelphia, would be "mainly a sales job." Given how the FBI was managed under Hoover, with constant attention to building a positive public image of the bureau and the director, there was a lot of truth to that statement. Salesmanship was a central part of the FBI. But a sales approach would not do the job this morning. Jamieson soon would be placed on probation because the burglary happened on his watch. That was minor compared with the punishment Tom Lewis, the agent in charge of the Media office, would receive.

Beginning that morning and continuing for a month, Jamieson headed the investigation. He called Washington headquarters before Hoover arrived. A memo based on that phone call was prepared for Hoover by a member of the director's staff:

SAC Jamieson telephonically advised that some time during the night the RA at Media, PA, had been broken into. Initial reports to Jamieson were that the file cabinets and desks were broken into but it does not appear that the unknown subject or unknown subjects got into the safe. . . . Media RA is located in the County Building, Room 203, Front Street and South Street, Media, PA. The building is privately owned.

ACTION: Agents of the Philadelphia office have instituted an immediate investigation. SAC Jamieson will keep the Bureau advised.

So they could fully inform the director about the burglary as soon as he arrived at the office that morning, Hoover's top aides prepared a memorandum based on all the information that agents in the Media and Philadelphia offices had phoned and telegraphed to headquarters. In the hour before he arrived, a sense of crisis grew among his aides. They sent a bulletin to all FBI offices in the country:

At 7:45 a.m., March nine, instant, forceful entry and burglary discovered at Media, PA. This RA located second floor . . . Front and South Avenue, Media. Office consists of five interconnecting rooms with three doors opening on to public hallway. Two of these doors locked permanently. One door used for normal entrance to office. Examination reveals entry made by jimmying one of two permanently locked doors and moving two supply cabinets immediately inside this door. Also evidence located of attempt to punch lock on one of two other doors.

Preliminary inspection reveals all agents' desks and locked file cabinets pried open. All serials [a term used by the FBI for files] and notes in these cabinets are missing. Total number and identity of serials being ascertained through review of pertinent Philadelphia files. . . .

Wire on radio console transmitter severed preventing all radio transmission from RA. . . .

. . . All offices promptly alert appropriate sources and informants. Furnish any positive information by most expeditious means to Philadelphia office . . . SAC affording on-scene supervision. End.

This was not how the workday usually started at the Media FBI office. Until this morning, the office was usually a quiet, calm working environment. Agents in Media spent most of their time on what they considered typical and preferred cases: bank robberies, stolen cars, and other stolen goods. The office seldom was in the news, which was the way the agents liked it. The last time the Media office was in the news prior to the events that started unfolding the evening of March 8, 1971, was exactly four years earlier on March 9, 1967, when the *Philadelphia Inquirer* ran a light feature story that reported that the FBI office that served Chester and Delaware Counties had been moved from Chester to Media.

The article noted that the four agents who worked in the Media office at that time were almost precise prototypes of the kind of men Director Hoover had told a congressional committee the previous year he wanted FBI agents to be: "I am not looking for 'collar ad types,' but I am looking for agents who are clean cut, mature and will measure up to the image which I think the American people feel an FBI man should be."

"They measure up in Media," the reporter wrote, also noting that a recent crime investigated by Media agents was typical of the work in the office: the robbery of furs, jewelry, and other items valued at $11,000 that belonged to Mrs. Ora Taylor of nearby Yeadon.

On the morning of March 9, 1971, the agents stationed at the Media office had to deal with a very different type of crime. It was a simple burglary—how it was described in the major Philadelphia newspapers in the first news stories about the break-in—that was not so simple. Unlike any other burglary, the one discovered in Media early that morning immediately consumed J. Edgar Hoover and his aides at FBI headquarters in Washington, and eventually attracted the attention of Attorney General John Mitchell. Agents from throughout the country were immediately put on alert to find the burglars and the files they had stolen. This definitely was not just a simple burglary.

By 8 a.m., the Media agents had thoroughly processed the five rooms in the office for latent fingerprints. They were pleased to find "what appeared to be an imprint of a right hand on the right side of the cabinet" that had been pushed when the door was forced open. This gave them hope for a fast arrest.

When McLaughlin discovered that the Speed Graphic camera had not been stolen, he grabbed it and photographed the crime scene, documenting each room in great detail. His photos corroborated the damage reported in the summary agents wrote that morning:

> . . . Examination of the door frame reflected that the wood had been splintered indicating the lock and or bolt had been broken away from the wooden door frame. . . . In each of the five rooms in the RA the cabinets and desks . . . had been broken into. . . . Lower lock on the door to room

203 (main entrance) had been damaged and was inoperable. . . . The door to room 204 had been broken open and the door jamb extensively damaged. . . . In room 205 . . . the five-drawer file cabinet had been ransacked and the serials and investigative notes maintained in the first three drawers were missing. In addition to serials and notes relating to these serials, it was reported the following items were missing from the third drawer in this file cabinet: Philadelphia office personnel list, law enforcement mailing list, list of staff of U.S. Attorney's office and U.S. Marshal's office, Philadelphia, and pamphlet entitled Correspondence with the FBI . . . missing from drawer of [another agent, named blacked out] his personal telephone directory. . . . It was noted that the only Directory of Students (for Swarthmore College) missing was that for the current school year. . . .

None of the office furniture had been damaged, according to the report. The supply cabinet, which contained blank office forms, had not been disturbed. Agents also noted that the burglars had left desk surfaces in neat condition.

McLaughlin immediately thought of the safe. He was relieved to discover that it was still there and that it had not been opened. There wasn't even any sign anyone had tried to open it. He remembers thinking that the burglars must have not taken it because it was heavy. That meant the firearms, handcuffs, and administrative manuals agents kept in the safe had not been stolen. He was especially relieved to know that the firearms were not missing. Agents kept their smaller pistols, called "detective specials," in the safe. That's what Davidon would have found if he had come to the office early that morning and succeeded in opening the safe. Pistols definitely were not what he had hoped to find.

IN A REPORT to Washington headquarters that morning, Media agents also described this missing item:

The personal autographed photograph of Director J. Edgar Hoover belonging to Special Agent [blacked out] was in a frame affixed to the wall in room 203 occupied by Special Agent [blacked out]. The photograph of Mr. Hoover had been removed from this frame and taken by unknown subjects. It should be noted that the glass of this picture was not broken but was found with the frame on a table approximately 30 feet from where it was hanging on the wall.

For most of Hoover's tenure as director, nearly all agents prominently displayed such pictures in their offices. They were photos of an agent standing beside Hoover on a day when the agent had visited FBI headquarters in Washington and had a brief meeting with the director. Hoover had the photos taken, and later he sent a signed copy to the agent so that the agent would have a memento of what Hoover assumed was a special occasion in his life—meeting Hoover. The near-reverential respect some agents felt for Hoover was evident in the home of a retired agent who for several months led the investigation of the Media burglary. Nearly the entire fireplace mantel and several other flat surfaces in his living room were lined with photos of the agent standing beside Hoover and other photos of Hoover with the agent's wife and children.

McLaughlin was that kind of agent—the kind who deeply admired the director. Meeting the director was indeed a very special occasion in his life. He told me he "met Mr. Hoover on a couple occasions. I was never so impressed by any other man in my life, other than my father." Like many devoted agents at that time, McLaughlin remembers the date he became an FBI agent with the same precision he remembers his birthday: "It was April 23, 1951." In retirement, he spoke warmly of the many years he worked in the bureau. "I really liked the bureau. I liked the bureau work. I liked the people. I liked everything."

McLaughlin was transferred from the New York office of the FBI to the downtown Philadelphia office in 1968. At first, he worked on the hijacking squad, a part of general criminal investigations. Soon he was sent to the Media office. He developed a special affection for the office. Often, when his workload was heavy, he would take two of his four children to the Media office after mass on Sundays at his nearby Catholic church. They would play—pretend they were writing documents on the typewriters and make up other office games—while he dictated reports on cases he had covered the previous week but had not had time to complete. "It was a busy place. But it was fun. I loved it. I really did." He would not work in the Media office after what he discovered the morning of March 9. It was now a crime scene and would not be an FBI office again. Like the other agents there, McLaughlin was soon transferred to Philadelphia and other offices in the area.

THE NEWS THAT FBI serials were missing registered as a Richter-magnitude earthquake when it reached FBI headquarters that morning. The serials were the heart of the bureau. They were the bureau's recorded history. They were the records of all communications—written accounts of exchanges between agents, exchanges between agents and informants, reports from informants, communications between and among high-level FBI officials in Washington and agents in the field, communications between the director and top officials in the field and at headquarters. Each office kept in its files locally generated serials, as well as those distributed by the headquarters office and other local bureau offices. Some of the serials were mundane, some were explosive, and, as agents knew, all were regarded as secret documents that should be protected and never be seen by anyone outside the bureau. Officials at headquarters immediately realized that morning that the possibility of any serials becoming public would consume the director.

Before Hoover arrived at his office that morning, his top aides agreed that W. Mark Felt should be asked to go to Media immediately. One of the people Hoover trusted most, Felt had been head of the bureau's Inspection Division since 1964. In that capacity, he enforced Hoover's stringent requirements for how field offices should be evaluated during what agents and many officials in the field regarded as dreaded periodic inspections. Part of his responsibility involved making sure the local offices carried out the secret political programs that would be revealed for the first time in the Media documents. That morning he was tasked to determine how this bureau tragedy, the burglary in Media, could have happened. Headquarters officials realized Hoover would be somewhat comforted at this very uncomfortable time by knowing that Felt would soon be at the scene of the crime. By then, Felt had been a close confidant of Hoover for many years. Just four months later, on July 1, 1971, Hoover would promote Felt to deputy associate director, the third-highest position in the bureau, with only Hoover and Clyde Tolson above him. Tolson was very ill by then, making Felt by default the second most powerful person in the FBI. By the fall of 1972, a few months after Hoover's death in May 1972, Felt would become Deep Throat, the most famous confidential source in history, for his role as source to *Washington Post* reporter Bob Woodward about Watergate crimes. Like Hoover, Felt regarded the Media burglary as a very serious crime against the

J. Edgar Hoover, director of the Federal
Bureau of Investigation, 1924–72.

bureau. He later wrote, in his 1979 and 2006 memoirs, that it was "the biggest blemish on the FBI's image."

As he shaved in his New York hotel room early that March 1971 morning, Felt wrote, the phone rang. "It was the night supervisor at the New York office: 'The bureau wants you to call as soon as possible,' he said. 'And they want you to call on the secure line.' I dressed, rushed to the office and picked up the phone." Felt was in New York that morning because he was in charge of the inspection then taking place at this, the bureau's largest field office and, it would be learned later, the FBI office that had long been most involved in political spying and dirty tricks.

"The bureau switchboard operator put me through to Edward S. Miller, my top assistant in the Inspection Division. He told me that burglars had broken into the FBI's resident agency at Media, Pennsylvania, near Philadelphia. 'Apparently they got away with a lot of serials,' Miller said. Within thirty minutes I was on the Metroliner for Philadelphia." Important as the New York inspection was, it was placed on hold while Felt rushed to Media.

HOOVER'S INITIAL ANGER focused on the fact that Tom Lewis, the agent in charge of the Media office, did not get the name of the woman who had interviewed him two weeks earlier, but Felt immediately focused on the safe in the Media office. He wrote in 1979 that his first thought when Miller called him that morning was to ask Miller to check whether Felt had purchased a large safe for the Media office the previous fall. He waited on the phone as Miller checked the records. "When Ed Miller assured me that I had, I breathed a sigh of relief."

Felt's official and unofficial writings about the safe provide contradictory accounts on the important point of the size of the safe in the Media office. His attitude regarding the safe when he arrived at the Media office the morning after the burglary angered agents in the office. If they had assigned him a nickname that morning, it would not have been Deep Throat, the nickname *Washington Post* managing editor Howard Simons gave Bob Woodward's anonymous source in 1972, after the title of a porn movie popular at that time. The Media agents might have named him Deep Scapegoater. That morning in Media Felt was covering up secrets, not revealing them as he did a little more than a year later to Woodward.

In his memoir, Felt wrote that he had played a pivotal role just a few months before the Media burglary in increasing security at the Media office after the director asked him to assess security at the bureau's 536 small FBI offices, including Media. "A midnight raid was not unexpected," he wrote, noting that draft board raids had stirred concern about a possible raid of an FBI office. Actually, an FBI office had been entered by burglars that September in Rochester, New York, but the burglars there were promptly arrested in the office, which was part of a suite of federal offices. Because 475 of the bureau's smallest offices were located in commercial offices where minimal or no protection existed, Felt said he told Hoover those offices should be provided "a good burglar-proof cabinet safe." But such safes cost $1,000 each, more than the FBI could afford, Felt wrote. Therefore, the "only workable solution," according to him, was to provide the few offices "close to college and universities with a great deal of activist ferment" with such safes. Because Media was close to several campuses—Haverford College, Bryn Mawr College, Swarthmore College, Villanova University—Felt said he ordered a large file drawer–type safe for Media.

But did he?

"When I arrived at the Media office," Felt wrote in his memoir, "the experts [FBI agents from the Media office] were looking for evidence to help identify the burglars":

> What I wanted to see, though, was the safe, and there it was—the biggest type of two-door, burglar-proof, fireproof cabinet safe that money

could buy—untouched and unscratched in the middle of the office. . . . I began my inquiry by asking Lewis to open the safe. Inside, where sensitive documents should have been stored, were several two-way radios, assorted Bureau firearms, handcuffs, a blackjack, and a copy of the National Crime Information Center operations manual, a public document. . . . The burglars did not even attempt to jimmy this monster. I suspect they stole away thinking that they had failed in their mission, that the really secret documents were locked away in the big safe. . . . The resident agents at Media completely missed the point, but the Citizens' Commission to Investigate the FBI did not miss a single important document.

In contrast, Media agents and the burglars—and also Felt's own official report written immediately after the burglary—described the safe as very small. In that official report, Felt criticized Lewis for not asking headquarters for a large safe. If he had done so, Felt concluded, the documents could not have been stolen.

One of Felt's accounts—the official one or the one in his memoir—has to be false. The safe could not have been a big "monster," as he described it in his memoir, and also too small to hold files, as he wrote in his official report.

A retired agent who worked in the office recalls that the safe Felt purchased for the office was so small that agents considered it useless. He remembers what happened in the fall of 1970 quite differently from the way Felt remembers it. He says Lewis, with the agreement of the agents in the office, thought there was an urgent need for security in the office, which essentially had no security. In September he asked the bureau for a large cabinet safe with lockable file drawers—similar to the type of safe Felt later claimed he provided for the office. But according to the Media agent, Felt refused to provide a large safe for the office. Instead, he approved the purchase of the very small one. At the same time, the agent said, Felt also refused to approve another important item Lewis asked the bureau to purchase: an alarm system. Felt refused that request, saying that because the Media office was relatively close to a local police station, a burglar alarm was not needed. Those details were not in Felt's official report on the burglary.

Felt's goals at the time of the burglary, as well as eight years later when he wrote his memoir, seemed to be to scapegoat Lewis and to conceal his own role in failing to provide security for the Media office. Remarkably, in both accounts he reached the same conclusion—Lewis was responsible for the burglary—yet with diametrically different claims about the size of the safe. In 1971, he wrote in his official report that Lewis had a small safe and was responsible for the burglary because he had failed to ask for a large one, where all the files could have been securely stored; in 1979, he wrote in his memoir that Lewis had a large safe and was responsible for the burglary because he did not store the files in it.

In his official report, Felt was silent on his refusal to increase security at Media. He accused Lewis of being negligent about security, but omitted the fact that Lewis had attempted to increase security at the office. In his memoir, Felt writes a misleading account of his own role, making it appear that he increased security at the office. His official conclusion, as stated in his memoir, was "The senior resident agent in charge had failed to protect Bureau documents by putting them in the safe."

Before Felt arrived at Media that morning, he promised Hoover he would have a recommendation on his desk by the next morning, and he did. He wrote to Hoover, "I recommend stern disciplinary action."

Hoover accepted Felt's recommendation and suspended Lewis without pay for a month and transferred him to the Atlanta field office. That meant that shortly after the burglary the agent who knew the most about the office and the area, Tom Lewis—who had been in charge of the office for fifteen years, first in Chester and since 1967 in Media—was forced to leave the area and not assist in the investigation. In the local community and among many FBI agents, the harsh treatment of Lewis was considered inappropriate and excessive. His transfer to Atlanta was a hardship for Lewis and his family. He and his wife, Catherine, and their six children had deep roots in the community near Media and did not want to leave. Local law enforcement officers respected him and even made entreaties to bureau officials not to transfer him. Their pleas were ignored. They organized a dinner in Lewis's honor, but he was forced to leave before it was held. His banishment was seen as such a great injustice that one of the first things L. Patrick Gray did when he was appointed acting director of the FBI on May 3, 1972, the day after Hoover died, was to quietly assign Lewis back to the Philadelphia area, where he and his family longed to be.

Given Felt's role as a key confidential source in the Watergate stories that revealed President Nixon's cover-up of Watergate crimes and contributed to bringing down the president, it is striking to realize that just a year earlier Felt covered up his own major role in contributing to the Media FBI office's being vulnerable to burglary. That there was no alarm system in the office was central to the Media burglars' decision to burglarize it. It is unknown if Felt ever acknowledged to himself the central role his misjudgment played in making possible the burglary that he later wrote "damaged the FBI's image, possibly forever, in the minds of many Americans."

THERE IS NO RECORD of Hoover's initial reaction when he was told the Media office had been burglarized and all serials had been removed. Given Felt's very close working relationship with Hoover, his account of the director's reaction undoubtedly is accurate. He reported that "Hoover was enraged, and so was I." This description matches a report in the *Washington Star* by Jeremiah O'Leary, one of the director's favorite reporters. He wrote at the time that when Hoover learned of the Media burglary he was "apoplectic."

Hoover's anger and concern about the potential impact of the Media burglary is not surprising. To him, the bureau's files were both secret and sacred. He had spent more effort than people outside the FBI knew creating what he thought would keep the bureau's files sealed and protected from outside scrutiny. His goal of being held accountable to no one but himself depended on his maintaining total control of his files. He knew that if they were exposed, the mythic legends he had created about both himself and the bureau over a lifetime would be endangered.

In the forty-seven years he had been director, as of 1971, even officials in the Department of Justice, technically his supervisors, and in the two houses of Congress had not seen his files. Only a very few select people outside the bureau knew anything about FBI files. They were the handful of people who occasionally were invited by the director to listen privately with him to salacious recordings his agents or informers had made of members of Congress or of other well-known people whom he could, through his files, blackmail. Over the years, few, if any, of these selected listeners revealed what they heard in the director's office. After all, an invitation to hear these private recordings, mostly of sexual indiscretions, was at least as much a threat of what the director could do to his guests as it was an invitation to share perverse amusement with a man who ironically had built a reputation as a strait-laced religious person who demanded that everyone who worked for the FBI reflect that same quality. He, and later his successors, would claim there were no FBI files on the personal lives of government officials or other prominent people. The few who knew with certainty that that was a lie didn't reveal the truth. Now Hoover was afraid the stolen files would reveal to the public what he had long protected and assumed would be secret forever.

Prior to March 1971, the only time internal FBI files had become public was during the March 1949 trial of Judith Coplon, a Department of Justice employee charged with stealing FBI secrets on behalf of the Soviet Union. Few documents became public then, but Hoover considered their exposure an outrageous and unacceptable intrusion into his power to totally control his secret operations.

Coplon's defense attorney, Archibald Palmer, succeeded in getting the Washington federal judge who presided over one of Coplon's two trials to order the federal prosecutor trying the case to submit FBI files in court. Because the prosecutor had described the files as a significant part of its case against Coplon, her lawyer argued that the government should reveal the documents in court.

J. Edgar Hoover did not see it that way, but the judge did. The court order that forced the FBI to show some of its files in open court rankled Hoover more than anything that happened to him prior to the 1971 burglary. He told Attorney General Tom Clark that never before in its history had the bureau publicly revealed any raw files, and it never would. He regarded the secrecy of the files as so important that he urged Clark—the future Supreme Court justice and the father of Ramsey Clark, appointed attorney general in 1967 by President Lyndon Johnson—to seek a mistrial. He even suggested that the prosecutor should seek a contempt citation against the defendant's attorney for making the request. The files, if revealed, he said, would endanger national security and would expose confidential informants, the Department of Justice, Attorney General Clark, and the bureau to embarrassment. That word, "embarrassment," was heard often in the bureau. "Don't embarrass the bureau" was the director's mantra throughout his tenure, easily outranking the bureau's official motto, "Fidelity, Bravery, and Integrity." It was taken very seriously. In the culture of the FBI, there was little if anything agents could do that would be considered worse.

Though Hoover insisted national security would be endangered if his files became public, actually it was his plan for permanent secrecy, not national security, that he feared would be endangered. His considerable influence over his immediate superior, the attorney general, was evident in the decision of the prosecutor, at first, to comply with Hoover's demand. The prosecutor told the court the continued secrecy of FBI files was so important that the government would drop all charges against Coplon rather than risk the exposure of the files. When that threat did not work and the judge again ordered the files be made public, Hoover took the extreme step of telling the attorney general he would resign as FBI director if the secret files were made public. It is believed to be the only time in his long career that he submitted his resignation. Clark convinced Hoover to stay. The prosecutor complied with the order and submitted the FBI files to the court. As Hoover bitterly regretted the exposure, he started planning how he could prevent such exposure from ever happening again.

Compared to the Media files that would become public twenty-two years later, those the bureau was forced to make public during the Coplon trial were relatively insignificant. Unlike the Media files, the files released at the Coplon trial did not include descriptions of secret bureau programs or guidelines. As Hoover predicted, though, the Coplon trial FBI files embarrassed the bureau, providing the first glimpse of the shoddy investigative methods it used. As such, they attracted considerable interest and criticism. One file labeled as "Reds" actors Fredric March, Helen Hayes, John Garfield, Canada Lee, and Paul Muni. The reports showed the bureau's disregard for verification and its interest in collecting salacious but irrelevant material about citizens. Various people, prominent and not prominent, were slandered without evidence. One file stamped "secret" was a report given to the bureau by an unknown Bronx man who told an FBI agent he had watched his neighbor walking around naked inside his own home, a fact that had no connection to national security or to suspicion of crime but was nevertheless placed in a permanent bureau file.

The result of "dossiers being laid out for public inspection," wrote *New York Times* reporter Cabell Phillips at the time, was that the FBI, which "has enjoyed an immunity from high-level criticism almost unparalleled among Government agents, found itself this week in a state of acute embarrassment as a result of public disclosure of some of its investigative techniques" that were made "over its strenuous, almost frantic, protests. . . . No one can recall a time in all that period of growth when the FBI has been subjected to a Congressional investigation, not an instance in which any appropriations committee has failed to give it all the money it requested. . . . The FBI enjoys an unusual autonomy. . . . It is a monolithic, tightly disciplined and intensely loyal hierarchy responsible solely to the director."

Coplon was convicted in both trials. Her convictions were historic, for they marked the first conviction of an American accused of spying for the Soviets. She was tried along with Valentin Gubitchev, a Soviet member of the United Nations Secretariat to whom she was accused of passing documents. As Hoover biographer Curt Gentry has written, the convictions also made the case for what Hoover had long been claiming: that the Soviets used

United Nations employees to conduct espionage on its behalf. But Hoover was so angry about a few of his files being exposed that he took no pride in being proven right on that point. In fact, his reactions demonstrate Hoover priorities that would have surprised the public. He was a leading cold warrior, a fact well known to the public through his speeches, articles, and books. But faced with a choice between convicting the first person charged with handing secrets to the Soviet Union and keeping a few FBI files secret, Hoover stood firmly for protecting his files even if it meant charges against Coplon would have to be dropped.

The FBI faced additional embarrassment in the Coplon cases. The historic convictions were overturned by the U.S. Circuit Court of Appeals. In light of the court's explanation for the reversals, the defeat was considered not only significant but also needless. In the unanimous opinion written by Judge Learned Hand, the court declared that Coplon's "guilt was plain." But the convictions must be overturned, the judges agreed, because of numerous illegal acts by the FBI in the course of the investigation that led to the charges. The illegalities included how the FBI made the arrests, lies by an FBI agent under oath during one of the Coplon trials, and illegal wiretapping of various phones, including ones on which the bureau listened to the defendant's conversations with her attorney.

Despite Hoover's humiliation over losing this important case, after the Coplon trial he provided more confirmation that he cared more about maintaining the secrecy of his files than about the outcome of prosecutions based on faulty FBI investigations. When the convictions were overturned, he successfully urged successive attorneys general not to retry the cases because to do so might require making public more illegal activity by the FBI. Though he didn't want Coplon to be tried again, he also did not want the failed charges against her to be dropped. For nearly twenty years after Coplon's conviction was overturned in December 1950, Hoover succeeded in keeping the charges against her from being dropped. With the charges hanging over her, her rights and movements were restricted. She was not allowed to vote, to drive, or to leave the New York City area, even to cross the Hudson River to view the unveiling of her father's tombstone. Finally, in an unusual family symmetry, Ramsey Clark, attorney general under President Johnson and son of the attorney general at the time of the Coplon trials, dismissed the charges against her. Hoover protested strongly but unsuccessfully against the attorney general he later dismissively called a "jellyfish" and described as the worst of all the attorneys general he had worked with.

After the Coplon trial failures, Hoover focused on creating a filing system he thought would permanently block future exposure of FBI files. It was this post-Coplon, super-secure system that he thought was totally sealed that was cracked open by the Media burglars.

From the time he became director in 1924 until 1949, Hoover's files had remained secret. But in light of the judicially forced exposure during the Coplon trial, he redesigned the bureau's filing system with more complex, deeper layers of secrecy. He ordered the chief agent in all field offices to keep "highly confidential" and "most secretive" sources and files isolated from general case files so they would not be "vulnerable to court-ordered discovery motions, congressional subpoenas, or requests from the Justice Department." He did this in part by ordering agent reports to be divided into two categories—investigative and administrative. Any part of a sensitive file that could cause embarrassment if it became public was to be isolated from the file and placed in a file labeled "administrative." Most, if not all, of the information he instructed to be placed in administrative files was in fact not administrative matter. Rather, these files included incriminating personal information regarding government witnesses; privileged medical records; sealed court documents; illegally obtained bank, telephone, and credit company records; and records of any form of technical surveillance— mail openings, break-ins, wiretaps, microphone installations, and the theft and deciphering of codes and information gathered from taps, break-ins, and code deciphering. In other words, the bureau would continue to gather information illegally but would file it in ways that would make it inaccessible to authorities.

The most sensitive files would be kept in special files in field offices, in the special file room in the director's office, and in a special file he designated the "blackmail file" and kept in what was known as the FBI's print shop in the basement of FBI headquarters. The most sensitive were to be kept in the director's "Official/Confidential and Personal files." Later, he continued to develop even deeper layers of secrecy in his file system, including one he labeled the "Do Not File" files.

Under Hoover's new and improved post-Coplon secrecy plan, sensitive materials were never to be seen by anyone outside the bureau—not even by Department of Justice attorneys, the people who prosecuted crimes based on FBI investigations. Hoover thought his new post-Coplon trial file system was so tightly sealed that it guaranteed the FBI's files would be beyond the reach of members of Congress, congressional committees, other federal agencies, and judges. He also intended for the files to be kept secret from his bosses, the attorney general, and the president, except as he chose to reveal secrets to them to serve his purposes.

During the very rare times prior to 1971 when Congress examined any aspect of intelligence operations, Hoover succeeded, with relative ease, in having the FBI excluded from examination. When the National Lawyers Guild issued a rare call for an investigation of the bureau after the revelations at Coplon's trial and tried to convince the Truman administration to pursue it, the director smeared the organization and destroyed its effort. Though Truman made it known inside the White House that he disapproved of some of Hoover's tactics, he refused to investigate how the FBI operated.

The Cold War was at a blazing point. People were afraid. Soon they forgot about the criticisms made against the FBI during Coplon's trials. Hoover did not forget. Protected by his sealed files and people's fears and forgetfulness, he continued his public roles as head of the country's most powerful law enforcement agency and leading fiery narrator of tales of the communist perils that faced Americans, as well as his private role as builder of secret files on organizations and on the personal and political lives of people he considered subversive.

It is believed that after Hoover locked his files in deeper secrecy in 1950, no journalist or official questioned him about FBI files, let alone sought access to them. Hoover's effort to maintain total secrecy succeeded. It went unchallenged.

Until the night of March 8, 1971.

FBI FILES—what Hoover thought he had assured would be forever beyond the reach of even the highest officials—were now in the hands of unknown burglars. Despite his elaborately deceptive labeling and other methods of maintaining secrecy, now a simple burglary could—if agents did not immediately find and arrest these burglars and seize and secure the documents—violate his secrecy in far more profound ways than he ever thought possible. Since creating the new filing procedures in 1950, he had put several large secret programs in place, programs he thought were necessary in order for the bureau to fulfill its mission. But he knew that if they ever became known, many people would criticize him.

How could it be that his elaborate secrecy system was protected from intrusions by federal judges, members of Congress and congressional committees, attorneys general, and even presidents, but it was not protected from intrusions by, of all people, burglars? It had never occurred to the director that some people cared so much about the Constitution and the right to dissent it guaranteed that they would be willing to risk their freedom in order to get access to his secret files to determine if he and the FBI were destroying that right. Since the Cold War, he had expected Americans to behave like lambs. The possibility that some Americans could be lions and break into his secret den was unimaginable.

Hoover realized that if the files stolen at Media became public, they were likely to have a much greater impact than the few that had become public at the time of the Coplon trial. His enemies—despite enjoying decades of nearly uninterrupted public adulation, he realized recently that he had acquired a few enemies—would be able to attack him with more than the rumors and speculation he had found easy to deny. If certain FBI files became public, people would be armed with official facts and policies rather than speculation.

The director wasted little time. He moved immediately to make that impossible. He and his top aides developed a two-pronged plan. First, he ordered an intensive investigation. He called it MEDBURG and gave it "major special" status. His daily memos to the key investigators and his top staff regarding MEDBURG usually were marked "urgent," "top priority," or "expedite." Nearly two hundred agents were transferred to Philadelphia to work on the case. Other agents at FBI offices throughout the Northeast and Midwest worked on it. Tips came in from throughout the country, from places as diverse as Los Angeles and a farm in North Carolina.

Second, bracing for what he then considered the remote possibility that the burglars might not be found quickly and might attempt to distribute the stolen files to journalists, he asked his top aides to consult with Department of Justice officials about the possibility of drafting a law he hoped the Nixon administration would support and Congress would pass quickly—a law similar to Great Britain's powerful Official Secrets Act. Such a bill would have made it a federal crime for anyone outside the bureau, including journalists, to possess or publish FBI documents.

Hoover wanted the burglars arrested and the documents seized and secured immediately. Speed was essential to achieving his chief goal: preventing the documents from becoming public. Operating under that sense of urgency, officials in FBI offices throughout the country were told to notify Philadelphia immediately by phone when they were ready to send photos of potential suspects "so arrangements can be made for transmittal by airplane."

For nearly a decade, FBI agents and informers had photographed thousands of people at peace marches and demonstrations throughout the country. Beginning immediately after the burglary, agents scoured those surveillance photos. Anyone who had been photographed at an antiwar rally instantly became a potential suspect in the Media burglary. The files also included photos that had been taken surreptitiously by the bureau at trials of antiwar activists. Agents were especially interested in photos taken in Rochester, New York, during the Flower City Conspiracy trial, the trial of the people who were arrested in September 1970 as they broke into a suite of federal offices in Rochester that included an FBI office. It was at that trial, for the only previous break-in at an FBI office, that Davidon started to think it might be possible to do so successfully.

By late afternoon the day after the Media burglary, the agents working the case had touched many bases in and near Media. A late report they filed that day stated, "Interviews have been conducted with local police, Delaware County Courthouse Police station across from the resident agency, residents in apartments above the resident agency space, custodial personnel, and neighbors. All interviews unproductive to date. Space being processed for fingerprints and crime scene in and around resident agency space being conducted."

It had been a long day. Then, at about 5:30, an agent in the Philadelphia office was surprised by a phone call from Bill Wingell, the Reuters reporter John Raines had called early that morning. Wingell wanted to know if it was true that the Media office had been burglarized the previous evening. He was curious. Needless to say, so was the FBI agent who took his call. Until that moment, FBI officials had no reason to think anyone—besides the unknown burglars and the FBI—knew about the burglary. The agent confirmed that the office had been burglarized. Wingell told him about the early-morning anonymous caller who had dictated a statement about why a group had burglarized the office.

Agents were more than eager to learn everything Wingell knew. He explained the somewhat unusual circumstance that led to his not calling them earlier. After taking the caller's dictated message, he said, he had called Reuters' U.S. headquarters in New York and told an editor that he had a potentially important news story. Not the expansive news agency that it is now, at that time Reuters did not report a wide range of U.S. news. That probably was why the editor told Wingell he was not interested in a story about a burglary in a small FBI office in a small town in Pennsylvania. Later that afternoon, Wingell realized he had not heard or read any local news about the burglary. He thought that was strange. While the British news agency might not be interested in an FBI office being burglarized, he thought, surely local news organizations would. He did not realize he was the only reporter who had been notified about the burglary.

The agent pressed Wingell for more details about his morning caller. Wingell said he had never heard the caller's voice before. He described him as a "male without any noticeable accent." The agent asked Wingell to provide the FBI with his typed notes of the statement the caller had dictated. He also asked Wingell to provide the bureau with his fingerprints. Wingell provided the statement, but he later balked at providing fingerprints, saying his refusal was a matter of principle. The FBI report indicates that Wingell promised to give them any future messages he might receive from the anonymous burglars.

That call by John Raines to Wingell, the burglars had hoped, would inform the public that the burglary had taken place. But the effort had failed. The burglars probably would have achieved their goal if the statement had been read to a local news organization. Instead, by calling an international news agency whose editors apparently didn't understand the significance of J. Edgar Hoover's files being stolen, minimal coverage of the burglary took place during the first two weeks after the burglary. Instead of breaking the story about the burglary, as the burglars had hoped, Wingell became a suspect in the case. Immediately after talking with him, agents searched bureau files. Red flags went up when they discovered that for nearly a decade he had photographed and written about Quaker organizations and other antiwar organizations in the Philadelphia area. They regarded with suspicion the fact that Wingell had not called them soon after he had been told the office was burglarized. Why did he wait until late afternoon? In a memo to the director after Wingell's call, an agent in the Philadelphia office wrote, "Wingell's long delay in contacting Philadelphia office appears unusual." They were skeptical that a journalist would wait several hours to confirm an anonymous caller's sensational claim that an FBI office had been burglarized. Eventually, they concluded he probably had no other role than the one he described, and they dropped him as a suspect.

Wingell was not the only person who was surprised there were no news stories about the burglary by that afternoon. Davidon was surprised and disappointed. Most of the burglars were busy at their day jobs that day, but as Davidon sat in his campus office trying to act normal, he kept checking radio news reports, and he went out to buy copies of the regional afternoon newspaper, the *Philadelphia Evening Bulletin*. He found no news about an

FBI office being burglarized. Frustrated, he found it impossible to maintain his silence. About the same time Wingell called the FBI, Davidon anonymously called a suburban editor of the *Philadelphia Inquirer*. According to the FBI report of a call received from the editor a few minutes later, the anonymous caller had asked the editor if he "had heard anything about ransacking of FBI office in Media." The editor told the FBI that the anonymous caller sounded as if he was "in his early 20s with a well modulated and educated voice." These two calls caused FBI officials to worry about press coverage. They assumed that if a long statement explaining the burglary had been given to Wingell by someone claiming to speak for the burglars, the same statement probably would be given to other news organizations and would prompt coverage. As it turned out, the bureau's worries were not justified. Not yet.

The next day, the two major local newspapers, the *Evening Bulletin* and the *Inquirer,* each published three-inch stories about the burglary. They were buried inside the papers and attracted very little attention, for they reported little more than the fact that the burglary had taken place: "Jamieson said something was stolen but refused to identify it." For two weeks, local news organizations showed little or no curiosity about the burglary. They accepted the FBI's statement that nothing important had been stolen. That was what the FBI wanted. The lack of interest by the Philadelphia news media in the burglary gave the FBI reason to be optimistic, to believe that without the spotlight of intense coverage the documents and burglars could be found quickly.

After the bureau learned from Wingell the content of the message John Raines had dictated to Wingell, Jamieson sent the director a memo that warned that the Media burglars might be part of a plan that endangered FBI offices everywhere: "It appears this group has instituted a program which to fulfill may involve similar break-ins and burglaries of other resident agencies or field offices. It is recommended by the Philadelphia office that the director alert all offices to the possibility that this may occur within their respective territories."

By the end of the day after the burglary, agents in the Philadelphia office had decided that in addition to the wide net they would cast to search for suspects among the thousands of people photographed at antiwar events by the FBI, the investigation should focus on the people associated with the Catholic peace movement who were identified in FBI files as the East Coast Conspiracy to Save Lives, or Eastcon. Because of the draft board raids, the FBI knew this large, amorphous group was capable of burglary. That fact elevated those believed to be part of that group in the hierarchy of likely suspects. In addition to questioning people in the Media area that first day about any unusual activity they may have seen or heard Monday evening, the agents closest to the investigation decided it would be crucial to establish the whereabouts Monday evening of the hundreds of people known by the FBI to be in the Eastcon group.

On the second day after the burglary, investigators named three people as key suspects: an "unknown woman" and two other people—Peter, the man who had abandoned the group just days before the burglary, and John Grady, the Catholic peace movement leader from the Bronx, the person all of the Media burglars had agreed must not be part of the Media group. The "unknown woman" was Bonnie Raines, but they did not know her name— only that a woman had interviewed Tom Lewis. These three people would remain prime suspects throughout the investigation.

The focus on Grady and the man who dropped out became intense very quickly. The New York field office was ordered to establish Grady's whereabouts the night of the burglary. Agents expressed certainty that he had not only participated in the Media burglary but was the leader of the group. They reasoned that if he had led several draft board raids where documents had been stolen, he must have led this FBI office raid where documents had been stolen. From the start, the director and the agents investigating the Media burglary let this important conclusion—and others—get ahead of their evidence. Their mistaken belief that Grady was the leader of the Media burglary led them down a path that, in the end, was destructive to the FBI—not only because it did not result in the arrest of the burglars, but also because it led agents to fund and direct a crime that would in the end humiliate the bureau and bring respect to the Catholic peace movement.

Hoover followed the details of the MEDBURG investigation closely. Indeed, he was directly involved in the case daily. He ordered agents to find out why the man who had abondoned the group had left the weekly Monday Resistance dinner early on the night of March 8. This suggested that Resistance dinners were covered regularly by an FBI informer—and with an eye for details, such as who left early. How else would the bureau have known that this suspect was at the dinner the night of the burglary? Interestingly, though, the absence of two Media burglars, Williamson and Durst, who usually attended the dinners, was apparently not noted by the FBI's source.

Ironically, the man who dropped out was the only member of the original Media group named a suspect during the earliest stages of the investigation.

Beginning the first day after the burglary, he was placed under twenty-four-hour surveillance that continued for months. Philadelphia agents parked in front of his home for endless hours. They followed him from city to city, watching him closely wherever he went, noting in their reports his frequent association with people who opposed the war and with "hippie type" people.

And then there was the "unknown woman."

Agents at the Media office immediately remembered the woman who called and said she was a college student and wanted to interview someone in the FBI office about hiring practices. Suddenly her February 24 interview with Tom Lewis came into sharp focus. Hoover was informed about her at once. In the early days of the investigation, he repeatedly emphasized the need to find her—at various times he referred to her as "that woman," "the girl," "the unknown walk-in," or "UNSUB," a bureau term for "subject with unknown name." He made clear in his early MEDBURG memos that he thought finding her was "imperative" to breaking the case. He was furious with Lewis for not getting her name. It didn't seem to occur to him that, given what they assumed was her purpose—to get information to help in burglarizing the office—if she had provided a name, it probably would have been a fictitious one. The agents who saw Bonnie Raines in the office that day prepared a written description based on what they remembered about her. Using their memories of her appearance, a Philadelphia Police Department sketch artist drew a likeness of her. Anyone seeing her could have easily matched Bonnie Raines with the drawing. The artist's sketch of her, along with this written description of her was shown to hundreds of people:

> She is white female, age 25, five-feet five-inches, approximately 120 pounds, dark brown hair parted in the middle, slender build, fair complexion, smooth fine facial features, high cheek bones, wearing black horn-rimmed prescription glasses, a crocheted tam, multi-designed, basically green in color, dark green overcoat extend below the knee, high leather or plastic knee length boots. . . . Both the tam and the overcoat appeared somewhat soiled . . . from what appeared to be long wear or use and were in need of cleaning and pressing. Her hair around the sides and back of her head were protruding from underneath the tam, the ends of which hair were somewhat wavy and curled but apparently were not well combed or well kept.

While the search of the bureau's thousands of photo files had turned countless antiwar activists into potential suspects in the Media burglary case, the search for the nameless woman made a special target of every woman with long dark hair who had ever attended an antiwar rally, plus an armed robber who probably never attended a peace rally but had hair matching the description.

In a final memo late the day after the burglary to the director and heads of field offices, Jamieson wrote:

> Press inquiries being answered by confirming burglary and theft of government property but not specifying nature thereof.
>
> Vigorous investigation being undertaken to identify individual or individuals involved.
>
> Each office is requested to give preferred investigative attention to this matter, and matter being handled as a special.

In an earlier memo to headquarters, it was noted that the doorjamb and the lock that had tool marks on it would be forwarded promptly to the FBI laboratory, along with fingerprints that had been lifted throughout the Media office.

IN WASHINGTON that morning, as if arranged by the gods of irony, about the same time J. Edgar Hoover and his top officials were learning that all the files, including secret surveillance files, had been stolen overnight from the Media office, a very good friend of the FBI was about to testify at a congressional hearing. Assistant Attorney General William H. Rehnquist, the future chief justice of the U.S. Supreme Court, was taking a seat in a Senate hearing room and was about to testify under oath that the government engaged in virtually no surveillance of Americans, and that the surveillance that did take place, he would assure his listeners, did not have a chilling effect.

The FBI had helped prepare the testimony of Rehnquist, who would be appointed to the Supreme Court by President Nixon six months later. He testified that although virtually no surveillance was being done, it was nevertheless essential that the government retain the power to do such surveillance. Rehnquist of course had no way of knowing that within two weeks the fruits of a burglary that had taken place in a small Pennsylvania town less than twelve hours before he testified would put the lie to his testimony.

Rehnquist's defense of surveillance was made that morning before the Senate Subcommittee on Constitutional Rights, which was chaired by Senator Sam J. Ervin Jr., Democrat from North Carolina. The committee had been in the limelight for several weeks as it heard testimony that revealed large-scale spying in the 1960s by U.S. Army intelligence operations against American activists. The Army hearings had been made possible largely through the substantial research of Christopher Pyle, a young Army captain, who revealed in 1970 after he left the Army that thousands of plainclothes Army agents surreptitiously collected information about American activists daily and filed it in databases at three hundred Army offices around the country. It was the first time evidence had been presented to the public about spying on civilians by any government agency.

The morning after the Media burglary, Senator Ervin, who would become renowned three years later as the tough chair of what became known as the Senate Watergate Committee, wanted the Department of Justice to agree to support legislation that would guarantee that citizens would not be abused by the collection of information by federal government agencies about their political opinions and private lives. Ervin was deeply concerned about political surveillance. As the use of computers by the government for collecting and storing data was about to become standard practice, the senator thought it was essential to anticipate the harm that could be done by such record-keeping and impose strong strictures that would prevent the abuse of citizens' rights. In public comments, Senator Ervin referred to the combination of spying on citizens and the use of what he called "electronic dossiers" as "warfare on the American people."

Speaking on behalf of the FBI and the Department of Justice that day, Rehnquist was combative in his opposition to the legislation Ervin proposed to protect Americans from such surveillance. Congress, Rehnquist insisted, must not restrict the government from collecting information about citizens. "Aide to Mitchell Opposes Any Curb on Surveillance" was the headline of the *New York Times* story on the hearing the next day. Rehnquist told the committee the department "will vigorously oppose any legislation which, whether by opening the door to unnecessary and unmanageable judicial supervision of such activities or otherwise, would effectively impair this extraordinarily important function of the Federal Government."

As Hoover wrestled that morning with how to find and secure the stolen Media documents and prevent them from ever becoming public, he could not have asked for more from Rehnquist. The future chief justice argued that "isolated imperfections" in surveillance and various forms of information collection should not be permitted "to obscure the fundamental necessity and importance of Federal information gathering, or the generally high level of performance in this area by the organizations involved," the FBI key among them. There should be no legislative restrictions, Rehnquist insisted, for "self-discipline on the part of the executive branch will provide an answer to virtually all of the legitimate complaints against excesses of information gathering."

New York Times columnist Tom Wicker wrote two days later that Rehnquist's claim that self-discipline by federal agencies adequately protected citizens from government intrusions on their rights should be viewed alongside Attorney General Mitchell's recent claim that the executive branch had an unlimited right to use electronic surveillance on any person or organization without seeking permission of, or notifying, any court. It was clear, wrote Wicker, "they are asking us to set a goat to guard the cabbage patch." Two weeks later, Americans would begin to learn what had happened as a result of relying on self-discipline by the FBI for a half century. They would learn about the goat's feast.

9

FBI and Burglars in a Race

DESPITE GETTING LITTLE or no sleep since the night before the burglary, most of the burglars took Davidon's advice and went to work or school the next day. By seven o'clock that evening they were back at the farmhouse. There was a sense of urgency as they convened again as the Citizens' Commission to Investigate the FBI. There had been no news stories about the burglary. As far as any of them knew, it was still a secret. Their planned public announcement seemed to have failed. They assumed the silence was a calm before a storm and that they were in a race to analyze and distribute FBI files before that storm hit.

Davidon arrived later than the others that evening. He was delayed by his phone interview with *Washington Star* columnist Mary McGrory about the Saturday meeting with Kissinger at the White House. Four days after the Media burglary, as the search for the burglars reached high gear, McGrory's interview with Davidon, along with a photograph of him, was on the front page of the *Star*.

For more than a week after the burglary, the burglars worked intensely as a cohesive group on thoroughly analyzing and organizing the files and preparing them for distribution. Under Davidon's leadership, they had developed a plan for release of the files. Unlike their failed strategy for announcing why the burglary had taken place, their distribution plan was handled so competently that it seemed like something that might have been organized by the best minds at J. Walter Thompson, a public relations/marketing agency then known as one of the best strategic marketers of information in the world. Davidon wisely concluded that the files would get much more attention if they were sent to journalists in small sets in successive mailings instead of in one big mailing. To draw maximum attention to the content, he made sure that each set included documents of significant news value and a cover letter from the commission.

Except for an unplanned ride to the city one day, the files were kept at the farm until the burglars were ready to copy them. They had agreed well before the burglary that it was important to review the files as far away from the city as possible, but at a place the burglars could travel to and from easily each day as they maintained double lives—normal life at work or school by day, commission life at the farm at night. They were grateful that Ron Durst was willing to stay at the farm and protect the documents full-time. But one day the pressure on him became too great. Alone in the house, he worried to the point of near panic about the possibility that law enforcement officers might arrive at any moment and discover him and the files. He felt compelled to take them and himself elsewhere. He loaded them in his car and drove to the city. Unfortunately, he went to Powelton Village, a section of Philadelphia where many members of the Resistance and some of the Media burglars lived. Because of its reputation as a neighborhood full of antiwar activists, the FBI had placed some Powelton residents—and eventually most of the neighborhood—under heavy surveillance almost immediately after the burglary. By the time Durst drove there, the neighborhood already was well on its way to becoming ground zero in the bureau's search for the Media burglars. When he dropped in on a couple of friends and asked if he could store some documents in their home, he realized from their silence and the strained expressions on their faces that he had made a mistake and should get out of the area immediately. The neighborhood felt radioactive. He drove back to the farm realizing anew that the nice secluded house, lonely as it was, was definitely the preferred hiding place for the files.

After the burglars finished organizing the files and cover letters, it was time for what they thought would be the easiest part of the post-burglary aspects of their work: copying the documents. Instead, to their great surprise, copying the documents was the most threatening aspect of anything they did, from the beginning of planning the burglary to distributing the files. They had what seemed like a very workable plan for making the thousands of copies they needed. Before the burglary, Durst bought a used tabletop Xerox copier at a very low price and set it up at the farm. They thought they were going to have a completely self-contained operation there: read, analyze, copy, package for mailing. None of them recalls years later how much the copier cost. Whatever it was, they agree it was too much. The copier was worthless. It operated so slowly that copying a document was like watching grass grow. This was not acceptable for people racing to copy and distribute documents before the FBI found them. In addition to copying slowly, much of the time the copier simply didn't work. Copies were so light it was nearly impossible to read them, and the ink had a foul odor—distinctive qualities that would be very helpful to FBI agents trying to trace copies to their source.

What to do? By the time they were ready to copy files, the burglars were well aware that a massive search for them was under way. Under the circumstances, it was of course not feasible to arrange for Xerox repair service at either the farm or at a Xerox repair center. Besides, the copier seemed to be beyond repair. This unexpected situation presented them with two problems that needed to be solved immediately: where to copy the files and how to get rid of the smelly, malfunctioning copier. They realized that though it was of no value to them, the copier could become a significant piece of evidence for the FBI. They found an easy solution to that problem. The philosophy professor who had turned down Davidon's invitation to be part of the group wanted to know if he could help them in any way. How was he at deep-sixing copy machines? He took on the job. He later told Davidon that on a weekend visit to friends in Ohio, he buried the copier deep in his host's densely cluttered garage. As he described the copier's resting place to Davidon later, it was one of those garages overflowing with what looked like a family's lifetime of discarded papers and old belongings. It seemed like a perfect place to conceal a fugitive copier. As far as is known, it never was discovered by anyone and may still be buried in that Ohio garage.

Once the burglars were rid of the copier, they made a decision that would bedevil them—and the FBI and the Xerox Corporation—for several months. Davidon and John Raines each took portions of the documents and copied them at their respective campus offices. Throughout this process—from casing through burglary, working at the farmhouse with documents, copying documents, and handling envelopes—the burglars continued to be very strict about wearing gloves. Davidon and Raines did so now as they stood for many hours at campus copiers near their offices copying and collating stacks of documents, separating them into precise groups. They copied files on a Sunday when colleagues and janitors were unlikely to be there and wonder why they were doing so much copying, not to mention why they were wearing gloves as they copied page after page. As far as they knew, no one saw them as they endlessly copied FBI files on overheated machines.

AS THE BURGLARS COPIED and fretted about distributing the documents as soon as possible, agents searched. From J. Edgar Hoover's perspective, the investigation was going badly. The "UNSUB" woman had not been identified, despite the fact that agents working the case continued to show the police artist's drawing of her to other agents, police officers, and countless other people they thought might be able to identify her. No one had. By a week after the burglary, lock-picking tools still had not been found in or near the Media office. FBI lab personnel were unable to identify precisely what tools were used on the locks. A locksmith brought in to evaluate the damaged locks offered no real help but offered high praise for the unknown lock picker. In his report he noted, "Lock obviously manipulated by person highly skilled in working with locks." Keith Forsyth chuckled many years later when he learned how highly his work had been regarded.

As the investigation continued, some top FBI officials in Philadelphia and Washington focused on determining which documents had been stolen. The task wasn't easy, but it was necessary in order for them to assess what damage would be done to the FBI if any of the documents became public. Simultaneously, the director kept insisting that the documents must be found and never become public. He was especially concerned about informers being identified. In a memo to a long list of field office supervisors around the country, he repeated his original demand: "This investigation must be given preferred investigative attention and all leads handled expeditiously."

During the first week of the investigation, reports from field offices included these:

- From Boston: Michael Kenney, editorial writer at the *Boston Globe,* received an announcement of the burglary and did not give agents original envelopes or copies of files he received. His articles, an agent wrote, indicate that "he has antiwar and anti-draft opinions. If efforts fail to get Kenney to hand over originals he received, will issue subpoena to Kenney to produce originals before grand jury." A March 13 memo repeated the plan to subpoena Kenney but noted that agents probably would be able to get documents from "friendly" Philadelphia newspapers. Kenney was later named a suspect in the case.
- From Newark: A possible suspect was found by the Red Bank, New Jersey, FBI office: a long-haired person sitting in a car near the office.

- From New Haven: The names of four persons were submitted as possible suspects "due to their adherence to views inimical to FBI and U.S. Government."
- From New York: A report said that John Peter Grady, key suspect and presumed to be the leader of the Media group, "keeps irregular hours and difficult to know when he will be home. . . . All logical informants and sources of the New York office are being contacted in this matter, however, to date with negative results."
- From Washington, D.C.: On orders from the director, bureau files were checked for all the people who had signed a letter to President Nixon in an advertisement that ran in the *Washington Post* on June 25, 1969: "Mr. President: End the war now." It had been placed in the paper by the End the War Now Ad Hoc Committee, based in Silver Spring, Maryland.
- From Indianapolis: The field office checked on the whereabouts on March 8 of a man from Bloomington, Indiana, who agents there thought might do such a thing.
- From New York: Agents investigated a man from New Paltz who on November 8, 1968, had sent a portion of his draft card to the Department of Justice.

The 33,698-page investigative record of the burglary conveys the impression that FBI officials in Washington and Philadelphia, beginning with Hoover, were frantic but not focused as they issued orders and reviewed findings. Consequently, ideas for new lines of investigation easily sparked new interest and swiftly diverted investigators' attention in new directions and away from earlier lines of investigation. Lines of investigation appear to have been both pursued and abandoned without justification for the shifts. Distraction, rather than analysis and insight, seemed to be the key driver during the early, most intense months of the investigation.

At first, the overriding assumption was that the burglary was done by people from the Catholic peace movement. Immediately, though, the field of possible suspects was expanded to include practically anyone who either looked inappropriate, according to FBI standards, or was known to have antiwar opinions. Those two descriptions covered a substantial portion of the population at that time. As the names of potential suspects flowed in from around the country, it did indeed seem as though any long-haired person, "hippie-looking" person, or known antiwar protester qualified to be considered a MEDBURG suspect. One insignificant tip led to the sudden investigation of communes throughout the Philadelphia area. The man-power employed by the bureau to investigate MEDBURG—approximately two hundred agents at the peak—was great, and so was the wasted energy.

The sense of urgency in the bureau increased as every lab report on fin-gerprints, as well as on the palm print on the cabinet by the door—the print that gave the Media agents hope for an early arrest that first morning—came back from the FBI lab negative. To the investigators' great disappoint-ment, all prints found in the Media office were those of FBI agents.

Agents questioned people who lived and worked in the immediate area of the office. They questioned more than once the people who lived above the FBI office. In the end, none of those interviews produced useful infor-mation. Other futile early efforts reported:

- On March 12, the Friday after the burglary, there was a "canvas [*sic*] of motels within five-mile radius of RA, canvas of taverns, restaurants and drug stores in Media area having employees and customers in area late night hours." During this canvas, agents apparently again did not notice that Davidon, an early suspect, had rented a room on March 8 in his own name.
- Records of rental car agencies in the area were reviewed but FBI agents did not discover that Davidon had rented a car from a local agency the day before the burglary.
- Owners of cars parked on streets near the office on the morning of the break-in were identified and "backgrounds secured. None identified as being connected with militant groups."
- Thirty-five post office employees on duty 2 p.m. to 11 p.m., March 8, contacted, and one all-night service station personnel interviewed.
- Contract employees of the company that managed the building where FBI office located were interviewed.
- Clients in community welfare office adjacent to Media Resident Agency up to 9 p.m. on March 8 interviewed without obtaining pertinent info.
- Former commune known to include numerous Swarthmore College students at time of raid [of commune] by bureau agents October 1970 at 1442 W. Baltimore Pike, Media. "Efforts being made to determine any possible involvement these individuals."
- Eighty-nine pieces of [military] deserter mail reviewed. Six disclosed information relating to FBI confidential sources in telephone companies in Philadelphia, Conshohocken, a town west of Philadelphia, Raleigh,

NC, and Wilmington, DE. More confidential phone company sources revealed later.

- South Carolina Employment Security Commission furnished "confidential employment information."

- A state employment agency in Delaware also provided confidential employment information.

A summary of those early efforts concluded, "All above could furnish no positive information. . . . Will maintain contact with sources on college campuses in area for any positive information."

An unusual news story came to the attention of the investigators. It surprised not only the FBI, but also the burglars. The *Delaware County Daily Times,* a newspaper in Chester, Pennsylvania, ran a story with this banner headline across the top of the front page on March 12: "Davidon Unveils Plot Against FBI." A smaller headline on the story, "Reveals ransackers of office," wasn't true. On March 11, Davidon had given a talk at the Swarthmore Presbyterian Church prior to the showing of a film, *The Holy Outlaw,* about Daniel Berrigan. Davidon had been asked weeks earlier to speak at the event. According to the news story, Davidon read the group a release he said he had received from the Citizens' Commission to Investigate the FBI. It was the group's announcement of the burglary, the one that John Raines read to a reporter the morning after the burglary. Until now it had not been reported by any news media. Davidon announced to the audience that he

Public remarks by William Davidon about the burglary were reported in a front-page banner headline in a local newspaper just four days after the burglary. As guest speaker at a meeting of clergy in Swarthmore, he read the commission's statement explaining why they broke into an FBI office. During the entire five-year investigation of the burglary, he was never questioned by FBI investigators.

was reading this announcement of an important event "because no news media had carried word of it." The story described the sixty-five people present at the forum as "startled" when Davidon read the "revelation." As the leader of the burglars, Davidon often had advised his fellow burglars on the need to be silent about the burglary. After the burglary, it seemed at times, especially when he made these public remarks, that he was not taking his own advice and was skirting too close to danger.

Other reports from investigating agents in the first week:

- "Members of Farkle Farm commune primarily engaged in drug and sex activities with little direct involvement in active resistance movement. Contacting Pennsylvania State Police and state narcotics officers regarding this commune is not sufficient. Possibility exists that members of the commune may have received information regarding this case. Immediately initiate direct contacts with members of this and other communes in your area to determine if information regarding burglary can be developed."
- "Locksmiths Philadelphia area being canvassed for clues . . . possible information regarding persons skilled in surreptitious entry."
- "Preliminary research under way for ex-servicemen similarly trained. Looking for those possibly associated with new left groups, having shown anti-Army bias after discharge."
- A commune of "unknown affinity" was interviewed. "Serious nature of burglary explained to them. They displayed extremely hostile attitude toward FBI."
- "Attempts being made to secure identity of unknown male who left nearby apartment at critical hour during early morning March nine last. He appears involved in illicit relationship and not related to this burglary. Further investigation required to identify him now being conducted."
- A resident of the Media building where the FBI office was located (her name was blacked out) "advised that she has been residing at this address with her husband since Feb. 28, 1971. She stated that she and her husband on the night of March 8, 1971, stayed up late and listened to the Frazier-Ali fight on the radio. They heard nothing downstairs. [Blacked out] advised that she is employed by the hardware store which is located to the rear of the resident agency, and that at no time has

she ever observed any unusual activist in the parking lot in back of the resident agency."

The frequent summaries by agents in the early weeks of the probe often ended with this notation: "investigation continuing intensively."

At the end of a March 12 report on the unknown woman, Bonnie Raines, sent by Jamieson to the director and SACs throughout the country, Hoover, in his characteristic broad handwriting, expressed a concern that he voiced repeatedly: "I don't understand why our resident agent at Media didn't get this person's name."

On March 17, when Hoover still thought the burglars would be apprehended and the documents found and secured at any time, he appeared before the House Appropriations Subcommittee. As usual, Hoover biographer Gentry wrote, "behind these closed doors, J. Edgar Hoover was treated like visiting royalty." He did acknowledge, though, that unusual criticism was in the air. Consistent with his past unproven assumptions, he told the members of the committee that student unrest was due to pro-Soviet and China-oriented dissident groups on the campuses, not the Vietnam War. "I think if the war in Vietnam ended today," he said, "they would find something else." As Hoover ended his presentation that day, the chairman of the committee, Representative Frank T. Bow, Republican from Ohio, told him, "It is a pleasure to have you here. We have great confidence in you and your associates. I think we sleep a little better at night because of your efforts." A short time later, Hoover learned that, as usual, he had received the increase he had asked for. Neither Hoover nor any member of the subcommittee said anything that day about the brief news reports that an FBI office had been burglarized.

IN ADDITION to the unknown female walk-in, the agents in the Media office also remembered Susan Smith. Unlike Raines, Smith was identified by Media agents soon after the burglary. They recalled that she had visited the office unannounced in January, used her real name, and said she was there to ask if one of the agents would be willing to speak to one of her classes. Agents remembered that she didn't tell them where she taught, but after the burglary, they quickly figured that out. They had her name and remembered her face. They scoured local college yearbooks and found her photo in one of them. Before they called her for an appointment, they searched their files and found a long roster of her activities and arrests at antiwar and civil rights demonstrations in various parts of the country, going back to the early 1960s. They found a report of an event where an agent had followed her and reported on her participation in a demonstration.

Smith was the first Media burglar contacted by FBI agents after the burglary. An agent called her at her campus office on March 17, the day before the burglars met for the last time, just as they completed copying the files and preparing them to be mailed. She didn't tell the others about the call, and she can't remember why she didn't. As she unfolds the tale, it seems evident that profound fear probably caused her to keep the visit a secret from everyone except two colleagues.

In a report on the call to Smith, she was described by an agent as "uncooperative and evasive." She refused during the phone conversation to make an appointment to meet with agents, "stating she had full schedule, and she inquired about reason for interview . . . asked agents not to contact her in person without first contacting her by telephone and was unwilling to give any assurance that she would then consent to interview in the future. . . . In view of uncooperative attitude, further background will be developed prior to further attempts to interview."

When Hoover was informed of her reaction, he ordered agents to go to Smith's office without prior notice. He gave them this advice: "This is a criminal investigation and unless some reason exists, it is not necessary to contact a suspect or a person who may have information on this case by telephone prior to conducting an interview. If interviewee is uncooperative upon initial contact, insure individual is aggressively advised on the criminal penalties involved in this case." That was a reference to Hoover's hope that people arrested in the case would be charged with espionage, not simply burglary. Agents working on the case had been informed two days earlier that because some of the stolen files were believed to be about foreign matters—one of the documents, for example, was about a visit to the United States by the Soviet Circus on Ice—the burglars could be charged with espionage, a serious accusation that could lead to many years in prison.

"If person refuses interview," Hoover continued, "develop names of relatives and associates and attempt to develop [as sources]. . . . Avoid harassment but do not hesitate to re-contact uncooperative suspects. . . . It will result in the solution of this case. . . . Locate and interview Susan Smith regarding her knowledge of this burglary."

Immediately after the message from Hoover, agents went to Smith's campus office and, following Hoover's advice, did so without calling in advance. "Bureau agents contacted Smith by surprise," according to the report on the visit. "She called in other staff, turned on tape recorder and refused to be interviewed."

Any of the burglars would have been very concerned if an FBI agent had come to interview them, as happened to three others over the next several weeks. But Smith had a unique problem. By outward appearances, she was her usual self-possessed, businesslike self before and after the burglary. She arrived at the farm each evening after the burglary and studiously read and commented on scores of pages of stolen files and made recommendations about how they should be categorized. Her calm appearance was a front. Actually, she was in a state of perpetual, intense fear. She couldn't sleep. Some days it was difficult for her to eat. She had no appetite. Her nerves went on alert every time she saw a police car. That instinct—Are they following me?—had been part of her life occasionally ever since she worked in Mississippi during the Freedom Summer in 1964, but it had pretty much disappeared. Now it was back and it was worse than it had ever been. That was true because of a question she could not answer. She was haunted by the question:

Did I take my gloves off inside the FBI office?

Two days after the burglary, the question arrived with such force and persistence that it felt like an interrogator had taken up residence in her head. She continued to be unable to answer the question. She tried repeatedly. She put herself through an exercise. In search of an accurate memory, she would try to relive every minute that she had been in the office the night of the burglary: *I touched the doorknob, I opened file cabinet drawers, I removed paper from drawers, I touched the side of file cabinets, I handled paper on top of desks, I opened desk drawers, moved chairs.*

There was no doubt about it. Given her role in the burglary, if she had removed a glove, her fingerprints would be found throughout the Media office.

Sometimes this replay of her time in the office went well, and she would start to feel that she had answered the question and resolved the problem that obsessed her. At such times, she would experience a period of calmness. She would remember herself wearing gloves the whole time she was inside the office. Near the end of this replay of crucial moments of the burglary, she would welcome a sense of relief and tell herself, *I'm sure I didn't take the gloves off.* But nearly every time she went through this scenario, the doubt returned, even before she had a chance to have the pleasure of a relaxing sigh of relief. The painful cycle would start again: *But did I, just before going through the door, take the gloves off? I remember pressing my hand on the door, just so, as I was leaving. Were my gloves on then?*

She never finished the exercise with certainty. Always, just as she was about to feel at ease, the painful uncertainty would return full force. Always a sound sleeper, she now spent hours staring into the darkness. Whether driving through the bucolic countryside between her home and the distant farmhouse or teaching one of her classes, her mind was often on two competing tracks—the things she would have preferred to be thinking about and the fear caused by the question that haunted her.

Years later, she remembers clearly how her fear intensified when an FBI agent called her and said he wanted to talk to her:

"About what?"

"About the Media burglary."

"It was terrifying," she remembers. Immediately the question was there as the agent was finishing his first sentence: *Did I remove my gloves?*

While he continued to talk, she was frantically thinking, *I can't remember whether I took my gloves off.* She was reassuring herself: *I'm sure I didn't take my gloves off.* She was asking herself again, *Did I take my gloves off just before going through the door, as we left? I remember I pressed my hand on the door just so.* Many years later, though her voice is calm, even soft, as she recalls this frightening moment, her brow furrows deeply and her eyes reflect the pain of her memory.

"It was like that feeling you have when you're thirty minutes away from home: Did I turn the burner off under the teakettle? Or, did I unplug the iron? But I couldn't go back to do anything about it."

When the agents showed up at her office the next day, Smith asked two other professors to be present. The agents were a mixture of cocky and angry. They were cocky about the fact that they had found her and, in doing so, had caught her in a lie. Why had she lied to them two months earlier, they wanted to know, when she came to the office? One of them seemed to relish describing how an agent at the Media office remembered the day after the burglary that a woman from one of the local colleges had come to the office, said she was a professor—Smith now thinks she said Temple University, though she's not sure—and asked if the FBI would send someone to campus to discuss the bureau's role in reacting to antiwar protests. She thinks she said, "We like to hear both sides of issues, and we are aware of a lot of accusations being made against the FBI, and we'd like to know what they have to say." The agent she met in the Media office was "very congenial," she recalls, and said the bureau would be happy to send someone from its speakers' bureau. Just let them know when. Her visit was, of course, a ruse. Smith was in the office that January day to case the inside of the office, though for considerably less time and in less detail than Bonnie Raines would case it a month later.

Now, in her campus office just days after the burglary, one of the agents was explaining to her, with pride, how they had managed to find her despite the fact that she had lied about where she taught. Taking pleasure in having blown her ill-disguised cover, he asked, "Why did you visit us? Why didn't you just call to ask if we would provide speakers?"

The agents' cockiness turned to anger when Smith told them she was going to tape-record the interview. They said they would not permit that. No interview then, she said. "We didn't tape-record you when you came to set up a speaker. Why would you want to tape-record us?" one of the agents asked. She recalls responding, " 'I don't trust you guys.' He said, 'Well, we're not going to talk if there's a tape recorder.' I said, 'Fine.' " And the agents left.

"But they got what they wanted," says Smith. As she tells the story of the meeting years later, she sounds like someone who has just confessed and fears the sheriff will arrive soon with handcuffs. "They had gotten across their message—they wanted me to know that they had figured out who I was. . . . And I had behaved very badly. I had panic in my voice. . . . Instead of seeing me as a self-righteous citizen, they saw somebody who was scared. . . . I think that was why they left so easily. That was all they wanted to know—my reaction, my emotions. I don't think they thought they were going to get any actual information from me."

She was right. In their report that day, the agents wrote that she was "visibly shaken during interview attempt."

From the wisdom of years of hindsight, she looks back on her "visit" to the bureau and regrets choosing "a ruse that was close to reality. I wasn't worried at the time I went in there. In fact, I thought I was clever. . . . I was pissed at myself that they had blown my cover, that I hadn't pulled that off."

As she faced them that day in her office, she felt certain they had her fingerprints. She felt sure then that the answer to the question that haunted her was yes, that she had removed her gloves. She had no way of knowing that no burglar's fingerprints had been found in the office and that she must have worn her gloves the entire time. She continued to toss and turn fitfully every night for months, waking and asking herself the question again and again: *Did I remove my gloves?* Because the burglary was a secret, she could not share this agonizing concern with close friends. During that time, the burglary was a heavy burden for Smith. Eventually, she would be proud of the accomplishment, but not then.

Surprisingly, she found comfort in something the FBI did shortly after they tried to interview her. A short time later, she heard from her parents. Retired and living in the South, they had been visited by the FBI. Then her brother told her he had been visited by the FBI. An aunt was visited by agents. Old friends in the West, including an attorney who represented her once many years earlier after she was arrested at a sit-in, were visited by the FBI. "They asked them all the same questions: What kind of person I was. What my politics were. Whether I'm the kind of person that would break the law like this. Would I break into an FBI office?"

As friends and family members called, one by one, and told her that FBI agents had attempted to interview them about her, Smith started to feel relieved. "That actually reassured me a little bit. . . . It seemed so dumb. If they really had evidence, why would they interview my parents? What's a friend on the West Coast going to know? It seemed that what they were doing was intended more as intimidation than as information gathering. . . . By that time I had read enough FBI documents that I knew they wasted their time on diddley squat a lot, so I thought that must be what they are doing to me. I figured if they had anything solid, they would have moved. The fear, or paranoia, continued, but their actions did reassure me."

She continued to puzzle over whether she had removed her gloves for a long time, but she asked the question of herself less often as she heard more about the kinds of questions the FBI agents were asking about her. "I always hated gloves," she says, either as normal attire or as burglar attire. She wishes she could have dismissed the question as flippantly after the agents came to her office.

BECAUSE EXPERTS TOLD investigators that the quality of the effort to pick the locks on the doors was superior, agents assumed a trained locksmith must have been involved. In an effort to determine if any of the people on the growing list of suspects had taken courses in lock picking, every locksmith training school in the country was contacted. The task was difficult. Some of the schools had very long lists of graduates. For instance, the Locksmithing Institution, a correspondence school, had 14,000 students in 1970. In this pre-computer age, it was extremely difficult to cross-reference hundreds of suspects with such large lists. Nevertheless, agents wanted the list.

Records show that officials at the school were reluctant to fulfill the FBI's request. They said they thought performing this function for the bureau would place them in a bad light with their graduates. In the end, though, they said they would do the research if the FBI provided a letter that set forth the reasons for providing the list and assured the school the list would not fall into the hands of its competitors. In the end, no suspects' names were found on the lists of graduates of any of the schools.

One name, Keith Forsyth, must have been missed. Forsyth was on the FBI's list of suspects for several weeks, but apparently his presence on the list of students enrolled in one of the schools was not noticed.

Faced with no progress one week after the burglary in the search for either burglars or stolen files, Jamieson suggested to the director that the bureau should attempt to forestall public disclosure by asking a judge for an order that would require judicial review of any "purported" stolen FBI documents that were made available to journalists or anyone else. This idea was proposed at the same time the burglars were frantically finding other ways to copy the documents. Jamieson thought requiring judicial review would "preclude the publishing, dissemination or disclosure of any data." His idea was welcomed at FBI headquarters. Al Rosen, a high official in the FBI, recommended to William Sullivan, the number three official in the bureau, that there probably was no precedent for such an order, but because of the significant potential "ramifications involved, it is felt we should explore the suggestion further." If approved, Rosen wrote Sullivan, representatives of both the bureau's Office of Legal Counsel and its General Investigative Division "will discuss this matter with appropriate Department of Justice officials." It was approved by Hoover, and was discussed at the Department of Justice, though not at high levels. This was an ironic step by Hoover. Years earlier during and after the Coplon trial, the director took steps to prevent judges from seeing FBI files. Now, in desperation, he wanted a judge to review stolen FBI files and order that they not be disclosed.

Hoover announced a radical decision to his top officials: To protect files, he would close all 538 of the bureau's small offices. His top aides shared his concern about the safety of these offices, many of them isolated, but they were aghast at this desperate suggestion. They strongly urged the director not to take that extreme step. They pointed out that closing all of the small offices would leave vast swaths of the nation virtually beyond the reach of the FBI, especially in the middle of the country and the West, where the distance between FBI offices in many places was already more than a hundred miles.

Reluctantly, the director agreed to a compromise. Instead of closing all 538 small offices, he would close the smallest ones, the 103 resident agencies. He imposed stringent conditions on the offices he left open. He ordered that all small offices that remained open be protected by security guards twenty-four hours a day. This unusual arrangement had unexpected consequences for agents in those offices. Because Hoover trusted no one outside the bureau to provide security for these FBI offices, he required that the security guards be FBI agents. In order to have agents on duty as agents during the day and as guards at night, the hours each agent worked increased substantially. It also meant a considerable reduction in time available for them to conduct investigations and arrests. So be it. In the aftermath of the Media burglary, the security of FBI offices was more important than law enforcement.

This unusual security arrangement led to special benefits for agents in those offices. Suddenly, they were earning a lot more money. Agents throughout the bureau had for many years been required by the director to submit phony statements of how much overtime they worked each month, for which they were not paid. The director used the cumulative phony overtime records when he annually asked Congress for a budget increase to help meet the bureau's critical need, as evidenced by the overtime hours, to hire more agents. He always got the increase, sometimes even more than he asked for. That overtime was fake. This overtime was real. Within a few months of the Media burglary, the agents at these offices were earning so much from overtime hours that some of them bought sports cars and better clothes for themselves and their families. They were living much better than they did on a typical agent's salary. An agent who worked in one of the small offices said the change was so obvious that people around town noticed that some agents had recently acquired spiffier wardrobes. Some even expanded their shoe supply beyond the Hoover-required wingtips.

Despite the increased security he put in place at small FBI offices throughout the country, Hoover continued to be afraid the bureau could not protect itself against more burglaries and more revelations. The investigation was taking much more time than he had expected. Increased protection at every office was absolutely necessary.

AFTER THE BURGLARS COPIED, collated, and packaged copies of stolen files, they had one more very important task: mailing them. John Raines agreed to mail the first set. Davidon would mail the second set and later arrange to place all the documents in the hands of Resist, a Cambridge, Massachusetts, organization that had agreed, without knowing who the burglars were, to send sets of the documents to a variety of people and organizations that Davidon and the Resist staff thought would give them wide public distribution. This arrangement resulted in nearly everyone who worked for Resist or served on its board becoming a MEDBURG suspect, including scholars Noam Chomsky and Howard Zinn and poet Grace Paley.

The day before the first documents were mailed, the Citizens' Commission to Investigate the FBI had a final meeting at the farm. By then—ten intense, work-filled days after the burglary—they were not as focused as a group as they had been. Forsyth remembers that he started to become disengaged just a few days after the burglary. He felt the older members of the group were more qualified for these post-burglary duties that involved strategic thinking about how news organizations and Congress should be informed. He was eager to move on to the next action that would help stop the war. After the documents were sorted, he didn't have any more responsibilities related to the Media burglary and its aftermath.

One of his main concerns when the documents were packaged and ready to be distributed was a missing document. It was a letter on FBI stationery to an official of the John Birch Society, an extreme right-wing organization that was then fairly active. He has no idea how the document disappeared but holds himself responsible for its loss. The gist of the letter, he recalls, was "I want to thank you for your kind support of the FBI. The John Birch Society and the FBI are supporting the same American values."

"It wasn't exactly a smoking gun," Forsyth recalls, "but it was a friendly, good ol' boy, we-think-you're-great kind of letter. It really stuck in my memory, partly, I suppose, because it disappeared. . . . I felt bad about that because I thought it showed the informal networks that exist between a fascist group like the John Birch Society and the government. There's no legitimate reason why a government police agency should be buddy-buddy with a group like that. . . . To me it was an artifact, a little emblem of the kind of shadow government that can exist that people don't like to think is possible. I wanted people to see it."

It was during that last time all the burglars were together—the day before the first set of documents was mailed—they agreed that now that their work was nearly done and the fruit of their efforts about to be given to the public, they would not meet with one another again, either as a group or as individuals. Some of them had given this a lot of thought and decided isolation was important in order to avoid the arrest of one of them leading to the arrest of another one. Despite the bonds that had developed among some of them, they kept that agreement. That meant they never shared with one another either the fears that shadowed some of them in the months after the burglary, the agonies at least two of them would endure in a few years, or the great sense of accomplishment most of them would experience privately years later when the expanding impact of the burglary became clear in news stories, congressional hearings, and trials. The agreement not to meet also meant that over the years only the Raineses talked freely to anyone from the group—each other—about this profound shared experience.

Several weeks after that last meeting of the group, when the FBI search for the burglars became so intense that it directly touched hundreds of people in the Philadelphia peace movement, the Raineses suggested to Davidon that the burglars should get together to learn how each of them was enduring the pressure and whether the FBI had visited them. Under the circumstances, Davidon thought that was a bad idea. The Raineses regretted the emotional disconnect, but they accepted the need for it and did not attempt to get in touch with others in the group again, though they occasionally saw some of them at demonstrations and trials during the next two years. They were particularly concerned because they heard that a woman in the Philadelphia peace movement who looked very much like Bonnie Raines had come under great pressure from the FBI. Thinking she was Bonnie, agents broke into her home by busting down the door of her Powelton Village residence. They used this tactic with another resident of the neighborhood. Neither break-in led to information helpful to the investigation.

Before the burglars parted at that last meeting, they reached another important agreement: They would take the secret of the Media burglary to their graves. If they were not arrested, no one would ever know who found and revealed the first documentary evidence of how J. Edgar Hoover operated—the first evidence that there was a secret FBI that suppressed dissent.

IT WAS TIME for the documents to be mailed. John Raines drove to Princeton the day after the burglars gathered for the last time. He dropped five packets of FBI documents into a mailbox. The return address on each was "Liberty Publications, Media, PA." They were addressed to Senator George McGovern, Democrat from South Dakota; Representative Parren Mitchell, Democrat from Maryland; Tom Wicker, columnist at the *New York Times*; Jack Nelson, investigative reporter in the Washington bureau of the *Los Angeles Times*; and this writer, then a reporter at the *Washington Post*.

The postmark, "Princeton," that was stamped on the envelopes that afternoon at the Princeton post office, set off a new line of investigation as soon as the bureau was given those envelopes by four of the five recipients less than a week later. Newark FBI agents swarmed into Princeton to check out local people who had long hair, looked "hippie-ish," or had ever spoken out against the Vietnam War. Soon, the official record shows, investigators focused on a young couple who operated a bookstore in Princeton. The FBI put them under twenty-four-hour surveillance and interviewed their friends and family members across the country. In the entire 33,698-page MED-BURG investigation, the only reported instance of an institution obeying the law or its internal regulations regarding privacy of records occurred during the investigation of this couple. Stanford University, unlike other FBI-queried institutions, refused to turn over the student records of the young man, a Stanford graduate.

After John Raines dropped the packets into a mailbox on a side street in Princeton near the university, he drove home to Philadelphia knowing he had just ended one chapter in the life of the burglary and set the stage for the next. Some of the stolen documents were now out of the burglars' hands. They had no idea what would happen next. Soon other people would receive the documents and determine whether the burglars' enormous risk would have any meaning.

10

To Publish or Not to Publish

S JOHN RAINES DROVE back to Philadelphia after mailing the first sets of Media files, agents working on the MEDBURG investigation at the Philadelphia FBI office got the best news—perhaps the only good news—they had received since starting the investigation. Jamieson, the agent in charge of the Philadelphia office, immediately informed the director about it in a memo: "[Blacked out] stated that Xerox Corporation would be most cooperative in assisting the bureau. . . . Bureau requested to direct Buffalo [FBI office] to contact Xerox at Webster, NY, with Xerox copy [of] press release, and request examination [of Citizens' Commission's] press release for all possible information to assist in solution of this case."

A local Xerox official had told the investigators these crucial facts: Every Xerox copier's drum leaves unique markings on each copy produced on it. Some of those markings make it possible to determine which model of copier produced the copy, and other markings make it possible to trace a copy to the specific machine on which it was made. Most copiers at that time produced copies that contained visible odd marks, but few people understood that those marks were evidence of which copier produced a given page.

A Xerox official examined a copy of the statement Raines read to reporter Bill Wingell the morning after the burglary, a copy of which the FBI got from Wingell after he subsequently received a hard copy of it in the mail. The official said the marking indicated the document had been copied on a Xerox model number 660 desk-type copier.

The next step was obvious. The bureau needed to collect sample copies that had been made on model 660 copiers, as many as possible. Finally, agents had new trails to follow, ones that seemed certain to produce valuable evidence, something totally lacking until now in the MEDBURG investigation.

The hope held out by Xerox was especially welcome now nearly two weeks after the burglary. All efforts to find the burglars and the documents had led nowhere. None of the fingerprints or dozens of interviews had produced a productive lead.

The amount of information technicians could ferret out of a copy was impressive. In addition to tracing a copy to the machine on which it had been produced, they could, Jamieson wrote, also determine "the quality of paper . . . and possibly the source using this quality of paper . . . the quality of toner used and whether it is a Xerox toner or another commercial toner."

Agents planned a new line of investigation, a search for suspect copiers. Now, "find that copier" became as strong a mantra as "find that woman." For Xerox technicians to determine which copier had produced a given copy of a document, they needed samples of copies made on model 660 machines so they could be compared to copies sent by the burglars. Unfortunately for the FBI, in the Philadelphia area there were thousands of model 660 copiers. They seemed to be the copier of choice, as abundant as spring flowers in the city that April. On that Friday afternoon, the FBI was glad to have that challenge. The race was on to find Xerox 660 copiers and get sample copies from them throughout Philadelphia and New Jersey.

THREE DAYS LATER, the spirits raised at the bureau by that good news from Xerox on Friday were severely dampened. On Monday, Hoover and the agents investigating the case received very bad news shortly after mail postmarked in Princeton was delivered in Washington. Hoover surely realized that afternoon that his major goal probably had been defeated—to prevent the stolen serials from becoming public. He was informed by the Washington field office (WFO) that at 3:30, "Jack Israel Garvey, administrative assistant to George McGovern, phoned WFO that the senator's office had that day received the first batch of stolen documents." A short time later, the WFO report continued, a letter from the senator was delivered "to Mr. Hoover advising that he was sending the material he had received 'purportedly' from the files of the Media FBI office." The files, the envelope containing them postmarked Princeton, March 19, and the cover letter were all delivered to the FBI. Garvey called back, an agent reported, saying that the senator's office had "inadvertently furnished [FBI] a Xerox copy of a copy of the Citizens' Commission's letter and would furnish original copy [of a copy] to the FBI the next morning." The WFO memo to the director ended, "All documents being handled carefully under separate communication to FBI laboratory for appropriate examination."

Later that afternoon, the FBI headquarters office got a call from Harlington Wood Jr., an attorney in the Department of Justice. He said Representative Parren J. Mitchell, a Democratic member of Congress from Baltimore, had called him to report that an envelope containing stolen FBI documents had been left anonymously at his Baltimore home. Later that day, the legislator told the FBI the documents and the envelope they were in could be picked up at his office. Mitchell said he would retain a copy of everything he received. He also said he and his staff had handled all the documents, and consequently their fingerprints were on them. He was reluctant when asked for his staff to be fingerprinted.

McGovern immediately condemned the burglary in a statement his office issued that afternoon. He said he refused to be associated with "this illegal action by a private group." He favored a full congressional investigation of the FBI. This burglary of an FBI office, he said, undermined "reasonable and constructive efforts to secure appropriate public review" of the bureau.

In a speech to a black police officers organization in Pittsburgh that evening, Mitchell, the first African American elected to Congress from Maryland, also emphasized that the files were the fruit of a criminal act. Unlike McGovern, though, he also commented indirectly on the nature of the stolen files. "I turned the information, which included a letter from the Citizens' Commission to Investigate the FBI . . . admitting it stole the documents, over to the Justice Department," said Mitchell. "The burglary was a crime and must be dealt with as such. . . . Surveillance of black student groups and peace groups, as indicated in the files, is equally criminal." Because the content of the files had not been made public, people could not fully understand Mitchell's statement.

That afternoon the director notified all SACs around the country that "late today WFO received information from Senator George S. McGovern that indicated he had documents belonging to FBI. These documents are being obtained." The director closed with this order:

"All offices make no comment if questioned by press or other sources. Advise bureau immediately of any information bearing upon this matter."

In another message to all SACs, Hoover reviewed the information about McGovern and Mitchell, and reminded the agents that if the documents became public, agents must immediately alert all "sources and informants . . . in view of current developments . . . additional disclosures may be made in future. Expedite and advise bureau by return teletype."

That Mitchell and McGovern, two of the most liberal members of Congress and among the very few members who had criticized him, immediately gave the copies of stolen documents they received to the FBI and quickly criticized the unknown burglars for their crime may have led Hoover to think he might have at least a reprieve from his greatest fears. Some FBI officials dared to think that if those two men—especially McGovern, then Hoover's strongest public critic—had refused to reveal the contents of the stolen documents, perhaps all members of Congress could be trusted to do the same. Perhaps this bit of magical thinking was caused by fear that the other shoe would soon drop and the hope that it could be prevented from dropping. Whatever the inspiration, William Sullivan, then associate director, dared to propose to Hoover, via a memo to Clyde Tolson, that the FBI ask a select group of members of Congress to help the FBI solve this important crime. The FBI, he proposed, would ask them to give the bureau any stolen documents they received, and in the event they were contacted at their homes or offices by people associated with the burglary or distribution of documents, report the people to the FBI. Such a request would likely lead to adverse comment from some members of Congress, Sullivan wrote. "Nevertheless, we have an obligation to seek their assistance as a criminal violation has occurred. If any members of the Congress should cooperate, it would afford us an opportunity to obtain information which might lead to the solution of the case."

There were a few problems with this idea. The only members of Congress Sullivan wanted to target were African Americans and liberal whites. If word got out that they had contacted only those people, Sullivan theorized, the FBI might be accused of regarding such members as prone to having contact with wanted criminals. FBI officials discussed eliminating that weakness in the proposed scheme by including a few white southern conservatives in the group. When it proved impossible to come up with an embarrassment-proof way of executing the plan, the idea was quickly shelved as unworkable.

An updated summary of the MEDBURG investigation, dated the next day, Tuesday, March 23, indicates that copies of stolen documents received the previous day from the two members of Congress were being examined by the FBI laboratory. The summary also noted, "If approved [by the director], letter will be forwarded to deputy attorney general to determine if any legal action can be taken to prohibit disclosure of contents of documents. It being noted [Congressman] Mitchell has made several statements to the press alluding to contents and has admitted possessing Xerox copies of serials."

DISCUSSION OF that new effort to prevent the stolen documents from becoming public must have taken place at FBI headquarters about the same time I arrived at the *Washington Post* newsroom that Tuesday, March 23, a little before 10 a.m. and picked up my mail. I had been off the previous day. That meant my mailbox was overflowing even more than usual with news releases. If it had not been for the interesting return address—"Liberty Publications, Media, PA"—I might have placed the envelope in a stack of mail to be opened later. But the return address caught my attention. I knew something, but I couldn't remember what, had happened in Media recently. Even I, who had left the *Evening Bulletin* in Philadelphia at the end of 1969 to join the *Washington Post* and continued to have a deep interest in news from Philadelphia, had not thought much about the burglary when I read the very short wire service story the *Post* ran shortly after the break-in. In the envelope were fourteen documents and a cover letter that looked like a mundane form letter, a somewhat faded copy of a copy. But the letterhead signaled it might not be mundane:

THE CITIZENS' COMMISSION TO INVESTIGATE THE FBI

I had not heard of the commission. Its letter began "Dear friend" and continued:

> Enclosed you will find copies of certain files from the Media, Pennsylvania, office of the FBI which were removed by our commission for public scrutiny. We are making these copies available to you and to several other persons in public life because we feel that you have shown concern and courage as regards issues which are, in part, documented in the enclosed materials.
>
> You will also find a statement which our commission prepared at the time of this action which may help interpret our decision to you and others. Please feel free to make copies of any or all of this material and disseminate it (or not) according to your own judgment.

About a week after you receive this material, our commission will
publicly announce this mailing together with the names of those to
whom we have sent it. We will, of course, make perfectly clear in our
announcement that our actions were entirely our own decision and
responsibility. Your degree of public association or disassociation with
our commission is entirely a matter of your own choice.

Sincerely,

The Citizens' Commission to Investigate the FBI

Unaccustomed as I was to receiving stolen FBI documents from either
known or anonymous sources, I started to read the documents with excitement but also with caution, the latter because I wasn't sure if they were
authentic. It had not occurred to me when I read the story about the burglary
two weeks earlier that files might have been stolen and sent to journalists—
any journalists, let alone me.

The first document I read after I read the cover letter was the one that
encouraged agents to increase interviews with dissenters "for plenty of reasons, chief of which are it will enhance the paranoia endemic in these circles
and will further serve to get the point across there is an FBI agent behind
every mailbox."

At first, I wondered if that document might be a joke, a bad one. Enhance
paranoia? An FBI agent behind every mailbox? I realized that questions had
been raised in the past year about the possible clandestine reach of the FBI
into the antiwar movement, but I found it hard to believe the FBI would
have paranoia as a stated goal. It seemed even more unlikely the bureau
would reduce such goals to writing and place them in a file.

The document continued, "In addition, some will be overcome by the
overwhelming personalities of the contacting agent and volunteer to tell
all—perhaps on a continuing basis." From what I had heard from various
sources who had been interviewed by FBI agents, the agent who wrote this
document seemed to have either a sense of humor or an exaggerated view of
the impression FBI agents made on the people they interviewed.

It was clear that if the FBI had paranoia as a goal of its intelligence
operations, it was significant news. Assuming the document was authentic,
here was evidence that the federal government, through Hoover's FBI, was
not simply spying. When William Rehnquist, the assistant attorney general,
testified two weeks earlier before a Senate committee, he said surveillance
by government intelligence agencies at that time did not create a "chilling
effect." But here was an FBI document that, if authentic, provided evidence

that the FBI went far beyond creating a chilling effect. The FBI, as a stated policy, wanted to freeze dissent.

I continued to read. As I did, the six colleagues with whom I shared a small office off the *Post's* main newsroom arrived one by one at their desks to start the workday. We were a somewhat motley crew of reporters with different specialties—science, medicine, education, and religion—crammed into a room not much larger than a walk-in closet in a large Georgetown house. Playing with the names of our specialties one day, managing editor Howard Simons had named our group SMERSH—for "science, medicine, education, religion and all that shit." I was one of the two religion reporters in SMERSH, though my reporting on religion in recent years, both at the *Evening Bulletin* in Philadelphia and at the *Washington Post,* often included coverage of education, the antiwar movement, and trials that were related to both religion and the antiwar movement. Since the previous November, I had covered developments in the case against the Berrigan brothers and others after J. Edgar Hoover made his sensational accusations against them at a hearing in November 1970. I also had written about the summer 1970 wedding of a former nun and former priest that was attended by more plainclothes FBI agents than invited guests. The wingtip shoes were the tip-off. But those assignments did not prepare me to easily believe what I was now reading.

Most mornings, I greeted each of my colleagues when they arrived. Not today. I was totally absorbed, hunched over the documents and not noticing what was happening around me. Every document told a story about FBI power that was unknown to anyone outside the FBI. One signed by Hoover, on November 4, 1970, had two subject headings—"Black Student Groups on College Campuses" and "Racial Matters." It was the first of numerous sets of stolen documents I would receive over the next two months that revealed Hoover's preoccupation with surveillance of black people and students, especially black students:

Effective immediately, all BSUs [Black Student Unions] and similar organizations organized to project the demands of black students, which are not presently under investigation, are to be subjects of discreet, preliminary inquiries, limited to established sources and carefully conducted to avoid criticism, to determine the size, aims, purposes, activities, leadership, key activists in each group to determine background and if their activities warrant active investigation. . . . Each office submit by airtel to reach Bureau by 12/4/70, a list of BSUs and similar groups by name and school which are or will be subjects of preliminary inquiries.

All higher education institutions, including two-year colleges, throughout the country were to be included in this plan to monitor black students
and black student organizations. "In connection with this program we must
develop network of discreet quality sources in a position to furnish required
information. Bear in mind that absence of information regarding these
groups in any area might be the fault of inadequate source coverage and
efforts should be undertaken immediately to improve this coverage."

Hoover conveyed a sense of urgency about the need to monitor black
students:

> Initiate inquiries immediately. I cannot overemphasize the importance of
> expeditious, thorough, and discreet handling of these cases. The violence,
> destruction, confrontation and disruptions on campuses make it manda-
> tory that we utilize to its capacity our intelligence-gathering capacity.
>
> Increased campus disorders involving black students pose a definite
> threat to the Nation's stability and security and indicate need for increase
> in both quality and quantity of intelligence information on Black student
> Unions and similar groups which are targeted for influence and control
> by violence-prone Black Panther Party and other extremists.

It was clear from the documents that black students were regarded as
potentially violent and therefore as appropriate subjects to be watched and
to have their actions recorded in FBI files. The details in another document provided evidence that the Philadelphia FBI office had followed up
on Hoover's instructions swiftly and comprehensively. Less than a month
after Hoover's directive, in a December 2, 1970, memo, Philadelphia SAC
Jamieson listed thirteen private and public campuses in the Philadelphia
area where the bureau already had established informants, as "per instructions" of the director. "Investigations are being opened or reopened." The
Philadelphia field office added private high schools to the list and established
informants in them. Another document reported that *every* black student at
Swarthmore College was under surveillance.

One of the files revealed that on some campuses the bureau had a network
of informers—called informants in FBI parlance—who provided reports to
the bureau about the activities of professors and students. They included
switchboard operators, letter carriers, the postmaster, campus security officers, the local police chief, and some college administrators.

In other evidence of the bureau's recently increased emphasis on campus investigations, in a September 16, 1970, memo, supervising FBI agents

throughout the country were informed that the director had approved hiring security informers aged eighteen to twenty-one. "We have been blocked off," it noted, "from this critical age group in the past. Let us take advantage of this opportunity."

The bureau's easy access to personal records was evident in the stolen files. The private records of Muhammad Kenyatta, the leader of a national black rights organization based in Philadelphia, were collected without regard for whether they were related to any potential criminal activity. An agent reported in one file that detailed confidential data on Kenyatta and his wife, Mary—phone records, checking account records—had been given to agents without subpoenas. The information was provided by sources with the agreement that if the bureau ever had an official need to use the information in a court proceeding, it would be sought again—at that time with the legally required subpoena and as though the FBI had not already illegally received the information. Documents released later by the burglars provided additional information about these cozy relationships, including ones between the FBI and employers and with government employment agencies. It appeared that whatever information the FBI wanted, it was given, without regard to privacy restrictions. Banks, credit card agencies, employers, landlords, law enforcement agencies, and military recruiters all opened their confidential files and their mouths when the FBI appeared.

When I finished reading the documents, I went to the main newsroom to tell the national desk what I had received. I didn't realize I was answering a question that had just been asked. Another editor on the national desk, Mary Lou Beatty, had just talked with Ken Clawson, then the *Post*'s reporter who covered the Department of Justice, a beat that included the FBI. At bureau headquarters the previous day, Clawson had learned about Senator McGovern and Representative Mitchell receiving and turning over copies of the stolen documents to the FBI. I approached the national desk right after he had called from the department press room to ask if anyone at the *Post* had received the documents. I promptly called Clawson and described what I had received.

Less than an hour later, a spokesperson in Hoover's office was unintentionally very helpful with our most critical need. On the basis of my description, Clawson confirmed that the documents were authentic and were the same ones McGovern and Mitchell had received. Officials were eager to confirm the documents were authentic because they wanted to convince *Post* officials that stories about the files would be dangerous and should not be published.

A short time later, the attorney general, John Mitchell, called *Post* editors—and did so at least twice again later that afternoon—to urge them not to publish stories about the contents of the documents. He first called the national editor, Ben Bagdikian, and then executive editor Ben Bradlee. Mitchell, who in 1975 would become the first attorney general to be convicted of a crime and serve time in prison—for approving funding of another historic burglary, the 1972 burglary of Democratic campaign headquarters at the Watergate complex in Washington—insisted that disclosure of the contents of the files from the Media FBI office would endanger national security and reveal national defense secrets. He made the same claims in a final call that day to publisher Katharine Graham.

Apparently assuming the *Post* was about to publish a story about the files, late that afternoon Mitchell issued a public statement urging anyone with copies of the stolen FBI files not to circulate or publish them. His statement received widespread coverage that evening, beginning at 6:45, when it was distributed by the wire services:

> Attorney General John N. Mitchell warned Tuesday that disclosure of information in files stolen from an FBI office in Media, PA, could endanger the lives of some federal agents and the security of the United States.
>
> He urged anyone with copies of the records to neither circulate them further nor publish them.
>
> The attorney general issued a statement after copies of the stolen FBI intelligence files were given anonymously to Sen. George S. McGovern, D-S.D., and Rep. Parren Mitchell, D-MD. Both congressmen returned the files to the Justice Department and condemned those who committed the act.
>
> "Disclosure of this information could endanger the lives or cause other serious harm to persons engaged in investigative activities on behalf of the United States. Disclosure of national defense information could injure the United States and give aid to foreign governments whose interests might be inimical to those of the United States," the attorney general said.
>
> The attorney general noted that copies of the stolen records "apparently" had been circulated to some members of congress and some members of the press.
>
> In his statement, the attorney general said, "The Department of Justice is investigating the recent burglary of FBI records at its office at Media, PA. It appears likely that these records included information which would

disclose the identity of confidential investigative sources and information related to the national defense. . . . The department urgently requests that those who have received copies of the material not to further circulate it or publish it."

Actually, when the attorney general issued his strong plea, he did not know if his claims were true. He had neither read the documents nor been briefed on them.

A memo Mitchell sent to Hoover the day he tried to stop stories about the stolen files suggests the attorney general did not even know until that day that an FBI office had been burglarized—despite the fact that the burglary had preoccupied FBI officials since the day it occurred two weeks earlier. Either in an effort to conceal the burglary even from Hoover's superior, the attorney general, or as a result of the bureau's single-minded, frenzied effort to find the burglars and prevent the documents from becoming public, FBI officials had not informed high Department of Justice officials that the burglary had occurred two weeks earlier. They had conferred with lower-level department officials in an effort to get support for seeking a judicial order to criminalize possessing or publishing the files but had not informed high-level officials. In the attorney general's memo to Hoover, he wrote, "According to press reports, numerous FBI documents were stolen in the burglary of the Media, PA, FBI office. . . . I would appreciate your advising me with all possible speed with respect to the nature and content of the documents you have identified as missing."

The highest-ranking assistant attorney general, Robert C. Mardian, called FBI associate director William Sullivan that evening after Mitchell had released his public statement and advised Sullivan he "was speaking for the Attorney General, who wanted, in addition to the stolen documents, a justification for information and activities of the FBI insofar as selected documents were concerned, which if published, could be damaging." It was a strange situation. Hoover had instructed his aides and all FBI officials in the field to make no comment to journalists about the burglary. Now he apparently was relying on the attorney general to comment, but neither Hoover nor his aides had informed Mitchell about the burglary.

In an angry memo sent to Hoover the day after the first *Washington Post* story on the files was published, Mardian—who, as head of the Internal Security Division of the Department of Justice, was the department official who would supervise plans for prosecuting whatever case might be developed against the burglars—in so many words accused Hoover of having been duplicitous about his communication with department officials about the burglary:

> The Attorney General has given me a copy of your memorandum March 24. . . . [It] contains numerous references to contacts with people in the Department concerning the March 8, 1971, theft. A cursory examination of memorandum would lead one to conclude that a close liaison did exist between the investigative [FBI] and prosecutive [Department of Justice] functions. Quite the contrary was true. No specific report of the burglary was in fact made to the Attorney General or to this Division.

After noting that a discussion between two FBI officials and department officials about seeking an injunction against public release of the documents took place face-to-face ten days after the burglary, Mardian wrote, "Other contacts were equally ineffectual vehicles to advise the department of the fact of the burglary."

As Katharine Graham and the *Post*'s lawyer struggled with the ethical and legal implications of publishing the secrets revealed in the stolen documents, no one at the *Post* realized the attorney general was bluffing when he repeatedly and forcefully urged the *Post* not to publish. He had used strong language—"could endanger lives"—in those conversations. That he had neither read nor been briefed on the stolen files was not known until exchanges between the Department of Justice and FBI officials, part of the official record of the investigation of the burglary, were made available to me by the FBI years later in response to a Freedom of Information Act request.

It was clear that the stolen files contained no information about national defense and that public knowledge of their contents could not endanger national security. Given the nature of the documents and the unusual way I had received them—stolen FBI files mailed by burglars who had stolen them—we of course carefully considered the ethical and legal issues involved in reporting on their contents. The impact of the attorney general's claims may have been diminished somewhat by the fact that he and other Nixon administration officials often had claimed that stories endangered national security. That threat had become a preferred Nixon administration means of trying to intimidate journalists from reporting information the administration wanted to keep secret. The threat was seldom, if ever, made because the story in question actually endangered national security. Usually it was made because the stories aired deception, wrongdoing, or other secret information the Nixon administration did not want the public to know. To be fair, the attempt to use vague but threatening national security claims to suppress stories had been used before Nixon was president and has been used since that time by nearly every administration, but the Nixon administration made a habit of using the claim. That left journalists in the difficult position of having to assess, each time the threat was made, whether it was genuine or empty. The possibility that publishing information from the stolen files could endanger lives was the most extreme claim made by Mitchell. After examining the documents carefully, it seemed that claim was a reckless attempt to intimidate and prevent important information from reaching the public.

What seemed likely was that publication of the secrets, in addition to delivering information to the public about the secret policies and actions of one of its most important institutions, would do what the *Post*'s legendary editorial cartoonist Herblock suggested in a cartoon published a couple days later in the newspaper. In the cartoon, two men in rumpled suits who bear a striking resemblance to John Mitchell and J. Edgar Hoover stand side by side in a battered large garbage can. The Mitchell character wears a Keystone Cop hat and the J. Edgar Hoover character wears a Sherlock Holmes hat. Both of them also wear sour expressions. Fish skeletons, empty tin cans, and other debris are falling out of the garbage can, which is marked FBI FILES. Mitchell holds a protest sign: PUBLICATION OF STORIES ABOUT PILFERED FBI DOCUMENTS COULD BE DANGEROUS. At the top is the caption "And Besides, It Makes Us Look Like Damn Fools."

The question of whether to publish the stolen files presented Graham with an unprecedented challenge. It was the first time a journalist had been given secret government documents by sources from outside government who had stolen the documents. Throughout history, inside whistleblowers have leaked classified information to journalists, but never had people not employed by the government stolen secret government records and given them to a journalist. Less than two years later, journalist Les Whitten, a colleague of investigative columnist Jack Anderson, would become the second journalist to receive secret government documents from a nongovernment source who had stolen the documents. The documents he received were stolen by activists who temporarily occupied the Washington headquarters of the Bureau of Indian Affairs. Whitten was arrested by the FBI and charged with possessing stolen government documents, charges that were later dropped.

For *Post* editors, the responsibility to reveal this information to the public far outweighed concern about how it had become available to us—as

"And Besides, It Makes Us Look Like Damn Fools"

PUBLICATION OF STORIES ABOUT PILFERED FBI DOCUMENTS COULD BE DANGEROUS

FBI FILES

©1971 HERBLOCK

This Herblock cartoon was published in the *Washington Post* and other newspapers shortly after the burglary.

the fruit of a burglary. How could we not publish this information? It was important for people to have access to evidence—no matter how we had acquired it—that the FBI, under Hoover's leadership, engaged in practices that had never been reported, probably were unconstitutional, and were counter to the public's understanding of Hoover and the FBI. The publisher did not agree.

As I wrote the story, I did not know that a different rationale was prevailing at the highest level of the newspaper. Throughout the day, as I wrote and called people who were named in the files—some of whom I had known as sources when I worked as a reporter in Philadelphia—top *Post* editors, Graham, and the company's legal counsel debated whether to publish. Not until I submitted the story close to the 6 p.m. deadline did I learn there was a possibility the story would not be published. Graham and the company's legal counsel opposed publication, primarily on the grounds that reporting on secret files that had been stolen had never been done before and was likely to be considered highly questionable ethically and legally. During the debate, Bradlee and Bagdikian continued to make the case that the significance of the information was such that it should be published, no matter who the source was. The debate continued until 10 p.m., when Graham agreed to publish. It was the first time Graham was confronted with a Nixon administration demand that she suppress a story.

After the decision was made to publish, Bradlee prepared a statement for release:

> After a painstaking review of the documents and the Attorney General's request, and with the advice of counsel, the editors of the Post decided to print those portions of the documents that:
>
> 1) clearly did not damage the national interest, and
>
> 2) did not unfairly damage individuals mentioned in the documents.

The story was distributed on the *Post*'s wire service shortly after Graham made her decision and was published prominently the next day on the front page of the *Post*. The same day the *Post* published the first story about the stolen files, the *New York Times* published a story reporting the attorney general's plea that stories not be published about them. The *Times* also reported that a spokesman for Mitchell said he was in "conversations" with the *Washington Post*.

Post executives were in untested waters that day. Given the unprecedented circumstance, it is understandable that the decision to publish was difficult for Graham. It was the first of the numerous difficult historic decisions she would make to publish stories that the Nixon administration had demanded she suppress. Some of her well-known decisions were heroic First Amendment defenses in the face of threats by the administration to damage the *Washington Post* economically, something it had the power to do through denial of the company's broadcast licenses. Just three months later,

The first story about the files stolen from the Media FBI office, published by the *Washington Post* on the front page on March 24, 1971. Many other news organizations, including the *Los Angeles Times* and the *Philadelphia Inquirer,* also ran the *Post* story on their front pages that day.

Stolen Documents Describe FBI Surveillance Activities

By Betty Medsger
and Ken W. Clawson
Washington Post Staff Writers

Copies of stolen FBI records sent to The Washington Post described the bureau's surveillance of campus and black activist organizations at one college as involving the local police chief, the postmaster, letter carriers, campus security officer and a switchboard operator.

One of the documents encourages agents to step up interviews with dissenters "for plenty of reasons, chief of which are it will enhance the paranoia endemic in these cir- cles and will further serve to get the point across there is an FBI agent behind every mailbox.

"In addition," continues the Sept. 16, 1970, document, "some will be overcome by the overwhelming personalities of the contacting agent and volunteer to tell all—perhaps on a continuing basis."

Late yesterday, Attorney General John N. Mitchell asked that the documents not be published on grounds that "disclosure of this information could endanger the lives or cause other serious harm to persons engaged in investi- gative activities on behalf of the United States."

Copies of the stolen records were received Monday by Sen. George McGovern (D-S.D.) and Rep. Parren J. Mitchell (D-Md.). McGovern and Rep. Mitchell gave the FBI the documents, believed to be identical to those received by The Washington Post.

Justice Department sources said yesterday there is no question that the documents are copies of files stolen in a burglary of the FBI's Media, Pa., office on March 8.

See FBI, A11, Col. 1

in June 1971, she made her second such decision when the *New York Times* and then the *Washington Post* decided to publish stories about the Pentagon Papers, the important secret history of the decisions that shaped the war in Vietnam and that had been given to the newspapers by former Pentagon and State Department analyst Daniel Ellsberg.

When copies of the same stolen FBI files arrived in the Washington bureaus of the *New York Times* and the *Los Angeles Times* the same day I received them, they were handled differently. At the *Los Angeles Times* bureau, someone intercepted the envelope, opened it, and did not deliver it to the journalist to whom it was addressed—prominent investigative reporter Jack Nelson. It is not clear whether Tom Wicker, the person to whom the files sent to the *New York Times* were addressed, received the envelope. He did not write about the files at that time. According to FBI records of what transpired, when the files arrived in the two Washington news bureaus, people in each office immediately called the FBI and reported that they had received the documents and then promptly delivered the files to the FBI. Someone at the *Los Angeles Times* bureau diverted the documents independently, not only without informing Nelson that they had arrived and without copying the files, but apparently also without informing the top editors at the home office in Los Angeles, where editors decided that day to publish the *Washington Post* story the next day, the same day it appeared in the *Post*.

Nelson was astounded when I told him years later that the FBI record of the MEDBURG investigation revealed files had arrived in his newsroom, addressed to him, and been intercepted and delivered to the FBI. He recalled being eager to get copies of the stolen files and, soon after the burglary, called sources in the antiwar movement in an effort to find someone who would provide access to them. As Nelson revealed in his memoir, *Scoop: The Evolution of a Southern Reporter*, published posthumously in 2013, during 1970 and 1971, Hoover was so furious about Nelson's coverage of the bureau that he conducted a campaign to get the *Los Angeles Times* to fire Nelson. When the *Times* was the only major news organization not notified when the FBI was about to arrest Angela Davis on October 13, 1970, Washington bureau chief David Kraslow asked why. Tom Bishop, head of the bureau's public relations operation, said Nelson's stories were the problem. Shouting into the phone, he told Kraslow, "When you get rid of that son of a bitch with a vendetta against the FBI, we'll cooperate with you." In 2011, the *Times* applied for Nelson's FBI file and found similar attacks on Nelson.

At the *New York Times,* the documents must have been copied before they were delivered to the FBI, for the *Times* published a story about the files, written by Fred Graham, the day after the *Washington Post*'s story. In 2013, Graham said Wicker probably received the files but turned them over to him because Graham regularly covered the FBI. Regarding his rationale for giving the files to the FBI, Graham said that would be "typical—write the story first and then be a good citizen and give the files to the FBI." Actually, he did it in reverse order.

According to FBI records, *Los Angeles Times* journalists also turned over to the FBI copies of Media files they subsequently received in the paper's Washington and Chicago bureaus. The FBI was appreciative of this gesture. All documents given to the FBI by journalists were subjected to lab tests for fingerprints and for the unique marks made by the copier used to make the copies.

After I learned years later from the FBI's MEDBURG investigative records that the files sent to the *Los Angeles Times* never reached Nelson— and may not have reached Wicker—I realized that the files may have reached me as the result of somewhat unusual circumstances. Given what happened to the files mailed to the other journalists, it seems reasonable to assume that the FBI had arranged after the burglary for mail addressed to at least Nelson to be monitored on the FBI's behalf at the newspaper's Washington office by someone who was, as the bureau described such people, "friendly" to the FBI. Because Nelson and Wicker were among the very few journalists who had written articles that raised critical questions about the FBI, bureau officials might have assumed that if the stolen files were distributed, those two journalists would be likely recipients.

What about the *Washington Post*? Whose mail there might have been monitored as part of an effort to secure the stolen files and prevent them from being reported? Clawson, the *Post* reporter who covered the FBI, was regarded by the bureau as a "friend," so his mail would not have been monitored. At that time, only one person at the *Post,* Alan Barth, a respected veteran editorial writer, had written commentary critical of the FBI. If anyone's mail there would have been watched with an eye to intercepting the files and preventing them from being reported, it might have been Barth's. It was unlikely my mail would have been watched because, unlike Nelson, Wicker, or Barth, I had no track record as a published critic of the FBI. That, plus my generally lower profile, probably made it possible for the envelope containing the stolen files to slip into my mailbox unnoticed. After I found the burglars years later, I learned that they did indeed choose

Nelson and Wicker as recipients because of their reputation for raising questions about FBI practices. I was chosen as a recipient because they respected my earlier reporting in Philadelphia and had followed my coverage of the Catholic peace movement after I moved to the *Washington Post*. Based on our past reporting, they thought the three of us and the heads of our news organizations would recognize that the files were newsworthy and push for publication.

A few weeks later, I too qualified for having my mail watched. One Saturday afternoon I went to the newsroom to see if the burglars had sent more documents. Envelopes containing more files arrived at random times, so I went to the newsroom every day in order to read and report on them as soon as they arrived. I found a new set in my mailbox that Saturday. As I started to read them, a tall white-haired man I had never seen before appeared at my desk. He said he worked in the mailroom, and as he glanced at the evidence on my desk, he said he had noticed that I had been receiving stolen FBI files recently. He also hastened to say he had "noticed you're from Johnstown, Pennsylvania." I thought that was strange and asked him how he knew that. "I see all those letters your mother sends you." My mother had never written to me at the *Washington Post,* and she probably never knew the address of the newspaper. My visitor from the mailroom that Saturday seemed to be making a ham-handed attempt to "enhance" my paranoia in the manner prescribed in the first Media file I had reported on. It was too late.

THE FACT THAT I did not know the names of my sources added an unusual twist to the ethics of my relationship with them. Not only is the identity of a journalist's confidential source usually known to the journalist, but that source usually asks the journalist to enter into an agreement to refuse to reveal his or her identity, even if the journalist is pressured to do so. My unknown sources had asked nothing of me except what they asked of other recipients in the cover letter that accompanied the files: that I consider making public the information they had sent me.

Like most journalists, I always have preferred to fully identify sources so their veracity can be judged, not only by me but also by readers on the basis of what is known about them. To casually grant confidentiality diminishes confidence in journalism. When a reporter uses confidential sources, she is saying "trust me," an arrogant request to the reader that should be made only when the information is of such great importance that it should be transmitted to the public even if the source must remain anonymous. My sources' credibility was not at stake; the authenticity of the files had been confirmed at the highest level of the government. The issue was whether I had an obligation to protect them. I possessed documents I assumed my sources had touched and that therefore might contain fingerprints that could be used by the FBI in its efforts to arrest them. That meant that though I did not know who my sources were and therefore could not reveal their names, I was nevertheless in a position to betray them if I gave law enforcement agents copies of the files they sent me. In recent years, numerous reporters had refused to obey government subpoenas that demanded that they name confidential sources before grand juries. Reporters refused to comply with such subpoenas primarily on two grounds—in order not to be questioned inside a closed grand jury chamber, where no one could know whether they revealed confidential information, and in order not to become, or be seen as becoming, an arm of law enforcement, except in very rare instances, such as when withholding information could lead to loss of life. The then recent case of *New York Times* reporter Earl Caldwell was a notable example. Caldwell had refused to name his confidential sources when federal prosecutors in the Bay Area subpoenaed him in connection with an investigation of the Black Panthers. In some such cases, the government persisted and journalists went to jail rather than name their sources.

The atmosphere in journalism by 1971 was such that many journalists, including me, had thought about what we would do if confronted with a government demand to reveal confidential sources. In fact, there were so many confrontations over journalists' legal and ethical responsibilities to protect confidential sources that a year earlier a group of respected editors, reporters, and lawyers, including Nelson, established the Reporters Committee for Freedom of the Press, to help journalists who faced such challenges get legal assistance. To some degree, being willing to pay the price of going to jail rather than divulge confidential sources had become simply another skill a reporter needed to develop if the journalist was going to report on controversial government issues.

While Graham and the editors discussed whether the *Post* would publish a story about the revelations in the documents, I, assuming they would publish, thought about what I would do if asked by the FBI to turn over what I had received from the burglars. I concluded that my unknown burglar sources deserved my protection as much as they would if they were sources known to me who had asked me to promise to protect their identity. They had passed an important confidential source test: They had provided me with information important to public discourse that was not otherwise available. I assumed that they, at great risk, had performed what eventually would be seen as a valuable public service, though I had no idea at the time how significant that service ultimately would be.

Years later, as I read the FBI's massive record of the investigation of the burglary, I discovered that when the bureau learned the *Post* had copies of the stolen files, FBI officials recommended to Hoover that *Post* editors be asked to hand over the copies I received. Of the five sets of files mailed by the burglars the previous Friday, four had been delivered to the FBI immediately. Hoover, reacting to the recommendation, ordered agents not to ask the *Post* for the files, at least not at that time. He said he was certain we would not turn them over. He was right.

11

Appropriate for the Secret Police
of the Soviet Union

REACTION TO the first stories about the Media files was swift and angry. Members of Congress who had never expressed anything but kind words for J. Edgar Hoover and the bureau now issued unprecedented calls for a congressional investigation of the FBI. Newspaper editorial boards that had consistently been full of praise for Hoover and the bureau now expressed shock at the revelations.

In an editorial the day after the first story about the files was published, the *Washington Post* explained why the newspaper had decided to reveal the contents of the stolen Media documents:

With due deliberation and with considerate regard for the Attorney General's objections, this newspaper yesterday published the substance of some FBI records—stolen by unknown persons from the FBI office in Media, PA, and sent to *The Washington Post* anonymously by mail. . . .

The records afford a glimpse, not often granted to the general public or even to committees of Congress, of some of the ways in which the FBI works and of some part of its concept of internal security. They indicate that the bureau focused a good deal of attention on college campuses and particularly on black student groups which, according to a memorandum issued by FBI Director J. Edgar Hoover, "pose a definite threat to the nation's stability and security." . . . Other documents indicated that students were used, sometimes on a paid basis, as informers.

This lifting of a corner of the curtain on FBI activity in the name of internal security . . . suggests strongly that an appropriate committee of the United States Congress ought to look much more thoroughly at what the bureau is doing. Disorder on college campuses undoubtedly presents a problem to the colleges concerned and perhaps to the communities where they are situated as well. But it does not rise to the level of a threat to the internal security of the United States.

Moreover, the intrusion of undercover operatives and student informers into the life of an institution which has the interchange of ideas and the conflict of opinion as its very raison d'etre introduces a disruptive element more deadly than disorder. The FBI has never shown much sensitivity to the poisonous effect which its surveillance, and especially its reliance on faceless informers, has upon the democratic process and upon the practice of free speech. But it must be self-evident that discussion and controversy respecting governmental policies and programs are bound to be inhibited if it is known that Big Brother, under disguise, is listening to them and reporting them.

In regard to the document that called for enhancing paranoia and the bureau's goal of conveying the sense that there is "an FBI agent behind every mailbox," the editorial noted, "The FBI is not only insensitive on this score; it is shown by these records to be callous and, indeed, deliberately corrupting":

That is a concept of internal security appropriate, perhaps, for the secret police of the Soviet Union but wholly inconsonant with the idea of a Federal Bureau of Investigation in the United States. A government of snoopers in a nation of informers was hardly the vision in the minds of those who established the American Republic.

We believe the American public needs to know what the FBI is doing. We believe the American public needs to think long and hard about whether internal security rests essentially upon official surveillance and the suppression of dissent or upon the traditional freedom of every citizen to speak his mind on any subject, whether others consider what he says wise or foolish, patriotic or subversive, conservative or radical. That is why we published the substance of the stolen FBI records.

After ignoring the burglary when local FBI officials initially told them that nothing important had been stolen, now the *Philadelphia Inquirer* and other news organizations in that region suddenly had a keen interest in every facet of the theft. The *Inquirer* ran the initial *Washington Post* story about the Media documents as a banner story across the top of its front page. There, on the turf where the burglary took place and where the general public soon realized a massive search for the burglars was under way, press and public interest became intense. The *Inquirer,* long a devoted admirer of Hoover on its editorial pages, now declared that the questions raised by the stolen documents "are questions too fundamental in a free society, with implications too suggestive of police state tactics, to be brushed lightly aside." The documents were so shocking, the paper stated in an editorial, that more than anything they revealed "the massive public ignorance about this super-secret national investigative organization":

> In nearly a half-century under the leadership of one man, who is somewhat of an enigma himself, the Federal Bureau of Investigation has become a legend in its own time—surrounded by an aura of romantic mysticism reminiscent of the best fiction that has been written about Scotland Yard and the Royal Mounted Police.
>
> There is no denying that the FBI very often gets its man—and sometimes in rather dramatic fashion, as people old enough to remember the Dillinger era will testify—but exactly what else the FBI does isn't so clear. . . .
>
> It is in the national interest for Congress and the people to know more about the FBI—its assignments, its objectives, its methods of operation. . . . If the FBI is doing a good job, let credit be given where credit is due. And if it isn't, let's find out about that, too. Most important of all, we ought to know more than we do about the nature of the job itself.
>
> A committee of Congress should conduct a public inquiry into these matters, not for vindictive purposes but to be sure there are adequate safeguards to insure that the FBI will always act in the national interest, with due regard for the constitutional rights and freedoms of all.
>
> All two hundred million of us in this country are in a bad way—and our freedoms may be in jeopardy—if we are dependent upon information from burglars to find out what the Federal Bureau of Investigation is doing.

The Media documents provided evidence that the bureau's mandate had been perverted, declared a *New York Times* editorial on March 29. "Little confidence is inspired by the security measures of a security agency whose files can be so easily burglarized." But more disquieting than the bureau's internal security is the evidence, provided via the stolen files, of FBI incursions into political surveillance which far exceed legitimate efforts to protect the national interest. One need not minimize the seriousness of certain violent and lawless episodes in the recent history of student unrest to be disturbed by the FBI's measures of campus infiltration, especially its apparent stress on surveillance of black students and their organizations. Such procedures assume undertones of latent racial prejudice. With rare exceptions, the protests by Negro students have been concerned with their personal place in the academic community rather than with the revolutionary excesses of the white (or black) radical fringe. . . .

Even more dangerous are the consequences—clearly intended—that flow from the widespread use of informers. These tactics, said an FBI newsletter, "will enhance the paranoia" among left-wing dissenters and "get the point across there is an FBI agent behind every mailbox."

The dictionary definition of paranoia is "a mental disorder marked by delusions or irrational suspicions." It is difficult to be paranoid over police surveillance which, far from being a delusion, is carried out with such plainly stated intent. . . .

Assistant Attorney General William H. Rehnquist recently denied that political surveillance as currently practiced has a "chilling effect" on free expression of dissent. Apparently the F.B.I., the Justice Department's investigatory arm, disagrees. Could anything be more chilling than the knowledge that the Federal Government allows law enforcement to be perverted into a deliberate process of spreading fear and suspicion, on the campuses or anywhere else in a society that wants to remain free?

Not everyone thought the Media files should have been published or that the revelations in them pointed to a crisis. Some readers, in published letters to the editor of the *Washington Post*, condemned the paper for reporting on the stolen documents. "How much more honorable would it have been," wrote Ralph Ostrich, "if *The Washington Post* had disdained the role of a 'fence' for the stolen property. If not by deed, then certainly by effect, The *Post* has given moral justification to the participants of this and future criminal acts."

"I for one am glad that the FBI is keeping tabs on the activities of radical students," wrote reader William E. Lynn Jr. "All of those who object to these security measures richly deserve the nasty little revolution that will doubtlessly be perpetrated on us."

Some readers praised the decision to write about the documents. William Hagen wrote that the *Washington Post*'s coverage of the documents "exemplifies the very highest ideal of journalism: to fearlessly inform the people."

The evidence in the documents emboldened some people who had been silent. Calls for a congressional investigation of the FBI were made repeatedly in editorials and by members of Congress in the month after the first story appeared. Such calls were unprecedented, for until now both reverential high regard and fear of Hoover's power to retaliate had kept most of his critics silent. "The quick succession of revelations and charges regarding the FBI has prompted the first high-level discussion of a general Congressional review in the bureau's history," wrote Christopher Lydon in the April 19, 1971, *New York Times*. By then, more Media documents had become public. Senators who called for such investigation included Edward Muskie of Maine, Gaylord Nelson of Wisconsin, Edward Kennedy of Massachusetts, Mike Mansfield of Montana, and John V. Tunney of California.

A communist threat was behind the stealing of the documents and behind their being made public by journalists, some Hoover supporters claimed as they adamantly opposed a congressional investigation of the FBI. Representative Roger H. Zion, Republican from Indiana, summed up that opposition: "A major Communist-front originated attack is taking place on America's top law official. Director J. Edgar Hoover of the FBI is now being subjected to relentless attack by the far left."

Most of the members of Congress who called for a congressional investigation urged Senator Sam Ervin and his Senate Subcommittee on Constitutional Rights to conduct the hearings. The *New York Times* editorial board did so twice. In view of his publicly declared abhorrence of government spying, including comments he made during his recent hearings that investigated spying against citizens by the Army, Ervin was seen as the best-prepared official to conduct such an investigation. He had a reputation for being Congress's fiercest defender of constitutional rights.

As the pressure for Ervin to conduct an investigation increased, he announced in late April that he would not do so. He said there would be political obstacles to such an investigation, and the committee would be "very much divided on ideological lines." Interestingly, he had not let that problem stop him from recently investigating the Army's domestic spying operations. Ervin also said he had seen no evidence that the FBI had exceeded its authority. "I am under the impression that Mr. Hoover's done a very good job," he said. The senator who just four months earlier had declared that political spying by the military amounted to "warfare on the American people" now said no to investigating the FBI.

The person who worked most closely with Senator Ervin at that time, Lawrence M. Baskir, his chief of staff on the subcommittee and since 1998 a judge on the U.S. Court of Federal Claims, privately encouraged the senator in the spring of 1971 to investigate the FBI. In those conversations, Baskir said, the senator adamantly refused. It was not until after Ervin chaired the Senate investigation of Watergate that he expressed his first concerns about the FBI. But again he expressed great respect for Hoover, by then dead, and once again balked at investigating the bureau. Ervin's refusal demonstrated the enduring power of Hoover and perhaps also the timidity of most members of Congress regarding intelligence matters, which they had long avoided. Ervin realized that his investigation of the Army had not resulted in the legislation he had hoped to achieve. Perhaps he thought it would be even more difficult to achieve anything beyond public awareness as the outcome of an investigation of the FBI. Whatever the causes of his hesitancy, such reluctance in Congress did not disappear until 1975. By then the public was so outraged by the accumulated information it had learned about the FBI and other intelligence agencies that a critical mass in Congress was willing to conduct the investigation that some members had called for when the Media documents first became public.

IMMEDIATELY AFTER PUBLICATION of the first stories about the contents of the files, the investigation of the burglary became much more intense. Investigators placed the man who dropped out of the group and the woman who looked like Bonnie Raines under what the FBI called FISUR, or physical surveillance. The most visible FISUR techniques used in the investigation were ones that involved agents sitting in parked cars along the tree-lined streets of the Powelton Village neighborhood in West Philadelphia, not far from the University of Pennsylvania. They sat there in several cars for many hours every day for weeks in front of these old brick row houses converted to apartments, physically surveilling people and street life in general. It was a strange technique. It was difficult to imagine how they thought such practices would lead to discoveries about Media suspects. The beards that some of them were growing failed to help them blend into the community. They continued to look like what they were: FBI agents sitting in cars.

The memos in the files of the official investigation say little about results gained from FISUR. They indicate that it was frustrating and ultimately unproductive. Whatever the people in charge of the investigation thought this technique would accomplish, for the agents in the cars it may simply have been a way to kill time away from the office in an investigation that seemed to stall every time it took a new and hopeful direction. Or perhaps this visible saturation surveillance from parked cars may simply have been the bureau engaging in a practice that echoed the prescription in one of the Media files: make people paranoid.

The residents of Powelton Village were not prone to becoming paranoid. From the beginning of the investigation, many of them were named as MEDBURG suspects or were believed to be connected to suspects. They did not know that, but most of them probably assumed as much, given the constant presence of agents near their homes. Residents of the neighborhood found the round-the-clock surveillance they were subjected to maddening. Being who they were—some were the same people who years earlier had put gags on the stone mouths of the statues of Ben Franklin and other historic figures in Philadelphia after the Boston trial where defendants, including renowned pediatrician Dr. Benjamin Spock, were convicted for assisting young men who resisted the draft—they looked for the humor in having the streets outside their apartments lined with parked FBI cars, usually with two agents in each car. They found the seeds for a humorous response in the fact that agents often slept in their cars.

One response was to perform street skits with the agents as unwilling actors. In one of them, a resident stood beside an FBI car and blew a bull-horn while another resident stood on the other side of the car with a tray of cookies and milk ready for the agents as they jolted awake from their inter-rupted afternoon nap.

Sometimes an announcement was made on a megaphone for all to hear during the agents' afternoon naps:

"This is your FBI at work!"

Bumper stickers reading THIS IS AN FBI CAR were pasted onto the back bumpers of FBI cars as agents slept.

No FBI agent was ever observed laughing at the residents' attempts at humor.

On June 6, 1971, a Saturday, Powelton residents went all out in their effort to turn the massive surveillance on its head with humor. They held what they called "Your FBI in Action Street Fair." All of the entertainment was FBI-centered. People, including Davidon and his family, stood beside a life-size cardboard cutout of J. Edgar Hoover and were photographed as they affectionately draped their arms around the director's shoulders. Copies of

Media documents were nailed to trees, and so were large photos of agents who had been photographed sitting in cars in the neighborhood. Copies of enlarged Media files also were auctioned at the fair. Neighborhood children had fun putting together jigsaw puzzles that had been made from pictures taken of agents who seemed to be living in their cars, like homeless people, in the neighborhood. At the perimeters of the neighborhood the day of the fair, posted notices welcomed FBI agents to the fair but asked them to leave their pistols at the 16th Precinct Police Station at the edge of Powelton. Surveillance may have been called off that day, but a resident reported seeing one of the regular neighborhood agents drive by on a nearby street and gun the gas pedal when he realized he had been seen.

In addition to finding a way to laugh at this disruptive situation, Powelton Village residents also sued the FBI, asking a judge to order a halt to the blanket surveillance of the neighborhood. They eventually won, but the surveillance continued for many months before the case was resolved. In response to the residents' lawsuit, the bureau acknowledged that it used forty to fifty cars to conduct surveillance in the neighborhood and brought agents from as far away as Jackson, Mississippi, to conduct it.

A strong impetus for the lawsuit came from the FBI's attack on the home of Anne Flitcraft. She was upstairs having dinner with neighbors when she heard a loud noise coming from the direction of her apartment. She ran to her apartment, but by the time she got there, FBI agents already had broken down the door with a sledgehammer and were inside removing copies of Media documents and ransacking every drawer, cabinet, and closet. She was researching Media files about police training for articles that were published a short time later by the Quaker-sponsored organization she worked for, NARMIC (National Action/Research on the Military-Industrial Complex). NARMIC had anonymously received the files at its downtown office. When agents left her apartment that day, they took the documents, her typewriter, books, and assorted office supplies.

As word spread about the FBI raid on Flitcraft's apartment, neighbors gathered at her home, including David Kairys, the lawyer who represented her and others in their successful lawsuit against the FBI surveillance of the neighborhood. He was just beginning a career in which he would successfully represent many people who had been treated unjustly by the government— including, in 1986, Donald Rochon, an African American FBI agent who endured extreme acts of racial harassment and discrimination in the bureau. The lawsuit inspired by the raid of Flitcraft's home was intended to let the FBI know that it could not conduct such raids with impunity. Soon after

Davidon and his family with "Mr. Hoover" at the "Your FBI in Action Street Fair" held in June 1971 in the Powelton Village neighborhood of Philadelphia. Residents organized the fair to draw attention to the intense round-the-clock surveillance conducted by the FBI in the neighborhood for months after the burglary. *From left:* Ann Morrissett, Davidon's wife; "Hoover"; Davidon; and daughters Sarah and Ruth.

the raid, neighbors created what they called an anti-FBI alarm system. They distributed boat horns that could be heard for about two blocks. Residents agreed to use the horns in the event of another FBI raid so neighbors could call lawyers and run to the scene as quickly as possible to offer support to the resident being raided.

Kairys and other neighbors delivered Flitcraft's badly damaged door to the Philadelphia FBI field office the morning after agents broke in through the door. A speechless group of agents watched as the door was carried off the elevator into the FBI office and a demand for repairs was made. When Hoover was informed about this, he wrote a memorandum stating that the Philadelphia field office should pay for repairs to the door from the office's "Confidential Fund."

MEANWHILE, the FBI's search for suspect Xerox model 660 copiers, once a source of great hope for the investigators, was at times even more intense and more demoralizing than the search for human suspects. At first, local

Xerox officials cooperated fully with the FBI. The company's maintenance personnel were instructed to visit the many offices that leased a model 660 and make sample copies for the FBI on each of those machines. Because collecting sample 660 copies took a lot of time, Xerox soon said it would collect the samples only during regular maintenance visits. They were collected surreptitiously at offices the FBI told Xerox were most likely to employ people who would break into an FBI office—campuses, nonprofit organizations, libraries, and also a surprising number of corporations. Copies were collected from thousands of copiers leased throughout eastern Pennsylvania, New Jersey, New York, New England, and the Midwest. At Xerox labs, the sample copies were compared with copies of FBI files and the cover letters distributed by the Citizens' Commission to Investigate the FBI. Eventually, overloaded by the volume of copies it was analyzing for the FBI, Xerox trained some staff members at the FBI lab to do the comparative analysis. Still the work taxed the company's offices on the East Coast.

The cooperative relationship between Xerox and the FBI came to a screeching halt a couple weeks into the effort. In interviews with two journalists—syndicated columnist Jack Anderson and Vin McLellan, a freelance writer whose story was published on April 15 in the *Washington Post*—Gerald A. Mulligan, manager of public relations operations for Xerox Corporation, at its Rochester, New York, headquarters, acknowledged that the corporation had complied with the bureau's request for a list of customers who leased the 660 copiers. But, Mulligan said, Xerox had recently ". . . decided at the very highest level" not to cooperate further with the bureau in the investigation. "What it came down to," Mulligan told Anderson, "was the ethical responsibilities of the business. If we were to do this, we had a responsibility to inform our customers it was being done, and this would have defeated the FBI's whole purpose." In addition to revealing the type of copier the FBI was looking for and reporting the company's decision not to cooperate further with the bureau in the investigation, the stories also disclosed that markings on copies could help the bureau track copies of the stolen files to the copiers used by the burglars.

Hoover was furious at Xerox for stopping its cooperation and for making public remarks. In a handwritten note on a copy of the Anderson column placed in the files of the investigation of the burglary, he scrawled, "This shows what happens when we issue <u>inadequate & ill-considered</u> instructions [underlines are his]. Certainly we should *not* have contacted a loud mouth like Mulligan. The approaches should have been properly evaluated as to security." Actually, it is unlikely that FBI agents had contacted Mulligan.

The reporters had. Hoover was angrily lashing out, as his next move made clear.

The decision by Xerox to halt cooperation was considered a major blow for the FBI. This part of the investigation had seemed to be working very efficiently and there were high hopes it would lead to arrests. Just as Hoover's immediate response after the burglary was to punish Tom Lewis, despite Lewis's efforts to make the office more secure, now Hoover decided to punish Xerox. He immediately issued an order that every FBI office must cancel its lease with the company. Managers at FBI headquarters pointed out that this would be nearly impossible, not to mention very expensive. The process of getting a new contract with another company would be long and cumbersome. Immediate cancellation, they said, would impede work throughout the bureau. Hoover was unmoved by their rationale. As his officials proceeded with the initial stages of preparing to cancel the Xerox contracts, the problem was solved when the CEO of Xerox returned from a vacation out of the country and was upset when he learned that one of his officials had withdrawn cooperation from the FBI. Concerns about spying on customers on behalf of the FBI vanished. He ordered Xerox employees to resume cooperating with the FBI and wrote a deeply apologetic letter to Hoover assuring him that Xerox was on board again and always would be at the service of the bureau. At that point, Hoover rescinded his order, all Xerox copiers remained in place in FBI offices, and, most important, copies produced on 660 copiers once again streamed into the FBI lab to be compared with copies of the Media documents.

The burglars had read the newspaper reports that Xerox had helped the FBI discover the model number of the copier they had used and that Xerox had indicated it was possible to match marks on the copies of the Media files with marks on the drums of Xerox copiers of that model. That was very frightening news.

John Raines discovered how frightening it was. Not long after the first stories about the documents were published and were being widely discussed in news stories, he was seated at his campus desk when he overheard a discussion in the hallway outside his office that might have seemed routine to anyone else. He quickly realized it was a discussion in which he did not want to participate. A man was telling the department secretary, "There's something wrong with your copier's drum, so I'm going to take it and replace it with a new one."

It was another one of those brick-in-the-stomach moments that Raines had experienced occasionally ever since Bonnie's visit to the FBI office made the burglars confident they should move ahead with their plans. Today's experience qualified as two bricks. He listened to the conversation in stunned silence as he stared out his street-level office window and saw a small white Ford car marked with a Xerox logo parked on the street at the end of the sidewalk that led to the door outside his office. A few minutes later he watched the man carry the drum of the Xerox 660 copier on which Raines had made hundreds of copies, perhaps even more, of stolen FBI documents. "I thought, 'Oh, God, there it goes,'" he remembers. The man carried the drum down the sidewalk and placed it in the trunk of the Xerox car. There was no doubt in Raines's mind that the drum had been moved because the FBI wanted to examine it in connection with the files that had been mailed, most of which were by then in the hands of the FBI in Washington, thanks to the news organizations that had forwarded the files they received to the FBI. The drum could, of course, have been removed and replaced by Xerox because it simply needed to be repaired or replaced. But under the circumstances, it was impossible for Raines to assume that.

The burglars had been very strict about being sure to wear gloves during the burglary and as they worked for days with the documents at the farm. It never occurred to them that they needed to protect against more than their own fingerprints—that the documents they copied had their own telltale markings that could reveal on which machine they had been copied. Not that they could have done anything about that. The documents had to be copied. But if they had known, perhaps they would not have made the copies on machines in their own offices.

As Raines listened to the sounds of the Xerox maintenance man replacing the drum in the outer office, he wondered why the man was taking the drum and not just making sample copies. Did that mean they already knew this machine was the culprit, and they were taking it away because they needed the drum as evidence? Was it all going to come to this—being unmasked by a Xerox copier? In that moment, Raines felt sure the drum on his department's copier, the drum carried down the sidewalk by the Xerox maintenance man, had become a smoking gun.

He called Davidon right away. Davidon acted quickly. He found a sharp metal object and made a bold scratch on the drum of his department's Xerox copier. This, he assumed, would change the footprint left by that machine and make it more difficult to match the many documents he had made on this copier. To decrease even more the chances of the copier being detected, the afternoon Davidon heard from Raines, he and another professor—the one person who had turned down Davidon's invitation to participate in the

Media group—after the president of Haverford College and his staff had left for the day, removed the drum from Davidon's department's copier and exchanged it with that of the copier in the president's outer office. Sure enough, Xerox workers came to Davidon's department a couple days later and made sample documents on the Xerox copier.

EXACTLY ONE MONTH AFTER the burglary, Hoover assigned Roy K. Moore to be in charge of the MEDBURG investigation. The appointment signaled Hoover's increased sense of urgency and the very high priority he gave the case. Hoover considered Moore one of the bureau's best investigators. Moore also was highly regarded by many of his peers. He had been in charge of several earlier high-profile investigations, including the 1964 murder of the three civil rights workers in Neshoba County, Mississippi; the 1963 Birmingham, Alabama, church bombing that killed four young girls; and the 1955 midair explosion of an airplane over Colorado that killed all forty-four people aboard. After he had settled into Philadelphia, Moore reviewed MEDBURG and immediately endorsed the continued search for the suspect copiers as crucial to the investigation.

The results of that search continued to be very frustrating, especially given the huge effort put into collecting thousands of sample copies. Like the search for human suspects, the one for suspect copiers went nowhere. None of the marks on the thousands of copies that were collected matched those on any of the documents released by the burglars. This seems strange, especially in light of the evidence presumably obtained from the copier Raines used. Either his department's copier actually was due to have its drum replaced—a striking coincidence of timing—or one or more Xerox officials had engaged in their own act of resistance and not reported that a match had been established between the markings on copies of stolen Media FBI documents and those on the machine Raines used to make hundreds of those copies. Or perhaps the matching test might simply have failed.

There were other frustrations inside the FBI. Just two weeks after the first Media documents became public, Hoover even offered to "step aside" if at any time the president or the attorney general felt that he might be "a burden or handicap to the re-election" of Nixon. The director described his offer to resign in a memorandum in which he summarized an April 6 phone conversation with Deputy Attorney General Richard Kleindienst. The conversation took place the day after Representative Hale Boggs, Democrat from Louisiana, claimed on the floor of the House that the FBI had tapped his phone. Boggs's public accusation, never proven, led to an announcement from the attorney general that the FBI had never wiretapped the phone of any member of the House or Senate.

Kleindienst reassured Hoover in their conversation that he was "a good American" and that "the thing is going to subside." But Kleindienst infuriated Hoover the next day when he announced, in an interview the deputy attorney general had sought on the CBS morning television news, that the Department of Justice would welcome an investigation of the FBI. He said he thought "the only way public confidence in the FBI can be restored is through a congressional investigation." To Hoover this was extraordinary. No member of any administration had ever called for an investigation of the FBI.

The impact was explosive, especially to Kleindienst's ears. Shortly after he returned to his office after the interview, he took a call from Hoover. The director denounced Kleindienst's public call for an investigation of the bureau so loudly that Kleindienst had to hold the phone away from his ear. Colleagues in his office could hear every word across the room as the director issued a threat:

"If I am called upon to testify before Congress, I will have to tell *all* that I know about this matter."

Kleindienst did not fully grasp what Hoover meant. He soon would. The director was alluding to the illegal wiretapping of phones that Henry Kissinger, supported by President Nixon, had asked Hoover to conduct beginning in May 1969.

It had all started when Kissinger, then Nixon's national security adviser, was beside himself the morning of May 9, 1969, when he read a story in the *New York Times* that revealed that the United States was secretly conducting bombing raids in Cambodia. He called Hoover immediately that morning to ask what could be done to discover who had leaked the secret. FBI records indicate he called the director two more times that day, pressing him urgently. By the end of the afternoon, a tap had been placed on the home phone of Morton Halperin, a senior staff member with responsibility for national security in Kissinger's office, and would remain on it for a year and a half, long after he stopped working for Kissinger.

As Colonel Alexander Haig, Kissinger's top aide, put it to an FBI official a short time later, Kissinger "considered the entire policy would be ruined unless these leaks could be stopped, and that damage to the country would be irreparable." In the end, seventeen people were tapped as part of this secret operation conducted by the FBI for Kissinger and the president.

Besides Halperin, those who were tapped included six other members of Kissinger's staff, four journalists, two White House advisers, a deputy assistant secretary of state, an ambassador, a brigadier general with the Defense Department, and one of the president's speechwriters. Hoover wrote in a May 9 memorandum about a conversation he had with Kissinger that Kissinger "appreciated this very much, and he hoped I would follow it up as far as we can take it and they will destroy whoever did this if we find him, no matter where he is."

Hoover had entered into this illegal arrangement on behalf of the president and Kissinger with great reluctance from the moment Kissinger's request was made. At first, the White House insisted there be no paper records of the project. Hoover, extremely fearful of being discovered carrying out this high-level illegal project, insisted that paper trails be kept. He ordered William Sullivan, then assistant director in charge of domestic intelligence, to make sure that each tap was authorized in writing by the attorney general. The whereabouts of the highly secret wiretap transcripts—kept at first in Sullivan's office under lock and key, then transferred to an office at the Department of Justice when Sullivan fell out of favor with Hoover in 1971, and ultimately placed in the office of presidential adviser John Ehrlichman at the White House—later became a major issue during the Watergate investigations.

When the taps were first put in place, both Kissinger and his top aide, Colonel Alexander Haig, went regularly to Sullivan's office to read the transcripts. They seemed to enjoy perusing the personal and political conversations that had been transcribed by FBI listeners who worked secretly in the heart of the bureau's electronic surveillance operations in the Old Post Office Building. The operations had been placed there years earlier rather than at FBI headquarters in the Department of Justice Building to make it unlikely an attorney general would accidentally walk in and discover them. Though Hoover required the attorney general to sign off on this high-level illegal operation being conducted for Kissinger and Nixon, he usually conducted such surveillance without the approval or knowledge of the attorney general. In the end, despite many months of daily transcripts of the conversations of seventeen highly placed government officials and journalists recorded around the clock, not a single clue emerged from the tapped phones about anyone leaking stories.

To Hoover, this project was fire, and he was determined it would not burn him. In his time of crisis in early April 1971, provoked first by the Media burglary revelations and then by Kleindienst's public call for an investigation of the FBI, he immediately realized he could use the Kissinger taps as blackmail against the White House. If there was an investigation of the FBI, he told the president, as he repeated to him the threat he had just made to Kleindienst: "I will have to tell *all* that I know about this matter." Unlike Kleindienst, the president knew exactly what Hoover was talking about.

Within two hours, Kleindienst was interviewed again on television—at his request, as before. This time he withdrew his call for an investigation of the FBI.

Less than a year earlier, Hoover had destroyed the president's plan to create a large domestic intelligence operation that would have been a secret collaborative effort by all intelligence agencies, with the FBI in charge. Not wanting to let go of the FBI's sole responsibility for domestic intelligence, Hoover said he would agree to the project only if each illegal operation was approved in writing by either the attorney general or the president. In anger, Nixon withdrew the plan, which all the other intelligence agencies had endorsed. Now, less than a year later, Hoover had defeated the president again by reminding him that he possessed evidence—signed authorizations of illegal wiretaps against the administration's own staff members and journalists—that could destroy Nixon.

The FBI had never been investigated. And Hoover had just assured it would not be investigated now. He did so as a chorus inside and outside Congress, in the aftermath of the publication of the first Media files, was calling for congressional scrutiny of the bureau. He must have felt confident that the blackmail he had just used against the president would guarantee that the president, for his own protection, would not only convince Kleindienst to retract his call but would also do everything he could to block any serious effort by Congress to investigate the bureau.

THE STORM THAT RAGED at FBI headquarters over the first Media revelations also hit CIA headquarters in Langley, Virginia. Hoover had recently ordered FBI officials to cut off relations with the CIA. Dealings between the two agencies had always been somewhat uncomfortable. When the CIA was formed, Hoover wanted it to be an expansion of the bureau. Failing to convince President Truman to do that, he occasionally engaged in dirty tricks against the agency when he thought it was conducting operations the FBI should have been directing—such as break-ins at embassies in Washington.

Now, in the spring of 1971, Hoover and the CIA director, Richard Helms, seemed to be in the same boat. The Media burglary had made the heads of both of these powerful agencies fearful that their most closely held secrets—elaborately hidden illegal domestic spying operations—would be exposed. At the FBI, the threat came from outside—the Media burglars and what they could continue to make public. At the CIA, the threat came from inside—CIA agents who wanted to know the truth about their own agency.

On March 25, 1971, the day after the *Washington Post* published the first evidence from Media files of illegal domestic intelligence operations by the FBI, Richard Helms received a forceful memorandum, labeled "CIA Domestic Activities." It came from a group of CIA agents who asked him if the CIA was conducting intelligence operations directed against American citizens despite the fact that its charter, issued when the agency was established by Congress in 1947, forbade it from engaging in domestic operations. The agents were members of one of five management advisory groups, or MAGs, as they were called inside the agency, small groups of CIA employees who occasionally advised superiors. The members of the MAG who wrote to Helms advised the director's office. That such groups had long existed at the CIA was a sharp contrast with the FBI. There was no system at the bureau for employees to send criticism up the line to Hoover and his top aides. In fact, it would have been anathema to his demands for devotion and total loyalty. However, in the end, the existence of formal internal channels to advise CIA officials did not seem to matter.

Noting that they were concerned because of the recent exposure of the domestic intelligence activities of "other federal agencies," the MAG members who sent the memorandum that day to Helms "through" William Colby, then the executive director and later the CIA director, addressed Helms with bold comments:

> We believe that there are CIA activities similar to those now under scrutiny which could cause great embarrassment to the Agency because they appear to exceed the scope of the CIA charter. . . . MAG opposes any Agency activity which could be construed as targeted against any person who enjoys the protection of the US Constitution—whether or not he resides in the United States. Except in those cases clearly related to national security, no US citizen should be the object of CIA operations.

If the required prohibitions were not being adhered to, the MAG members warned in their memorandum to Helms:

"One day the public and the Congress will come to have grave doubts about our role in government, and may severely restrict our ability to perform those tasks properly assigned to the CIA."

When written responses to the MAG from Helms were unresponsive to the concerns they stated, the group submitted more warnings. Helms, through other top officials, insisted in comments to the group that the CIA had no domestic operations. One official, Thomas H. Karamessines, wrote after he met with the group that he was "irritated" with them and had told them that "we must expect all kinds of irresponsible accusations in the press." Actually, no such accusations had been made about the CIA in the press yet; they were being made inside the CIA.

Less than a month later, Helms, in the only public speech he gave in his seven years as CIA director, told the annual convention of the American Society of Newspaper Editors, a venue guaranteed to result in widespread coverage of his remarks, that the CIA did not conduct domestic operations.

Stories about his speech appeared on the front pages of many newspapers the next day, including the *New York Times,* where the headline included the phrase "Rare Speech." Extensive excerpts from the speech were published in the *Times.* Helms made the case for an intelligence agency being essential in a democratic society. He said that "the nation must to a degree take it on faith that we too are honorable men devoted to her service. I can assure you that we are."

Helms insistently told the editors that day, "I emphasize at this point that the statute specifically forbids the Central Intelligence Agency to have any police, subpoena, or law-enforcement powers, or any domestic security functions. I can assure you that except for the normal responsibilities for protecting the physical security of our own personnel, our facilities, and our classified information, we do not have any such powers and function; we have never sought any; we do not exercise any. In short, we do not target on American citizens."

His speech to the editors was strange not so much because he was lying, which he was, but because the question he insisted on answering—whether the CIA had domestic operations—had not yet been asked publicly. It had been asked only within the agency, where compartmentalization of duties and secrets left many employees unaware of what happened beyond their realm of responsibility but now very worried about what was going on outside their immediate realm.

A few months later, in September 1971, Helms made similar remarks to an audience that probably was more skeptical than the editors were. At the annual CIA awards ceremony at the agency's headquarters, the director told CIA employees that he had spoken to the editors, "as you know, and I did it for only one purpose. That was to try and put in the record a few of these denials that we've all wanted to see put in the public record for some time. And you can rely on those denials. They're true, and you can use that as any text that you may need to demonstrate that we're . . . not trying to do espionage on American citizens in the United States, and we're not tapping telephone lines, and that we're not doing a lot of other things which we're accused of doing." As he spoke to those colleagues, Helms made a peculiar request. He told them he thought the "silly idea" that the CIA conducted domestic operations was perpetuated by jokes about the CIA and domestic espionage. "Although the jokes have no basis in fact," he said, "they never-theless give us a name which we don't deserve. . . . I would like to suggest that if you have it in your hearts to do so that you speak up when the occa-sion arises and try and set the facts straight."

Helms said all this despite knowing that some of the colleagues in the audience that day at the awards ceremony knew the jokes were true and that his claims were not. Some of them knew the truth.

The CIA had been conducting domestic operations since at least 1959, and since 1962 Helms had been in charge of these operations. The illegal domestic operations had in fact become so large by 1964 that the agency—in defiance of its charter that forbade domestic operations—had created a new branch called the Domestic Operations Division. And since 1967 these ille-gal domestic political operations had been given the highest level of priority, ranking with Soviet and Chinese operations.

Congress, playing no role in intelligence oversight, knew nothing about these operations. When Congress investigated the FBI and the CIA in 1975, it would become known that the CIA had created files on more than 300,000 Americans, compiled detailed profiles of more than 7,000 U.S. citizens and 1,000 organizations, and placed thousands on a watch list to have their mail opened and their telegrams read. Like the FBI, it had spied on, burglarized the homes and offices of, and carried out other criminal acts against thousands of American citizens, primarily because they were anti-war activists. Like the FBI, it also had placed antiwar members of Congress under surveillance.

Six months after their first memorandum to Helms, the MAG members wrote to him again, even more forcefully than they had before. The group had no power except to ask questions and state concerns. It did so, even boldly suggesting in its November 1971 memorandum to Helms that the viability of the CIA was at stake if he did not confront this issue. Noting that in Helms's speeches to the editors and to CIA employees he had made "rather categorical denials of Agency covert targeting on U.S. citizens," the group pointed out that "Agency employees aware of the various sensitive operations in question know that there is qualifying language explaining CIA involvement. . . . MAG believes that in the event of an exposé, such esoteric qualifiers will be lost on the American public and there is probably nothing the Agency could say to alleviate a negative reaction from Congress and the U.S. public."

Emphasizing the very serious potential damage his misleading statements could cause, the MAG wrote, "It is MAG's fear that such negative reaction could seriously damage our Congressional relations, affect our work against priority foreign targets and have significant impact on the viability of CIA."

They urged the director to review and halt illegal domestic opera-tions in order not to damage the agency's ability to carry out its mandated responsibilities. They warned there "are indications that the Agency . . . is collecting information on selected U.S. citizens both at home and abroad. In operational areas which are highly sensitive and potentially explosive—domestic radical or racial groups—this Agency must carefully weigh the needs of pressures for collecting and maintaining this information against the risk and impact of revelation should the operation become compromised or public knowledge. We therefore urge that all domestic collection and action programs be severely reviewed so that only those be continued which are of the highest priority and which absolutely cannot be undertaken by domestic agencies. CIA should not take on requirements of this type by default. . . . Our increasing concern and our intense interest in maximizing the Agency's ability to do its proper job, impel us to bring our serious appre-hensions to your attention."

Like Hoover's need to protect and hide COINTELPRO, the FBI's mas-sive political surveillance and dirty tricks operations conducted against Americans that eventually would be revealed, Helms's need to continue to hide the CIA's secret domestic spying program, MHCHAOS, was over-whelming, wrote Angus Mackenzie in his 1997 book *Secrets: The CIA's War at Home.* Helms was most concerned, even before MAG members con-fronted him in March 1971, about the fact that some CIA agents disap-proved of the programs.

In 1972, Helms called his top aides together and said he was adamant that MHCHAOS would not be "stopped simply because some members of the organization [the CIA] do not like this activity." He made changes in order to protect the program more now that the MAG was so determined to have it end. To the maximum extent possible, within the agency, the program and the agent then in charge of it, Richard Ober, would be identified with terrorism and not with American dissidents. The massive program would in fact have the same functions it always had, including the monitoring and destruction of the more than five hundred alternative newspaper staffs it had under surveillance. (At the same time, the FBI also monitored alternative and campus newspapers, sometimes suppressing them.)

Henceforth, Colby wrote in a memorandum after that meeting, the label "international terrorist" would replace "political dissident" as the target of the CIA's illegal domestic operations. As part of this image transformation, Helms did what Hoover had done many times—and would do again in April 1971 to protect COINTELPRO when he thought it was about to be revealed—to minimize the possibility that secret operations would be exposed. Helms ended MHCHAOS in name, but continued it in reality with a new name: International Terrorism Group. It would be much easier for people, including people within the CIA, to accept the domestic operations if they thought they were aimed primarily at stopping terrorism rather than at stopping dissent.

That simple burglary in Media now stirred panic in the hearts of the top officials in the country's most powerful intelligence agencies. Hoover knew that if his most important secrets emerged, the results could be disastrous. He did not live to see them become known. Helms, on the other hand, watched many of his secret operations revealed. He testified multiple times before various investigating committees as secrets surfaced—details of aggressive CIA plans to assassinate democratically elected leaders of other countries and to install dictators, as well as details of the agency's domestic political spying operations. After years of going to great lengths to protect the agency's secrets, in an interview for the CIA Oral History Program in 1988, Helms insisted the exposure and investigation of CIA secrets amounted to "just a congressional firestorm over nothing."

12

I'm Thinking of Turning You In

LIFE WAS FRAGILE for some of the Media burglars in the months right after the burglary. They felt they had little control. They were alone, not even in touch with each other. Before the burglary and while working with the files, they had felt secure in one another's hands, and most of the time they were relatively confident they could avoid arrest by being very cautious and staying concealed behind the curtain they had drawn around the group when they started planning the burglary. But after the burglary—especially after the first distribution of documents intensified both the FBI search and public interest—they had far less control. From news stories and the peace movement grapevine, they knew the search for them was intense and that it was touching the lives of countless people, cruelly in some instances. One misstep and one or all of the burglars could be arrested. Some of them also worried about the man who dropped out. Since he left the group, had he told anyone else who the burglars were?

Rumors about the burglary were swirling in the peace movement. Even among people who had engaged in acts of resistance themselves, including the draft board raids, people could not imagine that anyone they knew had enough courage to break into an FBI office. People still say that today. Philadelphia antiwar activists felt concern for the Media burglars, whoever they were, for they could see that the search was fierce and likely to end with arrests and severe penalties. Many local activists were paying a price themselves for the burglary because the FBI regarded everyone who was active in the peace movement as a potential suspect. In this anxious atmosphere among activists in Philadelphia, some of the burglars continued to think that it seemed inevitable that a mistake had been made during the burglary—or now as they hid openly—and that when that mistake became known, everything would come crashing down on them very quickly.

At such times, some of them found it hard to believe that J. Edgar Hoover's powerful FBI would not find them. It was widely believed that the FBI always got its man. How could that not apply to them, especially the women? The only Media burglars the FBI investigators thought they had actually seen were two of the three women in the group—Susan Smith and Bonnie Raines, both of whom had visited the office. The Media agents knew Susan's face and name. They knew Bonnie's face but not her name. The burglars didn't know, of course, that Hoover had taken a special interest in efforts to find Raines, but they became increasingly aware from news stories of the intensity of the investigation. One of the agents who investigated the burglary, Terry Neist, years later described the atmosphere inside the bureau at that time:

"It was like, 'This is the FBI. You have penetrated us.' It became almost a personal thing. . . . It became, for that reason, a very important case.

"Mr. Hoover was quite upset by this," said Neist.

BECAUSE THE BURGLARS had decided, for security's sake, not to be in touch with one another after they distributed the documents, none of them knew what was happening to others in the group. Did any of them think they were under suspicion? Had any of them been called or visited by the FBI? All of them wondered about one another, but the questions had to remain unanswered. Ron Durst and Keith Forsyth never heard from the FBI. For very unusual reasons, neither did William Davidon.

Susan Smith's anxiety about whether she had removed her gloves in the FBI office continued to ruin her nights. That agents called her within a week of the burglary convinced her that the FBI must have found her fingerprints. Agents told her the day they left her campus office in anger—after they refused to go along with her demand that she record their interview—that they would return. During the months, then years, when she thought they might return at any time, there were many days when she ached to remember with certainty whether she had removed that glove. She never was certain. And they never returned.

It was impossible to be sure, but some of the contacts initiated by agents seemed more like stabs in the dark than indications that the bureau had any evidence, let alone certainty, about any one individual's involvement in the burglary. It remains unclear whether the contact with Bob Williamson was a stab in the dark. He got an unexpected and unexplained ride home by two FBI agents one day, a trip that was one of two somewhat mysterious experiences he had soon after the burglary. Several months before the Media burglary, Williamson moved from a commune in a condemned house in North Philadelphia to Powelton Village. He lived near one of the Powelton streets where the presence of FBI agents was dense and constant. Every day, Williamson, like other residents of this friendly neighborhood, saw the very visible FBI presence on the streets near his home. But there was no indication that he was regarded any more suspiciously than any of his neighbors.

Until one day. He was sitting at his desk in the state building in South Philadelphia where he worked as a social worker. It was a very large room lined with many rows of employees at desks. Suddenly the public announcement system filled the room with this booming message: "Bob Williamson wanted at the front desk." He was being paged to go to the guard's desk on the first floor. It was nearly the end of the workday, so he cleared his desk and prepared to go home after he met with the person who wanted to talk with him.

At the guard's desk, two FBI agents were waiting for him. They flashed their badges, introduced themselves, and ordered Williamson to get in their car. "I took the ride. They said it in such a way that I didn't think I had a choice."

He can't remember years later what they said about the Media burglary, but he feels sure that it was mentioned. He also feels certain they didn't directly ask him if he was involved. He thinks he would remember that very well. He does remember that they talked about making progress in breaking the Media case. During that time, he thinks they tried to get him to talk about people who might have been involved. He remembers not saying much during the drive across the city from South Philadelphia to West Philadelphia. "I was scared," he says, more certain of his memory of the emotions he felt then than he is of the words spoken by either him or the agents. "Sometime during the ride their demeanor was almost friendly. . . . I may have even joked with them a little bit."

The intended message from the FBI for Williamson that day seemed to come from this: Without asking for his address, the agents drove directly to his apartment building and dropped him off. It felt like a fairly strong dose of the paranoia he and his fellow burglars had revealed as an FBI modus operandi. They wanted him to know they knew something, but it was impossible for him to know exactly how much they knew. Or did they just want him to think they knew something? He was never sure, not even after he questioned one of them in court two years later.

Not long after that lift home courtesy of the FBI, Williamson got a mysterious phone call at home. The caller "introduced himself, said he was new in town and was an 'old friend' of Dan Dougherty." Dan, the caller said, had told him to call Bob because "I would know what was happening in the movement in Philadelphia right now."

"My first clue," said Williamson, "was that he pronounced Dan's name wrong. He had pronounced it Doe-er-ty, but Dan pronounces it Dock-er-ty." Williamson's caution kicked in. When the stranger asked him if they could get together, Williamson said, "Sure, but why don't you call me tomorrow? I'm real busy right now." The caller agreed to call back.

As soon as he hung up, Williamson walked to a pay phone and called Dan Dougherty. He regarded him as "a real neat guy," someone who had never been involved in resistance actions but was very supportive of people who were involved in such actions. He lived in New Jersey and worked in a crisis center at Glassboro State College. "He was a friend of mine," says Williamson. "I didn't see him a whole lot, but I definitely considered him a friend. I knew he would not send me somebody like this, just off the wall."

He reached Dougherty and told him what had just happened. "Dan was an imaginative kind of guy, always a little bit adventurous," says Williamson. After telling Williamson he had never heard of the guy, he said, "Why don't we have a little fun with this?" Williamson agreed and followed Dougherty's instructions.

When the stranger called the next day, Williamson said he'd be happy to meet with him. They agreed to meet downtown at the Philadelphia Public Library. Then Williamson said, "I just happened to be talking to Dan, and he'd like to see you, too, 'cause it's been so long since you two have seen each other. So he'll be with me."

There was an awkward silence. The stranger quickly recovered by saying, "Sure, that would be great," and asked Williamson how he would recognize him. "I'll be wearing a yellow dashiki," he said. "And of course you know Dan, so you'll recognize him. See you tomorrow."

"Dan picks me up in his Volkswagen and we drive to the library," Williamson recalled. "We park at a parking meter and sit at the area in the library where the guy has agreed to meet us. . . . We talk a long time and then realize it's way past the time he was supposed to meet us. We wait a little longer, and then go out to the car. Dan's car wouldn't start." They opened the hood and found that someone had opened it and had stripped the distributor wires.

"So," says Williamson, "I guess we found out they have a sense of humor, too."

GIVEN HOW MUCH William Davidon spoke publicly about the burglary, it seemed remarkable that the FBI never got in touch with him. Even the press conference he held that spring to discuss the stolen documents didn't provoke a call or visit. He speculates the FBI did not get in touch with him because they viewed him in the way he hoped they would: as a person interested in the burglary but not involved in it. He was wrong. He was named a prime suspect within days of the break-in.

In a strange twist of fate, the Department of Justice immunized Davidon from being interviewed by the FBI about MEDBURG. During the first week after the burglary, an agent wrote in a report that Davidon's "possible connection with case being vigorously pursued." When his name came up as a likely suspect soon after the burglary, agents remembered, of course, that he was one of the unindicted coconspirators in the case that was still before a grand jury in Harrisburg, the case involving the kidnap and bombing conspiracy charges Hoover had made in November despite investigators having decided the accusations were groundless and should not be pursued. Soon after the Media burglary, Department of Justice lawyers told the director that MEDBURG investigators should not question Davidon because he was likely to be charged in a new grand jury indictment as a defendant in the Harrisburg case. The decision that Davidon must not be interviewed by FBI agents was made, Hoover told agents, by the chief prosecutor in the Harrisburg case, William Lynch, a department lawyer who usually worked on organized crime cases. However, when a new, superseding indictment was issued by a grand jury in late April 1971, Davidon was not indicted. He was again named an unindicted coconspirator, as he had been in January in the first Harrisburg indictment. Presumably, the department's prohibition against interviewing Davidon would have been lifted then, but the FBI never attempted to interview him then or at any other time in connection with MEDBURG, not even after the Harrisburg trial ended in April 1972 in a hung jury and prosecutors decided not to retry the case.

Though Davidon never was questioned by the FBI regarding MEDBURG and was not indicted in the Harrisburg case, he continued to be regarded by the FBI not only as a prime suspect in the Media case but also as a dangerous person. During the MEDBURG investigation, he was elevated to a higher level of danger status on the bureau's Security Index, the secret list of dangerous people the FBI planned to detain and incarcerate in the event of a national emergency—the existence of which was revealed in the Media files.

Davidon enjoyed drawing attention to the burglary. One of his boldest public efforts was distributing copies of the stolen files at the Conference on the FBI held at Princeton University in late October 1971. Two organizations, the Committee for Public Justice and Princeton's Woodrow Wilson School of Public and International Affairs, sponsored the event. In the invitation to selected constitutional scholars, lawyers, and journalists, three former FBI agents, and top officials who had served in high positions in the Department of Justice during John F. Kennedy and Lyndon Johnson's administrations, the sponsors said the conference was planned "as a scholarly effort to understand the structure of the FBI and its powers and role in American society. Apparently, no private or public body has before attempted such a study. This fact, we think, provides sufficient reason to do so now."

The organizers invited Hoover to send a representative to the conference. In a lengthy angry letter that was reported widely in the press, including on the front page of the *New York Times,* Hoover blasted the critical premise of the conference and refused to send a representative. Davidon learned about the conference when he read about Hoover's reaction. In his letter, Hoover wrote, "We are declining in view of our serious doubt that any worthwhile purpose could be served by an FBI representative attending an inquiry casting him in the role of defendant before even the first fact is brought out, and condemned by the 'judges' before trial begins.

"Basically, our position is that the FBI need tailor no special 'defense' of its own for this occasion," Hoover wrote. "The basic facts on how the FBI is organized and how it discharges its duties have been so well known for so long, and to so many responsible persons, that they are obvious to all except those who are so blind that they do not wish to see." This claim was predictable, but now, as a result of what had been learned about the bureau from the Media burglary six months earlier, it was not believable. It no longer was possible to expect people to believe something was true simply because Hoover said it was.

Scholarly papers were presented at the unprecedented conference by Aryeh Neier, then the executive director of the American Civil Liberties

Union, and others on these subjects—"Backgrounding the Bureau," "Less Than Perfect Performance," "Controversial Methods and Procedures," and "Question of Balance: Protection of Society, Protection of Individual Rights." Formal papers written for the conference and the papers presented during panel discussions contained the proper attributions and footnotes expected at scholarly gatherings. The invitation to the conference had said its overriding goal was "to explore the structure, role and powers of the FBI." But, the invitation stated, "Since we're private citizens, without access to all relevant information, this goal is difficult, but not impossible."

Access to FBI records was difficult, but, the planners might have noted, a few months earlier they had had some help obtaining access to original FBI files.

An event unusual in the annals of scholarly research—the burglary— provided the presenters with some information that otherwise would not have been available to them. Thanks to the Media burglary, the presenters had access for the first time to official FBI files that contained firsthand documented evidence of how the bureau worked, not just speculation and hearsay. Inside the ivied Princeton hall where the conference convened, sev- eral of the speakers, including eminent scholars, cited evidence from the Media files—and properly referenced them in their comments, in footnotes in their papers, and in the book on the conference, *Investigating the FBI,* that was published later—as they analyzed problems in the bureau and made the case for its reform. It was probably the first time burglars were the source of information discussed in such an august Ivy League setting, or in any aca- demic setting, and also the first time stolen files were the basis of footnotes in academic papers.

One of the people who presented a paper at the conference, Thomas I. Emerson, a professor at Yale Law School and the author of *The System of Freedom of Expression,* began his formal remarks with this stark observation: "The inescapable message of much of the material we have covered is that the FBI jeopardizes the whole system of freedom of expression which is the cornerstone of an open society. The philosophy and much of the activity of the Bureau is in direct conflict with the fundamental principles underlying that system."

As the conference participants vigorously discussed new evidence about how the FBI operated, surely none of them knew the identity of the quiet man with the warm smile who sat at a table in the hall outside a door open to the conference room, listening very carefully to the proceedings. Eager, as usual, to promote maximum awareness of the important information in the Media files, Davidon—their unknown footnote source!—sat there throughout the two-day conference with stacks of copies of some of the stolen Media files. As people approached his table during breaks, he greeted them with his gentle smile and offered them copies of the FBI files. Many of them had already seen the documents, and those who had not seemed to appreciate the chance to receive them.

JOHN RAINES HAD turned down Davidon's invitation to go with him to the Princeton conference. He and Bonnie did not think that was a good idea. They had experienced too many close calls since the burglary. Distributing copies of the stolen documents at such a high-profile event did not seem wise. They had been living in what one of them remembers as "a sustained period of worry and concern" ever since the burglary. Though the level of intensity varied, it was always there, not disappearing completely until about five years later.

Given the pressure they felt, the Raineses decided to stay away from peace demonstrations for an indefinite period. Beginning immediately after the burglary, they realized that agents were looking for the woman who had visited the office. So they decided that woman would not be seen at events where they knew FBI agents and informers were likely to be a constant presence.

A few key events made them think that their arrest, and possibly the arrest of all the burglars, was imminent. They first feared that the day John watched the Xerox maintenance person walk away from his office with the drum of the copier he had used to copy hundreds of the Media documents. Subsequent experiences felt even more threatening.

In early April 1971, they responded one evening to a knock at their front door and were both surprised and shaken, even before the visitor's threat. There stood the man who had abandoned the group shortly before the burglary. They liked him, but under these circumstances they were anything but happy to see him. They had no idea why he had left the group or what he thought now that the burglary had been done, but they invited him in. He had not come to congratulate them on a job well done. He was full of foreboding. He nervously told them he "was dealing with immense pressure." He told them he was very troubled about what he should do.

He said he was thinking of turning them in.

The Raineses were stunned. This was even worse than watching the Xerox repairman carry away the copier drum.

He told them someone had told him the Media files included defense secrets that, if revealed, would be disastrous to national security. When the Raineses told him they were sure such documents were not in the files, they could not tell if he believed them. After he left, the Raineses were very troubled about what they could do about what felt like a looming crisis. They thought he might hold the future of all the burglars in his hands. Given that they had not been arrested, they were convinced he had not revealed their plans to authorities before the burglary. But here he was, less than a month later, and he was telling them he was thinking of turning them in. The investigative record of the burglary contains no information about his visit to the Raineses despite the fact that the record includes considerable detail about the bureau's surveillance of him and investigators' belief that he was one of the Media burglars.

Bonnie and John Raines struggled with how to deal with this situation. When the man left that night, they were not confident they had convinced him not to turn them in. Sometime later that evening or the next day, they got an idea. Their kitchen did not really need a new coat of paint, but they thought painting it all day with him might give John Raines an opportunity to have a long and rambling conversation that would convince him not to turn the burglars in. Given the possible consequences of his threat, they felt something had to be done. This was all they could think of. They called him and asked him if they could hire him to help John paint the kitchen. He agreed and arrived for the job early Saturday morning.

Standing on ladders across from each other, the man and John Raines talked nearly all day. As they covered the kitchen walls with a coat of warm yellow paint, he revealed more about the source of his concern. He said he had no problem with the documents that had been released so far, the revelations about how the bureau operated, the spying on Americans. He thought those documents might even have a positive impact. But he was very worried about what his girlfriend had told him. It wasn't clear from what he said whether she knew he had once been part of the group, but John was left with the impression that she suspected he was close to the group, if not part of it. He told John she had convinced him that documents stolen at the Media office that had not yet been made public would reveal national defense secrets, including the location of missile defense systems. National security, she had told him, was now about to be seriously endangered because of the stolen documents.

John insisted this was not true. He told him he thought his girlfriend was working for the FBI and that she had gotten that idea from them. John emphasized that he had seen all of the stolen documents, and that none of them revealed defense secrets or posed a danger in any way to national security.

"I think he was on the verge of giving us up," said John Raines years later. "His girlfriend was really pushing him. He was very frightened." By the end of that Saturday, the kitchen looked fresh and new and John hoped he had convinced him not to turn them in. The Raineses convinced themselves that they had "quieted him down, cooled him down." That's what they hoped, but they were not sure and remained afraid he would turn them in. They never heard from him again, nor did any of the other Media burglars. According to the FBI's investigative files on the burglary, the man who dropped out of the group talked to the FBI about the burglary, but he did not do so until near the end of the investigation.

The Raineses were still worried about whether he was considering turning them in when two unwanted guests showed up on a warm afternoon in early May. John was dropped off in front of their home by a friend after a tennis game. As he said goodbye to his tennis partner and walked toward his front door, he was greeted by two men who were waiting for him on the porch. He recognized them immediately before they introduced themselves. They were FBI agents straight from central casting—short hair, white shirts, suits, ties, wingtip shoes—everything you would expect from watching Inspector Lewis Erskine, played by Efrem Zimbalist Jr. on *The F.B.I.* Sunday evenings. The agents showed John their badges and said they wanted to talk to him.

The burglars had agreed that they would refuse to talk with FBI agents unless a lawyer was present. That was the typical stance taken at that time by antiwar activists regarding contact with the bureau. For reasons John can't remember many years later—overwhelming fear being perhaps the most likely explanation—he violated that agreement and talked with the agents that day, but under rather unusual circumstances. He recalls welcoming them and telling them he would be glad to talk to them. He unlocked the front door and motioned for them to be seated in the living room. He apologized for being so sweaty from playing tennis and invited them to make themselves at home while he freshened up. He thinks he may have given them a cold drink of water or iced tea before he went upstairs. Once he was upstairs, he decided to shower.

His decision to welcome them and then let them wait while he showered was a split-second one. The shower gave him time to compose his thoughts. He thought hard about how he would respond. He thinks he may have decided as soon as he saw them that it might be more trouble not to talk than to talk. As he showered, he decided he would filibuster the interview.

After his shower, John joined his guests in the living room about twenty minutes after he had left them. As he looked at the two men he thought, "It's true. Just like everyone says, they do look like Mutt and Jeff." Their first comment as he sat down in a comfortable chair across from them must have stopped him from continuing to see them as comic figures.

"We're investigating the Media break-in, and we want to talk to you about it," one of them said. "Do you know anything about it?"

At that point, John recalls, he launched into the plan he had settled on while showering. He told them he thought he had read just about everything that had been written about the burglary and that he was appalled by what he had learned about the contents of the stolen documents. He described the documents. "That one about an FBI agent behind every mailbox . . . shocking. . . . Using campus switchboard operators. . . . Trying to scare politicians. . . . That was terrible."

After a rather lengthy rhetorical tour of the leading documents he had "read about in the newspapers," John recalls, he then tried to ask them questions. "All this time you folks are spending on political surveillance, aren't you kind of ashamed of your priorities?" The agents took it as a rhetorical question and answered with silence. John continued lecturing them. "Shouldn't you be out there looking at major crimes, like organized crime?" This was a touchy subject in the bureau, given the growing awareness outside the FBI of what had long been known inside the bureau—that the FBI director cared far more about conducting surveillance of civil rights and antiwar activists than he did about fighting organized crime.

John's spirited Socratic approach produced a mixed response. One of the agents frowned and looked somewhat angry as John lectured them. Occasionally, the irritated agent made a comment that made it clear he did not agree with John's assessment of the bureau. The other agent "was kind of apologetic." It was difficult, even under the pressure of this moment, for John not to see them as Mutt and Jeff, as the good cop and the bad cop. The good-cop agent would interrupt once in a while and say, "He [the bad cop] is actually a nice guy." In fact, the agent who was playing good cop seemed at one point about to confess that he agreed with John's opinion. Under the unusual circumstances, though, John may have been hearing more than the agent intended to convey. "As a matter of fact," the good-cop agent said, giving the impression that he was searching for the right words, "well, you know, we all have to work."

John Raines felt that he, rather than the agents, was in control of the conversation. In the shower, that had become his goal. He tried not to let silences develop. Every time one did, he filled it. After a while, he decided it was time for the conversation to end and announced that he would have to leave soon. The agents looked at each other and seemed to be preparing to leave when the agent playing the good cop looked directly at John and pointedly asked,

"By the way, did you have anything to do with this Media break-in?"

Though John had been willing to break the law and burglarize an FBI office, he recalls telling himself at that moment, "Remember, it's a crime to lie to an FBI agent." He thinks he may have missed only a very small beat before he returned to filibuster mode and replied indirectly, forcefully, and, in line with his goal, at length. "I feel so angry about what I found out from those stories about the documents about what you, the FBI, have been doing that I don't want to answer that. I don't want to make your search for people any easier, so I'm not going to say whether or not I was involved." He continued his lecture on the importance of what was revealed in the documents and how upset he was about the activities of the bureau.

For whatever reason—not liking being lectured, being bored by John's filibustering, or not really thinking he was a very likely suspect, or at least not likely to answer directly any question they posed—the agents thanked him and stood up to leave. There were no more questions and no suggestion there would be another visit.

From the living room window, a somewhat relieved but also puzzled John Raines watched the two agents walk to their car and drive away. They were gone. Thank goodness. Even now, he is not sure if he was wise or foolish that day. There was no mention of this meeting in the massive FBI record of the investigation.

He soon realized that one aspect of his drawn-out filibuster had been very foolish, perhaps nearly disastrous. While the agents were there, he did not pay attention to the time and did not think about the fact that Bonnie was likely to come home any minute. Only about five minutes after the agents left, she arrived. She was stunned to learn that FBI agents had just been there. Both of them briefly felt paralyzed when they realized what had almost happened—what almost certainly would have happened if she had come home just a few minutes earlier. The Raineses did not know, of course, that a very recognizable sketch of her, as she was remembered by the Media agents, had been distributed to agents throughout the country and that agents, especially the ones investigating the case, were constantly looking for her. Not finding her, in fact, was by then one of the most frustrating aspects of the case for Hoover and the investigators. Along with the women of the Weather Underground who had escaped the 1970 bomb factory explosion in Greenwich Village, where three members of the Weather Underground were killed and others went into hiding, she was one of the few women FBI agents were looking for at that time. The director had repeatedly expressed frustration and irritation that she had not been found.

The agents did not ask Raines anything about his wife. They did not mention her name. But if she had walked in while they were there, they surely would have recognized her as the woman in the police artist's sketch. The Raineses knew that the search for the woman who had visited the office was intense, because they had heard about what happened to a woman peace activist in Powelton Village who looked remarkably like Bonnie and apparently was believed by the FBI to be "that woman." They knew that the door to her home had been knocked down by the FBI. Because they were aware of that, Bonnie Raines's narrow escape that May afternoon—more than the visit itself and even more than the direct question to John Raines: "By the way, did you have anything to do with this Media break-in?"—shocked them as they reviewed everything that had been said by the agents. They were very relieved that she had not been seen, but the frightening thought of what might have happened was hard to shake. Bonnie sat in the living room where the FBI agents had sat. She was nearly transfixed, wondering what would have happened in that living room minutes earlier if she had not been stuck longer than usual in traffic at a stoplight, if she had not talked a few extra minutes with friends at the daycare center where she worked.

"They just missed me," she recalls years later. The memory brings back how she felt that day—frightened and also extremely lucky.

As of that day, the Raineses knew John was a suspect. They had no idea whether his unusual response to the agents convinced the agents he was not involved, or, they wondered, did the agents think—or know—that he was involved? And did they have a plan for approaching him again? The questions that came to mind were all frightening and impossible to answer.

Later that evening, after the children had gone to bed, they searched the downstairs rooms for hidden listening devices. John Raines's shower had given the agents time to move about on the first floor with ease. They could not be sure, but they saw no sign of listening devices. Finally, at the end of the day there was something to laugh at. In the kitchen, the one recently painted so beautifully by Raines and the man who dropped out of the group, they noticed the newspaper clipping they had taped to the refrigerator door weeks earlier. It was a boldly drawn editorial cartoon of a melting J. Edgar Hoover—a meltdown caused by the burglary of the Media FBI office. They liked that cartoon. Years later it was still on their refrigerator, a daily reminder of their big secret—and of their hope that the FBI agents didn't wander into their kitchen that day while they waited for John to finish his shower. They also wondered if their kitchen painter had had anything to do with the agents' visit.

The Raineses had another visitor in early summer, someone whose presence at their house must have raised the antennae of the FBI. John Peter Grady, the affable Catholic peace movement leader, showed up in late June or early July asking for a place to stay for a few days. They readily obliged. Though they had agreed with the other Media burglars that Grady should not be invited to be part of the Media burglary because of the need for especially tight security, they liked him very much and welcomed him into their home. He had just been mugged at 30th Street Station, the major railway station in Philadelphia, and felt pretty down and out by the time he knocked on their door. The warm family atmosphere of the Raineses' home must have been a healing balm during the few days Grady stayed there to rest and recover.

Within the space of a few weeks, they had been visited by two FBI agents and by two people who were prime suspects in the MEDBURG case—the man who dropped out and now Grady. The FBI investigators were still convinced that Grady not only was involved in the Media burglary but was its leader. Because the Raineses had no idea that Grady was a suspect in Media, nor that the FBI thought he was the leader of the Media burglars, they didn't realize that at that moment he was a radioactive guest in their home. To them, Grady was just a friend from the peace movement who needed a place to sleep and a calm and peaceful atmosphere. It never occurred to them that FBI agents might be stationed outside their home looking for him in connection with the Media burglary.

They also had no idea that a major recent development in the Media investigation had convinced Hoover and FBI investigators that the Media burglars would be arrested soon. New life had suddenly been breathed into the investigation when someone walked into the FBI office in Camden, New Jersey, with a tip about a draft board raid being planned for late that summer. He wondered if the FBI was interested.

Were they interested?!?

Does a cat chase a mouse?

This news again prompted the FBI to dramatically shift its MEDBURG investigation in a new direction. Now massive resources were focused on what they thought was going to happen in Camden. Ultimately, this decision would reveal one of the FBI's major weaknesses, then and now—excessive manipulation of informers to produce desired results. The bureau immediately went out on a limb, supporting one crime in order to solve another: MEDBURG.

Because Grady was deeply involved in planning the Camden raid, he probably was under constant surveillance at the time he was staying with the Raineses. The bureau must have taken a keen interest in the fact that John Raines, whom they had interviewed after a tennis game in May, and Grady were associated so closely that Grady stayed at Raines's home for a few days. Ironically, though, they still did not know Bonnie Raines was the "UNSUB," the other Media suspect they were searching for as intensely as they were searching for evidence directly implicating Grady in Media. Just as the Raineses did not know that Grady was a suspect in Media, Grady had no idea they had been involved in the break-in. Many other people in the Catholic peace movement had heard the rumors about a connection between Grady and Media, but the Raineses had not heard the rumors because at the time they were then staying away from gatherings of activists.

Actually, there was confusion about Grady's role in Media not only in the FBI but also among his fellow activists. Sometimes he responded to questions about rumors that he was involved in Media in ways that gave the impression he enjoyed hearing them. At such times, he often smiled his wide smile but was silent. He never said yes. He never said no. Many people close to him, even some family members years later, assumed that meant he was involved in Media. The FBI was sure he was, and later that summer they went after him in a very powerful way.

IN JULY, the Raineses' thoughts turned to Glen Lake, the beautiful spot in the Michigan woods where they had met ten years earlier and returned nearly every summer since then. The investigation of Media was like a continuous tornado in Philadelphia that summer. They were never at the center of the storm, but they never knew when it might edge toward them. They were eager to escape its ever-present threat. As a result, they were looking forward to their annual trip to Glen Lake more than they ever had before. It turned out that being a burglar was exhausting, especially in the aftermath. The time at the lake was also going to be special because it would be the first summer in several years that they would be there without a baby. Nathan, two and a half by the time of the trip, walked on his own now and didn't require constant attention.

As they did each year, they started the twelve-hour drive to Grand Rapids late one evening. They did it that way so the children, and their two dogs, Coco and her son Catcher, could sleep through the night in the back of the maroon Ford station wagon (a.k.a. the Media getaway car) all the way to Bonnie's parents' home, where they would spend three days before driving to the lake. They took turns driving that first night. The children and the dogs snuggled in the backseat, sleeping soundly. As they tunneled through the darkness of Pennsylvania, Ohio, and Indiana before turning north toward Michigan, they talked about what they would tell her parents about the burglary. They had a lot to tell them, as well as a big question to ask them.

They had decided before the burglary that they would ask the Muirs if they would be willing to raise the children if John and Bonnie were convicted and went to prison. They didn't like the idea of burdening them with their dangerous secret, but they also wanted to make sure that John's brother Bob and his then wife, Peggy, were not the only people willing to care for the children if they went to prison. They had wanted to discuss these important matters with the Muirs earlier, but they felt they couldn't risk discussing them on the phone or in letters that might be intercepted if they were under surveillance.

They felt safe telling Bonnie's parents what they had done. The Muirs had come a long way in their thinking since 1964, when they expressed concern about their pregnant daughter, Bonnie, going to Washington to protest the filibuster against the civil rights bill. Now, seven years later, they accepted, even approved, of their daughter and her husband being deeply involved in the peace movement. Now they themselves were very opposed to the war. They were worried in the summer of 1971 about whether their son, their only other child, would be drafted and sent to Vietnam.

Still, it seemed remarkable that Bonnie Raines's parents were not particularly surprised when Bonnie and John told them they had burglarized an FBI office. They told them about some of the important revelations in the files and that there was a national search for the burglars. Trying not to be alarmist, they told them they had no idea what the outcome would be, but they wanted to be prepared in case the worst—their arrest—happened. In case agents ever questioned her parents, they revealed few details about the burglary. They tried to convey this news in a way that would not cause Bonnie's parents to be consumed by worry. Bonnie remembers expressing more optimism to her parents than she and John actually felt at the time.

The Muirs readily agreed that they would raise the children if John and Bonnie went to prison. John and Bonnie talked with them about what might happen if they were arrested. Bail would be set by a judge and probably would be raised on their behalf, and then they would be free while waiting to go to trial. "We wanted them to know everything wouldn't come crashing down at one time," Bonnie recalls. "We wanted them to know that we had talked with Bob and Peggy. We also let them know that we had not told John's parents. We were protecting them as much as possible and did not share as much with them as we did with my parents. We thought his parents would be quite upset, particularly about my involvement, so we didn't want to tell them unless something happened."

Before John and Bonnie and the children left Grand Rapids, they were assured again by the Muirs that if they were arrested, they could be confident that the Muirs would care for the children as long as necessary. Bonnie recalls sensing at the time that "my folks assumed that everything was fine, that we could handle things." Her parents wished them a happy time at the lake, and her mother said, "Let's keep our fingers crossed and hope that nothing happens." Many years later, Dorothy Muir expressed great pride in what her daughter and son-in-law did in 1971. "I believed they wouldn't do it unless they thought it was important, and unless they thought they could get away with it. But I knew there was a risk."

As they drove away from Bonnie's parents' home, waving goodbye, the Raineses had an enormous sense of relief and gratitude for the promise and moral support they had just received. On the drive to Glen Lake and the respite it promised, they realized again that part of their original willingness to risk arrest and imprisonment came from the confidence they had that these loved ones, her parents and John's brother and his wife, "cared a great deal about us and our children, and that if the worst happened, those four people would strategize about how to care for the children." They also realized now—ten years after they met and nine years after they married—that they were able to take the serious risks they took at Media "because we thought our marriage could stand up under considerable stress and pressure."

In the backseat, unaware of the lofty thoughts of their parents, Lindsley, Mark, and Nathan couldn't wait to go swimming in the lake. Bonnie and John felt the same way. At his family's secluded lakeside home, they thought, at last they would push the pressure of being wanted by the FBI to the back of their minds. They would relax, soak up the sun, motor on the lake, and let the wonderful peacefulness of this green, tranquil, remote place soothe their souls. Exposing J. Edgar Hoover had by now brought on an exhaustion they hoped Glen Lake would cure.

It was great to see the familiar old red frame house come into view. As they turned up the dirt lane, even the memory that agents from the nearby Traverse City FBI office knew where the house was—they had come here the previous summer looking for Daniel Berrigan, then underground and refusing to voluntarily turn himself in to begin serving his sentence for his Catonsville Nine conviction—didn't diminish their certainty that they were about to begin the first truly relaxed and happy days they had had since long before the burglary.

Just twenty-four hours later, it turned into the worst vacation ever.

The day after they arrived, Bonnie and John, the children, and their two dogs leisurely walked down the hill to the dock after breakfast. They felt so good about being in this old familiar place and knowing that their children also loved being there. Their outboard motor was resting on top of the boat hoist. Nathan was walking behind them, so they aren't exactly sure how the catastrophe occurred. A two-year-old should not have been able to do what Nathan did. He released the safety catch on the boat hoist, causing the handwheel to whip around powerfully. Nathan's head got caught in the wheel and he was knocked out. The Raineses blanch many years later as they remember, as though it happened yesterday, the moment they turned around and saw Nathan unconscious on the dock. They thought he was dead. Later that day, a doctor told them that, given the great force that hit his head and whipped his small body, it was amazing he was alive.

Their station wagon was parked up the hill, near the house, impossible to reach quickly. But Chuck Knight, a neighbor, was at the next dock and, hearing their screams, ran over and said he would drive them to the hospital twenty-three miles away in Traverse City. His car was nearby. John carried the bleeding and unconscious Nathan to Knight's car. Off they went, speeding down country roads, John cradling Nathan in his arms. Bonnie gathered Lindsley and Mark and the two dogs together and walked with them as fast as she could up to the house, where she told John's parents what had happened, jumped into the station wagon, and sped away toward the hospital.

Meanwhile, as Knight raced to the hospital on narrow roads, his car ran out of gas. Bad luck was abundant that day. Knight flagged down a stranger, who drove John and Nathan the remaining miles to the hospital.

After a few hours at the hospital, they were assured that Nathan would live, but, they were told, he had been injured very seriously. He had sustained severe trauma on the left side of his head. For several weeks he remained paralyzed on his right side and could not speak. Compensating for the paralysis, he began using his left hand and would remain permanently left-handed. It was a very long and slow recovery. Immediately after they left the lake, it included a period of treatment at Johns Hopkins Hospital in Baltimore while the entire family lived for several weeks in the pool house on the grounds of Sargent and Eunice Kennedy Shriver's Maryland estate. They were there because John Raines had been hired by the Shrivers to help organize an international conference on bioethics in fall 1971 to mark the opening of the Kennedy Institute of Ethics, the international center for teaching and studying bioethics the Kennedy family had recently established at Georgetown University.

In the aftermath of Nathan's near-catastrophic accident, the Raineses felt a deep longing to provide endless love and safety for their children. During the month at the lake and during the time they lived at the Shrivers' place, Bonnie Raines remembers, "We gave that little boy a lot of tender loving care. . . . We realized how incredibly blessed we were that we still had him." They wrapped all of the children in a strong cocoon of love in an effort to make the memories of Nathan's tragedy go away and to help all of them feel completely secure. They did so knowing that at that time FBI investigators were frantically looking for the Media burglars.

They were just a few months beyond having dangerously lived out a principle that was very important to them: that parents' responsibility to protect and nurture their children should not exempt them from being activists and, in times of crisis, engaging in nonviolent resistance that could entail serious risks, including leaving their children and going to prison. They still believed in that principle now, even as they were more aware than ever of how much their children needed them. During this time, in the aftermath of Nathan's accident, the Raineses recall, they never regretted what they had done that night in Media, but their hearts ached at times as they thought about the pain their arrest would cause the children and themselves. Resisters together just four months earlier, now they were strong nurturers together desperately hoping they would never be arrested.

As far as they knew, their involvement in Media was still a locked secret,

During Nathan's long recovery from his serious injury the summer after the burglary, the Raineses felt an acute need to protect their children—at the same time they were afraid they might be arrested at any moment.

with the man who dropped out of the group the only person besides the other six burglars who had a key that could lead to the arrest of any of them. But Sargent Shriver, founder of the Peace Corps under John F. Kennedy, and of the Office of Economic Opportunity, the federal agency that created President Johnson's War on Poverty, shocked John Raines one day that fall. John and Shriver were in the backseat of Shriver's car, with then liberal and now conservative theologian Michael Novak a passenger in the front seat as all of them were being driven to a meeting related to the upcoming ethics conference. Out of the blue, Shriver, who less than a year later would be George McGovern's running mate in the presidential election, turned to John Raines and said, "John, I think you may have been involved in that Media FBI thing."

Raines was astounded. Under the circumstances, it didn't seem like an appropriate time to ask Shriver why he thought that. He decided it was better to let the subject die as quickly as possible. But he and Bonnie have always wondered what made Shriver, whose brothers-in-law John and Robert Kennedy often struggled with Hoover while they were in office, think John was involved in the Media burglary.

John remembers that after Shriver's comment that day he forced himself to try not to show his great surprise and said simply, "Sargent, I don't have the balls for that kind of thing." Shriver looked at him and said, "Yeah, I think you do."

THE RAINESES ALWAYS ASSUMED, based on the interview of John by the two agents, that he was a key suspect. He was, but perhaps his filibustering with the agents had an even deeper impact than he thought. The Raineses never knew, of course, that in a June 2, 1971, memorandum, John was eliminated by investigators as a MEDBURG suspect. That status was confirmed again when his name appeared on a June 28, 1971, list of MED-BURG suspects who had been eliminated.

13

Being American While Black and Other Insights from Media

THE MEDIA FBI FILES were significant for what they revealed about how Hoover operated the FBI rather than for what they revealed about the individuals and organizations the bureau spied on. Little, if any, of the information about people and organizations was about either the planning or the commission of a crime. Very little of it even revealed subversive expression. Much of it was extraordinarily mundane—like the transcription of a tapped conversation of a Philadelphia woman who called a friend and told him, in a phone conversation she did not know was being recorded by the FBI and would be transcribed and placed in an FBI file, that her baby was due in four months. Or the transcribed conversation of a man placing a collect call to "a female identified as Mom," as the FBI notes explain, in Illinois and asking her to send seventeen dollars so he could get a ride to visit her. She said she would.

A review of all the Media files revealed that efficient operations, governed by many rules, were created by Hoover to order, absorb, and maintain the bureau's collection of surveillance files on an ever-expanding number of people. But to what end? Ultimately, this information that outraged Congress and many other people when it was revealed by the Media burglars seemed to be, in a word, useless.

The spying constituted harassment, invasion of privacy, and violation of the right to dissent, but it had little or no connection to effective law enforcement or intelligence gathering—the important and only official missions of the FBI. The Media files provided the first evidence of what would become clear as much more evidence was gathered later: The FBI's spying operations did not lead to the prevention of any bombing, for instance, by the Weather Underground or any other group that planted bombs in that era. And the files led to few, if any, arrests after such bombs were detonated. Whatever the FBI was doing as it invaded lives, it was not preventing violent crimes or building cases on which arrests and successful prosecutions could be based. The carefully constructed spying system, aimed primarily against blacks and antiwar activists, seemed to create an illusion—to the FBI—that it was defeating enemies. The files seemed to indicate that Hoover lacked the capacity to shape an approach to either law enforcement or intelligence gathering that safeguarded civil liberties or protected Americans from violence.

MORE THAN ANYTHING, the Media files offered "the public and Congress an unprecedented glimpse of how the U.S. government watches its citizens—particularly black citizens," wrote *Washington Post* journalist William Greider in an analysis of all the files the summer after the burglary. Despite the fact that the files had been removed from a very small bureau office in a predominantly white area, they revealed details of the bureau's policies and actions that made it clear the FBI conducted massive spying on African Americans, most of it unjustified. It did so in ways, he wrote, that were as unreasonable as it would have been for the bureau to have spied on all lawyers who engaged in politics because, "as everyone knows, some lawyers in politics turn out to be crooks."

The overall impression in the Media files of how the FBI regarded black people was that they were dangerous and must be watched continuously. To become targets of the FBI, it wasn't necessary for African Americans to engage in violent behavior. It wasn't necessary for them to be radical or subversive. Being black was enough. The overall impression in directives written by Hoover, other headquarters officials, and local FBI officials was that the FBI thought of black Americans as falling into two categories—black people who should be spied on by the FBI and black people who should spy on other black people for the FBI. The latter group was to be recruited by the bureau to become part of its vast network of untrained informers.

The files also provided the first documentary evidence of Hoover's inability, or refusal, to differentiate people as individuals rather than as stereotypes of either a race or an ideology. One of the results of that failure on his part was that any organization devoted to racial equality risked being labeled subversive by the FBI and becoming subject to infiltration by the bureau. Local branch offices of organizations widely known to be constructive and nonviolent were infiltrated by the FBI: the Congress of Racial Equality, the Southern Christian Leadership Conference, and the NAACP. That pattern, it was learned later, was reflected in bureau behavior for years toward those and other nonviolent organizations throughout the country. It was learned later that NAACP officials had been under continuous FBI surveillance since 1923.

As required by directives from headquarters, African Americans came under the FBI's watchful eye everywhere—in churches, in classrooms, on college campuses, in bars, in restaurants, in bookstores, in their places of employment, in stores, in any social setting, in their neighborhoods and at the front doors of their homes. Probably few people suspected that the bill collector at their door was an FBI informer.

A blanket approach was used for both the spies and the spied-upon. All black people were eligible to be targeted, and in most parts of the country all agents were required to participate in operations designed to spy on black people—mostly by finding and hiring informers to do the spying.

New bureaucratic terms were created for these operations. Every field office was required to establish a "Racial Squad" to coordinate coverage of what the bureau labeled "Racial Matters." "Ghetto" informers were a subset of the group the bureau called "Racial Informants." These informants infiltrated groups the FBI considered to be black nationalist and black revolutionary groups, including in one category groups that were known to be violent as well as ones known to be nonviolent. "Ghetto" informers surveilled people who lived in black neighborhoods.

Every agent, not only agents on the Racial Squad, was required by headquarters officials to have at least one "ghetto informant" who reported to him. In Philadelphia, the bureau divided the city into fourteen areas, with agents required to establish "ghetto informants" in each. During that period, every agent in the Washington, D.C., office was required to recruit at least six "ghetto informants."

Exceptions could be made to the requirement that every agent recruit racial informers, but only under what, in the bureau's parlance, was considered a special circumstance—the absence of black people in the community served by the bureau office. Despite what would seem obvious as a result of demographics, an exemption from recruiting black people to inform on black people in a community that had no black people could not be taken for granted. A fairly elaborate bureaucratic process was required to assure that an agent who worked in a white area was not penalized for not having black informers. A bureau rule specified, "If an individual RA [resident agency, small FBI offices like Media] covers only a county which does not encompass any municipality containing a ghetto, so specify by memorandum form 170-6 with a copy for the RA's error folder, so that he will not be charged with failure to perform."

Most agents are believed to have taken these requirements seriously. They hired as many racial informers as the bureau stipulated, had frequent contact with their racial informers, and, as required, submitted reports at least once every two weeks on what the informers told them they had observed. There was some cynicism about these operations. Bob Wall, an agent who left the bureau during this era, said some agents "found" their racial informers by selecting names at random from phone books. They listed them in official files as their informers, but never contacted any racial informer and routinely wrote fake reports to fulfill the requirements. The reports—even the real ones—seldom involved serious discoveries that required law enforcement action or crime prevention responses. Perhaps numbed by the volume of reports, officials did not notice the contempt of some agents for this and other time-wasting work required by Hoover and other officials at Washington headquarters.

One of the assignments given to "ghetto informers" was to ascertain when riots would take place. In one Media file, an official in the Philadelphia office reminded local agents: "Whether or not a riot does occur, the Bureau holds us responsible to keep the Bureau, the Department [of Justice] and the White House advised in advance of each demonstration. The Bureau expects this coverage to come through informant sources primarily. In addition, we must advise the Bureau at least every two weeks of existing tensions and conditions which may trigger a riot." This information "can only come from a widespread grass-roots network of sources coupled with active informant coverage by individuals who are members of subversive and revolutionary organizations."

Once again, information flowed in, apparently without regard for whether it was accurate or served any purpose except to meet requirements that a certain number of informer reports be submitted to headquarters on a regular basis. No pending riot was discovered through these channels.

Bureau officials suggested the types of people who should be recruited as informers. A 1968 assignment to build a large network of informers throughout the black neighborhoods of Philadelphia included these recommendations about the types of people who should be hired for the "Racial Informant—Ghetto" category: "men honorably discharged from the armed services, members of veterans organizations and the like"; friends, relatives, and acquaintances of bureau employees; "employees and owners of businesses in ghetto areas which might include taverns, liquor stores, drug stores, pawn shops, gun shops, barber shops, janitors of apartment buildings, etc." The Bureau also suggested that agents establish contact with "persons who frequent ghetto areas on a regular basis such as taxi drivers, salesmen and distributors of newspapers, food and beverages. Installment collectors might also be considered in this regard."

The importance of recruiting people who would inform on black people was strongly and repeatedly emphasized. "It is essential," wrote Philadelphia SAC Jamieson in a February 1968 file found at Media, "that this office develop a large number of additional racial informants at this time and that we continue to add and develop racial informants and exploit their potential during the months ahead. In the inspection just passed, the Inspector pointed out, as we all know, that this is a problem of the entire office in which every agent and every squad shares responsibility."

Officials in the Philadelphia office also recommended where Philadelphia informers should find black people to be spied on. To get "maximum productivity from the racial informants," the agent in charge in Philadelphia advised informers to go to bars and cafés, bookstores, churches, and the headquarters of community organizations frequented by black people. At some restaurants and lounges, he wrote, "militant Negroes have been known to congregate." He suggested specific places: Green's Café, Wimpy's Burgers, South Street taprooms and luncheonettes, a luncheonette in Germantown, Foo Foo's Steak House, Mr. Silk's Third Base Lounge, and a settlement house in South Philadelphia.

Agents were told to monitor the Episcopal Church of the Advocate in North Philadelphia, then one of the most prominent churches in the city and known as a place where diverse opinions were welcome and where various community services, including free meals, were provided for poor people in the church's largely black neighborhood. Its pastor, the Reverend Paul Washington, one of the most respected clergy in the city, was named in some of the Media files.

As Greider wrote in his analysis, the files prescribing racial surveillance "sound like instructions for agents being sent to a foreign country."

Some of the assignments for agents and informers as they informed on black people in Philadelphia:

- "Attend and report on open meetings of known or suspected black extremist organizations. . . ."
- "Visit Afro-American type bookstores for the purpose of determining if militant extremist literature is available therein and, if so, to identify the owners, operators and clientele of such stores."
- "Identify black extremist militants who attempt to influence the Negro community and report on the effect of such efforts."
- "Report on changes in the attitude of the Negro community toward the white community which may lead to racial violence."
- "Report on all indications of efforts by foreign powers to take over the Negro militant movement. In those cases where you have an exceptionally intelligent and knowledgeable informant, such an informant may be given the assignment of reporting on the general mood of the Negro community concerning susceptibility to foreign influence whether this be from African nations in the form of Pan-Africanism, from the Soviet or Chinese communist bloc nations, or from other nations."

The suggestion of foreign influence in the black community undoubtedly came as a shock—or joke—to most, if not all, black Philadelphians. Their efforts for equality were rooted in their own experiences and needs, not inspired by "outsiders"—a term Hoover often used to express his lifelong perception that most protest by Americans was the result of foreign influence.

In addition to the Media files revealing that the FBI had easy access to the personal bank and other records of Muhammad Kenyatta, a prominent young civil rights leader in the Philadelphia area in the late 1960s and early 1970s, the files also revealed that the bureau maintained detailed reports on his daily activities. Kenyatta had campaigned the year before the Media burglary, as head of the National Black Economic Development Conference, for churches to contribute "reparations" to fund programs that served poor black people. He succeeded in getting such donations from, among other institutions, the local Episcopal diocese. A Baptist minister, he later graduated from Harvard Law School and was teaching constitutional law at the University of Buffalo Law School at the time of his death in 1992. FBI files on Kenyatta revealed that his bank records were handed over to FBI agents by a bank cashier as well as by the executive officer of Southeast National Bank. They provided access to copies of canceled checks and monthly statements of his personal account. When it was determined that the bank's computer system did not furnish complete information about "the nature and source of deposits and credits to this account," the bank provided the FBI with microfilms that contained full information about him. The phone company, equally obliging, provided the bureau with Kenyatta's unlisted phone number and information about his calls.

Kenyatta and his family moved to Philadelphia from Mississippi in 1968 because of a threatening letter that he thought at the time was written by a committee of students who purportedly were his rivals in a student organization at Tougaloo College near Jackson. He learned the truth about the letter in 1975: It had been fabricated by three FBI agents in a successful effort to force him to leave Mississippi.

THE BLACK PEOPLE WHO may have been targeted most in the Philadelphia area were students. They were easy targets because they stood out as very small and visible populations on campuses, all of which in eastern Pennsylvania at that time were overwhelmingly white except for Lincoln University, a predominantly black campus. Whether or not black students were peaceful, they came under the bureau's watchful eyes.

The director regarded the need for black informers on campuses as urgent. In a November 4, 1970, memo, he declared that "increased campus disorders involving black students pose a definite threat to the Nation's stability and security and indicate a need for increase in both quality and quantity of intelligence information on Black Student Unions and similar groups which are targets for influence and control by violence-prone Black Panther Party and other extremists."

He required agents to investigate and, if possible, infiltrate every black student organization at two-year colleges as well as four-year colleges and universities, and to do so without regard for whether there had been disturbances on such campuses. ". . . We must develop network of discreet quality sources in a position to furnish required information. Bear in mind that absence of information regarding these groups in any area might be the fault of inadequate source coverage and efforts should be undertaken immediately to improve this coverage."

In addition to campus-by-campus surveillance of black students, the FBI sent informers to the first national convention of the then new Washington-based National Association of Black Students, a loosely knit group of students from across the country. Every field office in the country was assigned in 1970 to send some of its local informants to the first NABS convention in Detroit.

If a black informer was about to enroll in college, that made him or her especially attractive to the FBI. Agents were ordered by headquarters officials to "immediately ascertain among all Negro informants, including ghetto informants, which informants are planning to enter college this fall and would be in a position to infiltrate black power groups on campuses. . . . Any agent who has a Negro informant who is contemplating college attendance should immediately report such."

The Black Student Union at Pennsylvania Military College in Chester was reported by school officials to be peaceful and loosely knit, but that did not discourage the FBI from placing its members under surveillance. An FBI file notes that after a months-long investigation by the bureau, it was evident that the union was "a somewhat disorganized group of students, possibly having a membership and/or following of no more than 30 students and possibly as few as a half dozen, who have not displayed radical or militant ideas, and do not appear to be aligned with any radical or black militant groups." The report noted that the union's purpose, in addition to encouraging black awareness, was to encourage black high school students to enroll at the college. Administrators at the college told an FBI representative that the Black Student Union "is a legitimate organization . . . that . . . is recognized by the school administration as a proper school activity." Nevertheless, the bureau concluded that it would "open cases" on the two leaders of what the bureau acknowledged was a "basically dormant" group.

THOUGH THE PUBLIC did not realize it until the full history of the FBI started to emerge in the mid-1970s, campuses had always been a venue for clandestine FBI operations. In addition to documenting the blanket coverage of black students on campuses, the Media files documented that every college and university was to be investigated and infiltrated by agents and informers. A file labeled STAG—for Student Agitation—listed the sixty-seven such institutions in the area served by resident agencies in the counties immediately west of Philadelphia. Given how expansive the demands for university infiltration were, agents based in these offices must have spent a substantial portion of their time monitoring campuses.

In a September 1970 memo, a supervising agent in the Philadelphia field office ordered "each Resident Agent" to inform the head of Squad 4 within a week of the following information in regard to every college or university in his area:

- The number of "sources" the FBI had "on the academic or administrative staff" on each campus, including security officers";
- The number of "current student security informants, or PSIs," on each campus;
- Other "current sources" of information regarding student agitation on each campus;
- The identity of any of the above—professor, police officer, student— "who can provide you with advance information on student agitation";
- A "listing of what information of Bureau interest cannot be obtained from the university or college";
- "Steps you propose to increase, strengthen and improve your coverage with respect to STAG";
- The cultivation of informers who could move into high levels of leadership in radical organizations on campuses and elsewhere.

The director announced in the fall of 1970 that informers could be hired as young as age eighteen. Now not only would older informers from off-campus be hired to inform on campuses, but more students would be hired to spy on one another. This lowering of the age of informers was greeted as a positive step. "We have been blocked off from this critical age group in the past," wrote one official. "Let us take advantage of this opportunity."

Stressing the importance of collecting information on campuses, Special Agent William B. Anderson Jr. of the Philadelphia field office sent this message to the agents in the small regional offices near Philadelphia:

"I want facts, not double talk. This information is not for statistical purposes or to reassure RA accomplishments. We have a job to do and cannot get where we are going until we know where we are." The promotion of paranoia must have been a major accomplishment of the campus operations. Agents and informers were a frequent presence on all of the campuses— known to those who supplied them with information, unknown to the professors and students on whom files were being developed.

Some campus conferences prompted elaborate coverage by the bureau. One that involved saturation coverage was the August 1969 conference of War Resisters International at Haverford College. A file found at Media stated that "in view of current international situation and the Paris Peace talks [regarding the Vietnam War]," twenty-two "security informants" were assigned by the bureau to the conference and told to determine its scope and "whether or not there are any indications it will generate any anti-US propaganda."

Agents and informers who covered the conference were unaware that a then relatively unknown man FBI agents would be searching for in two years was present. Once a hawk who advised the Pentagon on the conduct of the Vietnam War, Daniel Ellsberg attended the conference in the hope of learning from the pacifists there what he could do to help end the war. It turned out to be a pivotal point in his life. Inspired by participants' commitment to nonviolence as a way of life and as a political tool, Ellsberg decided by the end of the conference that, having risked his life in Vietnam when he supported the war, he would now risk his freedom to oppose it. Soon after that conference he decided he would do that by making public the secret history of the Vietnam War, the Pentagon Papers, which he had helped write. He hoped public access to this official history of the war, which he released in June 1971, would convince more Americans that the war was a serious mistake and should end.

Another Media file illustrated the bureau's attempts to convince college administrators that they should exert more control over student protesters. This memorandum from Hoover instructed agents throughout the country to deliver the article attached to it, "Campus or Battleground? Columbia Is a Warning to All American Universities," an article from *Barron's*, to campus administrations. It was to be delivered personally to administrators who were "established" sources of the FBI, and it was to be mailed "anonymously to college administrators who have a reluctance to take decisive action against the 'New Left.'" In his handwriting at the end of the memorandum, Hoover wrote, "Let me know of disposition, and any results." The article was written by Robert Hessen, then a graduate student at Columbia University's School of Business and later an economic and business historian at Stanford University's Hoover Institution, a think tank named after the late president Herbert Hoover.

At the bottom of the routing slip attached to the article, in the handwriting of someone from the Philadelphia FBI office, is this note to Tom Lewis, the resident agent at the Media office: "Tom: Can you handle Swarthmore, Haverford, Villanova."

A term at the top of that routing slip, COINTELPRO, set off a state of near panic inside FBI headquarters when officials realized this file had been distributed by the burglars. It would be more than two years until the significance of the term would be even partially understood outside the bureau.

THE ARRAY OF EMPLOYEES at Swarthmore College who were described in Media files as "established" sources who had worked with the FBI in the past made people on other campuses wonder who was invading their privacy and reporting their conversations and actions to the bureau. The FBI sources at Swarthmore included a campus security officer, a switchboard operator, the town's chief of police, and the postmaster. In one instance, they had been engaged to spy on a philosophy professor who agents thought might have been visited by suspects in a violent Boston crime. The professor, never contacted by the FBI, said he had no knowledge of the suspects.

According to FBI records of their collaboration with the Swarthmore switchboard operator, at the bureau's request she checked the records of his calls and found none related to the suspects. Agents noted in the professor's FBI file, however, that the operator said the professor was not highly regarded on campus. The police chief, contacted by the bureau because he lived near the professor, said he knew nothing about the suspects ever visiting the professor but expressed concern that hippies visited the professor's home. He told agents he was also concerned about the fact that the professor had converted his garage into a print shop with equipment sufficient to publish a newspaper. Agents noted all of that information in a file, plus the fact that the police chief would keep a close eye on what happened at the professor's house.

The Swarthmore College student daughter of a member of Congress, Representative Henry S. Reuss, Democrat from Wisconsin, also was under FBI surveillance at Swarthmore—apparently because she was his daughter and because she, like her parents, opposed the Vietnam War. The records gathered on Jacqueline Reuss included her grades and details of her travels when she was a student in France. When the Media file about her became public, her father protested the surveillance of his daughter and others. The FBI, he said in a public statement, had no business compiling dossiers on "Americans who are accused of no wrongdoing." According to the Media file on Reuss, information from her college records was provided confidentially to the FBI by the secretary to the registrar at Swarthmore College. The secretary, like other campus workers named in the FBI files, was described as an "established" FBI source.

Campus-related files found at Media suggest it may have been routine for campus administrators to readily give FBI agents student information that was supposed to be private and that had no connection with potential criminal activity:

- The acting chancellor of the Eastern Shore campus of the University of Maryland gave the FBI extensive information about the president of the student government association, none of it related to potential criminal action.
- An administrator at Rutgers University provided the FBI with information about students that was unrelated to potential criminal activity.
- The dean of student affairs at Lincoln University, a black campus in eastern Pennsylvania, provided the FBI with information about students who had engaged in no wrongdoing.

A professor at the University of Pennsylvania came under FBI surveillance after an investigation of his fourteen-year-old son was closed. At first, according to a Media file, Herbert L. Shore's son was the main subject of the surveillance. Phone conversations between Shore, director of performing arts at the Annenberg School of Communications at the university, and his son were tapped while the boy attended summer camp in East Germany. The FBI files on the case include transcripts of father and son discussing a family member's health. Guessing who they were discussing, an agent wrote in the report on the taped phone conversation that they talked about "Mom, who presumably is the subject's mother." Military intelligence agents also intercepted and read letters exchanged between Shore and his son that summer.

The FBI investigation of this junior high school student continued for several months. Then an FBI agent wrote, "The case on Norman Jon Shore should be closed inasmuch as the individual is only 14 years old." But, the agent added, the investigation would now turn instead to the father. A file was opened on him. It grew easily, thanks to an "established" employee in the university's personnel records department who, when contacted by an FBI agent, told the agent that because Professor Shore held a high university post, he had an extensive personnel record. She made that record available to the FBI. "I think it's a sad commentary on this country . . . that there is this paranoia because a kid goes to camp in a socialist country," Shore told a reporter when the document about him and his son became public after the Media burglary. When Shore died in 2004, he was described as an expert on

African theater who "worked his entire life for peace and democracy in the United States and in Africa."

AMERICANS WHO PARTICIPATED in academic and cross-cultural exchanges with counterparts in other countries, including communist countries, found themselves in a contradictory situation: to spy or not to spy on their exchange colleagues. To participate in these programs, even ones organized by the State Department or other U.S. government agencies, meant Americans, including even teenagers, risked being targeted by the FBI. For instance, Americans who visited the Soviet Union for at least a month were questioned by the bureau upon their return to the United States. The purpose of such investigations, according to a file found at Media, was to "determine whether any of them were approached for recruitment by the Soviet Intelligence Services" either in the USSR or in the United States after they returned. But they were also questioned by the FBI to determine if they could be turned into spies for the bureau. Agents were instructed to assess people returning from Sino-Soviet bloc countries, especially those who were employed in the news media, entertainment, religious organizations, and education, and also people who were public officials, "labor leader or prominent person," for their potential to work as informers for the bureau during their travels. Such requests were carried out as part of a special program, DESECO—Development of Selected Contacts. Attached to the memo about this program was a long list of potential informers—Americans, mostly scientists, scheduled to attend various upcoming international conventions, including the Twelfth International Conference on Low Temperature Physics in Kyoto, Japan; the Third International Symposium on Fresh Water from the Sea at Dubrovnik, Yugoslavia; the Seventh World Congress of Sociology; the International Iron and Steel Conference in Japan; and the International Astronautical Federation and Aerospace Conference in Constance, West Germany. They were asked to spy on their fellow scientists while at these conferences.

MEDIA RECORDS REVEALED that FBI files on some people spanned decades, even if nothing was ever discovered about the person that indicated even a hint of wrongdoing. One man's ongoing file started with a five-dollar fine for breach of the peace in 1954, a minor law enforcement issue that usually would not concern the FBI. The man was still being monitored by the bureau at the time of the burglary in 1971. He had come to the attention of the FBI in 1967 because he was a conscientious objector. The bureau investigated his past extensively. As they did, agents discovered the fine and built his file beginning at that point. In the course of their investigation, agents placed in his file statements from unnamed informers who worked with him at Bellevue Medical Center in New York City in 1957. Into the file went statements that he was "described as 'queer fish,' 'screwball,' 'smarty pants'"; a report that he volunteered for risky research experiments and was described by the psychiatrist who was in charge of the research as "altruistic, sincere, believer in God, but not in conventional religion"; reports from police intelligence files in Haverford, Pennsylvania, that he distributed antiwar leaflets in 1968; and a report that he was present at a rally at which *other* people said the war in Vietnam was "unconstitutional" and "illegal." Item after item was added to his FBI file, none of them indicating that the man ever was a suspect in any crime.

The mindless nature of how FBI surveillance files were initiated is illustrated in a file found at Media that was based on an informer's report about an evening he spent productively, from his and the bureau's view, at what the FBI called the Bernheim Commune in Philadelphia. The informer had been assigned to clandestinely observe a political meeting at the commune. When the informer arrived for the meeting, he learned that it was scheduled for another day. While there, though, the informer noticed that a women's liberation meeting was taking place in another room. Having struck out with the political meeting, the informer, being entrepreneurial and wishing to be paid for an evening's work, saw the women's meeting as an opportunity not to return to his agent handler empty-handed.

In the report he submitted, the informer referred to the people in the commune as intellectual revolutionaries who were not part of organizations. Among the observations he regarded as worth reporting to the FBI—and that his handling agent thought worth memorializing in FBI files—was that one of the women "kept going in and out of the meeting to attend her small child in the kitchen" and that a number of other "rather hippie-type individuals were observed coming and going from the upper floors and it would appear that the three-story house is being operated as a commune."

As a result of the informer going to the commune for a meeting that did not take place and attending a meeting of women where, as he reported, little took place, an FBI file was nevertheless opened on every member of the commune who was at the house that evening.

Detailed reports were prepared by informers and agents about demonstrations, even if very few people attended. An FBI report about a peaceful demonstration in Philadelphia noted that it was attended by "100 demonstrators and no spectators." They had gathered to protest research on chemical weapons used in Vietnam. The official report notes that the demonstration—organized by none other than William Davidon, future Media burglar—was covered by eighteen Philadelphia police officers, plus a group of police photographers, and police in seven cruising police cars.

In another Media file, officials expressed concern about informers who went too far. The subject was discussed in the same bureau newsletter in which agents were advised to increase paranoia.

"There have been a few instances where security informants in the New Left got carried away during a demonstration, assaulted police, etc." The key word in this area, the official wrote, was "control." "The [bureau headquarters officials] define this to mean that while our informants should be privy to everything going on and should rise to the maximum level of their ability in the New Left Movement, they should not become the person who carries the gun, throws the bomb, does the robbery or by some specific violative, overt act becomes a deeply involved participant. This is a judgment area and any actions which seem to border on it should be discussed." The statement was far from a clear rejection of such behavior.

One Media file recounts a bureau correspondence with Canadian counterparts that must have left the FBI disappointed, or perhaps perplexed. According to an official response from the Royal Canadian Mounted Police found in the Media files, when asked by the FBI in 1969 to locate Americans believed to be in the Union of American Exiles in Canada, the RCMP intelligence office responded, "At the present time, we do not have a source in the position of positively identifying the individuals mentioned."

Most reports in the Media files were about clandestine investigations with harassment as the goal. The only files that were about developing evidence for prosecution were investigations of antidraft organizations and people who were engaged in "counseling, aiding and abetting in the antidraft movement." Hoover wrote in 1967 that he "cannot stress too strongly for prompt expeditious handling of these cases." He assured agents that journalists would be sources of information when developing evidence in these cases. "If it is ascertained that the news media has obtained items of an evidentiary nature, such as photographs or statements," he instructed agents, they "must be contacted promptly in order that the evidence may be securely maintained for possible future use."

Advice in a file on recruiting future agents emphasized that military veterans were especially valuable recruits. "Catch the veteran almost before he is home," advised an official in a file on recruitment. The Philadelphia office, he wrote, had excellent success with approaching such people as soon as they were discharged. Veterans were prized as FBI employees because they "are mature, have already been relocated certainly at least once and have no fear of Washington, DC. They have been subject to discipline and order." But there were some drawbacks with veterans. "Because the discharged veteran is several years further along than the current high school graduate, some may have had a 'wild oats' period." Because of this, the investigations of veterans should be "more demanding" than the investigations of other applicants.

The physical appearance of FBI agents—at the time they were hired and throughout their employment—was extraordinarily important to the director. This preoccupation was evident in the smallest details, not to mention the oddest ones.

In one Media file, a high FBI official discussed facial hair standards when hiring clerical employees:

> I recently saw a photograph of a favorably recommended clerical applicant. This photograph reflected long sideburns and long hair in the back and too full on the sides. Please, when interviewing applicants be alert for long hairs, beards, mustaches, pear-shaped heads, truck drivers, etc. We are not that hard up yet. . . . In connection with long hair and sideburns, where you have an applicant that you would like to favorably recommend, ask the applicant to submit to you a new photograph with short sideburns and conventional hair style. I have not had one refuse me yet.

The reference to "pear-shaped heads," strange as it might seem, was not casual advice. Nor was it a joke. It was well known in the bureau that Hoover would not tolerate people with such heads. One had suffered a terrible fate when he met the director. One day, as new agents who had recently graduated from the FBI Academy were paraded into the director's office one by one for a quick handshake with the director—a ceremony that took place after each class of new agents graduated—Hoover promptly ordered that one of them be dismissed from the bureau immediately. The young agent had passed the sweaty palm test—any agent who shook Hoover's hand with a sweaty palm was fired on the spot—but he had failed the pear-shaped head test.

Weight requirements were strictly enforced. This is evident in a January 4, 1971, memo to all Philadelphia-area agents from Philadelphia SAC Jamieson. He reminded agents and other employees in the Philadelphia field office of their responsibility to follow the demands made by the director in a 1965 order: that every July, October, January, and April "each Special Agent must be weighed and the Bureau advised of the results by the last day of such months." He reminded them their weight must be recorded in the office of Mrs. Lee Landsburg, the nurse in the FBI field office. Reverting to capital letters, he wrote, "ANY MAN FOUND TO BE OVERWEIGHT WILL BE REQUIRED TO LOSE THE WEIGHT, AND WILL BE WEIGHED WEEKLY BY HIS SUPERVISOR UNTIL HIS WEIGHT IS BROUGHT WITHIN BUREAU STANDARDS." Heads of resident agency offices, such as Media, were to be weighed every time they came to the Philadelphia field office, but not more than once a month. Jamieson concluded by noting, "I expect every agent and male clerical employee to maintain his weight within the desirable limits at all times."

Read today, Jamieson's memo sounds like it might have been written for a segment on Jon Stewart's *Daily Show* on Comedy Central. Actually, weight gain, even slight weight gain, was treated as a serious issue in the bureau. Some agents were fired for being only a few pounds overweight. Some were clever in how they deceived the director about weight gain. One agent, who had to meet with Hoover not long after he had been found to be overweight, bought a suit for the occasion that was too large in order to make it appear that he had recently lost, not gained, weight.

FEW PEOPLE LAUGHED when they discovered in news reports about the Media files that they had been monitored by the FBI. The members of one group managed to do so. When it was reported that Media files revealed the FBI was intercepting the mail of the Friends Peace Committee of the Philadelphia Yearly Meeting, the Quaker organization publicly announced that it would put the FBI on its mailing list and make the interception of its mail unnecessary. There was no response from the FBI—unless breaking down Quaker employee Anne Flitcraft's front door with a sledgehammer, invading her apartment, and removing her personal and professional papers, books, and typewriter should be regarded as a response.

Another organization, the Philadelphia-based Women's International League for Peace and Freedom, also responded publicly to reports that the FBI had surveilled the league's fiftieth anniversary celebration in 1965. Dr. Martin Luther King was the keynote speaker at the event. The heading on the file about the event was "COMMUNIST INFILTRATION OF WOMEN'S INTERNATIONAL LEAGUE FOR PEACE AND FREEDOM." In addition to clandestinely covering the gathering, the bureau distributed biographical sketches of the candidates for the national board of the organization to FBI offices in thirty-seven cities.

After the bureau's file on the group became public, the group released "An Open Letter to the FBI." In it, Naomi Marcus, the chair of the league's policy committee, wrote, "We neither appreciate nor need the FBI's snooping on us or our members. We have always operated in an open manner. We welcome as members all who believe in working by nonviolent means to create the conditions which will make peace and freedom possible. We do not inquire into the political affiliations of those who wish to join us. . . . We . . . recognize that there are merits as well as imperfections in all existing forms of political and socio-economic systems. We do not believe in 'devil' theories. . . . We call for a curb on Big Brother, and resolve that we will not be intimidated by those who seek to discredit us or to distract us from our goals."

In the large Philadelphia FBI office, the Media files revealed, monitoring antiwar activists and black people dominated the FBI's workload throughout the 1960s and early 1970s. That was true until 1975 when Neil Welch, as the new special agent in charge brought an approach different from Hoover's, shifting the emphasis of investigations at the Philadelphia office to organized crime and government corruption, areas that had been of little interest to Hoover but were ones most Americans probably assumed had always been at the top of the FBI's agenda at all times.

AFTER I RECEIVED the first two sets of Media files, I was eager to see all the files that had been stolen. I wanted evidence of whether the burglars were distorting the overall nature of the files by distributing only files that matched a biased goal. FBI and Department of Justice officials had claimed that was the case. I called a source in the Catholic peace movement, someone I thought might have been involved in some of the clandestine draft board raids. At a coffee shop near the *Washington Post* offices, I asked if she knew anyone who could help me get access to all of the Media files. She agreed to explore the possibility. A few days later she called and we met again. She had talked to someone who said he thought he would be able to arrange for me to go to a place where I would have access to all of the Media files. Someone would be in touch with me about arrangements.

When I returned to the newsroom, I did something very stupid. I was delighted—actually, I was very excited—that my search for all of the Media files might be successful. As I passed the desk of Ken Clawson, without thinking I stopped and impulsively said, "Ken, guess what? I think I'm going to get to see all of the Media files." It was Clawson who had shared a byline with me on the first story about the documents because he had gotten confirmation from the bureau that the files were authentic. When I saw his expression instantly change from relaxed and casual to fierce and hardened, I was surprised and realized I had made a mistake. "I'll go with you," he said rather sternly. No longer so excited, I told him that wouldn't be possible because I was dealing with confidential sources who would deal only with me. Trying to act as though nothing important had just been discussed, I walked to my office. About thirty minutes later, Clawson appeared beside my desk. "I will go with you," he said, a heavy emphasis on "will," as though he was giving an order, something he was not in a position to do. He turned and walked away as though the matter was settled. I knew then that it was settled, but not in the way he intended.

I gave myself a day to think about my strong gut reaction to Clawson's demand. I could not be certain about why he reacted so strongly. I thought there were two possible explanations. He could have been acting simply from fiercely competitive instincts and thought that if the cache of Media files was going to be found, it would be a significant story, one he was determined to report. Or—and this seemed to be the more likely cause of his reaction—after months of writing about the bureau he had perhaps developed such a close working relationship with the director's staff, or even the director, that he might be willing to notify the FBI that I, or we, as he intended, were going to meet either the burglars or people who might be very closely associated with them. The search for the burglars and the stolen files was at a fever pitch at this time, so I assume that details from Clawson about my plan to travel to the files would have been of keen interest to the FBI, especially because the bureau's search for the burglars and the files had failed so far. I decided I could not take a chance. In order to eliminate the possibility of jeopardizing my anonymous sources, I concluded I had to undo my chance to see all of the Media files. Whoever the burglars were, I was not going to be used to guide the FBI to them.

Two days after Clawson made his demand to me, I met my source and explained my error in judgment and withdrew my request for access. Needless to say, my source agreed that that was necessary under the circumstances. This time, when I returned to the newsroom and stopped at

Clawson's desk, I told him there would be no trip to see the Media files. I told him my sources had called it off. He looked very disappointed.

Less than a year later, Clawson quit his job at the *Washington Post* and became deputy director of communications in the Nixon White House and later director of communications. Soon after he moved to the White House post, I got some insight into his relationship with Hoover. Another *Post* colleague, White House correspondent Don Oberdorfer, told me what he had observed one day as Clawson assembled his new office in the White House. He unpacked and put on prominent display a framed and warmly inscribed photograph of J. Edgar Hoover.

A special relationship had developed between Hoover and Clawson as a result of an interview Clawson had with him on November 16, 1970. As Curt Gentry wrote in his biography of Hoover, since "his outburst before the women's press club in 1964, when he'd angrily denounced the Rev. Martin Luther King, Jr., J. Edgar Hoover had not held a press conference or given a personal interview" until the one with Clawson.

The interview had come about under circumstances that endeared Clawson to Hoover. Thus the warm inscription. Clawson's efforts to get an interview with the director started in the summer of 1970 when he was transferred from covering the White House to covering the Department of Justice. *Post* executive editor Ben Bradlee playfully bet Clawson a lunch that he could not get an interview with Hoover. Clawson was determined to win the bet. A written request to the director produced a perfunctory rejection. He tried other approaches. All failed. Then, thanks to a hallway encounter with Hoover in the Department of Justice Building that was set up by Attorney General John Mitchell, Clawson directly asked him for an interview. Hoover said no then, but he remembered the request a few days later when reviews of a book by Ramsey Clark were published in Sunday editions of newspapers. The reviews had noted that the book included scathing criticism by Clark of Hoover and the bureau. Clark had written, for example, that the bureau suffered from "the excessive domination of a single person, J. Edgar Hoover, and his self-centered concern for his reputation and that of the FBI."

When Clawson arrived at work that Monday morning, the day after the reviews appeared, he had eight urgent messages from the FBI director's office. That interview Clawson wanted? He could have it now. Clawson raced to the director's office. The director said he could have twenty minutes. It seemed as though he couldn't stop talking. Hours passed. Clawson said later his writing hand got tired. The director missed lunch for the first time in the memory of anyone in his office.

In Hoover's anger over Clark's book, he sputtered to Clawson that Clark was a "jellyfish"—the worst attorney general he had worked with in all his years as director. Clark was even worse, the director told Clawson, than Robert Kennedy. Given how much Hoover disliked Kennedy, that was quite a criticism. With Clark, said Hoover, "you never knew which way he was going to flop on an issue." About Mitchell, the current attorney general, "There never has been an attorney general for whom I've had a higher regard."

Hoover expressed his fury regarding Bobby Kennedy urging him to hire black agents, something Hoover automatically assumed meant he would have to "lower the standards." He said he had told Kennedy he would resign rather than do that. With pride and apparently no shame, Hoover told Clawson he "didn't speak to Bobby Kennedy the last six months he was in office." The director could not have been more pleased with Clawson's story. And Bradlee, loser of the bet, took Clawson to lunch at Sans Souci, then a fashionable Washington restaurant.

As it turned out, over a period of about three months the burglars did release all of the Media files, excluding, of course, routine blank forms and files about criminal investigations they had no interest in hampering, such as organized crime.

In the last set of files sent to journalists by the Citizens' Commission to Investigate the FBI, on May 3, 1971, the burglars included a statistical analysis of the files they had removed from the Media office, excluding the 30 percent of the total that were manuals, routing forms, and similar procedural materials. They described the investigative files as follows:

1 percent—organized crime, mostly gambling.
7 percent—leaving the military without permission.
7 percent—draft resistance, including refusal to submit to military induction.
20 percent—murder, rape and interstate theft.
25 percent—bank robberies.
40 percent—political surveillance and other investigation of political activity. Of these cases, 2 were about conservative individuals or organizations and 200 were about liberal individuals or organizations.

THE MEDIA FILES WERE case histories that demonstrated for the first time that the FBI used its hidden and unlimited power to monitor many people on the basis of their opinions—or the opinions of their associates, or on the basis of what their appearance or lifestyle suggested to the FBI their opinions might be. Lives were imprisoned in these secret FBI files. People could neither access nor assess the files created about them by the FBI. Until the Media files became public, no one outside the bureau knew that people stood secretly accused by the FBI in files. The people who were the subjects in the files had no chance to see their FBI record, no chance to correct false information that had been placed in the files by untrained informers, and no chance to expunge this secret record of their lives.

The FBI had assumed that the people sealed inside its files did not have the basic rights of access and review that even people charged with the most serious crimes have regarding government evidence collected about them. The most powerful law enforcement agency in the country was secret judge, secret jury, and secret warden of years-long secret investigations of countless people.

The number three official in the bureau at the time of the burglary, William C. Sullivan, said later that "the documents they stole from us and released to the press caused a national uproar. . . . The documents relating to our security investigation proved beyond a doubt that the FBI was investigating students as if they were criminals."

By creating such records, the bureau was neither fighting crime nor protecting national security. Instead, it was—just as Davidon had feared when he decided to risk his future, and to invite others to join him in doing so—building massive files intended to intimidate people from exercising their right to dissent.

The files stolen at Media revealed many important secrets the public needed to know, but they were just the beginning. If those secrets were found in a remote office in suburban Philadelphia, people wanted to know what was in files located in other FBI offices, including at headquarters. Except for the part of the secret FBI that was revealed at Media, most of the bureau's secrets were still securely protected inside the FBI headquarters in Washington and in FBI offices throughout the country. Not until the chain of events set off by the Media burglary resulted in investigations of the bureau was it learned that the bureau's operations often led to actions that harmed—and were intended to harm—the activists who were targeted. The impact often was much more than simple harassment.

The bureau struggled mightily to make it impossible for Congress and the public to learn more about the secret FBI than was revealed in the Media files. Ultimately, the bureau would fail in that effort.

14

The Subterfuge Continues

FBI OFFICIALS DREADED discovering which secrets might show up next in news reports. As the Media burglars continued to release a new set of files every ten to fourteen days until mid-May 1971, the internal files of the bureau's investigation of the burglary reveal that the FBI reacted feverishly throughout that time as one shoe after another dropped. The director and his aides waited helplessly for news they could not stop and to arrest burglars they could not find.

Accustomed to being in total control of the bureau and its public image, the director lost control for the first time. He wanted to keep all bureau files secret, as he always had, but now that his secrets could emerge at any time, Hoover and his top aides deemed the exposure of some secrets to be much more important than that of others. They dreaded most the damage that would be done by public exposure of two programs: SI and COINTELPRO. The director had put these programs in place many years earlier. COINTELPRO operations were regarded in the bureau as the ones that could cause the greatest damage if they became known. Hoover and his top aides had gone to great lengths to make sure that the existence of COINTELPRO was known only inside the bureau, and they were determined that would remain the case. But after the burglary, determination did not count for much. That spring the Media burglars, not the bureau, were in charge of what the public learned about the FBI.

The other program FBI officials urgently wanted to keep secret was SI—the Security Index. It had been started by Hoover in 1939 and had a tumultuous history. Some attorneys general had been aware of the index. One had ordered Hoover to eliminate it, but Hoover never did so. It had survived that attorney general's order, and it had continued to grow through World War II and the Cold War. Now, in the spring of 1971, it seemed possible it might be exposed and endangered by the Media burglary.

So they could plan damage control, officials at the Intelligence Division at FBI headquarters in Washington and in the Philadelphia field office worked daily throughout the spring of 1971 to try to reconstruct the Media files so they could be prepared to comment—or not comment, as it turned out—if queried about specific files. Despite their efforts, it proved to be nearly impossible to reconstruct the Media files with precision. To some extent, they were guessing what files had been kept at Media and might emerge. That Hoover had punished the head of the Media office, the person who knew most about the files in the office, by exiling him to Atlanta hindered the reconstruction effort. Because of the difficulty of knowing what secrets would emerge next, bureau officials were uncertain for weeks whether files about the two programs they thought would be most endangered by public exposure, SI and COINTELPRO, were in the Media files.

They were.

The names of the two programs eventually surfaced in Media files that spring, but when they did they were not understood. That provided some relief to FBI officials, but only temporarily. Most of the stolen files were fairly straightforward, such as the report that said informers should be placed in all black student organizations at colleges. That document was clear and easily understood. Not so with SI and COINTELPRO. They were acronyms without clear reference points in the files. It took a lawsuit by a relentless television reporter, a demanding attorney general, and congressional investigations over the next five years to force into public light the files that would reveal what the COINTELPRO operations were.

The mysterious acronyms—SI and COINTELPRO—were like messages in bottles that had washed ashore but could not be opened—dark, sealed bottles that shielded the terms from being understood even after they had surfaced. "SI" first appeared in a memo found at Media in which agents were ordered to place members of the Jewish Defense League on SI. The term appeared again in a February 26, 1971, memo that summarized an effort to have a University of California at Berkeley student placed on SI. In both instances, the meaning of the term was not clear. An FBI informer in Washington described the Berkeley student as "an inveterate Marxist revolutionist . . . far out," and he recommended she be placed on the SI. After having the student monitored by informers in Berkeley, an agent there wrote, "Due to lack of information and activities of subject, San Francisco is not submitting a summary report at this time. Subject is not being recommended for inclusion on the Security Index as it is felt additional investigation is acquired [*sic*] before this evaluation can be reached." Despite the agent's reservations, however, the student was placed on the Security Index.

In Hoover's confidential memo to Attorney General Mitchell on March 25, the day after the first story about the Media documents was published, Hoover expressed concern about SI being revealed. It is evident he assumed the attorney general was not familiar with the term, for he explained it to him, though incompletely: SI is "a listing of individuals deemed a threat to the internal security." If SI were revealed, Hoover informed him, "it could open the door to inquiries regarding the propriety and purpose of maintaining lists of subversives." The danger that exposure of bureau programs aimed at subversives would cause public controversy was the director's persistent concern as the Media secrets emerged.

The full explanation of the Security Index was first revealed by *Washington Post* reporter William Greider in a June 13, 1971, article:

> Unknown to the general public or even to Congress, the federal government maintains a super-secret listing of so-called potential subversives—a file which would be the basis for federal arrests in the event of war or an "internal security emergency."
>
> It is called the "Security Index," compiled and kept up-to-date by the Federal Bureau of Investigation, supervised by the Justice Department's Internal Security Division.
>
> Though it has been in existence since at least the 1930s, the government does not admit it, even when Congress makes an inquiry. Both the FBI and the Justice Department refuse to concede even that there is something called the "Security Index," much less explain what it is.
>
> The index is a closely held list of the names, addresses, jobs and phone numbers of thousands of Americans considered potentially dangerous as spies or saboteurs if war or national insurrection developed. How many thousands is not known, but the list has been expanded in recent years as New Left radicals and militant black leaders were added to the rolls, joining the Old Left types from the Communist Party and Trotskyite organizations. A conservative guess based on public figures on subversives is that more than 10,000 people are kept under scrutiny as index subjects.

It was later revealed the index included the names of more than 26,000 Americans.

Just a year earlier, in 1970, Greider reported, Senator Sam Ervin's Senate Judiciary Subcommittee on Constitutional Rights had asked all federal departments, including the Department of Justice, to report on all of the "law enforcement–oriented or intelligence-type files" which the agencies maintained on citizens. The Department of Justice did not report the existence, let alone the details, of the Security Index at that time. Interestingly, the index was probably the only FBI collection of intelligence data on citizens that the department monitored—or was supposed to monitor—and was therefore in a position to report to the senate committee. But given that Hoover informed the attorney general about some of the basic facts concerning the Security Index soon after the Media files started to become public, it seems likely that the Department of Justice had forfeited oversight of the list much earlier.

HOW HOOVER MANAGED the index from 1939 until the fall of 1971 is a case study in how he maintained tight control and was able to run a secret FBI within the FBI. It also illustrates the tension between his desire for protection by officials and his desire for total independence. While there was only one FBI director from 1924 to 1972, there were sixteen attorneys general—the people who technically were his direct supervisors but whom he thought of as his protectors rather than as his bosses. Bending each of them to his will usually was easy, but not always, as is seen in the reluctance of some of them to authorize illegal FBI programs in writing, including approval of his maintaining a list of Americans to be arrested and imprisoned without trial in the event of a national emergency.

Hoover started the Security Index early in his career as director. Over the lifetime of the index, he changed its name twice. He succeeded in keeping its existence secret from the public from 1939 until the Media burglary. But that success was marked by tumultuous struggles from time to time. In the beginning, it was called the Custodial Detention Index. It became the Security Index in 1943 and then the Administrative Index, or AMDEX, in the fall of 1971. The name changes were related to increasing secrecy and had nothing to do with alterations in the nature of the program or in how it was conducted.

The list was started the day after Germany invaded Poland in September

1939. FBI agents throughout the country were ordered to prepare reports on "persons of German, Italian and Communist sympathies," as well as other persons "whose interests may be directed primarily to the interest of some other nation than the United States" for listing on the new Custodial Detention Index. The names were gathered, according to FBI historian Athan Theoharis, not from knowledge about individuals' subversive activities but primarily from the subscription lists of German, Italian, and communist newspapers; from membership lists of organizations; and from informant and agent reports on who attended meetings and demonstrations. This casual and imprecise method of harvesting alleged subversives' names for such a serious purpose—to get names of "both aliens and citizens of the United States, on whom there is information available that their presence at liberty in this country in time of war or national emergency would be dangerous to the public peace and the safety of the United States Government"—was striking in view of the fact that placing names on the list could lead to their loss of freedom and, in varying ways, the destruction of their lives.

Hoover was clear about intending to keep standards loose in regard to which people should be placed on the list of alleged subversives considered dangerous enough to be stripped of their freedom by the FBI at the time of a national emergency. People whose names were placed on the list, he instructed, should be "watched carefully . . . because their previous activities indicate the *possibility but not the probability* that they will harm the national interest." Hoover's language here—"possibility but not the probability"—reflects the elasticity he used to determine who should be included on the list. Over the years that elasticity was stretched more and more.

Because there was no law authorizing such lists, Hoover warned agents from the time the list was established that its existence must be "entirely confidential." When the full history of the director and the bureau started to emerge in the 1970s, it became known for the first time that the director never had been shy about breaking the law. Any concerns he expressed about operating outside the law were not about respect for the law or regret about breaking it but instead about the possibility of embarrassing the bureau if the violations became known.

In June 1940, Attorney General Robert H. Jackson alleviated Hoover's concerns when he agreed with Hoover that there was a critical need for such a list and assured the director that in the event of an emergency he, as attorney general, would authorize warrants for the arrests of those on the list. But Jackson imposed a stipulation Hoover regarded as an intrusion on his turf. Jackson insisted that the Department of Justice should review the list regularly. Hoover agreed, but he did so only after the attorney general agreed that the department would not prosecute anyone on the list because to do so might lead to exposure of FBI informers.

Efforts by Jackson to require Hoover to use only lawful methods in the bureau caused a conflict between Jackson—the future U.S. Supreme Court justice and prosecutor at the Nuremberg trials—and President Franklin D. Roosevelt. Discovery of instances of attorneys general and presidents not reining in the FBI led the Church Committee to conclude in 1975 that the major failures it uncovered in the FBI were largely the result of a failure of oversight by Congress, attorneys general, and presidents. Too often, in fact, presidents had been enablers of the wrongdoing, the committee concluded, beginning with Franklin Roosevelt.

Through private directives to Hoover and orders to Jackson to keep hands off Hoover, Roosevelt gave the director reason to believe he could operate without regard for the law, especially without regard for the protection of civil liberties. Like Presidents Johnson and Nixon, Roosevelt instructed Hoover to gather intelligence about the president's political enemies. From then on, on those rare occasions when Hoover was asked to justify his illegal operations, he cited Roosevelt's approval of such actions, claiming years later that FDR's secret memorandums and oral directives should be regarded as Hoover's permanent license to operate as he wished. Years later, Hoover sometimes even doctored the language of Roosevelt's written directives to make them match Hoover's desire for authorization to go beyond the law.

An example of Roosevelt's freewheeling attitude toward Hoover was evident in his response to a Jackson memorandum on the need to limit the FBI's methods to legal ones. In the memorandum, Jackson stated that though the president condoned questionable FBI procedures, such evidence would not be admissible in court. Jackson pointed out to the president, "The subject matter of investigation which the FBI has authority to undertake do not extend beyond charges of suspicion of crime, or of definite subversive activity which does not consist of views or expressions of opinions, but of overt acts of incriminating evidence."

Roosevelt, in angry response, forced the attorney general to withdraw that interpretation and to give Hoover free rein. Jackson reluctantly ate his mandate to Hoover in this April 4, 1941, memorandum: "I had no thought to restrict or alter in any manner the internal operation of the FBI or the

Department of Justice, or its right to proceed in all the fields in which it has been operating." He agreed to remain quiet about his opposition to Hoover's intelligence operations.

GIVEN THE FREE REIN Hoover assumed he had, an extraordinary development took place in his life in 1943. For the first time—one of very few times in his half century as FBI director—an attorney general, assuming his role as Hoover's boss, ordered him to terminate an operation. When Attorney General Francis Biddle learned about the index—known then as the Custodial Detention list—he was deeply disturbed that the program existed and ordered Hoover to eliminate it. Such lists, he told Hoover, were illegal, and so were the bureau's plans for emergency arrests of the people whose names were on the list.

Biddle stated his orders to Hoover in a July 16, 1943, letter:

"There is no statutory authorization or other present justification for keeping a 'custodial detention' list of citizens." He challenged the reliability of the evidence used to compile the list, and he attacked the central underlying premise of the program:

"The notion that it is possible to make a valid determination as to how dangerous a person is . . . without reference to time, environment, and other relevant circumstances, is impractical, unwise, and dangerous." In his order, he told Hoover that the FBI files on individuals who already had been given a "detention" classification must henceforth include a card stipulating, "This classification is unreliable. It is hereby cancelled, and should not be used as a determination of dangerousness or of any other fact."

Biddle's order was forceful, but it contained a flaw. Expecting Hoover to carry out his order, he did not require oversight of how the director executed it. In the absence of oversight, Hoover immediately defied the order. He carried out no part of it.

Deeply angered by the attorney general's action, within a month of the order, Hoover confidentially announced to FBI officials and agents that the bureau would secretly defy it. He lied to Biddle, telling him that the Custodial Detention Index no longer existed. In his world of truth by language technicality, that was accurate. The Custodial Detention Index no longer existed, but its complete content and purpose remained in place. Hoover kept it functioning and simply renamed it. The FBI continued to add names of alleged subversives to the index as though Biddle had never issued his order.

Hoover's defiance of Biddle's order deepened the culture of lawlessness that continued to flourish in the FBI the rest of Hoover's life. The public did not know that culture existed until after the revelations that started with the Media burglary. FBI agents were, of course, a necessary part of the director's elaborate plan to violate the attorney general's order. In an August 14, 1943, letter marked "personal attention strictly confidential" and sent to agents in charge of all FBI field offices, the director announced the continuation of the list, despite the attorney general's order, and also announced the deceptive name change: The "character of investigations of individuals who may be dangerous or potentially dangerous to the public safety or internal security of the United States shall be 'Security Matter' and not 'Custodial Detention.' The phraseology, 'Custodial Detention,' shall no longer be used to designate the character of the investigation, nor shall it be used for any purpose in reports or other communications."

"Henceforth," Hoover told FBI officials, "the cards known as Custodial Detention cards will be known and referred to as Security Index cards, and the list composed of such cards will be known as the Security Index. . . . The fact that the Security Index and Security Index Cards are prepared and maintained should be considered as strictly confidential, and should at no time be mentioned or alluded to in investigative reports, or discussed with agencies or individuals outside the Bureau, other than duly qualified field representatives of the Office of Naval Intelligence and the Military Intelligence Service, and then only on a strictly confidential basis."

Subterfuge accomplished.

Hoover regretted no longer having an attorney general acting as a shield to protect him in regard to the secret list. But through his determined deviousness he demonstrated to everyone inside the bureau that he, not the attorney general, set the rules. He demonstrated inside the FBI that he was in full control of the bureau files and that his asserting control of what the bureau did, including in matters of national security, outweighed his responsibility to obey his superiors, to be truthful, or to obey the law. He demonstrated he was, indeed, a law unto himself—willing to operate without statutory authorization, without approval of the attorney general, and without integrity—in order to accomplish his goals.

Two years later, to Hoover's relief, he got his shield back. He once again had the kind of attorney general he wanted when Tom Clark was appointed by President Harry Truman in 1945. Clark, who would be appointed to the U.S. Supreme Court by President Truman in 1949, created the Security Portfolio, a secret emergency detention program inside the Department of Justice but carried out by the FBI. Under this program, Hoover was authorized to do what he already had been doing: maintain the Security Index in defiance of Biddle's order. The Security Portfolio program called for the issuance of a master arrest warrant by the attorney general at the time of an emergency and for the suspension of the writ of habeas corpus at such times. The FBI was authorized by the attorney general to summarily arrest up to 20,000 people and place them in national security detention camps.

This arrangement gave Hoover control of the list and how it would be used. Once again he was privately assured that the attorney general would protect him, even in conducting illegal programs. However, this arrangement was soon flummoxed by an unexpected development—the passage by Congress of the Emergency Detention Act of 1950, also known as the McCarran Act. This landmark legislation mandated that the FBI create and maintain lists of subversive citizens to be arrested in times of national emergency, what the FBI already had been doing since 1939. During hearings and public debate on the proposed bill, Hoover and the attorney general strongly supported the proposed legislation, but neither of them revealed to Congress that such a program already existed.

The law passed with solid support because of a strong liberal-conservative consensus on national security, a consensus very similar to the one that quickly developed between Democrats and Republicans in Congress after the attacks of September 11, 2001. During hearings on the detention act, liberal leaders in the Senate, including Hubert Humphrey, were emphatic in their admiration for and confidence in Hoover.

Congress achieved important goals for itself and for the FBI when it passed the Emergency Detention Act. By passing the law, Congress increased its public support for strong internal security, considered a political necessity at the time, given the circumstances that year—fear stirred by the arrest the previous year of Judith Coplon for allegedly passing secret documents to the Soviet Union, the arrests of Julius and Ethel Rosenberg for passing secrets of the U.S. bomb-building program to the Soviet Union (they would be executed in 1953), and the entry of the United States into the Korean War. Until this time, internal security had been the nearly exclusive—and in large part secret—bailiwick of the executive branch. Now Congress took a strong stance on internal security but did so while making the executive role in national security even stronger. It required the executive branch to create a security apparatus that would assure that the detention and arrest of subversives would be isolated from the political pressures of the legislative branch. At the same time, Congress detached itself by not establishing congressional oversight of the internal security apparatus it mandated.

There was a strange twist. Hoover was upset about the new law. Congress had just authorized what it thought was a great increase in power for the bureau. It had done so without establishing oversight over how Hoover would use that power. What more could he have wanted?

Members of Congress did not realize that because the director already had unilaterally assumed so much power for years in regard to national security matters, that he regarded what Congress and the public thought was an expansion of his power as the opposite. Publicly, he warmly embraced the passing of the Emergency Detention Act of 1950 and happily accepted the respect and adulation he received from members of Congress during the hearings that led up to the passage of the law. Inside the bureau, however, this law that was widely regarded among civil libertarians as a disastrous infringement on rights was seen as a disastrous infringement on the FBI's power.

Once again he had a solution: Just as he had defied Biddle's order, now he would defy Congress.

As soon as the measure became law, Hoover started developing secret plans to evade it because he thought it was not sufficiently repressive. In his mind, there were now two detention programs—the one Congress had just established and the one he had long been operating—and they were at odds with each other. The secret detention plan he had been carrying out without statutory support was more repressive, and he was determined to continue using those harsher standards, no matter what was now required by the new law.

Many defenders of constitutional rights thought the Emergency Detention Act would lead to the suppression of speech and to unfair accusations against people who were merely liberals, not communists. Like Congress, these opponents of the law didn't know that Hoover had long carried out, and would continue to carry out, a secret and much more repressive program than the one Congress had just made the law of the land. To the liberals in Congress who joined conservatives in passing the law, the Emergency Detention Act was the forceful measure they believed was needed at this time when anticommunism, especially as embodied in the hearings recently started by Senator Joseph McCarthy, had made many people fearful about whether domestic communists were penetrating the federal government. But to the FBI and the Department of Justice, the new law was too weak. Under its provisions, people could be placed on the detention list and apprehended only if they had been active in subversive organizations since January 1, 1949. Under the secret Justice/FBI program already in place, people could be added to the list if they had at *any* time been engaged in what the FBI regarded as subversive activities and whether or not they belonged to a subversive organization. Another difference was that under the new law, habeas corpus was not suspended, and individual warrants would be required. Under the FBI's secret program long in place, habeas corpus would be suspended and blanket arrest warrants would be issued.

Without Congress knowing, Hoover secretly took the strongest possible action against the new law. He asked Tom Clark's successor, Attorney General J. Howard McGrath, to order the FBI to ignore the will of Congress. McGrath agreed, but he was reluctant to put such an order in writing. However, just two weeks after the law was passed, McGrath verbally directed Hoover to disregard the new law and to "proceed with the program as previously outlined." Hoover was advised that "all persons now or hereafter included by the bureau on the Security Index should be considered subjects for immediate apprehension" during a national emergency. Two years later—after more prodding by Hoover—in 1952, McGrath gave Hoover what he wanted: written approval to violate the new law. In a memorandum, he fully endorsed the "bureau's concepts of the Detention Program and the Security Index standards." In early 1953, President Dwight D. Eisenhower's attorney general, Herbert Brownell, also agreed that the FBI should ignore the requirements of the Emergency Detention Act of 1950 and should continue using its own more repressive standards in preparing for the detention of the people Hoover considered the most dangerous Americans.

That Hoover could, with the support of attorneys general from both political parties, disregard this major new law meant his superiors had placed him beyond the reach of the law. That was the kind of protection he liked. William W. Keller, an international security scholar, sees this as a seminal moment in the establishment of Hoover's power over internal security matters. After the bureau "achieved sufficient insularity of operations to apply detention standards that were at variance with those mandated by law," Keller says, the power wielded by the director was so great that it "suggested the emergence of an agency that resembled more the model of a police state."

From then on, Hoover assumed he could expand his authority in internal security matters and that he could get away with secretly shaping and loosening the standards for selection and detention of subversives.

It was during debate of the detention bill, Keller has concluded, that Congress "shut the door to a more sophisticated view of domestic communism and the actual magnitude of the threat it posed after 1950 to American government and society. They adopted the bipolar thinking that came to dominate the field of internal security for a generation. The actions of the liberal senators in introducing the detention legislation and their consistent support for the FBI, the backing of the liberal press and the attitude of liberal organizations all buttressed the view that internal security powers should be centralized in the FBI as administrative functions."

LACK OF OVERSIGHT was essential to Hoover's growing power. So was his popularity. Recognizing that, he became a master of public relations. The FBI did not enter American consciousness as an important and popular government agency until it successfully defeated John Dillinger and other criminals who had terrorized the country, particularly the Midwest, briefly in the early 1930s. Until then, the average American was hardly aware of the bureau. Hoover grasped that moment of public enthusiasm and turned it into a public relations bonanza that transformed the FBI and the director into popular icons. Iconic stature provided a shield that immunized the director and the bureau from criticism. So great was his public adulation after the killing of Dillinger that the director briefly considered running for president. When a private straw poll revealed, to his surprise, that he would not have the support of law enforcement agents outside the FBI, he settled instead for becoming one of the best-known and most powerful public officials in the country.

Determined to expand and sustain this new popularity, Hoover opened a public relations division within the bureau. The public relations arm soon became nearly the largest and most productive such operation in the federal government, second only to the one operated by the U.S. Marines. Knowing that some members of Congress thought it inappropriate to fund a public relations operation in the federal law enforcement agency, he called it the Crime Records Division—which it was not. "A propagandist more than a cop," wrote historian and media studies professor Stuart Ewen, "Hoover helped inaugurate a merciless publicity environment that again and again depicted the United States as a society under siege." Under Hoover's byline, his staff and freelance ghostwriters penned dozens of books and hundreds of articles in a wide variety of magazines and newspaper columns where he expressed his views on countless subjects. He turned himself into the go-to government man for thoughts on crime, communism, war, religion, child-rearing, and even on how to make the best popovers. The material created by the division ranged from manifestos against communism to children's coloring books on crime to *Mickey Mouse Club* television episodes broadcast from the director's office to confidential tips, true and untrue, to "friendly" journalists about the personal lives of powerful people the director considered enemies of the bureau. His goal was achieved: During the presidency of Harry Truman, polls showed that Hoover was more popular with the public than the president was.

One of the most important ways the heroic brand of the FBI and its director was made forever a part of American popular culture was through the strong liaison Hoover established with Hollywood studios immediately after the killing of Dillinger. Seven FBI-centered feature films were made in 1935 alone, including Warner Brothers' *G-Man* starring James Cagney. The public didn't realize that the FBI often was fighting serious crime much more in the movies than it was in real life. With a few notable exceptions, the bulk of criminal cases solved by the FBI, especially after World War II, were the easiest types of cases, bank robberies and stolen cars, crimes usually solved by local and state law enforcement agencies.

Scripts of proposed movies and all segments of *The F.B.I.*, ABC network's hit prime-time Sunday evening dramatic series about the FBI that ran from 1965 to 1974, were carefully controlled by the director himself. He required that all scripts be approved by him, and all actors and other people who worked on network and studio film projects be investigated by the FBI.

The director's close ties with Hollywood also served his political purposes well in the 1950s, when Hollywood executives became the first employers to blacklist employees on the basis of unverified FBI surveillance of alleged communists and alleged associates of communists.

The combination of no oversight of his operations and his large and successful public relations operations led to his achieving the distinction of being one of the most powerful appointed officials—many have said *the* most powerful—who has ever served in the federal government. His popularity was widely recognized over many years, but how he used that power—much of which was wielded secretly—would not be known to the public until the Media burglars released files.

FROM 1953 THROUGH 1971, when the Security Index was revealed in the Media documents, the list of alleged subversives was continuously expanded by the FBI, and so were the criteria by which people were chosen to be placed on the list. Increasingly flexible standards were used in the 1960s to decide what types of Americans would be added to it. Hoover was particularly concerned by the mid-1960s that not enough New Left people were being added. He was stumped by how to categorize them. Many, he lamented, were anarchists who were not joiners. Previously, harvesting names from membership and subscription lists had been an efficient way to expand the lists. Nonjoiners made that old method useless. "In many instances," he complained in an April 2, 1968, letter to agents at all field offices, "security investigations of these individuals are not being initiated." Sometimes, he said, "subjects are not being recommended for inclusion on the Security Index merely because no membership in a basic revolutionary organization could be established." He told agents not to let that stop them. "Even if a subject's membership in a subversive organization cannot be proven, his inclusion on the Security Index may often be justified because of activities which establish his anarchistic tendencies. . . . A subject without any organization affiliation can qualify for the Security Index by virtue of his public pronouncements and activities which establish his rejection of law and order and reveal him to be a potential threat to the security of the United States."

Later that year, Hoover made the standards for adding names to the list even more nebulous: "It is not possible to formulate any hard-and-fast standards by which the dangerousness of individual members or affiliates or revolutionary organizations may be automatically measured because of manner revolutionary organizations function and great scope and variety of activities. Exercise sound judgment and discretion in evaluation of importance and dangerousness of individual members or affiliates. . . . Where there is doubt an individual may be a current threat to the internal security of the nation, the question should be resolved in the interest of security and investigation conducted."

WHILE THE INTENSE SEARCH for the Media burglars continued in 1971, Hoover still assumed he could operate the bureau with disregard for the law. He was outraged that files were being revealed, but he—with the attorney general, John Mitchell, as his enabler—was defiant. This time Hoover's defiance was in response to the repeal of the Emergency Detention Act of 1950.

In the fall of 1971, just months after Congress, the press, and the public had learned about the bureau policies and practices revealed in the Media documents, Congress repealed the Emergency Detention Act of 1950 with wide bipartisan support. A national campaign promoting repeal of the act had been conducted by the Japanese American Citizens League. The 25,000-member organization set out to convince Americans that because of the detention act every American lived with the threat of being unjustly and indefinitely incarcerated in the manner that 110,000 Japanese Americans, two-thirds of them American citizens, had been incarcerated in remote camps after Japan attacked Pearl Harbor in World War II. They were incarcerated despite the fact that there was no evidence that Japanese American citizens or Japanese immigrants had engaged in any subversive action against the United States. Only the repeal of the 1950 law, the league claimed, could remove the threat of the government taking such repressive steps again. Another impetus for repeal came from widespread revulsion to a 1968 report by the House Un-American Activities Committee that recommended the establishment of camps to detain black nationalists and communists. This radical recommendation by the House committee raised fears that the 1950 law could indeed be used, as many people had feared, to detain people on the basis of race or political opinion. There also were rampant rumors that the government was preparing the six detention camps that were established under the 1950 detention act to be used to detain subversives.

During the hearings on repeal of the Emergency Detention Act, Nixon administration officials in the Department of Justice spoke forcefully in support of its repeal. Their positive public stance, however, stood in direct contradiction to what the attorney general would do immediately after the law was passed. Prior to the vote on the bill, at a hearing of the House Judiciary Committee, Assistant Attorney General Robert Mardian testified that the Department of Justice was "unequivocally in favor" of repealing the law. Deputy Attorney General Kleindienst, in a letter to the committee, said continuation of the act would be "extremely offensive to many Americans."

In what seemed like a triumph for basic rights and the erasure of a stain, Congress repealed the Emergency Detention Act of 1950 and replaced it with the Non-Detention Act. The new 1971 law declared, "No citizen shall be imprisoned or otherwise detained by the United States except pursuant to an Act of Congress." When President Nixon signed the measure on September 25, 1971, he said the repeal was "wholeheartedly supported by this administration":

No president has ever attempted to use the provisions of this act. . . . Nevertheless, the mere continued existence of these legal provisions has aroused concern among many Americans that the act might someday be used to apprehend and detain citizens who hold unpopular views. . . . I have supported and signed this repeal in order to put an end to such suspicions. In taking this action, I want to underscore this Nation's abiding respect for the liberty of the individual. . . . There is no place in American life for the kind of anxiety—however unwarranted—which the Emergency Detention Act has evidently engendered. . . . We do have a great deal to fear if we begin to lose faith in our constitutional ideals. The legislation I have signed today keeps faith with those ideals.

The cumulative crimes known as Watergate had not yet started to be revealed. Consequently, Nixon's expression of reverent regard for constitutional ideals was not received at the time with the cynicism that would have greeted them in little more than a year when his lawless White House operations started coming to light. Interestingly, the meaning of the Non-Detention Act was contested in litigation in the aftermath of the 9/11 attacks. President George W. Bush claimed the Non-Detention Act of 1971 was intended to restrict imprisonment and detention by the attorney general but had no impact on the authority of the president or military authorities to detain and imprison. An analysis conducted in 2005 at the request of Congress by its Research Service concluded, "Legislative debate, committee reports, and the political context of 1971 indicate that when Congress enacted Section 4001(a) it intended the statutory language to restrict all detentions by the executive branch, not merely those by the Attorney General. Lawmakers, both supporters and opponents of Section 4001(a) recognized that it would restrict the President and military authorities." The law was generally interpreted that way when it was passed in 1971, except by the two people most responsible for enforcing it—the FBI director and the attorney general.

J. Edgar Hoover, as usual, interpreted the new Non-Detention Act his way.

Just as he had in 1950, after the president signed the act in 1971, the FBI director did what he had done twenty-one years earlier when the Emergency Detention Act of 1950 became law. He set in motion secret plans to defy it.

Plans for his new subterfuge started the day after Congress voted to repeal the act, when the head of the FBI's Intelligence Division, Richard Cotter, made the case in a September 17, 1971, memorandum to the director for continuing to maintain the Security Index. "The potential dangerousness of subversives is probably even greater now than before the repeal of the Act, since they no doubt feel safer now to conspire in the destruction of this country." Bolstering the case that Hoover would make in his request that the attorney general approve an order for the bureau to flaunt the law, D. J. Dalbey, head of the bureau's Office of Legal Counsel, wrote in a memorandum that repeal of the Emergency Detention Act did not affect either the bureau's "basic investigative authority" or its right to carry "in its files an assessment of each principal subversive which would be sufficient to mark him for Government attention should need arise in a national emergency." Despite bureau officials' certainty about their conclusion, once again they wanted the attorney general to give them a secret protective shield for the operations they now planned to carry out in defiance of Congress. The bureau needed clear authority, Dalbey advised Hoover, to "protect" it if "some spokesman of the extreme left" claimed the repeal undercut such investigative authority.

Ironically, the authority Hoover and other bureau officials now felt they had lost by the detention act being repealed was the authority that they had thought in 1950, at the time the Emergency Detention Act was enacted, was inadequate. But now they felt naked, unprotected. With the repeal of the Emergency Detention Act, there was no detention law—not even the one they regarded as inadequate because it was not sufficiently repressive. But as long as a detention act was in place, it was possible for the FBI to hide behind it, even as the bureau went beyond what it mandated. Now there was no law to hide behind—only a law to defy.

Despite the shifting nature of their relationship in the past year, the director appealed to Attorney General Mitchell. Hoover told him that, in the absence of the law just repealed, he could rely instead on old presidential directives as a rationale for creating lists of subversives—something he had done many times in the absence of laws. But in the event of public disclosure, Hoover thought reliance on those old directives was a dangerous option. He told Mitchell he preferred to have the official backing of the attorney general for maintaining lists of subversives.

Mitchell, who, along with his top aides, had publicly supported the repeal, now privately became an enthusiastic accomplice in Hoover's plan to defy it. The two highest law enforcement officials in the country secretly agreed that the FBI could ignore the repeal. The bureau would continue to choose people it considered to be dangerous and place them on detention lists. In a secret October 22, 1971, memorandum, the attorney general assured the director that the FBI could do everything it had done before. The FBI's authority in this area, Mitchell wrote, "remained unaffected by repeal of the emergency detention title. . . . The repeal . . . does not alter or limit the FBI's authority and responsibility to record, file and index information. . . . An FBI administrative index compiled and maintained to assist the Bureau in making readily retrievable and available the results of its investigations into subversive activities and related matters is not prohibited by the repeal of the Emergency Detention Act." Mitchell also gave the FBI exclusive control of the index. That meant the bureau no longer would have to submit the names of alleged subversives to the department for review, except for a monthly report on the federal employees the bureau added to the list.

Hoover won. The sixteenth—and, as it would turn out, the last—attorney general under whom he would serve gave him carte blanche to disobey a new law that had been designed, in part, to wipe out this part of his intelligence operations. That was quite an accomplishment. Not only could the bureau secretly continue to maintain and build the index of subversive Americans, but it would, wrote Mitchell, make the "sole determination as to which individuals should be included" on the list. Vetting of those people by the Department of Justice officials often had been perfunctory, and now, under Mitchell's new order, it would not exist at all.

Following the pattern of subterfuge he had established many years earlier, as a guard against discovery of the bureau's defiance of the law, Hoover now changed the name of the index again. This time it was changed from the Security Index to the Administrative Index, or ADEX. In 1943, he had changed the index from the Custodial Index to the Security Index to hide his refusal to enforce Attorney General Biddle's order to destroy it. This time the name change was done to hide his deception of Congress. In case anyone ever asked, technically there no longer was a Security Index. With the magic of language, Hoover had once again eliminated the index while actually keeping it. No one outside the FBI would know the index was still there and continued to grow. Under his new plan, no one would know that the significant public consensus and nearly unanimous congressional decision that the Emergency Detention Act should be repealed had been secretly upended by the FBI director with the approval of the attorney general.

Subterfuge accomplished again.

IN 1971, J. Edgar Hoover experienced both the cold shoulder and the warm embrace of Attorney General John Mitchell. The attorney general's support of Hoover's defiance of Congress's Non-Detention Act just days after it was passed contrasted sharply with how he treated the director in March 1971. At that time, Mitchell ignored the director's request that he

seek a court order to make it a crime to publish stories about the stolen files
or to possess copies of them.

The explanation for his contrasting treatment of Hoover in the spring
and fall of 1971 probably is rooted in the complex, secret, and dangerous web
in which Hoover, Mitchell, and Nixon were entangled, beginning in the
summer of 1970. The three men were ideological soul mates, but they had
markedly different priorities then.

By the time the Media burglary took place in March, Mitchell and
Nixon undoubtedly still resented what Hoover had done to them a year earlier when he took steps that defeated Nixon's major effort to expand intelligence operations against the people he regarded as enemies of his war plans
and his reelection plans.

A year later, at the very time Congress, the press, and the public were
learning from the Media files for the first time about the FBI's spying on
antiwar and other activists and about the bureau's goal to make Americans "paranoid," the president and the attorney general were involved in a
highly secret effort to create an alternative to the expanded domestic intelligence plan Hoover had forced Nixon to kill in 1970. Some of the practices
exposed by the Media files—as well as some of Hoover's practices not yet
exposed—were similar to dirty tricks programs the attorney general and
the president had by that time been desperately trying to expand for more
than a year. The then still deeply secret White House plans involved bizarre
and shocking criminal operations that would be conducted from the White
House. They included the plan to burglarize Democratic National Committee headquarters at the Watergate Hotel and the plan to break into the
office of Daniel Ellsberg's psychiatrist. Among the crimes White House
staffers planned then but did not execute were the bombing of the Brookings Institution, a liberal think tank in Washington, and the assassination
of columnist Jack Anderson.

Not until 1973, as investigations of Watergate crimes commenced, did the
public learn about either the intelligence agency collaboration plan Nixon
tried to put in place in 1970 or the wild crimes that were being planned
in the White House in the spring of 1971. Both efforts were driven by the
president's intense desire to target people he regarded as enemies, primarily
antiwar activists and journalists, even more than they already were being
targeted by multiple intelligence agencies.

Hoover and Nixon had been close friends since the director and Nixon,
as a young member of Congress from California from 1946 to 1952, worked
together closely in choosing who the House Un-American Activities Com-

mittee would accuse of being communists, or fellow travelers with communists, often on the basis of secret unverified FBI informer files provided confidentially to the committee by Hoover. The two of them had been close collaborators ever since then. In 1970, though, Nixon was furious when his old friend Hoover forced him to kill his intelligence collaboration plan. Most, if not all, presidents under whom Hoover had served as director had used the FBI to gather political intelligence on their behalf, often against their political opponents, but no president before Nixon had pressured Hoover to collaborate with other intelligence agencies. Hoover was willing to do just about anything presidents asked him except that. He despised working with other agencies. He had always been a lone wolf, not a collaborator. He wanted to keep all domestic intelligence work under the bureau's exclusive control and within the walls and files of the FBI.

The two old friends, Nixon and Hoover, played a convoluted series of potentially explosive tricks on each other in 1970 and 1971. Their divergent priorities came between them. Nixon was obsessed with a desire to quash the antiwar movement. Hoover shared that obsession, but his other obsession, fear of losing his job, was his top priority. Given his friendship and political collaboration with Nixon over many years, he undoubtedly expected Nixon to endorse his continued service as FBI director at least as enthusiastically as President Lyndon Johnson had. In 1964, President Johnson had issued an executive order exempting Hoover from compulsory retirement at age seventy. Johnson hailed him then as "a quiet, humble and magnificent public servant . . . a hero to millions of citizens and an anathema to all evil men. . . . No other American now or in our past, has served the cause of justice so faithfully and so well." Johnson's high praise for his former neighbor was easily believed by the public, for by 1964 Hoover had long been an American icon. Under Nixon, the platitudes about Hoover continued, but the atmosphere was more treacherous, for neither Hoover nor Nixon felt an ethical imperative when loyalty competed with self-interest.

Immediately after Nixon's secret plan for intelligence agencies to collaborate—known as the Huston Plan for Tom Charles Huston, the young White House aide who designed it on Nixon's behalf—was approved in 1970 by the heads of all intelligence agencies, Hoover informed the president he would not go along with the plan unless every request for illegal work by the FBI under the joint operation—bugging, wiretapping, home or office burglary, all of which the FBI secretly had been doing for many years—was first authorized in writing by the president.

That did it. Rather than agree to Hoover's demand for written presidential authorization for illegal projects, Nixon killed the intelligence col-laboration plan before it started, as Hoover must have been sure he would. The president was unwilling to create a paper trail that would be evidence he had asked intelligence agencies to engage in illegal activities. Interest-ingly, Nixon did not exert the same caution with the massive recorded trail of evidence his White House tapes created daily—the definitive record that later contributed to public certainty about his criminal behavior and thus to his decision to resign.

When the dispute between the president and Hoover became known years later, it was speculated that by that time in his life Hoover had become opposed to breaking the law. Comments he wrote to Sullivan make it clear that was not the case:

> For years and years and years I have approved opening mail and other similar operations, but no. It is becoming more and more dangerous and we are apt to get caught. I am not opposed to doing this. I am not opposed to continuing the burglaries and the opening of mail and other similar activities, providing someone higher than myself approves of it. . . . I no longer want to accept the sole responsibility. [If] the attorney general or some other high-ranking person in the White House [approves] then I will carry out their decision. But I am not going to accept the responsibil-ity myself anymore, even though I've done it for years. . . . I am not going to do that anymore.

IN HOOVER'S DEALINGS with the attorney general and the White House during the Nixon administration, he had found ways, as he often had in the past, to have his cake and eat it too—creating an impression that he was abiding by the law when actually he was conducting illegal opera-tions. Even as he told the president he was unwilling to make unilateral decisions for the bureau to engage in illegal intelligence activities, he was in fact continuing such projects and initiating new ones, including treacherous dirty tricks.

Mitchell's refusal to respond to Hoover's request at the time of the Media burglary that the Department of Justice go to court in an effort to criminal-ize distribution and publication of the Media files might have come from a desire to prevent discovery of the crimes then being planned at the White House. Seeing the high public interest in the information revealed in the Media files, the attorney general would have realized that this first public glimpse of the FBI's domestic intelligence operations revealed the tip of a very large hidden domestic intelligence iceberg. As someone involved in both the failed 1970 intelligence collaboration plan and now, in the spring of 1971, in the plans for crimes to be carried out by the White House, Mitchell, and also the president, probably were desperate for the intelligence iceberg not to become visible, especially while they were in the process of making the iceberg bigger. That may have made them fear that an effort in court to suppress distribution and publication of the Media files might stimulate new interest and lead not only to more revelations about secret FBI intelligence operations but also to exposure of the unprecedented and bizarre criminal operations then being developed in the White House.

Whatever caused the attorney general to ignore Hoover's March 1971 request that he seek an injunction against publication of the Media files— excessive pique at Hoover's 1970 behavior, excessive caution about exposing criminal operations being hatched in the White House, or excessive fear of the damage Hoover could cause because of what he knew and could reveal about demands for illegal operations he carried out at the president's request—a few months later, in the fall of 1971, Mitchell gave the director reason to be optimistic when he gave him written approval to defy the law Congress had just passed requiring an end to the bureau's maintaining lists of subversives to be detained.

Hoover's secret FBI had trumped Congress just seven months after the Media burglary. From inside the FBI, it appeared Hoover's subterfuge might continue, despite the Media revelations. Even before the burglary, however, Hoover's world had started to change. Some critics had surfaced, including a few former agents. They had aired complaints, but they had not revealed details of the bureau's operations. Hoover thought he had easily discredited them as just a few disgruntled agents. Nevertheless, he no longer felt completely secure. He was seventy-six in 1971 and, bureau insiders later reported, feared his enemies might learn about his illegal actions and use that information to force him out of office. He had become meticulous about appearing to be abiding strictly by the law. But the Media files were a profound challenge. They provided the public with firsthand evidence—some of it in his own words—of how he operated the FBI. He was still able to fool Congress and to engage the attorney general as an enabler in violating the law, but he could not refute the truth of his own secret files now on display for the first time.

15

COINTELPRO Hovers

ONE OMINOUS "message in a bottle" from the Media burglars remained a secret—COINTELPRO. Despite having demonstrated inside the bureau in September 1971 that he was still a master at subterfuge, it was not possible for the director and his top aides to rest easy that fall. They were determined to stay the course, but they also feared daily that the worst was yet to come. What if someone was able to figure out what COINTELPRO was?

COINTELPRO hovered over the FBI.

The possible exposure of the program was regarded inside the bureau as the most dangerous bureau operation that could be exposed. It was assumed by bureau officials that the public's reaction to it would be much more explosive than the reaction to the Security Index had been. As threatening as the Security Index was, people inside the FBI realized that if COINTELPRO became known, people would realize that the bureau conducted operations far more controversial and damaging to Americans' rights than creating lists of alleged subversives to be arrested during a national emergency. For that reason, FBI officials desperately hoped in the spring of 1971 that COINTELPRO never would become public, that it would remain buried in the bureau's most secret files. But they lived with a grim truth throughout that spring: The Media burglars were still free and were able to distribute files at any time, and for all FBI officials knew, the burglars might have a file that would reveal the existence of COINTELPRO.

Clever as the director had been through the years in protecting himself and the bureau, he would have realized that if COINTELPRO records became public, it would be impossible for him to avoid responsibility. Unknown outside the bureau, there was a long trail of secret files that provided detailed evidence that Hoover himself created the COINTELPRO operations, sought proposals for them, and had authorized and monitored most of them. Not only that, but he had put a premium on the development of COINTELPRO projects. Only the best agents were to be permitted to conduct them, and they would be rewarded for doing so. He had kept these operations a secret from most attorneys general he served under, including the current one—not that Attorney General Mitchell would have opposed them.

The only Media file that mentioned COINTELPRO arrived in my mailbox on April 5, 1971. The term was near the top of a routing slip that included the request that agents distribute the attached article that had been published in *Barron's,* the weekly financial publication, on how campus protests should be handled more forcefully by college presidents. There was no

This document, a simple routing slip, had more impact than any other file stolen from the Media office. The term at the top, COINTELPRO, had never been seen before outside the bureau. It was the name of one of Hoover's most carefully guarded secrets—dirty tricks operations conducted against dissidents.

clue about what the term "COINTELPRO" meant, but simply reporting about the file that contained the term set off an alarm inside the FBI. To bureau officials, a very important shoe had just dropped. As soon as my story about that file—written without the unexplained "COINTELPRO" term—was published on April 6, headquarters officials realized that one of their worst fears, public exposure of COINTELPRO, had just come closer to being realized. They had been waiting to see if that file would be released by the burglars. When it was, they knew then with certainty that the term existed outside the FBI for the first time. Something had to be done. My story on the files that arrived that day from the burglars emphasized the one with the COINTELPRO routing slip and was headlined "FBI Secretly Prods Colleges on New Left." On a copy of the story included in the MED-BURG investigative file, Hoover handwrote three brief notes, each one a request for documents mentioned in the story.

He acted quickly. On the same day the story was published, he wrote to the heads of all the field offices then conducting COINTELPRO operations and told them that the program's "90-day status letters will no longer be required and should be discontinued." That change suggested that the director was trying to increase secrecy about the program by eliminating one of the layers of reporting that documented progress in COINTELPRO operations. But in that same memorandum to field offices he also made it clear that COINTELPRO was still an important program despite the potential danger that could result from its name now being known outside the bureau. He told the agents in charge of the field offices that they must "continue aggressive and imaginative participation in the program."

Two days after he learned that the COINTELPRO routing slip had been released by the burglars, Hoover wrote a letter to the attorney general. His April 8 letter to Mitchell seemed to be designed as a warning that something new and controversial might emerge at any time from the Media files. Specifically, he expressed concern that the burglars might make COIN-TELPRO public, but he did not mention the routing slip that already had been released. He informed the attorney general that the term, used alone, did not make the program "readily comprehensible." Perhaps still hoping that the routing slip would spark no interest and COINTELPRO would remain secret, even from the attorney general, Hoover did not explain the nature of COINTELPRO operations, only that they existed.

By three weeks after the bureau learned from my story that the COIN-TELPRO routing slip had been released, concern at FBI headquarters apparently had increased dramatically about the possible exposure of the program. Hoover made a radical decision: he eliminated those programs he had started in 1956 and that he regarded as so important to his intelligence operation.

He took that extreme step after FBI official Charles Brennan wrote a memo to him on April 27, 1971, recommending the closure of COIN-TELPRO. This should be done, Brennan wrote, in order "to afford additional security to our sensitive techniques and operations. . . . These programs involve a variety of sensitive intelligence techniques and disruptive activities, which are afforded close supervision at the Seat of Government [a bureau term for the national FBI headquarters in Washington]. They have been carefully supervised with all actions being afforded prior Bureau approval and an effort has been made to avoid engaging in harassment. Although successful over the years, it is felt they should now be discontinued for security reasons because of their sensitivity." Beginning three years later, as some COINTELPRO operations were revealed for the first time, it would be discovered that the operations not only did not avoid harassment but were designed specifically to be harassment, often of law-abiding Americans, sometimes for years and sometimes by provoking violence.

The director immediately agreed with the recommendation to close COINTELPRO. On April 28, he sent a memorandum to field offices ordering the immediate discontinuance of all COINTELPRO operations. Given the importance of COINTELPRO to the FBI, this would appear to have been a profoundly significant decision, one that would be disruptive to some of the major operations of the bureau. That was not a problem, however, for just as changing the name of the Security Index and its predecessor, the Custodial Detention Index, were ruses to cover his earlier defiance, the internal announcement that COINTELPRO was being closed was not what it appeared to be.

When the details of COINTELPRO started to be revealed, more than two years later, reporters at first accepted the FBI's official statement that the program no longer existed, that it had been canceled on April 28, 1971. That was not true. Consistent with past Hoover practice, his order to eliminate COINTELPRO was designed to protect and to deceive. Once again the devil was in Hoover's nomenclature. The program was no longer called COINTELPRO, but the program itself, with all the same qualities and practices, continued. From now on, Hoover wrote when he notified FBI officials that he had "closed" COINTELPRO, such operations would be conducted on an ad hoc basis, each approved by the director. That was exactly how they had been operated before. The only difference was that now the operations did not have the COINTELPRO designation. Therefore, if someone asked—as people did, beginning a year after the burglary—FBI officials would be able to say—as they did—"That program doesn't exist anymore." But it did.

New COINTELPRO-like operations, in fact, continued to be initiated at that time in 1971, including efforts to destroy the reputation of John Kerry, after he testified before Senator J. William Fulbright's Senate Foreign Relations Committee and called the war in Vietnam "a tragic mistake." The FBI eventually created a 2,934-page file on Kerry—the future Massachusetts senator, 2004 Democratic presidential candidate and secretary of state— and a 19,978-page file on Vietnam Veterans Against the War, the prominent organization of veterans returning from Vietnam he led in 1971. In fact, many such operations were conducted against individuals and organizations throughout the mid-1970s.

Given that the COINTELPRO operations had not been revealed by May 2, 1972, the day Hoover died, a little more than a year after the term surfaced on a Media file, he may have remained confident until his death that the program, perhaps his darkest secret, would remain hidden forever. That COINTELPRO had not been revealed by then may have convinced Hoover that the legacy he had spent a lifetime developing might not be redefined by what the Media files revealed or by the accusations a few former agents made against him in the last two years of his life—or by the powerful secrets he knew had not yet been revealed. Maybe those secrets would remain sealed.

HOOVER'S STRONGEST SUPPORTERS pulled out all the stops in the spring of 1971 to buoy his spirits. They encircled him with warm support and angry defenses in that year that was marked by harsh public criticism—a time that was what *New York Times* columnist Tom Wicker described in an April 15, 1971, column as "the worst period of controversy Mr. Hoover has encountered in his 47-year career."

Thanks to a campaign by the bureau's public relations office, on May 10, 1971, the forty-seventh anniversary of Hoover's becoming director of the bureau, seventy-one members of Congress placed tributes to him in the *Congressional Record*.

Some of the extremely critical reaction that spring was from unexpected sources. Two publications that over many years had written only laudatory commentary about the director, *Time* magazine and *Life* magazine, delivered harsh criticism after the burglary. There was evidence, *Time* reported, that Hoover's "fiefdom," the FBI, was "crumbling, largely because of his own mistakes. The FBI's spirit is sapped, its morale low, its initiative stifled." The FBI had become, according to *Time,* "a secretive, enormously powerful Government agency under dictatorial rule, operating on its own, answerable to no authority except the judgments—or whims—of one man."

On April 9, just a month after the burglary and two weeks after the first stolen files became public, *Life* ran a striking image of the director on its cover. It was a portrait of a sculpture of Hoover as a Roman emperor, complete with toga, with the title "The 47-year Reign of J. Edgar Hoover: Emperor of the FBI." Inside the magazine, the headline was, "After almost half a century in total and imperious charge: G-Man under fire." Pointing to reaction to recent revelations, *Life* noted that "the thrust of the criticism appears to be changing, and Mr. Hoover has drawn the attention of more powerful critics. Now he has been challenged—of all places—on the floor of the House. It has been widely charged that the director's imperious disregard for any but his own views of the national interest diminishes his Bureau's effectiveness and has even become a serious infringement on civil rights."

A month after the *Life* cover appeared, Hoover made a rare public appearance. He spoke at a dinner sponsored by the American Newspaper Women's Club in Washington. He had accepted an invitation to introduce the person who would be honored that evening, Martha Mitchell, the wife of the attorney general. She was a prominent personality and a favorite of the Nixon administration at the time because of her frequent brash and funny public comments about whatever was on her mind. Later, when she called reporters in the middle of the night with inside secrets about Watergate crimes, she was considered a liability to the Nixon administration who had to be hushed. But now, in the spring of 1971, when Hoover warmly introduced her, she was still considered an amusing asset. She urged the audience to look at Mr. Hoover carefully that evening, for "when you've seen one FBI Director, you have seen them all."

In a rare jovial mood, Hoover nearly matched Martha Mitchell's ability to draw laughs. "I know that those of you who subscribe to an alleged national magazine may have had some difficulty recognizing me in the conventional clothes I am wearing this evening. But, like ordinary people, we emperors do have our problems, and I regret to say that my toga did not get back from the cleaners on time."

President Nixon defended Hoover a month after the burglary when he answered questions at the annual convention of the American Society of Newspaper Editors, the same convention where CIA director Helms denied the CIA conducted domestic spying. Asked by one of the editors to comment on the fact that "J. Edgar Hoover very recently seems to have become one of the favorite 'whipping boys' of a number of prominent Americans," Nixon responded angrily. The criticisms of Hoover, he said, "are unfair . . . and malicious. . . . I would ask the editors of the nation's papers to be fair about the situation. He, like any man who is a strong man and an able man . . . has made many enemies. . . . He has been nonpolitical . . . nonpartisan. Despite all of the talk about surveillance and bugging and the rest, let me say I have been in police states, and the idea that this is a police state is just pure nonsense. And every . . . paper in the country ought to say that. . . . As long as I am in this office, we are going to be sure that not the FBI or any other organization engages in any [surveillance] activity except where the national interests or the protection of innocent people requires it, and then it will be as limited as it possibly can be." As Nixon made those comments that day, his own secret plans to greatly increase political surveillance and dirty tricks against his perceived enemies were well under way.

The hundreds of newspaper editors assembled in the convention hall that day with Nixon accepted the president's observations without questioning him. Many of them may have been surprised when Washington journalists later reported stories about not only the dirty tricks of Hoover's FBI but also those of the Nixon Plumbers team.

Throughout that awful year in Hoover's life, he was defended repeatedly by former FBI agents—individually and by the Society of Former Agents of the FBI. Organized in 1937, the society now rallied around him at meetings throughout the country. Members in chapter after chapter unanimously passed resolutions backing the director. With 5,500 members at the time, the society had been fairly independent of FBI headquarters until 1964, when the director and the society decided they needed each other and established a formal bond. They entered into an agreement that members of the society would be deputized to help the bureau round up the thousands of people listed on the Security Index in the event of a national emergency. Otherwise, the society was primarily a source of fellowship and was an informal but very valuable high-level employment agency for former agents. It found jobs for former agents in security positions and high-level executive positions in American corporations, where many former agents landed. For example, John S. Bugas, the former head of the Detroit FBI office, upon retiring from the bureau became vice president of Ford Motor Company and a close friend and aide of Henry Ford II. Such connections often were either a personal or a professional benefit to the bureau. One of the benefits of the close connection with Ford was that the corporation paid for various special events for the FBI, including a banquet at the society's 1970 national convention at Disneyland, where the guest of honor was Efrem Zimbalist Jr., star of the *The F.B.I.,* the very popular weekly television series sponsored by Ford. Hoover was there and, as usual, treated Zimbalist like he was not only a real FBI agent but FBI agent number one. At Hoover's invitation, Zimbalist often spoke at various gatherings of agents, including the graduation ceremony of new agents.

The society's members tended to be politically conservative. Some were extremely right-wing, such as Willard Cleon Skousen, a John Birch Society official who wrote *The Naked Communist* in 1958 and whose ideas have been promoted in recent years by commentator Glenn Beck and by some Tea Party leaders. Some other former agents in the society created private organizations that specialized in using the skills they had learned in the bureau, including planting rumors about politicians Hoover did not like. Senator William Proxmire of Wisconsin, Senator George McGovern, Senator William Fulbright, and Senator Edward Kennedy were favorite targets.

After the Media burglary, Hoover could not have asked for more from ex-agents. On April 17, 1971, the North Central chapter of the society adopted a resolution that praised the director's record and deplored the allegations of his critics. Given extensive coverage by the press, the resolution said there was no basis "to the criticism by some" that "the FBI has become oppressive in its investigative activities and is becoming a threat to the civil liberties of citizens. . . . We know without any question that the FBI, under the most explicit direction of Mr. Hoover, has jealously protected the nation against any invasion of these liberties."

The president of the North Central chapter, Duane Traynor, released this statement: There was "no fairer man who ever lived or was more attuned to the needs of the nation than Mr. Hoover." In the society's spring 1971 newsletter, the *Grapevine,* a column charged that a "strongly suspected undercover conspiracy" to smear Hoover had been hatched by everyone from "anarchist revolutionaries" to "bleeding-heart liberals." At the former agents society's annual national convention in Atlanta that year, the members passed a vote of confidence in Hoover against "vicious and unwarranted attacks" that were "politically motivated."

So many people signed up in the spring of 1971 to support the director by attending the society's annual Congressional Night dinner in Washington that the event had to be moved from the Rayburn House Office Building to a larger space at the Shoreham Hotel. The *Grapevine* reported that the April 1971 Congressional Night dinner, attended each year by society members and members of Congress, "developed into an evening of serious commentary about numerous recent scurrilous attacks against the FBI and Director J. Edgar Hoover." Those present included former FBI official and then head of the Defense Intelligence Agency Joseph F. Carroll and seven members of Congress who were former FBI agents. Hoover didn't usually attend this annual dinner, but he did now when he was under attack. When Carroll introduced the director that evening, he received a standing ovation that lasted several minutes.

Hoover spoke harsh words that night. He attacked the "few journalistic prostitutes" who could not appreciate the FBI. He assured the former agents and others in the audience that the FBI would not compromise its standards "to accommodate kooks, misfits, drunks and slobs."

"It is time we stopped coddling the hoodlums and the hippies who are causing so much serious trouble these days," he said. "Let us treat them like the vicious enemies of society that they really are, regardless of their age."

The director was given more public accolades from President Nixon two months after he had defended him to the newspaper editors. He and Attorney General Mitchell both spoke at the ceremony that marked the graduation of police officers from the FBI Academy on June 30, 1971. The president told the young police officers from throughout the country that more than twenty years earlier, as a young member of Congress from California, he had worked with Hoover on "major investigations of various subversive elements in this country." Regarding current attacks on the director, the president said, "Anybody who is strong, anybody who fights for what he believes in, anybody who stands up where it is tough is bound to be controversial. . . . The great majority of the American people back Mr. Hoover."

In what Nixon later said was the strongest part of his defense of Hoover that day, he told the graduates that "he is a man who has never served a party, he has always served his country." Nixon assured the police officers that, like the director, he and the attorney general "back law enforcement officials in their attempts to reestablish respect for the law."

A remarkable series of expressions of both contempt and respect for the law took place in exchanges at the White House that day and the next. After telling the young police officers about his deep respect for the law and the need to reestablish the rule of law, the next evening the president, according to White House tapes, ordered White House chief of staff H. R. Haldeman to have someone break into the Brookings Institution and steal material related to the conduct of the Vietnam War. The president was forceful in his recommendation: "Just break in. Break in and take it out! You understand? Just go in and take it! . . . Go in around 8 or 9 o'clock . . . and clean it up."

White House aide Charles Colson was recorded that day proposing that the Brookings burglary be accomplished by firebombing the think tank. As firefighters would rush to the scene, he said, they would supply cover for FBI agents, working on behalf of the White House, to enter the building and steal the documents, presumably while the firefighters were putting out the fire. That criminal favor would be done by the FBI, aides confidently predicted, on the orders of the FBI director the president had just publicly insisted to young police officers never served the interest of a political party.

Only a few hours before Nixon gave bold advice on how to break into Brookings, he and Hoover discussed the events of the previous day in a phone conversation. Hoover thanked the president for his generous remarks at the graduation ceremony. He said the president's remarks were especially meaningful at this time when he "was being attacked from many sides." They commiserated with each other about the U.S. Supreme Court decision that was issued while Nixon was at the ceremony at the FBI—the decision supporting the right of the *New York Times* and the *Washington Post* to publish the Pentagon Papers. The decision inspired them to air their mutual low regard for the court:

PRESIDENT NIXON: I wanted to tell you I was so damn mad when that Supreme Court had to come down. . . . I didn't like their decision.

DIRECTOR HOOVER: It was unbelievable.

PRESIDENT NIXON: You know, those clowns we got up there. I'll tell you, I hope I outlive the bastards.

DIRECTOR HOOVER: Well, I hope you do, too.

PRESIDENT NIXON: I mean politically, too. Because, by God—we've got to change that court.

DIRECTOR HOOVER: There's no question about that whatsoever.

They both expressed regret that Nixon's praise of Hoover at the FBI ceremony was not the leading story in newspapers the next day.

The president explained why it wasn't:

PRESIDENT NIXON: If it hadn't been for that stinking [Pentagon Papers]
court decision we'd have been the lead story.

DIRECTOR HOOVER: And it should have been. Your remarks were simply
wonderful.

Hoover told the president his praise was so wonderful that he had ordered
that it be published in *Law Enforcement Bulletin*, a publication the bureau
then distributed regularly to 15,000 police departments in the country.

PRESIDENT NIXON: Oh, heck.

They ended the conversation criticizing someone each of them obviously
held in as low regard as they held the Supreme Court—*Washington Post*
publisher Katharine Graham:

DIRECTOR HOOVER: I saw her on the TV last night. Mrs. Graham.
I would have thought she's about 85 years old. She's only about,
I think, something like 57.

PRESIDENT NIXON: She's a terrible old bag.

DIRECTOR HOOVER: Oh, she's an old bitch in my estimation.

PRESIDENT NIXON (LAUGHING): That's right.

The president thanked the director for the cuff links, emblazoned with
the FBI seal, he had given him the previous day.

BY THE FALL OF 1971, Hoover had two major fears. On October 1, Sullivan, after a series of raging arguments with the director, arrived at work and
found that his name had been removed from his office door and the locks
changed. He had been fired. Hoover knew that Sullivan, after more than
thirty years of devoted service to him, including creating some of the worst
of the COINTELPRO operations, knew essentially everything that could be
used to destroy Hoover. Given that, Hoover added Sullivan, a loose cannon
now that he was fired, to his other greatest fear at that time: the Media burglary. "Only those who worked for him," wrote Gentry, "knew how shaken
Hoover had been by the burglary of the small Pennsylvania agency."

Comments about Hoover in the White House during those months often
were not as generous or flattering, to put it mildly, as either the president's
public remarks or his private comments to Hoover had been. White House

tapes that later became public reveal that the president and his top aides were eager for Hoover to retire. Their grievances against him were mounting. They thought he was too old for the job and was becoming senile. They resented him for letting his fear of being forced out of office make him less amenable to their requests for illegal operations.

They were downright harsh in their private assessments of him. "He should get the hell out of there," Nixon said in an October 8, 1971, conversation with Mitchell. They considered asking him to retire, and if he would agree to do so, they would have a grand public celebration of his service as FBI director. Nixon had a meeting with Hoover in July 1971 for the purpose of asking him to step down. Hoover apparently anticipated what was afoot and spent the entire meeting filibustering Nixon about the past and about how well things were going at the FBI. Nixon said not a word to Hoover about retiring. As the director had done the previous year, he now outmaneuvered Nixon again. He left the Oval Office with his job intact and the president feeling doomed to live with Hoover as FBI director forever. Nixon also had a meeting with Hoover in October 1971 that he hoped would lead to his retirement. It did not.

The president was afraid of Hoover. He undoubtedly had the director's April 1971 threat to blackmail him in mind in October 1971, when he said of Hoover, "We may have on our hands here a man who will pull down the temple with him, including me." Finally, the president was told that he should not force Hoover to retire because of how the Catholic peace activists would capitalize on such a move.

It was G. Gordon Liddy—the former FBI agent then on the staff of the White House and one of the planners of the burglary of the 1972 break-in, for which he was convicted, at Democratic National Committee headquarters at the Watergate—who ultimately convinced Nixon it would be dangerous to force Hoover to retire. Liddy wrote a detailed memo for the president that listed the pros and cons of removing Hoover from office, concluding that it would not be in the "best interest of the Nation, the President, the FBI and Mr. Hoover, that the Director retire before the end of 1971." Fearful of the harm Hoover might do to him if he forced him to retire, the president concluded that Liddy had made a strong case for not removing Hoover. One of the reasons Liddy had given for not removing Hoover was that doing so would be seen during the 1972 Harrisburg trial of the Catholic peace activists whom Hoover had accused of plotting to bomb tunnels and kidnap Henry Kissinger as lending "weight to what are sure to be defense contentions of a conspiracy to justify Hoover's accusations against the Berrigans."

WHEN THE PRESIDENT LEARNED on the morning of May 2, 1972, that J. Edgar Hoover had been found dead in his bedroom early that morning, he immediately started to plan the funeral as a grand public occasion that would be televised. He would give the eulogy himself. The timing was not quite right. Nixon would have preferred that Hoover had died earlier in his first term so the appointment of his replacement would not become a battleground over Nixon's law-and-order politics or over the FBI's past. "The house cleaning [at the FBI] is going to come, but it should not come now because we can't have any flaps about that now," Nixon told L. Patrick Gray in the White House just hours after Hoover's funeral. He had plucked Gray from the Department of Justice and appointed him acting director of the bureau the day after Hoover died. Newspaper commentary the day after Hoover's death focused on the fact that now that Hoover had died, the bureau was likely to face "the most thorough public investigation in its history."

As Nixon and H. R. Haldeman, White House chief of staff, discussed Hoover's funeral, Nixon, in the absence of Hoover having a family, took over. Nixon said he would like for Hoover to be buried at Arlington National Cemetery. Haldeman suggested that was inappropriate inasmuch as Hoover in death, as in life, "the last thing he'd want is to be anywhere near Bobby Kennedy." Both Robert Kennedy and his brother John were buried at Arlington. Nixon settled for what Hoover wanted, burial beside his parents in the family plot at Congressional Cemetery in southeast Washington, not far from his childhood home.

Hoover's remains lay in state in the Capitol Rotunda the day after he died. He was only the twenty-second person, and the first civil servant, accorded that honor since the Rotunda was completed in 1824. Most of the others who had been given that high honor were presidents and select members of Congress and the military. A thousand people an hour filed past Hoover's closed casket. Outside the Rotunda, a few hundred protesters quietly read the names of the thousands of Americans who had been killed in the Vietnam War. It was not reported whether they were being photographed by FBI agents or informers, as such demonstrations routinely were.

In the front pews at Hoover's funeral at National Presbyterian Church in northwest Washington on May 4 were Chief Justice Warren Burger; Mamie Eisenhower, whose husband had been buried from the same church just two years earlier; John Mitchell, who recently had resigned as attorney general to become the director of the Committee to Re-elect the President; and Vice President Spiro Agnew, who would be forced out of office the next year and charged with political corruption and income tax evasion. Agnew released a statement saying Hoover was dear to Americans because of "his total dedication to principle and his complete incorruptibility." Among the other dignitaries seated near the front of the church were two new Supreme Court justices, William Rehnquist and Lewis Powell, and Frank Rizzo, then the mayor of Philadelphia, formerly the police commissioner, and a longtime admirer of the director.

Among the couple thousand attendees were hundreds of FBI agents. Seated in the midst of them was Efrem Zimbalist Jr., the actor selected years earlier by Hoover to be the star of *The F.B.I.* Mark Felt, Hoover's man at Media the morning after the burglary, was seated among the agents and was an honorary pallbearer. As of the previous day he had become the second-highest-ranking person in the bureau, taking the place of Tolson, who retired within hours of Hoover's death. Felt, very disappointed that he was not appointed to succeed Hoover, would soon expand his power over day-to-day operations of the bureau while Gray was acting director. Felt also took over Hoover's responsibility for editing and giving final approval to scripts of *The F.B.I.,* sometimes spending several hours a day writing multi-page single-spaced elaborate edits and critiques. He did this throughout the time he served as a high administrator at the bureau, including, beginning the following fall, during the period when he met *Washington Post* reporter Bob Woodward occasionally late at night in a dark garage in Arlington, Virginia, complicating the life of the man who gave the eulogy at Hoover's funeral.

In his eulogy, Nixon expressed the highest praise for his longtime friend. "America has revered this man not only as the Director of an institution," he said,

> but as an institution in his own right. For nearly half a century, nearly one-fourth of the whole history of this Republic, J. Edgar Hoover has exerted a great influence for good in our national life. While eight presidents came and went, while other leaders of morals and manners and opinion rose and fell, the Director stayed at his post . . . helped to keep steel in America's backbone, and the flame of freedom in America's soul.
>
> He personified integrity; he personified honor; he personified prin-

ciple; he personified courage; he personified discipline; he personified dedication; he personified loyalty; he personified patriotism. . . .

The United States is a better country because this good man lived his long life among us these past 77 years. Each of us stands forever in his debt. In the years ahead, let us cherish his memory. Let us be true to his legacy.

The president concluded, "He loved the law of this country."

Within the next two years, Americans would learn that neither of these two very powerful leaders, the president at the podium or the FBI director in the coffin, seemed to love the law very much.

16

Victory at Camden

FOR TWO MONTHS in the summer of 1971, the FBI prepared to arrest the Media burglars. Bureau officials were sure they were going to raid a draft board in Camden, New Jersey. Kept informed by a local building contractor who infiltrated the group planning the raid, FBI officials secured the approval of the Nixon administration's Department of Justice and planned for the arrests with meticulous care, seeming to leave nothing to chance.

As preparations for the arrests were under way, William C. Sullivan, the third-highest official in the bureau, expressed certainty that the Camden burglars were the Media burglars. In a July 1971 memorandum to assistant director Al Rosen, he wrote:

> . . . We found out that the same group of dissenters who broke into our Media office was planning an entry into another federal office building nearby. We knew who the members of the group were—and we knew their leader, John Grady.
>
> It is evident that this is an extremely important case for the Bureau. If successful, it will do an enormous amount toward offsetting some of the difficulties we have had in the past. It could have national impact. . . . It will be a very complex sensitive operation. . . . We cannot be too careful or take too many precautions, or plan too thoroughly in order to make this successful.
>
> Because of the extreme importance of this action to the Bureau and

to this country, I conclude that no stone should be left unturned in order to make this operation successful.

For Hoover, the elaborately planned Camden arrests promised victory in a case that so far seemed impossible to solve. He had expected the Media burglars to be arrested soon after the burglary and the documents secured. Even with the bureau's highly regarded Roy Moore in charge of the investigation, no progress had been made. Now, at last, victory seemed to be at hand. It looked like Hoover might restore his half-century legacy to the well-burnished gloss it had before the Media burglary, to the prestige he had long assumed he would hold forever in history books: the country's greatest crime fighter, the country's greatest defender against enemies both internal and external.

Before the summer of 1971, Camden probably was not a place where Hoover would have expected to retrieve his legacy. In 1971, as now, the small, blighted city across the Delaware River from downtown Philadelphia via the Ben Franklin Bridge was one of the poorest, most damaged, and most dangerous in the nation. It was second only to Newark as the most likely place in the nation to be mugged or killed. It was a city where industries, stores, and schools had closed and where the people who could not leave struggled to survive.

But on June 25, 1971, Camden became J. Edgar Hoover's source of hope. It was then that FBI officials thought that, at last, they would finally be able to arrest the Media perpetrators. It was on that day Robert Hardy first went to the Camden FBI office and told an agent he had learned about plans for a draft board raid being planned there. Agent Terry Neist remembers the moment Hardy walked in. "I have some friends," Hardy said, speaking rather hesitantly. "Some people I know . . . want me to get involved in something. And I don't think it's right, and I don't know what to do about it."

"Well, what is it?" Neist recalls asking. Hardy told the agent his friends were planning to break into a draft board.

Neist made a crucial decision immediately. He hired Hardy as an informer within minutes of meeting him and, as he recalls, told him, "What we'd like you to do is tell them you're going to join the group, and then I will meet with you regularly, myself and someone else, so we can keep track of what they're doing."

For Hoover and the agents investigating the Media burglary, Hardy's news was like Christmas morning and winning the lottery wrapped into one grand occasion.

Hardy made that first fateful visit to the FBI the day after his close friend Mike Giocondo, forty-two and a former priest, had told him about the group's plans and about their deep frustrations about how difficult the raid would be. Because he regarded Hardy as a good manager of small construction projects, Giocondo thought Hardy might be able to help the group solve some of the problems they were having with plans for the break-in. When Hardy first talked to Neist, he knew the names of only two members of the group, Giocondo and the Reverend Michael Doyle, a thirty-three-year-old Camden priest who had emigrated from Ireland eight years earlier. Doyle was a friend of Giocondo and also of Hardy and his wife, Peg, and their children. Just a year earlier Doyle had guided Hardy through his decision to convert to Catholicism.

Hardy strongly opposed the war in Vietnam, but he rejected protest that involved breaking into government offices. In an interview with filmmaker Anthony Giacchino, Hardy recalled being at the U.S. naval docks in Philadelphia when refrigerated ships arrived from Vietnam with the bodies of dead troops. "This one day they had 440 caskets they were unloading. I remember longshoremen and myself and other men and women who were there greeting the caskets and putting them into hearses. How we wept. At that time, I said I would do whatever I could to stop that war."

At their first meeting, Neist asked Hardy, an ex-Marine and an officer in the local Junior Chamber of Commerce, who the leader of the group was. He said he didn't know but he would find out. They agreed Neist would meet Hardy at a carnival that evening on the grounds of St. Joseph's Catholic Church, where he would be staffing a booth. When Neist approached the booth, Hardy handed him a small piece of paper.

On it he had written, "The group's leader is John Peter Grady."

Grady. The man believed to be the mastermind of countless draft board raids. The man FBI officials believed, from nearly the moment agents discovered the Media office had been burglarized, was the mastermind of the Media burglary.

"Well, when we heard this," Neist recalled years later, "I mean, Mr. Grady was someone who . . . the FBI was aware of and thought might be involved in some of these draft board break-ins. . . . So, with this we realized that maybe this group will lead us to the individuals who broke into the FBI office in Media, Pennsylvania."

This news was greeted as a golden break in the MEDBURG case. Despite investigators' certainty that Grady was the leader of the Media group, after enormous effort by agents they still had no evidence of his—or anyone else's—involvement in Media. Nevertheless, they were still confident of their original assumption, and now, thanks to Hardy, they thought they would be able to arrest Grady and the other Media burglars. Bureau officials were so certain that Grady and other people in the Camden group were the people who had burglarized the Media FBI office that during this time they merged the two cases into one: MEDBURG-CAMDEN.

Hardy's news that Grady was leading a group that planned to raid the draft board in Camden infused the investigation with renewed optimism. In a July 7, 1971, memorandum to William Sullivan, headquarters official Al Rosen wrote, "It is our intention that by careful planning we may be in a position to apprehend those participating in this new break-in—15 to 25 individuals—during the actual attempt. We hope to link many of these individuals with the Media break-in."

Rosen noted that the bureau had discontinued electronic surveillance plans at a cabin in the Pennsylvania mountains where they thought Grady was supposed to appear recently, but, to MEDBURG investigators' disappointment, he had not. In a recommendation that was accepted, Rosen suggested that plans to take the Media case before a grand jury should be shelved because "any grand jury action would obviously adversely influence Grady's plans for his newest actions." The bureau's plans for successful arrests of Media burglars at Camden were so important, Rosen advised, that no information about the plans should be disseminated outside the bureau and only on a very limited basis inside the bureau.

Among headquarters officials and with Roy Moore and his large team of MEDBURG investigators, there was a this-must-not-go-wrong attitude about the pending Camden arrests. Hoover was determined that the arrests would be a source of pride, not embarrassment. By the time the Camden arrests were being planned, he had felt a powerful sting from a series of deeply embarrassing episodes. It was an embarrassment that an FBI office *could* be burglarized. It was an embarrassment—and disaster, in the director's opinion—that the stolen files distributed by the burglars had uncovered, for the first time, his secret political spying operations. It was an embarrassment that the hundreds of FBI agents assigned to the investigation of the case, MEDBURG, had not found either the burglars or the files they stole. It was an embarrassment that countless draft board burglars, who had stolen thousands of Selective Service files in the last two years, had eluded arrest. The bureau had also endured significant embarrassment as a result of the criticism directed at the director after his sensational public accusations in November 1970 that Philip Berrigan and seven other people in the Catholic peace movement were conspiring to kidnap President Nixon's national security adviser, Henry Kissinger, and to bomb tunnels under Washington.

Now that Hoover believed the Media burglars were within reach, he was determined the arrests at Camden would be carried out perfectly. The FBI would not be subjected to criticism or embarrassment for what it was about to do in Camden.

BEGINNING THE DAY Hardy appeared in their Camden office, head-quarters officials, including Hoover, agreed that agents would closely watch as plans for the Camden draft board raid unfolded before hidden FBI eyes. Moore assured Hoover that agents were monitoring Grady and "his associates" seven days a week and developing plans to "neutralize Grady's activity at critical time." The "associates" were typical of the mix of people who had raided other draft boards—Jesuit priests from New York City, a local Irish-born Catholic parish priest, a local Lutheran minister, elementary school teachers, a Navy veteran, a sociologist, and a local doctor. Most of them were working-class Catholics in their twenties and thirties from Philadelphia and other northeastern cities, some of whom had dropped out of college to protest the war in Vietnam, and others who had a variety of jobs and were raising young families.

Hardy easily moved into his role as an informer. He was accepted immediately as a member of the group and worked with them every day for the next two months. According to Hardy and official FBI records, the FBI paid him an amount equal to his usual daily earnings as a self-employed construction worker. He became a leader in the group and reported the details of the evolving plans for the raid to his FBI handlers at least once a day for two months. "Usually I met them in the morning in diners or parking lots," Hardy said later. "Each day I collected my thoughts on everything that had happened and had been said, and then dictated it into my contact's tape recorder. It was transcribed daily by two stenographers at the FBI. Also, a radio was installed in my van so whenever the ignition was on, the conversations would be directly broadcast to the FBI. The FBI recorded these conversations and had them transcribed. I saw to it that many conversations took place in my van."

As agents listened to the conversations between Hardy and Grady, they collected extensive documentary information about the Catholic antiwar movement. They listened as Grady bragged about his accomplishments, describing one draft board raid after another he claimed he had been involved in. Grady told Hardy that as a longtime friend and supporter of the Berrigans, he was personally responsible for moving the Catholic peace movement away from the Berrigans' "jail-term martyr kind of situation to a strike force action group," such as what he now was planning at Camden.

Agents must have been particularly interested when Grady talked about Media in one of his first conversations with Hardy. He told him the FBI office in Media "was unguarded and that the files were there in sort of a home-type atmosphere. He implied that it was very simple." Such comments led the listening FBI agents to think Grady was indeed what they thought he was, the leader of the Media burglars.

In recorded conversations between the two men, Grady told Hardy he thought Hardy was bright and that he hoped he would continue working with the group after the Camden raid because he "had the type of talent that was needed in the underground." Grady told him there were "very few people in the movement who could think and work at the same time, and that Hardy was one of those people." Because Hardy knew Camden well, and most of the burglars did not, Grady asked him to establish where getaway and blocking vehicles would park the night of the raid and to teach some of the burglars how to quietly and quickly remove glass from the window that would be the burglars' entrance into the draft board office. Grady was protective of Hardy. He warned him not to park his van in an alley the night of the raid because he did not want to see Hardy "get busted" during his first movement action.

Hardy's FBI handlers must have realized that Grady thought of Hardy as a leader of the group when they heard the code name Grady gave him. He called Hardy Moses. If the agents and officials at headquarters had a sense of irony, a sense of humor, or recall of Old Testament history as they watched the relationship evolve between the informer and the leader of the group, perhaps they thought about the wilderness they hoped "Moses" was leading the FBI out of, and the wilderness they hoped he would lead the Camden burglars into.

Three weeks before the burglary, Grady unintentionally gave the FBI what it regarded as a treasure trove of evidence. As he prepared to move from one Camden apartment to another, Grady asked Hardy to remove and temporarily store his personal possessions, including all of the photos, maps, and slides related to the Camden plan, plus material about other raids and his book business. He asked Hardy to keep his belongings until a few days later when Grady and his wife and children had moved into another apartment. Hardy readily obliged and immediately drove Grady's possessions directly from Grady's apartment to the FBI field office in Philadelphia, where agents promptly photographed every item, including every page of Grady's personal notebook.

As more and more invaluable evidence accumulated, officials at FBI headquarters established unusually tight security regarding all information related to Camden. Orders went out that there must be no leaks. The usual way of distributing internal memos was forbidden. Communication security was made so tight that memos about Camden could be distributed only by one official handing a memorandum to another official. Only a few officials at the highest levels of headquarters had access to Camden information— Hoover, Clyde Tolson, William Sullivan, and Al Rosen, an assistant director, and D. J. Dalbey, head of the bureau's Office of Legal Counsel. Secrecy was recognized as "imperative" from the outset, Rosen wrote, "both from the standpoint of protecting our source who has successfully associated himself to a very close degree with Grady and, more important, insuring there be no leak which would scare off Grady and his group."

Hoover wanted written support and advice from the Department of Justice for the arrests, but he did not trust Robert Mardian, the assistant attorney general in charge of the department's Internal Security Division, to maintain security regarding Camden. Acknowledging Hoover's concerns, Mardian assured the director in writing that he recognized "the need for the utmost secrecy in this case." In his August 12 "Depredations of Government Buildings" message to Hoover, Mardian approved the planned Camden arrest operation and gave the director advice regarding procedures. In an indication of the importance the department placed on the Camden case, Mardian told Hoover he had assigned Guy Goodwin, the Internal Security Division's well-known convener of antiwar grand juries, to be on the scene in Camden during the arrests. Mardian assured the director that he himself would be available by phone at any time that night. He continued to discuss arrest plans with the director on a regular basis.

Mardian recommended that the bureau deal with Nixon-appointed federal judges "personally known" to Mardian when getting search warrants in New Jersey in connection with the case. He need not have worried about judges being cooperative. The first federal judge assigned to the case during preliminary proceedings was so helpful to the bureau that he may have been in violation of judicial ethics. The Philadelphia field office reported to Hoover on September 2 that "District Judge Mitchell H. Cohen in Camden is extremely well disposed toward the Bureau and has been most helpful with respect to matters coming before him in this case. He is most anxious that departmental attorney Guy Goodwin should be the trial attorney with respect to Camden Action." He urged the bureau to ask to have the first prosecutor assigned to the case replaced because the judge thought the prosecutor was too inexperienced. The prosecutor was replaced, but not with Guy Goodwin. Later, Judge Cohen removed himself from the case because the FBI, with his permission, had used his chambers as a vantage point from which to monitor and photograph the defendants as they conducted dry runs. Another judge, also someone favored by Mardian, recused himself because he was a former FBI agent.

AT FIRST the Camden operation, from the FBI's perspective, looked like it would be easy. The bureau would essentially just stand by and watch the burglars fall into a trap of their own making. But it soon became evident that the arrests might be more difficult than expected. Not long after the surveillance started, with Hardy firmly in place as the FBI's ears and eyes, agents learned rather startling news. Originally scheduled for mid-July, the raid was postponed by the burglars three times. The dry runs did not go well. At times the group even considered canceling the raid altogether.

Some of the participants were ambivalent about proceeding because this raid involved unique problems. Unlike other draft boards that had been raided, this one was on an upper floor of a closely guarded building in the center of a city. The raid was complicated in other ways. It involved scaling a fire escape while not setting off an alarm at the base of the fire escape. And windows on the fifth floor had to be quietly and skillfully removed in order to enter the draft board from a narrow parapet outside the window. The raiders felt fortunate that the new member of the group, Hardy, had taught them how to do that and also had figured out how to avoid setting off the alarm, which none of the rest of them had even noticed.

FBI officials, originally certain this raid would result in arrests that would amount to a huge victory for the bureau, were alarmed when they learned the raid might be canceled. Moore became so fearful the raid might never take place that he proposed a drastic change in FBI strategy in order to make sure arrests would take place even if the raid did not. Instead of assuming, as the bureau had from the outset, that the Camden burglars would be caught red-handed as they broke into the board and destroyed government property, Moore thought the bureau should be prepared to arrest them instead as they conducted a dry run or as they prepared to enter the building. This would mean charging them with a lesser crime, conspiracy to commit crimes, rather than with the actual commission of crimes. Making the case for conspiracy charges, Moore wrote Hoover:

> As Bureau is aware, the principal source [Hardy], Camden action, has been under direction and control of the Philadelphia and Newark offices since June 25 last. He has attended nightly meetings and participated in the on-the-street surveillances and quote dry runs unquote, has identified participants involved, and will be in key position during break-in and/or quote dry run unquote. Source is willing to testify. In corroboration of his testimony, agents can supply the following hard evidence:
>
> One. Have actually observed participants and surveillances.
>
> Two. Have photographed them.
>
> Three. Have recorded their conversations on transceivers.
>
> Four. Have obtained copies of their notes, plans, charts, photographs in furtherance of their plan to burglarize offices in the Camden Post Office Building, and can testify to identity of a large number of the participants and their cars.

It was a plea from Moore for arrests before this group slipped away, the FBI's opportunity to arrest them perhaps gone forever.

Rosen was assigned to consider Moore's proposal. In an August 5 memo to Sullivan supporting Moore, Rosen wrote that he agreed with Moore: "While it would be desirable to arrest these individuals red-handed in the act, the possibility of additional delays exists. Rather than risk the possibility conditions will change, requiring Grady and his group to postpone their planned break-in, SAC Moore's recommendation appears to have merit and we recommend it be followed."

To support Moore's conspiracy proposal, Rosen described how frustrating the repeated postponements by the Camden burglars were for the FBI:

"We have observed through our intensive investigation of Grady and associates . . . that because of the perversity of these people they are inclined to procrastinate. In fact, it has been reported by our informant that should the break-in fail to take place this weekend, the actual 'hit' could be delayed until some time in the fall."

Crime prevention definitely was not the FBI's goal in regard to this burglary.

Mardian agreed with Moore's conclusion that if the crime itself didn't take place, the mountain of recordings and photographs gathered by the FBI demonstrated "solid evidence of conspiracy," but he had serious problems with settling for conspiracy charges. In a memo to Hoover he urged him to consider "the anti-Government position which we can expect from the press" if the raiders were charged with conspiracy rather than with actual commission of a crime. Hoover wrote this tart observation on Mardian's memo: "If this is going to be the controlling factor at all times, our work and efforts are futile."

Finally, in that same memo to Hoover, Mardian ordered that "no arrests should be effected absent an actual unlawful entry by one or more members of the group." Only criminal charges, he said, would be acceptable to the Department of Justice.

The burglars' reluctance to move ahead would bedevil the FBI until the moment the break-in took place. Just two days before the raid, Grady expressed doubts. Hardy reported that Grady had said that evening, "We're tooling up for Saturday night. If it doesn't go Saturday, we're all leaving town." A bulletin from Moore to Hoover marked "urgent" reported Grady's ambivalence. Even the Friday night before the Saturday night raid some of the burglars thought it should be canceled. Everyone—burglars and FBI officials and arresting agents—was extremely insecure about whether the raid would take place. The FBI agents were ready and eager. The burglars were reluctant and fearful.

LOGISTICALLY, it seemed the FBI could not have been better prepared. Numerous bureau clerks were brought to Camden the day of the raid to prepare papers on each defendant to be used at the arraignment the next morning. Twenty-five interview rooms were set up in the federal building for agents to interview each person after they had been searched following arrest. Thanks to agents' surveillance and Hardy's reports, they had precise information about plans: a map drawn by Hardy showed the time and place where each of the twenty-eight burglars would be stationed at the time the raid was to begin; where each of the group's two vans and eight cars would be positioned on streets near the federal building, some of them faking intersection accidents; when and where Grady would be standing when he gave the "go" hand signal for the ladder to be placed against the federal building.

Early that afternoon, more than eighty FBI agents from throughout Pennsylvania and New Jersey, plus more than a dozen federal marshals, arrived in Camden. Sullivan wrote later that agents hid in a nearby funeral home from early afternoon until the time they got in position to make the arrests. Like the burglars, the agents also planned to move to locations near the federal building without being noticed. "So as not to attract attention," Sullivan wrote, "we took the agents in and out in a hearse. . . . The men were forced to wait for the break-in among the corpses."

As FBI agents were arriving in the city, the burglars started stage one of their plan. According to a minute-by-minute log maintained by the FBI, the burglars started casing the federal building at two o'clock on Saturday afternoon. With the FBI listening in as the burglars arrived, the burglars gathered at a downtown apartment to finalize plans at 6 p.m. They left the apartment at 10:50, and by 11:15, according to the FBI log, "all break-in units observed in place."

The break-in was scheduled to begin at 11:50. In Washington, Sullivan was seated at his desk at FBI headquarters with an open phone line to Moore in Philadelphia. In Camden, all FBI personnel were in place and ready to move in.

Suddenly, FBI observers watched and listened in shock as each cluster of burglars broke up and left the scene. In that moment, Moore must have deeply regretted that Mardian had not approved his suggestion that the burglars be arrested for conspiracy instead of breaking and entering. Had the last chance to arrest these people just evaporated? Hardy soon reported to his handlers that the burglars discovered at the last minute, as they were in place and waiting for Grady's hand signal, that the entry crew had forgotten to bring the ladder needed to start the climb to the fire escape. Back at the Anderson apartment, Grady severely reprimanded the people who'd forgotten the ladder.

At 2:30 a.m., the burglars returned to the federal building area, this time with a ladder. Grady roamed the area in a camper-type truck. He gave his hand signal, and the entry team went into action. They placed the ladder against the building, climbed up to the fire escape, and then swiftly and quietly ran up the fire escape, gently removed the window to the fifth-floor Selective Service office, in the way Hardy had taught them, and stepped over the windowsill and into the dark office.

The agents were ready. It was time for their signal. But they received a signal to stay in place, not to move ahead. Sullivan later wrote that the agents had to be held back.

The agents surrounding the federal building, like Hardy, thought the arrests would take place as soon as the burglars went inside the draft board office. " 'No, not yet,' " Sullivan said he ordered. " 'If we move in now, all we'd have against them is trespassing in a federal building. Let's give them time and get them for destroying federal property.' . . . The men were edgy, ready to move in at once, but I made them wait almost two hours before I gave the signal to go." As they waited, in the distance they could hear the sounds of a riot that had been taking place since two nights earlier in response to the shooting death of a Puerto Rican man from the community by a local police officer at a traffic stop.

Sullivan was as eager for the arrests to take place as the agents were. In fact, he had wanted to be at the scene to direct the operation, but Mark Felt, by then more powerful than Sullivan as Hoover's close adviser, recommended that the director reject Sullivan's request to be on the scene the night of the raid. He told Hoover, "SAC Moore is eminently qualified to handle on the scene supervision, and Sullivan should be here to coordinate at the Seat of Government." Reluctantly, Sullivan directed operations from Washington, occasionally receiving instructions from Department of Justice officials and passing them on to Moore. He wrote about the experience in his memoir, *The Bureau: My Thirty Years in Hoover's FBI,* which was published posthumously in 1979 after he was killed early one morning in November 1977 near his home in New Hampshire by a young hunter who said he mistook Sullivan for a deer.

"We didn't interfere with their new plan," Sullivan wrote, "because we wanted to catch them red-handed." That decision not to arrest the burglars immediately and to give them time to destroy draft records—a decision made at the highest levels of the federal government right before the raid that evening—had powerful unintended consequences later on the case against the Camden defendants.

Finally, it was time. Sullivan's order to make the arrests was issued by him through Moore at 4:31 a.m. on Sunday, August 22, 1971. By that time, the eighty-plus FBI agents had been waiting in place for more than five hours. When the signal was given, agents ran up the five-story fire escape and stepped through the dark opening where the burglars had removed the window. "There were agents everywhere," Sullivan said. "They found Grady's friends busily smashing file cabinets and promptly arrested them."

Simultaneously, agents ran into the courtyard of St. Paul's Episcopal Church, as other agents entered a nearby Lutheran minister's home. At these three locations in downtown Camden the FBI arrested twenty people by 4:36. Eight others were arrested in Camden hours later. The people arrested early that Sunday morning would become known as the Camden 28. The people arrested in the fifth-floor draft board office vividly remember the moment. Six of them were quietly removing Selective Service files from drawers, tearing them, and stuffing them into large canvas mailing bags, while two other people were lifting the filled bags to the ledge outside the window they had entered.

Suddenly, Giocondo recalls, someone outside the open draft board window shouted, "Freeze, it's the FBI!"

The burglars were surprised when they saw Guy Goodwin, the attorney from the Internal Security Division of the Department of Justice, standing above them. Staring down into their faces, he gloated. "Hello, Ro-Ro," Goodwin casually said to Rosemary Reilly, and "Hi, Cookie," to Kathleen Ridolfi. He seemed to take pleasure in letting them know he knew their nicknames. By then, Goodwin was widely considered in antiwar circles to be a sort of circuit-riding prosecutor of antiwar activists. His specialty was convening grand juries that indicted antiwar activists, often as a result of subpoenas many thought were fishing expeditions that substituted for weak FBI investigations. He seldom, if ever, tried the cases. After indictments were issued, Goodwin left town and local prosecutors took over. Knowing that background, some of the Camden raiders were surprised that morning that they merited the attention of this nationally known antiwar prosecutor.

John Swinglish, a Navy veteran from Washington, D.C., and one of the burglars, remembered noticing from his off-site lookout location that the lights were on in the draft board office. "And I thought, why are they turning the lights on. This is crazy."

Father Michael Doyle, one of the people arrested inside the office, also thought what was happening was crazy: "Three guys jumped me, and they were just miserable. I mean, I couldn't believe it. They just threw me to the ground. One guy jumped with his two knees into my chest. . . . I looked up at them, and I said, 'So this is the FBI?'" Some agents pointed guns at the burglars as they ordered them down. Neist denied later that guns were used, but defendants, including Ridolfi, a professor now at Santa Clara University Law School in California, insist the agents used guns.

One agent must have been embarrassed when, after pressing Father Doyle to the floor as if he were dangerous, he was reduced to explaining to the priest that because the agents forgot to bring enough handcuffs he wanted the priest's belt so he could restrain him with makeshift fetters. Like all the other defendants, Doyle had been trained, in the revered tradition of nonviolent resistance, not to resist arrest. Now he was not only not resisting arrest—he was asked to provide the means of his restraint. He obediently removed his belt and handed it to the agent so it could be used to restrain him despite his passive reaction to being arrested, thrown to the floor, and stepped on.

This was not where Roseta Doyle, the priest's mother back in Ireland, expected to see her son in the United States—on the floor, trampled on by an FBI agent. Then again, though both she and her son knew well the concept of resistance as a result of living through the troubles in Ireland, she did not expect him to be resisting the American government, at least not by raiding a draft board.

Doyle himself had not expected this destiny in his adopted country. When he arrived in the United States in 1963 at age twenty-five, he was assigned to teach in a Catholic high school in Cape May, a beautiful seaside resort town on the southern tip of New Jersey where the streets are lined with pretty Victorian houses. A couple years after his arrival, he spoke openly in opposition to the war in Vietnam. His bishop did what many Catholic bishops did at that time. He punished Doyle for expressing views the bishop regarded as inappropriate by firing him from his teaching position and assigning him to work in a very poor inner-city church in Camden. Doyle, like many other Catholic priests who were punished by being sent to a "ghetto," soon regarded the transfer as the opposite of punishment. In the inner city, he says, "I found my mission." In that community, he worked to improve the circumstances that perpetuated poverty, and he became deeply committed to the welfare of the members of his congregation, most of them African American and Hispanic people. To this day, more than forty years after being arrested in Camden, Doyle has lived and worked in the very poor inner city of Camden, with time out only for an occasional trip to Ireland.

Doyle's opposition to the war grew stronger in the late 1960s. He saw connections between the deteriorating conditions in the city and the increased spending on the war. He also became aware of the disproportionate killing in Vietnam of young men from poor places like Camden. Given his strong opposition to the war, it probably was inevitable that he would notice when, as he puts it, "Dan and Phil Berrigan began to make their moves in those years of the '60s. I was interested in what they were doing. The Sermon on the Mount, and turn the other cheek and all of that kind of thing. . . . I began to rethink my ideas. . . . And say, well, if the Christian truth is to be preached, it's got to be without guns, it has got to be without killing. And that Jesus would have died for the ones who killed him, and that would be the only solution. So that's how it kind of got going." Eventually, he concluded that the usual forms of protest were having little or no effect. Nonviolent resistance seemed to be the only avenue left to draw attention to the terrible impact of the war in both Vietnam and the United States. Two years after his arrest in the Camden draft board, when Doyle faced the jury, in his intense and lyrical Irish brogue he posed rhetorical questions that explained the dilemma that led to his becoming a resister:

"What do you do when a child's on fire? We saw children on fire. What do you do when a child's on fire in a war that was a mistake? What do you do? Write a letter?"

THE ARRESTS AT CAMDEN gave the FBI an enormous sense of satisfaction. The bureau's sense of triumph was evident immediately. Just hours after the arrests, FBI director J. Edgar Hoover and Attorney General John Mitchell held an unprecedented joint press conference in Washington where they announced their victory at Camden. Hoover told journalists the people were apprehended at night in the Camden Selective Service office as they destroyed draft board records. He said they were carrying binoculars, radio transceivers, pry bars, and "flashlights with the lenses taped to emit a thin beam of light." He did not mention the unusual source of that equipment. That would be revealed at the trial. The charges against them, the director said, included committing a crime on a government reservation, breaking and entering, destruction of government property, removal and mutilation of public records, theft of government property, unlawful interference with the administration of the Selective Service Act, and conspiracy to commit the crimes listed. If convicted on those charges, he said, they "could receive sentences ranging up to 40 years imprisonment." Actually, the potential sentence for each defendant was forty-seven years.

"Raids and arrests impressive and successful," Moore wrote Hoover soon after the arrests. "Widespread national radio, TV and press coverage . . . continuing. Highly favorable and complimentary to FBI."

About the same time the high-level press conference was taking place in Washington, the defendants were being arraigned in Camden on the third floor of the building where they had been arrested. The government asked for high bail for John Peter Grady because he was the "ringleader and mastermind" of the group. Bail for the defendants totaled $605,000, ranging from $5,000 for some to $150,000 for Grady. A lawyer asked U.S. magistrate Charles L. Rudd, who presided, for lower bail for Grady because he was the father of five children. Judge Rudd angrily responded, "I'll set the bail. I don't want to see my country destroyed." He praised the FBI then, as he did several times during the hearing: "God bless them. They've done a wonderful job."

Exuberant about the advance in the Media case that FBI officials thought the Camden arrests represented, assistant FBI director Al Rosen sent this message to Sullivan two days after the Camden arrests:

"We now have key subjects in custody and must keep pressure on them to obtain admissions. . . . There is no physical evidence or witnesses to FBI-Media burglary—Matter can only be resolved by admissions." Moore later proposed plans for getting them to confess to participating in the Media break-in.

In his post-Camden arrest memo to Sullivan, Rosen emphasized the significance of finally arresting Grady, whom they had wanted to arrest ever since the morning of March 9. He wrote, "Grady, according to several sources . . . is directly responsible for the Media Resident Agency break-in." The arrest of "Grady, avowed instigator of many of the raids on draft boards in the last two years by Berrigan supporters and East Coast Conspiracy to Save Lives members, is an irreparable loss to this segment of the New Left."

Hoover personally informed high-level Nixon administration officials about the Camden arrests the day after they occurred. He sent letters to the attorney general; H. R. Haldeman, the White House chief of staff; and Henry Kissinger, President Nixon's national security adviser, drawing attention to the bureau's success at Camden. In a September 2 letter, Kissinger thanked Hoover for keeping him informed: "I appreciate having additional background on this very effective operation."

THE TWENTY-EIGHT PEOPLE arrested at Camden had no clue that their arrests were scripted to serve grand purposes. To the FBI, the arrests were finally a chance for victory in the MEDBURG case. In Moore's strategy, the arrests also offered a chance to solve several of the other draft board cases, in addition to solving MEDBURG. But to the Camden defendants the arrests were a very depressing matter. Few other draft board raiders had sat in holding cells contemplating many years in prison. Most had walked away from draft boards and never been caught. Worse, from the perspective of some of them, now they had been arrested for a raid they thought never should have happened and in which they regretted participating.

Both before and after the raid, the problems were obvious to many of the raiders. Hardy reported to his handlers that "members of the group say that this action will be the most difficult one that they have ever performed."

The group was too big and too disorganized. Making matters even more complicated, veteran draft board raiders were brought in from New York to help shortly before the day of the raid, allowing little or no time for them to participate in dry runs. Two women, responding to a last-minute call for more participants, tried to get a bus from New York to Camden, but they discovered that because of the riot taking place in Camden, bus service to the city had been canceled. Determined to get there to help their friends, they hitchhiked from New York. When they arrived during the riot, they couldn't find the group and had to search for them in the midst of what one of them, Joan Reilly, later described as "violence and chaos."

The FBI agents who endured the long lead-up to the arrests also had complaints. In a memo written soon after the raid, SAC Moore expressed a mixture of lament and praise for what his agents endured throughout the operation. From the day Hardy walked into their office, Moore informed the director, agents conducted surveillance of "Grady and associates" seven days a week. They kept track of—photographed and recorded—the raiders at a command post and at twenty fixed locations during dry runs. It was necessary, he wrote, to overcome many difficult obstacles—"conducting investigation and surveillance in hippie neighborhoods dominated by communes . . . in ghetto type area." Because the raiders kept postponing the event, he wrote, it was necessary to assemble the eighty arresting agents on three different weekends, only to have two of the raids canceled mid-raid. They "were moved into Camden area early in the afternoon each Saturday and held their positions in hot, humid and close quarters from approximately 2 p.m. to 6 a.m. the following morning. Outstanding performance."

As the arrested men sat in a crowded holding cell in the basement of the federal building while they waited to be taken to their arraignment, they looked at one another. They knew something had gone terribly wrong. They soon agreed that someone in their midst these last months had been an informer. It did not take long for them to realize that one member of the group was not there: Bob Hardy. In the two years Catholic antiwar activists had been raiding draft boards, no group was known to have had an informer in its midst. Facing the fact that Hardy had informed on them was especially difficult for the two men who had known him for years, Giocondo and Doyle. They found it nearly impossible to believe that their good friend had turned them in.

Hoover was grateful for what Hardy had done. A short time after the arrests, Hardy got a letter from the director. Hardy reported what he wrote: "He said, 'Dear Mr. Hardy, I wish to take the time to thank you for what you've done. You've done in ten weeks what would have taken 200 agents a year to accomplish. Our country is very grateful.' And in it was 50 one hundred dollar bills. I took the money. I thought it was a reward. Well, it was."

There was strong agreement among FBI officials that they could not have pulled off the arrests without Hardy. "To a large degree, the success was attributed to Hardy," Moore wrote to headquarters. The informer had done the work for the bureau, he wrote, at "great personal inconvenience. . . . He suffered great financial loss . . . serious and detrimental effect on his ability to secure necessary contracts for continuous income purposes."

At a bail reduction hearing not long after the arrests, according to a report by an agent, "one of the women subjects [a Camden defendant] suspects Hardy is the informer and gave him an obscene gesture, which he returned." After this, the report notes, the possibility of relocating Hardy to protect him was suggested to him by FBI agents, and he responded, "Run from these bastards? Not on your life."

AS THE DEFENDANTS ABSORBED the shock of having been turned in by an informer and having their arrests announced at a major press conference by none other than the attorney general of the United States and the director of the FBI, they tried to focus on how to move forward, as individuals and as a group. Some of them had assumed that eventually one of the draft board raids might go wrong, but they never thought one would go quite this wrong.

As the Camden defendants contemplated how to deal with their new status as criminal defendants, they were shaken by tragic news just a few weeks after their arrests. For a few of them, it challenged the deeply humane instincts at the heart of their philosophy of nonviolent resistance. Bob Hardy's nine-year-old son Billy was critically injured. One day Sandy Grady, a reporter from the *Evening Bulletin* in Philadelphia, dropped by to chat with Hardy at his Camden home. Billy had been waiting to go out with his dad. When Grady arrived, Hardy asked Billy to wait. Billy went out to play and, as Doyle put it, being a boy, climbed a tree. He fell from the tree and was impaled on the sharp-pointed top of a metal fence. An older boy who lived next door ran to Billy and lifted him off the fence and screamed for help. Hardy and Grady came running from the house.

For three weeks, Billy was unconscious in the intensive care unit at Cooper Hospital in Camden. By this time, Doyle had partially, though reluctantly, removed the large wedge that Hardy's role as informer had brought between them. When the Camden defendants first got out of jail, Swinglish, the Navy veteran, had challenged the priest to put into action his belief in love and forgiveness and to be willing to "go see the man who had betrayed us." Doyle had to push himself hard to do what normally would have come naturally to him, but he did it. He walked the one block from his rectory to Hardy's home. They had an awkward conversation, but at least they talked, and, by doing so, they crossed a barrier. They talked a couple more times, in fact, before Billy was injured. At no point, though, in the few conversations Doyle and Hardy had before Billy's accident did Doyle and Hardy discuss what Hardy had done to the group. It was as though they could have a connection now only if they detoured around that awful shared experience. Doyle wondered if their friendship could ever be restored.

Doyle considered little Billy a friend. He remembers him, as others do, with great fondness. "He was a wonderful boy, and I knew him very well." So it was natural that Doyle would visit Billy at the hospital. The first time he went to see Billy, "sitting there in the waiting room outside the intensive care unit were Bob Hardy and Michael Reimer, the FBI agent who was one of Hardy's contacts for the Camden 28 surveillance. He was there to support Bob Hardy, and I, as the priest of the parish, was there, too, to support him.

"And I remember the three of us sitting on a couch. Somehow my mind was twisting in some kind of unreality. There was only one thing that was real and that was that a child was dying. But the situation of our relationships on that couch. . . . I just felt I was in Twilight Zone. And I remember walking out of that hospital that day and banging on the front of my car and trying to feel, to feel something that was there and real."

Some of the surreal nature of the relationships vanished for Doyle as he focused on the acute needs of the Hardys as their son suffered. He was particularly concerned about Peg Hardy. Fear nearly paralyzed her and kept her from visiting her unconscious son. Doyle implored her to go see him. "I told her that if he died and she had never fixed his hair or rubbed his face that she might forever regret it." Finally, she agreed, and Doyle took her to see Billy. They stood beside his bed, "and I got her to talk to him."

"It was a time of enormous emotional upheaval. Billy slowly died. They couldn't save him because infection set in. He died October third."

Three days later, Doyle conducted Billy's funeral at St. Joseph's Cathedral Church in Camden. A funeral for a sweet nine-year-old child is always an unspeakably sad occasion. Certainly this one was. Doyle remembers looking into the faces of the people sitting in the pews in front of him. "The family was there, and the Camden 28 and their supporters were there. . . . Maybe twenty FBI agents also were there showing support for the family." The FBI agents and the people they had arrested were sitting near each other. Each group grieving. Each group looking slightly awkward. Each group managing to put their concern for the Hardys above their antipathy for each other.

"I don't remember what I said that night," said Doyle, "something, I'm sure, like, 'What can I say about a nine-year-old boy who died?' I tried to talk about the sadness of it all and the tragedy of it all. It was a bewildering, roller-coaster situation of reality and unreality, tragedy. It was a terrible tragedy. Relationships that were not reality. I found it extremely tearing inside. Just twisting without adequate expression."

After the funeral, Peg and Bob Hardy showed Doyle two pieces of wood they had found in Billy's dresser drawer. With a nail and hammer Billy had chiseled the word "peace" in one and "love" in the other. Doyle had the pieces of wood mounted as a hanging for the Hardys "as a remembrance of Billy and his two great words for his world."

For some of the defendants, perhaps especially Giocondo, the defendant who had known Hardy longest, it was very difficult to think of forgiving Hardy for being an informer against him and the others. How could someone so close to you do that? The idea of linking Hardy with trust now felt like an oxymoron. Nevertheless, the bond had been so strong when Hardy worked with them that the desire to support him and his family in some way at the time of their extreme loss rose above their overarching anger. It was impossible, though, for most of the defendants to erase the thought that someday soon at their trial Hardy would testify against them and help send them to prison.

17

Defeat at Camden

THE FBI WAS EAGER to use the Camden arrests to keep the momentum moving toward the arrest of the Media burglars. But that was impossible. The public didn't know it, but the triumphant announcements by the FBI after the arrests were hollow. What had appeared in June to be a great opportunity for the bureau to establish that John Peter Grady was what the FBI had thought he was since the day after the Media break-in—the leader of the Media burglars—never materialized.

By the time the Camden burglars were sitting in jail the morning of August 22, 1971, after they were arrested—at the same time that J. Edgar Hoover and Attorney General John Mitchell were jointly announcing the arrests at a news conference in Washington—the FBI had no more evidence of who burglarized the Media FBI office than it did when agents jumped with joy when the Camden informer, Robert Hardy, showed up on their doorstep in June 1971.

The promise of Camden had vanished. The FBI had no evidence linking Grady—or anybody else from the Camden group, or anyone at all—to the Media burglary. This was true despite the fact that agents had listened to and transcribed hundreds of hours of the informer's conversations with Grady, including responses to the questions they had primed Hardy to ask Grady about his involvement in the Media burglary. They had photographed and analyzed the large cache of personal possessions that Grady had entrusted to the informer for a few days, including his extensive personal notebook, address book, and business records. From coast to coast, agents were given contact information for the people listed in Grady's address book and told to interview them. His name was not known to some of the people. Others thought they might have ordered books from him, but they did not remember ever meeting him. Most important, none of them knew anything about a connection between Grady and a place called Media. Not even a conversation with a brother from whom Grady was somewhat estranged produced any valuable information. The brother lamented to the FBI that their mother had always loved John Peter more than she loved him, but he seemed to know little if anything about Grady's activities.

Still, the investigators continued to think Grady was responsible for Media and that the other Media burglars were among those arrested at Camden. Roy Moore, the star investigator in charge of the MEDBURG investigation, insisted in a memo to Hoover four days after the arrests, "These people were involved in FBI-Media break-in and later distribution of FBI records."

But, contrary to Moore's claim, there was no certainty, only a belief. Investigators and bureau officials expressed frustration to one another soon after the initial glow produced by the Camden arrests. They did so while expressing contradictory assessments of the MEDBURG case. In internal memos, they repeatedly stated their belief that they knew who the Media burglars were. But, remarkably, at the same time they repeatedly acknowledged that they had no evidence pointing to any of the Media burglars. They were deeply disappointed that their entire Camden effort had reaped no evidence related to Media—despite accumulating an astounding 25,000 pieces of evidence from the Camden defendants, including Grady's records and a mountain of debris they collected from other defendants, even perfume bottles and chewing gum wrappers.

Moore confessed to Hoover the total lack of progress in MEDBURG while simultaneously expressing certainty that the bureau could take advantage of the momentum set in motion by the Camden arrests. "There is no physical evidence or witnesses to FBI-Media burglary," he wrote, just four days after the Camden arrests and after he had written to Hoover about the great public relations benefit of the arrests for the bureau. Apparently deeply frustrated, Moore wrote, "Matter can only be resolved by admissions. We now have key subjects in custody and must keep pressure on them to obtain admissions."

He described his new strategy to the director:

"Direct, positive and prompt action is the best way to defeat the group—hit them hard and turn the spotlight of public opinion against them now and stop future offenses. This action should also hinder them from recruiting new personnel." And, he noted, it would deplete their money by requiring them to "put up huge sums of money for bail and attorneys."

Moore recommended two new approaches, both involving pressing Camden defendants to confess to their involvement in Media. First, agents should conduct pointed interviews with the Camden defendants, and second, they should put them under oath in the closed confines of a grand jury and press them with questions about the burglary. Moore wanted the Department of Justice to empanel a grand jury soon for this purpose.

He summed up for Hoover what he thought would be necessary to arrest the people he was sure were the Media burglars. He was confident they were among thirty-nine people who had been targeted by agents and could be smoked out now by bringing indictments against them for three draft board raids that were unsolved crimes. The thirty-nine people he thought should be indicted had been winnowed down from four hundred "New Left activists" the MEDBURG squad had investigated in the Northeast in their search for the Media burglars, beginning the day after the burglary. He described the dimensions of the herculean effort that had taken place. For each of those four hundred people, agents had developed complete backgrounds, information about their associates and activities. "Informants were developed and directed seven days per week. . . . Voluminous files developed."

By the time of the arrests at Camden, he told the director, the people believed to have conducted the Media burglary had been winnowed down to thirty-nine suspects, most of whom had been arrested at Camden. A focus now on these thirty-nine people, Moore told the director, would unlock Media.

The fact that the Camden defendants were now facing sentences of up to forty-seven years in prison, Moore thought, meant that if they were forced to testify in secret before a grand jury it was likely they would be intimidated into revealing what they knew about their own or others' involvement in Media—presumably because they would be willing to exchange information about their own or other people's roles in Media for reduced sentences for their roles in Camden. Pointed interviews, plus "prompt additional indictments," Moore predicted, "will bring heavy pressure on entire Berrigan movement and . . . will likely serve as the means to obtain admissions regarding the FBI-Media burglary."

Hoover liked Moore's plan. In a memorandum to his four highest aides—Tolson, Felt, Sullivan, and Rosen—shortly after the Camden arrests, he wrote, "Moore feels as I do. If we proceed with . . . Selective Service cases, we could break the Media case. . . . Mr. Moore stated that nothing would make him happier than to make the arrests this week." The grand jury would be disguised as an investigation of draft board break-ins, but its real purpose would be to smoke out the Media burglars. If subpoenaed witnesses refused to testify, Hoover said, "the judge could fine them for contempt," bringing even more pressure.

To Hoover and Moore's great disappointment, Department of Justice officials refused to convene a grand jury now in response to their request. Use of the subpoena power of secret grand juries by the department to compensate for weak or failed FBI investigations had been strongly criticized in the past year. The MEDBURG investigative files reveal how this strategy that had been used repeatedly in the recent past haunted the bureau in this case. It wasn't that department officials had scruples about using grand juries as fishing expeditions when bureau investigations failed; the Nixon Department of Justice had in fact convened several such grand juries and based prosecutions on the results. But Justice officials expressed concern that doing so now might generate so much criticism that it would jeopardize the bombing–kidnap–draft board conspiracy case, which was scheduled to go to trial in January 1972 in Harrisburg, Pennsylvania. This case, designed to rescue Hoover from his embarrassing November 1970 accusations against the Berrigan brothers and others, rested nearly entirely on very slender evidence that had been brought before a grand jury. Moore's grand jury proposal targeted at the thirty-nine people was tabled until after the Harrisburg trial.

With this decision by Justice officials, Hoover found himself in the unusual situation of not being permitted to move forward in his preferred way on this case that was most important to him—the Media burglary—because of a case that had been created to defend baseless claims his top aides had pleaded with him not to make in November 1970. To all other causes of failure to solve the MEDBURG case, add Hoover being hoist by his own petard.

Now, as throughout the MEDBURG investigation, the official record indicates that investigators and headquarters officials did not confront their failures and reassess their strategies. Instead, Moore and other investigators, with Hoover's approval, remained wedded to their original assumptions about who had committed the crime, and stayed focused on that track. Even when they explored what could be learned from the behavior of Camden defendants that might point to similar behavior by the Media burglars, they stuck with their original assumptions. They had observed that the Camden burglars usually drank in local bars late at night after they finished casing duties. That prompted visits by agents to every bar in Media and its environs in the fall of 1971, armed with photos of possible suspects. Bartenders did not recognize any of them. They also examined local apartments near the FBI office that had been either vacant at the time of the burglary or vacated soon afterward. Fingerprints lifted from surfaces, cigarette butts, and an empty beer can found in those apartments were sent to the FBI lab with no positive results.

In an attempt to uncover new evidence in Media, a team of agents who had not participated previously in the investigation was assigned to survey the community. When they were done, their work, combined with work by earlier agents, meant that eighteen hundred local people who lived or worked in thirty-five square blocks, an area that must have included nearly the entire town, had been interviewed. Result: "No information of value was developed."

Following Moore's advice to press Camden defendants for information about Media, agents arranged for two women who worked in the Selective Service Board office next door to the Media FBI office to observe the Camden defendants when they were arraigned. As the women tried to discreetly survey the defendants and their supporters in the courtroom, Cookie Ridolfi's facial features attracted their attention. They moved close to her. They looked at her eyes, facial structure, hair coloring, and overall stature and told agents that her features precisely matched those of the woman who had come to their office and asked when the FBI office was open. MEDBURG investigators had already assumed Ridolfi was one of the Media burglars. The assertion of the Selective Service staff workers reinforced that assumption.

After Ridolfi was selected by the women, two agents went to interview her at her South Philadelphia home, where she lived with her mother. In a memorandum to the director marked "urgent"—for unclear reasons, given the lack of information agents got from Ridolfi—agents reported that they told Ridolfi immediately that they were there to discuss Media, not Camden, because they thought there was a connection between the two burglaries. They informed the director that she "made no verbal response to this assertion but did indicate by her general demeanor that the statement had some effect on her. Cookie then stated that she had to take a bath and wash her hair" and accompanied the agents to the door. As they left, they reported, one of them told her he had been reading the writings of the Berrigan brothers, and he thought she didn't adhere well to their teachings.

A few other Camden defendants were interviewed about Media. Contrary to what Moore had predicted, none of them confessed to breaking into the Media office. In fact, all of them said they knew nothing about Media beyond what they had read in newspapers. When FBI agents interviewed Father Michael Doyle about Media, the priest told them he knew nothing about it and was glad he didn't. He told them he thought their use of informers was abhorrent. He also used the occasion to ask them if he would be deported to Ireland if he was convicted on the Camden charges. They said they didn't know.

Now, as before, agents persisted in assuming that the people they interviewed about Media were lying when they said they did not know who broke into the FBI office. They could not imagine that the Media burglars had not bragged to other people—people the FBI hoped would now snitch on them—about what they had done.

Consistent with that assumption, one MEDBURG investigator predicted that in addition to the pressure brought by the Camden arrests, "it is almost a certainty that there is a wide circle of individuals in the various New left groups and among the Berrigan adherents who have some direct or hear-say knowledge about Medburg. It is highly likely that others among the Camden 28 were Medburg participants. Well-handled interviews of these people and their associates should eventually lead to someone with first-hand knowledge who is willing to testify for one reason or another."

Investigators continued to apply Moore's strategy after he left the investigation in October 1971 when he was assigned to be in charge of the Chicago FBI field office. It is not known if he asked to be removed from MEDBURG, but it is known that he was very frustrated by the case. Many years later he told me the investigators knew who the burglars were, but "we could not get their friends to talk." Files he gave me indicated he was wrong—at the end of the investigation only one of the Media burglars was a suspect.

AS THE MEDIA INVESTIGATION continued, some of the investigators' techniques, as in the earliest months, seemed more like either make-work or incompetence than sophisticated criminal investigative methods. For instance, hundreds of staples were removed from copies of Media files that had been sent to journalists and others. With assistance from a staple expert, agents established that approximately twenty different types of staplers had been used to staple the five different types of staples they removed from the copies. Scores of pages of detailed reports on the staples were prepared, consuming considerable time. But because the earlier search to find the Xerox 660 copier that had been used by the burglars had failed to link the files to a particular copier and therefore failed to link them to any individual—after collecting sample copies from more than 4,000 such copiers—there was no way to use the staple evidence.

A wild-goose chase at Yale Law School was halted by the New Haven FBI field office. In October 1971, the director asked that field office to break into the Yale Law School office of civil liberties attorney Frank Donner. The effort concerned a stolen Media document that Hoover thought might not be authentic and may have come from Donner's office and therefore might be a lead to whether he was involved in MEDBURG. The agent in charge at New Haven reported to Hoover that employees in the administrative offices at Yale Law School were not acquainted with Donner. The agent told the director that New Haven agents did not believe the file in question originated with Donner and that "it is not believed feasible to make an attempt to enter the office of Donner . . . to secure typewriter samples or make any further open or discreet inquiries." Two months later, Hoover was back with the same request. This time the New Haven field office responded even more forcefully:

"Any attempted investigation of Donner's material at Yale . . . in his office would be extremely inadvisable due to the potential for embarrassment to the Bureau."

At the time, Donner was conducting a massive study, based at Yale, of government surveillance of citizens for the American Civil Liberties Union. Then as later, he was widely regarded as the leading scholar on government surveillance of citizens. He later wrote the leading books on the subject, including his 1981 landmark book *The Age of Surveillance: The Aims and Methods of America's Political Intelligence System*. Donner had no connection to the Media burglary, but the stolen files and the information that later flowed from them during and after congressional investigations of intelligence agencies expanded the scope of his scholarly work on government surveillance. Just a month after the Media burglary, on April 22, 1971, he wrote a major article in the *New York Review of Books* in which he said the documents stolen at Media were evidence of a relatively new and "formidable way of responding to political and social movements—a system of political intelligence" as a means of controlling dissent. That public statement was probably more than enough to prompt Hoover to think Donner should be viewed as a potential suspect in the Media burglary.

There were signs that agents in other FBI field offices also were growing weary of being asked to conduct MEDBURG investigations that seemed more likely to be foolish than fruitful in the search for the burglars. In Louisville, agents, at the director's request right after the burglary, had instructed the warden at the Federal Youth Center in Ashland, Kentucky, to read and copy all incoming and outgoing mail and monitor the visits and phone conversations of a young pacifist whose wife the bureau mistakenly assumed for months was the "UNSUB," Bonnie Raines. The man, a conscientious objector, had been convicted in the fall of 1970 for a break-in at federal offices in Rochester, New York. The daily reports on him had been forwarded to the bureau since March 26, 1971. In November, the agent in charge of the Louisville field office reported that because nothing from the excessive coverage of this prisoner had been developed "pertinent to the break-in of the Media" office, "it is not felt that a current report . . . would be meaningful or necessary. Consequently, no report is being submitted by Louisville."

In Washington, that message generated this fierce underlined, bold, all-caps response from Hoover:

ALL INDIVIDUALS INVOLVED IN NEW LEFT EXTREMIST ACTIVITY SHOULD BE CONSIDERED DANGEROUS BECAUSE OF THEIR KNOWN ADVOCACY AND USE OF EXPLOSIVES, REPORTED ACQUISITION OF FIREARMS AND INCENDIARY DEVICES AND KNOWN PROPENSITY FOR VIOLENCE.

However maddening and frustrating the burglaries by the Catholic peace movement were to the FBI, Hoover had much evidence that these activists were strong advocates of nonviolence. It was at the root of their dissent. Recently, in fact, the informer in the Camden case, Hardy, had "tested" some Camden defendants' commitment to nonviolence, even offering one of them a pistol. He refused to touch it. None of them were willing to consider possessing a gun when the informer offered them one for their protection. They went to great lengths to avoid encounters that could provoke violence and to train themselves to react passively if they were confronted by law enforcement officers, as the Camden defendants did. Hoover's assumption that the Catholic peace movement activists—or all New Leftists, to use his broader term—should be assumed to be armed and violent starkly illustrates his refusal throughout his tenure as director to differentiate between various types of dissenters. In his mind, all dissenters were equally dangerous whether they advocated violence or nonviolence.

The Chicago field office was reluctant to follow up on a request from the Philadelphia field office that agents there find a man believed to be affiliated with Bethany Theological Seminary in nearby Oak Brook, Illinois, and ask him how he had disposed of his nametag in 1969 when he attended the War Resisters International Conference at Haverford College. A facsimile of his nametag was on one of the stolen Media files. It was clear that agents did not appreciate being told in advance of interviewing him that "his cooperation could be elicited by concentrating on both his anti-communism and zealous religious emotional feelings" and "best chance of success . . . is in isolating him and implanting in his mind the thought that . . . his problems were the result of actions on the part of godless communists, that the FBI was not responsible for his problems." When found, the man was running a Baptist organization that was a precursor of Jews for Jesus. The interview produced no helpful information. He did not know how his nametag had ended up in an FBI file three years earlier. The most likely possibility, of course, was that he had lost the tag and its sticky back had accidentally adhered to papers carried by one of the twenty FBI informers who covered the conference for the bureau.

The Philadelphia field office realized by December 1971 that the MED-BURG case was taking over the office. Literally. "In view of the intensive investigation given this case and the number of reports submitted, much file space is consumed by material pertinent to this case," wrote J. Clifford Ousley, who supervised MEDBURG after Moore was reassigned. To conserve filing space, he ordered, in FBI bureaucratese, that "informant channelizing memoranda are destroyed after pertinent information has been incorporated in report form." Ensure, he urged, that "no material is destroyed which would be pertinent to your future prosecutive needs." Given what emerged at the Camden trial, it seems likely that order was issued more to save face rather than to save space. The bureau had files about its Camden investigation that, if they had become public, would have been damaging to the FBI. They included transcripts of the many hours of conversations between the informer and the defendants and conversations between the informer and agents, all of which the FBI refused to produce in court.

THE CAMDEN TRIAL OPENED on February 5, 1973, in a third-floor courtroom in the downtown Camden federal building where the burglary had taken place. By that time, much had changed. The Harrisburg trial had ended in April 1972 in a hung jury. Once determined to win this case designed to protect Hoover's reputation, Department of Justice officials decided not to retry the defendants when, even in deeply conservative Dauphin County, they did not get convictions.

Another crucial change since the Camden arrests: J. Edgar Hoover had died in May 1972. He had written memos pushing agents to solve the Media case nearly daily beginning the day after the burglary and continuing until the day before he died in his sleep. He continued to be eager for the Camden case to result in convictions for the twenty-eight defendants. He was confident that that would be the outcome despite a major obstacle to the case that arose in March 1972 and infuriated him.

That obstacle: Two months before Hoover died, the FBI lost its chief Camden witness, informer Robert Hardy.

At about the same time that FBI agents in Philadelphia followed instructions in December 1971 to destroy some of the files related to Hardy's work as an informer, Hardy was thinking more deeply about the morality of what he had done for the FBI at Camden and how it would be used to prosecute the defendants. After he and his wife discussed the matter at length, he decided he needed to tell the truth: that the FBI had used him as a provocateur. He met with Father Doyle and Philadelphia attorney David Kairys to reveal his role. He told them he had decided to tell the truth because of Billy. It "is a matter of spirit to me," Hardy told the two men. "It's Billy living on. I want to do what's right."

In a step that became significant news and was profoundly important to the defendants, Hardy stated in an affidavit in March 1972 that, at the FBI's request, he had become the leader of the Camden group, and in the process, he had become an agent provocateur. He said he had advised the group on how to break into the draft board office and taught them techniques they had not needed in earlier draft board raids and therefore did not know. His role was so significant, he said, that the burglary could not have happened without him. Furthermore, the FBI had paid for most of the tools used by the burglars to carry out the burglary and had even paid for the burglars' groceries during the two months they prepared for the break-in—"right down to every potato chip."

Hardy said his worries about the meaning of what he had done had started minutes after the Camden raid got under way. He was alone in his pickup truck, at a location agreed to by the burglars and known to the FBI. His truck was one of the blocking vehicles. He was assigned by the burglars to be ready to tell police he was having engine problems if an officer questioned him. He was assigned by the FBI to make sure he informed them about every move by the burglars. As he sat there, listening in on the conversations taking place among the burglars on their walkie-talkies, he realized as minutes passed that no arrests were taking place. He couldn't understand why nothing was happening. The communication surveillance system the FBI had installed in his truck was only for one-way communication, so Hardy couldn't use it to ask agents what had gone wrong. He was surprised because, he later said, he had been told repeatedly that "his friends" would never go to jail, that they would be arrested at the outset of the raid and charged with only minor crimes. "They reassured me, even up until the night of the break-in, that they would never go to jail. And, of course, they lied."

As he sat in his truck faking that his truck was broken down, he realized that criminal charges were mounting the longer his friends were inside the draft board office removing and destroying files. But he couldn't do anything. He felt helpless. "The next morning, I talked with my two agents, Mike and Terry. I said, 'You guys really screwed us. You lied to me all the way through.'

"And that's when Mike Ryman said, 'Well, the decision was made at the little White House in California: John Mitchell, Mr. Hoover and Mr. Nixon, they made the decision to let these people break in and lock their butts up for as long as they could.'"

"I don't say Terry Neist and Mike Ryman lied, but those who made the decision at the higher levels—their intention was to destroy the Catholic Left," Hardy said.

From the start, what the FBI wanted from Hardy, he said, was "everything I could find out, particularly about Grady. He was their main target. They thought he did the Media raid." They "asked me to find out who had done it." He said he tried, but "that's the one thing I could not get out of Grady, or anybody that worked with him." Hardy thought that if he had found who burglarized Media, it would have been as important to the FBI "as finding out today where Jimmy Hoffa is buried."

Hardy testified later that he did not agree with the defendants' philosophy of breaking the law as a means of protest, but that he also came to disagree with the government's use of illegal means to entrap the defendants.

After Hardy's affidavit became public, and the bureau felt a deep frustration about this case that was supposed to end in triumph at Camden, an official at Washington headquarters, R. J. Gallagher, wrote a memorandum to other bureau officials at headquarters. It was a long lament about how much everything related to solving the Media burglary seemed to be going wrong at that point:

> From the moment during June 1971, when we first became aware of the intended plan of John Peter Grady, avid revolutionary and Berrigan Brothers admirer, to mastermind a burglary of Federal space in the Camden, NJ, area, it was obvious as a result of our continuous investigation into the Media incident that both activities were inexorably entwined. Grady, who was eventually caught red handed with his associates as they broke into the Selective Service Office at Camden, New Jersey on August 22, 1971, has been identified through several sources and independent investigation as having masterminded the Media break-in [author's note: an assertion that was fabricated either by FBI agents or by their sources, though in the end the bureau admitted it had no sources with direct knowledge about the burglary].
>
> An all-out investigation was initiated immediately upon determining that our Media Resident Agency had been broken into. . . . The investigation from the outset was handicapped by the almost total lack of physical evidence. A thorough crime scene search was conducted followed by another search in order to insure that all possible evidence was brought to light. . . .
>
> We have constantly attempted to develop new avenues of investigation aimed at developing evidence to support prosecution under Medburg. Supervisors responsible for Medburg and the Camden action have on a regular basis reviewed and double checked all aspects of the investigation.
>
> Recognizing many of the Grady group in the Camden action were responsible for the Media burglary, we have continually, through regular contacts with the U.S. Attorney's office, Camden, NJ, and the Internal Security Division, pressed for early prosecution in the Camden action. In spite of our pressure . . . the Camden Action prosecution is still pending. No trial date has been set. . . . Now possibly due to some extent to the delay in prosecution, Robert Hardy, the informant in the Camden break-in, has soured and has given an affidavit to the defense indicating the break-in was financed to a large extent by the FBI and that he, as an FBI informant, was instrumental in revitalizing the planned break-in which was doomed to failure because of disorganization and ineptness on the part of Grady and his group.

Hardy's allegations are false, and Newark and Philadelphia agents involved are analyzing same and submitting affidavits.

No such affidavits were submitted by agents or FBI officials.

AS THE CAMDEN TRIAL got under way in the courtroom of a Nixon-appointed judge, Clarkson Fisher, on the surface it looked like it might be a typical antiwar trial of that era where judges, fearing defendants would create a disruptive atmosphere, took steps to prevent such behavior. Known as a tough, pro-prosecution judge, Judge Fisher ruled in favor of the government in nearly every pretrial motion, even refusing to order the government to provide the defendants with the reports based on Hardy's meetings with his FBI supervising agents.

Fairly early in the trial there were signs that he might not be as inflexible as he appeared at first. In a significant decision, he ruled that the defendants and their lawyers could be "cocounsel"—a ruling that meant all defendants and defense lawyers would be permitted to actively participate in the trial. The right to self-representation was often recognized by judges, but the right of defendants to be cocounsel, as lawyers are, was unusual, if not unheard of. Judge Fisher also granted the defendants' unusual request that jurors be permitted to ask questions of witnesses. He even had no problem when defendant Paul Couming arrived in court with pads and pencils the day after that permission was granted and asked to distribute them to jurors so they could write questions. The judge said he could. In the course of the trial, every juror asked questions.

The judge seemed to recognize early in the five-month trial that these defendants—whose courtroom dress ranged from blue jeans, dashiki, suit and tie, skirt and sweater to clerical black—treated him and the trial proceedings with respect and were unlikely to cause the disruptions he had feared. The judge in turn went out of his way to be respectful to the participants. According to an FBI report, early in the trial Judge Fisher invited one of the government's witnesses, Joseph E. Ziel of the FBI's Newark field office, to his chambers after he was cross-examined for five and a half days by sixteen defendants and three defense lawyers. He told Ziel he had been a "magnificent witness." Much later in the trial, the judge told Robert Good, one of the defendants, in his chambers that he was going to have a very hard time if Good was convicted. He also told Good that he regretted he knew so little about the Vietnam War, and now, inspired by the defendants and their witnesses, was studying the war.

In contrast, at the same time these convivial exchanges were taking place with the Camden judge, the MEDBURG investigative record documents that the FBI agents assigned to assist prosecutors at the trial sent an "all offices expedite" message to FBI offices around the country asking them to "furnish any derogatory information . . . to discredit . . . witnesses." The New York field office, for instance, was asked to check whether its records included documentation that historian Howard Zinn, a defense witness at Camden, had attended the 1948 New York State Communist Party convention. One of the Camden prosecutors later told me the derogatory information about defense witnesses collected by the agents and presented to prosecutors was obnoxious and irrelevant.

At the outset of the trial, for more than two months a parade of FBI agents testified about the details of what had happened at Camden. In cross-examination, defense attorney David Kairys pushed FBI agents on why they did not prevent the crime from taking place. Given the overwhelming man-power they had, it would have been easy to have prevented the destruction of government property, the crime for which the defendants were now being tried. Why did agents wait hours to arrest? They said they didn't know where all the burglars were, and for safety reasons delayed arrests until they could locate everyone. That answer was not believable, for it was clear that thanks to Hardy's detailed reports, agents knew in advance exactly where every burglar was and also had the benefit of listening to their conversations at the time. Each agent was asked by defense attorneys if he had taken any step at any time while he was attached to the investigation to prevent the crime. Each said he had not. None of them testified to what the investigative file attests: The agents expected to arrest the defendants before they destroyed property, but were prevented from doing so by orders issued from FBI headquarters in Washington—the orders that Hardy said he was told originated with the attorney general and the president.

On the witness stand, Hardy testified for the defense. Frank Donner, the expert on political surveillance, was in court to observe this historic occasion: the first time in U.S. history that a government informer was a witness for the defense rather than for the government. Hardy described the details of his role as planner, morale booster, creator of schematic drawings of the office where the break-in would occur, and supplier of tools and food at FBI expense. There were numerous dramatic moments in Hardy's testimony. Perhaps the most powerful were his responses to Kairys's questions about the tools used during the break-in. Kairys says he had "thought a lot about how I could most convincingly bring home to the jurors what Hardy and the FBI had done." He did it with vivid visual elements.

"Mr. Hardy," he began, "I have in front of me all of the tools that the defendants were caught with inside the draft board. These are the burglars' tools the FBI agents testified were used to break into the draft board office in the middle of the night. I'm going to show you each one and ask you where it came from and who paid for it. Then I'm going to make two piles with these items on the floor directly in front of the jury. One pile will be items you or the FBI provided or paid for; the other will be items the defendants provided or paid for. Include in the second pile—the defendants' pile—items that you are uncertain about or that you can't say for sure were provided by you or the FBI."

"Okay," said Hardy.

"One thing before we start. Your own personal tools that you gave to the defendants, were you reimbursed for them?"

"Yes, I was reimbursed for anything at all that I provided."

"So if you say an item was from your shop and you provided it to the defendants, that also means the FBI reimbursed you and paid for it?"

"That's right."

"Okay. Exhibit G-11. What is this?"

"These are bolt cutters. I bought them."

"You bought them for the defendants to use, and the FBI reimbursed you, so these go in the FBI pile?"

"Right."

"How about these three screwdrivers, Exhibits G-608, 609, and 604?"

"The black-handled one, 604, is my own personal screwdriver. The other two were bought."

"So the FBI pile. How about G-615?"

"These are utility knives, several of them. One was mine, and the others were bought."

"And this, G-610?"

"It's a plumb hammer. That was bought."

"G-659?"

"This is duct tape that we used from the fifth-floor fire escape to tape over the glass before we drilled it and broke it out. This is my personal tape."

"G-707, 102, and 104?"

"Walkie-talkies. These I purchased, and the FBI paid me."

"Okay, D-101?"

"A prying tool. Purchased."

"D-111?"

"Two drill bits for glass. I didn't buy these. I told them what to get and where to get it, but I think they paid."

"D-103?"

"A portable drill. That isn't mine, but I gave it to them."

"How about D-100?"

"This is my rope, a long rope."

When Kairys finished questioning Hardy, the attorney recalls, there were two distinctly different piles. "The FBI pile had a large number and variety of tools and equipment, covering a large portion of the rug in front of the jury. The defendants' pile had two drill bits, a small flat piece of metal, and a small V-8 juice can."

Kairys had one more question for Hardy. He walked to the piles on the floor and picked up Exhibit D-103 and said, "Mr. Hardy, this portable drill you had me put in the FBI pile, whose is it?"

"That drill belongs to an FBI agent."

"An FBI agent. How did it get here?"

"My plan required one of those new kind of drills, portable, run by battery, but I couldn't find one in stores around here. The group had waited for me to get them one. A few days before the raid, I called my FBI guys and told them I had to have a portable drill right away or the action would be called off. They told me to meet later that day at a parking lot we used in Merchantville. My lead control agent, Mike Ryman, met me there. I asked him where he got the portable drill. He said one of the FBI agents in the office had one in his personal shop. That agent went home to get it so Agent Ryman could give it to me and I could give it to the defendants."

After that testimony, there was little doubt about whether the FBI had taken steps to make sure this crime happened.

The prosecution made no attempt to rebut Hardy's testimony.

When the defendants met shortly after their arrest to discuss trial strategy, there was disagreement on whether they would claim they had been entrapped by Hardy. Pride prevented some of them from acknowledging that they had depended on him. When Kairys first brought up Hardy's role with Grady, he said, "Nah, he was nothing. He's a blowhard. You know, hundreds of draft boards have been raided. We didn't need him."

The defendants who shared Grady's opinion wanted to rely on jury nullification—ask the jury to refuse to convict them because the defendants had engaged in civil disobedience—broken the law—in order to protest the

Vietnam War and to take a stand to preserve life rather than cause death. Kairys and the other two lawyers working with the defendants, Marty Stoler and Carl Broge, respected the rich history of jury nullification as it had been used throughout American history to fight unjust laws.

In the end, the defendants agreed to meld two defenses—jury nullification and a defense based on a legal theory that the government had over-reached in its effort to make sure the crime took place. That combination of approaches was carried out in a rare collaboration between attorneys and defendants.

Judge Fisher permitted the defendants to explain how their opposition to the war had caused them to commit an act of resistance. He also permitted them to call as witnesses a wide range of people who supported resistance to the war, including both Daniel and Philip Berrigan. One by one, defense witnesses spoke of resistance to the government's war policy as an admired virtue central to an understanding of American history and to maintaining a just society. One of the most surprising witnesses was Major Clement St. Martin, the commander of the New Jersey State induction center in Newark from 1968 to 1971. Files under his control had been destroyed by the defendants. Nevertheless, he testified in their defense. He said he had become completely frustrated after years of making futile complaints through appropriate channels about the gross corruption in the way the draft forced the sons of the poor to serve in Vietnam and released the sons of the rich and sons of state and federal officials from service. His frustrations had grown particularly deep, he testified, in 1969 when a "very high" Selective Service official, responding to complaints filed by the major, told him, "Mind your business. We have twenty million animals to choose from."

But, prosecutor John Barry asked the major, did the inequities in the system justify "private individuals breaking into the buildings in the middle of the night"? It is unlikely that Barry, or anyone else in the courtroom, could have anticipated the answer. The major startled nearly everyone when he said, "If they plan another raid, I might join them."

Howard Zinn told the jury that civil disobedience seems like an outrageous outlaw idea but actually is "at the center of American democratic philosophy." Called by Ridolfi as an expert witness on civil disobedience and the history of the Vietnam War, he testified that the Camden defendants had acted in the tradition of the people who defied the Fugitive Slave Acts and freed slaves before the Civil War. Such actions, he said, have been necessary "all through history in order to win justice for people." He warned against clinging to the idea that "we must obey the law . . . that the law is holy. . . . It's a very bad education we all get because it misses the distinction between law and justice."

Zinn's greatest impact that day may have been how he profoundly saddened but also inspired Betty Good, mother of defendant Bob Good. Testifying on a Friday, Zinn said the Pentagon Papers "showed very clearly that the United States was not in Vietnam for purposes of liberty and democracy and humanitarian and self-determination reasons." The secret memos in the Pentagon Papers, he said, "were saying again and again, when talking about why we were in Vietnam, and why we were interested in Southeast Asia—they were talking about tin, rubber and oil . . . about the resources of Southeast Asia."

As Zinn emphasized that idea again—that the United States was in Vietnam for resources: tin, rubber and oil—Mrs. Good, seated in the front row, could not suppress the impact of this revelation. She left the courtroom and sobbed in the hallway. She was inconsolable. That weekend she asked her son to put her on the stand on Monday. A few other parents of defendants had testified about the values they had imparted to their children. Bob Good was not sure what his mother would say. She and his father had strongly questioned his decision to become a conscientious objector and his later decisions to engage in acts of civil disobedience to oppose the war. She had come to Camden to offer moral support but without fully approving of what her son had done in Camden. He was cautious as he stood before her in the courtroom and asked her a general question about how she and his carpenter father had raised him on their farm near Sharpsville in western Pennsylvania.

Never in a courtroom until she came to Camden to provide moral support for her son, Betty Good faced the jurors and first told them the story of two of her ten children, Bob and Paul. Bob, she said, for three years had lived as though the Vietnam War was next door, as though he could see the killing, hear the bombs, as though he was responsible for it and responsible for stopping it. And Paul, who she said was Bob's closest brother, had proudly joined the Army and gone to Vietnam.

She described driving Paul to the airport in Pittsburgh six years before the day she was testifying. She and her husband were proud their son wanted to serve his country. As Bob would say when he testified, "That's what you did where we came from." Paul's flight to Vietnam that day marked the first time he was on an airplane. Less than two months later he was killed in the Mekong Delta and brought home to Sharpsville, where he was buried with full military rites.

Mrs. Good told the jury that, like her son Paul, she had not paid much attention to the world outside Sharpsville and also had not paid attention to what the U.S. government was doing in Vietnam. She had just assumed officials knew what they were doing and that the war was necessary to keep communists from attacking the United States. She looked at jurors steadily as she said, "We ought to be ashamed of ourselves. I know I am. I am ashamed of the day I took my son to that airplane and put him on. I'm ashamed of any pride that I had when taps were played. And I did have pride then. I am proud of my son because he didn't know. A kid that never had a gun in his life. . . . And to take that lovely boy and tell him, 'You are fighting for your country.' How stupid can we get? He was fighting for his country! Can anybody stand there and tell me now he was fighting for his country?"

Mrs. Good told the jury that the realization that her son Paul had not died for his country had come to her only as she listened to Zinn three days earlier in the courtroom. "Tin, rubber and oil" had been echoing in her mind ever since she listened to him discuss the history of the war. "And the public was told the main U.S. interest was in saving Vietnam from Communism" and "to save Americans from attack."

She apologized for her past tendency to blame every new idea Bob had on communism. "I was hung up on it. I feel that is the way most of us middle-class Americans are. We're so hung up on communism . . . that we don't know what our own government is doing. . . . I can't understand what we're doing over there. We should get out of this. But not one of us raised our hand. We left it up to these people—the defendants—for them to do it."

Betty Good surprised her son and transfixed many, if not everyone, in the courtroom, including Judge Fisher. Bob Good asked his mother if there was anything else she wanted to say. "Well, yes," she replied. "There's one thing I had in mind to say, that when you were arrested you sent me the most beautiful letter. And if I thought I was going to be up here, I would have brought it." Turning to look at the jurors again, she said, "He spelled it out for us, why he was doing this, how he felt it was something he had to do and indeed put the blame back on us because of the way we brought him up: that he was doing this for the country, not against the country."

Bob, moved deeply by his mother's words, was about to tell her she could step down from the witness stand when he realized he had forgotten to invite the prosecutors to cross-examine her. When he did so, the judge nodded to Barry that he could proceed. "We have no questions, your honor," said the prosecutor. Mrs. Good's testimony was uncontested.

IN HIS SUMMATION to the jury, Barry reminded the jurors that at that time in Washington another burglary, the Watergate burglary, was the center of controversy. Those burglars, like the Camden burglars, he said, thought they were doing something that served a greater political good.

Kairys emphasized the FBI's complicity in the crime in his closing remarks: "Neither the FBI nor the defendants placed any value on those pieces of paper in the draft board office. To the defendants, they were non-living matter that had no right to exist. To the FBI, they were part of the machinery of war but a part of that machinery that was expendable to discredit antiwar movements." He urged jurors to realize that, as Judge Fisher would say in his charge to the jury, "they could acquit if they felt government participation in setting up the crime had gone to 'intolerable' lengths that were 'offensive to the basic standards of decency and shocking to the universal sense of justice.'" As the judge noted in his charge to the jury and Kairys said in his closing remarks, under a new U.S. Supreme Court ruling, a decision to acquit could be reached on the basis of government overreaching activity even if the defendants had a predisposition to commit the crime.

Making the case for nullification by the jury, Kairys told the jurors that the defendants, out of passionate opposition to the Vietnam War, had engaged in civil disobedience because "they saw a conflict between law and morality, between law and life. . . . They made the same choices we would want German people to make when Jews were being killed, the same choices we would want Americans to make when black people were in slavery."

AS THE DEFENDANTS WAITED for the jury's verdict, some of them were optimistic. Others were fearful. They knew they had had a fair trial, one where they, unlike the defendants in most antiwar trials of that era, had been permitted to make the case against the war and the case for their decision to engage in nonviolent civil disobedience in protest of the war. But from the beginning defense attorneys had warned them that the chances of all jurors agreeing to acquit all defendants was highly unlikely. It had not happened in any antiwar trial to date. Kairys had cautioned them that acquittals were especially unlikely for crimes committed during wartime that involved breaking into a federal building in the middle of the night and destroying war-related government property. He firmly believed they should be found not guilty on the basis of the standards of nullification and because the government had wildly overreached when the FBI reignited plans for the break-in and forced it to take place despite defendants' repeated wishes that it be canceled, but he thought acquittals were unlikely.

The defendants thought Michael Doyle was clever but unrealistic when he, during closing remarks to the jury, told the jurors they would have the last word, and then, pausing, smiled and amended his statement: "No, you will have the last two words."

On the fourth day of jury deliberation, word went out on a telephone tree that the jury had reached verdicts. Over the next few hours, defendants and their supporters, lawyers from both sides, U.S. marshals, court staff, and journalists drove on that gray and rainy Sunday afternoon from their homes throughout the greater Philadelphia area to be present to hear the verdicts announced.

The atmosphere was tense and somber as the Camden defendants and many supporters gradually filled the large courtroom to capacity. Unable to find seats, latecomers lined the perimeter of the room. In the front, the defendants sat, as they had throughout the trial, around long tables clustered on the left front side, angled so all of them faced the judge. On the right side, the four prosecutors sat at a single long table.

The hum of conversations stopped when Judge Fisher entered the courtroom. From the bench, he prepared the audience for a tedious process. "Ladies and gentlemen," he said, "I am going to bring the jury in in a minute. Before I do, I just wanted to request of everyone, if they would, we have to go through this by defendant and by count, each individually, and it will be quite a bit of time consumed. If we could have no demonstrations, no matter what the verdict is on any defendant or on any count, out of courtesy to the jury, because they are very tired, and we just wouldn't be able to get through it if there was a lot of noise. So I especially request that.

"Okay. Bring them in."

The jurors filed in and took their seats. Kairys remembers searching jurors' faces for clues. Some of them established eye contact. A good sign, he thought. But, he realized, mostly they just looked wiped out.

The court clerk asked the jury foreman, James Lomax, if the jurors had agreed on a verdict. "Yes," said Lomax.

"How say you? How do you find the defendant, Terry Edward Buckalew, on count one of the indictment?"

"We, your honor, find him not guilty."

Asked about each of the other six counts as to Buckalew, Lomax responded "not guilty" six times.

The defendants, who were standing as the foreman read, some with their heads bowed at first, were now glancing at one another. Their faces were filled with surprise and hopeful could-it-be expressions.

Judge Fisher, apparently sensing a trend, interrupted the process. "Mr. Lomax," he asked, "do you have any different verdicts than that on any count for any defendant?"

"None different, your honor."

A slight smile creased the judge's face.

The courtroom was silent for a split second. Then there was an explosive gasp as the striking result was absorbed: all twenty-eight defendants had just been acquitted of all the crimes for which they had been tried.

Someone started to sing "Amazing Grace." Neither the judge nor the prosecutor objected. It was clear neither of them considered it a disruption. People found it difficult, though, to sing through their tears, soon evident on faces throughout the courtroom.

The defendants moved, at first almost as if they were in a stupor. They could not believe what they had just heard. They hugged one another. Their faces were portraits of disbelief, relief, and, finally, overwhelming happiness.

As though in another universe, directly across from the defendants, the four prosecutors stood at their table, looking slightly out of place as they motionlessly watched the defendants' moving reactions to their unexpected triumph. Carolyn Ellis, one of the assistant prosecutors, impulsively turned and hugged a spectator in the front row as she said, "Tell them congratulations for me." And then she rushed from the courtroom.

Chief prosecutor John Barry stood at his place at the prosecutors' table for a few minutes. Three defendants who were hugging one another realized, as they released their embrace, that Barry had approached and was standing in front of them. Most of the other defendants paused and watched in silence as this improbable scene unfolded. Barry, who had presented the case against them for five months, at first put his hand forward to one of the defendants and shook hands in what looked like a typical end-of-trial formal courtesy congratulatory gesture. But he and the defendant soon dropped this hesitant formal approach and warmly embraced. Awkwardly at first and then more easily, Barry moved from defendant to defendant, each time his handshake turning into an embrace. He had seemed testy at times during the trial and determined to get convictions. Now that had dissolved.

Barry returned to the prosecutors' table. There were tears in his eyes as he walked up to where I was standing in the first row, directly behind the prosecutors' table. We had never met, but he knew that, standing there with pad and pencil, I was a journalist. He reached for my hand. As he shook it, he said, "It ended the way it should have ended."

In numerous ways, the trial was historic. It was, said Supreme Court justice William Brennan, "one of the great trials of the twentieth century."

LARGELY UNNOTICED in the middle of this jubilant crowd celebrating this, the first acquittal of all defendants in any antiwar trial, were Media burglars John and Bonnie Raines. Like everyone else in the courtroom, they were radiant—smiling widely, thrilled, amazed at the verdicts, and shedding a few tears of joy. They had special reasons to be so happy.

This was the case that was supposed to have led to their arrest. These defendants had endured the threat of forty-seven years in prison for crimes the FBI had aided and abetted, all in order to find and arrest the Media burglars. John and Bonnie felt relief and joy for the Camden defendants. They also felt relief and joy for themselves. It was as though these defendants had been stand-ins for them—which, in a way, they had been.

As they quietly shared the warm spirit of the spontaneous courtroom celebration of the Camden defendants' victory and freedom, John and Bonnie couldn't help letting themselves wish, just briefly, that they might be arrested and have a similar trial in which their stealing and revealing FBI secrets would be on full display in a courtroom—their rationale for the burglary would be explained, their trove of important documents would be discussed. Their testimony, they dared to think, would change hearts and minds in the courtroom and in the public as news stories reported to the outside world what transpired during their trial. For people who had been keeping their involvement in the Media burglary a secret for more than two years by that time, and who expected to continue to keep it a secret the rest of their lives, as all of the Media burglars had promised one another they would, this was quite a fantasy.

John Raines let his fantasy of a great trial—a trial similar, he liked to think, to the Camden 28 trial—roll in his mind several times in the next few years. In his fantasy trial, he hoped the burglars would be represented by John Doar, the distinguished lawyer who during John's summers in the South had played a powerful positive role there as an attorney for the Civil Rights Division of the Department of Justice. As their attorney in the Media case, according to John's fantasy, Doar would help the burglars develop a defense that would make clear that they had burglarized the Media FBI office in order to reveal information to the public and Congress about FBI practices that were illegal and dangerous to democracy—practices that suppressed dissent.

John Raines's fantasy was a mixture of hope moderated by fear: hope that if they were arrested they would have a good trial, and fear that they might actually be arrested. He thought he should prepare in case they were. He had gained weight in recent years and decided he should become a thin person. For about a year, he stayed on a strict diet of cottage cheese and fruit and lost sixty pounds. He is proud that he never gained weight again. He resumed playing tennis during that year of dieting and has played regularly ever since. Once he lost the weight, he bought a fine dark suit. If the need arose, he was ready to make a good appearance in court as a defendant.

John and Bonnie enjoyed thinking that if the Media Eight—what they assumed their group would become known as if they were arrested—went to trial, there surely would be a great concluding moment when they, too, would be acquitted for what they had done. They hoped a jury would recognize that the burglary they had carried out should be regarded not as a crime but as a service to their country.

WHEN THE CAMDEN TRIAL ENDED, the Philadelphia FBI office was still investigating the Media burglary. In this third year of the MEDBURG investigation, FBI officials still claimed they were certain Grady was the leader of the burglars and that evidence would be found to link him to the Media break-in. After Hoover's death in May 1972, acting FBI directors had tried to keep the MEDBURG investigation on track, but bureau officials' attention inevitably was diverted by other crimes that were center stage in Washington by the time the Camden defendants were acquitted. In addition to the Watergate burglars facing trials, the top Department of Justice officials who played major roles in both the MEDBURG and Camden cases—Attorney General John Mitchell, Assistant Attorney General Robert Mardian, and Attorney General Richard Kleindienst—had resigned their government positions and soon would be charged and eventually most would be convicted in connection with their roles in Watergate-related crimes.

As the Watergate investigations led to convictions of high-level officials in Washington, other officials in Congress and in the Department of Justice, informed by the Media revelations, were preparing for the next big Washington investigation: the first-ever investigation of the FBI.

18

The Secret FBI Emerges

THE MEDIA FILES were the essential beginning—the opening of
the door to the secret FBI. To the immense frustration of J. Edgar
Hoover's closest bureau allies who assumed responsibility after his
May 1972 death for protecting his secrets and keeping the bureau as it had
always been, the door the Media burglars opened in March 1971 could not
be closed. As it opened more, at first in small increments, the impact of the
burglary expanded. FBI officials kept trying to push it shut, but that became
impossible as more truth about the FBI's past—the secret FBI—became
known.

When the bureau's secret COINTELPRO programs were first revealed,
it was clear why Hoover and his successors feared the bureau's reputation
would be seriously damaged if those operations became known. From the
Media files, people had learned that the FBI purposely encouraged the
growth of paranoia, was consumed by a perceived need to monitor black
people, and had spied on people for years without justification. Later, as a
judge and then other officials ordered the FBI to open COINTELPRO files,
Americans learned that some FBI operations aimed at dissenters went far
beyond spying. Some were designed to hurt people physically and to destroy
reputations by planting derogatory information that had been fabricated by
the bureau.

How the records of the secret FBI were forced open after the Media files
became known is a story of the persistence and dedication of numerous
people in the face of strong resistance from the FBI. They included a journalist, members of both houses of Congress, members of the Socialist Work-

ers Party, and, ultimately, two attorneys general and a few FBI officials. A remarkable chain of events was in play in this effort. It was a rare, perhaps unprecedented, instance of an act of resistance by people willing to lose their freedom empowering government officials to do what generations of public officials had failed to do: exercise oversight of the FBI.

At first, Department of Justice officials worked shoulder to shoulder with the bureau, standing together as a united bulwark against efforts to expose Hoover's deepest secrets. But by late 1973, some officials in the department thought it might not be wise, or even possible, for them to continue to protect Hoover's secrets. They realized they could no longer blindly defend the FBI. They too wanted to know what was in those files that earlier Justice officials had ignored for decades despite the fact that the FBI was part of the department and, as such, came under the authority of the attorney general.

As interest in investigating the FBI grew, the relationships among the key players were uneasy at best. Relationships were uneasy between the FBI and Justice officials. They were uneasy between the top officials in the bureau and Clarence Kelley, who became Hoover's successor in July 1973. Kelley was pushed and pulled by three groups: the Hoover loyalists who wanted him, their boss, to join them in protecting Hoover's secrets from scrutiny by anyone outside the bureau, successive attorneys general who urged him to open the Hoover files, and some members of Congress who were edging toward accepting responsibility for oversight of the FBI.

For Kelley, those years were torturous. A person who didn't like conflict, Kelley was in the center of it constantly. He went along with the Hoover loyalists' defense of the past most of his first year as director. He publicly stated that Hoover had done nothing wrong. He defended COINTELPRO, saying it was necessary during what he called a revolutionary time. Under pressure from the Hoover loyalists, he even asked an attorney general to seek a presidential directive empowering the FBI to continue conducting COINTELPRO-like operations. The attorney general refused. When compelled by members of Congress and Justice officials to open secret files, Kelley refused at first, and then did so, but very reluctantly, knowing the Hoover phalanx would, to say the least, make his life miserable. They did. Occasionally, for instance, they gave him false or misleading information to use in remarks he made at congressional hearings. Later, embarrassed, he retracted such comments. Eventually, when he had more fully absorbed how Hoover had misused the bureau, Kelley, a former FBI agent and former chief of police in Kansas City, stopped being Hoover's protector. Eventually, he formally apologized to the American people for the FBI's past.

Even in death, at first Hoover seemed to win the battle for no more disclosure after the Media files were disclosed. Some members of Congress, as well as newspaper editorial boards, called for an investigation of the bureau immediately after the Media files were released, but most members of Congress were not yet willing to investigate or oversee the FBI. For instance, in April 1971, a few weeks after the first Media revelations, Senator Gaylord Nelson, Democrat from Wisconsin, proposed the creation of a joint congressional FBI oversight committee. His resolution failed to muster support then and each of two more times he proposed it.

Representative Hale Boggs, Democrat from Louisiana, may have described the deep timidity of Congress most clearly in comments he made on April 22, 1971: "Our apathy in this Congress, our silence in this House, our very fear of speaking out in other forums has watered the roots and hastened the growth of a vine of tyranny which is ensnaring that Constitution and Bill of Rights which we are sworn to uphold."

By the end of 1973, the tide had started to turn. The traditionalists in the FBI were kicking and screaming as they tried to keep Hoover's secrets sealed. They no longer were confident they could trust either the new director or Justice officials to support their efforts.

Absorbed in reports about the Watergate investigations, the public developed a keen interest in the country's intelligence agencies. Previously, Americans had shown little interest in how they operated and had seldom questioned their practices. The Media revelations stimulated interest in intelligence operations, and the Watergate investigations greatly increased that interest, especially after reports about the Nixon administration's wild secret intelligence operation, the Plumbers, based in the White House.

It was the persistence of Carl Stern, a legal affairs reporter for NBC television, that led to COINTELPRO being exposed. Without his efforts, FBI officials might have been able to close the door permanently on more disclosure. The Media burglars revealed the term. Then Stern pressed to find out what it meant. What he forced the FBI to reveal, as the result of a lawsuit, made it impossible for Department of Justice officials to continue to support the bureau's efforts to keep Hoover's past off-limits to the public.

The department and the FBI said no to Stern more than once. Finally, a judge ordered the bureau to release the files Stern sought. When he reported what those documents revealed about the purpose of COINTELPRO, the Justice officials who had tried to prevent the files from being released saw them for the first time themselves, at the same time the public first saw them. Added to the Media revelations, Stern's revelations greatly increased pressure for records of operations conducted inside Hoover's secret FBI to be opened to public scrutiny.

Stern had become interested in determining what COINTELPRO was a year after the Media files were released. While in the office of the Senate Judiciary Committee in March 1972, he noticed on someone's desk a copy of the Media file that included the routing slip with the "COINTELPRO–New Left" label. When Stern asked what the term meant, no one in the office knew. Sensing it was important, Stern decided to find out. On March 20, 1972, in a letter to then deputy attorney general Richard Kleindienst, he applied under the Freedom of Information Act of 1966 for the FBI documents that established and defined COINTELPRO. In a written response, Kleindienst told Stern that the COINTELPRO documents were "exempt from disclosure" and that information about the COINTELPRO operations must "be kept secret in the interest of the national defense and foreign policy." (It was learned later that none of the COINTELPRO files concerned either national defense or foreign policy.)

Stern then appealed directly to acting FBI director L. Patrick Gray, who refused to provide the files. In a letter in September 1972, he told Stern, "This matter involved a highly sensitive operation. It has now been discontinued, but I do not feel that details concerning it should be released since such disclosure would definitely be harmful to the Bureau's operations and to the national security." Actually, only the name of the operations had been discontinued. The operations themselves were still being conducted.

Stern persisted. In an October 26, 1972, letter to Kleindienst, he renewed his request "for the umpteenth time for whatever documents authorized and defined the FBI's COINTELPRO–New Left program." He was turned down again in what Kleindienst described as "a final denial by the Attorney General."

On January 31, 1973, Stern sued the Department of Justice and the FBI in federal court, claiming that under the Freedom of Information Act (FOIA), the COINTELPRO documents should be made public. Stern's suit was filed by attorney Ronald L. Plesser representing him through the newly formed Press Information Center. With his lawsuit, Stern would become the first journalist to sue the government for files under the FOIA and the first journalist to receive FBI files as a result of the act. The only FBI files made available to journalists before this were ones that the director provided to "friendly journalists" in an attempt to smear individuals or organizations.

Department of Justice lawyers claimed the judge could have no say in the matter because, they said, the federal judiciary lacked jurisdiction over intelligence matters. U.S. district judge Barrington Parker thought otherwise, and on July 24, 1973, he ordered the documents be released to him for private inspection. When department officials submitted the files to Judge Parker, it was the first time COINTELPRO files had been seen by anyone outside the FBI. On September 25, 1973, Judge Parker ordered Justice officials to release the files to Stern. At first, the department appealed the order, but acting attorney general Robert Bork withdrew the appeal and turned four pages of COINTELPRO documents over to Stern on December 6, 1973.

From Stern's story broadcast on NBC—the first story reported about COINTELPRO—people learned that in a May 1968 memorandum Hoover had informed officials at FBI headquarters in Washington and in key field offices that he had opened COINTELPRO–New Left to "expose, disrupt and otherwise neutralize" the New Left movement. He emphasized that the operations would be carried out in heavy secrecy and that they would be aimed at "disrupting the organized activity of these groups. . . . No opportunity should be missed to capitalize upon organizational and personal conflicts of their leadership. . . . The devious maneuvers and duplicity of these activists must be exposed to public scrutiny through the cooperation of reliable news media, both locally and at the seat of government [Hoover's term for bureau headquarters in Washington]." He ordered heads of selected field offices throughout the nation to take advantage "of all opportunities for counter-intelligence and also inspire action in instances where circumstances warrant." Activists in these organizations, he instructed, "must not only be contained but must be neutralized."

In the memorandum, Hoover emphasized again the clandestine nature of the operations: "The nature of this new endeavor is such that under no circumstances should the existence of the program be made known outside the bureau and appropriate within-office security should be afforded this sensitive operation."

Agents in charge of field offices were instructed by Hoover to send proposals for COINTELPRO programs to Hoover. They were reviewed by officials in the Domestic Intelligence Division and by Hoover himself. Coming up with a COINTELPRO proposal the director liked was a career booster for agents. In addition to proposals from agents in the field, COIN-TELPRO proposals also originated with officials at headquarters and with Hoover himself.

There was no going back after Bork's crucial decision to release the files rather than appeal the court order to do so.

Bork, who became well known in 1987 when he was rejected by the Senate in 1987 after President Ronald Reagan nominated him to serve on the U.S. Supreme Court, ordered the FBI to release the COINTELPRO files to Stern soon after Bork became acting attorney general as a result of the Saturday Night Massacre, the evening, October 20, 1973, when Nixon, within a matter of hours, fired one attorney general and one deputy attorney general and, through Bork, fired the Watergate special prosecutor. At the end of the evening, Bork was the last domino standing at the top of the Department of Justice. He released the COINTELPRO statement-of-purpose files to Stern in the midst of that intense Watergate atmosphere, and as he did so, he urged attorney general–designee William Saxbe, who became attorney general on January 4, 1974, to investigate the FBI's COINTELPRO operations. Reluctant at first, Saxbe did order an investigation, but he had a difficult time convincing Assistant Attorney General Henry E. Petersen to conduct the inquiry. Though limited in scope, it was the first investigation of the bureau by any agency.

When the first glimpses of COINTELPRO operations emerged as a result of that limited investigation, the *Washington Post* declared in an editorial, "Mr. Hoover's Dirty Tricks," that what had been revealed so far about Hoover's FBI showed that he had made "meaningless the rule of law." The *Post* called on FBI director Kelley and Attorney General Saxbe to make sure that steps would be "taken to see that such outrages against the Constitution are not allowed to be repeated." The editorial focused on the FBI's treatment of black people, including the bureau's plans to prevent "the rise of a messiah" and to prevent black leaders from "gaining respectability" by discrediting them with bad publicity, ridicule, and whatever means could be thought up by what Hoover called "imaginative" FBI agents. The editorial blasted the revelations in recently released files that Hoover had praised one American city's officials for placing all its black militant leaders in jail for a summer on successive trumped-up charges until "they could no longer make bail."

In the past, the FBI had succeeded in stopping the only congressional effort to make the FBI accountable—a hearing in 1965 that was limited to an examination of the use of electronic surveillance by the FBI and other federal agencies. Senator Edward Long of Missouri asked the FBI and other federal investigative agencies to provide records of their electronic surveillance activities to the Senate Subcommittee on Administrative Practice and Procedure. Determined not to reveal any information from FBI files, especially about the bureau's investigative methods, Hoover said he would provide the committee with *all* its electronic records, including ones that contained recordings of Long allegedly being offered money by the Teamsters union. With that threat, Hoover achieved his goal. Long issued a statement that certified that the FBI did not wiretap, and the bureau was dropped from the list of agencies being investigated. After meeting with Long about this matter, FBI deputy director Cartha "Deke" DeLoach told Hoover that Long had been "neutralized." But he suggested that Long should be watched. He was. The bureau continued to investigate Long and initiated investigations of all members of the subcommittee and their legal counsel. In contrast, in the mid-1970s, as a series of investigations of the FBI were getting under way, no deals were made to make it possible for the FBI to escape investigation.

While FBI agents were investigating the crimes of the Nixon administration in 1974, some officials in the Department of Justice were preparing to investigate the FBI's past. A new attitude had developed among officials in the department after Nixon and the high-level department officials who were partners in his corruption left the government one by one and, in most cases, were indicted and then convicted. William Saxbe, the last attorney general appointed by Nixon, and Saxbe's successor, Edward Levi, who was appointed attorney general by President Gerald Ford, played major roles in forcing open wider the FBI door the Media burglars had opened.

FBI director Kelley opposed the department's investigation of the bureau. He was in fact still very reluctant to criticize the FBI's past when Saxbe did so in 1974 in a setting that for Kelley was public, personal, and very embarrassing—the June 20 graduation ceremony of 250 police officers from the United States and a few foreign countries who had just completed three months of training at the FBI National Academy in Quantico, Virginia. Sanford Ungar, author of *FBI: An Uncensored Look Behind the Walls,* observed this ceremony that was attended by notable present and past FBI officials, military officers, members of foreign diplomatic missions, and the proud families of the young police officers who were graduating that day.

Introduced by Kelley, Saxbe used his keynote address to make his first public remarks about the FBI's past. As FBI officials listened from seats scattered throughout the audience, Saxbe referred to the "recent memoranda released"—a reference to the files released to Stern—that revealed the FBI had "sought to expose, disrupt, misdirect, discredit, or otherwise neutralize" a number of organizations and their members. The FBI, Saxbe told the graduates, had leaked "detrimental information" and "spread dissension through partially fake and entirely fabricated documents." Disruptive tactics used by the FBI, he said, with or without the knowledge of the attorney general, should not occur. "The national security can be protected without resorting to such practices." Then came his kicker. He told the young police officer graduates,

"When you return to your various police departments, I hope you will take the word with you and pass it along that the dirty tricks are over—not only in campaign tactics, but in law enforcement as well. The public is demanding that we find ways to enforce the laws that do not violate standards of decency and fairness."

The silence was heavy, Ungar remembers, as Saxbe told his audience that his "point in discussing certain FBI programs is not to criticize a man who is no longer here to defend himself. . . . The purpose of my remarks is to stress that all of us with criminal justice responsibilities must continually examine and reexamine every aspect of our work to make certain it is fair—as well as legal. There is no person who should be immune from criticsm and no practice that should be shielded from healthy skepticism."

These remarks by Saxbe were the first public criticism ever made by a sitting attorney general of Hoover or his secret operations. The tide was indeed shifting.

After the speech, a ranking FBI official believed by Ungar to be representative of bureau reaction to Saxbe's comments said to him, "When you invite someone into your home, do you expect him to take a crap on the living room floor?"

Meanwhile, Assistant Attorney General Petersen was so hesitant to take on Saxbe's assignment to investigate COINTELPRO operations that he asked the FBI to provide him with summaries of COINTELPRO files rather than access to the original records of the programs. This meant that the department's first investigation of COINTELPRO was far weaker than it would have been if it had been based on the bureau's original files. When original files were released later to the Senate committee that investigated the FBI in 1975, it became clear that the FBI-prepared summaries had minimized the toxic nature of the COINTELPRO reports.

Four months after Saxbe's unwelcome speech at the FBI Academy, the recent first glimpses of COINTELPRO were the subject of fierce debate at an open congressional hearing of the House Civil Rights and Constitutional Rights Subcommittee of the Committee on the Judiciary, chaired by Representative Don Edwards, Democrat from California and a former FBI agent. Hoover's appearances before congressional committees on Capitol Hill had been lovefests at which few questions were asked—except an implied "How much more can we do for you?" Director Kelley did not get much love on the Hill. In comparison to Hoover's appearances there, his were more like facing a firing squad. He was pressed repeatedly to reveal and condemn the past and to agree not to repeat it. Kelley seldom appeared alone at these hearings. The ghost of Hoover usually was nearby.

That attitude was evident at the November 20, 1974, hearing of Edwards's subcommittee—the first congressional hearing at which COINTELPRO operations were discussed. In addition to Kelley, the committee also had compelled Justice officials to be present. Standing in for Attorney General Saxbe were Assistant Attorney General Petersen and Deputy Attorney General Laurence Silberman.

The circumstances were unusual: As FBI investigators continued to search for the Media burglars in Philadelphia and elsewhere, the director of the FBI was seated before a congressional committee that had compelled him to be there to answer questions about the controversial program whose existence was known because its mysterious name had been revealed by the burglars still being searched for by his agents.

Edwards drew attention to that anomalous circumstance when he opened the session. In his opening remarks, he gave credit to the Media burglars for the fact that the committee and its witnesses were gathered to discuss the FBI's past. "The subcommittee's attention was first directed to allegations of questionable FBI activities when materials surfaced after an FBI office was broken into in Media, PA, in 1971. Following that break-in, a suit was brought under the Freedom of Information Act by NBC newsman Carl Stern. After an 18-month court battle, the FBI recently released a number of memoranda, which surfaced the so-called COINTELPRO operations. The potential for invasions of constitutionally protected rights was apparent."

Edwards then turned to the director and blasted his recent defense of COINTELPRO:

Regardless of the unattractiveness or noisy militancy of some private citizens or organizations, the Constitution does not permit federal interference with their activities except through the criminal justice system, armed with its ancient safeguards. There are no exceptions. No federal agency, the CIA, the IRS, or the FBI, can be at the same time policeman, prosecutor, judge and jury. That is what constitutionally guaranteed due process is all about. . . .

I suggest that the philosophy supporting COINTELPRO is the subversive notion that any public official, the president or a policeman, possesses a kind of inherent power to set aside the Constitution whenever he

thinks the public interest, or national security warrants it. That notion is
the postulate of tyranny. Law enforcers cannot be lawbreakers.

Two days before this hearing, Saxbe had released key parts of the Petersen
investigation at a press conference where he told reporters that some of the
COINTELPRO operations were "abhorrent in a free society." Despite the
fact that the report was based on files that had been watered down in summaries prepared by FBI officials, some of the harsh aspects of the operations
still were evident. Kelley and all other top officials at the FBI had joined
together to urge the attorney general not to release the report. Public disclosure, the director told Saxbe, would cause "catastrophic damage" to the FBI.

Even Senator Sam J. Ervin Jr., Democrat from North Carolina, then
deep in investigating Watergate in televised public hearings that were riveting the country, advised Saxbe not to release the report. He was widely
regarded as a strong defender of constitutional rights, especially the right to
privacy and the right to dissent. But presented with evidence of what the
FBI was doing in this area he cared about so much, Ervin and all members of the Senate Subcommittee on Constitutional Rights, the committee
he chaired, advised Saxbe to keep the COINTELPRO report secret. Ervin
reacted as he did when he refused to investigate the FBI when asked to do
so shortly after the Media files first became public.

Despite nearly unanimous advice from the FBI and members of Congress that he should suppress the department's COINTELPRO report,
Saxbe released it. Petersen had recommended that on the basis of his report
no FBI agents should be prosecuted for operations they had carried out.
Nevertheless, Saxbe considered recommending that a special prosecutor be
appointed to investigate the FBI. That idea also was strongly opposed by
everyone Saxbe consulted, including Senator Ervin. In the end, Saxbe did
not recommend the appointment of a special prosecutor.

When Saxbe released the COINTELPRO report at a press conference
shortly before the Edwards committee hearing, Kelley issued a news release
defending COINTELPRO: "FBI employees acted in good faith and within
the bounds of what was expected of them by the president, the attorney
general, Congress, and, I believe, a majority of the American people."

Now, at the House subcommittee hearing, Edwards praised Saxbe's
conclusion that some of the COINTELPRO actions were abhorrent and
strongly criticized Kelley's defense of the operations. Paul Sarbanes, Democratic member of the House from Maryland, turned to Kelley and asked if
he agreed with the attorney general's conclusion that some of the COIN-

TELPRO "activities involved isolated instances of practices that are abhorrent in a free society."

The director responded, "I do not."

Kelley told the committee he thought the attorney general had authority to allow the FBI to go beyond investigating, monitoring, and employing counterintelligence to take action to disrupt the activities of particular organizations. His comments sounded remarkably like Hoover's justification for COINTELPRO. Where was the statutory basis for such an executive order? asked the Reverend Robert F. Drinan, Democrat from Massachusetts.

"It is inherent," responded the director. That claim inevitably brought to mind President Nixon's recent claim that he had inherent rights as president, and that crimes committed by him, therefore, were not crimes. "I do not want to argue about anything that happened in the past," Kelley said at one point, clearly frustrated with the line of questioning.

Silberman stepped into the crossfire and acknowledged that Department of Justice officials "do not have power to authorize the bureau to disrupt domestic groups." At the same time, he practically pleaded for mercy for the director. "I would like to tell this committee that the attorney general and I have absolute confidence in Clarence Kelley. He is put in a very awkward position here and you all ought to realize it. He was not there when these acts were engaged in and he has an obvious personal reluctance, it seems to me, to have to be in a position to condemn his predecessor."

When Drinan asked if Justice officials "have any intention of seeking out the FBI agents who engaged in this criminal conduct and bringing disciplinary or criminal action against them," Petersen said the matter was open to consideration, but because the program "was directed by the Director of the Federal Bureau of Investigation . . . it would be somewhat incongruous to single out . . . the grade 10 agent on the street level for doing what he was directed to do by the director of the Federal Bureau of Investigation."

Petersen's remark placed the ghost of Hoover at center stage. ". . . If discipline were to be meted out," he continued, "it would have to be meted out to one who is no longer alive. . . . We do not intend . . . to discipline agents . . . for actions which, indeed, the entire bureau and the director were responsible."

THE TIPPING POINT that led to the first extensive investigation of the FBI and other intelligence agencies was a story written by then *New York Times* reporter Seymour Hersh on December 22, 1974: "Huge CIA Operation Reported in U.S. Against Anti-War Forces." Hersh's front-page story that day reported that the CIA had collected surveillance files on thousands of activists in violation of its charter, which prohibits the agency from conducting domestic operations. The programs that CIA director Richard Helms had denied existed, after select CIA staff members pressed him, the day after the first Media files were reported, to confirm or deny whether such programs existed inside the agency, were now confirmed in Hersh's story. They existed, they were extensive, they were illegal—and, it would be learned later, they had been directed by Helms.

By January 1975, Congress no longer could avoid what was by then considered a potential crisis in intelligence operations. A string of revelations— the Media files, Stern's reports on the files that defined and established COINTELPRO–New Left, Petersen's report on the bureau's watered-down files, Watergate revelations about the manipulation of intelligence agencies by the Nixon administration, and now Hersh's report on the CIA's domestic operations—together led to widespread concern that there were serious problems in the nation's intelligence agencies that needed to be examined. That month the Senate passed a resolution establishing the Senate Select Committee to Study Governmental Operations with Respect to Intelligence Activities. The committee would be known as the Church Committee for its chair, Frank Church, Democratic senator from Idaho. At the same time, the House established a similar committee. Unfortunately, its extensive work ended up having little impact. Most of its hearings were closed and its final report ultimately was suppressed.

As questioning of the behavior and values of Hoover grew in the 1970s, the many people who relied on Hoover's perception of who was dangerous and what thinking was appropriate must have been shocked. Writer Jim Edwards got some insight into how people relied on the director for guidance on such matters when he reviewed the bureau's 1,700-page file on George Seldes, an investigative journalist who, after a career as a *Chicago Tribune* reporter, published his own newsletter, *In Fact*. In it, Seldes reported many important developments long before the mainstream press did. For instance, he published evidence of the deadly power of tobacco in 1941, decades before the mainstream press. As Edwards reviewed Seldes's file for an article he wrote for *Brill's Content* in November 2000, in addition to discovering that the bureau had followed and harassed Seldes and his wife, Helen, including secretly opening and copying mail sent to their Norwich, Connecticut, home, he reviewed files that offered insights about the relationship between Hoover and the public.

"It was not uncommon," Edwards found, "for members of the public to write to Hoover. They asked his advice, inquired as to whether their neighbor was a communist, turned in their friends as Reds and occasionally wrote proclamations of innocence if they believed that they might be suspected of something." For example, a person who wrote on stationery with the letterhead of the architecture department of Pennsylvania State University, and whose name was blacked out, informed Hoover that "he was receiving Seldes' *In Fact* against his will." He told Hoover he had not subscribed to the publication, preferred "not to have it enter my home," but had been unsuccessful in attempts to have his name removed from the mailing list. "In case of any eventuality [it's not clear what he thought that might be—perhaps an FBI agent someday finding an issue of the newsletter near his dead body in his home] I wish to state now that I have never subscribed to *In Fact*." In his response, Hoover replied and "assured the worried academic that 'you may be sure that your letter will be made a matter of permanent record.'" Everyone in the files of the secret FBI could count on that.

19

Crude and Cruel

SOME OPERATIONS carried out by the secret FBI were crude. Others were cruel and life-threatening. Antiwar activists' oranges were injected with powerful laxatives. Agents hired prostitutes known to have venereal disease to infect campus antiwar leaders. Prostitutes were hired in an effort to entrap leaders of the Fair Play for Cuba Committee. Some plots were designed to destroy specific individuals and institutions—providing an apartment diagram that guided a Chicago police shooter to "Fred's bed" so Black Panther Fred Hampton could be killed, taunting the Reverend Martin Luther King Jr. to commit suicide.

Some of the plots would have been considered beyond the bounds of humane conduct if carried out by any agency or individual, but they were regarded as even worse—nearly beyond belief—when it was discovered such operations had been executed by the nation's most powerful law enforcement agency, and that it did so under the leadership of a director who repeatedly spoke of the need for strict moral behavior. And who would fire an agent for simply having sweaty palms.

The Media break-in changed the whole dynamic, says historian Athan Theoharis. Then, when COINTELPRO was revealed, "that finally exceeded what the public would support."

Widely exposed during the Church Committee hearings in 1975, these secret FBI operations—COINTELPRO and others—utilized the tools of espionage. Tools usually reserved for clandestine use against foreign enemies were employed under Hoover against a wide swath of Americans in efforts to stop dissent. The methods used by the FBI inflicted pain, anxiety, and humiliation—forms of torture.

The operations were, in the words of respected surveillance scholar Frank Donner, "an embryonic version of officially instigated terrorism."

Wrote Donner, "The bureau constituted itself the secret instrument of a tribal system of justice directed against people it had itself defined as enemies and outcasts." These investigations were "highly personalized . . . unfettered by professionalism or, for that matter, the norms of legality and accountability."

"It seemed like a good idea at the time."

That's how Cartha "Deke" DeLoach, deputy director of the FBI from 1965 to 1970, assessed COINTELPRO operations in his 1996 book *Hoover's FBI: The Inside Story.* DeLoach defended Hoover until his own death in March 2013. When the nature of these operations was first revealed in the mid-1970s, probably few, if any, people thought such methods of intelligence gathering or law enforcement were a good idea.

The operations were carried out as part of Hoover's overall vision of his duty not only to enforce the law—which could not be done with these programs because most of the FBI actions involved were illegal and, therefore, could not be presented in court—but also to maintain the status quo and quash new ideas by harassing people into silence and passivity. Files were maintained and actions taken against people in nearly all movements: the civil rights movement, the antiwar movement, the women's movement, the gay rights movement (then referred to as homosexual groups), and the environmental movement. The Ku Klux Klan was added to the list after President Johnson ordered the director in 1964 to investigate a series of brutal murders against civil rights workers in Mississippi.

Sanford Ungar, to this day still the only writer to whom an FBI director (Clarence Kelley) granted wide access to FBI officials and internal information about their operations, in 1975 described some COINTELPRO methods and the impact of these secret illegal operations on the FBI's official responsibilities:

As the director saw that he was on to an issue that was stirring considerable emotion in the country, he embarked on a veritable crusade. . . . Once an organization or activist . . . had been put into the category of a threat, they were pursued with a vengeance almost unknown in FBI annals. Their phones were tapped, their every movement watched in the hope that some basis could be found for charging them with a local or federal crime.

The manpower assigned to such domestic intelligence was sometimes doubled, tripled or quadrupled—even at the expense of the bureau's responsibilities for genuine counterintelligence efforts against foreign espionage—as the FBI pursued the director's new public enemy number one.

The COINTELPRO operations were started by Hoover in 1956. Frustrated by recent U.S. Supreme Court decisions that made it no longer possible to prosecute people for radical political speech or Communist Party membership, the director circumvented the court's decisions and created COINTELPRO as his secret means of punishing, through harassment and dirty tricks, people who could no longer be punished under the law.

He had always secretly used such unscrupulous methods, it would be learned in the 1980s, but the 1970s investigations provided the first evidence of what he created, starting in 1956—COINTELPRO operations directed against specific types of individuals and organizations. He opened successive COINTELPRO programs, including ones that were directed against the Socialist Workers Party, the Puerto Rican Independence Movement, the Black Liberation Movement, the New Left, the American Indian Movement, and black and white hate groups. In all, there were twelve COINTELPRO umbrella programs. Within each category, the director used wide discretion as to which individuals and organizations would be targeted. As with the infiltration of black groups in Philadelphia that was documented in the Media files, organizations that professed violence, such as the Black Panther Party, and organizations that professed nonviolence, such as the Southern Christian Leadership Conference, all qualified as targets of COINTELPRO programs.

The Church Committee investigation presented the country, for the first time, with a substantial body of information about how the secret FBI and other intelligence agencies operated. Memorably, the hearings revealed the CIA's attempted assassinations of Cuban president Fidel Castro and its attempts to overthrow democratically elected leaders. But in the end, Frederick A. O. Schwarz Jr., the chief counsel to the Church Committee, concluded, after examining all the evidence gathered by the committee, that the worst abuses were committed by the FBI. "The FBI abuses were much more dangerous. They undermined American democracy, violated the law and subverted the Constitution." The pervasiveness of domestic intelligence, he noted, was "reflected in the sheer volume of Americans spied upon. The FBI opened more than 500,000 domestic intelligence files, each typically including several individuals' names."

On the first day of the Church Committee's hearings, Schwarz stated the key role of the Media files in exposing abuses by the bureau:

"Let me observe that whatever effort there was to turn off COIN-TELPRO occurred only after it had been exposed . . . by the theft of documents from the Media, Pennsylvania, office of the FBI, and exposed in the press, pursuant to a Freedom of Information Act lawsuit [a reference to Carl Stern's suit]."

The evidence collected by the Church Committee revealed the very wide scope and impact of the secret power and influence Hoover assumed belonged to him. No part of the government or American life was outside his reach. He used his secret power to destroy individuals and to manipulate and destroy organizations, including a major American university. He secretly punished people he regarded as wrong-thinking—civil rights leaders, senior members of Congress who questioned war policy, and also average people who wrote letters to a member of Congress or dared to express their dissent by appearing at an antiwar demonstration. In Hoover's world, the evidence showed, any American was fair game.

In addition to the evidence gathered and testimony given before the Church Committee about abusive actions carried out by the FBI against people because of their dissent, the committee's hearings also were notable for the insights elicited from FBI officials about the rationale for Hoover's abusive intelligence operations.

When asked if, during the execution of COINTELPRO operations, anybody at the FBI had discussed the operations' constitutionality or legality, the former head of the bureau's Racial Intelligence Section, George Moore, answered,

"No, we never gave it a thought."

William C. Sullivan, the head of the FBI's Domestic Intelligence Division for ten years and the person responsible for some of the worst elements of the bureau's long campaign to destroy Martin Luther King, confirmed that analysis when he told the Church Committee:

Never once did I hear anybody, including myself, raise the question: "Is this course of action which we have agreed upon lawful, is it legal, is it ethical or moral?" We never gave any thought to this line of reasoning

because we were just naturally pragmatic. The one thing we were concerned about, will this course of action work, will it get us what we want,
will we reach the objective we desire to reach.

Schwarz has concluded that the "assumption of everlasting secrecy" was
the key to understanding why the director assumed he could get away with
abusing Americans and could create an atmosphere where integrity was not
an issue. "The expectation of permanent secrecy and no effective oversight
led many to ignore the law."

In its final report, the Church Committee's conclusions about COIN-
TELPRO included this observation:

> Many of the techniques used would be intolerable in a democratic society
> even if all the targets had been involved in violent activity, but COIN-
> TELPRO went far beyond that. The unexpressed major premise of the
> programs was that a law enforcement agency has the duty to do whatever
> is necessary to combat perceived threats to the existing social and politi-
> cal order."

Among all of the political operations conducted by the bureau, surely
the most egregious was the one conducted against the Reverend Dr. Martin
Luther King. Hoover's attitude toward King can be described as a nearly
savage hatred. That extreme quality is evident in many COINTELPRO
operations, but may be most evident in the records of FBI plots against
black people, especially the years-long multifaceted operation designed to
destroy King, the best-known and most respected civil rights leader. The
plot involved office break-ins, use of informers, mail opening, wiretapping,
and bugging of King's office, home, and hotel rooms. In one of the most
extreme operations against King, the bureau attempted to convince him to
commit suicide just weeks before he was to receive the Nobel Peace Prize in
Oslo in 1964. In another extreme measure, Hoover instructed agents not to
inform King about advance notice it had received about threats against his
life. Hoover told President Johnson he regarded King as "an instrument in
the hands of subversive forces seeking to undermine our nation."

As King delivered his "I Have a Dream" speech, widely considered one
of the greatest speeches of the twentieth century, on the steps of the Lincoln
Memorial on August 28, 1963, before 250,000 people who had come to the
March on Washington to support civil rights and urge passage of the Civil
Rights Act, top officials of the FBI listened to the speech in their offices

a few blocks away at FBI headquarters and decided it was the speech of a demagogue who should be toppled by the bureau. It was then that Hoover and other officials at headquarters started to plot King's demise. They also had the audacity to assume the FBI should surreptitiously select someone to replace King as the leader of black Americans.

Hoover's tendency to be particularly cruel to African Americans was also evident in the planting of false rumors that set off violent confrontations between black organizations. It was evident in his seemingly casual, callous attitude toward setting up the murder of one black man, Fred Hampton, and allowing another black man, Geronimo Pratt, to be falsely convicted for murder. Chicago Black Panther leader Hampton was shot dead in his sleep in his apartment by Chicago police after a diagram of his apartment, including where he slept, was given to police by an FBI informant with a spot on the diagram marked "Fred's bed." In internal documents, the FBI took credit for the killing. The information the informer provided, wrote an agent, was considered to be of "tremendous value" to the "success of the raid." After the raid that resulted in the killing of Hampton and Mark Clark, a member of the Panthers' Peoria chapter, the FBI installed wiretaps on the phones of the survivors of the raid so agents could listen to them talk with their lawyers. The bureau gave the FBI informer who provided the floor plan a bonus.

Pratt, a much-decorated Vietnam veteran and Black Panther leader in Los Angeles, spent twenty-seven years in prison for a murder conviction that was overturned in 1997 by an Orange County judge who ruled that evidence that could have led to Pratt's acquittal was concealed by the FBI at his trial. He was convicted on the basis of testimony of an FBI informer who lied at the trial.

The FBI's approach to investigating the Black Panther Party was in the spirit of the worst of the COINTELPRO operations—set up people to destroy one another. Testimony at the Church hearings revealed that the bureau's national effort to destroy the Panthers involved using informants and disinformation to promote gang warfare between Panthers and other black organizations and also to promote intramural violence within branches of the party. These bureau efforts were believed to be responsible for the deaths of at least four Black Panthers who were shot to death.

Violence was promoted by the FBI in black organizations so often in the late 1960s and early 1970s that it is impossible, in retrospect, to know whether any given violent confrontation that took place in that era was instigated by genuine animosities among actual members of the groups or was instigated by FBI agents or informers, many of whom infiltrated such groups and promoted violence.

The sad conundrum of whether the FBI was the source of violent episodes and internal distrust in organizations in that era came to light in 2012 in two communities. People knowledgeable of the history of the Black Panther Party in Northern California were shocked when journalist Seth Rosenfeld reported FBI documentation that the late Richard Aoki, a deeply respected leader in ethnic studies in the Bay Area and a member of the Black Panther Party in Oakland, was an FBI informer for many years, including at the time he armed the Oakland Panthers and taught them how to use the weapons he supplied.

In Memphis, people were stunned in 2013 when the FBI confirmed that the late Ernest Withers, the best-known and beloved photographer of the civil rights movement and of life in Memphis, was an FBI informer during the years he photographed all the major events in the movement from 1958 until 1972. Throughout that time he worked closely with key people in the movement, including Martin Luther King. During that time he filed reports with the FBI, including ones on King at the time of the sanitation workers' strike that brought King to Memphis the week he was killed there in April 1968. Withers secretly supplied the FBI with photographs of King and others in the civil rights movement and also filed reports with agents about conversations he heard among movement members.

MANY FBI OPERATIONS reflected Hoover's apparent obsession with the details of the private lives of people whose opinions he disliked or of powerful people he threatened to blackmail by virtue of the secrets he kept on them in his files. A file on a COINTELPRO operation focused on Puerto Rican independence activists documents something he often did—lift his crude personal fascinations to an official mandate in intelligence gathering. An informer was instructed by the bureau "to report even the slightest bits of information concerning the personal lives" of the activists. It also illustrates his approval of cruel outcomes. During a COINTELPRO "disruption" of one Puerto Rican organization, the target of the disruption suffered a serious heart attack. In a report, FBI agents described his heart attack as a "positive result" of the bureau's effort.

A Los Angeles agent received enthusiastic approval from the director for a plan to punish actress Jean Seberg in 1970 for giving a contribution to the Black Panther Party. The plan was tragically successful. The agent proposed to Hoover that Seberg, then several months pregnant, be publicly humiliated by planting the false rumor that her baby's father was a Black Panther leader. The planting of such a rumor, the agent wrote in his proposal, "could cause her embarrassment and serve to cheapen her image with the general public." The director approved the proposed plan, noting in his response that "Jean Seberg has been a financial supporter of the B.P.P. [Black Panther Party] and should be neutralized." He advised Los Angeles agents to increase the effectiveness of the operation by waiting a couple months so Seberg's pregnancy would be more obvious when the rumor was planted. Apparently eager to move ahead, agents in Los Angeles planted the rumor with *Los Angeles Times* gossip columnist Joyce Haber as soon as the director approved the plan. Haber wrote that an international movie star who supported the "black revolution" was expecting and the "Papa's said to be a rather prominent Black Panther." With other details, Haber made it clear the unnamed star was Seberg. Soon after reading the rumor, Seberg went into premature labor and three days later gave birth to a dead white baby girl. After Seberg committed suicide on the anniversary of the birth of the dead baby in 1979, her husband, Romain Gary, the French novelist-diplomat, said Seberg had suffered severe depression ever since the published rumor and the birth of her dead child. He said she had tried to commit suicide each year on the anniversary of the birth.

Shortly after Seberg's suicide became known, then FBI director William Webster issued a contrite statement: "The days when the FBI used derogatory information to combat advocates of unpopular causes have long since passed. We are out of that business forever."

Hoover even felt free to secretly manipulate elections. When he learned in June 1967 that a Peace Party ticket might be formed for the 1968 presidential election, he approved a plan to destroy the effort by, in his words, labeling "as communists or communist-backed the more hysterical opponents of the President on Vietnam question in the midst of the presidential campaign [which] would be a real boon to Mr. Johnson." He added in this note, sent to all of the bureau's field offices, that in regard to New Left activists, "every avenue of possible embarrassment must be vigorously and enthusiastically exploited."

If Muhammad Ali had known about either the FBI's surveillance of him or that he and Frazier unwittingly provided cover for the burglary of the Media FBI office, he might have thought the cover was a sort of poetic justice. The bureau built a file on Ali, beginning with its investigation of his Selective Service case. Some of his phone conversations were tapped, and

FBI informers gained access to, of all things, his elementary school records in his hometown, Louisville, Kentucky. They discovered that little Cassius Clay liked art. They recorded every grade he made from elementary through high school. A minor driving citation, as well as family disagreements over his becoming a Muslim, were noted in the file. His appearances on *The Tonight Show* with Johnny Carson were monitored and summarized by agents, at taxpayers' expense, for the FBI director. Hoover had concluded, regarding Ali's claim that his refusal to serve in the Army rested on religious grounds, that Ali's beliefs "were a matter of convenience rather than ones sincerely held." The U.S. Supreme Court rejected that claim on June 28, 1971, in a unanimous opinion that supported Ali's claim that his "beliefs are founded on tenets of the Muslim religion as he understands them."

FOR HOOVER, from the beginning, much of his motivation in intelligence operations flowed from his conviction that all dissent and all movements for basic rights flowed from communism. There was a time when it was important for the FBI to competently investigate the infiltration of Soviet spies in the United States, including in government agencies where real harm could have been done. Unfortunately, this specific need in a precise period was transformed by Hoover into a vast and unending conspiracy. His focus on pursuing actual enemies evolved into seeing and pursuing enemies everywhere, even in the expression of the mildest liberal ideas. In the process, dissent was in effect secretly criminalized by the bureau. This resulted in countless numbers of innocent people being victimized while some actual enemies may have gone unnoticed. Tragically, for the bureau and the country, his obsession with communism cost him his competence.

Hoover played major public and major private roles in the anticommunism movement. Publicly, he was the ringmaster of the movement, much more so than Senator Joseph McCarthy, whose name is most frequently connected to anticommunism. In fact, Hoover provided McCarthy much, if not most, of the material McCarthy used as the basis of his reckless investigations. Hoover wrote books and articles and gave speeches on communism, and he advised the powerful House Un-American Activities Committee to expose communists and communist sympathizers, "fellow travelers," and liberals, who he often said were more dangerous than communists. He gave HUAC that advice in a major speech, known as the "Communist Menace" speech, on March 26, 1947.

In that speech, Hoover prescribed the pattern for how alleged communists and others should be rooted out. He urged HUAC to publicly "expose" communists and other people whose politics were suspect. Exposure by HUAC, he said, would lead the public to "quarantine" such people in their communities. Indeed, that is what happened.

Hoover's two-punch plan—"expose" and "quarantine"—was carried out repeatedly throughout the country by HUAC and state and education committees in what Victor Navasky, former editor of the *Nation,* astutely described as "degradation ceremonies."

The job of HUAC and the other "shaming" groups, Navasky wrote in *Naming Names,* "was not to legislate or even to discover subversives—that had already been done by the intelligence agencies and their informants—so much as it was to stigmatize."

Hoover's major private role in the anticommunism movement included giving HUAC the FBI's unverified surveillance files to use as the basis of its hearings in Washington and around the country. Those unverified FBI files were the basis of most efforts throughout the country—in federal, state, and local government agencies; in universities; in public school boards; in businesses and other private organizations—that led to the public humiliation and dismissal of thousands of people from their jobs during the anticommunist era. The accused were not permitted to face their accusers or defend themselves.

HUAC and other agencies "exposed" people by using the unverified FBI files. Often the accused were, as Hoover predicted would happen, quarantined. People who refused to testify were found in contempt, and some of them were imprisoned. Many lost their jobs or were shunned in their workplaces and communities. The accused had no access to the secret FBI files used to condemn them.

In addition to placing himself in charge of searching for Americans who had suspect political opinions during the anticommunist years, and turning their names over to the various agencies that then exposed them to public scorn and loss of employment, Hoover played another very important role during this era. As the fiery prophet of anticommunism, he contributed significantly to shaping the national narrative on anticommunism. He did so in ways that made Americans deeply fearful, and, ironically, at the same time contributed significantly to Americans being intellectually defenseless against communism. His rhetoric often consisted of raw hatred of communism and of the Soviet Union. He encouraged blind, religious allegiance to the hatred, but he imparted little or no understanding of the ideology and its history. Consequently, average Americans tended to rely on the warnings

Hoover preached repeatedly. As a result, if a serious communist threat had in fact developed in the United States, many, if not most, Americans would have been inadequately equipped to understand or oppose it. He drummed up fear and convinced people the FBI would get rid of the enemies that, he said, were penetrating the country's major institutions, even elementary and high schools.

The FBI files that were the basis of these anonymous accusations were the product not only of spying by FBI agents and untrained informers, but also of reports by members of the American Legion who from 1940 to 1966 spied for the FBI in their communities as part of a formal agreement with the bureau. The large contribution made by Legion members to the FBI's massive trove of unevaluated informer files was first reported by FBI historian Athan Theoharis in 1985 in *Political Science Quarterly*. From the 16,700 American Legion posts in the country, a network of 100,880 untrained volunteer informers was created. They regularly reported information to the FBI about their fellow citizens, their neighbors. This augmentation of the FBI's spying capacity was the closest the FBI came to being like the much-despised Stasi, the spying agency in the former East Germany, where people lived in constant fear of being informed on by their neighbors, even by their spouses. East Germans, however, knew such a system existed and dreaded it. In contrast, Americans lived in innocence with no idea that the American Legion member next door might be spying on them on behalf of the FBI.

With the establishment of COINTELPRO and other operations that encouraged the use of the best and brightest agents to devise high-impact actions, supported by an extensive network of untrained informers, a culture of carelessness and lawlessness penetrated the bureau. That was admitted by Sullivan, the longtime head of the Domestic Intelligence Division. In an internal memorandum, Sullivan wrote that many of the COINTELPRO operations were "clearly illegal."

Lawlessness had been part of the FBI culture for many years. In a reversal of what would be expected to be the norm in law enforcement integrity, an agent's expressed concern about the illegality of certain practices could have serious negative consequences in Hoover's FBI. That is illustrated in the reaction of FBI officials at Washington headquarters to a New York agent who expressed concern at a training class in Washington in 1951 about whether break-ins by FBI agents at homes and offices were unconstitutional. Headquarters officials were startled that an agent would raise such a question and ordered officials at the New York office to determine whether that agent's "mental outlook might be present" among other agents on the New York office's break-in squad. Washington officials urged the New York FBI officials to "determine which of these men should be retained on this type of activity and which should be deleted." Officials in New York and Washington were relieved to learn, after an examination of New York agents' attitudes, that no other member of the New York break-in squad had scruples about the constitutionality of break-ins.

ANYONE COULD BECOME a target of the FBI's political operations, but files suggest that intellectuals were among Hoover's chief targets—professors, artists, scientists, clergy. To be an intellectual, like being black, was to be regarded as a potential subversive, if not an active one. The director's wide brush rather than precise approach to investigations and to intelligence gathering is indicative of how the bureau monitored intellectuals of various kinds. Files were maintained on nearly all well-known writers and artists. Reading a list of writers who were in the FBI's files gives the impression that all the leading writers were there. To name a few: Sinclair Lewis, Pearl S. Buck, William Faulkner, Ernest Hemingway, John Steinbeck, Thomas Mann, Carl Sandburg, Dashiell Hammett, Truman Capote, Thornton Wilder, Lillian Hellman, Robert Frost, Graham Greene, Hannah Arendt. It is an endless roll call of the best novelists, nonfiction writers, poets, essayists, and playwrights, including Nobel laureates. Science fiction writers, including Ray Bradbury, also were regarded with suspicion and placed in the files. So were some publishers, including Alfred A. Knopf. His file was active for forty years primarily because of FBI interest in the authors Knopf published, some of whom Hoover considered subversive. One entry in Knopf's file involved a loyalty check conducted by the FBI when he was nominated to be on the advisory board of the National Park Service. A wide array of scientists, including Albert Einstein, were monitored.

Playwright Arthur Miller wrote extensively about the atmosphere of fear that permeated the lives of artists during the Cold War. "The politics of alien conspiracy soon dominated political discourse," he wrote in a 1996 article in the *New Yorker* about the late 1940s and early 1950s, a period "in our lives" when there was no "point of moral reference against which to gauge the action. . . . The left could not look straight at the Soviet Union's abrogations of human rights. The anti-Communist liberals could not acknowledge the violations of those rights by congressional committees."

Miller recalled what happened when he submitted a screenplay, *The Hook,* to Harry Cohn, the head of Columbia Pictures, in 1951. It was about union corruption, including murders, on the Brooklyn waterfront. "Something that would once have been considered unthinkable" happened. "He showed my script to the FBI." They wanted Miller to change the gangsters in the script to communists. Miller refused. Cohn chastised Miller for being unwilling to make the change that Cohn told him would have made the script "pro-American." The American Legion, then in its formal working relationship with the FBI, organized a boycott of Miller's play *Death of a Salesman.*

In 1952, Miller wrote a play that confronted the paranoia of that time, *The Crucible.* In it, he surveyed the tactics of the current political investigations through the prism of the Salem witch trials that took place in Massachusetts in 1692. *The Crucible* received tepid reviews when it opened on Broadway in 1953, but it became a classic, produced all over the world to this day. It has been produced, wrote Miller, "wherever a political coup appears imminent. . . . From Argentina to Chile to Greece, Czechoslovakia, China . . . the play seems to present the same primeval structure of human sacrifice to the furies of fanaticism and paranoia that goes on repeating itself as though imbedded in the brain of social man."

Miller lamented that the "accused were unable to cry out passionately." Few did, but historian Bernard DeVoto did so in his "Easy Chair" column in *Harper's* magazine in October 1949. An early and outspoken conservationist and historian, DeVoto also wrote occasionally in defense of civil liberties. It was in that last capacity that "he tangled with the FBI," wrote Tom Knudson in *High Country News* in 1994 after reviewing DeVoto's FBI file.

DeVoto's biographer, novelist Wallace Stegner, once said DeVoto was a "literary department store" who wrote "aisles of fiction, shelves of history, bins of criticism and an entire warehouse of contemporary essays, conservation polemics and political musings." For one of the books in his three-volume epic history of the American frontier, *Across the Wide Missouri,* he won a Pulitzer Prize. The most famous of his many columns was "Due Notice to the FBI," a "stinging attack," Knudson writes, "on the government spying, Red-baiting, blacklisting and Communist witch hunts that swept across America after World War II."

DeVoto had been interviewed by the FBI about someone he refused to identify in his article. The FBI also had asked questions of acquaintances of DeVoto's about the same person's politics and personal life. The FBI interview inspired this response from DeVoto in his column:

We have occasional qualms. . . . We find that the FBI has put at the disposal of this or that body a hash of gossip, rumor, slander, backbiting, malice, and drunken invention which, when it makes the headlines, shatters the reputations of innocent and harmless people and of people who our laws say are innocent until someone proves them guilty in court. We are shocked. Sometimes we are scared. Sometimes we are sickened. We know that the thing stinks to heaven, that it is an avalanching danger to our society. But we don't do anything about it.

They ask, "Have you—has he—ever been present at a meeting or a party where anyone sympathetic to Communism was also present? Did you—did he—belong to the Liberal Club in college? Did you—did he—escort to a dance a girl who has read Lenin or is interested in abstract painting? Have you—has he—ever recommended the *Progressive* to a friend?"

. . . I say it has gone too far. We are dividing into the hunted and the hunters. There is loose in the United States the same evil that once split Salem Village between the bewitched and the accused and stole men's reason quite away. We are informers to the secret police. Honest men are spying on their neighbors for patriotism's sake. . . .

None of us can know how much of this inquiry into the private lives of American citizens and government employees is necessary. Some of it is necessary—but we have no way of knowing which, when, or where. We have seen enough to know for sure that a great deal of it is altogether irresponsible. . . .

Representatives of the FBI . . . have questioned me, in the past, about a number of people and I have answered their questions. That's over. From now on, any representative of the government, properly identified, can count on a drink and perhaps informed talk about the Red (but non-Communist) Sox at my house. But if he wants information from me about anyone whatsoever, no soap.

Predictably, Hoover was furious at this rare public rebuke of his methods. He ordered an investigation of DeVoto that went on for years, and immediately notified heads of all FBI field offices across the country, "This article reflects the necessity of constantly being on the alert."

New files were born. In addition to investigating DeVoto, the FBI investigated the people whose letters approving of DeVoto's column were published in *Harper's*. His file filled with rumors about his politics and also with reports that he was "a fallen away Catholic" who had a "frontier childhood" in Utah. He was, according to one report placed in the file, a "shabbily dressed author" who once taught literature at Northwestern and Harvard universities. He was placed on the "no contact" list, probably without irony about the fact that that was the point: DeVoto did not want to be contacted.

Criticism was not tolerated. Sullivan explained years later to the Church Committee how the bureau routinely handled censure: "Anyone who wrote a book or was writing a book or we knew was going to be critical of Mr. Hoover and the FBI, we made efforts right then and there to find out anything that we could to use against them."

In the midst of that atmosphere, a visceral reaction against, rather than knowledge of, writers seemed to guide the director's conviction that authors should be watched and dossiers created about them for FBI files. For instance, when he read a newspaper report that Jean-Paul Sartre, who was internationally known as a French novelist, playwright, and philosopher and had recently been awarded the Nobel Prize for Literature, had said he would take an active role in the French "Who Killed Kennedy Committee," Hoover wrote on the routing slip attached to the clipping, "Find out who Sartre is." His reported lack of reading may explain why he did not recognize the name of one of the most best known authors in the world. It was widely believed inside the bureau that he did not read even "his" books, the ones written under his name by ghostwriters. It is stunning that such a person presumed he was capable of branding writers as subversive, let alone that it was legal for him to do so.

Suppression of writers' free expression was a continuous bureau project, but it probably was most aggressive during the 1960s, when the bureau forcefully and secretly—and sometimes violently—attacked campus and underground newspapers. They did so with various goals: forcing the publications to close, infiltrating them with informers, and threatening the credibility—and sometimes the lives—of their staff. The FBI often worked with the CIA and Army intelligence agencies in operations against these newspapers. In all, at least 150 such newspapers were the targets of these operations, according to Angus Mackenzie, who studied the scope of the operations in 1981 for *Columbia Journalism Review*.

The bureau's systematic approach to suppressing First Amendment rights involved convincing advertisers, including Columbia Records, to cease advertising in the underground press and campus papers—an idea that originated in the San Francisco FBI office and was used elsewhere with success. Banks that held the accounts of the newspapers were successfully recruited by the bureau to help in efforts to shut them down. Upon requests from the bureau, banks provided records of advertising income and contributions that had been deposited by the newspapers. The FBI used the information to convince people to stop supporting the newspapers.

The FBI also set up phony newspapers that hired radical young writers, giving the bureau wide ability to spy on them. It set up a photo agency, New York Press Service, that posed as an agency that served underground and campus newspapers. The person in charge, paid by the FBI, successfully solicited business with this letter to the newspapers: "The next time your organization schedules a demonstration, march, picket or office party, let us know in advance. We'll cover it like a blanket and deliver a cost free sample of our work to your office." Every response and every photograph shot went to the FBI.

Probably the most aggressive operation against an alternative news organization was the one conducted against Liberation News Service (LNS), a national service that distributed stories to alternative and campus newspapers. By 1968, Mackenzie reported, the FBI had assigned three informers to penetrate LNS, while nine informers reported on it from outside. The FBI used various counterintelligence techniques in attempts to destroy LNS. Within the antiwar movement, informers used disinformation to make LNS appear to be an FBI front. The bureau created friction among staff members and once planned to burn its offices in Washington, D.C., while the staff slept upstairs.

CONSISTENT WITH Hoover's assumption that intellectuals often were subversives, campuses were important playing fields for the FBI during the Cold War and the Vietnam War. Professors and students were targets of the FBI throughout that long period, but the emphases were reversed during the two wars. During the Cold War, professors were the main targets. During the Vietnam War, students were the chief campus objects of scrutiny, in massive numbers. And of all campus targets, black students were considered the greatest threat. On some campuses, as the initial Media files revealed, all black students were targeted by the FBI.

To deal with professors, whom Hoover considered to be among the country's worst internal threats, in 1951 he created the Responsibilities Program. Officially it was closed after four years, but like his nonclosing of

COINTELPRO in 1971, the Responsibilities Program continued to operate after the director "closed" it—removed its name—a gesture he thought would make it more difficult for this secret program to be discovered.

Hoover informed state governors about the program at a closed meeting in his office in 1951, where he swore them to secrecy. He spoke to them about two targeted groups, teachers and union members. Regarding unions, he informed them he had more than 12,000 informers in various industrial plants. He recited the number of subversives in each governor's state. He also told them that the bureau had a list of 4,463 Americans who were "the most potentially dangerous." Those people, he said, the FBI kept "under surveillance at all times." He told the governors that his authority for conducting such operations derived from the "responsibility of the bureau for the internal security of the country as a whole."

In response to the governors' interest in what was being done about subversives on campuses, Hoover told them about the Responsibilities Program and its principal goal, the firing of professors, lecturers, and other university employees. The emphasis in the program was on state universities, but faculty at some private universities also were targeted. Even elementary and high school teachers and schools' nonteaching staff members were subject to FBI investigation under the program.

By Hoover's standards, the Responsibilities Program was effective. It led to the dismissal of more than a thousand professors without due process. The program was one way he succeeded in creating an atmosphere during the peak of the Cold War in which the basic tenets of academic freedom were ignored on some of the nation's campuses. Former FBI agents and local American Legion members were hired by university administrators or governing boards to investigate the political activities of their own students and faculty members. Some universities, including Columbia, literally opened their faculty and student files to FBI agents. Professors and students spied on one another—sometimes at the request of the FBI, other times at the request of campus administrators and boards of regents or trustees. This, of course, fostered a poisonous learning and teaching environment. For campuses in small towns and cities, community life also was affected as selected professors were targeted for having suspect opinions.

Entire academic disciplines were affected, especially in the social sciences. The annual conventions of anthropologists and sociologists were peppered with FBI agents and informers who wrote secret reports for FBI files on speeches and academic papers presented at the conventions. A 1958 study of social scientists found that two-thirds of the approximately twenty-five hundred social science faculty members surveyed had been visited by the FBI at least once, and one-third of them had been visited three or more times. The threatening atmosphere created by the monitoring of social science researchers and their work is believed to have had a significant impact on the type of research done in some academic fields for nearly two decades as some professors engaged primarily in quantitative research and statistical analysis that was less likely to be regarded as politically suspect by the FBI than was work based on qualitative research.

In one of Hoover's largest projects, the FBI directed successive sustained clandestine operations against the University of California, with an emphasis on that system's Berkeley campus. The operations there involved hundreds of agents and informers spying on thousands of faculty and students from the late 1940s through the early 1970s. On the Berkeley campus, one of the most prestigious universities in the world, the bureau "mounted the most extensive covert operations the FBI is known to have ever undertaken in any college community," according to Seth Rosenfeld, author of *Subversives: The FBI's War on Student Radicals and Reagan's Rise to Power*, published in 2012. The University of California may, in fact, have been the largest organization of any type Hoover targeted for disruption by the bureau. These documented FBI actions were not known until Rosenfeld researched them over a period of thirty years for his comprehensive book on the FBI's role at Berkeley.

The files on the Berkeley operations suggest that Hoover was far more concerned with the political ideas of professors and students and the president of the university, Clark Kerr, than he was with what logically would be assumed to be the FBI's chief interest at Berkeley— the security of the federally funded campus program that played a major role in developing nuclear weapons, including development of the atomic bomb.

In 1960, Hoover assigned FBI agents to search for derogatory information about each of the university's 5,365 faculty members. Staff members, even at the lowest levels, also were investigated. At one point, a sixty-page bureau report was prepared on the university. It included a list of Berkeley professors to be placed on the secret Security Index, the list of Americans to be detained without warrant in the event of a national emergency. It included reports on fifty-four professors whose families subscribed or contributed money to what the bureau considered "subversive publications," information apparently gathered as a result of the bureau's large secret mail-opening program.

The special report also discussed Berkeley faculty members' involvement in "illicit love affairs, homosexuality, sexual perversion, excessive drinking, or other instances of conduct reflecting mental instability."

The FBI had been deeply embedded on the Berkeley campus for more than twenty years by the time the Free Speech Movement started in the fall of 1964 in response to the university's enforcing for the first time a little-known rule that barred students from speaking on campus about off-campus political causes, such as civil rights, an issue of deep interest to many Berkeley students. Mario Savio, who became the most widely known leader of the movement, had returned to campus in the fall of 1964 after working in Mississippi during Freedom Summer. Like many students who had worked there that summer and faced violence while helping black people register to vote, Savio was shocked that officials at his California campus barred students from speaking about the most important issues of the day. Having suffered physically to help black people assert their right to vote in Mississippi, he now defended Berkeley students' right to speak freely on campus.

With the birth of the Free Speech Movement, the FBI had many new targets: the protesting students and faculty who supported them. The students who participated in the movement lived under FBI surveillance for years. Savio was followed by the FBI long after the movement and his days on campus had ended. Even students' families and some reporters who covered the movement were investigated by the FBI.

Hoover's anger at the protesting Berkeley students, from the Free Speech Movement through opposition to the Vietnam War, fueled his long-simmering distaste for Berkeley, especially his dislike of Clark Kerr. Kerr, who had been head of the Berkeley campus from 1952 to 1958 and head of the entire University of California system from 1958 to 1967, was remembered when he died in 2003 at age ninety-two not only as the creator of the highly esteemed California higher education system but also as a very significant influence on the reform of higher education nationally and internationally as chairman and director of the Carnegie Commission on Higher Education. But Hoover despised him because he was, as an FBI report identified him in 1958, "a 'liberal' in the education field." A Quaker, as a young adult Kerr had worked for the American Friends Service Committee on various projects that served poor people. In Hoover's opinion, such an affiliation automatically made Kerr a subversive who should be removed from his position of influence.

"I know Kerr is no good," Hoover once wrote in a memo to top aides.

An economics professor and a labor arbitrator, Kerr also was against communism. He had in fact signed the controversial loyalty oath that many University of California faculty members refused to sign in the 1950s. But Kerr defended the rights of professors who refused to sign it when the university system's governing board of regents moved to fire them. That support of his colleagues' rights increased Hoover's dislike of Kerr. When President Johnson requested a routine background check of Kerr when he planned to appoint him to his cabinet as secretary of health, education, and welfare, FBI files reveal, Hoover sabotaged Kerr by telling Johnson that Kerr was disloyal—an accusation the bureau had investigated and knew was not true.

Hoover's determination to have Kerr fired from the University of California went into turbo speed just two weeks after Ronald Reagan was inaugurated as governor of California in January 1967. For Hoover, as for Reagan, getting rid of Kerr was a priority. When he campaigned against Governor Pat Brown in November 1966, Reagan promised to "clean up" the University of California. Like Hoover, he thought Kerr was too soft on student protest.

After Reagan was inaugurated, he immediately asked the FBI agent in charge of the San Francisco office for a briefing on what the bureau knew about professors and students on the Berkeley campus. The agent, Curtis O. Lynum, was somewhat aghast about the request and recommended to Hoover that the bureau not brief Reagan because the controversy at the university was too politically sensitive. But Hoover saw Reagan's interest in Berkeley as an "opportunity" and ordered Lynum to share the bureau's abundant Berkeley files with the new governor. It was not the first time Lynum had opposed Hoover over Berkeley matters. Two years earlier, Hoover had ordered him to write a report that would indicate the demonstrations on the campus were controlled by the Communist Party. That order and Hoover's reaction then to Lynum were indicative of Hoover's willingness not to let facts shape his interpretation of reality. Lynum told him there was no evidence that communists controlled the demonstrations. The director insisted the party was involved and asked him two more times for a report that would state that. Much to Hoover's annoyance, each time Lynum refused to write what would have been a false report.

Against his own judgment, Lynum obeyed Hoover's order to brief Reagan on Berkeley soon after his inauguration. Plans moved quickly, thanks largely to the fact that Hoover and Reagan already had a trusting and effective working relationship, and also because Hoover had already laid the groundwork for Kerr's firing. FBI files obtained by Rosenfeld reveal that

Hoover and Reagan had worked together much more than was previously realized on blacklisting alleged subversives in the movie industry in the 1950s. Now they joined forces once more, this time against Kerr.

The high level of power that was brought to bear in the effort to fire Kerr is striking. It involved the head of the FBI, the head of the CIA, and the new California governor. Hoover often treated the CIA with contempt, sometimes even ordering agents to have no contact with the agency and once, during World War II, sabotaging a clandestine action by the CIA's predecessor, the Office of Strategic Services. But for the sake of getting rid of Clark Kerr, Hoover collaborated with CIA director John McCone and welcomed him to a secret meeting in his office at 3:30 on the afternoon of June 28, 1965. It was the last of several high-level meetings McCone attended that day, including a national intelligence briefing, where he presented a plan for an immediate substantial increase in U.S. troop strength in Vietnam, and a meeting where he briefed members of the Atomic Energy Commission about foreign nuclear weapons development.

That afternoon, after a meeting at the State Department, where McCone discussed new turmoil in Africa and the Middle East, he came to Hoover's office to plot what to do about Kerr. These two heads of the nation's most powerful law enforcement and intelligence agencies huddled in intense discussion about how to remove Kerr. It may have been the only time the director ever happily collaborated with the CIA. The quality of the education system Kerr had created in California and was renowned for was not part of their agenda. The fact that he was a liberal who did not take strong action against students protesters was.

McCone, a 1922 graduate of Berkeley, had some ideas about how to accomplish their mutual goal. He knew well a member of the university's board of regents he thought might influence other regents to oppose Kerr. Over the next two years, Hoover provided secret FBI files on faculty members and students to that regent. Finally, with Reagan elected governor, the plan conceived by Hoover and McCone went into play. On January 20, 1967, at the first board of regents meeting after Reagan was inaugurated, and with Reagan attending, the board voted to fire Kerr.

When the FBI's role in events that led to the firing of Kerr was first revealed by Rosenfeld in a June 9, 2002, article in the *San Francisco Chronicle*, Senator Patrick Leahy, chairman of the Senate Judiciary Committee, said at a hearing of his committee that the bureau's role was "outrageous and some would even say criminal conduct."

The FBI fought strenuously to keep information about the FBI's Berkeley covert actions from being released to Rosenfeld. In his thirty-year pursuit of the files, each time Rosenfeld asked for relevant FBI files, the bureau refused to supply most of the ones he requested. When documents were released, many were nearly totally redacted, making them meaningless. Like Carl Stern forty years earlier, the only way Rosenfeld was able to obtain the files he requested—and have some redacted information restored—was by suing the bureau. He did so five times. In each suit, federal trial and appellate judges ordered the FBI to release the files requested by Rosenfeld. In the end, he received nearly 300,000 pages that documented the long history of Hoover's campaign to cleanse Berkeley of people he thought were subversive.

The FBI spent more than a million dollars trying to prevent Rosenfeld from obtaining the files that document this history. When his book was published in 2012, Rosenfeld compared the FBI's actions against Berkeley during the Cold War with its recent efforts to refuse to release files about that history: "During the Cold War FBI officials sought to change the course of history by secretly interceding in events, manipulating public opinion, and taking sides in partisan politics. The bureau's efforts, decades later, to improperly withhold information about those activities under the FOIA are, in effect, another attempt to shape history, this time by obscuring the past."

Senator Dianne Feinstein, Democrat from California and chairman of the Senate Intelligence Committee, asked Robert S. Mueller III, the FBI director since September 2001, if the bureau purposely "pursued litigation as a means to prevent or delay Mr. Rosenfeld from obtaining information to which he was entitled under the FOIA." In response, Mueller instructed the bureau's general counsel to examine the record to determine if that was the case. In a letter to the senator, Mueller said he "abhorred any investigative activity that targets or punishes individuals for the constitutional expression of their views. Such investigations are wrong and anti-democratic, and past examples are a stain on the FBI's greater tradition of observing and protecting the freedom of Americans to exercise their First Amendment rights."

Rosenfeld requested, again under the FOIA, and eventually received the general counsel's report Mueller had ordered. All the findings were deleted. But in the very brief text that was not redacted was a revealing comment by Howard Shapiro, then the FBI's general counsel. He stated that in the bureau's failed appeal to the Ninth Circuit Court of Appeals, "it appears that we were advancing arguments that bordered on the frivolous in order to cover our own previous misconduct."

HOOVER'S PERCEPTION that he could intrude into and influence the inner workings of institutions beyond his mandated responsibility even included forays into the U.S. Supreme Court. He expected members of the judiciary, the branch of government that is supposed to be the most independent, to bend to his will. Justices of the U.S. Supreme Court and court staff members should, he thought, be willing to violate laws and their codes of ethics in order to serve his interests. Members of the court staff and at least one justice did so.

During court appeals in the espionage cases of Ethel and Julius Rosenberg, who were executed in 1953 for conspiring to pass atomic secrets to the Soviet Union, Hoover received daily intelligence reports from inside the court, where all information exchanged that is not filed publicly is supposed to be confidential. According to a 1953 FBI memorandum, during the Rosenbergs' appeals, the captain of the Supreme Court police "furnished immediately all information heard by his men stationed throughout the Supreme Court building. He kept special [FBI] agents advised of the arrival and departure of persons having important roles in this case." As soon as the Rosenbergs were executed, the director authorized sending a letter of appreciation to two Supreme Court officials "for their whole-hearted cooperation in this case."

A 2,076-page FBI file on the U.S. Supreme Court reveals that in addition to using Supreme Court employees as sources, the bureau investigated Hoover's suspicions of communist influence on the court in the 1950s, when Earl Warren was chief justice of the court. The file became public as a result of a Freedom of Information request by Alexander Charns, a Durham, North Carolina, attorney and the author of the 1992 book *Cloak and Gavel: FBI Wiretaps, Bugs, Informers, and the Supreme Court.*

In 1965, a high-ranking FBI official, acting on Hoover's behalf, secretly asked for and received direct assistance on Hoover's behalf from Supreme Court justice Abe Fortas regarding a case then pending before the court that involved the bureau. After Fortas, in response to Hoover's inquiry, violated a court rule that prohibits justices from discussing pending cases with anyone outside the court, Hoover wrote in a memo to the FBI official who consulted with the justice that Fortas had demonstrated he was "a more honest man than I gave him credit for being." It was a strange interpretation of honesty. Hoover said he had feared Fortas "would try to weasel out [of helping Hoover] on grounds it was improper for him as a member of the court to even discuss the matter"—as, of course, it was. To Hoover, it was more important that the justice serve Hoover's interest than it was that he maintain the integrity required by the court.

IN THE ANNALS of both national law enforcement agencies and intelligence agencies, the roles Hoover played and the adulation he sought and received were unique. He repeatedly stretched his responsibilities into areas that were not part of his official responsibility. As Ungar wrote, "The FBI acted as if it had an entire way of life to protect." With the growth of protest, the bureau "became ever more frightened and confused until it saw itself as a bulwark against the lawlessness and disintegration of the American way of life. The FBI felt it had a mission to set things right again, and if that meant its own escalation of tactics and some desperate measures in the name of law, then so be it."

Hoover's roles in regard to the Vietnam War and racial issues—the two most important issues in the country in the twentieth century—were the most far-reaching of all his self-appointed intrusions into important areas of American life.

From the beginning of the Vietnam War, he made himself the watchdog of dissent against the war. His efforts got under way in the summer of 1964, as the Johnson administration was still trying to determine whether a U.S. Navy ship had been attacked by North Vietnamese forces in the Gulf of Tonkin. Acting as though it was certain the attack had occurred, members of the administration urged Congress to authorize President Johnson to send troops to Vietnam to retaliate against this attack. The measure authorizing those first troops, the Gulf of Tonkin Resolution—an extremely important piece of legislation that would be relied on for a decade by both President Johnson and President Nixon as Congress's ongoing blank check authorizing the war—passed unanimously in the House of Representatives. In the Senate, only Senator Ernest Gruening, Democrat from Alaska, and Senator Wayne Morse, Democrat from Oregon, voted against the measure. Gruening warned his colleagues they were signing "a predated declaration of war." Morse predicted that "history will record that we have made a great mistake by giving the president war making powers in the absence of a declaration of war. What is wrong with letting the Constitution operate as written by our constitutional fathers?"

The FBI director was watching closely as this first Vietnam War authorization legislation was being debated. He, of course, had no professional responsibility in relation to legislation or to war planning. But he regarded those who did not support the war to be subversives who should be targeted by the FBI, and he used the bureau to enforce that position from the time of those congressional debates on the first war legislation in 1964 until he died in 1972. He had agents collect the names of people who sent telegrams to Senator Morse expressing support for his stand against the war resolution and started files on them. That was the beginning of the lists he collected in connection with the Vietnam War. Later, he expanded COINTELPRO to include operations against antiwar activists.

Two years after the Gulf of Tonkin Resolution was passed, Senator J. William Fulbright, Democrat from Arkansas, convened hearings on the progress of the war. Hoover and his agents were listening and watching again. At President Johnson's request, Hoover placed Fulbright under constant surveillance, including when he dined at embassies. Hoover assigned agents to find evidence that Fulbright, one of the most respected senior members of Congress at the time, "was either a communist agent or a dupe of the communist powers."

Throughout the Vietnam War, the FBI supported the assumption of Presidents Johnson and Nixon that opposition to the war in the United States was not homegrown but was made possible by financial support from foreign—most likely communist—governments. It was difficult for American intelligence operators to let go of the idea that foreign governments were providing the antiwar movement with financial support because they knew the United States, through the CIA, had provided aid for years to antigovernment groups in Eastern Europe and elsewhere. Because of that, they "easily calculated," wrote former CIA agent Vincent Marchetti, that "somehow the communist countries were now getting even by using American groups to stir up trouble in the United States." Hard as the CIA and FBI tried to establish evidence of foreign support for American activists, such evidence never was found, according to Marchetti and officials of both the CIA and the FBI. Ungar, in his extensive research, reached the same conclusion: "Despite many investigations, no such link ever was found."

WHEN MEMBERS OF the Socialist Workers Party (SWP) learned in 1973 that the party had been the target of one of the major COINTELPRO programs, they sued the government for violating their constitutional rights. Their lawsuit produced shocking revelations about FBI conduct. As the revelations poured out in the courtroom, the attorney general imposed new restrictions and forced the FBI to abandon its harassment of the party that was still taking place during the trial.

During the thirteen years the suit unfolded in federal court in Manhattan, the FBI was forced to reveal how it had systematically harassed the party for decades, damaging the lives of hundreds of individuals and preventing members of the party from participating in public discourse. At the end of the trial, the Nixon-appointed judge who presided over the case, U.S. federal judge Thomas P. Griesa, ruled in August 1986 that the FBI's forty-year program of continuous harassment and abuse of the party and its members had "no legal authority or justification" and "was illegal and patently unconstitutional."

In response to a series of orders from Judge Griesa, the FBI was forced to turn over massive evidence that documented the bureau's four decades of surveillance and dirty tricks operations conducted against the SWP. As the FBI finally conceded during the trial, and as the judge wrote in his decision:

"There is no evidence that any FBI informant ever reported an instance of planned or actual espionage, violence, terrorism or efforts to subvert the governmental structure of the United States." In fact, the bureau found no evidence of any type of criminal activity by party members. When the massive secret records of the forty-year intense observation of the party were reviewed by Judge Griesa, he found "a consistent recital of peaceful, lawful political activities, peaceful, lawful personal activities and a total absence of any criminal activities or plans of any nature whatever."

When the judge ordered bureau officials to submit written rationale for why the long and multifaceted SWP operation was conducted they wrote: Individuals in "subversive groups were presumed to recognize that the use of violence as a potential tool is inevitable," and "all members are investigated sufficiently to assess their willingness to use violence for their cause." In other words, FBI officials believed that a radical idea inevitably would lead to violent behavior—even, apparently, after forty years of being nonviolent.

Evidence produced during the case about the FBI's operations against the SWP revealed the following:

- From 1960 to 1966, specially trained teams of FBI agents burglarized the New York offices of the SWP at least ninety-two times, an average of once every three weeks. Homes of party officers also were burglarized. Each burglary involved a team of twelve FBI agents, six working inside and six providing security outside the scene of the burglary. Fearful of being discovered by police, they carried no FBI identification and were told to "take a fall" for the bureau if they were arrested. Inside the SWP offices, they photographed and stole more than 10,000 documents. Because they had no legal right to the documents—such as financial records, membership lists, personal correspondence—they could not have obtained a search warrant to get them legally.

- During the burglaries, agents placed electronic transmitting devices and microphones in the walls of offices so agents could listen to SWP members at any time. In such instances, waiting for plaster to dry absorbed many hours.
- Auditoriums and hotels where the party held events were electronically bugged.
- Agents routinely received commendations and financial rewards from Hoover for each burglary because they involved "the highest degree of security."
- Agents created millions of pages of dossiers on the party and individual members.
- More than sixteen hundred informers were used to infiltrate and take actions against this party that had twenty-five hundred members at its peak and a thousand members at the time it sued the government in 1973.
- In 1961, despite having never found any mention of a plan to engage in violent action, the bureau nevertheless switched from a program of harassment against the SWP to a program designed to destroy the party.
- Hundreds of members were publicly humiliated by false information the bureau planted with news media about the party's candidates for public office, including members who ran for president of the borough of Manhattan and president of the United States.
- A man was forced out of being a scoutmaster in the Boy Scouts in Orange, New Jersey, because his wife was a member of the party.
- Members lost jobs as public school teachers, postal workers, and aerospace employees as a result of employers being told they were members of the party or as a result of derogatory false information provided by the bureau.
- A member was turned down for a government job after the FBI notified the employer the person had attended an SWP meeting—fifteen years earlier.

- FBI agents caused SWP members to be arrested for minor offenses, such as littering.
- Dirty tricks projects included physically attacking party members in their offices, making anonymous bomb threats in calls to party offices, and firing shots at an SWP office.

Three years into the SWP trial, Attorney General Edward H. Levi ordered the FBI to end its decades-long operations against the SWP. Much evidence had accumulated by then—"the largest disclosure of internal FBI workings since the theft of FBI documents in Media, PA," reported the *New York Times*. FBI director Clarence Kelley just weeks earlier had announced that he had transferred the case from the bureau's Intelligence Division to its General Investigative Division. That wasn't enough for Levi. Two internal Department of Justice review committees he appointed recommended he should step in and stop the FBI's actions against the SWP because, both concluded, the party's activities did not justify bureau scrutiny.

Remarkably, until the attorney general ordered the investigation halted, FBI informers continued to operate clandestinely inside the SWP even during the trial, submitting regular reports to the bureau on the SWP's evolving legal strategy in the case.

It was during this trial that Levi, in another unprecedented action, issued the first FBI guidelines. They required the bureau to open and continue investigations only if they were related to evidence of commission of a crime or suspicion of planning to commit a crime.

While the truth about Hoover's secret FBI was emerging during the SWP trial and official investigations, there also were continuous efforts then by bureau officials to hide the truth. In 1980, in the course of the SWP case, it was revealed that FBI officials concealed considerable information about the bureau's illegal break-ins in responses to Department of Justice inquiries, in response to subpoenas issued in both the Senate and House investigations of the bureau, and in responses to orders from Judge Griesa during the SWP case. When evidence of this continuing subterfuge became public, William H. Webster, the federal judge who succeeded Kelley as FBI director in February 1978, issued a public announcement that statements made by FBI officials about illegal break-ins the bureau conducted were "grossly inaccurate" during those official investigations.

ATHAN THEOHARIS MAY KNOW more about the FBI than any other person. His extensive examination of the bureau started with major research he conducted for the Church Committee. Since then, as an historian on the faculty of Marquette University, he has written extensively about the bureau. From that deep knowledge, he has concluded in regard to COIN-TELPRO and similar bureau operations: "I know of no case where there was a benefit to society. . . . The FBI gathered no information that had anything to do with finding out, say, that Joe Smith is going to bomb the Capitol, something that could have been stopped. . . . I can think of no crime that was stopped by information gained during COINTELPRO and COINTELPRO-like operations. . . . It was harass and destroy rather than investigate, prosecute and convict."

Given the information the bureau gathered in those operations, says Theoharis, "there was no way it could have been used. It was obtained illegally, and it was worthless information. What was gathered for forty years in the campaign against the Socialist Workers Party is evidence of this."

In these programs, said Theoharis, "Hoover moved the FBI away from law enforcement. . . . The person in charge of law enforcement created a culture of lawlessness."

JOURNALISTS AND SCHOLARS have found that forcing the FBI to comply with the Freedom of Information Act can take a long time and be very costly. Their difficulties pale, however, in comparison to those of four Boston men as they spent nearly forty years trying to gain access to the FBI files they needed to exonerate them and free them from death row.

The four men—Peter Limone, Joseph Salvati, Louis Greco, and Henry Tameleo—were convicted for the 1965 murder of Edward Deegan. Three of them were sentenced to die in the electric chair. All of them proclaimed their innocence from the time they were arrested. The record shows that the FBI willfully sacrificed these innocent men as part of the bureau's ill-conceived approach to fighting organized crime in New England. For years, Hoover ignored organized crime, even saying it did not exist. When he finally acknowledged its existence, he created a law enforcement approach that failed, as this Boston case tragically illustrates.

When the crimes perpetrated by the FBI in this Boston organized crime–related case in the 1960s became known, it was evident that Hoover could be just as lawless and inhumane in criminal cases as he was in intelligence matters, perhaps more so. In the intelligence cases, dissent was trampled. In this criminal case, the truth about life-and-death matters was trampled and the FBI knowingly caused innocent people to be falsely convicted and sentenced to die. Unfortunately, in 2002, forty-year-old efforts to gain access to the crucial files that contained exonerating information continued to be rejected—by the FBI, by the Department of Justice, and by President George W. Bush.

The astonishing truth about the case remained secret for four decades: that those four men were framed by the FBI. They were convicted and kept in prison for more than three decades—where two of them died—on the basis of the false testimony of an informer the FBI knew was lying, and who, worse, actually had been coached by the FBI in his lying. FBI agents had precise advance information they had gathered from illegal electronic surveillance about plans for the murder in 1965, but they did nothing to stop it. They knew two of their informers said they would commit the murder but did nothing to stop them. One of the killers later told agents he would falsely accuse the four innocent men. FBI agents helped him carry out that plan.

The FBI presented its perjured informer to a state prosecutor, vouched for his honesty, and urged the prosecutor to try the case. At the trial the bureau in essence set up, one of the agents testified that Joseph "the Animal" Barboza, the witness he had prepared to give false testimony—and who was the only source of evidence against the four men—was an honest person whose testimony could be trusted.

On the day the four men were convicted for this crime the FBI knew they did not commit, agents in the organized crime unit of the Boston FBI office celebrated. Hoover sent commendations and financial awards to the two agents who guided the witness with his perjury. The director apparently did not blink when, a few days later, the agent in charge of the Boston office, in a memorandum to the director, praised the continued development of Barboza as an informer in the bureau's elite Top Echelon group of inform-ers and described him as "a professional assassin responsible for numerous homicides and acknowledged by all professional law enforcement represen-tatives in this area to be the most dangerous individual known."

Then, for three decades, the FBI compounded the grave injustice per-petrated against the four men by refusing to submit the only evidence that could have exonerated them, the evidence in the FBI's files, as the four men used every legal avenue available to them to gain their freedom and clear their names—repeated requests for a new trial, efforts to have their sentences commuted, requests for clemency. The injustice was compounded for many years after Hoover had approved it and long after he died.

Hoover was informed of, and approved, each step of the framing of the men, beginning with knowing about the planned murder before it took place and through the steps that sustained the injustice after the men were convicted until he died. The injustice continued to be sustained in 2002, when, at the request of Attorney General John Ashcroft, President Bush issued an executive order requiring the Department of Justice not to turn the requested FBI files over to the four men because the release of the files would "politicize the criminal justice process" and "would be contrary to the national interest." Astonishingly, Hoover's secret FBI was being protected at the highest levels of the federal government at that late date in a case where the opening of the files was desperately needed to right severe injustices perpetrated by the bureau more than forty years earlier. Former FBI director Robert Mueller—first as an assistant U.S. attorney in Boston and then as the acting U.S. attorney there—throughout the 1980s, *Boston Globe* journalist Kevin Cullen reported, wrote letters to the parole and pardons board opposing clemency for the four men framed by the FBI as they repeatedly proclaimed their innocence.

This justice-denying secret role of the FBI in this case finally was broken open by the efforts of Representative Dan Burton, Republican from Indiana, and Vincent Garo, a Medford, Massachusetts, attorney who, as the lawyer for one of the four men, worked for more than twenty years to get access to the bureau files that eventually led to the men being exonerated, two of them posthumously, at a federal trial against the government.

The cruel official attitude toward injustice perpetrated against the men by the FBI was on display during 2004 testimony by Paul Rico, one of the two FBI agents responsible for causing the case to be brought to trial with the perjured informer-witness. When Rico was asked at a hearing of the House Committee on Government Reform, convened by Burton, chair of the committee, if he had any remorse that four innocent men went to prison, he replied, "Would you like tears or something?"

In contrast, at the same hearing, the man who prosecuted the case had much remorse, and also anger at the FBI. "I was outraged—outraged," said Jack Zalkind. "I certainly would never have allowed myself to prosecute this case having that knowledge. . . . This information should have been in my hands. It should have been in the hands of the defense attorneys. It is outrageous, it's terrible, and that trial shouldn't have gone forward."

In 2007 in the U.S. District Court in Boston, Judge Nancy Gertner ordered the federal government to pay an unprecedented $102 million judgment for the FBI's role in what is known as the Deegan murder case—for "intentional misconduct, subornation of perjury, conspiracy, the framing of innocent men" in the murder of Edward "Teddy" Deegan.

The misconduct in this case ran "all the way up to the FBI director," Judge Gertner declared in her order that damages be paid to the surviving two falsely charged men and to the families of all four men. This case "was not the work of two renegade agents. It was known to, supported by, encouraged and facilitated by the FBI hierarchy all the way to the FBI director. FBI officials up the line allowed their employees to break laws, violate rules and ruin lives, interrupted only with the occasional burst of applause."

IN THREE FEDERAL COURTROOMS, Hoover's secret FBI has been confronted: in Judge Clarkson Fisher's Camden courtroom in 1973 for essentially entrapping twenty-eight people in the bureau's desperate effort to find the Media burglars; in Judge Thomas P. Griesa's New York courtroom in the 1980s for violating the constitutional rights of the members of a political party for more than forty years; and in Judge Nancy Gertner's Boston courtroom in 2007 for concocting a murder trial that sent four innocent men to death row for decades on the basis of information in FBI files that would have exonerated the men.

Another federal judge, Laurence H. Silberman, has called for Hoover's legacy to be confronted. So far that hasn't happened. Judge Silberman's conviction that steps need to be taken to stop the likelihood of FBI officials ever again using the FBI as Hoover used it arose from the revulsion he felt in 1975 when he was forced to read a collection of Hoover's derogatory files about members of Congress and other well-known people. The House Judiciary Committee demanded that Silberman, then deputy attorney general, testify before the committee about Hoover's "secret and confidential" files. It had been assumed those files had been destroyed by Hoover's secretary, Helen Gandy, immediately after he died. Apparently she missed some. Without FBI director Clarence Kelley realizing it, they were in a file cabinet near his office.

Silberman spent three weekends at FBI headquarters reading those files that were the result, he wrote in a column in 2005 in the *Wall Street Journal*, of Hoover tasking "his agents with reporting privately to him any bits of dirt on figures such as Martin Luther King or their families—information

Hoover sometimes used as blackmail to ensure his and the bureau's power." It was a sickening experience for Silberman, the worst experience he had, he said, in all his many years in public service. He wrote that he intended "to take to my grave nasty bits of information on various political figures— some still active." But, "bad as the dirty collection business was, perhaps even worse was the evidence that he allowed—even offered—the bureau to be used by presidents for naked political purposes," said Silberman, who was appointed to the U.S. Circuit Court in Washington, D.C., in 1985 by President Ronald Reagan.

Silberman has made two recommendations for confronting Hoover's legacy. First, he proposes that all new FBI recruits be required to study "the nature of the secret and confidential files of J. Edgar Hoover." Only knowledge of what happened in the FBI for forty-eight years under Hoover, he thinks, will assure that the FBI's past will not be repeated.

He also recommended that J. Edgar's name be removed from the FBI's massive national headquarters building in Washington. Representative Burton has joined in this call. The longtime director should not be honored, both firmly believe, especially in such a prominent way. "The country and the bureau" would "be well served" by removing Hoover's name, said Silberman. "It is as if the Defense Department were named for Aaron Burr. Liberals and conservatives should unite to support legislation to accomplish this repudiation of a very sad chapter in American history."

Considered a classic example of brutalist architecture, the mammoth concrete FBI headquarters on Pennsylvania Avenue between the Capitol and the White House was dedicated by President Gerald Ford on the day it opened, September 30, 1975. At that time, at $126 million, it was the most expensive federal government building ever built. Hundreds filled the courtyard as the United States Marine Band played, among other selections, the "J. Edgar Hoover March," a song composed for the occasion by Al Nencioni, an FBI agent in the Alexandria, Virginia, field office.

Since that sunny dedication day, the J. Edgar Hoover Building has honored Hoover by boldly bearing his name. Conclusions of investigations and court rulings by judges that have declared his actions unconstitutional and shocking to the conscience have revealed the depth of his shame.

20

Closing Cases

FBI HEADQUARTERS FELT like a war zone in July 1976. The attorney general, Edward Levi, and the Church Committee were pushing Clarence Kelley to get the domestic intelligence files under control. Levi thought Kelley had made a bad decision when he appointed one of the strongest Hoover defenders as his associate director. Levi eventually ordered Kelley to fire him. Inasmuch as Kelley realized by then that the person he had appointed was sandbagging him in regard to intelligence operations—hiding files, giving him inaccurate information to pass to Levi and the Church Committee, thereby humiliating him—he wasn't unhappy about complying with Levi's demand. The people who saw their main mission as protecting Hoover's files were, of course, very unhappy with the firing.

Then Neil Welch, the special agent in charge in the Philadelphia field office, arrived to conduct a special assignment for Kelley. That upset the old guard even more.

As evidence mounted about the true nature of J. Edgar Hoover's secret FBI, Levi demanded that Kelley force the Intelligence Division to review its files and decide whether continuing them could be justified. In response to Kelley's assignment, the intelligence bureaucrats quietly but firmly rebelled. They simply stopped reviewing the files. Kelley analyzed the situation and concluded he would appoint someone from outside headquarters to take control of this problem. It was not the kind of task Kelley liked. He suffered now even more than he had in his first year at the bureau from being pushed and pulled on the one hand by the staunch Hoover loyalists and, on the other hand, by the reformers, the Church Committee, and the attorney general. He also suffered from serious back pain and wanted to return to Kansas City, where he had been police chief before he became FBI director, for treatment of his back problem.

Enter Neil J. Welch.

For a variety of reasons, Welch seemed to be the perfect person for the job that needed to be done. He had been called by the new associate director, Richard G. Held. "Come immediately," said Held. Welch said later that Kelley wanted someone who could "take charge . . . someone tough enough to handle the headquarters bureaucrats. In short, 'the toughest SOB we have because the whole bureaucracy is going to fight this effort.'"

A somewhat gruff man with a sardonic sense of humor, Welch took pride in thinking he fit that bill well. But what gave him unique qualifications for Kelley's assignment was that Welch openly hated COINTELPRO and for years had refused to let agents in his office participate in it. That, of course, was anathema to Hoover. In 1971, at the time the Media burglary took place, Hoover placed Welch on probation because of his refusal to let agents in the Detroit FBI office, where he was then SAC, participate in COINTELPRO.

He was in fact the only SAC in the country who refused to let agents under his supervision be involved in such operations. He maintained that policy in every city where he was the SAC—Detroit, Philadelphia, and New York. He made an exception in Buffalo, where he was in charge of the FBI office before going to the Detroit office. Every Russian official who came to the United States seemed to insist on visiting Niagara Falls. Given that situation and pressure from headquarters about the presence of Soviets, Welch relented and permitted an intelligence crew to go to the falls regularly to watch Russians watching the falls.

There were other SACs who were not enthusiastic about having their agents participate in COINTELPRO operations, but it is believed that only Welch drew the line and said his agents could not be involved in them. "It was a serious problem," he said; "not only was that stuff ridiculous and silly and unjustified and all that. It's also terribly disruptive in an office to have eighty-five percent of your people working according to proper guidelines and statutes, with everything you do provable in court—guys enforcing the law because they were sworn to uphold the Constitution and the laws of the United States. And then, at the same time, you got a little backwater place over here [in the office] where you got guys that are out doing all kinds of inventive things for none of which can any possible authority be found. It doesn't belong in there. It's a bad fit."

Even with his rule against COINTELPRO operations being carried out by agents in the Detroit office, Welch still had to go to great lengths to prevent some agents from proposing them to Washington behind his back. Every time young agents went to Washington headquarters for in-service training, they "returned to Detroit with bizarre counterintelligence schemes so regularly" that Welch started requiring agents who went to bureau headquarters to be debriefed when they returned to Detroit. "Those hopelessly poisoned by the bureau instruction were summarily reassigned to the bank robbery squad where they could do no harm." But one agent's propensity for COINTELPRO must have slipped through Welch's debriefing unnoticed. Welch got a call from someone in the Domestic Intelligence Division in Washington who wanted to make sure Welch would be able to provide security for the quart of foul-smelling distilled pig feces liquid the Detroit office had ordered for a COINTELPRO operation against the local Black Panther organization. Welch recalls that he went wild. There was a lot of screaming and yelling. He canceled the operation and made sure the liquid, which was supposed to have a potency that would belittle the best efforts of the biggest skunk, was not delivered to the Detroit FBI office.

In addition to thinking such programs were cruel and stupid, Welch thought few, if any, of the COINTELPRO programs were constitutional, a crucial factor that, until the time he arrived at headquarters on orders from Kelley, had not been given much attention in the bureau. "As soon as you get into an area where you are dealing with people's ideas," he said, "you are dealing with something extraordinary. . . . Domestic intelligence is prone to abuse unless tightly regulated. . . . As soon as you gather intelligence you are making some hard decisions. You are impacting people's rights to associate without Big Brother and his ears. As long as they're not breaking any laws, they should be free from government surveillance and . . . from being on some government list . . . free from intrusive informant operations and things more inventive, such as flattening their tires."

In perhaps his most devastating comment about Hoover's massive intelligence operation, Welch said it was "mindless."

WELCH ACCEPTED Kelley's special assignment to come to headquarters in July 1976 in order to, as Kelley had put it, "get this domestic intelligence caseload closed down to a defendable level."

Since being transferred by Kelley to Philadelphia in 1975, Welch had been called to Washington several times on special assignments from Kelley. The most frequent ones were to teach advanced courses to agents at the FBI Academy in investigating organized crime and political corruption. That was the work he liked most and that he thought should be the bureau's primary work. During Hoover's lifetime, he had to do such cases almost surreptitiously. He is proud that when he was assigned to Philadelphia he "almost immediately upon arrival completely shut down the domestic intelligence program there, which had been operating prior to that moment in a timeless and mindless manner as in days of old. I reassigned all the agents to criminal work." That was possible now that Kelley was director. When he did that in Detroit, under Hoover, he "encountered warlike resistance," including a threat to remove him as SAC. Welch was punished by Hoover for his firm resistance to COINTELPRO, but he survived. That may have been possible because Hoover surely knew that Welch's leadership in the new Jackson, Mississippi, office in 1964 played a major role in the bureau's solving some crucial Ku Klux Klan murder cases when President Johnson ordered Hoover to investigate those cases.

Unlike Hoover, Kelley regarded Welch as a model FBI field office administrator. As Kelley gradually moved the bureau away from an emphasis on domestic intelligence operations and into a greater emphasis on investigating organized crime, government corruption, and police brutality—areas that Welch was emphasizing in Philadelphia—Kelley relied on him for advice. The shift meant the bureau, like Welch's office, also moved from an emphasis on quantity to an emphasis on quality. Hoover had placed a major emphasis on the quantity of crimes solved, and for that reason concentrated on easy bank robberies and stolen car cases. That approach built the numbers he used to impress Congress at appropriations time. However, it prevented the bureau from attacking the crimes that were most damaging to the country.

What Welch saw when he arrived at headquarters in July 1976 was not pretty. "The place looked like it was under siege. The Department of Justice was there gathering information on sundry topics . . . taking statements from bureaucrats. . . . I was just another unwelcome investigator, and, as I understood, one particularly unwelcome, both because of the unusual nature of my mission and because of my known views on the 'usefulness' of that bureaucratic empire."

Kelley had left for Kansas City, so Welch received his orders from Kelley through Held as soon as he arrived. Held walked Welch through the executive office suites, repeating Welch's assignment to each FBI executive: "SAC Neil Welch has the director's orders to undertake a special assignment immediately. You are to cooperate with him in every way. Consider his orders those of Director Kelley, without question of any kind." Shock was obvious on every face, Welch remembers.

For several weeks that summer, he and Norm Rand, Welch's friend and formerly an agent in Detroit, sat across from each other in a room that contained only their large desk and intelligence files. The files were wheeled in, cartload after cartload, and stacked, as Welch remembers, on their desk and in floor-to-ceiling piles throughout the room. The assignment involved reviewing intelligence files housed in Washington headquarters as well as at bureau offices throughout the country. At the outset, Welch sent a telegram, followed by a phone call, instructing every field office SAC to review the intelligence files in their offices. When they balked, Welch told them he would fly to their office the next day to do the task. They fell in line without him having to do so. The domestic intelligence files were flown to Washington.

Surreptitiously, the two highest officials in the Domestic Intelligence Division tried to discourage people in the field from cooperating with Welch. He says he reacted as he thought Kelley would want him to react in what the director had described as an emergency situation. "The ship was about to flounder," said Welch, so he transferred the two men out of the Intelligence Division. When the head of the personnel office told Welch it would not be possible to arrange transfers quickly, he did it himself, in Kelley's name, effective immediately. "That was that. All resistance collapsed."

Well, almost all. A few days later another person from the Intelligence Division approached Welch with a plea that he stop reviewing and closing intelligence files. "He made the case for resistance," Welch recalls, "with an argument . . . that a change now would undercut our previous positions, we needed to keep solidarity with the past, he said. And we should hold out and wait for a more friendly administration and Congress. To go along with Levi, he said, would serve to aid communism and the enemies of our country.

"I didn't say much to him," said Welch, "except that the decisions had been made by higher authority, and all, soundly so in my judgment, were final, and in any event were those of the director and the attorney general on behalf of the president. His job, I told him, was to follow orders, or resign if he couldn't do so for whatever reason." Some people in the Domestic Intelligence Division were, as a matter of fervid belief, devoted to keeping the cases alive because, like Hoover, they saw a danger in opinions different from their own, subversive opinions, and they thought people who held opinions they considered subversive should be carefully watched. Others in the division had no particular interest in the intelligence itself; they wanted to maintain the caseload simply because their jobs depended on maintaining it until they retired. Their attitude, said Welch, was "It's what we do. And we have to keep doing it because we're too old to learn to do something else." Neither of those two groups, the ideologically dedicated or the retirement-calendar watchers, liked what Welch was about to do to the intelligence files.

He and Rand read each of the intelligence files delivered to them. The number of people or organizations who were named within each file varied, for many of the thick files included dossiers on several people. These files were the fruit of COINTELPRO and COINTELPRO-like operations. As Welch and Rand reviewed them, they answered these questions about each file:

> How long has this investigation of the individual or group been going
>   on?
> Was there a violation of a criminal law?
> Does he or she pose a criminal threat to society?
> Do we have an actual bombing case on this guy?
> The bottom line: Does this investigation meet AG guidelines?

Under Levi's new guidelines, only cases that involved actual criminal conduct or clear and present danger would remain open—all others were to be closed.

Some of the cases they reviewed were relatively new, only a year or two old. Others had been started in the 1930s. "I can tell you I have never given the closing of any of those cases a second thought and doubt we made any mistake that came back to endanger the nation," said Welch years later.

Asked what the standards were for opening the cases, Welch says, "God knows. It was the product of perceived threats at earlier times. The process got out of tune with the passage of time. And the bureaucrats, for their own selfish reasons, chose to ignore changing times." An investigation that might have been of real concern at a particular time in the Cold War, but should have been closed, was often reinvestigated periodically and maintained just to keep the number of cases up. What appeared to be dangerous forever may have stayed in the files out of inertia, not because of continued danger.

In the end, of the 4,868 cases Welch and Rand reviewed, they decided only 636 qualified to be left open. Welch stipulated that the open cases were to be reviewed in sixty days. Convincing evidence would have to be presented to justify continuing an investigation beyond that time. Otherwise, if there was no reason to continue the investigation and insufficient evidence to present it to a prosecutor, the case must be closed.

Welch's overriding goal was to apply the standards of criminal investigations to intelligence cases. Doing so would make it impossible for the cases to live forever. "If they could convince me that the subject of a case had committed a felony, or was about to do so, they got thirty days to wrap it up. Otherwise, it's over now and for evermore." He moved the 636 open cases to the Criminal Division. That meant each of them had to be investigated quickly and decisions made about whether the case should live or die. The cases could not linger in the files.

"The name of the game henceforth was not endless intelligence gathering, surveillance, and intrusion by informants or wiretaps," said Welch, "but handling the case like any other crime: Develop the evidence and go to a prosecutor to either prosecute or close it and go to something more pressing."

This emphasis on applying criminal investigative standards to intelligence cases would be criticized years later, especially after the September 11 attacks, as having weakened the capacity of the bureau to discover and capture terrorism plotters. Defenders of the system promoted by Welch claimed the opposite: that approaching terrorism as a criminal rather than an intelligence problem intensified investigations and made it more likely that they would lead to important information. Without using criminal investigation standards, they claimed, such investigations were more likely to become victims of bureaucratic inertia, as intelligence files often had.

"I suppose I knew it was a thankless job, one that would incur a lifetime of enemies," Welch said years later about his special assignment to clean up the intelligence files of J. Edgar Hoover's secret FBI in 1976, "but, nevertheless, one that needed doing and one I probably was uniquely qualified for." He says he thought at the time that taking this assignment "will ensure they never bring me into this headquarters again."

Just a year later, though, a blue-ribbon search committee appointed by President Jimmy Carter wanted Welch to come back to headquarters—as the next director of the FBI. They recommended three finalists, but he was their unanimous choice. Among the qualifications the committee established was that the new director must not have had connections with or approve of the bureau's COINTELPRO operations. In a sign of how the FBI was regarded then, the committee decided it could not trust the FBI to run checks on the candidates and did not ask them to do so despite the usual practice of relying on FBI checks on candidates for high-level federal appointments.

Welch, characteristically, was blunt with the committee. They seemed to like that and also that he was a favorite of agents on the street, many of whom had longed for years for leadership that focused on real crime and not on useless intelligence gathering and secret dirty tricks. The committee members were very aware that he was openly critical of headquarters, having recently told a reporter that "you could put sandbags around the building and shut off the phones and the bureau's criminal investigative work would be better off for it."

J. Edgar Hoover understood the problem, Welch wrote in a book assessing his experience in the FBI, "but not the solution. He strove for efficiency and was near genius in devising methods to measure individual and group effort, time and productivity. . . . The result was a bureaucratic stalemate which generated bushels of statistics without much meaning."

In the letter of application the committee asked candidates for director to write, Welch told the committee, "I feel that what has developed at our FBI headquarters over the years is a ponderous, ineffectual, costly bureaucracy which does not contribute substantially or materially to the essential work of the FBI." That attitude may have endeared him to Carter's committee, but it did not win applause at FBI headquarters.

As the selection process was unwinding, Welch heard that one of the intelligence supervisors he had unceremoniously transferred out of the Domestic Intelligence Division at the outset of his evaluation of intelligence files a year earlier "tried to undo my candidacy for FBI director by ordering a search for any writings I may have made . . . thinking they might show me to be some kind of secret communist sympathizer. . . . The domestic intelligence old boy network was working on the [Capitol] Hill to torpedo me."

"I'm quite sure that the only writings they found," said Welch, "over 5,000 strong, were: 'Close this file permanently. NJW for Dir. C. Kelley.' "

Carter didn't choose any of the five people recommended by his blue-ribbon search committee. Instead, he appointed William H. Webster of St. Louis, then a judge on the U.S. Court of Appeals for the Eighth Circuit, as FBI director in February 1978. That year Webster appointed Welch to be in charge of the New York field office.

When he accepted the New York job, Welch said he planned "to take this office apart brick by brick and reassemble it." He had in mind what he knew he would find in New York. Over the years, that office, like the Philadelphia office prior to his arrival, had diverted its workforce from organized crime investigations to intelligence investigations of radical organizations. When Welch arrived in New York, agent Paul Cummings, an old friend who was about to retire, told him, "When I leave, Chief, you can turn out the lights." He was the only FBI agent then doing organized crime investigations in New York City.

As he settled into the New York field office, Welch discovered that the FBI's "war against the Weatherman Underground had been won by La Cosa Nostra." Responding to headquarters' demands, the New York office had transferred its best undercover agents from the organized crime unit, Squad 47, to investigate the Weather Underground. The result, he said, was a triple failure: members of the FBI squad were indicted for their alleged illegal tactics, "FBI penetration of New York's crime families had disappeared," and the Weather Underground people were still at large.

WHEN THE MEDIA FBI OFFICE was burglarized, Welch, as someone who detested the intelligence operations the stolen files revealed, was intrigued. When J. Edgar Hoover complained that the published Media files presented a distorted picture of FBI activities, Welch thought instead that the documents showed that the FBI's priorities were distorted. "The burglars probably have no idea what they caused," he said. "The fallout was immense. . . . They spent millions to transfer agents from those offices and spent millions on the unproductive work of agents guarding FBI offices day and night" when they were afraid another burglary would occur. "It was insane."

When Welch became SAC in Philadelphia, the Media case was under his authority. Actually, by that time, 1975, the FBI was not paying much attention to the case. The last entry in the investigative file was made on January 14, 1975. But entries had started to be made less frequently much earlier, shortly after the Camden trial ended in May 1973.

By September 22, 1972, MEDBURG investigators reported that "more than 400 suspects had been developed and individual files opened on each during the investigation of the MEDBURG case. Most were eliminated as MEDBURG suspects by establishing their whereabouts during the pertinent period, or by interview." That memorandum included the last list of prime MEDBURG suspects prepared by the FBI—the seven people they had concluded probably were the Media burglars. Only one of the people on that last list of suspects, Bob Williamson, was actually a Media burglar. What six of them, including Williamson, seemed to have in common was that they were close friends of the seventh person on the list, John Peter Grady, the person FBI investigators thought, beginning the day after the burglary, was the leader of the Media group. That makes it difficult to know if investigators had any more reason to think Williamson was a Media burglar than they did any of the other six. In addition to Grady, the final Media suspects were Paul Couming, Peter Fordi, Edward J. McGowan, and Cookie Ridolfi, all of them Camden defendants, and Joseph O'Rourke.

All of the Media burglars, except Bonnie Raines—the person in the group on whom the investigators focused most attention, though they never knew her name and, therefore, could not name her as a suspect—were listed as suspects at various times during the investigation. The other six burglars had been eliminated sometime before this final list was prepared.

In December 1972, agents interviewed a key person, the man who abandoned the Media burglary group just days before the burglary, but they didn't seem to realize he had been part of the group. Immediately after the burglary, he had become a key MEDBURG suspect and was placed under twenty-four-hour surveillance. In the report of their 1972 interview with him, agents wrote that they did not think he "knows who the MEDBURG subjects are." Actually, he knew everything about who they were and what they had done. A few weeks after the burglary, he had told the Raineses he was considering turning the burglars in. But when he talked to agents he did not indicate he had any direct knowledge about the Media burglars.

In the aftermath of the failed investigation, some FBI agents gave the impression they knew much more about the burglars than they did. Strangely, an FBI source told at least one journalist an account of the burglary that was a complete fabrication. Speaking to Sanford Ungar, in an interview for his 1976 book *FBI: An Uncensored Look Behind the Walls,* an FBI agent stated these "facts" he claimed to know were true: that there were twenty Media burglars; that they modeled their group on modern revolutionary groups in Latin America and knowledge of what each knew about the other was kept as limited as possible; that not all of them lived in the Philadelphia area; that they were divided into three groups—the thieves, the sorters, and the distributors. The initial operation, he said, went smoothly, but there was a personal crisis and the person who was supposed to provide storage space the first night withdrew the offer. The sorting took place in New York and Boston. The files were copied over a period of weeks. Investigators identified as implicated in the burglary a sister of one FBI agent assigned to Philadelphia and the priest brother of another agent.

Not a single fact in that list of claims about the Media burglary is accu-

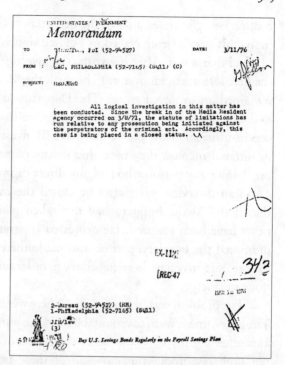

The MEDBURG investigation was closed by Neil Welch in 1976 with this memorandum to Director Kelley.

rate. And none of those claims appears in the official investigation of the burglary. The reason for passing on such a detailed fabrication is inexplicable. Perhaps an agent did so only because he thought the truth about who the burglars were would never emerge, and, therefore, he could tell a tale that would never be discovered to be false. Still, why did they spin it?

One mystery was cleared up when the *Philadelphia Inquirer* published an article on the thirtieth anniversary of the burglary. Throughout the investigation, investigators continued to think John Peter Grady was a member of and leader of the Media burglars. Grady often was noncommittal with friends about whether he participated in the break-in. In an interview with an *Inquirer* reporter for that 2001 story, Grady for the first time publicly stated emphatically that he had nothing to do with the Media burglary.

The five-year anniversary of the burglary, the date on which the statute of limitations on burglary charges expired, was March 8, 1976. Three days later, Welch, in his capacity as SAC of the Philadelphia office, closed the MEDBURG case. In a memorandum to Director Kelley on that day, with the subject MEDBURG, Welch wrote, "All logical investigation in this matter has been conducted. Since the break in of the Media Resident Agency occurred on 3/8/71, the statute of limitations has run relative to any prosecution being initiated against the perpetrators of the criminal act. Accordingly, this case is being placed in a closed status."

And that was it. After five years, the investigation was closed. Despite all the fierce efforts of Hoover until he died, the Media burglary was closed and remained an unsolved crime. The Department of Justice had long before told FBI officials it could not take the case to a grand jury because there was insufficient evidence. Actually, as FBI investigators repeatedly admitted in internal memos, they never found any physical evidence related to the break-in or any person who had any direct or indirect knowledge of it.

In an interview years after he closed the case, Welch said he thought that if the Media burglary had not taken place, COINTELPRO might never have been revealed. He expressed frustration over the situation that prompted the burglary, and he also made the extraordinary assertion that the break-in may have been necessary in order for the truth about FBI operations to emerge.

"The problem was," he said sadly, "there weren't any checks and balances. The government wasn't accountable." Of the burglary, he says, "There wasn't any other means to know what the government was doing. Probably—not probably, unquestionably—all of these people were aware of things that had happened. People had lost their jobs, or some unfortunate circumstances had mysteriously overcome them in their activities, or they came to know that they were being infiltrated, or informants were spying on them. . . . Most of them probably were very intelligent people. They had to know the government was probably doing something with them.

"The system ought to provide for some other mechanism," he said, "so people don't have to resort to these extraordinary—to criminal acts! There ought to be other avenues available to them. We had people taking acts of civil disobedience. They had to resort to this kind of activity—criminal acts against the government—in order to get some exposure of the government's wrongdoing. What I'm saying is that they wouldn't have to do that if there were some proper method of accountability on the part of the government."

Welch became slightly gruff. He wanted to make it clear that despite his sympathetic statements about civil disobedience as related to the burglary, he doesn't believe in burglary as an investigative tool. If they had done it on his watch, he insists, and they had been caught, he would have "locked every one of them up. . . . Tell it to the court. You're not justified . . . to burglarize a government office."

As I left his Sarasota home after the interview, he added another thought: "If they had been convicted, I would have recommended that they should be given suspended sentences because of the major contribution they made to their country."

BY THE TIME Welch formally notified Clarence Kelley in March 1976 that he had closed the Media burglary investigation, Kelley had gone through a profound change. From the time he became director in 1973, he had been compelled repeatedly by numerous investigators to answer countless questions about Hoover's past at official hearings. By the spring of 1976, Kelley had abandoned his initial total commitment to the Hoover traditionalists. As files he had earlier tried to prevent from becoming public were exposed, he realized that many of Hoover's actions could not be defended. By 1976, Kelley felt so strongly about what he had come to think of as Hoover's abuses that he decided to apologize to the American people. He did so in a speech two months after. Welch closed the MEDBURG case, on May 8, 1976, at Westminster College in Fulton, Missouri:

> During most of my tenure as director of the FBI, I have been compelled to devote much of my time attempting to reconstruct and then to explain activities that occurred years ago.
>
> Some of those activities were clearly wrong and quite indefensible. We most certainly must never allow them to be repeated.

Welch agreed.

21

Dumbstruck That It Meant Something

POST-BURGLARY LIFE varied greatly for the Media burglars. Because they kept their promise not to be in touch with one another in order to minimize the likelihood of arrest of one leading to arrest of any other member of the group, they never knew the struggles each of them endured.

For Bob Williamson and Keith Forsyth, the youngest burglars, it was difficult to move ahead into normal lives after their resistance ended. It turned out that age made a difference in resistance. Unlike the older burglars, Forsyth and Williamson had to rebuild their lives and start over. The process involved profound changes, including disengaging from people and from issues they had cared about deeply. Rebuilding was at times a painful challenge. In different ways, each of them crashed before they found a satisfying new life.

For several years, both Forsyth and Williamson became so detached from their resistance past that they didn't even realize what the Media burglary had accomplished—the chain of important revelations and reforms the burglary initiated. The other burglars privately experienced a growing sense of accomplishment throughout the 1970s as they absorbed the unfolding story of change and revelations at the FBI. In contrast, it would be more than a decade until either Forsyth or Williamson fully understood the significant impact of the burglary. Consumed during their resistance years with informing themselves daily about what was happening in Vietnam and Washington, after their resistance years they turned inward and took less interest in what was going on in their former world of antiwar political activism.

The different impact of the burglary on the younger burglars can be understood, to some degree, in the very different nature of the post-burglary daily lives of the older and younger burglars.

The older burglars were cushioned by daily obligations. They continued to go to work each day, all of them advancing in their careers over time. They continued to pay mortgages, make home repairs. They continued to nurture their children, play with them, watch their progress in school, watch their minds become curious, watch them learn to love. The daily tasks and responsibilities that absorbed them before the burglary continued to absorb them afterward. In a sense, there was no break for them.

For the younger burglars, there was a big break between their past in resistance and their unknown future. When their resistance ended, Williamson and Forsyth had no answer to the basic question, "What next?" The very thing it was assumed would make resistance easier for younger people—a lack of personal obligations and responsibilities—was actually what later made their lives more difficult. They had none of the daily obligations that often are not only a heavy burden but also the threads of the fabric that holds a life together, that gives a person a sense of purpose and fulfillment.

Because Williamson and Forsyth had dropped out of college to work to build opposition to the war, they had no traditional formal higher education degree, no career or even career plans, no commitment to an ongoing relationship, and no children who depended on them. When they gave up nearly everything to oppose the war full-time, they sacrificed developing the threads that weave a life together. As they made that sacrifice, it didn't seem to matter to them. Their goal—waking up Americans to what was happening in Vietnam—was so important to them that they thought little at the time about what they were forgoing. They may not have even thought they were making a significant sacrifice. Forsyth and Williamson, like other people who dedicated themselves then to nonviolent resistance to the war, willingly lived modestly, reducing their needs so they could live on small incomes—Forsyth as a cabdriver, Williamson as a caseworker for a state agency—while they spent most of their time working on their primary commitment.

Williamson and Forsyth were also different from the older burglars in other ways. They did not grow up hearing about the Holocaust and having a burning desire to prevent such atrocities. They had no memories of the United States bombing Hiroshima. They were children during the early years of the civil rights movement in the South, though racial justice had become part of their burning desire to fight injustice. The roots of their resistance grew primarily from the Vietnam War and the tumultuous events of the late 1960s.

As Williamson puts it, they "came of age in a time of assassinations and war." They grew up with a vague, and later gnawing and raw, awareness that major disasters were taking place: first the assassination of President John F. Kennedy in 1963, then the assassinations in 1968 of Martin Luther King and Robert F. Kennedy; the massacre of hundreds of unarmed civilians at My Lai; and the killing of students at Kent State and Jackson State in 1970.

Forsyth and Williamson were children of American small towns that were supposed to be idyllic in every way, including lack of controversy. In Williamson's Catholic home in Runnemede, New Jersey, and Forsyth's Baptist home in Marion, Ohio, the Vietnam War—the issue that drove their resistance—was avoided. The war seemed to always hover in their families, as it did in homes throughout the country as sons and daughters started contesting their parents' views of it. In such homes, the war often sat at the edges of family conversations, a subject that could cut and injure at any time.

With World War II a vivid memory, their parents desperately hoped war never would take place on American soil. That hope contributed to their solid support of the Vietnam War and to their belief, an echo of national leaders' statements on war policy, that the United States should fight communism "there" so it would not have to fight it "here."

Williamson and Forsyth stood out from the other Media burglars in another striking way. Five months after the Media burglary, both of them were arrested at Camden. Despite being acutely aware that even as they agreed to raid the Camden draft board, hundreds of agents were then frantically searching for the Media burglars—most intensively in the Powelton Village neighborhood where they lived—they decided to be part of the Camden group. They did so, of course, without knowing the FBI believed the Media burglars were part of the Camden burglars.

Camden affected Williamson and Forsyth in very different ways. Williamson immersed himself in the case, enjoying many aspects of trial preparation and the trial itself. Forsyth abandoned the group. He wanted to have as little connection as possible to the case. He was angry at himself for agree-

Federal agents arrest Keith Forsyth
(third from right) the morning after
the raid on the Camden draft board
in August 1971. *(Photo:* Camden
Courier-Post*)*

ing to participate in the raid. He regretted his decision to do so. He thought
it was perhaps the most foolish thing he had ever done, especially in light
of the fact that, almost from the moment he said yes, he thought the group
was disorganized and headed for disaster. But for reasons not entirely clear
to him, even years later, he did not drop out, not even after the informer,
Robert Hardy, offered him a gun as they sat in Hardy's truck, where conversations—unknown to Forsythe, of course—were piped directly to an FBI
office and overheard by agents. Hardy suggested Forsyth might like to use
it. Forsyth refused to touch it.

After the arraignment of the Camden defendants, Forsyth had very
little contact with anyone in the Camden group and immediately started
establishing a different focus in his life, a process that Williamson didn't
start until after the Camden trial. Forsyth stayed away from the trial. He
did not even regularly follow news reports on the unusual developments
taking place in the courtroom. He wanted to be away from it, both physically and emotionally. He chose to avoid thinking about the fact that he
might be convicted for something he thought was ill-conceived and that he
should not have joined. When the Camden trial ended, he was surprised
and, of course, glad that he was acquitted instead of convicted. Still, he had
little interest in what led to the unexpected acquittal. His interest would be

rekindled in the group and the trial twenty years later. He would become involved in community and union organizing. He continued to oppose the war until it ended, but he no longer was an antiwar activist.

WILLIAMSON CONSIDERED CAMDEN his enduring safety valve. Media was a big secret he could not discuss, and living with that secret was sometimes an uncomfortable burden. Camden, on the other hand, was the opposite. Everything about it was completely open. Camden, especially with its not-guilty verdicts for all, was something very special he could discuss with anyone. He did so until, eventually, he got immersed in a new life.

He later looked back on the trial as having many positive aspects, including being fun. He enjoyed developing trial strategy, he enjoyed philosophical exchanges with all involved, and especially he enjoyed the warmth of the community of defendants. But the beginning of Camden, the night of the arrests, was not fun. Williamson doesn't remember the details of some incidents from that period of his life, but he recalls his arrest that night with keen precision. He was standing on the parapet outside the window of the dark draft board office. From inside, other burglars were handing him large canvas bags stuffed with Selective Service records. He knew the file drawers and cabinets were almost empty and the job was about to end when suddenly—as he grabbed another large stuffed bag as it was hefted out the window and added it to the stack of bags on the parapet—he heard a loud clatter of feet below getting closer and closer as they rushed up the fire escape. He turned slightly and there, facing him, was a man, an FBI agent, pointing the barrel of his gun at Williamson. He recalls that it nearly touched his nose. The man and the other agents behind him yelled, "Freeze!" Again and again they yelled, "Freeze!"

"Just like in the movies. I mean really yelling. Deep guttural level. And so I did—I pretty much froze at that point."

"I remember the feeling of being in shock and being numb." One of the agents arrested him on the parapet. Then somehow, he doesn't remember how, they pulled him through the window. The next thing Williamson remembers is that "we're all laying on the floor." He was facedown, with an FBI agent's foot in the center of his back.

Williamson was stunned, but not surprised.

He had assumed that something like this was bound to happen since June 1969, when he attended the crucial meeting at Iron Mountain—the name John Peter Grady gave an old Episcopal church, St. George's, in the

Bronx, where some of the Catholic resisters occasionally met and where Grady's unsuccessful 1968 campaign for Congress was based. It was at this meeting that some people in the Catholic peace movement decided to move from symbolic actions like the Catonsville Nine action in 1968 to clandestine actions, such as draft board raids conducted at night with the goal of actually—as opposed to symbolically—damaging the draft system and fleeing rather than waiting to be arrested.

Knowing that discussion of this critical change in strategy would take place at this meeting, Williamson immersed himself in the writings of highly respected advocates of nonviolent resistance—Henry David Thoreau's essay "Civil Disobedience," Louis Fisher's biography of Mohandas Gandhi, and several writings by Martin Luther King. "I knew Gandhi had been a mentor to King, so I wanted to understand him. . . . It was against that backdrop that I went to this meeting. I went strongly committed to nonviolence and determined that nothing I would do would cause harm to anybody."

He remembers that after lengthy and sometimes tense discussion, about half of the approximately twenty people there agreed that they felt they were likely to have more impact if they moved away from symbolic acts of resistance and engaged instead in clandestine actions designed to actually slow down the government's ability to draft young men. People who attended the meeting recall that Daniel and Philip Berrigan opposed that change in strategy and continued to believe that symbolic public actions followed by immediately accepting responsibility were likely to have a more positive impact on the public.

As Williamson absorbed the thoughtful but difficult discussion, he decided to cast his lot with the group that wanted to do clandestine actions. He was impressed by the case made for that approach by various people, especially John Peter Grady. The Berrigans' ideas still continued to permeate Williamson's thinking about conscience and about the war, as they did for other people in this part of the peace movement, including the other people who went to Media.

After it was settled that some people supported and other people opposed the new strategy, Williamson recalls, the people who made a commitment to clandestine action stayed to discuss how they would move ahead—the caution needed, the potential dangers to such resisters and to people they might encounter inside draft boards. They discussed at length the harm they might inadvertently cause guards in federal buildings. They wrestled with the question of "what would happen if a guard walked in and caught us while we were in a draft board." That concern arose from their belief, based on observation, that most guards in federal buildings were older men, people they assumed never expected anything to go wrong on the job. Given that, they feared the guards might be so shocked if they found burglars inside a draft board office when offices were closed that they would have a heart attack. That led to a lengthy discussion on how to be a calming influence in such a situation, on how to assure someone they were not being threatened. He does not recall that they discussed the possibility of a guard being armed and therefore a threat to burglars. Finally, Williamson says, Grady hammered home then and many times after that day the importance of being realistic about the personal consequences of these more aggressive nonviolent acts of resistance: that they might be arrested and pay a very heavy price. Williamson took that to heart and waited for it to happen. Arrest and imprisonment, he felt certain, would be the inevitable consequences of the decision he made that day.

WILLIAMSON'S THINKING had changed radically from the time he left Runnemede, his suburban hometown in the southwestern part of New Jersey, until the day of the meeting in the Bronx. He appreciated his hometown and realized his parents had provided what seemed like the perfect environment, a good home for their children in a community that had good schools and streets where children could ride their bicycles any time of the day and be safe. The perfect nature of his world was pierced for him for the first time when President Kennedy was assassinated. "Until that time I was very insulated and protected. . . . I had the sense that nothing bad would ever happen in the world. . . . I grew up in such a way that I wasn't aware that bad things happen." The assassination of President Kennedy "planted the seed of a kind of—the word that comes to mind is 'realism.' I really did live a very insulated life as I was growing up. Children think in almost magical terms. Well, I guess I had a sort of magical sense that God was looking out for all the good people, and that they would all be protected. . . . So when Kennedy was killed it was a tremendous shock. I think it was the beginning of a realization that the world was not always a nice place. That there was in fact evil and it could touch our lives."

Williamson absorbed and expressed the dominant views of his small town. As a high school junior, he wrote and delivered a speech critical of draft card burners for the American Legion Oratorical Contest.

Short and very thin then as now, after Williamson was introduced at a Legion speech competition, he would slowly walk toward the center of the

At St. Joseph's College, Bob Williamson (left) was on the committee that invited prominent people to speak on campus, including the Reverend Martin Luther King Jr. and Vice President Hubert Humphrey, pictured here with Williamson, 1968. *(Photo:* Philadelphia Evening Bulletin, © *Temple University Libraries)*

stage, pausing to sniff dramatically as he looked all over the stage for the source of an odor. Then, in a strong voice, he would announce, "I smell smoke!" After a dramatic pause, he would look squarely into the faces of the audience and declare, "It is the smoke of burning draft cards, and it hangs over our nation like poisonous smog." He would then make a case for the justness of a war to prevent the spread of communism, the importance of the rule of law, the duty of citizens to respect it, and the dangers posed by the draft card burners' open defiance of it. He was fervently dedicated to this message. His speech won at the county and district levels, and he won second place at the state level, winning a college scholarship from the Legion that helped pay for his education at St. Joseph's College in Philadelphia.

By the time he said yes to Davidon's invitation to consider burglarizing an FBI office, Williamson saw the war very differently. The change started when he wrote a paper on cluster bombs during his freshman year at college. In his research, he discovered that the manufacturer of these weapons, then being used in Vietnam, pointed out in corporate literature that the "advantage" of the cluster bombs was the widespread and diffused destruction they caused (including the killing of civilians). That assessment jolted Williamson and prompted him to start asking questions about the war. He had similar objections to the indiscriminate destructive power of napalm. When Martin Luther King spoke at St. Joseph's in January 1968 and gave his reasons for opposing the Vietnam War—even in the face of criticism from his colleagues in the civil rights movement—Williamson took his message to heart.

A few months later, the night King was assassinated, Williamson was playing pool with some friends. One of them laughed and made a racist remark about King as they listened to the news that he had just been killed. Williamson burned with anger and sadness. He made a decision. "I realized that night I was getting to be a person whose principles were real important to me. I was at the point where I realized you had to take a stand for your principles."

Now, after that meeting in the Bronx, he was committed to living his principles in ways that involved very serious risks. Instead of dressing up as Death, as part of an antiwar street theater group he had been performing with in the past year in Philadelphia, Williamson now prepared to raid draft boards. He took Grady's warning seriously. He thought he would probably be caught the first time he broke into a draft board, but to his amazement, after raiding four draft boards and an FBI office, he still had not been arrested.

That luck changed at Camden. The expected finally happened on the parapet. He assumed his arrest in Camden also meant that his plan to have no plan for his future also would prove to have been wise. Feeling absolutely

Bob Williamson thought he would be convicted in Camden. Between his arrest and trial there, he visited New Mexico.

certain he would go to prison for years, he thought he would have plenty of time to think about the rest of his life.

When it was clear the Camden trial would not get under way for at least a year, Williamson decided that after two years of continuously opposing the war and moving from one act of resistance to another, "It was probably time for me to have a little bit of fun before I went away to prison for forty years." He went west. Some feminist friends he had lived with in Philadelphia were visiting Albuquerque. They liked the area and urged him to join them. That trip and the beautiful countryside it introduced him to transformed the geography and purpose of his life.

He had never been west of Ohio. Instead of going the fast interstate route, he purposely took a slow scenic route, watching the topography of the country change for two weeks as he drove. He camped in Oklahoma, where he saw a truly big sky for the first time. After he arrived in Albuquerque, he joined his friends near Taos. They left the campsite after a few days, and he spent a couple weeks alone there, soaking in nature.

For the first time in about three years, something besides the war grabbed and held his attention. "For a young guy who hadn't been noticing nature for many years, if ever, the absorption with it now was healing," he says. "It was cool in the morning. It warmed up throughout the day. And there was always a thunderstorm right before dusk. And then a magnificent sunset. They were orange and purple and red. . . . The sunsets really were magnificent. . . . The area was unspoiled and very beautiful. It was very quiet, and so it was good for me. I let my hair grow, and I enjoyed where I was."

He continued to assume he would be going to prison and decided he should get ready for it. With that in mind, he hoped he could store memories of the peaceful and spectacularly beautiful New Mexico landscape so he would be able to retrieve and relive them for solace during the long days ahead in prison. He began what became a lifelong meditation practice. That too, he thought, would come in handy in prison. His time in that mountain meadow provided a rich respite.

In late 1972, the Camden trial beckoned and Williamson drove east. He became deeply absorbed in doing legal research and helping develop trial strategy. During the trial, he enjoyed cross-examining some of the witnesses, especially the FBI agent who had arrested him at Camden. Judge Fisher permitted him to use copies of some of the stolen Media files as the basis of questions he posed to at least one agent. He referred to the Media files again when he testified, claiming that reading the files and learning about the illegal activity of the FBI had convinced him to continue raiding draft boards. That's why, he testified, he said yes when he was asked to participate in the Camden raid.

Williamson played a significant role in the defendants' efforts to gain the judge's trust and make him feel at ease with them. When the trial opened in February 1973, Williamson, as well as others, sensed that Judge Fisher was afraid this large group of defendants would be unruly. Memories were still fresh regarding the raucous nature of the 1969 Chicago Seven trial of people for allegedly conspiring to incite riots at the 1968 Democratic convention in Chicago. Each new antiwar trial after that one was seen as a potential repeat of the Chicago trial with defiant defendants and defiant judges in the mold of the Chicago judge, Julius Hoffman. "I could understand his concern," says Williamson of Judge Fisher's rigidity in the early days of the trial. "There were so many of us. Most of us were representing ourselves. I had hair all the way down my back and often wore my dashiki. We were very different-looking—from each other and from the people who usually appeared in court. . . . Our goal was to tell our story, to explain why we had done what we had done, and to call on the jury, as an act of conscience, to make a statement about this war by finding us not guilty. . . . We had to get him to see that we had no intention of turning his courtroom into a 'circus,'" a term Judge Fisher had used in a warning to the defendants right before the trial opened.

With that goal in mind, Williamson met with Judge Fisher shortly after the trial started and told him that he was going to do something tangible to reassure the judge that the defendants were sincere, reasonable people. He would be on a juice fast for the duration of the trial. It was a private gesture, not a publicity stunt, Williamson assured the judge. No one would know about it except the judge, the defendants, and the lawyers. He recalls that the judge's "demeanor changed. . . . His first reaction was concern. He didn't want me to hurt myself . . . he frequently asked me, in the hall or in chambers, how I was."

Judge Fisher's visible apprehension about the defendants melted fairly quickly. Each morning, as he took the bench, he scanned the faces of the defendants, their attorneys, and the prosecutors, establishing eye contact with many of them. His relaxed and expectant look suggested he was looking forward to whatever might happen in court that day.

Williamson maintained his secret juice fast throughout the three-month trial. Already very thin, he lost twenty pounds during the trial, but he remained healthy and energetic. He remembers savoring the celebratory spaghetti dinner, cooked by codefendant Peter Fordi, that broke his fast a few hours after the verdict was announced. Pasta may never have tasted so good.

Throughout the trial, Williamson felt he and his fellow defendants were creating an important record—not only about what they had done but also about the important role of resistance in American history and about the history of the Vietnam War and how that history had driven them to raid the Camden draft board. He was grateful the judge allowed them considerable leeway in giving testimony about their motivation. But despite how well the trial had gone, Williamson had no illusions about winning. "I don't think any of us expected what happened."

"When they said 'not guilty' after 'not guilty' after 'not guilty,' it was just the most unbelievable experience. I'll never forget the exhilaration we felt, and the gratitude we all felt toward the jury, and their courage in returning those 'not guilty' verdicts. And it was also a very humbling experience. . . . Thoreau's essay on civil disobedience was a guide for me, and part of the deal is that if you do the crime, you do the time. So, again, I expected to be arrested. I expected to go to prison. . . . I don't think there was anyone, certainly at the defense table, who expected it to be an acquittal. We had no idea. None. I can't stress that too much because it was just such an incredible shock to be found not guilty by these people. . . . It was deeply moving, it was very emotional." He remembers hugging fellow defendants and being approached by the prosecutor, who shook his hand and wished him well. "I don't remember what he said. I just remember what he did. He was very gracious."

Then, several minutes later, one of the FBI agents who had been involved in the case from the beginning "came up to me in the men's room and congratulated me and wished me luck. It was as though he was saying, 'It's okay now. We're going to let this go. We're going to move on now.' . . . I didn't feel triumphant. That wasn't really the feeling. It was more like grateful."

Even in his toughest times years later, Williamson was always able to evoke again the emotion of that moment when he suddenly realized that the jury had acquitted him and all of the defendants. In his living room many years later in Albuquerque, as he recalls the moment when verdicts were announced, his eyes fill with tears, as they did that day in Camden. He still finds it hard to believe that the jury voted as it did. "It was really something. . . . It was an unbelievable thrill."

SOON AFTER being acquitted at Camden, Williamson was faced with a new question: Now what? "The expected ending—that I would go to prison—didn't happen. I was free. The war by then was clearly coming to an end. . . . Watergate was well under way. And I had no idea who I was. I didn't know what I wanted to do with my life. My assumption had been that I would go to prison, that I would spend however many years in prison and those years would give me ample time to reflect on the next step. Instead, the government wasn't going to be providing me with room and board, and I needed to find some way to more or less take care of myself."

About three months after the trial ended, Williamson had a deep realization that he needed to "get away from all these people. As much as I loved them, as much as we'd all been through together. . . . My friends, almost without exception, were like, 'It's on to the next battle.' But I wanted the war to be over."

In Philadelphia at that time, he recalls, "What you do all day is you're figuring out . . . how to stop the government. . . . It's nonstop. I mean, it just never ends. It's one meeting after another. . . . As spirited as those discussions were, there was also an element of groupthink. I felt I would lose myself if I stayed there any longer. And, fortunately, I had this place to come to."

"This place" was New Mexico. The beautiful mountains, deserts, and glorious sunsets lured him west again. Life had been good there in the months between the arraignment and trial. As soon as Williamson had enough money, "I decided I was going to New Mexico. I came out here and got a job driving a school bus part-time, lived in a cabin up in the mountains, chopping wood, carrying my own water . . . and I lived alone for, oh, a good year and a half."

He felt content at first in New Mexico. Years later, he said New Mexico rescued him all those years ago. If he had not moved west, Williamson feels he would have become frozen in time. But there also were very difficult times during his earliest years in New Mexico. He spent a lot of time meditating. He smoked a lot of dope. He had some friends. But he didn't have a purpose. And he was very lonely.

When he read years later about how NASA prepared astronauts for life after traveling in space, Williamson wished the resistance community could have done what NASA did. As astronauts were being trained for a trip to outer space, they were also required to have a second goal, one they wanted to achieve after they returned from their dramatic voyage in space. NASA learned, says Williamson, "that when people have set their sights on something for a long period of time and . . . devoted themselves to achieving it, and when that goal has been reached and is over with, a lot of people . . . then go into a deep depression because they don't know who they are without the definition they got from the original goal.

"Well, that's what happened to me. My entire self-image was that of an antiwar crusader, an antiwar resister."

Williamson found that most of the people he met in Albuquerque didn't seem very interested in his resistance past, and they weren't as consumed with politics as he had been. He had mixed feelings about this reaction. On the one hand, he had just been through several extremely eventful and dramatic years. From his perspective, it was, if nothing else, quite a story. But on the other hand, there was something very refreshing about living among people who were more interested in who you were now than in who you used to be, and more interested in your character than in your political views. Eventually, he reached the point where he rarely talked about "the old days."

It was difficult to decide what he was going to do with his life. He no longer could accept the conclusions of many of his old friends in the resistance movement. "Since the world is unfair, they thought we should be in rebellion against 'the system' and not cooperate with it in any way, live our lives blaming the system, speaking out against it at every opportunity and being in resistance to everything it stands for." Williamson no longer was willing to live that way.

As he struggled with his first steps toward a new purpose in life, he nearly hit bottom once when a relationship that meant a great deal to him didn't work out. He decided to leave New Mexico. "I wanted to get as far away from Albuquerque as I could get and still be as far away from Philadelphia and New Jersey as I could get." He jumped at the chance to drive to Miami when a friend wanted to relocate there.

It was the winter of 1974. Williamson had no money and no food by the time he arrived in Miami, and he pawned his guitar for cash. He was living in his Volkswagen, trying unsuccessfully to find a job. One night, he got "an unbelievably bad toothache, the worst pain I had ever felt." Sitting in his car, he started feeling very sorry for himself. Reflecting back on his life to that point, he remembers complaining to God: "I'm a good person. I risked my freedom to try to stop a war and make my country a better, a more just place. Here I am, and I'm alone, I don't know anyone here, I'm broke, I'm hungry, I'm in pain, and no one cares."

As he sank deeper into his misery that night, he suddenly had a power-

While he was a college student, Williamson and other students who lived in
North Philadelphia did volunteer work for an organization that helped renters
negotiate with landlords to repair their apartments.

ful insight, which he describes as a spiritual experience. He realized that
he alone was responsible for his situation. He had chosen to be alone in a
strange city. He had no money because he hadn't earned any. No one else
was responsible for his situation; he alone was. If it was going to change, it
would be up to him to change it.

Almost forty years after that night, he still had trouble putting the experience of that insight into words. "I wasn't sitting there, calmly and rationally
thinking through my dilemma and devising a solution. I was in excruciating
pain, sobbing, one of the absolute lowest emotional points in my life. And
suddenly, I was filled with this awareness of an idea, and everything sort of
stopped for a minute.

"I have tried to put the realization into words, but my words don't really
do it justice. Since that night, I have had my share of bad days, but on that
night something fundamentally changed in me. Since that night, there have
been times when I wanted to feel sorry for myself, but I just couldn't sustain
the self-pity anymore. From that night on, at some level, I knew better."

This insight was followed by the quick realization that his toothache
had gone away completely. The next morning, Williamson walked into a
small newspaper and got a job. That soon led to a job at a larger newspaper
in Miami Beach, where he developed skills as a production manager, skills
he used later when he returned to Albuquerque and started a graphic arts
business.

During Williamson's search for new meaning in his life, he says he got tremendous value from participating in what was called "est"—Erhard Seminar Training, intensive seminars created by Werner Erhard in the 1970s and attended by thousands of people. Williamson found est particularly helpful "because it emphasized personal responsibility, which it defined as neither blame nor credit, but rather a willingness to operate from the assumption that I am responsible for the way I experience life. This was not presented as a truth or a dogma. It was simply a way of looking at life that I found empowering. I realized that if I lived my life from the point of view that I was truly the author of my own life, I might end up being right or wrong about that, but in the meantime, I would have been far more resourceful than if I had acted as if the outcomes in my life were determined by outside forces. . . . As a result of est, I understood and accepted myself— warts and all—far more than I had up to that point in my life. I also found that it became possible for me to be far less judgmental of others as well— particularly people in public life whom I had never met and had no actual personal experience of."

For the past twenty-five years, Williamson has worked as a business coach, holding online meetings and seminars to help clients achieve per-

Bob Williamson with his daughter, Jessica, age six, in 1984.

sonal and business goals. He does some pro bono coaching and has served on nonprofit boards in his community.

He has been married and divorced twice. The graphic arts business he started in 1975 eventually failed after twelve years, leaving him $80,000 in debt. As a matter of principle, he refused to go into bankruptcy and instead scrimped and saved for years until he paid all his debts. He says, "I think I have had my share of struggles in life, and made more than my share of mistakes. During the most difficult times, I have even experienced depression and near despair. I am not what most people would call a wealthy man, but my needs are met and I have been able to give something back. I have a passion for my work and it gives me great satisfaction. So while my life has not been a bed of roses, I am grateful for an underlying sense of optimism and good humor which has always carried me through the tough times."

A tremendous source of his happiness is being part of the lives of his daughter, Jessica, born in 1978, his son-in-law, Mike, and his two granddaughters—Aelea, born in 2004, and Raven, born in 2008.

As he started to erase his old identity as a resister, Williamson says, "it was clear to me that what I thought about the way the world should work really didn't make much difference to the world, and that the world was a lot bigger than I was. . . . I was going to have to figure out some kind of way to make peace with it. And that," he says, "was the beginning of an odyssey for me which was about the ending of my focusing on the world and trying to fix the world's problems and the beginning of my turning that vision inward to try and discover whether I was the best person I could be.

"I stopped blaming my parents, and I stopped blaming society, and I stopped blaming the economic system and I stopped blaming people's indifference and I stopped blaming racism and sexism and everything else for the way things were, and I started thinking more and more . . . about who I was, and whether I was becoming everything that I could be. That began to be the question around which I framed my life."

During this evolution, he apologized to his parents and siblings for the anguish his resistance against the war had caused them. From the time he left college to live in a poor neighborhood in North Philadelphia, through his years as an antiwar activist, his parents were repeatedly shocked by his actions. When he was arrested in Camden, they were mortified, a reaction that was deepened when an official in their small community wrote a letter that was published in the local newspaper stating how ashamed he was that someone from Runnemede was involved with people who broke into draft boards. With sadness, he recalls, "My parents felt shamed in their own community."

Williamson moved from being an intensely engaged political activist to becoming apolitical and then later a conservative with libertarian leanings. He worked behind the scenes in 1982 as a speechwriter for the Republican candidate for governor of New Mexico. He laughs as he suggests, undoubtedly correctly, that he is probably the only Media burglar who voted not only once but twice for both Ronald Reagan and George W. Bush. The writings of conservative economists Friedrich Hayek and Thomas Sowell have strongly influenced his thinking in recent years.

There was a time, Williamson says, when he was tempted to enter politics himself, but he cured himself of that delusion by considering the spectacle of trying to explain to voters how someone who opposed the Vietnam War by breaking into draft boards—and the FBI—could have become a conservative. "Virtually every voter would be able to find something completely distasteful about me in either my past or my present."

AS WILLIAMSON REBUILT his life, he seldom thought of his acts of resistance—including the Media burglary. At times he viewed them as having little significance beyond whatever their personal meaning was to each individual burglar. With the passage of time, the memories and the personal meaning of his own resistance became a smaller part of the "odyssey I've been through since then."

One evening, about fifteen years after the burglary, he was perusing the Albuquerque television listings and noticed that one station would be broadcasting a documentary on the FBI. His reaction was a little like the interest stirred by reading a news item about an old high school friend one hasn't seen in many years. He decided to watch it.

As the program started, the narrator announced that in 1971 a group of people, who were never found, burglarized the small FBI office in Media, Pennsylvania. Williamson was puzzled. He wondered why the reporter was talking about "our burglary." The reporter went on to say that much of what is known about how the FBI operated under J. Edgar Hoover is a result of the Media burglary—that the burglary was seminal in the passage of changes to the Freedom of Information Act and various reforms in the FBI.

"Well, I remember being dumbstruck that somebody apparently thought that our little action was that important. . . . Until that moment, I never thought it had any long-range impact."

By the time the program ended, he was seeing the Media burglary in a somewhat different light. "The thing that impressed me about it was that here I am, just some guy, and my friends and I pulled this thing off. And it had an impact.

"I still get chill bumps when I realize that the Media burglary started a long chain of events that caused reforms. . . . And we didn't even know what we were doing. We had no idea whether our risk would result in anything. . . . It's very gratifying to know that people . . . think that we performed a service to our country. That's what we intended to do. I know our hearts were pure in that regard."

His gratification that the Media action produced some positive results in terms of more openness in the FBI in particular and government in general has also been tempered by his sobering view that the law of unintended consequences works both ways. Williamson thinks the revelations that came out as a result of the burglary probably also contributed to the increasing cynicism and distrust Americans felt then—and continue to feel now—about their government. He thinks much of that distrust is probably deserved. But he also thinks that, in some ways, it has made it more difficult for leaders at every level of government to do what they think is right. "Four American presidents believed the Vietnam War had to be pursued. They may have been wrong about that on any number of levels, but I have

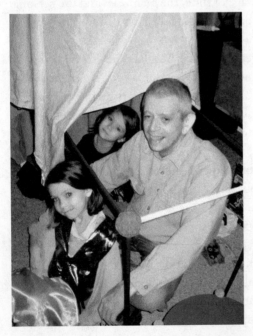

At the center of Williamson's life in Albuquerque are his daughter, Jessica; her husband, Mike; and their two children, Aelea (*foreground*) and Raven, seen here in January 2012 with Williamson.

come to respect the fact that they had more information than I did, and I have come to believe they all did what they thought was right. That does not change the fact that I also did what I thought was right, and so did all of the other people I worked with back then . . . but it tempers it with a big dose of humility."

Since the night Williamson shined a taped flashlight's narrow beam on open FBI file cabinet drawers, guiding fellow burglars in the dark, he has become a much more conservative person. Nevertheless, he views his radical act of burglarizing an FBI office as a patriotic act that gave him a sense of accomplishment then and now, notwithstanding his concerns about unintended consequences. "That was an exciting time," he says, "and it was one of the times in my life when I felt most alive. I don't regret it."

While he would not presume to offer advice to anyone now considering action as extreme as what he participated in at Media, he hopes such people would give it long and careful thought. "That burglary is an example of what someone can do, or try to do, as a citizen. But when you take an action like that, you own the consequences. I was not prosecuted for the break-in, or for distributing those FBI files to the media. Nevertheless, the consequences for me—personally, emotionally, spiritually—have been fairly significant. I know that at the age of twenty-two, I acted with a clear conscience. I also know that I could not possibly have foreseen the full range of effects of my actions then. Over the last forty-plus years, as I have grown older, thinking about this has made me more careful about how my actions are likely to affect others. Still, in spite of that, I think I can make a pretty good case that, on balance, the Media burglary produced more good than harm."

22

Unconditionally Positive

SUPPORTING THE VIETNAM WAR was as natural for Keith Forsyth as getting up in the morning. Like Williamson, he followed his
father in such important matters, giving hardly any thought to it.
Then, in the first semester of his freshman year at the College of Wooster
in Ohio, his mind was split open by a small book. It caused him to give the
war a great deal of thought. In fact, he spent that entire semester searching
for evidence that the war was justified and should be supported. He wanted
to continue supporting it, but now he wanted to do so on a sound, rational
basis rather than simply as an echo of his father.

If the U.S. State Department had not failed to provide him with the
government's rationale for the war and why it should be supported, Forsyth
might not have been standing outside the Media FBI office trying to pick
the lock on the night of March 8, 1971.

Only a couple weeks after he arrived on campus in the fall of 1968,
another freshman, a guy named Chuck who lived down the hall from Forsyth, gave him *Peace in Vietnam: A New Approach in Southeast Asia* and
urged Forsyth to read it. Today he can't remember Chuck's last name. He
has no idea where Chuck is, what work he does, or what kind of person he
has become, but Forsyth is certain of one thing about Chuck: He owes the
opening of his mind to him.

Forsyth took Chuck's advice. He read the book with a great deal of interest. "I remember saying to myself, as I was reading the book, 'This can't be
true. This is America.'" The book set forth the contemporary history of
Vietnam and made the case, in a straightforward, nonpolemical way, that

the United States should not be at war in Vietnam, had no vital interest in being at war there, and, beginning with its support of the French colonial interests there, had worked against, not for, the best interests of—or even the possibility of—democracy in Vietnam.

This made Forsyth so angry that if it hadn't been for two aspects of the book, he thinks he would have dismissed its message immediately. First, its tone was reasonable, and it was heavily documented, qualities that appealed to this serious college freshman who loved science and philosophy. Second, it was published by the American Friends Service Committee, a Quaker organization. Forsyth was raised as what he calls "a plain vanilla Protestant," first a Baptist and then, as his parents moved up economically, a Presbyterian. "I was raised in a very religious family. By that time I was still interested in religion, but I felt organized religion had problems with hypocrisy." But Quakers were another matter. In contrast to other Christian denominations, Forsyth thought, Quakers had "very high moral principles and a relatively low level of hypocrisy. . . . They had a reputation for being really honest and living up to their beliefs.

"So, I'm thinking to myself, 'They wouldn't be saying this stuff if it wasn't true.' . . . Here are these people who couldn't possibly tell a lie because their consciences wouldn't permit them, here they are saying all these horrible things about what our government, the land of the free, the home of the brave, is doing to these defenseless people in Vietnam. . . . It clashed with all the things I had been taught about America. My father's a very patriotic guy. He's one of those rags-to-riches stories. . . . And he supported this war. I had all this patriotism. That's the way it was in the '50s and the '60s, especially in the Midwest. That whole aura of conformity, patriotism, the whole thing. I believed it all. So now the Quakers were saying something else. They were describing how we were behaving someplace else, Vietnam. It didn't fit with my ideas of what this country was like.

"It changed my life."

The profound shift in his opinion about the war did not take place until later, after he searched to either verify or dispute the claims made in the book. At first, Forsyth didn't accept what he read. He couldn't. He remembers that his sense of my-country-won't-do-wrong was too deep to allow immediate acceptance of these critical claims. He thought the Quakers must have made a mistake, that perhaps this book represented uncharacteristic behavior on their part. Surely they had misunderstood the history of Vietnam and the actions of the U.S. government there.

Published in 1966, the book was a report by a special working group appointed in 1965 by the board of directors of the American Friends Service Committee, a Quaker organization founded in 1917 that conducts service programs throughout the world, one of which recruits conscientious objectors to work in war zones with war victims. As he read, Forsyth learned that the AFSC first expressed its concerns about Vietnam in 1954, warning at that early date that Quakers were "profoundly disturbed with the pressures for United States military intervention in Indo-China. On the basis of long Quaker experience in international service we are convinced that nothing but disaster lies down this road."

From the public record, the working group documented the United States' rejection of at least seven efforts prior to 1966 to negotiate an end to the war. It documented lies made to the public about the war by the Johnson administration five years before such lies were revealed in the Pentagon Papers, the secret official history of the war that became public in 1971. Forsyth felt demoralized when he read that a series of "false premises and mistaken assumptions . . . have shaped United States public opinion and policy toward Vietnam and much of Southeast Asia for years." In an analysis that bears a striking resemblance to criticism of the U.S. invasion of Iraq in 2003, the study group wrote:

> It is not the military credibility of the United States that is lacking, but credibility in matters of rationality, political maturity and legal and moral responsibility. In the eyes of a large part of the world, United States conduct in Vietnam has already brought its credibility with respect to these nonmilitary qualities into question. Much can be done to restore American credibility and honor if the United States will abandon its clearly calamitous policy of reliance upon military means to achieve impossible political ends.

The freshman from Marion, Ohio, was riveted. He had not been paying much attention to the war. That was for adults. And all the adults he knew had subtly conveyed the impression that he should always trust his country to do the right thing. Now he was reading something that conveyed a very different impression. With policies built on false premises and mistaken assumptions, he read, "it is understandable how the United States can be moving inexorably down the road of no return. But this is not the only path open. The *politically relevant* [italics in original] alternatives now facing the Administration are to continue escalating the war or to start de-escalating immediately and, in accordance with political realities, to make an effort to negotiate a ceasefire and a political settlement calling for the orderly withdrawal of United States military forces."

After a series of specific recommendations for changes in war policies, the working group urged that "American understanding must go beyond turning from destructive to constructive approaches. It must become aware of the subtle and dangerous assumption that the United States can determine the course of the whole world. . . . We must refurbish the American dream and seek ways to enlarge it into a world dream. But we must remember that we Americans are only a small portion of the dreamers."

IF THE CASE made by the Quaker group was true, a rather shaken Forsyth thought, then his country had made some very big mistakes that had resulted in millions of unnecessary deaths, not to mention deaths still taking place. Though the book seemed to be well documented, Forsyth still found the claims very difficult to believe. This former member of Youth for Christ, an international evangelical group that focuses on converting young people to Christianity, did not easily slide out of his unquestioning patriotic assumptions, even when presented with facts.

Now, for the first time, he raised questions about the sweeping patriotism he had inherited and blindly accepted. He wasn't a very political per-

Keith Forsyth and cousins at their maternal grandparents' home in Marion, Ohio.

son, but he thought about political issues, and "to the extent that I had any politics, it was pretty much what rubbed off from my parents. They were politically conservative . . . and I was conservative. I handed out flyers for [Republican presidential candidate Barry] Goldwater in 1964. . . . I had accepted the high school civics propaganda that America can do no wrong and has done no wrong. I had no reason to doubt it."

He decided he needed to know more—much more. Because what he had read challenged his basic assumptions, he set out to learn what reputable scholars, government officials, and other war analysts had written on this subject. At the campus library he made a list of all the books in print on Vietnam and the war there. He bought a few of them. He borrowed others from the library. At his request, the campus librarian got more books on Vietnam via interlibrary loan from other campuses in the Midwest. The books poured in, twenty-some altogether. In his search to find the truth about American involvement in Vietnam, he became a constant presence at the campus library that fall. He devoured every book he could find on the history of Vietnam and the American war there. Forsyth read them cover to cover. He wasn't studying what the College of Wooster wanted him to study as a freshman, but he was studying very hard. He had become a student of the Vietnam War. His regular studies suffered, but he didn't care. He thought it was more important to learn whether his country had become something altogether different from what he thought it was.

Forsyth finished reading the books on Vietnam four weeks after he finished *Peace in Vietnam*. They were written by U.S. and foreign scholars. The books did not make a pitch for pacifism, and they were not overtly political. He described them as "mostly dry academic tomes," books written by historians and other scholars and experts. More to the point of what was on Forsyth's mind, these books corroborated the historical facts and analysis in the Quaker book that led to his research. "This is really far out," Forsyth remembers thinking. He was surprised and confused at the general agreement he found among writers. He was upset. He did not want to believe what he was reading: that his country was fighting an unjust war. He thought there must be other books that would make the case *for* the war. He remained convinced that despite all the evidence he had read, there must be more to this. "I couldn't believe this whole thing had happened with absolutely no merit whatever to why we're there.

"So I called the State Department."

When he called the main State Department number provided by an operator, in the usual ways of large government bureaucracies, he was transferred from one office to another several times. As each new person came on the line, he explained that he was a college student calling with a request for information about the U.S. government's policy on the Vietnam War. It was not clear if his question was a puzzle, unexpected, or unwanted, but no one seemed to be able to respond to it. The patriotic kid from Ohio persevered until he was finally transferred to someone who listened to his question.

He recounts the conversation this way: "Look, I'm a college student and I'm studying Vietnam. I'm reading all these books by all these professors, and they are telling me that we have no moral right to be in Vietnam. I assume you guys must not agree with that." He asked for the names of articles and books that supported the government's position.

"He told me he'd send a few pamphlets they had. I said I would appreciate that, but, 'Besides the stuff that the government publishes, is there any independent material, anything written by human beings out there who don't work for the government who think this war is a good idea?'" There was a pause as the official asked the question of someone else in the office.

The official came back on the line and gave Forsyth the name of one book. Forsyth thanked him and said he was surprised there weren't many books that supported U.S. policy. An eager student, he found the State Department–recommended book and immediately read it, hoping it would provide the well-reasoned justification for the war he was looking for.

"Now, I was eighteen at the time," says Forsyth as he recounts his quest to understand U.S. credibility in Vietnam, "and I remember saying to myself, 'I would be ashamed to publish a book of this quality.' It was full of unsubstantiated assertions. By this time I was used to reading very elaborately documented books about the war, about the country. This book that they had referred me to had no documentation and made wild statements, such as 'All of a sudden the democratic government of Vietnam appears.' . . . It was poorly written in every sense of the word. And this was the only book he referred me to supporting the other side."

Forsyth called the State Department again and reached the man who had recommended the book. He told him he had read the book and that he was disappointed in the quality of it and wanted to read more books. He asked the man if he could provide a list of books by authors who supported the U.S. military role in Vietnam. To Forsyth the logic was simple: If the United States had decided to fight this war, its officials must have very strong and respectable reasons for doing so, ones that would make all

Americans understand and support the war. The official said he would call him back. When he did a few days later, he said, "There aren't any more. That's the only one."

After Forsyth failed to get the Department of State to recommend books that made the case for the war, he searched more on his own. "I looked hard. I'm a pretty thorough guy." He came up with nothing. At that point, Forsyth finally was willing to believe and trust what he had read about the case against the Vietnam War.

What happened next, he says, was a reaction, not a decision. He explains the difference. "If you are walking down a street and see somebody walk up to a stranger and blow their brains out for no reason, you would have a reaction to that. You wouldn't decide what you thought about it. You would know immediately, you would react." That, he said, happened to him at the end of his long search to find convincing arguments in support of the war in Vietnam. He felt as though he did not have a choice. Once he had completed as much research as he thought it was possible to do through the written material available in English at that time and through his source at the State Department, he reacted. He went from being an apathetic college student from suburban Akron who didn't think much about the world beyond himself and his friends to figuring out how he would accomplish the goal that now was his deepest concern:

Stop this war.

His doubts removed, he had come to believe the war represented values that were the antithesis of what he had assumed were American values. For Forsyth, "From then on, the Vietnam War was about 90 percent of what I was interested in."

Challenged about his claim that he had no choice except to act, he acknowledges that his reaction was not inevitable, that he could have made a choice—that he could have read the same information and chosen to disagree with it or be either neutral or apathetic. Sure, he says, "when I read the book I could have stopped after the first few pages and said, 'Yeah, the war in Vietnam is wrong, but it's so depressing I don't want to hear about it anymore,' and thrown the book away. Or I could have said, 'I got courses to take and coeds to chase, too bad about this.' But I don't see what I did next, becoming part of the peace movement, as a choice. I'm a person who takes things seriously. . . . When I read something that went against my opinion, I was shocked and had to find out if I was wrong. I did everything I could to learn both sides. Then, after I did that, I had a new opinion. I had no choice at that point." He was then an eighteen-year-old freshman with, as he looks back on it, a corrected opinion, a lot of anger, and a strong need to do something about what he had discovered.

In addition to feeling angry, he said, "I felt hurt. I felt personally manipulated, lied to. It still pushes my buttons. I felt a lot of righteous indignation that somebody would be saying one thing and doing the opposite—protecting democracy in Vietnam while they are instead destroying the possibility of democracy—I immediately started wondering what was the story with all these grown-ups that put us in this situation. It wasn't my responsibility to have to read this book prior to being eighteen years old. But here are all these other people that are grown up, and they don't seem to be asking any questions. The war's been going on for years by then. What's the story with them?"

Forsyth tried to talk with his father about the war. He always has considered himself to be a lot like his father. "He's a relatively independent, critical thinker. That's where I picked up that quality. And I just couldn't fathom how he could be going along with this. . . . Part of what I was thinking was that if I didn't have a college deferment [from military service], my ass would be over there with people shooting at it. And, I thought, if you're going to send your son over to a war, you'd better be damn sure that it's right to send me."

In these conversations, Forsyth remembers, his father used to bring up World War II, "as though it was the same. . . . And I would say, 'That's totally irrelevant. World War II was a just war. We had to do what we did then. What you did was right and it was good. What we are doing now is the opposite.'" He felt a deep respect for the heroic way his father's generation had met their obligations during World War II, but he couldn't understand why they seemed to be blind to the injustice of this new war.

FORSYTH DROPPED OUT of college in spring 1970 and lived at home while he thought about how he would work to stop the war. He considered transferring to a larger campus that would have a larger peace movement. He was thinking about his options when President Nixon made his announcement on April 30 that the United States was invading Cambodia. Later that night, a friend from Wooster called and asked him to return to campus to help organize demonstrations against the invasion. The campus was not very politically active, he recalls, but, as on countless other quiet campuses, many people there were furious about Nixon's announcement and protested, many of them for the first time.

Nixon announced the invasion of Cambodia on a Thursday evening. Protests started late that evening and continued through the weekend. On Monday, Forsyth was with friends in the newsroom of the Wooster student newspaper, mimeographing leaflets advertising a protest on campus. The teletype machine started click-clacking loudly, a sign that a story was about to come over the wire. Forsyth can't remember now whether it was a scream, a cry, or a curse. He just remembers someone reading the story being transmitted let out a strong reaction. Everybody in the room quickly gathered around the teletype machine. They couldn't believe what they read: Student protesters had been killed just minutes earlier and just forty-six miles away at Kent State University. Four had been killed and nine wounded by National Guardsmen who shot into the crowd gathered on the campus green.

Until that moment, Forsyth's rage against the war had been intellectual, based on what he had learned during his deep research. Now his rage was a visceral reaction—nearby students had been killed. People who probably had the same antiwar opinions he had.

Ten days later, other killings accelerated Forsyth's transformation to resister. He was still at Wooster organizing protests against the Cambodian invasion and the killings at Kent State when he woke in a friend's dorm room to awful sounds on a radio. Other people were in the room. Whatever they were listening to was interrupted by a special news report. Everyone in the room hushed, trying to understand what they were hearing.

"They played a tape," Forsyth recalls. "A reporter or somebody had a tape of what happened. . . . They played this tape, and there was all this talking, and you could hear some cop on a bullhorn . . . and then, all of a sudden, it wasn't like bang, pause, confusion. Instead, it was just like, all of a sudden, all this shooting started. I found out later it was individual weapon fire, but it sounded like one or two automatic weapons. . . . It was ten or twenty rifles and pistols and shotguns all being fired at once. The story that circulated later was that somebody shot at them and they shot back, which obviously was bullshit because there was not a bang and then a pause and then a bang. . . . It was just all of a sudden a big barrage that sounded like machine-gun fire." Indeed, that was the case that night at Jackson State College in Mississippi. Students had fired no shots, but every window on one side of their dormitory was broken by police gunshots.

Forsyth is emotionally drained after he recounts the memory of how he felt that night as he listened with Wooster friends huddled around that radio. In the moments that followed, he learned what it was he had just heard on tape: Two black students had been killed and twelve wounded as

Mississippi State Police fired on students in a dormitory at Jackson State College, a black college. He pauses, and with a sense of finality, says, "And that was it for me."

"After Jackson State—" He loses his voice briefly, the anger and sadness present now as he remembers.

"That was the moment when I really decided that something more than just the end of the Vietnam War was called for. There was a larger evil at work. I was already mad. I was already feeling enraged and betrayed. And after that it just multiplied."

When he learned what had happened to those black students and, over the next several days, as he saw how people reacted—and didn't react—to their deaths, he experienced an epiphany about how little awareness he himself had of race. It had not been a part of his consciousness. He had grown up totally shielded from an awareness of race. Now, as he absorbed what the Mississippi police had done to these black students, he mourned them and also his own lack of awareness of how differently, how unjustly black people were treated in the United States. He thought of the omissions in his experience and knowledge about race. "There had been zero black people in my neighborhood or high school. In the town I grew up in, Marion, a

Keith Forsyth, age fifteen, on one of many fishing trips he took with his maternal grandfather, Robert Delno Hickok, a relative of Wild Bill Hickok. They caught northern pike this day on the north side of Georgian Bay on Lake Huron, in 1965.

small town in Ohio, there were black people, but I didn't even find out about that until I was fourteen. I thought the whole town was white. I went downtown all the time, walking all over—well, I thought all over. Then, a friend, one summer day he and I went on a longer than usual walk. We found black people, a whole community of black people in that little town, and we didn't know about them. They were really segregated. They didn't go downtown to shop. . . . Nobody mentioned them. They just didn't come up. As I thought about them after Jackson State, I thought about the fact that ever since I was a little kid, I knew all the best places to fish fifty miles around there, but I didn't know there were black people three miles from my home. Isn't that incomprehensible?"

He also remembered then what happened his senior year of high school when Martin Luther King was assassinated. "I had a civics class, and we didn't even talk about his death, if you can believe that." In the aftermath of the Jackson State killings, he remembered King's assassination and asked himself: Why did they not talk about this event, King's death, that, he now realized, had traumatized the country and at the time was discussed throughout the world?

"All these memories hit me in the face after I listened to that tape. It started to wake me up. I started visualizing those black kids. . . . I knew I didn't want to be shot, and I was sure they didn't want to be shot. . . . I had a vague awareness of racism. I knew, for instance, some pillars of our church who were particularly racist. But it didn't have the same importance to me as the war. It didn't have the same impact. I didn't think something needed to change. . . . Until Jackson State happened, it didn't burn."

His idealized view of American society was now not just in question, as it had been when he first read *Peace in Vietnam*. Now it was in shreds. Whereas before he had assumed that American society was generally one giant middle class, with variations based largely on terrain, climate, and tastes, now he saw a society torn by racial injustice and by a herd mentality that caused many people not to question their government and its policies. "I started thinking more in terms of tactics and political effectiveness. I started reading books on political strategy and tactics and how to organize. . . . 'Effectiveness' was a big word for me. I don't remember my rationale, but resistance seemed like the next thing to do, the thing that would be effective. And I felt that it had to be nonviolent resistance to be tactically effective." He wasn't a total pacifist, but he was a pacifist by personality and strategy. He believed war could be justified and necessary, as he thought

World War II was. But he believed violent protest was not only inhumane but also strategically counterproductive.

His transformation now accelerated—from organizing demonstrations on the Wooster campus to deciding he was willing to break the law in order to protest government policies. His sense of personal responsibility for the war, aroused by his study of it, now dominated his thinking. "It's *our* government, it's *our* money going over there, it's *our* policy, and they're *our* politicians who are doing this," he thought. "It's *our* responsibility to do something about this.

"I got that from my parents. I was raised with a strong sense of personal responsibility for things, everything from 'Don't sit in the mud with your Sunday clothes on' to 'Don't take other people's things.' I had learned that you're responsible for what you do, and while the content of some of my views had changed, that sense of responsibility had not changed. That's still the centerpiece of my life."

BY THE END of May 1970, Forsyth had reached the point of awareness that the older Media burglars had reached before 1968. His awakening had begun in the fall of 1969. Until then, he had little concern about the traumatic events that transpired the previous year—the assassinations of Martin Luther King and Robert F. Kennedy, the demonstrations and riots at the Democratic convention in Chicago, and the election of Richard Nixon as president. "I was aware of all that [1968] stuff," he says, "but I was still a kid from the Midwest. All that stuff wasn't nearly as important to me as what impression I was making on girls."

After Cambodia, after Kent State and Jackson State, he made three decisions simultaneously:

Get out of Ohio.
Go to Philadelphia.
Do resistance.

Forsyth may not have known that W. C. Fields had written a famous epitaph for his tombstone that has fueled countless insulting jokes about Philadelphia: "On the whole, I'd rather be in Philadelphia." It was not W.C.'s favorite place, except as an alternative to death. The jokes that followed included such gems as the one about the travel contest: The first prize is a week in Philadelphia, and the second prize is two weeks in Philadelphia. If Forsyth had known this harsh humor about the city, he would not have cared. Philadelphia was where he wanted to be. He had been told, correctly, that it was one of the best places for a would-be resister to go in 1970. People told him there was a big peace movement there. They were right.

Forsyth went home after the campus demonstrations. A few days later, he went to the eastern edge of Akron and put out his thumb. With no apologies to W. C. Fields and lots of optimism about finding a place for the next stage of his life, he was on his way to Philadelphia. "I knew Philadelphia was a big city, so obviously there would be an antiwar movement of some size. I knew the Quakers were out here, so I figured this sounded like good, fertile ground for doing what I needed to do and learn what I needed to learn."

Not long after Forsyth arrived in the city, he picked up a flyer distributed by a group of people claiming responsibility for raiding a series of Philadelphia draft boards. When he saw that flyer, Forsyth says, "I knew I had found the kind of resistance I was looking for. . . . I got to the people I wanted to meet very quickly after that. I was introduced to people who introduced me to people . . . and pretty soon I met people who were also interested in doing acts of resistance against the war. . . . They were doing what I wanted to do. They had experience doing it, and they weren't afraid of getting arrested. That's all I needed to know." That was the beginning of Forsyth's nearly full-time resistance work.

He applied the same methodical approach to preparation for resistance that he had applied earlier to studying the war. He assumed he should be prepared, as much as one can be, to face the possibility of arrest, trial, and short- or long-term imprisonment. He read studies on what happens to people when they go to prison, about how police treat people when they arrest them. "I thought about how I would feel about this. If I were to get arrested and sent to jail for five years, would I then change my mind and decide it wasn't worth it? What would it be like to be in a cage for five years? Would I change my mind about the risk I had taken? What would I do every day? . . . I went through this in great detail with myself. I wanted to make sure if I was going to chicken out, I wanted to chicken out before and not during or after. And so I decided that it wasn't going to be any fun, but it was no big deal. . . . I'm not a fragile personality type, so I decided I would be okay. I wasn't worried."

———

FORSYTH REGARDED his chosen resistance base, the Catholic peace movement, as more like an amoeba than a disciplined political action group. Most of the time, he says, you felt "it wasn't really an organization at all. It was just a bunch of people that felt the same way. I remember reading something in the paper by some PR turkey that portrayed us as this organization that was run by Dan and Phil Berrigan. . . . It was the antithesis of that. There were a lot of people involved who never met Dan and Phil. And there were a lot of people who should have met them because they could have learned something from the Berrigans. It was very loose and spread out, and different people did things in very different ways. Some wanted to get arrested. That was their philosophy—especially those close to Dan and Phil had that orientation. They felt, 'We're going to do this, and we're going to take responsibility publicly and get arrested on purpose.' They felt that increased the political impact to force the state to put them on trial and put them in jail. . . . That was a perfectly legitimate philosophy. I didn't happen to agree with it, but I respected it."

Given his view, it was fortunate Forsyth became involved in this movement after it had switched from symbolic actions to clandestine burglaries of draft boards. "I wanted to disable draft boards. I wasn't interested in being arrested. I wasn't afraid of being arrested, but I wasn't interested in being arrested. I wanted to be free so I could destroy as much of the Selective Service system as I could, or the Army. . . . I would have rather done it on Army bases"—destroyed records, made it hard to fight the war—"but they had barbed wire around bases. . . . Security was tight. And the only way you could do any damage there would involve injuring people, and I wouldn't do that. My only choice was the draft boards."

It was his only choice until Davidon asked him, in December 1970, what he thought of burglarizing an FBI office, an option that of course had never occurred to him and perhaps not to anyone else except Davidon.

Unlike some of the Media burglars, Forsyth says he didn't live in fear of being found by the FBI after the Media burglary. All of his fear was concentrated in those intense hours he spent breaking into the office and thinking they should call off the burglary. Later, he thought the job had been done well and was confident no trails could lead to them. Consequently, in the aftermath of the burglary, he did not have sleepless nights, he did not worry about a knock on the door. He was never visited or called by the FBI.

He remembers being "totally happy" hours after the raid when the group gathered at the farmhouse to begin the next stage of their work, sorting the documents they had stolen. But even as it became clear during the ten days the burglars read and sorted the stolen files that they had been successful beyond their wildest hopes, Forsyth started to disengage from the process. The satisfaction he felt soon after the burglary dwindled fast. "I really felt good about Media," he said. "It was a great thing, but within a week after it was over, the effect on me had worn off. I knew we had done a good thing, but I quickly felt, 'What am I going to do now?' And I really didn't know what to do now." At movement parties, he was silent as he listened to people discussing in excited detail what the Media documents had revealed. "People were very pleased. But I wasn't that excited about it. It didn't have that much meaning for me. We did this and it was over, and now it was time to go back to work the next day," he says. "That's what it was like. You go to work and you do something and the project is finished and it's successful. Your boss gives you a pat on the back. Well, you don't quit your job then. You go back to work the next day and start up the next thing. That's sort of how it was for me."

Within a short time, though, moving on to the next resistance project became difficult for Forsyth. "I was hoping somebody smarter than me would come up with a good idea and suggest it to me. But nobody did. And I came to realize the limitations of that whole draft board thing. . . . There are so many draft boards in the country. It was clear what we were doing was not causing them to suffer from a soldier shortage over there. The reality that we were this mouse gnawing on the elephant's toenail was coming home to me more and more, and I got more and more frustrated. And very unhappy. . . .

"In the beginning it was more satisfying," Forsyth says. "In the beginning just the act of resistance was enough. As that started to wear off, the opportunity to do Media came along, and that escalation was enough. But then, once that was over, it was, 'What do we do now?' And the only good ideas I remember after that were about things that were not feasible because of the security.

"I think in some ways Media made the draft board raid work even less satisfying because it seemed kind of like going backwards to a lower level. . . . My frustration level was rapidly increasing immediately after Media."

In late June or early July 1971, Forsyth was recruited to be part of the group that was planning the Camden draft board raid. It wasn't the great idea he was looking for, but he agreed to participate. "Camden was bad news from the beginning, and I knew it was bad news. . . . I knew it was something I was getting myself into that I shouldn't. But I was just frustrated, mad at myself and at everybody else, and said, 'I'm gonna do it. I don't give a shit.' He felt awful afterwards. He felt that many of the people in the Camden raid never should have been there, that they had not been properly prepared. "And, of course, I had as much responsibility as anyone else to bring that up and try to deal with it, but I didn't do it."

After Forsyth was released from jail and arraigned for the Camden raid, he said goodbye to this phase of his life. "Camden was my last contact with the Catholic Left. . . . I had just had it with that stuff. I felt like I had to do something different. . . . I had been with them a year, a very long year. . . . It seemed like forever. I decided that grassroots work was going to be more effective. I think my thinking was something like this: Resistance is not effective, it's not working in the short run. We need to dig in for the long haul instead. I had a sense of accomplishment, but not a big one. Not a big one at all." He readily acknowledges that his post-resistance attitude probably developed in part from the intense impatience often typical in youth. He had made a major change in his life in order to stop the war. When the war didn't end, and he felt he might not be able to do more to make it end, he felt compelled to move on, to use his intense drive for another purpose.

"I told the people in the group, 'I'm not going to do this anymore.' There weren't any long goodbyes. I just said, 'This is the end for me, see you later.' It sounds kind of cold, but I wasn't in it for the social aspect. . . . I felt closer to the people I lived with than I did to them. . . . They [the people he lived with] were all involved in some kind of progressive politics, though some were more into macramé than they were into anything else. But to the extent that I had emotional attachments, it was to the people I lived with. . . . The resistance work was strictly business as far as I was concerned. I think I was atypical. I think to most people in the Catholic Left, the group was like a family, but not to me."

Not until years later was he able to feel deep satisfaction about what he accomplished in those days. Like Williamson, he did not fully recognize the significance of what the Media burglary revealed, and the large public reaction to the revelations, until several years later, after he had rebuilt his life. "It took me five to ten years to figure that out.

"In terms of the antiwar movement and that period of my life, it was downhill from then on. That was the beginning of my period of frustration. Actually, I was frustrated from the day I read that book in 1968 on, but I mean really frustrated [by mid-1971]. As long as I was doing more, and more, and more, somehow that helped to keep my frustration at bay. The war was still going on, and it didn't look like it was going to end anytime real soon. I couldn't think of anything to do except to get down in the grass-roots and try to change people's minds about things. . . . At the time that seemed the most effective thing to do.

Forsyth put away his lock-picking tools, which were rather well worn by mid-1971. He returned the standard items to the various toolboxes from which he had borrowed them. He kept the ones he had made for a while and then threw them away. Almost immediately after he got out of jail following his arrest in Camden, he called someone who was doing community orga-nizing. A short time later he moved to Kensington, then a largely working-class and poor neighborhood in Philadelphia.

For most of the next ten years, Forsyth was first a neighborhood orga-nizer and later a union reform organizer in a factory owned by the Budd Company, a metal fabricator and major supplier of body components for automobile manufacturing companies. During these years, he said many years after he left organizing, "I wanted to change America. I was fired with the zealot's vision." But after a few years, Forsyth found the work less and less satisfying. His lack of satisfaction may have come in part from the nature of the particular group he was working with. Members consumed themselves with constant criticism of one another, a sharp contrast to the warm, friendly atmosphere of the Catholic peace movement.

By 1981, Forsyth said, he knew "this is not me anymore." By that time, "the most immediate thing was how personally painful it was, the way we were attacking each other and expecting perfection. . . . A lot of the people I was working with, I started wondering what it would be like if they were in charge of the government, and whether that would be such a good idea. . . . I was the most zealous of the zealous, and when I finally woke up to what I was like, from a human point of view, I just couldn't do it anymore."

Finally, the "missionary attitude" drove him out of organizing. Increas-ingly, he was bothered "by the relationships we had with the people we were supposedly organizing. The missionary thing was always there . . . that sense that Father knows best, that we knew best. . . . We said we were try-ing to empower people, but we were pushing our own agenda, and there was always an undercurrent of not being completely up front about exactly what we were doing. . . . You say you're trying to save the world. . . . But we treated people like recruitees. . . . It's still a source of pain to me now when I think of that missionary attitude."

At the end of this period of his life, Forsyth again "didn't know what I was going to do, but I had to get out, so I did." In 1981, at age thirty-one, he was a veteran of intense political involvement, with thirteen years of experience under his belt: campus organizing at Wooster, long-term community and union reform organizing in Philadelphia, an acquittal in the very unusual Camden trial, and no arrest in his biggest coup, the Media FBI burglary. "If I have any regrets, it's that I wasn't able to keep up. . . . I just got real tired and real discouraged."

AS HE CLOSED the organizing chapter of his life, Forsyth decided to build a new life. He analyzed his skills, his interests, his needs. He decided to utilize his strong penchant for being precise and methodical. He went back to college and earned two degrees—a bachelor's degree in physics from the State University of New York at Albany and a master's degree in electrical engineering from Drexel University. He became an electrical engineer, his father's profession.

He likes this work. It provides him with a refreshing contrast to an aspect of political work he found extremely distasteful. In political life, he found, "if you're fanatic enough, you can justify anything in the name of some principle. If you're a good enough arguer—and I met some champion debaters—you can make green red and red green. I'd go home after some debates and say, 'What the hell did I just agree with? Am I out of my mind?'

"That's one of the reasons why I gravitated toward engineering. . . . What I do now, when it's all done and it comes time to turn on that switch, it either works or it doesn't. . . . If smoke comes out, you screwed up, you're wrong, you made a mistake, and you can't blame it on anybody else. If it works, I get the credit. If it doesn't work, I get the blame, and that's the way I like it. You can't bullshit your way around."

Since then he has worked for companies and also worked independently, operating his own consulting business, Forsyth Electro Optics, from his home in Manayunk, a neighborhood high on a hill above the Schuylkill River on the western edge of Philadelphia. His work has included such projects as designing equipment that uses light in the operation of lasers, fiber-optic systems, electronic cameras, and other devices. He advises companies and individuals on the feasibility of systems they have designed.

Forsyth hastens to point out that though he is not active politically, he hasn't rejected his progressive beliefs. "I have a lot of bad things to say about the left and about my own involvement in the left. I'm not active, and I'm very cynical about the prospects for change, but I have no sympathy for these reconstructed people who say, 'We made a mistake. Nixon was right all along.' . . . That stuff makes me puke. I'm not reconstructed in that sense."

His relations with his parents have improved. He often has differed with them on politics. Usually, "I find that they don't convince me, and I don't convince them. . . . My attitude now is that I'm not going to try to convince them. . . . If they say something that I really disagree with . . . I'll say something about it, but I don't get hot about it anymore. I just stop and think, 'There probably is another side to this,' and let it go. At that time, I couldn't let it go. At that time, what they thought was really important to me. . . . When you're a kid, especially if you grew up in a real close family, your parents' beliefs have a weight that they don't have after you've become an adult. At that time I felt betrayed: How can you support this war, how can you do this to me?"

Forsyth finds pleasure in the fact that he and his parents have found one common ground: They agree that most people in elected office are scoundrels. He doesn't think most are taking money from dubious deals. They are scoundrels, he believes, because "they are gutless. Their purpose in life is to get reelected. They are afraid to stand for something."

The most important part of his rebuilt life is his family. He cherishes them. He found it difficult when his sons—Adam, born in 1983, and Micah, born in 1986—were growing up to imagine how he could devote time to political work as well as to nurturing the family he and his wife, Susan Grossinger, created. He worried about the impact on his children of his lack of political engagement, but it seemed necessary to at least take a breather, if

Keith Forsyth and his wife, Susan Grossinger, in 1987.

not a permanent leave, from being political in order to build the professional and personal parts of his life, those parts he ignored until 1981.

Forsyth hopes Adam and Micah will not be afraid to make hard decisions, such as ones that might involve making a sacrifice in order to help other people. As soon as they were able to listen to stories, he started telling them his story. Since they were very little, they've known that Daddy went to jail once for being against the war. "I told them there was a war going on and that . . . a lot of people thought it was a good idea, and a lot of people thought it was a bad idea. And Daddy thought it was a real bad idea. I tell them that a lot of innocent people were getting killed and that when things like that happen people ought to try to stop it. I tell them that I tried to do that."

The portrait Forsyth paints of himself in those early years of protest and organizing includes patches of frustration, anger, and personal distress. It's obvious that some of the memories are painful. "The frustration is still there," he says. "I don't access it very often because it gets me upset, and there's no point to it. Today he analyzes politics in a different way from how he did in the early 1970s. While he still has strong opinions about various issues, he sees more ambiguity now than he saw during the Vietnam War. He has also shifted in his view of the public. "I don't regard our problems today as solely the fault of the leaders. I think that at that time I tended to see the American public as a bunch of gullible little lambs who were being led down the primrose path by these nasty, manipulative politicians and chairmen of General Motors and other companies. . . . My opinion of the population is different now. Let's put it this way: I think the American people, the majority of them, are sufficiently well educated and free from worrying about whether they are going to be carried out in the middle of the night by secret police and free enough from starving to death that they can take more responsibility for the way they vote and for the way their government is run."

That's the attitude he hopes Adam and Micah will have, that sense of being responsible that he acquired from his parents and that he then redirected into his work against the war after *Peace in Vietnam*, the book Chuck gave him, set him on a new course.

AT SOME POINT—while Forsyth was getting an education, building a profession, becoming a husband, nurturing two sons with his wife—he made peace with his past, with his assessment of the people he walked away from after Camden and with the person he was then. His frustration and feelings of futility about failing to stop the war gradually dissipated. Forsyth's memories of those years still can evoke powerful traces of the frustration and pain he felt then, but those reactions now take a backseat. They have been largely replaced by a deep pride and satisfaction in what he and the people he worked with then, especially his fellow Media burglars, did in those days when millions of Americans wanted their government to end the war in Vietnam.

In a sign of his acceptance of his past and of his renewed respect for his former colleagues in the Catholic peace movement, Forsyth was present in 2003 when the federal judges of New Jersey, in an extraordinary act, sponsored, on the thirtieth anniversary of the Camden verdict, a daylong reunion of the Camden 28 defendants and others associated with the trial—prosecutors, an FBI agent, some witnesses, the son of the deceased judge, the widow of the deceased chief prosecutor, a federal judge herself, and even the informer. It took place in the same courtroom where the trial occurred, with the graying defendants sitting in an expanded jury box. During the 1973 trial, Forsyth had no interest in working with fellow defendants to create the open courtroom atmosphere in which the judge permitted them to explain the history of the war, the basis of their opposition to the war, and why they had broken laws in order to draw attention to what they regarded as an unlawful action—the war itself. Now, on the thirtieth anniversary of the trial, Forsyth was fully engaged in this courtroom he had shunned then. He sat with his fellow defendants in the jury box. It was obvious that now he was proud of what the defendants had accomplished in the trial, and he was happy to join them in celebrating and examining the unusual trial, that era, and the personal commitments that had spawned their resistance.

In contrast to all the other people who commented at the reunion, Terry Neist—the only FBI agent at the reunion and one of the two agents in charge of the Camden informer in the months leading up to the arrests and also one of the agents who investigated the Media burglary—made it clear at the reunion that he was still angry about the verdict. "We are a nation of laws," he said. "They broke the law. They should have been found guilty."

Forsyth spoke up. He was diplomatic as he responded to Neist in an agreeable but firm voice that was heard clearly throughout the courtroom. "Terry raised important points," said Forsyth. "We *are* a nation of laws, and for good reasons. Most of us take that very seriously. Deciding when to break the law is not a trivial decision or a light decision. I hope that if I was presented today with the same issues, I would have the courage to make the decision I made when I was a child of twenty-one. I hope the young people out there listening will try to make the right decision today." His comments were greeted with murmurs of approval throughout the audience that packed the reunion courtroom.

The frustration and sense of failure that once dominated Forsyth's assessment of that period in his life were completely absent one day as he summed up what the acts of resistance he carried out in his youth mean to him now:

"It's one of the few decisions I made, one of the few things I ever did, that I feel unconditionally positive about. . . . I had to decide whether it was going to be just an opinion about which I would shoot off my mouth and not do anything, or was I really going to be serious and do something? . . . I spent a lot of time thinking about that. . . . I weighed the personal risk. I asked myself how much risk I was willing to face for an opinion. . . . That's one of those times when people were called on to take a position one way or another. I'm proud of the position I took. . . . There are a lot of other things in my life that are just sort of neutral. I get by from day to day like everybody else . . . sometimes doing things I'm ashamed of. . . . But I feel great about what I did then."

23

Very Pleased . . . Missing the Joy

RON DURST REMEMBERS the pleasure of hearing people talk about the burglary. "I remember being proud and not being able to tell anyone. . . . That was okay. The action spoke for itself." But the secrecy the burglars imposed on one another led to some unusual ways of getting approval. "It was a funny thing. I was getting indirect feedback through the news media and through people at parties. . . . They'd comment on what a wonderful thing had happened with Media, and they'd say it was incredible what this was doing to the FBI. People thought it was absolutely wonderful. They would wonder who had done it. I would have liked to have said, 'I was one of the people who did it.' But I didn't. I knew I was getting compliments and a lot of support—though they didn't know they were giving it to me. . . . I was getting a lot of feedback from seeing the stories in the news media. . . . I was excited and very pleased.

"I was always looking over my shoulder, but it was a funny thing to be in a situation where you have done something that was against the law and yet you are proud of it. I'd look over my shoulder in a kind of fearful way, but the fear was attached to a feeling of pride and not to shame or guilt." Durst was briefly considered a suspect, but he was never called or visited by the FBI.

The roots of his willingness to say yes when Davidon asked him what he thought of burglarizing an FBI office grew from tragic family stories that started shaping his conscience and his resolve to stop injustice when he was a child. The stories were horrendous. Whole generations of both his father's and mother's families were killed during the Holocaust. His parents escaped and brought with them stories of Nazi brutality that were permanently etched in his mind. These stories of profound loss filled many family conversations when Durst was growing up. As a small boy, he felt sorrow and anger for the enormous loss of life, including aunts and uncles he never had the chance to know. His anger about that tragic loss stayed with him, and as he became an adult it helped shape his decisions about the kind of life he would live. He could not believe average Germans after the war when they said, "I didn't know." Nor could he accept the claim of Nazi soldiers that they should be excused because "I was taking orders."

Later, his family lessons echoed in his response to the war in Vietnam. As the number of people killed added up to many thousands of Americans and millions of Vietnamese and Cambodians, he examined his anger about the Holocaust in new ways. He raised questions with himself that he had not considered before. "It's very easy to live in the United States and point at Germany and say, 'Why didn't you follow the laws of your conscience?' That's easy to do. It's harder to do it in the present, in your own situation." He thought about the passivity of German bystanders, of average German citizens, and he compared their reactions to the reactions of Americans to Vietnam. Sure, many Americans cared, but, he thought, not enough of them. Too many Americans were passive and seemed satisfied to let the killing continue, or not to explore why it was happening.

Earlier, Durst had easily adopted the fierce cry about the Holocaust: "Never again!" As his outrage about the Vietnam War grew, he heard the same cry in a new way. He told himself that the cry should also mean that such brutal killing must never happen again against *any* people—not in Auschwitz, not in My Lai, not in Cambodia. This compelling demand fueled his resistance to the Vietnam War.

As Durst edged closer to more serious resistance, he was perplexed by what he saw as a fundamental change in official American policies as reflected in its aggression in Vietnam in contrast to its role in creating the Nuremberg trials after World War II. In those trials, judges from Allied countries—including U.S. Supreme Court justice Robert Jackson—from 1945 to 1949 presided over the trials of more than one hundred Nazis for leading a war that was in violation of international treaties and involved brutal crimes against humanity. For the first time, the international community, organized primarily by the United States, agreed it had a moral and legal obligation not to let perpetrators of war crimes get away with impunity; they would be held responsible for their crimes. The United States and those grand principles established at Nuremberg seemed to be synonymous. Until Vietnam, said Durst.

By 1970, Durst was puzzled that the United States could have gone to such great lengths to enshrine those principles at the end of World War II but twenty years later was waging a war in Vietnam that increasingly was seen, in the eyes of more and more Americans and the international community, as one that could not be justified and that was needlessly causing the killing of thousands of people each year.

"There comes a time," he decided, "when one has to break the laws of the land, when well-thought-out civil disobedience is necessary to maintain a righteous and reasonable state. . . . I couldn't stand seeing all those people dying for a war that didn't make any sense." His determination not to be a passive bystander increased when Davidon focused his attention on the possibility that the FBI was spying on activists and suppressing dissent. He had engaged in smaller acts of civil disobedience in the past year. He decided it was time for him to take a bold step. He was ready to follow one of the principles enshrined at Nuremberg: that sometimes laws should be broken.

In the years since the burglary, Durst has become relatively prosperous. Living for many years far from the Philadelphia area, he says he still has essentially the same values he had then. As an investor, for instance, he said he refuses to invest in companies that profit from war. In other ways, his priorities have changed. He gradually focused more on personal needs, family needs. "After a while I didn't pay as much attention to issues." He hopes he still has the capacity to refuse to be passive in the face of great injustice—to act again as he did at Media, "in a way that made a difference."

Like an artist who feels as though he has just created a fine painting, perhaps his best, Ron Durst was radiant one day as he recounted in careful detail the execution of the Media burglary and then summed up the satisfaction he felt years later. "It was a wonderful, well-conceived act of civil disobedience. It was much more than we hoped it would be. It's something that I'm really proud of. It's not something that I can put on my résumé, but to me it's one of the most significant things I've done in my life."

FOR SUSAN SMITH, the agony of never being sure if she had removed a glove and left fingerprints while she was in the FBI office continued for many years, as did her yearning to be able to share the experience with friends. The yearning "gradually faded but never went away," she says. "There was no time when there was a clear break, and I suddenly felt, 'Well, it's over now.' Instead, it thinned out and became a thin line."

But she thinks "the Pandora's box we opened" was well worth the price of whatever torment she endured. "The immediate impact, the unraveling of what the FBI was doing, would have been enough. But the long-term impact, the revelation of COINTELPRO, the legitimizing of the complaints that had been made but ignored. The image of the wonder boys shattered; they no longer were the invincible. Even those on the left who regarded the FBI as an enemy tended to regard them as all-powerful. After the burglary, one of the things we achieved was to show they were not."

Like John Raines, Smith was a veteran of Freedom Summer in Mississippi in 1964. She didn't talk about her time there very much, but it had been a powerful experience—life-threatening but ultimately very gratifying.

While she worked in the northeastern corner of Mississippi, Smith lived with three other civil rights workers—one of them black, two white—in an old unpainted, dry-as-kindling farmhouse. It had four rooms, an outhouse, and an outdoor water spigot. It was down a dirt road near a wooded area. No other houses were within sight. Two weeks after they moved into the house, they were wakened one night by a series of explosions—gasoline bombs, they learned later—on the front porch. Tall flames quickly engulfed the front of the old house, a perfect tinderbox. Each of them woke up shouting to the others to get out of the house. But, Smith remembers, "as soon as we stood up and started shouting, gunfire—rifle and shotgun fire—hit the front of the house. We ran to the back and dove out the back windows and hit the ground." They stayed flat until the gunfire ended. When they inspected the house after the gunfire stopped, they saw that the walls were pockmarked with bullet holes, all just above waist level. It was difficult to think the fire had not been set so the four of them would become easy to target as they fled the raging fire.

A few weeks later, a mechanic removed a brake pin in her car, something that could have led to a serious accident. One day, as she stood beside her broken-down car along a country road, she was told to get out of Mississippi or face the fate of James Chaney, Andrew Goodman, and Michael Schwerner, the three civil rights workers brutally killed a few months earlier. She was frightened, but she refused to be intimidated. She stayed through the autumn.

When she went to the South, there was clarity, even purity, she thought later, about what she did. Your actions were laid out for the entire world to see, to judge, to accept or reject. Those conditions met the criteria for what she thought was the ideal political life—a life that was visible and could be judged by your actions. By contrast, though the burglary was done for the public, it was hidden from the public.

Smith's conflict over the type of resistance Davidon now invited her to participate in arose in part from what she learned as a college student from the writings of Hannah Arendt, a leading political philosopher of the twentieth century. Arendt left Germany in 1933, settled in New York, and wrote about the struggle to grasp the origin and import of totalitarian movements and how they affected moral and political judgment. With Arendt, Smith shared the conundrum posed by having both a respect for the rule of law and also a certainty that the law, as either applied or ignored by a government, sometimes needed to be changed, challenged, or disobeyed.

As she thought about whether to participate in the Media burglary, an unusual kind of fear—that prison would be worse than death—haunted her.

Smith, thirty-seven at the time, looked at it this way: She thought that she would rather be dead soon than be in prison forever, that she would rather sacrifice her life than her freedom. "In Mississippi all that was at risk was my life. In the burglary, all that would be at risk was twenty to thirty years in prison. Now, this may seem strange, but I don't have any problem risking my life. . . . When you're dead, you're dead. I mean, that's it. It's over. But when you're in prison, you're spending twenty to thirty years in prison. What does it mean to live in prison? Now, obviously, lots of people with long sentences have made a lot out of their lives in prison. But I couldn't quite see spending twenty to thirty years in prison as being a really good thing."

When Smith thinks about her two main resistance experiences, she regards Freedom Summer in Mississippi as the most important experience of her life and the Media burglary as the most difficult experience of her life. She still appreciates the purity of helping register black people to vote in Mississippi. She's always felt regret about the secrecy surrounding the Media burglary even though she understood then and now that it was necessary.

For Smith, something profoundly important was missing in the months and weeks after the burglary.

Public resistance, she knew from past experience, "generated a powerful sense of community and solidarity." Because the resisters were hiding, the Media burglary could not do that. "That was a loss. There wasn't that sense of solidarity waiting for you, that kind of euphoria. I missed the joy. I think about the freedom songs we sang in Mississippi. There even was a joy in facing the tear gas together. But that definitely was not true for what we did at Media. There could be none of that. That was very hard, that sense of isolation."

24

Building Little Pockets of Life

THE LOVE OF DISSENT that propelled William Davidon in 1971 to protect dissent with fierce devotion almost seems to have been part of his DNA. In 1938, at age eleven, he traveled by bus from his home in the Weequahic neighborhood of Newark, the same neighborhood where novelist Philip Roth grew up, to a rally in nearby Jersey City to protest Mayor Frank Hague's decision to forbid Norman Thomas, a pacifist and socialist and one of the leading orators of that time, from speaking in Jersey City because the mayor did not like Thomas's ideas.

Little William Davidon could not understand why the mayor would want to stop someone from expressing his ideas. Beginning with that early inspiration, he's never stopped cherishing the freedom to dissent.

In his bedroom, Davidon listened daily to his family's radio as he taught himself how to take the radio apart and reassemble it. As he did, he occasionally heard speeches by Thomas. He was affronted in a simple but profound childlike way that anyone would try to keep Thomas from speaking. The eleven-year-old Davidon had no idea, of course, that the man whose disregard for dissent he had protested was even more corrupt and powerful than Tammany Hall bosses across the harbor in New York City. Nor did he realize at such a tender age that the attack on dissent he had protested made national headlines and that a lawsuit brought by Thomas and the American Civil Liberties Union resulted in the U.S. Supreme Court declaring the mayor's prohibition against Thomas's speaking to be unconstitutional.

Mayor Hague often discussed his bizarre hatred of basic rights. His strange rationale matched ones expressed years later by J. Edgar Hoover.

"We hear about constitutional rights, free speech and free press," Hague once said. "Every time I hear these words, I say to myself, 'that man is a Red, that man is a Communist.' Whenever [you] hear a discussion of civil rights and the right of free speech and the rights of the Constitution, always remember you will find [him] with a Russian flag under his coat."

Davidon's very early appreciation of dissent was learned among friends and from what he observed in his community, not from his parents. Neither of them, either by example or by words of encouragement, expressed an interest in their son's support of the right to dissent. He remembers neither of them endorsing his evolving political interests. His mother, Ruth Simon Davidon, was apolitical. When her son went to city hall that day to protest, she "wasn't unhappy, but she wasn't supportive either. She just was not too concerned," Davidon recalls. His father, Jack, an itinerant civil engineer who worked for companies that built harbors and other major construction projects, was away a lot, traveling from town to town during the week and coming home only on weekends. Davidon remembers being told that his father had to travel because few companies hired Jewish engineers then. Consequently, the only way his father could get work was by driving many miles from job to job. When Davidon searches his memory, he cannot recall that he and his father ever talked to each other about the crucial issues of the day that were unfolding and starting to be of interest to him. He likes to think his father had views similar to his. He remembers him as a good man, but someone who was silent most of the time and who revealed very little about what he was thinking.

There was much silence in the Davidon home, but the streets of Newark spoke volumes. Davidon thinks the nature of that early World War II period, so full of tragedy in the United States and around the world, was the crucial early incubator of his values and interests. In his Weequahic neighborhood, where his family moved shortly after he was born in 1927 in Fort Lauderdale, Florida, he remembers "a lot of poverty and conspicuous injustice." The impact of the Depression and the war was very visible in Weequahic. People were out of work. Beggars were on the streets. There was a lot of sadness, as countless families grieved the loss of their sons at war and the horrific tragedies taking place in Europe and Asia.

He continued to be interested in such matters as a freshman at Purdue University, but he thought the university was primarily interested in producing as many engineers as quickly as it could for the war effort. A friend suggested the University of Chicago would be a more compatible environment for his intellectual and political interests. He transferred there and earned all of his degrees—bachelor's, master's, and doctoral degrees in physics—at the University of Chicago. His undergraduate studies there were interrupted when he enlisted in the U.S. Navy.

It was on August 6, 1945, that the direction of Davidon's lifelong protest was set. It was on that day that the United States dropped the atomic bomb "Little Boy" on Hiroshima, destroying the city and killing 150,000 Japanese people. Three days later the United States dropped another bomb, "Fat Man," on Nagasaki, killing another 70,000. Countless thousands of people in both cities were permanently disabled, as were future generations of children whose parents carried genes damaged by radiation.

For a great many people, the dropping of those first atomic bombs was cause for celebration. Japan surrendered and World War II ended. Davidon did not celebrate. He felt more like grieving than celebrating. He wanted the war to end, but not in this brutal way.

He immediately recognized the enormous threat that existed, beginning that day, when the United States unleashed a force that from then on would endanger the world. If nuclear arms were not stopped, the war of the future, he realized, could lead to no future. As a young physicist, he understood the scientific knowledge that had been used to build the bombs. He was beginning to realize that national leaders, even those with stated peaceful intentions, might decide to use nuclear weapons, the mightiest known to humanity, to destroy their enemies, and in the process also destroy circles of life far beyond their real or perceived enemies. His opposition to nuclear arsenals was increased by a realization the theologian Reinhold Niebuhr later expressed: that the danger of atomic war was as great from miscalculation as it was from intentional provocation.

After those bombs were dropped on Hiroshima and Nagasaki, Davidon lived with—and lived to stop—the possibility of annihilation. His dissent became that simple and that complex. It was about a decade later, he said, that he grew more politically sophisticated and became affiliated with other physicists who spoke at public gatherings in Chicago about the dangers of nuclear power. He gave speeches about the enormous military power government leaders now held and could use in the public's name.

The unsettling, ugly modern truth Davidon lived with after August 1945 evoked in him an enduring clarity about the potential for the annihilation of humankind that most Americans probably never felt until September 11, 2001, the day the Twin Towers were struck and destroyed. As arms analyst Jonathan Schell wrote in the *Nation* a month after 9/11, "When the attacks occurred, the thought that flashed spontaneously into millions of minds was that our world has changed forever. . . . It was . . . a bone-deep recognition of the utter perishability of all human works and all human beings in the face of human destructive powers. . . . The destruction of the Twin Towers . . . was a taste of annihilation, a small piece of the end of the world." As in 1945, when the United States bombed Japan, Schell wrote, on 9/11 the most profound question was asked by millions: "What was safe?" The damage, of course, was much greater in the Japanese bombings, but for Americans, who had never experienced an attack on the mainland until 9/11, the fear seared into the nation's psyche was profound.

Fear, of course, was not new to Americans in 2001. It has stalked the American landscape many times, including during the years of the Vietnam War. Some Americans feared that enemies of the United States would use nuclear weapons against the country and thought that the United States should be prepared to retaliate against such attacks—either at home or in other countries, such as in Vietnam—and therefore must maintain large stockpiles of such weapons and build ever more powerful nuclear weapons. But Davidon and many other people who opposed the United States' use of nuclear weapons also were afraid. They were afraid not only of the possibility that other governments might use nuclear weapons, but also of how their own government might use its vast supply of such weapons in Vietnam.

During the 1950s, the time when Cold War fears intensified, Davidon also became concerned about the power of the evolving values of his generation. They were building suburbia, acquiring more money and possessions than any previous generation had. They were proud that they had saved the world from fascism. At the same time, perhaps because of Cold War fears, they fell silent, rarely asking questions of government officials about important policies and actions taking place then, including the expansion of the country's nuclear arsenal.

Davidon thinks the silence of his generation after World War II, especially in the 1950s, diminished an important part of the American spirit—the impulse to question and to understand what the government is doing in the name of its citizens. He sees a sad irony in the fact that many of the people who made up what became known a few decades later as the Greatest Generation were largely silent when leading American officials—Senator Joseph McCarthy and FBI director J. Edgar Hoover key among them—labeled citizens who questioned government policies as un-American in the 1950s and early 1960s. His generation's silence, he thinks, created a habit of silence that by 1964 contributed to the fact that most Americans accepted without question the major decision by the administration of President Lyndon Johnson to send troops to Vietnam.

DAVIDON THOUGHT of silencing his own protest after the Cuban Missile Crisis in 1962. He had moved to Haverford College the year before and was looking forward to life as a scholar and researcher. So determined was he to remove himself from the scene of protest that he accepted a position as a professor of physics in New Zealand, thinking that was the only way he could escape deep engagement in protest over U.S. nuclear and war policies would be to leave the country. When he realized that such a move would mean being unable to see his son Alan, who lived with Davidon's first wife in the Chicago area, for extended periods of time, Davidon resolved to stay at Haverford College.

Having made that decision, he threw himself into activism on campus and in the Philadelphia area. He often contemplated theoretical physics matters during his years when resistance dominated his life, but his physics research, started at the University of Chicago, the Enrico Fermi Institute for Nuclear Studies, and Argonne National Laboratory, was put aside until after the Vietnam War. Probably few, if any, of the activists he worked with closely knew that their pleasant physics professor companion spent some of their long silent waiting periods together doing challenging mathematics and physics problems in his head. "One of the nice things about theoretical work is that you can do it wherever you happen to be," he says, smiling mischievously as he thinks of some of the places where he contemplated mathematical problems—in parked cars on side streets while monitoring late-night light patterns in the windows of federal buildings and in a closet while waiting for a security guard to walk by on his last round of the evening.

After the Media burglary, it was as though Davidon could not stop his activism, despite the potential jeopardy he had accumulated. In both small and large ways, his resistance activities continued for a little more than a year. Perhaps because he had read the burglars' initial statement of purpose at a public gathering just days after the burglary—remarks that led to the first story published about the burglars' explanation of what they had done—journalists called him from time to time that spring to inquire about getting documents from the Media files. He never said he had the files, but he told them he would see what he could do. Invariably, they anonymously received what they wanted. Only once did a reporter ask him if he was involved in the burglary. It was a student reporter for the Haverford campus newspaper. Davidon remembers evading the question and advising the student to write only what he knew. He continued to anonymously mail packets of copies of previously unseen stolen files to journalists about every ten days through mid-May.

Nothing Davidon did after the FBI burglary would have as much impact as the burglary had, but he continued to feel compelled to find new ways to oppose the war. He did so in two daring acts, neither of which involved other people from the Media group. In March 1972, a year after the Media burglary, Davidon was standing in an unlikely spot—by a railroad car filled with bombs in the middle of a field in the rich and gently rolling farmland of York County in southeastern Pennsylvania. This unusual circumstance was, of course, not an accident. Someone who lived in that farming community had told Davidon he had noticed that bombs destined for Vietnam were stored in open railroad cars that appeared to be accessible.

Earlier, Davidon and others had made it more difficult for a few thousand men to be drafted by stealing draft records. Now he warmed to the idea of making the bombs inoperable and, in the process, drawing the attention of local people to the fact that their local economy depended in part on producing weapons used to kill Vietnamese people. The bombs had been manufactured at the nearby American Machine and Foundry Company (AMF) plant and were going to be shipped to Vietnam.

Davidon and two other people went to the field a few times and walked along the tracks, surveying the surrounding area and examining the bombs. They developed a plan to damage as many of them as they could. Following Forsyth's example at Media, in order to avoid having tools that could be traced to a hardware store, they made their own, including modified pliers designed to strip the threads on the bomb casings. New tools in hand, one evening they climbed into the dark railcars and worked for hours among the MK82 bombs, removing the caps and stripping the threads on the casings of hundreds of them. They carefully watched their surroundings inside and outside the railcars and talked softly and as little as necessary as they worked in the dark. Their concerns for security seemed to be unnecessary. They saw no guard—no one, in fact—near the plant or the railway cars during casing or as they worked inside the cars.

A few days later, several reporters, including this one, received a small bulky manila envelope that contained a news release typed in the same italic font that appeared on the letters sent a year earlier with each new packet of stolen FBI documents sent to journalists. With the release was a copy of one of the documents that had been stolen from the Media office and a dark green threaded disk. The last item, as the news release explained, was the plastic cap of one of the 500-pound bombs that a group that called itself the Citizens' Commission to Demilitarize Industry had removed when its members stripped bombs at the AMF plant and "rendered [the bombs] unusable."

In the news release prepared and sent anonymously by Davidon, he wrote that there were links between the FBI burglary and the damaging of the bombs. First, he noted the similarity of their names—the Citizens' Commission to Investigate the FBI and the Citizens' Commission to Demilitarize Industry. "Our two commissions," he wrote, "are responsible for these actions," the burglary of the FBI and the damaging of several hundred casings for MK82 bombs made for the U.S. Navy by the AMF Company. "In addition to objectives and methods, we also share the typewriter on which this and other statements have been typed."

That message must have infuriated the FBI agents who were still searching for the people who had burglarized the FBI office. Now, a year after the break-in, not only had the FBI not arrested the Media burglars or found the typewriter or copiers the burglars had used, but here were anonymous people publicly announcing that they had just used the typewriter the FBI had failed to find in connection with yet another invasion of government property.

Writing for himself and the others, Davidon said the new commission members were not grandiose in their assumptions about the potential impact of their sabotage:

We realize all too well how small our accomplishments are when measured against what must be done to free our society from the forces that sponsor repression and mass murder. We have made public a few secret files and have neutralized a few bombs. But for every FBI file we have made public there are thousands that remain secret. For every bomb we have sabotaged there are tens of thousands yet to be assembled. In themselves, our actions will neither stop governmental repression nor the terror it rains on the people of Indochina. But we have acted and, within the limits imposed upon us, we have succeeded: files have been made public, bombs have been damaged, and the government has been stymied in its efforts to find us, let alone stop us. Our success, we hope, contributes to a new kind of resistance movement in this country—a movement that rejects terror and violence yet is not afraid to deny forcefully the instruments of terror and violence to others.

Like Albert Camus before us, we have chosen to be "neither victims nor executioners."

In his continuing acts of resistance, Davidon wanted officials and the public to know that despite the government's power, it could be confronted in ways that embarrassed it and diminished that power, even if just a little. He wanted people to see that the giant Goliath was vulnerable to small Davids, especially when Davids joined together. He and some other Davids surprised Goliath one more time before Davidon ended his resistance.

A HEADLINE IN the Wednesday, May 31, 1972, *Philadelphia Evening Bulletin*—"3 Air Force Jets Are Sabotaged at Willow Grove"—topped a story that was prominently played in all local news media that day. The previous day had not been a routine Memorial Day at the Willow Grove Naval Air Station. In the wee hours of the morning, three U.S. Air Force Hercules C-130 transport planes, each large enough to carry ninety-two people or up to thirteen tons of cargo, were sabotaged at the station, eighteen miles north of Philadelphia along a main highway. Such planes were routinely used in Vietnam for carrying a wide variety of missiles, and the planes on the station grounds were ready to be sent there.

Electrical and hydraulic lines were cut on the four-engine turboprop transports and some parts were removed sometime after 11 p.m. on May 30. Officials were shocked when they discovered the sabotage at about 6 a.m. when ground crews tried to run routine preflight checks of the planes. They were inoperable. A tool compartment in one plane was open. Hydraulic hose lines to the brake systems and electrical wiring exposed around the undercarriage had been cut. On the exterior of one of the planes, someone had painted in bold red letters BREAD NOT BOMBS along with a large peace symbol.

The public information officer at the base told reporters the next day that whoever the saboteurs were, they knew how to cripple the planes. He said officials feared the sabotage might have been an inside job. An inspection of the two-mile perimeter fence showed no evidence, he said, that anyone had broken through or climbed over the fence. Officials were perplexed about how anyone could have entered and left the field undetected. "It is not known how these people got aboard the base or managed to elude Navy and

Air Force security patrols," the PI officer said. "I am certain they did not come through the main gate," he told a reporter. "Visitors at night must be cleared by a telephone call from the person they wish to see." He also said there was "no evidence that the saboteurs broke through or went over the fence." The damaged green-camouflaged planes were parked that night on a concrete ramp about half a mile from the busy north-south highway that was the eastern border of the fenced field. They had returned from flights at 11 p.m. that night. When the sabotage was discovered, security was tripled immediately at the base.

Yet another Citizens' Commission anonymously took responsibility for this sabotage. This one, the Citizens' Commission to Interdict War Materiel, anonymously announced that it had damaged planes at Willow Grove as a protest of the Vietnam War. A person who said he spoke for that group called the *Evening Bulletin,* as well as other Philadelphia-area news media outlets, and described the damage the group had done. The details he provided matched the damage described by the Navy public information officer when he was contacted a short time later.

The anonymous caller, Davidon, read a statement that later was mailed to news organizations:

> Our Citizens' Commission to Interdict War Materiel has carefully chosen ways which endanger no one for grounding these planes. . . . This action occurs appropriately on traditional Memorial Day, for we best remember those killed in war by protecting the lives and rights of those who are not yet its victims. If we had not acted now, these planes would have continued to supply the current U.S. war machine which is devastating four countries in Indochina. The way we chose was carefully done so no one would be injured. There was no fire or explosion, in sharp contrast to the daily murder of hundreds of people by the Nixon Administration in its desperate effort to impose the Thieu regime on South Vietnam.

Group members had spent several evenings at the field developing their plan. Their first and most important discovery was that the Navy used only a standard padlock on the gate in the chain-link fence near the planes. They hacked off the old padlock and replaced it with one exactly like the one in place but with a key only they possessed. After repeated observation of the field, they established the precise timing of the frequent patrol rounds made by security guards in a jeep that passed very close to the parked planes on each patrol. They decided they needed two cycles of rounds by the security guards to accomplish their goals. That night, they waited for the jeep to pass, unlocked the gate, and ran to the planes, one of them armed with a can of red paint, the others ready to use the tools inside the planes. They hunkered down inside the cockpits so they couldn't be seen as the jeep passed. After the second time it passed, they jumped out of the planes, ran to the gate, locked the padlock, and ran to their cars. All was done, of course, while wearing gloves.

Between stripping threads on bombs in York and sabotaging planes in Willow Grove, on April 24, 1972, Davidon went for a canoe ride on Sandy Hook Bay in northern New Jersey. Not surprisingly, it was not just a pleasant outing. He and forty-four other Philadelphia antiwar activists in seventeen aluminum canoes and light rowboats rowed out to conduct what they called a blockade of the munitions ship USS *Nitro*, which was departing for the Atlantic to transfer ammunition to aircraft carriers bound for Vietnam.

From their tiny canoes, they yelled to the many sailors looking down at them from the *Nitro* and urged them to jump ship and refuse to go to Vietnam. It was just a symbolic action, but seven of the sailors accepted the invitation and jumped over the side of the ship and swam to the boats. All the Navy men were captured and returned to the *Nitro,* and some of the demonstrators were arrested.

The day after the sabotage at Willow Grove, the commanding officer of the 913th Tactical Air Lift Command, which operated the planes, said a joint investigation of the sabotage was under way by the FBI and the Air Force Special Investigation Division. Once again, Davidon was never questioned by investigators. No arrests were ever made.

By the time the sabotage at Willow Grove was being investigated, Davidon had been avoiding arrest for break-ins and sabotage for three years. The only time the FBI got in touch with him and questioned him during the entire period of his protest was in July 1970, when they queried him regarding a surprise appearance by Daniel Berrigan when the poet-priest briefly emerged out of the underground, with help from Davidon, and gave a sermon at a Methodist church in Philadelphia. It took place just weeks before he was found by FBI agents on Block Island, Rhode Island, and taken to prison to begin serving his sentence for his Catonsville conviction. Davidon willingly talked with agents then, but he told them only what was already publicly known about Berrigan's appearance.

Beginning in 1977, however, the FBI was in touch with Davidon regularly—on his initiative. He took advantage, as any citizen could by then, of Congress's 1974 strengthening of the FOIA, one of the transparency reforms set in motion after the burglary. He submitted a written request for his FBI file. Letters were exchanged between him and officials in the FOIA office of the FBI for at least four years.

He received only a few files initially, and they were not very revealing. He suggested there might be more. More trickled out to him. One of the documents he received noted that he was on the FBI's Security Index, the existence of which had been revealed in the stolen files. In a January 26, 1978, letter to Allen H. McCreight, chief of the Freedom of Information/ Privacy Acts Branch of the FBI, Davidon wrote, "The material you sent me on January 5 indicates that I was placed on a 'Security Index' by the F.B.I., and I would like to know if such an Index is still maintained, what its significance is, and whether I am still listed on it. Thank you for your help." Davidon does not remember receiving answers to those questions, and a search of the files he received does not include any.

On February 1, 1979, a letter to Davidon from Thomas H. Bresson, the acting chief of the bureau's FOIA office, noted that pursuant to a phone conversation a few days earlier between Davidon and someone in the FOIA office, the investigative file of the burglary of the Media FBI office, the MEDBURG file, would be processed and eventually would be available for his perusal at FBI headquarters. Sometime later, he was notified that it was taking more time than expected to process the very large MEDBURG file—nearly 34,000 pages. The official apologized to Davidon for the delay and assured him he would be notified when the file was available. That the MEDBURG file had not been processed until Davidon requested it suggests that the first person who asked to see the MEDBURG file must have been none other than the mastermind of the burglary.

DAVIDON SEEMED to be almost surprised by his realization years later that during his years of intense antiwar activity he "never thought through the implications" of his actions on his family. "In some vague sense I knew what the implications might be, but I did not give much weight to the possibility of getting caught or of having my life disrupted. I never made plans with regard to Ann and the kids in terms of anything long-lasting happening to me. I knew it was a possibility. I knew that was one of the things that could occur, but I did not plan on it." Without thinking about it very much, he compartmentalized his life in ways that made it easy for him not to think much about how his actions might affect his family.

By the time he moved to Haverford, he and his first wife, the mother of his oldest child, Alan, a future prosecutor in Phoenix, had been divorced several years. In 1963 he married Ann Morrissett, who, like him, was active in the peace movement. She served on boards of various peace organizations and often attended rallies with Davidon and their young daughters—Ruth, who was born in 1964, and Sarah, who was born in 1967.

In recent years, Davidon has thought often, and sometimes with great sadness, about how he handled the potential impact of his resistance on his family. He finds it a perplexing dilemma, a balancing act, even many years later. On the one hand, he thinks it is very important for people who risk arrest in resistance to think about how their actions may affect the people closest to them. On the other hand, he thinks, as he did then, that perhaps they should not do so too much. He worries that too much time spent contemplating the possible painful impact of one's resistance on others could lead to refusing to take a risk. "In some sense," he said, "it's like walking across a very narrow walkway over a high place. You don't want to spend too much time looking down at the ground twenty stories below. If you do, you won't go." He recalls that he seldom looked down during his resistance years.

But now, in his eighties, he wonders if he did not think much about such matters because he may have "had too much confidence" in those days. After the first draft board raids were successful, he recalls no longer being very fearful. "That was foolhardy," he says now, "given all the things that could have gone wrong." He remembers that he never thought the Media burglary would not be successful. He never really thought anyone would be arrested. "I knew it was a possibility, but I didn't plan for it. At times, I thought about the possibility of going to prison. I thought that life in prison might take place for me, but I think I just pushed it aside." He thinks now that that attitude was a mistake.

He doesn't recall being aware at the time that there were others in the group, especially John Raines, who were very fearful about what might happen to their families as a result of the burglary. "I think I was probably more irresponsible in that respect," he says. "I know John and Bonnie did do a lot of thinking about these matters. I wasn't really thinking through the consequences of getting caught. I was assuming it wouldn't happen."

Actually, Ann Morrissett said she did not want to talk with Davidon about his resistance activities. In an interview, she told me she paid as little attention as possible to that part of her husband's life. She regarded the burglaries with disgust, as an egotistical macho exercise. She was particularly disgusted by the burglary of the FBI office. Her rejection of such resistance was evident at their home the morning after the burglary. When Davidon left for Media early the evening of the burglary, he reminded her that the break-in would take place that night and that he might not be home until the next morning. He arrived home about 6:30 a.m. He remembers telling Ann at breakfast that "everything went well last night." Both of them think she may have said nothing in response. He had just experienced what was one of the most important accomplishments of his life, and it was not discussed. That was a stark contrast to the spirit of jubilation and relief the Raineses experienced as they sat at breakfast that morning with their children.

According to both Morrissett and Davidon, they had few heart-to-heart conversations about important matters, including Davidon's resistance activities. They had very similar worldviews but disagreed on some of the methods of accomplishing their goals. As Davidon has searched in recent years for an explanation of how he handled these matters, he has often been sad but also philosophical. "Families that are close share things naturally," he said. "Some families don't have that kind of close relationship. . . . Too close an involvement of people who are not directly involved can in some situations interfere with what you really want to get done," he says as he assesses why two people, he and Ann, who had very similar values, did not talk much about his resistance activities. "Building the warmth and closeness within the family is a crucial value but not the only value." They were divorced in 1978 after fifteen years of marriage.

Interestingly, during that time, Davidon said, he got a glimpse of what a warm household could be like from some of the Catholic activists. The large Davidon-Morrissett home on the Haverford campus was strategically located midway between Washington, D.C., and New York, and several times small groups of the Catholic resisters stayed at the house on their way to those cities. Many years later, Davidon still remembers their visits warmly. When they were there, he said, the house would come alive with the "great life, great spirit of these people. It impressed me. I suppose because it was a contrast, both from the specifics of my life at home at that time, and also, I guess, from my personality."

In 1987, Davidon and Maxine Libros, a psychotherapist, were married. They talked freely with each other about their pasts. Libros was proud of Davidon's resistance. She didn't know him at the time he was an activist, but she knew of him through her long friendship with his brother and sister-in-law. She admits that if she had been married to Davidon in 1971, she, like Morrissett, may not have had much enthusiasm for, or at least may have

Davidon and Maxine Libros married in 1987. She did not know him during
his resistance years, but she was proud of what he accomplished during that
time. *(Photo by Betty Medsger)*

been frightened by, the prospect of his burglarizing an FBI office. It was
good, she said, to be in love with him and share his life many years after his
resistance when she was free to admire his courage and accomplishments
but not have the burden of worrying about the risks involved.

During their years together, Libros and Davidon often talked about the
Vietnam War and resistance to it. One evening during a joint interview, as
they discussed the Media burglary, Libros's pride in his role was obvious.
She smiled warmly as Davidon described some of the methods of resistance
he and others used. She admitted that she questioned the value of some of
them. As she searched for the words to describe her reservations, he helped
her. "You aren't quite sure that this was the best way to build opposition to
the war?" he asked. She nodded yes. So did he. "Even I wasn't always sure
this was the best way to build opposition," he acknowledged. He paused
as he contemplated what both of them had just said. Then he described
the pained conclusion he reached years ago. Sure, he disliked some of the
methods he had used, perhaps especially burglary, but he refused to let himself become frozen by such concerns. He was humbled, even troubled at
times, but never frozen. She understood. Despite her minor reservations, she
applauded what he did then.

At the time Davidon married Libros, he was still very interested in various social issues, but he was not consumed by them, as he had been years earlier. He now cherished personal happiness as he never had before, and experienced it with Libros until her sudden death in July 2010 from an aneurysm. By that time, he had Parkinson's disease and, unable to live alone, moved from Philadelphia to a residence for seniors near his daughter, Sarah Davidon Hoover, who lives in Colorado. (Her former husband, Alex Hoover, is not related to the late FBI director.)

In his renewed close relationship with daughter Sarah, a member of the pediatrics faculty at the University of Colorado School of Medicine, Davidon occasionally talks with her about the profound impact his resistance could have had on his wife and daughters. Sometimes he cries as he thinks about how his actions then "might have drastically changed our lives." She comforts him at such times by dwelling on her appreciation of what he did and on the fact that she is grateful to have this chance to renew a close relationship with him. Davidon is deeply pleased that Sarah is appreciative of his past. After studying the impact of the Media burglary, she told him she was proud of his place in history, not a description he ever would use for what he did, but one that brought a smile to his face when she said it.

Daughter Sarah was amused when she read the word-by-word transcripts of the FBI recordings of conversations on the family's home phone, the bugging a result of an order by Attorney General John Mitchell. Their home phones were tapped from November 24, 1970, through January 6, 1971—precisely the period when Davidon was recruiting the Media burglars and making arrangements by phone for meetings with each of them. After the tap had been on for about two weeks, the FBI director informed the attorney general in a memo that "this surveillance has produced highly significant information to corroborate Davidon's involvement" with the Catholic activists. However, Hoover and bureau investigators thought the conversations they recorded were related to the Harrisburg case, when in fact they probably were related to the burglary of the Media office. In any event, agents in the Philadelphia office, where the transcripts were made, apparently thought the tap was not productive and succeeded in convincing the director not to reinstitute it after January 6, 1971. By then the burglary team had been formed and casing was about to begin. One recorded comment by Davidon—that he had been up all night lately and needed to collapse—could have been taken as a clue but apparently was not.

One of the transcripts is a precise record of Ruth Davidon, then seven, talking with a little friend about her birthday party and asking if the cake would be vanilla or chocolate. In another transcript, Bob Williamson is recorded briefly chatting with one of the Davidon daughters and asking her when Davidon would be home.

Ruth Davidon did not learn about her father's role in the Media burglary until 1992. Now an anesthesiologist in San Francisco and twice a finalist for the U.S. Olympic women's rowing team, she eventually realized that she had learned some lessons from her activist parents that most children probably do not pick up from their parents. For instance, "I was an adolescent before I realized that being apathetic was an option." Their approach to life has made her take for granted that "when you see something wrong, you should act to try to fix it." Even some of her games were affected by her parents' activism. When other kids played phone, Ruth remembers that they might say, "I can't talk now, I have to go shopping." Not Ruth. When she pretended she was an adult who didn't have time to talk on the phone, she would say, "I can't talk now. I have to go to a meeting."

As a little girl in 1971, Ruth remembers, she kept hearing a strange term used to describe her father—"unindicted coconspirator." "We, the family, would go to parties at friends' houses, and people would come up and say, 'Oh, here's the unindicted coconspirator!' They were laughing and treating him well. So I went to school and said, 'My dad's an unindicted coconspirator.' The teacher looked amazed and said, 'Indicted? Your father's been indicted?' I could tell that the teacher didn't think it was a good thing. I started to be quieter about my parents.

"I remember asking my dad, 'Are you going to jail?' When he would say he might, I would cry and say things like, 'It's not worth it. Can't you just stay home with me and don't do this stuff anymore?' . . . The concept of jail was so scary."

When Davidon told Ruth years later that he was one of the Media burglars, she was proud. "I feel good about what he did, but it's easy for me to sit here now and say that because I'm so happy and healthy and have a great life. . . . It's easy for me now to say, 'I'm glad he did it because it was for such a good cause.' I think he did the right thing, but if he had gone to jail for twenty years, and I was in drug rehab today, I might think differently."

Like her sister, Ruth Davidon hopes she "would have the courage he had if something drastic happened that needed a response. I'd want to be able to make sure my children were okay, cared for and emotionally okay, but I want to be able to take risks." Perhaps the most important lesson she learned from him: "I want what I say and what I do to be consistent."

Sarah Davidon Hoover remembers sitting in a backpack on her father's back at several antiwar rallies. Even when he was not a speaker, she had a vague sense that he was liked and respected as a leader. People would gather around him to ask his opinion. When she discovered later the seriousness of some of his endeavors, she said, she realized that "pretty typical people can do atypical things and make a difference."

FEARFUL THAT decreased opposition to the war would encourage Nixon and his war advisers to think the American people didn't care about the war, Davidon thought it was important to keep pressing the point—this war must stop—even after all the jeopardy he had accumulated at Media. He continued to move from one action to another, some of them potentially very dangerous, in order to remind people that the war still raged in Vietnam. These actions, he said, flowed from his commitment to Albert Camus's belief that it was necessary "to keep alive a living society within the shell of the dying one."

At critical times, Davidon believed, a life should be useful. Without realizing it, he had forced himself to answer the profoundly challenging question posed by Dietrich Bonhoeffer in the midst of his deep despair about the Third Reich. As Bonhoeffer, the German theologian and resistance fighter who was hanged by the Nazis on orders from Adolf Hitler, contemplated the very heavy responsibilities of conscience posed by being aware of extreme injustice, he wrote in a letter sent from prison in 1943: "We have been silent witnesses of evil deeds; we have been drenched by many storms; we learnt the art of equivocation and pretense; experience has made us suspicious of others and kept us from being truthful and open; intolerable conflicts have worn us down and even made us cynical."

Finally, Bonhoeffer asked, "Are we still of any use?"

Davidon asked himself that question throughout the Vietnam War. He concluded that to be of use during the war he should keep trying to find ways to oppose it and to invite others to do so as well. It was that desire to defeat despair and keep hope alive in the midst of a seemingly endless war that made him push fear aside and move from one act of resistance to another. He continued during those years of repeated resistance to dislike the idea of breaking and entering, of destroying property, of risking personal confrontation with a guard. He hated the use of deception. But he hated the escalation of the war more. He hated the possibility that the FBI had created a police state and that no government officials would act to determine if that was true.

"When you feel, as I did, not only in the case of the prosecution of the Vietnam War, but also in many things being done by your government," Davidon said, "it feels as though the forces you are fighting are so huge in comparison to what we can influence. At times like that, how do you keep alive the struggle to influence? It was a matter of keeping alive a sense of purpose and accomplishment when the forces seemed so overwhelming.

"Not just Media, but a lot of other actions were important to me, to others, in just building that sense that the struggle isn't futile. . . . Sometimes we accomplished more than we had reason to expect, as in Media. It was a long shot. We didn't know if we would find anything important. Other times, we never knew if we accomplished anything—the draft boards, deactivating bombs, we didn't know. But it gave voice and a sense of purpose. It built little pockets of life that made sense at a terrible time."

On November 8, 2013, after having had Parkinson's disease for many years, Davidon passed away in Colorado. His daughter Sarah was with him as he died a peaceful death.

25

You Didn't Do That

NAH, you didn't do that."

When a stunned Nathan Raines was finally able to speak, that's what he said to his parents when they told him that one night, a couple days after his second birthday, they were part of a group that burglarized an FBI office. As they told him, Nathan, in his late teens by then, could not believe what he was hearing. He took it in slowly, disbelieving but also realizing that his parents—this good-looking, hardworking couple, people he knew so well, the people who had nurtured him through physical disaster as well as very happy times—were not joking.

"To me it was like some World War II spy novel. I couldn't believe my parents . . . four children, a station wagon . . . had been involved in something this elaborate." They once were burglars? Nah.

Bonnie and John Raines revealed their big secret to each of their four children separately. After initially expressing shock, each child moved through a range of reactions as they absorbed this stunning information from their parents. The Raineses told them the basic information and then provided more details as each child asked questions. They had always planned to tell the children at some point. "It was such a significant part of our lives," says Bonnie Raines. "I think we felt that there really wasn't any way of their finally understanding their parents without knowing that."

After learning their parents' secret, each of the children asked questions over weeks, even years. None of them could imagine their parents carrying out a burglary. They could not imagine their mother, wearing gloves, her beautiful black hair hidden under a stocking hat, casing an FBI office.

Or their dad waiting in a getaway car—the old family station wagon they remembered so well—in a dark parking lot. Though the children were adults when the Raineses finally told them, even then they didn't tell them the most frightening parts—for instance, that the FBI came to the house shortly after the burglary and directly asked John Raines if he was involved in Media. They saved that news for later.

Like his three siblings, Nathan thought often about what his parents had told him. He kept asking questions. It was like adding pieces to a complex mosaic: what they did, how they did it, why they did it, what it meant to them, and what it meant to the country. Then, like his siblings, he moved beyond the basic facts and questions to profound questions:

How could they have been that brave?
How did they develop the skills necessary to succeed in pulling off a
    burglary?
How was it possible for them to care so much about a cause that they
    were willing to risk going to prison for many years?

That question led to the most difficult one of all:

How could they have cared so deeply about anything that they were
    willing to risk having the family severed?

The Raineses explained the promise they had made to each other to try to find the courage to resist great injustice together. They told the children they had made arrangements for them to be raised by Uncle Bob and Bonnie Raines's parents, Dorothy and Andrew Muir, if they went to prison. The children loved Uncle Bob, and they loved the Muirs, but they could not imagine what it would have been like to live for years with them while their parents were in prison. More precisely, they could not imagine what it would have been like to grow up without their parents.

When they were first told about the burglary, each of the children asked if their parents were still in danger of being arrested. They were relieved to hear that they felt sure the FBI was no longer interested in them and that their freedom no longer was threatened. But just imagining what might have happened was very painful for each of the children, as it was for the Raineses. "Thank God things didn't go wrong," says Nathan.

Lindsley admits that despite her pride in what they did, occasionally she

Bonnie with Lindsley, the oldest Raines child, age eight, in 1971, the year of the burglary. The Raineses told her about the burglary when she was in college. They did not tell the other children until many years later.

feels "a little bit angry when I think about what could have happened . . . that they were willing to take that risk." As a mother of three now, she cannot imagine doing the same.

She and Mark, age eight and seven at the time of the burglary, searched for clues they might have seen then. The children didn't know where their parents and the other people went when they left the house early each evening. Nor did they know what happened late at night in the attic. Bonnie Raines remembers telling them during that period, late 1970 through March 1971, that they must never go to the attic. Despite that warning, they recall that they did go up there. They saw maps and drawings on the wall of the forbidden room where, they now realize, people they knew as their parents' friends developed the strategy for the FBI burglary and its aftermath late at night while Keith Forsyth practiced speeding up his lock-picking skills. They thought what they saw on the wall was just part of their parents' work.

As she tried to remember that time, Lindsley recalled something that seemed highly relevant. Her mother once told her that because the FBI might be tapping their phone it was important to be careful about what she said on the phone. Lindsley didn't understand what the FBI was, or why it might be interested in what she said, but she remembers thinking at first that it was "kind of cool" that the FBI, whatever it was, might be interested in her conversations. But then she had a second thought: "What if I say a curse word? Am I going to get in trouble?"

She also remembered Bob Williamson, but as her troubadour, not as a burglar. She has fond memories of him playing his guitar as she sang along. He would sing her favorite songs and also make up songs just for her. Sometimes he played until she fell asleep.

After Mark learned about the burglary, he read some of the stolen documents. He was angry about what the FBI was doing, and he was very proud of his parents' role in revealing it.

The three oldest children always knew their parents were politically engaged. Even when the children were very young, the Raineses talked to them about the civil rights movement, about the war in Vietnam. They took the children to the trials of friends and to demonstrations. They hoped such experiences would plant seeds that would make the children aware of injustice and the need to do something about it. Once the children went with Bonnie Raines to get their father out of jail when he was arrested and jailed at a military base in New Jersey in 1970 as he tried, along with other activists, to block a freight train loaded with napalm that was on its way to a port to be shipped to Vietnam. After she got a call saying he was in jail, Bonnie Raines corralled the children into the station wagon and drove to the office of Uncle Bob, then pastor of a prominent Methodist church in Philadelphia, to get the $300 in cash she needed to pay John's fine. Mother and children then sped off to rescue him.

As the youngest child, Mary did not have such experiences. She was literally the embodiment of the confidence they had by 1975 that they probably were not going to be arrested for Media. By the time she was growing up, they seldom went to demonstrations and trials. Perhaps because Mary did not have Vietnam-era memories of her parents and their friends, it may have been even more difficult for her to imagine them burglarizing an FBI office. As she talked with Mark and Nathan months after learning about the burglary, she searched for words to describe the conundrum their secret posed for her. "You look at your parents as being, you know—"

Nathan gently suggests, "Authority figures?"

"Yes," Mary readily agrees that's what she means. "And here they were doing crazy things like I think happens only in movies. Mom's telling about how she walked in and was wearing those gloves and scoping out the place. It was all like a big spy movie to me. I could not believe that my parents actually did something like that." As she sorted it out with her brothers,

Mary seemed to be proud, amazed, and confused all at once. "I don't think I can feel what they were feeling, but I think I understand now how strongly they felt in order to put so much at risk. . . . Somebody needed to do it. . . . Maybe no one else thought of it. Once they knew it needed to be done, they had to go ahead. They had to take things into their own hands. Still, I could not believe that my parents did something like that."

Nathan shares her sense of amazement. Learning what they did that night, he said, "made me look at them in a different light.

"I have nothing but pride about what they did," he said years after his initial shock. "Pride and a sense of duty that I have to sort of try to carry on what my parents started. . . . I think we all have felt a need to continue what they've started. . . . They risked everything. But they knew that this information was important enough that the public needed to know about it." A counselor in a very poor public middle school in North Philadelphia, Nathan says that "if there was a situation where I felt the government was overstepping its bounds, I would absolutely consider doing something similar to what they did."

Each of the Raines children echoes the pride Nathan expresses. "I definitely was proud of them," says Mary. "It was kind of like having a rock star parent, but in a cooler way. I don't really idolize . . . except for people like Martin Luther King." At some point, she realized that her parents, like the few people she idolized, also put a lot on the line. They "did something for the country. . . . They risked a lot." As the mother of two small children now, she can't imagine taking the same risk. But they "fueled the fire for us to . . . make our own individual choices based on the values that they taught us." Mary's most recent job was as an attorney investigating police misconduct for the Independent Police Review Authority in Chicago.

The Raineses shared their secret first with Lindsley. She knew it for several years before her siblings were told. The day they told her is etched very clearly in her mind. They had come to visit her on parents' weekend one autumn when she was a student at Denison University in Granville, Ohio. "We went for a walk down the hill. There's this quiet place." As the three of them sat down in a beautiful sheltered spot, one of her parents said, "We have something to tell you."

Lindsley, now a social worker in the trauma unit of Cooper Memorial Hospital in Camden, New Jersey, remembers thinking, " 'My God, they're getting divorced.' . . . They told me the story. And I just remember thinking, 'Oh my God.' I really had no idea that this had happened. . . . I was amazed and awestruck. . . . I just remember being blown away, like . . . I can't believe that they did it, first of all, and that they got away with it. . . . The consequences didn't cross my mind then. . . . And then they said, 'But you can't tell anybody!' I'm like, 'Okay.' . . . I was the oldest and the first one to know, and so that was kind of a little prize, a little package for me that I could hold on to. . . . I was happy to know. . . . They were acknowledging that I was old enough and mature enough to sort of deal with it and appreciate what they had done."

AT FAMILY GATHERINGS in the Philadelphia row house where the Raineses moved after the children were all on their own, or at the old house in Glen Lake in northern Michigan, where their children, and now grandchildren, all like to gather every summer, questions still come up occasionally about the biggest family secret, the night John and Bonnie Raines burglarized an FBI office. Many stories have been told. They laugh when they remember the story about Nathan's best friend. When Nathan told him the big secret about his parents, the friend did not believe him. "You're making this story up, just to look cool, to make your parents look cool," he said. "I suppose you'll tell me next they're art thieves."

"We laugh and shake our heads at the same time," says Lindsley. Though the children have now been privy to the big secret for years, a sense of wonderment occasionally still emerges when they talk about what their parents did that night in 1971, and they still can't quite imagine how it was possible.

The stories that piece together how it was possible for Bonnie and John Raines to say yes when Davidon asked them what they thought of burglarizing an FBI office begin with John filling out a form that came across his desk in the spring of 1961 at the small Methodist church where he worked in Setauket, a community on the North Shore of Long Island. It was an invitation from the Congress of Racial Equality (CORE) to travel to the South that summer as a Freedom Rider. At the time, his decision to participate did not seem particularly consequential. He had no plans for the summer and thought this might be an interesting thing to do.

Little did he know. Becoming a Freedom Rider that summer introduced him to an America he did not know and transformed him into a person he had not planned to be. It led to his marriage to Bonnie Muir, to their unusual commitment to joint participation in acts of nonviolent resistance, and ultimately to their driving to Media in March 1971.

CORE planned the Freedom Rides to force open the access to transportation the U.S. Supreme Court had ordered when it ruled, in *Boynton v. Virginia* in December 1960, that segregation in interstate transportation facilities was illegal. After that court decision, government agencies did not move to enforce it, and the facilities remained segregated. CORE officials concluded that transportation facilities would remain segregated until people forced authorities to apply the new law, just as public schools remained segregated until brave black people enrolled in previously all-white schools, despite angry whites standing in schoolhouse doors barring their entrance. After much violence and the intervention of federal troops, local authorities were forced to abide by the 1954 Supreme Court ruling that required integration of public schools. Now CORE's Freedom Riders would force access by black people to public transportation with a similar method: teams of black and white people would ride buses together. If attempts were made to deny black people that right, the integrated team would insist that the new law be enforced. In the end, 450 people, including John Raines, volunteered and made up sixty teams, each half black and half white, that traveled throughout the South that summer and fall. They endured arrests and beatings, the burning of some of their buses, and even attempts to burn the Riders themselves. In one town, angry white women broke through circles of white men surrounding the Freedom Riders and madly clawed their faces until they drew blood.

At the end of the suffering, the Riders achieved their goal: In November 1961, the Interstate Commerce Commission issued rules on how the law established by the U.S. Supreme Court would be enforced.

This was new territory for John Raines. He had not been very interested in the civil rights movement. He was aware of Rosa Parks's heroic role in the Montgomery, Alabama, bus boycott in 1955, but he had not been either intellectually or emotionally engaged in such issues. He had never, for instance, preached a sermon on civil rights or racial issues. Shortly before the CORE invitation reached him, he had made an important decision about his future. He had notified officials at the Setauket church that he was leaving his post as pastor, a position he had held for two years, to return to Union Theological Seminary to study for a doctoral degree in Christian social ethics. He had finalized arrangements to work as an assistant at the seminary to Professor Reinhold Niebuhr, one of the most respected theologians of the twentieth century. Then twenty-seven, Raines had decided that the academic life, rather than life as a pastor, was the life he preferred. This decision was a detour from family expectations. Raines's father was then a prominent Methodist bishop, based in Indianapolis, and his two brothers were both ordained Methodist ministers. But he was looking forward to the change. He longed for the rich intellectual life of the seminary in Morning-side Heights, adjacent to Columbia University, and to preparing for a career as a professor.

He was planning to teach social ethics, not planning to apply them to the point of subjecting himself to arrest, something that would be very likely now that he had agreed to become a Freedom Rider. Before he left for the South, he knew Freedom Riders on the first buses that went south had been attacked and their buses set on fire. There also had been news reports about the threatening attack one evening at a crowded African American church in Montgomery, Alabama. As local black people held a special service to thank the Freedom Riders for their bravery and commitment, an angry white mob circled the church and threw rocks and Molotov cocktails at it. The scene was hellish—black people inside the church, including the Rev-erend Dr. Martin Luther King, singing joyously as they thanked black and white Freedom Riders for their courage, and white people outside the church puncturing the inside music with explosions that threatened to destroy the church and those in it. Federal marshals arrived to control the mob, but they were unable to do so. It was not until National Guardsmen arrived that many hours later the people who had been kept inside the church all night to protect them from the mob were freed.

What had been a relatively casual decision about how to spend his sum-mer turned out to be much more for John Raines. Whatever he originally thought about whether CORE was overreacting by requiring every Freedom Rider to attend workshops in how to maintain nonviolent behavior no mat-ter how badly one was treated, he soon realized such training was necessary. After he finished the training, he flew to St. Louis in early July to meet his fellow Freedom Riders for a bus ride to their first destination, Little Rock. His fellow Freedom Riders included one of the organizers of the Freedom Rides, the Reverend Benjamin Elton Cox, then twenty-nine and the African American pastor of Pilgrim Congregational Church in High Point, North Carolina, and Janet Reinitz, then twenty-three, a white artist from New York City.

As they traveled south into Arkansas, word spread in Little Rock that an integrated bus was on its way to the local bus station. When the Freedom Riders' bus pulled into the bus terminal, an angry white mob was waiting inside. As the Riders walked into the terminal they quickly realized the game they were expected to play. In a not very subtle attempt to be techni-cally in compliance with the new federal law that required racially integrated transportation facilities—while simultaneously maintaining segregation—

the old "white" and "black" passenger areas had been renamed "integrated" and "segregated." The "integrated" area was for black people, and the "segregated" area was for white people. Police tried to guide the Freedom Riders toward the area designated for black people. The Riders conferred briefly about how to deal with the subterfuge, and then, led by Cox, they slowly and calmly walked together into the area designated for white people.

Raines remembers the white mob screaming at them furiously at that point. The police chief, Paul Glascock, was surprised and enraged at the Freedom Riders. He had apparently thought the riders would go along with the transparent trick. He promptly arrested them under a state breach-of-the-peace statute and took four of the five to jail. The fifth, a high school student, obeyed his order to return to St. Louis.

Actually, no Freedom Rider was supposed to be arrested in Little Rock. Local and state officials were desperate to prevent the city from being in the spotlight again. In 1957, it had received international notoriety when the governor, Orval Faubus, supported white segregationists when they publicly defied efforts of African American students to integrate the city's Central High School. Shocking scenes of violent white mobs attacking African Americans and using their bodies as barricades to keep black children from entering school were broadcast nightly on national network news and abroad.

In anticipation of the Freedom Riders coming to Little Rock, orders had gone out from officials that there should be no repeat in 1961 of those 1957 scenes. Even Governor Faubus was upset about their arrests. As the local *Gazette* editorialized while the riders were behind bars, "The quicker the defendants can be freed the better for the community."

The judge assigned to their case, Judge Quinn Glover, told them he would suspend their sentences if they returned to their homes. No way. They had more bus rides to take. They refused his offer. Days later, he ordered that they be brought to his chambers for a private meeting. "I know you have a right to do what you did. I know the mob, not you, was the threat to the peace," John Raines recalls the judge telling them, "but if I don't find you guilty, I won't get reelected." Trying to appeal to their racial justice instincts, Judge Glover said, "And the other guy is worse on niggrahs than I am." He told them he would set them free if they agreed to get out of town. Unwilling earlier to promise to go home, they were willing now to agree to get out of town. After all, they wanted to ride to their next assignment, and it seemed as though they had made their point in Little Rock. They grabbed their new freedom, left the courthouse, and boarded a bus for Louisiana.

CROWDED BUS STOP. Crowd mills about Negro and white Freedom Riders, upper right, who arrived last night in Little Rock, Ark., and were soon arrested. At far right is Rev. John C. Raines, former pastor of Setauket Methodist Church on Long Island.

Pastor From LI Jailed As Little Rock 'Rider'

(Special to Newsday)

Little Rock, Ark.—Freedom Riders arrived in Arkansas for the first time last night, were greeted by a menacing crowd and arrested without any outbreak of violence. One of the four riders jailed for refusing to leave a white waiting room was the Rev. John C. Raines, 27, who just completed a two-year term as pastor of the Setauket, L.I., Methodist Church.

The rider, two Negroes and two whites, were held in $500 bond under a state law enacted in 1959 to prevent disturbances due to sit-in demonstrations. It outlaws creating a threat of breach of the peace. A fifth rider, an 18-year-old Negro girl, waited outside the station. She was taken into custody, but later released. Little Rock was the scene of one of the earliest and most violent demonstrations against public school integration.

The Freedom Riders arrived last night on a Midwest Trailways bus from St. Louis. They were met by a crowd of about 250, most of them teenagers, who surged toward the waiting room—jeering and holding up soft drink bottles. Police Chief R. E. Glasscock told the riders to leave because they threatened a breach of the peace. They refused to go and were taken in police cars to the city jail.

The Rev. Mr. Raines left Setauket last week to join the program of the Committee on Racial Equality (CORE) in St. Louis. The Rev. Harrison Davis, Methodist district superintendent for Long Island, said he had just completed "a fine and happy ministry" at the Setauket church, where he served for more than two years. He is a graduate of Union Theological Seminary in New York and plans to return there this fall to begin work for a doctorate degree. His father is the Rev. Richard C. Raines, Methodist bishop of the Indiana area. Freedom Riders arrested with the Rev. Mr.

Raines were the Rev. B. Elton Cox, 30, of St. Louis, field secretary of CORE, a Negro; Ann Bliss Malone, 23, St. Louis, a Negro, and Mrs. Janet Reinitz, 23, New York City, who is white. Miss Annie Lumpkin, 18, of St. Louis, a Negro, was not held. She said she was instructed not to go inside. She stayed at the home of a Little Rock Negro minister.

Cited of four who were arrested were arraigned until tomorrow in Municipal Court today to give their attorney time to prepare a defense. Negro attorney Thad Williams asked for the trial delay and said the four would remain in jail and no attempt would be made to raise bond. Williams said he was retained by CORE. "I think they were surprised that they were arrested here," Williams said. "I've been in that (bus station) waiting room myself." The maximum penalty on the misdemeanor charge is a $500 fine, six months in jail, or both. The riders were originally scheduled to travel from Little Rock to Shreveport, La.

Meanwhile, in Jackson, Miss., a three-judge federal panel—with one dissenting—yesterday postponed hearing a suit asking for a halt to the arrest of Freedom Riders in Mississippi. The National Association for the Advancement of Colored People (NAACP) filed the court action and the Justice Department yesterday joined the case as a "friend of the court."

Despite objections lodged by Chief Justice Elbert Tuttle of the United States Fifth Circuit Court of Appeals, the panel postponed the case until Aug. 7 because of the illness of a Mississippi assistant attorney general.

The Justice Department's "friend of the court" brief asked for an injunction to stop Mississippi from enforcing state statutes calling its racial segregation of travelers, and called such laws clearly unconstitutional.

Story in *Newsday*, a Long Island newspaper, about the young local minister, John Raines, who became a Freedom Rider in the South in the summer of 1961.

Raines being booked at the Little Rock jail. Days later, a judge freed him and his fellow Freedom Riders on condition that they leave town.
(*Photo from Orval Eugene Faubus Collection, University of Arkansas Libraries*)

As the Freedom Riders emerged from a bus in Shreveport, they looked up and saw police snipers lining the edge of the roof of the bus station, their rifles aimed at the Freedom Riders. Local police had completely sealed off the bus terminal. No tests of laws would take place there that day. Dave Dennis, a local man who had just been released from Mississippi's Parchman State Prison where he had been imprisoned for his role as a Freedom Rider just days earlier, took them to a meeting with local black clergy who invited them to stay at their homes that night. But when it became clear that the local clergy felt threatened by the strong measures taken by local authorities, the riders feared their presence in town would add more danger to what already was a very dangerous situation for local black people. They thanked the black ministers for their offer of hospitality, but told them they would ride through the night to their next destination. The next day, the riders were turned away at the Baton Rouge terminal.

JOHN RAINES'S BASIC ASSUMPTIONS about crucial aspects of American life were challenged for the first time by what he observed as a Freedom Rider. For one thing, it was the first time he met people who looked like him—white—who wanted to kill him, all because he supported the yearnings of black people for equality. Before that experience, he had no idea that some government agencies in the United States were instruments of repression against their own people. He had no idea that countless black Americans were prevented from exercising their basic rights, such as riding on a public bus or voting. He had thought going on a Freedom Ride would be a nice way to spend his summer. It turned out to be a transforming experience.

The day after his Freedom Ride ended, Raines traveled to visit his parents at Glen Lake. It took nearly all day to make the journey by plane and car. He was looking forward to a quiet respite with his parents by the lake. As he traveled that day, he felt a need to decompress and think about what he had just experienced. He knew his parents' lake house would be the perfect place to do it. It had been a family gathering place since they bought it in 1951. His parents had not been active in the civil rights movement, but he grew up knowing they hated racism. While he was in the South, his father, in an interview with Robert Caro, then a reporter for *Newsday,* a newspaper on Long Island, said he respected his son for being a Freedom Rider.

When he arrived at the old cottage—which the family called the "pea-green shack on the damn hill" because years ago cars often got stuck on the unpaved road that led up to the cottage—nestled in trees above Glen Lake, he was tired but also eager to talk. He had stories to tell. He was also hungry. His parents were happy to see him, but they had finished dinner much earlier. They were tired and ready to go to bed by the time he arrived. They suggested he have dinner at the Homestead. They would hear his stories in the morning.

With that suggestion, Richard and Lucille Raines unintentionally set the stage for the next life-changing development in their son's life that summer.

John liked the Homestead, a stately resort hidden in the woods on the northeastern edge of Lake Michigan, just a few miles from his parents' cottage. There weren't many people in the Homestead dining room by the time he arrived that evening. That made it easy for Bonnie Muir, his waitress, to spend more time talking with him than she usually did with customers. As she served him dinner, she learned two things that pleased her—that he had just returned from being a Freedom Rider and that he was about to move to New York. As he answered her questions about his time in the South, he struck her right away as "a great alternative to the sort of all-American guys that I had dated before that." They were "very nice, but not very interested in the world." Muir *was* interested in the world. A news junkie, she had read about the arrests of some of the Freedom Riders a few weeks earlier. She was not an activist, but she admired people who were. She was happy to meet such a person, especially one as handsome and charming as John Raines.

It was clear they both enjoyed their conversation that evening. Both later said they felt a meshing of values in their conversation that night that they seldom, if ever, had felt before. In the two weeks before Raines left for New York, they enjoyed what they later called "three or four intense dates." On one of those evenings, he took her home to meet what she still calls, after fifty years of marriage, his "exuberant" family. All of them gathered after dinner, as they often did, on the front porch and sang. "They were great singers. They sang four-part harmony . . . some hymns, barbershop quartet songs. I thought it was wonderful." She was starting to fall in love not only with Raines but also with his family.

Crazy about each other by the time they parted in late August, Raines and Muir arranged to meet several weeks later in New York. They agree that, as Bonnie Raines put it years later, "It was really there, in New York, that we fell in love." For hours, they walked the streets of Morningside Heights and Harlem, ecstatic in their new love and also in their affection for the city on those clear, beautiful autumn days. Many years later, John Raines suggests, with a grin, that Bonnie would not have married him if he hadn't lived in

New York. She laughs and counters that she might not have married him if he hadn't been a Freedom Rider.

Anyone observing the couple with the striking all-American good looks as they dated that summer at Glen Lake, or several weeks later in New York, might have predicted that if they married they would be likely to root themselves in a few years in one of the nation's expanding lush suburbs. Surely no one would have predicted then that ten years later they would be driving a getaway car through the Philadelphia Main Line district after committing what J. Edgar Hoover, the director of the FBI, considered one of the worst crimes in the bureau's history.

ON THE SURFACE that summer at Glen Lake, Bonnie Muir seemed like a quintessential summer lodge waitress. Her long, shining black hair framed an engaging and warm face. She had a radiant smile and was a dreamy version of Hollywood's girl next door. She had just finished her sophomore year at Michigan State University and was earning money for her education by working at the Homestead. She had grown up in Grand Rapids, the daughter of loving parents Dorothy and Andrew Muir. At the university she was a good student, a pretty cheerleader who cheered the Spartans on at every football game, and an enthusiastic Kappa Kappa Gamma sorority sister. But there was much more to her than those visible signs of the happily conforming midcentury coed. Like most middle-class American women of her generation, when she thought of her future, she had these expectations: She would graduate, she would marry, she would have children, and, if she worked outside the home, she would be an elementary school teacher. Within two years, Muir would envision a future radically different from those expectations.

John Raines, tall and blond with radiant blue eyes and an easy, hearty laugh, had, like most men of the educated class, grown up close to the establishment and with a certainty that a variety of professions would be open to him. When he was a child, his parents were part of the liberal Minneapolis elite during the years his father, the future Indianapolis bishop, was pastor of the large Hennepin Avenue Methodist Church. Hubert Humphrey, the mayor of Minneapolis during some of those years, lived on the same street as the Raineses and was a friend who dropped by their home occasionally. Raines realized later that he had grown up accustomed to being connected to power. It was an environment, he recalls, that gave him and his brothers "an impression that all was right with the world, and that they would inherit it and run it." Protestant clergy in top-tier appointments, such as bishops or pastors of large, prestigious congregations, were not rich by virtue of salaries. Rather, church officials made it possible for such clergy to live like the rich by buying large homes for them in the best neighborhoods and paying for them to send their children to superior schools. This was the case for the Raines family.

One year after they met, John and Bonnie were married, on August 17, 1962, in Grand Rapids. She left Michigan State at the end of her junior year. They started life together in New York the next month, and she immediately enrolled in City College of New York as an elementary education major. Their first child, daughter Lindsley, was born on September 10, 1963. Several months later, when she was pregnant with their second child, Mark, she and John went to Washington and stood with thousands of people in a round-the-clock vigil at the Lincoln Memorial protesting the filibuster then taking place on Capitol Hill in an attempt to block passage of the 1964 Civil Rights Act. That was the first time Bonnie Raines participated in a protest.

After they married, John kept going south. "Bonnie knew I would be going south again, and she wanted me to go," John recalls. Each time he prepared to leave, "Bonnie never said, 'I wish you wouldn't go, but go if you have to.' Instead, it was always, 'Go. I wish I could go too.'" She stayed behind in their small student apartment in Morningside Heights, near Union Seminary, alone the first year, but later with the company of their two babies.

John Raines was present at some of the pivotal events of the civil rights movement, beginning with the Freedom Rides in the summer of 1961. In 1964, he was in Mississippi during Freedom Summer. In April 1965, he answered Martin Luther King's plea for people to come to Selma, Alabama. King's plea went out after local black people were attacked by whites, led by state and local law enforcement officials on horseback, after local black people, including schoolteachers, were denied the right to register to vote and fired from their jobs for trying to do so. In the summer of 1965, Raines went to Baker County in southwest Georgia. That turned out to be his most unforgettable trip south.

In Mississippi in 1964, the most violent of the civil rights summers, John Raines walked the streets of Hattiesburg and drove country roads with black people as they tried to register to vote under extremely hostile conditions. Black leaders from Mississippi predicted months earlier that the situation might be explosive that summer and begged for federal protection. A new organization had been formed—the Association for the Preservation of the White Race—by white people who wanted an organization even more aggressive in its support of racism and segregation than the Ku Klux Klan and the White Citizens' Councils. The new organization boldly and openly described itself as anti-Negro, anti-Catholic, and anti-Semitic. Thirty thousand members had signed up in fifteen counties across the state. In addition, the state legislature passed laws that spring designed to make it extremely difficult for civil rights workers to have a public presence. The new laws prohibited people from picketing any public buildings or demonstrating on public streets and sidewalks or on any property belonging to cities, counties, or the state. Enraged at the possibility of black people registering to vote, white people burned black homes and churches that spring with impunity. Local law enforcement officers not only didn't investigate the crimes, they often participated in them.

Black community leaders from Mississippi went to Washington to plead for the Johnson administration to send two hundred federal marshals to protect civil rights workers that summer. Their plea was made at the same time southern senators were conducting their filibuster against the 1964 Civil Rights Act. Historian Howard Zinn, writing about the refusal to send the marshals, said the request for two hundred marshals to protect civil rights workers and local black people as they tried to secure one of their most basic rights as Americans, the right to vote, was a pretty small request, especially when compared to the fact that by that time the government had 40,000 troops in Vietnam in a war U.S. officials said was being fought to secure basic rights for Vietnamese people.

The fears of Mississippi black people turned out to be more than justified. The tragedy that, more than any other during those summers, came to symbolize the extreme violence southern whites used against black people and their supporters took place that year: the murder of James Chaney, a local young African American civil rights worker, and Andrew Goodman and Michael Schwerner, two young white civil rights workers from New York.

It was in the midst of that terrible cauldron in Mississippi in summer 1964 that John Raines started thinking seriously about the role of the FBI. Like many civil rights workers, he wondered why the FBI was not on the scene there and elsewhere in previous years when violence was threatened against civil rights workers. Records that emerged years later showed that skepticism about FBI director J. Edgar Hoover's attitudes toward the civil rights movement was well placed. When asked to investigate threats against civil rights workers, he repeatedly claimed that the FBI could not intervene—even when there was evidence that violence against civil rights workers was likely—because the bureau was an investigating agency, not a crime-fighting agency. This claim was the opposite of how the FBI had responded historically to predicted crime. Hoover and the bureau, in fact, gained their greatest fame for being crime fighters. The bureau's dramatic crime-fighting, crime-preventing efforts in the 1930s, when the FBI stopped the violent sprees involving John Dillinger, Bonnie and Clyde, and other well-known crime figures of that era, had been used by Hoover to build the reputation of the FBI. Hoover proudly trumpeted the bureau's crime-fighting image. In contrast, when civil rights workers were threatened in the 1950s and early 1960s, Hoover refused to be involved until he was forced to by President Johnson.

A few days after the three young men disappeared and were feared murdered, the White House recognized that the situation in Mississippi was at least as grave as black people had told them it would be when they asked for protection in May. At a planning session at the White House that involved Attorney General Robert Kennedy and his aides Burke Marshall and Nicholas Katzenbach, President Johnson summed up the law enforcement problem then in Mississippi this way: "There are three sovereignties involved. There's the United States, there's the state of Mississippi, and there's J. Edgar Hoover."

President Johnson ordered his old friend the FBI director to take action in Mississippi. With that, the FBI opened an office in Jackson, the first in the state. Agents there—led by Roy Moore, the same agent the director appointed to be in charge of the MEDBURG investigation in 1971—conducted an intensive investigation. Forty-four days after the three men disappeared, their bodies were found. They had been ambushed, shot dead, and then buried in an earthen dam near Philadelphia, Mississippi, the town where Ronald Reagan launched his 1980 presidential campaign. They were victims of a conspiracy by local law enforcement agents and the Ku Klux Klan. The FBI arrested eighteen men in October 1964.

From 1961 through 1965, on each of Raines's trips south, he faced the seething hatred of southern whites many times as they tried to prevent black people from registering to vote and from entering bus stations, restaurants, schools, voter registration offices, and other public places. He was in the center of angry white mobs and was arrested several times, but his most threatening experience took place in 1965, when he spent a night alone in a jail in Newton, Georgia. What happened that summer in Newton, a rural area in Baker County in southwest Georgia, was not a touchstone moment of the civil rights movement as, say, Freedom Summer in Mississippi or the Selma-to-Montgomery march in Alabama had been. It was, however, a touchstone moment for the black people in that isolated part of Georgia and for John Raines.

He went to Newton in response to a call for help from Charles Sherrod, his former classmate at Union Seminary in New York. Sherrod had left the seminary and gone to Baker County to establish a chapter of the Student Non-Violent Coordinating Committee, then one of the most effective organizations supporting grassroots efforts by black people to claim their basic rights. By the time Sherrod asked Union Seminary for help in the summer of 1965, he had been working in Baker County for five years. It felt, he later wrote, as if there had been virtually no change. Segregation in southwest Georgia seemed to be total. Nearly every public institution was still off-limits to black people.

As violence against African Americans increased as they tried to register to vote that summer, Sherrod realized he needed public exposure of the attacks. He called Union Seminary president John Bennett and said, "Get us a couple whites." A familiar pattern went into play. Sherrod, Bennett, and students at the seminary, including Raines, knew that if northern whites came and were beaten along with local blacks, reporters would come. That meant the beatings might be shown on national television, and that, in turn, made it more likely that protection from the federal government might arrive.

When Bennett put word out at Union Seminary that Sherrod needed help, Raines and a few other seminarians responded—as they had in the past to calls from the South—as they would have if a member of their own family had asked for help during a crisis. They flew to Georgia immediately. As with the seminarians' earlier trips, travel costs were paid by the seminary.

A few days after he arrived, Raines was arrested at a rally in Newton and incarcerated. Instead of being placed in a jail inside a courthouse, where many southern jails were located, he was placed in a building behind the Baker County Courthouse. He remembers the space was very small and very dark. Given his isolation and the fact that the sheriff was someone who was known for turning a blind eye to violence against black people and their supporters, Raines realized he was in a dangerous situation, but he didn't realize how dangerous. He was completely helpless to do anything about it.

Without Raines knowing it, word spread in the local black community during the night that a civil rights worker was in trouble—that the local White Citizens' Council was planning to attack him in jail. Frantic to save him, leaders in the black community convinced a local black farmer to put up his modest farm for the bail needed to get John Raines out of jail. To this day, Raines is profoundly grateful for that act of generosity that may have saved his life. In that experience, more than any other, he said he learned how important the embrace of a community of resisters can be.

DURING HIS SUMMERS in the South, Raines gradually realized that southern black people were giving him what he came to call his "second education." It changed him forever. This new education was, in some ways, in opposition to what he calls his "first education." Prestigious schools— Carleton College in Minnesota and Union Theological Seminary in New York before he became a minister on Long Island—were the venues of his "first education." The lessons taught there, he recalled, were primarily "an education in deservedness. We were all being trained to be leaders of our generation—liberal leaders who would help others become more like us. . . . We were taught to want to become judges, to go to Washington and become part of Foggy Bottom [the U.S. State Department]. . . . We were taught to aspire to what privileged white males should aspire to—which was leadership of the country."

In his first education, Raines was taught to accept the world as it is, full of the coming together of ambiguity and tragedy. "We felt comfortable. We saw the everyday injustices of life, but we were persuaded that life had tragic moral limitations and that we were well qualified to become leaders because we did not bring impossible and disruptive expectations to the social system."

Learning how to change, rather than accept, official systems was not part of Raines's first education. In fact, he had never thought about that concept—until 1961 as a Freedom Rider. It was foreign to him. His motivation for going to the South had been to go help those poor people, but he discovered there was much more to it than that. It was a matter of "being invited into danger" in order to change powerful unjust systems. "I was exposed immediately to the power of a resisting community, people who were committed to being nonviolent, despite being treated very violently. . . . They were willing to expose themselves to great danger. They invited me into that danger with them while also protecting me from danger—the man who put his farm up, for instance. It was a very powerful experience for me. . . . I wandered in and was grasped by the movement."

This "second education," taught in the crucible of those summers in the

South, led, Raines said, to a major shift in "my whole understanding of the law. . . . Judges had always been friends of the family, and we knew policemen were there to protect us, and they did. Now I began to see another face of law and order: control over powerless people, such as the black majority in the South that couldn't vote. I began to get a different sense of how power is used in society. . . . I saw the law used to inflict injustice upon many people." Until then, he had no idea that black Americans experienced profound injustice. Repeatedly, on each trip south, he saw firsthand evidence that law enforcement agencies—local, state, and federal—failed to protect African Americans, not only from having their basic rights withheld, but also from violent attacks.

Eventually, he defined his second education as an education "in how America looks from below and how it is lived from below." That was the reverse of his first education, which he now saw as "an education that did not want you to ever experience America from below except as a situation where you might go and help once in a while."

Raines's new education, he said, "made me look, from then on, at the government in a different way." He looked at the government more carefully. He inspected power—the power of individuals and the power of institutions—for whether it was causing harm. "Without that experience, without what black people taught me about resistance," says Raines, "I would have been a very different person ten years later. I would have been a different kind of teacher, a different kind of ethicist, a different kind of theologian." Without that experience, the Raineses both agree, it is unlikely they would have driven to Media on that March evening in 1971.

Interestingly, the two primary influences that convinced the Raineses that sometimes it is necessary to resist government injustice, even if great risk is involved, were the same influences that convinced the German theologian Dietrich Bonhoeffer, one of the most revered resistance figures in modern history, to join the German resistance to Adolf Hitler and the Third Reich. Bonhoeffer and Raines both worked closely with Union Seminary professor Reinhold Niebuhr and learned from his thinking—Bonhoeffer in 1930, John Raines in the early 1960s. Both Bonhoeffer and Raines also counted their firsthand experience with African Americans as a powerful influence on their becoming willing to resist official power.

When Bonhoeffer arrived at Union Seminary in 1930 for a year of study, he had a firm conviction that churches, in Germany and in the United States, should not speak out on public issues. He thought Christians should accept the conditions of the world and not try to change them. In their ongoing friendly debate, Niebuhr insisted that churches as institutions and individual Christians had a responsibility to be involved in social action. Earlier, as a young minister in Detroit, Niebuhr had spoken against the poor housing conditions of black people and the working conditions of autoworkers. After coming to Union in 1928, he spoke out on nearly every major issue, from support for the United States entering World War II to opposition to dropping bombs on Japan to opposition to the war in Vietnam. Another theologian, the late Robert McAfee Brown, wrote in 1986 that Niebuhr was "the troubler of our national conscience." It would be learned years after the Media burglary that Niebuhr's activism had earned him a hefty FBI file.

By the time Bonhoeffer returned to Germany from New York, he had rejected his earlier belief that Christians should be disengaged and had fully embraced Niebuhr's belief that Christians should actively oppose injustice. As the Third Reich extended its grip on Germany, Bonhoeffer watched its control permeate most institutions, including the large state church, the Lutheran Church. Conforming to Hitler's condemnation of Jews, the church forbade study of the Old Testament and forbade the belief that Jesus was a Jew. As Hitler's willing handmaiden, the church undoubtedly contributed significantly to many Germans being silent as the Holocaust took place.

Bonhoeffer attributed much of the evolution in his thinking not only to Niebuhr but also to insights he gained from becoming immersed in Harlem clubs and a Harlem church. The connections between religion and injustice, especially racial injustice, often were at the center of discussions he had with Franklin Fisher, a black seminarian from Alabama who became his close friend. This subject was new to Bonhoeffer. So were the sounds of jazz and Negro spirituals, music that was exciting to the ears of this German classical pianist and theologian. The two of them visited Harlem clubs and the church that would become Bonhoeffer's home in New York, the Abyssinian Baptist Church, where the Reverend Adam Clayton Powell Sr., the father of the future member of Congress, was then the pastor.

From members of the congregation, who warmly welcomed Bonhoeffer, he learned for the first time the legacy of American slavery and about African Americans' ongoing struggle for freedom. He later wrote that his hatred of anti-Semitism and his courage to resist the Nazis came from lessons he learned from African Americans who befriended him in Harlem. Like Raines, Bonhoeffer received an unexpected second education from black Americans in how to how to fight injustice with courage and strength.

After he returned to Germany and later joined the resistance to Hitler, Bonhoeffer described the impact of his Harlem experiences on his commitment to resistance very much the way John Raines described the impact of his experiences in the South. Bonhoeffer wrote, "We have for once learnt to see the great events of world history from below, from the perspective of the outcast, the suspects, the maltreated, the oppressed, the reviled—in short, from the perspective of those who suffer."

When Bonhoeffer returned to Germany in 1931, he took with him several 78 rpm recordings of jazz and Negro spirituals. As the juggernaut of Nazism tightened, he played, again and again, that music he first heard and came to love in Harlem. At Finkenwalde—a seminary in exile that the Gestapo closed but that Bonhoeffer continued to operate in the underground—during the darkest times he played those records. He, his students, and other fellow resisters closed windows and doors, gathered close to a Victrola, and listened surreptitiously to the deep and powerful voice of Paul Robeson singing, "Go down. Go down, Moses! Way down in Egypt's land. Tell old Pharaoh, Let my people go!" The Harlem days that had been so satisfying—the music and memories of the black people who shared with him their personal stories and the history of their people—all became, during the increasingly brutal years of the Third Reich, a sustaining balm, even a source of some small hope when hope was nearly dead in Germany.

Drawing strength from his New York memories of conversations with Niebuhr and with black people in Harlem, when Bonhoeffer was imprisoned by the Nazis, he secretly wrote some of the most eloquent literature ever written about resistance to government authority. He was hanged on April 9, 1945, at Flossenbürg, a German concentration camp where the Nazis killed 73,000 people, including Bonhoeffer, shortly before the camp was liberated by the Allies on April 23, 1945.

Both Raines and Bonhoeffer, after they studied with Niebuhr at the seminary, lived the essence of Niebuhr's central teaching: Don't accept limits—push limits.

BONNIE RAINES'S AWAKENING to the potentially powerful impact of nonviolent resistance was fueled at first primarily by John's experiences. Later, her own experiences led to her commitment to resistance. She supported and admired what he did. At the same time, her reality was quite different from his. In the South and at the seminary, John Raines met men, including other young fathers, who were rethinking their values and considering whether they would be willing in the future to risk their freedom in order to oppose injustice. The men's shared experiences reinforced their evolving thinking. When John Raines rejected the expectations many people had of him—for instance, the assumption that he would accept a comfortable place in the church establishment—other avenues, including life as an academic, were considered acceptable for him.

Like other men who changed as he had, his basic judgments about himself and his relation to his family were not questioned. That was not the case for Bonnie Raines. So strong were the expectations of what a woman should be that she felt she dare not speak to many people about the new and different life she hoped to have. The early 1960s was still a time when hardly anyone expected women to have choices about the direction of their lives. She felt she had to keep her dreams hidden and share them only with her husband.

She loved being a mother, but she also wanted to be able to be a serious activist. Sometimes she wondered how her dreams had become so different from what she assumed were the dreams of most women her age. Part of the answer could be found in a childhood that was peppered with experiences that encouraged her to think beyond the usual expectations of what a woman should be. Her parents, unlike many parents of girls in mid-1950s America, had not wrapped her in a cocoon and isolated her from the world. They had encouraged her to read books, to read the news, to become an informed and questioning person. At the church her family attended in Grand Rapids, the Fountain Street Church, a nondenominational liberal congregation, she started to develop an appreciation for dissent. When a local group invited Eleanor Roosevelt to speak, the announcement sparked a controversy that closed most doors in the city to her. During the subsequent debate, many hateful letters opposing her speaking in Grand Rapids were published in the local newspaper. Though Bonnie Muir was only fifteen at the time, she recalls being upset by the effort to silence Mrs. Roosevelt. In the end, the only place in town where she was welcome to speak was the Fountain Street Church. Bonnie went with her parents to hear Mrs. Roosevelt and sat near the front of the church so she could see this woman who had been the subject of so much controversy. She remembers being impressed by her comments, especially ones about peace and justice.

Two books Bonnie read shortly after hearing Mrs. Roosevelt speak encouraged her interest in justice and equality. John Steinbeck's *Grapes of Wrath* introduced her to the realization that some powerless people were not protected by the government. Reading Anne Frank's diary had the biggest impact on her then. She read it when she was about the age Anne was when she wrote the book. From it, Bonnie first learned about the tragic consequences of ethnic hatred. She remembers looking at photos of Anne and thinking that, with their dark hair and dark eyes, they looked a little like each other. Starting then, she became an avid reader, particularly of history, with a keen interest in resistance, including the important role of resistance in freeing slaves. She admired the French people who stood up to the Nazis during World War II.

After she and John married in 1962 and moved to New York, she recalls, she could almost feel her mind opening. Her ideals had been planted in Grand Rapids, but they were richly nourished to maturity in that small student apartment in Morningside Heights. In that loving environment, where John and Bonnie frequently discussed the importance of the search for justice, she challenged herself to think about how she would lead a life that mattered.

Just as John's experience in the South had informed him about the depth of inequality that existed in the United States, Bonnie's experiences as a young teacher in East Harlem provided her with similar lessons. That was her first close exposure to profound inequality. In one class she taught there were forty-four children, most of whom could not speak English. She continued to believe a dedicated teacher could make the difference students needed, but she realized the public school system put up barriers to successful teaching. Each new experience—as a student, as a new teacher in city schools, as a politically aware person—strengthened her resolve to become an activist. She was confronted repeatedly with evidence of injustice and inequality that made her react: "This just can't go on. People have to stand up. I was angry at the abuse of power—in the South, in the education system, in the war policies."

She thought carefully about how to weave together diverse roles—how to be a student, a new teacher, a new mother, and a committed political activist. Very happy personally, she found she was otherwise angry and idealistic at the same time, two qualities that continued to be demanding and constructive forces throughout a life that has been dedicated to improving the lives of children.

In the absence of choices, she concluded she would have to create them in order to invent the life she wanted. She discovered that doing so often was difficult and lonely. She was acutely aware in those early-1960s days of the warning that was repeatedly announced, including in her own head: "Women don't do that." She decided that before she could commit herself to taking part in acts of resistance to fight injustice, she needed to establish in her own life the foundation that would make it possible for her to be the

fully engaged woman she was determined to become—personally, profes-
sionally, and politically. That meant going "against my socialization."

"My first act of resistance," Bonnie recalls, "was to pull it all together
before there was a women's movement, a feminist movement." She revolted
with a determination to come out on the other side "sure that I didn't have
to feel there was something wrong with me. I was stubborn, and I decided
at some point in the early '60s, I was going to advance this life."

As part of that effort, she concluded she "could not just be involved in
liberating myself and making sure that my daughters were going to have
more opportunity and choice." She wanted to have the courage to take risks
"for something larger than just my own self-actualization and my daughters'
self-actualization."

IN THOSE EARLY YEARS of their marriage in New York, the Raineses
talked with each other often about how both of them could be good parents
and also engage in resistance together. Contemplating how to be that kind
of couple was no less difficult—perhaps even more so—than figuring out
how Bonnie could be the kind of woman she wanted to be. Their goal of
dual activism posed profound practical and moral questions. Most of the
people they met in movements, first in civil rights and later in the antiwar
movement, were single. "They were living an ascetic lifestyle and feeling free
to take risks. That was so different from our situation," she said. "We talked
a lot about the tendency when you marry and have children to feel a certain
level of comfort and sense that you will work your way through the rest of
your life like that," in a protective family shell. They were concerned about
the fact that soon after people had children it was assumed they should exit
from the parts of civic life that needed the most commitment. This meant
that as far as activism was concerned, a sizable part of the population was
essentially on hold until they became middle-aged or older, if not forever.

The absence of engagement by parents during the child-rearing years,
they thought, had a heavy impact on society. They concluded, said Bonnie
Raines, that "each generation seems to have its own version of tyranny and
needs to know how to resist it. We thought that just because we had children didn't mean that we were exempt from the responsibility of our generation to address these things. . . . There was a real temptation to let other
people, say, religious people, take care of those things. It was a temptation
to say, 'Let them carry the banner for the rest of us. We'll applaud them and

bail them out of jail when they are arrested, but we'll not engage in the same activities.' We thought about that a lot. We thought it would be a cop-out."

It was then, in those New York years, that the Raineses made the promise to each other that made it possible for them to say yes to William Davidon's December 1970 question about burglarizing an FBI office. After much reflection in that New York apartment nearly a decade before his question, they promised each other that when injustice reached extreme levels, they hoped both of them, not just John, would be willing to risk their freedom to fight injustice. It was extremely difficult to make this promise, for their children were at the center of their lives. But so was their love of justice and their belief that *all* citizens should take responsibility for opposing injustice in times of crisis. They forced themselves to face a painful challenge that few people contemplated—joint resistance.

After John Raines completed his doctoral studies at Union Seminary in 1966, the Raineses moved to Philadelphia, where he became a tenure-track professor in the new Department of Religion at Temple University, where he still teaches part-time after retiring in December 2011. It was an exciting academic environment that suited him well, unique in the diversity of its faculty and courses: Protestant, Catholic, Jewish, and, a few years after he arrived, Muslim studies. Within little more than a year after he started teaching at Temple, Raines created one of the first courses offered in the United States on the Holocaust. Later he would be instrumental in the department's adding the study of Islam. It became a favorite place for Muslim graduate students from predominantly Muslim countries to study comparative religions and then encourage universities in their home countries to offer comparative religion studies instead of only the study of Islam.

Soon after they moved to Philadelphia, the Raineses were drawn to the large antiwar community there. Before long their home in the Germantown section of the city was a gathering place for antiwar activists who, over casual dinners prepared by Bonnie, discussed how to end the war in Vietnam. Bonnie's role as earth mother expanded. Often nearly everyone else talked strategy while she cooked big meals for them. She loved this environment, but sometimes a depressing thought gnawed at the edges of her soul: "You know you really aren't as good as they are."

Though the Raineses found it difficult not to feel hopeless as the war continued, they also were still essentially optimistic people. That was part of why they had become activists. They believed that active dissent could cause change. But after 1968, they had lost much of their optimism. Increasingly, confidence in the federal government was replaced by alienation. For them and many other people, Vice President Hubert Humphrey, more than anyone, symbolized the loss of hope in the government. In 1964, as a senator, he had been crucial in the development and successful passage of the Civil Rights Act, which outlawed racial discrimination in public facilities. But as the war in Vietnam continued, Humphrey tumbled precipitously from being a source of hope among liberals to being a source of despair and anger. In a forceful private memo to President Johnson in February 1964, he had strongly opposed the war, but, his opinion coldly rejected by Johnson, Humphrey soon publicly reversed his position, condemned people who opposed the war, and openly speculated, as Johnson did—despite contrary evidence—that antiwar protests were supported by money from foreign governments.

Like William Davidon, the Raineses felt hope was becoming scarce. Like him, they also were looking for more powerful nonviolent ways to protest the war. Their path into more serious resistance was very similar to Davidon's. One of John's graduate students—Sister Sarah Fahy, a nun who was the daughter of Judge Charles Fahy, a senior judge then on the U.S. Court of Appeals in Washington, D.C.—introduced them to people in the Catholic peace movement. The Raineses found their optimism renewed, as Davidon did, by the Catholic resisters. John remembers being impressed by the fact that the Catholic peace movement resisters were "angry, but they also were optimistic and hopeful." The Raineses—whose protest and resistance grew originally out of a "deep liking for the country rather than a deep hatred of the country"—came to feel they shared common ground with the Catholic activists. "They wanted to do something that would have effect, not just cause havoc," says John. "They wanted to do things that would have real consequences."

The Raineses joined about two dozen people organized by the Catholic peace activists in a draft board raid in North Philadelphia in February 1970. Less than a year later, they accepted Davidon's invitation to consider burglarizing the Media FBI office. In doing so, they did indeed do something that had real consequences for the country.

THE MEDIA BURGLARY had real consequences for the country and also in the Raineses' lives. They felt direct pressure, probably more than any of the burglars, from a series of events. There was the visit from the man who abandoned the group and told John and Bonnie he was thinking of turning all of the burglars in to the FBI. There was the Xerox technician who carried away from John Raines's office the drum of the copier he had used to copy hundreds of the stolen files. There were the two agents who came to the Raineses' home about two months after the burglary and asked John directly if he was involved in Media and left just minutes before Bonnie returned home. Each of these incidents gave them reason to fear that arrest might be imminent.

The personal toll was heavy at times, so much so that they decided never to take part in an act of resistance again, at least not one that involved such great risk. "Not long after Media," John recalls, "Bonnie and I began to realize that was the end. . . . Media would be the last thing we would do. We had taken on all the jeopardy we could."

Though they would add no more new jeopardy, their old jeopardy remained a frequent companion, often touching and scaring them. Bonnie describes their lives after the Media break-in as "a sustained period of worry and concern. That went on for five years." Though the level of intensity varied, it was always there. Throughout the first six months after the burglary, she said, "we talked a lot with each other about what we had done. Every morning, when you went to get the paper, you'd wonder if you would read that you were a suspect, or read that someone's fingerprint had been found. Maybe there will be an article on some angle the FBI has picked up. Maybe someone was brought in for questioning. There was always that half expectation that something was going to crop up. You were always waiting for the other shoe to drop."

Bonnie dreamed about the search for the Media burglars. The dreams were more like nightmares. She would dream agents were closing in on them, surrounding their house, about to knock or break in. Then she would wake up, groping in the first moments to understand what was a dream and what was reality. Then relief. FBI agents were not breaking into their house. But the fear always lingered.

She remembers seldom driving during those years without looking in the rearview mirror and wondering if the driver behind her was an FBI agent. If there were two men in the car, she really worried; FBI agents usually traveled in pairs. Both she and John often thought they were being followed, were about to be pulled over, arrested, and, in a moment, their lives changed forever. She remembers sometimes being in the middle of a conversation with one of the children—"You dropped your teddy bear, sweetheart"—and noticing that there were two men in the car behind her and that the car seemed to be awfully close. She often drove, in those post-burglary days, with one eye on the road, one eye on the car in the rearview mirror, her heart with the children in the backseat, and a knot of fear in her stomach.

Over the years, when friends occasionally commented in the presence of the Raineses about the "amazing revelations" in those FBI documents stolen at Media, the Raineses would nod in agreement, and then share with each other what they hoped looked like meaningless glances. They kept their egos in check. They depended on their inner confidence and each other for the approval that might have come from other people acknowledging their significant accomplishment. Bonnie thinks the need to live as though the burglary always would be a secret "induced a certain level of maturity in us." But sometimes they wished they could share their big secret. Keeping the secret meant Bonnie never was able to tell her feminist friends about her great breakthrough—that years earlier she had taken risks that led to very important information becoming known to the American people about their government. She could not tell them she had discovered that she could be brave.

Gradually, they slipped into completely normal lives. Like many of their friends, said Bonnie, "we became a dual-career couple trying to hold things together." Each of them found different outlets for professional work that satisfied their need to improve society. She finished her long-time-coming master's degree at Temple University and moved eventually from working in daycare centers to a series of top leadership positions in organizations where she worked with teachers, social agencies, and legislators in developing policies and legislation designed to improve the lives of children, especially poor children. One of her accomplishments later in her career was convincing high school administrators to provide instruction in parenting—the most important role most people are likely to have in life, but a role for which there is little or no formal preparation.

As life became more normal, John Raines focused on publishing in order not to perish on the path to academic tenure. A book he wrote for that purpose, *Attack on Privacy*, published in 1974, included research that was far more original than the people who evaluated it during his tenure review may have realized. It was a treatise on the various organized forces in society, including the FBI, that invade citizens' privacy and change people from citizens to what he called "passive system inhabitants." He included his analysis of direct excerpts from at least four of the documents stolen from the Media office—properly footnoted, of course.

On the book jacket, John is described as a professor who has "given a great deal of attention to the intersection of public issues and matters of conscience and spirit." Indeed, he had given a great deal of attention—not to mention action—to such matters. Perhaps none of his readers, except his wife and other Media burglars, understood that he had specific actions, not only profound ideas, in mind when he wrote the last paragraph of the book:

> Freedom and dignity . . . remain fragile accomplishments. They depend upon rules and conventions and self-restraints, most of which cannot be systematically supervised. They depend upon persons who have many opportunities of corruption and are daily exposed to the retribution of angered interests and powers. In the end they depend upon the few who stay alert and who are able when necessary to pay prices, and upon the many who pay their prices in other ways but are willing to say "no" when the trespass of liberty becomes sufficiently blatant and the times sufficiently critical.

During this time, John also participated in home duties more than he had in the past. Until then, Bonnie had assumed responsibility for multiple roles at home and at work. Now John did more work in the home, including more childcare. They both enjoy recalling that he was so deeply involved in taking care of Mary when she was an infant that when she cried out in the night, often it was Daddy she asked for.

IN THE MORE THAN forty years since the burglary, the Raineses have continued to find pleasure in talking with each other about it. Eventually they talked about it less frequently, but once in a while they look at each other with a special look—a mixture of satisfaction and amazement. Each of them recognizes the look. The memories bring a smile. One of them breaks the silence, usually with a laugh, and says, "Can you believe we did it?" At such times they again feel a deep, quiet incredulity. And happiness.

Sometimes, in those special moments, one of them says, "How could we have possibly expected to get away with it?"

"It just seemed impossible," says Bonnie, "that somebody didn't make some huge mistake, or somebody didn't spill the beans. . . . We just had to go on faith that nobody would spill the beans and that none of us had made some awful mistake. But you couldn't help wondering."

At other times, they talk simply of their "wonderful secret."

They both agree that they became savvier about power because of the burglary. They think they are more certain than most people that it is possible to cause change, even in very large and powerful institutions. John thinks the experience made him a different academic than he otherwise would have been. Beginning with the Freedom Rides in 1961 and through Media in 1971, he said, "I think I've been in moral places that most of my colleagues haven't been. I was less obsessed with authorities. . . . I think it meant that it was hard to scare me. I've never kissed ass in the department, even when it was made pretty clear that if I wanted this or that I needed to kiss ass. I just didn't do it. They didn't have the power to punish and reward me. Fear and the need to please authority were not a part of my adult life after those experiences. That probably was to my disadvantage. I would have gotten promoted earlier, perhaps, if I'd been willing to play some of the smaller politics of academic friendship, but that was simply uninteresting. Academic politics became very boring for me. I was interested in the larger political scene, not in academic politics."

Despite the heavy impact of the burglary on their lives, Bonnie Raines sees the burglary as an aberration in an otherwise rather normal and law-abiding life that continued to be fueled by a sense of urgency about injustice and lack of equity. The burglary was, for her, a stepping-stone toward confidence. "It made me know," she said, "that I can do something in the way of social change. It was an important step in that direction. I came to realize I have a lifelong need to be contributing to social change. I think it also made me fairly realistic about the limits of our government and the abuse of power."

As the political temperament of the country became both more conservative and more apathetic, beginning in the late 1970s, the Raineses realized that what they did in 1971 might now seem "outrageously risky." Some people, says John, might think, "How could you be so foolish? My God, you were not only husband and wife; you were father and mother of three children. How could you have put them in that kind of jeopardy?"

"I live with that," says John. "The answer I have to that is, if all of us simply did what we thought was safe, that would let people who want to take our government away from us do that." There are different ways to protect children, your own and other people's children and grandchildren, he says. Sometimes it means protecting them from having their freedoms taken away by powerful institutions. That, he says, was part of what motivated them in 1971. Thinking of the arrests and sentences that never happened, he says, "But is it nice forty years later . . . knowing that we got away with it? Sure. . . . That's great."

At the time, they recall, it did not seem unreasonable, let alone outrageous to engage in such a radical act. It felt like an appropriate response to the outrageous behavior of the government in terms of both the war then being waged and the massive spying they thought was being done against American citizens.

Resistance was not really such a big deal, says John. "Courage was natural. It was all around you. What now might look courageous to some people, and outrageous to others, seemed more natural then." Sure, he was afraid, "stomach-knotting" afraid in the South and in the days right before the burglary and the night of the burglary. Even so, he looks back on those actions and regards them as having been "nearly natural" things to do under the circumstances.

"It was an utterly different climate then," he recalls, warming to the memories. "There were deep divisions then, but thousands of people jeopardized their freedom—refusing the draft, burning draft cards, blocking railroad cars loaded with napalm bound for shipment to Vietnam, walking from Selma to Montgomery, sitting in bus stations. . . . There was an entirely different climate about being a public person." By a decade later, he recalled, politics was regarded as "dirty and not something to try to influence." People stopped, he said, being willing to pay a price to change something they thought was wrong.

"*That* was not the strange time," he likes to think. "*This* is the strange time. We stole FBI files and gave them to the press because we had confidence in the public, in the processes of public discourse. And we were right. The government did take the material we stole and eventually conducted hearings and tried to change how the FBI operated. . . . I think we desperately need to have a rebirth of our sense of the importance of politics and the importance of public discourse. And gain confidence that good things, not just corrupt things, can come from that.

"It is important to understand that we did not think of ourselves as especially heroic or courageous. We probably didn't even think of those words. We thought of ourselves as taking an important risk that would be well received by many people and that would be used to bring about change if we were right about what we would find. And we were.

"We did not, for a minute, think of ourselves as being Don Quixotes. We thought of ourselves as being very accurate about the political possibilities. . . . And we would not have undertaken the action if we had not thought it was in tune with the times, thought it would not be received by many. It would have been utterly foolish to have taken on that kind of action if we thought the world was not prepared to receive it. . . .

"We did not feel helpless. We were not an island different from the sea around us. We never felt like isolated islands. We felt like part of the sea of that time." It also helped that "we were young, we had incredible amounts of energy and idealism. We felt potent and felt we could manage almost anything."

Bonnie Raines agrees. When asked how it was possible to move forward with the burglary despite seemingly forbidding obstacles—among them fear that the FBI knew about the burglary and had placed that second lock on the FBI office door they thought was not there before that night and the abandonment of the group just days before the burglary by someone who knew every detail of their plans—she, like John, finds the explanation mainly in the nature of that era. "The times called for and supported bold actions," she said. "We were just conceited enough to believe that we were smart, strategic, and patient, and also that perhaps it fell just to us and not others to expose the FBI in a credible and compelling way."

Perhaps more than any other Media burglar, John Raines enjoys recalling the spirit of that earlier time, the years that prepared them for Media. As he and Bonnie sit in the old Glen Lake home of his parents, where by now

Bonnie Raines (front row, right) and John Raines (behind her, third from right) with their four children, three of their seven grandchildren, plus their childrens' spouses and friends. Throughout their lives, such gatherings have made them acutely aware of the family life they would have lost if they had been found and imprisoned. *(Photo by Betty Medsger)*

their children and their grandchildren have developed an abiding affection for the old house and the fun and family closeness they experience there every summer, he looks out from the screened porch, across the tops of the fruit trees on the slope that rolls down to the lake, and he lets the memories flow. A bit of the preacher he turned away from becoming and the resister and professor he became all rise to the surface and blend as he reflects on the times and spirit that nurtured and motivated eight people in 1971 to risk their futures to protect dissent.

"It was a time when a president could say, 'My fellow Americans, ask not what your country can do for you; ask what you can do for your country.' He could say those words not in a vacuum, but in a country that was ready to hear those words.

"It was a time when the Peace Corps was formed and people were waiting to join it.

"It was a time when southern cops were shown on national television on Sunday night beating up people in Alabama, and by the next day so many people were trying to fly to Alabama that major airlines had put extra planes on, getting thousands of people to Montgomery by midday Monday.

"It was a time when LBJ could announce a war on poverty. Think about that. Poverty was something to go to war against. It was a war to win, to spend millions and billions to win. And he could get the votes in Congress because they thought there were enough people in this country then who believed poverty was an enemy that should be defeated rather than something that should be blamed on the poor.

"It was a time when literally hundreds of thousands of people would get in cars and fill East Coast highways, get on trains, and travel to New York and Washington, again and again, for massive rallies against the Vietnam War.

"It was a time of the best music we've produced. . . . It began with the freedom songs in the South, then the Beatles. The energy that was in the music and the counterculture—along with the drugs and some of the craziness—the sheer energy of that time was astonishing.

"It was a time when I found Catholics could be radical, and nuns could be the most radical of all.

"It was a time when I discovered the wonderful liberality of the Jewish conscience.

"It was a time when black people in the South taught me courage.

"It was a time when I as a WASP finally discovered and became close to the moral resources of all these other communities.

"It was a time when [Senator Eugene] McCarthy's delegates to the 1968 Democratic convention were gassed by Chicago police, beaten by them on national television, and chanted to the cameras, 'The whole world is watching,' and knew that the world *was* watching.

"It was a time when Hubert Humphrey, even after the huge disaster of the Chicago '68 convention, would have won the election if the liberal antiwar folks like myself had had better political judgment about how much was at stake in that election."

A look of profound despair crosses his face—his deep regret—for what he now regards as a profoundly foolish belief he held then: that it was more important to punish Humphrey for his failure to take a strong stand against the war than it was to prevent Nixon from being elected. This memory moves him to shift to the painful memories of what flowed from that election—more war and more certainty at the Nixon White House about staying the course in Vietnam.

"It was a time when Richard Nixon rimmed the White House with Washington, D.C., buses, bumper to bumper, while thousands of antiwar demonstrators filled the Washington Mall. And he bragged to the country that while he was protected by the buses he watched a football game."

Most important, though, says John Raines, "It was a time when we still believed we could and should be a good nation, not just a powerful nation."

Near the end of his vivid recall of that time, he is high from the memories he has evoked. "What an exciting time it was," he says, almost sounding as though it's a surprise that such a good time existed, a time when people were passionate about justice.

Bonnie Raines agrees, but she is slightly uncomfortable with his occasional emphasis on the past. The woman whose sketched face became well known to FBI agents throughout the country—the woman J. Edgar Hoover believed was the key to solving this case that he considered one of the worst things that ever happened to the bureau in his forty-seven years as its director—hesitates to dwell too much on the past.

"Yes, it was exciting," she says, "but we differ on that. You can feed off that more than I can. I tend to say, 'Well, okay, but what do we do now?'"

"Now," says John.

His soft echo of her last word is not a question but rather is recognition of being pulled back to reality, something Bonnie occasionally does when she thinks he is sinking into too deep an appreciation of the past, however remarkable and important it was. He acknowledges the wisdom in her concern. He, too, is realistic. He acknowledges that the accomplishments of the burglary and its aftermath are fragile. "Government intimidation and surveillance are never farther away than the next unpopular war or movement."

He sometimes despairs about "now." "America has lost some of the freedoms that we fought for and thought we had won back in the '60s and early '70s. We're back to square one. We're back to having to fight. We the people, once again, have to fight for an America that belongs to all Americans, not to just the special few Americans who have a lot of money and can use that money now freely to influence elections and drown out the voice and the meaning of the vote of . . . the people."

Bonnie agrees. "I worry. I worry very much about what it's going to take to change the climate in this country right now. And the silence of the ordinary people who just accept. Even when certain activities are exposed, they are just accepted. . . . It's not just about what's going on in America. It's global—the huge inequality gap of wealth in the world and in this country. . . . There has to be a generation that picks those problems up and says, 'These are the ones we're now going to attack.'"

Despite the realities of "now" that Bonnie often introduces into their conversations, she savors the big secret of what they did on March 8, 1971, as much as John does. That special smile that has appeared countless times over the years when they reminisced about the burglary is on their faces now.

"That was a fairly good moment in time, wasn't it?" says Bonnie.

John couldn't agree more. "It was wonderful."

26

Fragile Reform

AFTER ALL of the evidence of abusive behavior by the FBI had been placed on the table—the Media files, the COINTELPRO files Carl Stern sued to have the FBI release, and the massive documentation and testimony gathered by the Church Committee—efforts were initiated to prevent such abuses from taking place again. Reformers soon discovered it was nearly as difficult to put reforms in place as it had been to compel the FBI to open the files of J. Edgar Hoover's secret FBI.

At the end of its work, the committee made 180 detailed recommendations with two major goals—curbing abuses and simultaneously increasing the capacity of intelligence agencies to fulfill their lawful missions. The effort to turn key recommendations into legislation was slowed somewhat at the outset when the relatively halcyon bipartisan work of the committee was deliberately recast by some opponents of reform in ways that stretched and denied the truth.

One of the first attacks on the committee was a vicious false accusation made by George H. W. Bush, the future president. Shortly after he was confirmed in January 1976 as the new director of the CIA, he appeared before the Church Committee and angrily stated that the committee was responsible for the assassination on Christmas Day 1975 of Richard Welch, the then new CIA station chief in Greece. The committee had honored its agreement with the CIA not to name agents involved in any of the wrongdoing it revealed. In fact, as Senator Fritz Mondale, a member of the Church Committee, pointed out to Bush, the committee did not even have Welch's name. The CIA, for reasons unrelated to the committee, had warned Welch not to move into the house of the previous station chief's home, but he had done so.

Later, Bush returned to the committee and conceded there was no evidence that the Church Committee had any impact on Welch's cover in Greece, nor did the committee have "any relationship to his tragic death." But the original accusation made a strong impression that was never completely erased. Some members of Congress repeated it seemingly without regard for the fact that the director of the CIA had retracted his accusation.

Such attacks on the Church Committee have echoed through three decades. On September 11, 2001, James Baker, secretary of state in President George H. W. Bush's administration, issued an angry broadside against Frank Church. The late senator and the committee, he said, could be blamed for the horrendous disaster that had just happened hours earlier when more than 3,000 people were killed in New York, at the Pentagon, and in a field in western Pennsylvania. The Church Committee hearings, he said, had caused the United States to "unilaterally disarm in terms of our intelligence capabilities." In the same vein, a short time after 9/11, the *Wall Street Journal* asserted in an editorial that the opening of the Church hearings was "the moment that our nation moved from an intelligence to anti-intelligence footing." Given the very powerful influence the CIA had under successive presidents, beginning with President Reagan, such claims were not sustainable.

In March 2005, George H. W. Bush, despite his decades-old apology to the Church Committee, apparently could not resist taking a swipe at the committee again. In opening remarks at a conference on counter-intelligence, he said, "It burns me up to see the agency under fire." Recent criticism, he said, reminded him of the 1970s, when Congress "unleashed a bunch of untutored little jerks out there" to investigate the CIA.

IMMEDIATELY AFTER the Church Committee hearings, despite efforts to turn the public and Congress against the committee, a spirit of reform carried the day in Congress. That spirit changed over the next five years as Congress tackled these major reforms the Church Committee had recommended:

- Limit the FBI director's term to ten years.
- Establish permanent intelligence oversight committees.
- Create a Foreign Intelligence Surveillance Act court to control electronic surveillance.

- Write a binding charter that specifies requirements and limits on FBI conduct in investigations.

Setting a ten-year limit on how long an FBI director could serve was approved in 1976. Hoover had made that reform easy. Given what had become known about how he abused his position, even the strongest defenders of the FBI were hesitant to keep in place a system that had made it possible to appoint a twenty-nine-year-old and give him freedom to build and maintain a fiefdom without accountability for a half century, as Hoover had.

Congress also embraced the Church Committee's recommendation to establish permanent congressional oversight of the FBI. Such committees were created in both houses of Congress. Members of several existing committees—Armed Services, Appropriations, Foreign Affairs, and Judiciary—fought this effort, claiming that oversight of intelligence agencies should be only their responsibility. Given the considerable evidence that showed that none of those committees had in the past exercised the oversight powers they now claimed were theirs, these turf claims did not succeed. During the debate on establishing oversight committees, a few senators, including Senator Milton Young, Republican from North Dakota, argued that Congress could not be trusted with oversight of intelligence agencies. But voices that claimed the FBI must no longer be an autonomous agency, free of checks and balances, won the day.

In 1978, Congress passed the Foreign Intelligence Surveillance Act, regarded by many as the most important reform to emerge from the Church recommendations. It established a secret federal court to review applications for warrants for electronic surveillance for foreign intelligence or counterintelligence purposes in the United States in which communications of residents might be intercepted. The law rejected the claim of presidential inherent authority in such matters, as well as the use of ambiguous terms, such as "subversive" and "national security," to justify electronic surveillance. The court would set time limits on warrants in order to stop the FBI's practice of placing people under endless electronic surveillance. A popular measure, the act passed in the Senate 95 to 1. It was this court that, in the years after 9/11, the administration of President George W. Bush attempted to evade.

A fierce debate erupted over another major reform recommended by the Church Committee, the creation of a legislative charter for the FBI. For many people inside and outside the bureau such a charter was a major goal.

A charter that would spell out, as a matter of law, what the bureau could and could not do, they thought, would be the strongest possible guarantee that the bureau could never again flout the law. FBI director Clarence Kelley was a strong supporter of the charter concept, but he retired before the charter proposal was debated and ultimately rejected.

As the draft of the charter evolved, it became something completely different from what was originally planned by reformers. In the end, goals of charter supporters varied greatly. Some wanted a charter that would deepen reform of the FBI. Others wanted a charter that would thwart reform.

The charter that ultimately was proposed was, in fact, the opposite of what the Church Committee had recommended. Instead of inhibiting overreach and violation of civil liberties by the FBI, the charter endorsed and protected such behavior. Thomas I. Emerson, a constitutional law professor at Yale Law School and a strong advocate of preventing the FBI from continuing its past behavior, called for either rejection or serious revisions of the charter. As written, he said, it would make matters much worse: It could legalize and ingrain more deeply the worst FBI practices instead of preventing them. Senator Edward Kennedy noted when he introduced the charter bill that it had essentially been written by the bureau. In the jawboning that led to the compromise, the reformers had lost. Consequently, Emerson pointed out, the proposed charter would continue to allow "highly intensive methods of investigation that are incompatible with democratic institutions." It did not require judicial warrants for investigations of political organizations, nor did it provide for oversight by the attorney general.

As Aryeh Neier, former head of the ACLU and then law professor at New York University Law School, said during the debate, "It belatedly grants to the bureau to operate, as it has all along, as our national political police."

Former attorney general Ramsey Clark also strongly opposed the charter. "We are considering a law that, far from preserving and enlarging freedom, puts the imprimatur of positive law on police practices and abuses developed over the years that are irreconcilable with the ideas of freedom." He wondered how such a charter even could be proposed at that time. "Now, in the wake of Hoover's career, and knowing of the revelations about COINTELPRO, and the outrageous violations of individuals' freedom, from the Black Panthers to Martin Luther King Jr., from Ethel Rosenberg to Jean Seberg, Congress contemplates memorializing the practices by legalizing them."

Some ACLU officials supported the charter in the belief that a charter, *any* charter, was essential. They agreed that the one proposed in 1979 had major flaws, but they maintained that simply getting a charter in place would pave the way for reform in the future. Once in place, the imperfect charter could be amended.

For many, approving a charter that essentially retroactively made Hoover's FBI lawful was too great a risk. They were not willing to count on amending it in the future. The effort to establish a charter for the FBI failed. Those who initially wanted a charter the most were the people who were most opposed to the one that was proposed. The politics of intelligence had changed again, and compromise was not possible.

With Congress's failure to agree on a charter, the guidelines promulgated by Attorney General Edward Levi in 1976 were the only external rules governing how the FBI should operate. As the first FBI guidelines ever promulgated by an attorney general, they marked a departure from the practice of most past attorneys general forfeiting their supervision of the bureau and its director to the director. At the time, some FBI critics saw Levi's guidelines as a way of heading off a charter—as a way to keep control of the FBI in the executive branch. Critics also saw guidelines promulgated by an attorney general as fragile because they would be subject to being changed every time a new administration took office.

But the guidelines Levi put in place, after conferring with the Church Committee and the FBI, could not be dismissed by reformers. In contrast to the rules-free past, the Levi guidelines required the bureau to have "specific and articulable facts giving reason to believe that an individual or a group is or may be engaged in activities which involve the use of force or violence and which involve or will involve the violation of federal law" in order to open a full investigation. They embodied the idea that "government monitoring of individuals or groups because they hold unpopular or controversial political views is intolerable in our society." Time limits were set on each phase of an investigation. FBI headquarters had to approve the use of informers, and the attorney general had to approve the use of mail covers and other invasive investigative methods.

In 1980, a year after the charter effort died, there was more evidence that the reform pendulum was reversing. That year FBI reform was an issue in the presidential campaign. Ronald Reagan, the Republican candidate, promised that as president he would unleash the FBI. Soon after he became president he took his first step in that direction. In September 1980, just two months before Reagan was elected, W. Mark Felt and Edward Miller had become the only high-ranking bureau officials ever to be convicted of criminal charges. They were convicted for ordering FBI agents to illegally break

W. Mark Felt on CBS's *Face the Nation,* August 30, 1976. *(AP Photo)*

into the homes of families and friends of Weather Underground members. Shortly after he was inaugurated, Reagan pardoned Felt and Miller. It was a sign that as far as his administration was concerned, intelligence reform was over.

Break-ins like the ones Felt and Miller admitted they had approved and directed had been standard practice at the FBI for many years as part of COINTELPRO and other operations. Until their trial, no agent had been prosecuted for such crimes. In the aftermath of the Church Committee revelations and the illegal bureau actions revealed as part of the Socialist Workers Party lawsuit, the Department of Justice investigated dozens of street-level agents, many from the New York field office, who had conducted break-ins and other crimes on behalf of the FBI. Prosecutors decided to charge the high-level officials who had conceived and ordered the crimes rather than the agents who carried out their orders. Some aspects of the crimes were particularly egregious. For instance, Jennifer Dohrn learned years later, when she received her FBI file under the Freedom of Information Act, that in the course of planning the numerous break-ins that were conducted at her apartment and at various places where she worked, Felt suggested agents should kidnap her infant son as a way of pressuring her sister, Bernadine Dohrn, one of the members of the Weather Underground being sought by the FBI, to turn herself in.

When Reagan pardoned Felt and Miller, he likened the pardon to what President Carter had done for draft resisters: "Thousands of draft evaders and others who violated the Selective Service laws were unconditionally pardoned by my predecessor. America was generous to those who refused to serve their country in the Vietnam War. We can be no less generous to two men who acted on high principle to bring an end to the terrorism that was threatening our nation."

When Felt's history emerged more fully, it was evident that in many ways he embodied key aspects of the FBI and its director during its first half century. Like Hoover, Felt spent his entire professional life in the FBI, much of it at Washington headquarters working very closely with Hoover. Like Hoover, he had a public image as a hero—Watergate's Deep Throat and Reagan's terrorism fighter—and managed to evade public scolding for engaging in crimes and dirty tricks.

As the FBI official in charge of inspections of FBI field offices for years, Felt had helped manage the bureau's illegal COINTELPRO operations throughout the country. Like Hoover, he promoted the public image of the FBI by editing or censoring scripts for Hollywood movies and network television dramatic series based on FBI cases. In the two years before Hoover's death, Felt was locked in a bitter contest for Hoover's favor with another top official, William C. Sullivan. Felt won. After Hoover's death, Felt served as the second-highest official, under interim director L. Patrick Gray. In 2005, Felt complied with his family's wishes and briefly emerged from retirement in California to confirm that he was Deep Throat—the mysterious man who met *Washington Post* reporter Bob Woodward in a dark garage and provided or confirmed clues about Watergate crimes.

Not until 2012, in *Leak: Why Mark Felt Became Deep Throat* by Max Holland, did it become widely known that Felt had other important secrets, ones that cast him in a very different light from his heroic image. During his last year in the FBI, Felt leaked information not only to Woodward, but also to other reporters, sometimes on the same day. More significantly, some of what he leaked was not true. Most of this behavior, Holland concludes from extensive research, was motivated not by an idealistic desire to expose corruption—the image promoted by his family and by Woodward and fellow reporter Carl Bernstein—but by an intense and almost reckless desire to be appointed FBI director. Holland also reveals that the two enemies who vied for Hoover's anointment as his successor, Felt and Sullivan, managed to end each other's FBI careers with COINTELPRO-like dirty tricks. Such actions were consistent with Felt's use of deception in reports on the Media burglary to misrepresent the crime scene there in ways that provided Hoover with the justification he wanted in order to blame and punish Tom Lewis, the head agent in the office, for the burglary.

Reagan's pardon of Felt and Miller was the first step he took to turn back the clock at FBI headquarters to the Hoover days. The next step took place in August 1981 when a little-noticed voluminous report by a Department of Justice task force on crime called for the attorney general to take "whatever action is necessary" to eliminate impediments to effective performance of federal law enforcement. After that report, Attorney General William French Smith considerably loosened the controls Levi had put in place. Now the bureau had fewer restrictions on what could prompt and continue an investigation, and the need for attorney general approval of certain investigative methods was eliminated. Those who had predicted Levi's guidelines were fragile and would be short-lived turned out to be right.

In hindsight, perhaps the results were predictable. In 1988, documents released to the Center for Constitutional Rights under the Freedom of Information Act revealed that beginning in 1981, the FBI did indeed assume that the "impediments" on investigations had been lifted. That year it opened a five-year investigation of individuals and organizations that opposed Reagan's policies in Central America. The investigation—which included widespread use throughout the country of informers at political meetings; break-ins at churches, members' homes, and organizations' offices; and surveillance of hundreds of peace demonstrations—started under FBI director William Webster and continued under his successor, William Sessions, both of them former federal judges.

The massive five-year investigation involved fifty-two of the fifty-six FBI field offices and included investigations of the National Council of Churches, the Roman Catholic Maryknoll Sisters, the United Auto Workers, and the Southern Christian Leadership Conference. The focus was on the Committee in Solidarity with the People of El Salvador, known as CISPES.

The ghost of Hoover seemed to be in charge. The investigation was carried out almost precisely as it would have been by him. But there were new elements—ones Hoover never had to confront. Despite Reagan's efforts to unleash the FBI, there were mechanisms in place for holding the FBI accountable, thanks to the Church Committee—recommended reforms that had been enacted. Levi's guidelines had been gutted, as many had feared they would be, but the congressional intelligence committees were in place. Those committees also were subject to political winds, and sometimes they, like Reagan, had the unleashing of the FBI as their goal. At other times they conducted investigations.

In the CISPES case, Director Sessions was grilled by the Senate Intelligence Committee. At first, he defended the program, saying it was justified as part of an international terrorism investigation. That idea had been the brainchild of an informer, Frank Varelli, who told FBI agents that CISPES was linked to the Soviet KGB intelligence agency. Sessions later confessed to the Intelligence Committee that mistakes had been made by the bureau, including continuing to rely on Varelli despite realizing early in the investigation that he was unreliable. Files indicated that officials at headquarters several times warned agents involved in the CISPES operation not to abuse people's First Amendment rights. But agents continued to do precisely that. The warnings had not been followed by internal oversight. For instance, despite such warnings, the New Orleans office moved beyond surveillance to "a plan of attack against CISPES and specifically against individuals who defiantly display their contempt for the U.S. government by making speeches and propagandizing their cause."

At the White House, in contrast to the FBI director's confessional comments about the CISPES investigation, President Reagan said he believed the FBI had conducted a proper investigation against groups opposed to his policy. In the tradition of Presidents Franklin Roosevelt, Lyndon Johnson, and Richard Nixon, Reagan was willing to use the FBI to spy on Americans who opposed his policies.

Little in what was learned during the Senate hearings or from the FBI's internal investigation imparted optimism about internal oversight by leadership at the FBI regarding the CISPES case. But the fact that there was a congressional investigation and hearing constituted a striking change. It was now more difficult for the FBI to hide questionable behavior. A director could be compelled by Congress to testify. It was, in fact, so shocking for an FBI director to testify about such matters that his mere appearance before the committee stirred excitement. A *New York Times* editorial referred to Sessions's "remarkable admission of mistakes in probing opponents of Washington's Central America policy. Such a confession was unimaginable in J. Edgar Hoover's time." Moving beyond surprise that an FBI director could confess mistakes, the editorial writer advised that his "confession ought to remind Congress to take its F.B.I.-monitoring function more seriously." It was time, nine years after the failed attempt by Congress to establish a charter for the FBI, to reopen that effort in order "to shore up its flagging self-regulation," the *Times* editorial urged. That never happened.

THE CONGRESSIONAL INVESTIGATION of the CISPES case unfolded in ways that are indicative of a pattern that has been repeated numerous times over the years since those mid-1970s efforts to curb FBI abuses. The pattern often has included these elements, occurring in this order:

- Abuse by the FBI became known when an organization, a few years after it suspected abuse, managed to get files under the Freedom of Information Act that proved such abuse had indeed taken place. Because it usually took at least a few years, often longer, for such files to be released, abuses usually did not come to light until years after they occurred.
- News stories based on the files were published in one or more major newspapers.
- Editorial writers and officials of civil liberties organizations called for an investigation by Congress.
- A congressional oversight committee investigated the charges and announced it would hold hearings, including testimony from some of the people whose rights were abused.
- The committee compelled the director—fill in name of person at the helm at any given time—to appear before the committee.
- During questioning, the director defended what the bureau had done and said the bureau had not violated civil liberties.
- Weeks or months later, depending on when additional confirming information emerged, either from the press or newly released FBI files, the director appeared again before the committee and acknowledged that the bureau had gone too far, that it had in fact violated civil liberties, that there was no intentional harm, and that the inappropriate behavior would not happen again.
- The committee expressed regret about the abuse and expressed gratitude to the director for eventually being forthright.
- Invariably, a member of the committee remarked that the committee was glad the director was, unlike J. Edgar Hoover, willing to admit error.
- Usually, no one was held responsible.

To some extent, simply not being J. Edgar Hoover was sufficient when it came to how successive directors were perceived by Congress and the presidents who appointed them. But none of the directors developed and carried out plans to change the bureau in ways that truly melded strong respect for the Bill of Rights into the values and skills required in order to be either law enforcers or intelligence gatherers. And Congress seldom, if ever, insisted that such transformation take place. As important as each of the mechanisms put in place by Congress to provide oversight of the FBI was, inertia and lack of political will often made such efforts sluggish and unsystematic.

The single most important reform that has led to exposure of FBI abuses and provided an impetus to continued reform was not any of the actions specifically aimed at changing the bureau. Rather, the single most powerful source of reform has been the Freedom of Information Act, as it was strengthened by Congress in 1974 to require government agencies to respond to requests for government records. Most investigations of FBI abuses have been initiated because information that became known as a result of average citizens, journalists, or civil liberties organizations, such as the ACLU and the Center for Constitutional Rights, requesting FBI files that were so compelling that Congress could not avoid investigating the bureau.

Hoover understood the potential power of the exposure the FOIA would cause. That's why, when the act was first passed in 1966, he ordered FBI officials not to comply with requests made under this new law. And thus his multiple layers of protection of secret records about the bureau's dirty tricks operations, such as COINTELPRO. Hoover's fear of exposure was a compliment to Americans. He thought that if Americans knew what he was really doing—as opposed to the image he had promoted for so long—they would insist that the FBI be investigated. Hoover was right. When some of the essential facts about how he operated were revealed, first by the Media burglars and then by the court-ordered release of more secret FBI files, the public insisted that the FBI be investigated. From a different perspective, William Davidon had that same confidence in Americans: that if they were given evidence that the FBI was suppressing dissent, they would demand an investigation.

Only after changes were made to the FOIA in 1974 did the bureau comply with requests, and then reluctantly. It had done so in one instance before—under court order in 1973 when journalist Carl Stern asked for the first COINTELPRO files. The need for easier access to files was clear "in the immediate aftermath of the Watergate hearings," says leading FBI scholar Athan Theoharis. As the author or editor of several books on the

FBI, he has obtained thousands of FBI files under the FOIA to develop a historical record of the FBI that was impossible to document until original files became available as a result of the 1974 amendments that strengthened the FOIA. Trials and hearings related to Watergate, as well as revelations from the Media files and news stories about the CIA's unlawful domestic operations, Theoharis says, made clear "the extent to which national security claims are political security claims, not legitimate claims." In the face of becoming aware of the monumental harm done by government secrecy, not to mention lies, about the Vietnam War and about intelligence practices, there was a strong consensus in 1974, says Theoharis, that "we need to ensure access to records if we're going to understand what the federal government is actually doing."

At first FBI officials negotiated with Congress to weaken the proposed 1974 FOIA reforms. Then they decided to stop negotiations because the bureau "wanted the bill to be 'as bad as possible' to make the case stronger for presidential veto," according to a National Security Archives report. The effort to defeat the 1974 FOIA reforms was supported inside Gerald Ford's administration by Donald Rumsfeld, Ford's White House chief of staff; Dick Cheney, the deputy chief of staff; and Antonin Scalia. The future Supreme Court justice was then head of the office of legal counsel at the Department of Justice office. Scalia rallied opposition to the measure, urging the CIA to push the White House to veto it. As a young member of Congress in 1966, Rumsfeld had supported the original Freedom of Information Act. In 1974, concerned about leaks from the Ford administration, he opposed strengthening the law.

Ford was inclined initially to sign the law, realizing that, as one aide put it in a memo, to veto a Freedom of Information law might be a political disadvantage in an administration that, in the wake of Watergate, had openness and candor as its theme. Nevertheless, Ford vetoed the bill. The public consensus for more disclosure was so strong that his veto was easily overridden: by a vote of 371–31 in the House and 65–27 in the Senate.

ANY ASSESSMENT of the FBI's history should acknowledge that the bureau has endured unprecedented circumstances. No other government agency was shaped by and in the image of one individual. Workers in no other agency worked, willingly or unwillingly, in the rigid and secret world of a single leader for so long. Also, no other agency has been forced to reveal elements of its unsavory past and been forced to change after having been told forever that it was a model law enforcement agency, the world's best. In the wake of the 1970s investigations of the FBI, many agents must have felt whiplashed, caught between the spirit of the reformers of the 1970s and the spirit of the past. Many retired as soon as they could, rather than deal with change. Many decided simply to hunker down and change as little as possible. Others thought the reforms made them better agents because the new rules set limits that led to stronger evidence for prosecutions and to more precision in intelligence gathering.

But whatever the bureau had become by September 11, 2001, it did not seem to matter. On September 12, the FBI was confronted and ordered to change. Drastically. Immediately. The turmoil that roiled the bureau, beginning then, may have surpassed even the tumult that took place when Hoover's loyal followers resisted the investigations and bureau reforms of the 1970s. Now, in the aftermath of 9/11, the changes were fast and furious and threatened the bureau in fundamental ways, including a push to remove one of its major missions.

Robert S. Mueller III, on the job as director only a week by 9/11, had spent most of his career as a prosecutor or supervisor of prosecutions. He assumed that would be his job now, leading the FBI in investigating what had happened and contributing to the Justice Department's future prosecution of the people who had planned these horrific crimes. Attorney General John Ashcroft had news for him: Forget prosecutions. His order to the new FBI director was huge:

"This must not happen again."

Describing a similar encounter at that time with President George W. Bush, Mueller said in an April 2013 address at his alma mater, the University of Virginia School of Law, "I felt like a high school kid who had done the wrong homework assignment. I got it wrong."

Mueller said he realized then that the course of the bureau had to change. Shortly after those encounters with Bush and Ashcroft, Mueller sent this message to the special agents in charge of the fifty-six FBI field offices:

"The FBI has just one set of priorities: *Stop the next attack.*"

Overnight, the FBI's mandate was to transform itself from a law enforcement and domestic intelligence agency into primarily a domestic intelligence agency, just as the CIA had a new mandate to greatly expand its paramilitary capacity. There were threats from Congress to force the Bush administration to entirely remove intelligence gathering from the FBI and establish a new domestic intelligence agency.

While Americans assumed the FBI was going into high gear to do everything it could to save the country from the next attack, the bureau had a double focus. It was trying to guard against another attack while also fighting for its continued existence. Hoover's instant reaction to any circumstance that reflected badly on him or the bureau had been to find a person who could be scapegoated. In the aftermath of September 11, some bureau officials felt the bureau itself was the scapegoat.

Top bureau officials may have felt somewhat cynical when they became aware of Ashcroft's demand that their mission shift dramatically in order to prevent another attack. In the months immediately before 9/11, Ashcroft had blocked the bureau's efforts to increase its counterterrorism efforts. It was later discovered that though the FBI may have failed to see crucial signs that pointed to terrorist attacks, some bureau officials, including Thomas Pickard, who had become acting director when Louis Freeh resigned as director in June 2001, were pressing the issue urgently in the months before 9/11. When Pickard submitted the bureau's annual budget to Ashcroft that summer, he asked for an increase in only one area, counterterrorism. On July 18, Ashcroft sent a letter to Pickard in which he not only rejected the increase but also reduced the bureau's existing counterterrorism budget. Determined to reverse that decision, Pickard immediately appealed it and made the case for the urgent need for an increase in the counterterrorism budget. In a letter dated September 10 that arrived on Pickard's desk the morning of September 12, the attorney general notified Pickard that his appeal had been rejected. The bureau's budget for counterterrorism would be cut, not increased.

Ashcroft's striking lack of interest in fighting terrorism was made astonishingly clear to Pickard in other ways in the months before 9/11. In an early-summer conversation with the attorney general, Pickard told Ashcroft that chatter picked up by the CIA about possible attacks was very strong. Ashcroft told him then he was not interested in hearing about terrorism. On July 12, Pickard met with Ashcroft with the goal of convincing him that terrorism was a serious threat that needed his attention, not to mention the critical attention of the bureau. "We're at a very high level of chatter that something big is about to happen," Pickard later recalled telling the attorney general that day. "The CIA is very alarmed." At that point, Ashcroft interrupted him: "I don't want to hear about that anymore. There's nothing I can do about that."

Feeling a desperate need to convince Ashcroft of the urgency posed by terrorism, Pickard continued to try to press his case. As he did, Ashcroft jumped to his feet and angrily told him, "I don't want you to ever talk to me about al-Qaeda, about these threats. I don't want to hear about al-Qaeda anymore."

After 9/11, Ashcroft sang a different tune. What he had insisted Pickard not discuss, he now demanded the FBI turn its full attention to: "This must not happen again."

BY THE TIME the National Commission on Terrorist Attacks upon the United States, known as the 9/11 Commission, issued its final report in July 2004, Mueller had saved the FBI. He succeeded in convincing the commission that the bureau should remain intact and continue to be responsible for domestic intelligence gathering. Congress also stopped demanding that the bureau should forfeit that major function. The commission, in fact, had harsh words for Congress. In the years before 9/11, the commissioners concluded, congressional oversight of intelligence and counterterrorism issues had become "dysfunctional" and divided among too many congressional committees. The legislators were urged to take their oversight responsibility more seriously, to conduct "robust oversight."

Though Mueller had saved the bureau from being gutted, it was unclear if he was succeeding in transforming it in ways that would make it possible for the FBI to meet the demand that it prevent another attack. Even under the best of internal circumstances, the bureau could not, of course, guarantee that it meet that demand. The pressure to do so was enormous. Every tip that streamed in was supposed to be followed, no matter how insignificant some of them seemed. The fear of missing a big one was agonizing. One FBI official at headquarters shot himself to death at home after receiving an alarming call in the middle of the night from an agent in New York.

In the midst of Mueller's efforts to transform the bureau, evidence emerged that the bureau had indeed missed clues that, if followed, might have prevented the 9/11 attacks. Information that the average person, let alone a counterterrorism agent, might regard as a blinking red light had not led to investigations. Crucial information had not been communicated from one intelligence agency to another, despite, in at least one instance, an FBI agent assigned to the CIA formally requesting CIA permission to provide crucial information to counterterrorism specialists at the FBI. Inexplicably, he was denied permission. Even more unexplainable, counterterrorism officials at the FBI failed to communicate some crucial information about potential terrorist threats to one another, and sometimes did not communicate it to the acting director, Pickard, despite his known priority regarding such threats.

The bureau's pre-9/11 failures came to public attention most forcefully in June 2002, when Coleen Rowley, a longtime FBI agent and a lawyer in the bureau's Minneapolis office, testified in Congress about the refusal of officials at FBI headquarters in August 2001 to seek the judicial emergency search warrant Minneapolis agents formally requested in order to search the laptop and other possessions of Zacarias Moussaoui, a French-born man who had been arrested in Minnesota for overstaying his visa after he finished a course in flying commercial jetliners at a local flight school. From discussions with European intelligence agencies, Harry Samit, an agent in the Minneapolis office, learned that Moussaoui was a recruiter for a Muslim extremist allied with Osama bin Laden. That information, combined with knowing that Moussaoui recently had paid $8,600 in cash for his flight training, alarmed Samit about the threat Moussaoui might pose. He thought it was imperative to review the files on Moussaoui's computer as soon as possible. With a sense of growing urgency, he and Rowley made repeated attempts to get the necessary warrant. Each time counterterrorism officials at headquarters refused their request, seeming not to take Samit and Rowley's concerns seriously. They were turned down again early the morning of September 11. After the fourth plane crashed in Pennsylvania on 9/11, counterterrorism officials at headquarters relented and obtained the warrant that made it possible for Minneapolis agents to inspect Moussaoui's belongings.

Their suspicions had been justified. On his computer they found, among other information of interest, the German phone number for the roommate of Mohamed Atta, the ringleader of the 9/11 plot. They also learned that Moussaoui was the paymaster for the 9/11 hijackers. Moussaoui later pled guilty to conspiring in the 9/11 plot and was sentenced to life in prison. He is the only person who has been tried in a U.S. court on charges of involvement in the September 11 attacks.

In that instance, it was not simply a matter of the bureau not connecting the dots, a criticism that has been leveled against it many times since 9/11. It was a matter of officials at bureau headquarters not listening to the warnings of agents who did connect dots and who repeatedly tried to push through the inertia at Washington headquarters to avert the tragedy they feared might happen. Years later, the Minneapolis agents continued to think of the failure to get permission to investigate Moussaoui earlier as what former *New York Times* reporter Philip Shenon later called "the terrible missed chance."

In her testimony before a Senate committee in June 2002, and in an earlier letter to Mueller, Rowley criticized his public claim after September 11 that the bureau had known nothing before September 11 that could have prevented the attacks that day. He stopped making that claim.

That extreme example from the Minneapolis field office, as well as other pre-9/11 missed opportunities, illustrate Mueller's challenge as he set out to reinvent the FBI. The challenge was complicated not only by continuing emergency circumstances that put the bureau under great pressure, but also by haunting mistakes during the recent past and by ingrained habits from the more distant past. As Shenon concluded in his 2008 book *The Commission: The Uncensored History of the 9/11 Investigation,*

"The problem was mostly with the agency's sclerotic, hierarchical bureaucracy in Washington—at its core, unchanged since the days of J. Edgar Hoover—as well as the FBI's unmatched arrogance in dealing with other government agencies."

That analysis was reflected in an investigation of the bureau's pre-9/11 failures by Glenn Fine, the Department of Justice inspector general. He found "significant deficiencies in the way the FBI handled these issues." The FBI, he reported, was stymied by bureaucratic obstacles, communication breakdowns, and a lack of urgency. His investigation confirmed that before 9/11 crucial warnings related to possible future terrorist attacks were not acted on. When his report was released, Fine told a reporter he did not "believe it was misconduct on the part of the individuals so much as systemic problems" at the bureau.

While part of the bureau struggled to adapt to the new mandate, the part of the bureau that relies on street agents and informers easily slipped into old Hoover-era habits that were first exposed by the Media burglars, habits that may never have been lost. Unproductive and invasive investigative methods from the Hoover era, such as closely monitoring nonviolent antiwar protesters, were dusted off. An inspector general's investigation found that FBI officials had made false and misleading statements to Congress in 2002 about the fact that it had placed under investigation several organizations because they opposed the war in Iraq. The groups included pacifist organizations—the Catholic Worker movement, the Thomas Merton Center, and the American Friends Service Committee. In the aftermath of 9/11, such protesters were classified as terrorists.

In some parts of the country, mosques were infiltrated by a greatly expanded army of FBI informers, many with the misunderstanding—one actually taught in FBI workshops for a while after 9/11—that most Muslims should be regarded with suspicion and therefore as investigative targets in the effort to prevent another 9/11. Instead of focusing on developing truly knowledgeable sources in Muslim communities, some bureau officials followed what had proven in the past to be an easy but usually time-absorbing, unproductive, and invasive investigative method—blanket surveillance. Muslim communities, including the congregations of some mosques, were saturated with surveillance without regard for whether a given mosque was known as a place where radical jihadists gathered to plot future attacks. The use of such methods also is evidence that the FBI's historic difficulty in understanding other cultures has persisted at a time when such understanding has been perhaps more important than at any time in the bureau's history.

The expanded use of invasive surveillance was made possible by the passage, shortly after 9/11, of the Patriot Act, which considerably loosened restraints on the FBI. As the Bush administration was about to leave office, Attorney General Michael Mukasey, a former federal judge in New York, issued new attorney general guidelines for the FBI. As of his rewriting of the guidelines, first put in place in 1976 by Attorney General Levi and modified repeatedly since then, the FBI could operate with even fewer restrictions. Agents could target individuals without a clear basis for suspecting they were planning a crime. Mukasey validated the casting of wide nets that pulled people into investigations on the basis of their race, religion, or political activities, as long as they met any additional criteria that drew suspicion. It was widely assumed that Eric Holder, attorney general in the Obama administration, would revise Mukasey's FBI guidelines and restore some of the restrictions. Instead, the Obama administration loosened some FBI guidelines more. It also deepened secrecy about national security policies and practices, including secrecy about policies and laws governing its greatly increased use overseas of unmanned drones to kill suspected terrorists and conduct surveillance.

AS THE BUREAU STRUGGLED to transform itself after 9/11, it was forced to embrace new methods and new tools in order to fulfill its greatly expanded intelligence-gathering mission. New data collection and analysis systems were installed. The new equipment and data systems were to be used by agents who, because of wrongheaded decisions by directors in the 1980s and 1990s, had little familiarity with even minimal computer use. The computers in their offices were so old that agents could not send or receive email, and they could not do basic research of bureau files from their computers, let alone conduct searches on the Internet. Millions of dollars were spent on failed attempts to update and integrate the bureau's computer systems.

Current technology was not the only important element missing at the FBI in 2001. So were crucial language skills. Thousands of hours of Arabic-language phone conversations recorded by the bureau before the 9/11 attacks had not been translated because the bureau had few translators who understood Arabic.

By three years after 9/11, a report by the inspector general revealed that so many recordings believed to be relevant to terrorism had not been translated that, as Senator Charles E. Grassley, Republican from Iowa, said at the time, the FBI was still drowning in information about terrorism activities. Even with a great increase in the number of translators of Arabic, Farsi, and other languages, the influx of new material from wiretaps and other intelligence sources vastly outpaced the bureau's translation capacity. By 2004, more than 123,000 hours of audio recordings collected since 9/11 in languages associated with terrorism had not yet been translated. For all languages, nearly half a million hours of audiotapes, or 30 percent of what had been collected since 9/11, had not been translated. A bureau rule required that audio recordings directly related to active al-Qaeda investigations be transcribed within twelve hours of interception, but because of the backlog, such transcriptions routinely were not made until at least a month after they were recorded. Computer problems also aggravated the translation problems. Without FBI officials realizing it, as computer drives filled with recordings to be translated, older recordings, including many that had not been translated, were automatically deleted, never to be heard. In an understatement, the inspector general's report said the bureau faced "significant management challenges" in developing quick and accurate translations.

The bureau got more money, more agents, more informers, more translators, more analysts, more computers, and much, much more data to use in its effort to prevent another terrorist attack—an effort that by now has continued for more than a decade.

As this growth took place, the bureau became part of the vastly expanded national security system that has burgeoned since 9/11 in government and private industry, a system that *Washington Post* journalists Dana Priest and William M. Arkin call "Top Secret America." In their series and book based on their extensive examination of the expansion and quality of the nation's security system a decade after 9/11, they concluded that "the top-secret world the government created in response to the terrorist attacks of September 11, 2001, had become so large, so unwieldy and so secretive that no one knows how much money it costs, how many people it employs, how many programs exist within it or exactly how many agencies do the same work."

The influx of information became enormous. Priest and Arkin reported in 2011 that the National Security Agency, the government's major surveillance system, "now ingests 1.7 billion pieces of intercepted communications every twenty-four hours—telephone calls, radio signals, cell phone conversations, emails, text and Twitter messages, bulletin board postings, instant messages, website changes, computer network pings, and IP addresses."

As large digital haystacks have grown in the FBI—and in other intelligence agencies—from a constant inward rush of new data from collection systems, other government agencies, and private industry, so has frustration about developing the capacity to extract valuable information from these digital haystacks. The increasing flow of data, and consequent greater demand to analyze data, was developed to increase the capacity of the bureau to discover and piece together crucial information that, if acted upon, might prevent another attack. But some people question whether that endless flow may instead decrease the bureau's capacity to succeed at that task. The sheer volume is overwhelming at times, much of it duplicative and much of it ignored or never seen. A system meant to send alerts to its users often instead produces a numbing effect.

Assessing the impact of the volume of undifferentiated information intelligence agencies receive daily, Richard Clarke, who served as chief counterterrorism adviser on the National Security Council under both President Bill Clinton and President George W. Bush, said in a 2013 interview, "More is good. A hell of a lot more can be bad."

THERE HAVE BEEN alarming signs that the systems put in place have not worked well at crucial times. For instance, available clues were not connected, or were not taken seriously, in two major attacks, one that happened and one that failed—the rampage shootings by an Army psychiatrist at Fort Hood that resulted in the deaths of thirteen people, and the failed attempt by a Nigerian radical, Umar Farouk Abdulmutallab, to bomb Detroit as the commercial jet in which he was a passenger landed there on Christmas Day 2009. In the latter case, the would-be attacker's father had informed officials at the American embassy in Lagos, Nigeria, about his son's radicalization and interest in attacking the United States. In the end, no steps were taken to prevent him from entering the country. His effort to bomb Detroit failed because he was tackled by a passenger who observed the man trying to ignite explosives hidden in his underwear. Explicit information about the Christmas bomber's plans was missed, Priest and Arkin reported, because, as an official admitted to them, "the system had gotten so big that the lines of responsibility had become hopelessly blurred." As far as the FBI was concerned, the information in its own files about Abdulmutallab was a secret—a secret that was inaccessible to the FBI.

After the Senate Intelligence Committee investigated the handling of the failed Detroit bombing, it issued a report that was a sweeping indictment. The problems included failure of agents to communicate with one another as well as mistakes in computer programing. A counterterrorism analyst at the FBI never received relevant information sent to her about Abdulmutallab because the incorrect configuration of her computer profile blocked reception of the information. Commenting on the glitches that prevented intelligence agencies from stopping the Christmas bomber before he nearly succeeded, former Senator Christopher S. Bond, Republican from Missouri, then the vice chair of the Senate Intelligence Committee, summarized the persisting problem:

"We cannot depend on dumb luck, incompetent terrorists and alert citizens to keep our families safe."

In another Senate report, "A Ticking Time Bomb"—this one an investigation of intelligence agencies' handling of the Fort Hood attack by the Senate Committee on Homeland Security and Government Affairs—it was found that crucial information the committee concluded might have averted the attack was mishandled as it moved among FBI offices and in exchanges between the FBI and military intelligence offices.

JUST AS Hoover's secret FBI's emphasis on conducting political surveillance and dirty tricks—along with his emphasis on solving easy crimes, stolen cars and bank robberies, while neglecting the crimes that damaged society most, organized crime and government corruption—distorted the mission and competence of the bureau while he was director, the difficulty of accessing and analyzing the enormous data collections of Top Secret America has threatened bureau competence since 9/11. When the bureau does not know what dots it has, it cannot connect dots.

The new FBI secrecy is potentially dangerous to the public in two ways: first, in regard to what the FBI needs to know but cannot find, and second, in regard to what the FBI does not need to know but that it has been collecting since 9/11 and storing in the vast databases shared across the nation's seventeen intelligence agencies. That information about millions of Americans—much of it needlessly collected, much of it duplicative, much of it irrelevant to the mission of the FBI or any other intelligence agency, much of it so overwhelming in volume that it is ignored—sits there, available, as Hoover's secret files were, for potential abusive use at any time, including invasion of privacy and inhibiting civil liberties.

Since 9/11, many people in the FBI have engaged in near-heroic efforts to keep the bureau an effective and law-abiding agency in the face of major operational changes and massive internal and external pressures to succeed in its assignment as the nation's chief bulwark against another terrorist attack in the United States. To some degree, struggles inside the bureau reflect conflicting public concerns. Many Americans are very afraid of another attack taking place in the United States and want maximum protection from the bureau, even if liberties must be sacrificed. At the same time, many other Americans feel conflicted. They too are afraid, but they do not want fear of enemies, external or internal, to overwhelm either the bureau's capacity to protect the country or its ability to function as a lawful intelligence and law enforcement agency that also protects privacy and civil liberties.

27

The NSA Files

W HILE THE FBI was spending millions of dollars in the years immediately after 9/11 on repeated attempts to create a useful bureau-wide computer system, one that would make it possible for agents to be able, finally, to send email messages to one another and do basic searches of the bureau's own files, the National Security Agency (NSA) was executing a far more advanced high-tech plan. During that time the agency put in place sophisticated equipment and software programs that allowed it to monitor and absorb the world.

The most startling aspect of that expansion was the NSA's decision less than a month after the 9/11 attacks to aim its powerful electronic surveil-lance equipment at Americans' communications and take it all in, literally. Until then, the mission of the NSA, the nation's largest intelligence agency, had been limited to surveillance of enemies overseas. Now it was targeting law-abiding Americans, hoping to find the few terrorists among them, and also conducting blanket surveillance of the citizens of some of America's closest allies.

Phone calls by landline or cell, email messages, Internet searches, text messages, Facebook messages, audio messages, video streaming—the NSA was accessing all of it and storing it.

As the NSA exponentially increased its surveillance powers, so did the FBI. As the NSA's main partner in surveillance operations, the FBI now had access to the vast array of domestic intelligence retrieved by the NSA. This data was the primary source of the huge new haystacks of data that grew inside the FBI after 9/11. With the bureau's capacity expanded by the NSA developing cutting-edge surveillance equipment, it was now able to sweep up more information than the late FBI director, J. Edgar Hoover, could have imagined as a capability.

The extent and nature of the NSA's expansion since 9/11 had only been hinted at before June 2013, when a former NSA contractor, Edward J. Snowden, released to journalists Laura Poitras, documentary filmmaker, and Glenn Greenwald, then of *The Guardian,* NSA files that provided extensive evidence of the vast NSA expansion and how it operated. The evidence in the NSA files raised profound questions. In addition to important personal and political questions about the impact of mass surveillance of Americans and the residents of other countries, the evidence of the penetrating capacity of the new NSA—and by extension, of the new FBI— also raised profound questions about the possibility that Internet freedom was being seriously damaged by its use by powerful intelligence agencies as a giant surveillance machine. Equally important were questions about the Internet now being seen by the government as a mechanism for new forms of warfare and, indeed, as a new landscape for war. As one top-secret memo put it, cyber operations will be turned into "another capability alongside air, sea and land forces."

At first, intelligence officials denied the reports that the NSA was conducting massive surveillance of Americans' communications. Eventually, they admitted that it did but that doing so was essential to preventing the next terrorist attack. Director of National Intelligence James Clapper, in response to questions at a hearing of the Senate Intelligence Committee in March 2013, said the NSA did not collect data on millions of Americans. After the release of secret NSA files that contained evidence that contradicted Clapper's congressional testimony, he wrote a letter to the committee in which he admitted that his prior testimony had been "clearly erroneous— for which I apologize." Some members of Congress have called for him to be prosecuted for lying to Congress.

In attempts to justify the massive sweeps, intelligence officials and President Barack Obama insisted that the agency was collecting metadata from the phone calls—information about where each call was made and its destination, when each call was placed and its duration. Such information, they said, could be extracted from data banks and used to establish connections between terrorists and potential terrorists. The content of the calls, they insisted, was not collected or listened to.

Additional NSA files, however, provided confirmation that, indeed, the content of calls was being collected and could easily be retrieved. In fact, the vast amounts of additional material being stored by the NSA for the possible future use of either metadata or the content of individual communications was a key reason for the current expansion of the NSA's physical facilities, or data warehouses, in the United States and around the globe. Elaborating on the files that documented that the NSA and the FBI now tapped directly into the central servers of at least nine leading U.S. Internet companies to extract whatever the user had produced, or was producing, Snowden said, "They can literally watch your ideas form as you type."

The NSA files revealed that expansion of the NSA's reach was greatly aided by its collaboration with foreign intelligence agencies and communications companies here and abroad. For instance, the NSA has greatly increased its international surveillance capacity by working closely with its longtime British counterpart, GCHQ (Government Communications Headquarters). With massive funds from the NSA, GCHQ created Tempora, a system American and British agencies use to collect the phone calls and web traffic that travel through fiber-optic cables under the sea. According to an NSA file, major American and European phone companies have secretly given GCHQ and the NSA unlimited access to their network of undersea fiber-optic cables. The capacity of the cables is extraordinary. They can convey more than 21 petabytes a day—equivalent to transmitting all the information in the 14 million books in the British Library 192 times every twenty-four hours.

The two intelligence agencies also are perfecting their existing cell phone surveillance capability. The stated goal of the project is to "exploit any phone, anywhere, any time." This plan includes developing the ability to "attack" phone apps and increase capacity to track the patterns of unlimited numbers of emails, conversations, Internet searches, and any other use of cell phones.

After reviewing the scope of the NSA's capacity, it is not surprising to learn that the vision of the agency and its British collaborators is "to tap directly into the nervous system of the 21st century and peer into the lives of others."

AMERICANS' REACTIONS to these revelations have been mixed, becoming increasingly critical of the NSA as more evidence has been revealed. Many ardent defenders of the right to privacy and of civil liberties are grateful that some organizations, key among them the American Civil Liberties Union, have strongly opposed these new intrusions into Americans' lives. Others accept the assurances of President Obama and intelligence officials that all of this expansion has been necessary in order to prevent the next terrorist attack.

The contrast between public attitudes during the Hoover era and now is interesting in regard to how people have reacted to evidence of intrusive invasions by intelligence agencies. For decades, many Americans accepted Hoover's pronouncements that communism was at the heart of every new movement for rights that came along, and, therefore, such movements should be regarded as potentially subversive. But when Americans were presented with evidence—from the Media burglars and subsequent investigations—of the true nature of what the bureau did under his leadership, a national consensus developed that his methods were not only unacceptable but must be guarded against in the future. Given evidence, few thought it was acceptable to place members of nonviolent groups, such as various Quaker organizations or the Southern Christian Leadership Conference, under constant surveillance. Few thought it was acceptable that actress Jean Seberg should be harassed by the FBI's planting false rumors about the race of the father of her unborn child, a dirty tricks operation that resulted in the death of her premature baby and, ultimately, in her suicide. And few thought it was acceptable for the FBI to secretly decide that Martin Luther King was a demagogue who should be displaced by the bureau as leader of the civil rights movement and in the process be harassed for years by the bureau, including sending him a message suggesting he should kill himself.

By contrast, Americans have had a more muted reaction to the evidence presented to them about overreach by the NSA and the FBI. The evidence of overreach by intelligence agencies arrives now while many people still fear that there is an enemy who might hit again at any time. That fear has been encouraged by presidents and intelligence officials as they have reminded Americans often that they should be afraid, and should also be confident that they are being protected by increased security measures.

Uncertainty about the new enemy, as well as uncertainty about whether officials are leveling with Americans about the enemy, has made it difficult to ask questions during discussions of national security. It is especially difficult to discuss whether the government has taken steps that may have increased the vulnerability to attack.

Many politicians, like the citizens they represent, have felt paralyzed by this issue. They have been afraid to ask questions because they fear that if there is a terror attack tomorrow, those who questioned increasing the capacity of the security apparatus will be blamed for the attack and voted out of office at the next election. Consequently, Republican and Democratic administrations and leaders in Congress have found since 9/11 that the only deeply bipartisan issue has been the expansion of national security.

That's why it was striking news two months after the secret NSA files became public when a bipartisan group of members of the House of Representatives nearly succeeded in defunding the NSA's telephone data collection program. The measure, proposed by Representative Justin Amash, Republican from Michigan, and cosponsored by Representative John Conyers, Democrat from Michigan, failed, but by a surprisingly narrow margin, 205–217. Both opposition and support for the measure were strongly bipartisan. The Democratic and Republican leaders of the House, in rare agreement, pushed the president's strong request that the measure be defeated. The signal sent by the close vote was so strong that two days after the vote, sixty-one House Democrats who had voted no on the measure, including House party leaders Nancy Pelosi, Democrat from California, and Steny Hoyer, Democrat from Maryland, sent the president a letter signaling that they had stood with him on that vote but that they would now join the effort to roll back the massive government surveillance.

A crucial moment in the debate on the move to defund NSA phone surveillance came when Representative James Sensenbrenner, Republican from Wisconsin, told his colleagues that as a primary author of the Patriot Act and its various extensions since 9/11—the law intended to give intelligence agencies more leeway, but not as much as it was now widely understood they had taken—he and his coauthors never intended to allow the wholesale vacuuming up of domestic phone records, nor did they envision that their legislation supported data dragnets that would go beyond specific targets of terrorism investigations. "The time has come to stop it," he said as he urged the members to vote to defund.

Because of his deep involvement with the legislation that is supposed to govern the intelligence agencies, Sensenbrenner's remarks were regarded as a pivotal moment. Politicians also said their move toward reining in the agencies reflected a gut-level concern about personal privacy that had been growing among their constituents since the release of the NSA files. When the files were first released, Congress and the public focused mostly on bringing the leaker to justice. Some, including House Speaker John Boehner, Republican from Ohio, and former vice president Dick Cheney, called Snowden a traitor. But, as more revelations of penetrating surveillance emerged, the emphasis switched from punishing Snowden to confronting the implications of the files he revealed.

Two senators, Senator Ron Wyden, Democrat from Oregon, and Senator Mark Udall, Democrat from Utah, had repeatedly asked the NSA in recent years if it could quantify the number of Americans it was surveilling. Agency officials first told the senators the agency did not have the technological capacity to extract the number. Later it told them that expending time searching for the number would divert time and money from surveillance, "likely impeding the NSA's mission." In the NSA files that Snowden made public was the answer. Yes, the agency could find the number. An appropriately named NSA program, Boundless Informant, was created for the purpose of quantifying how many people were being surveilled in any country at any moment. NSA slides released showed that the agency kept ongoing records of this information and that the level of surveillance in any country could be accessed at any time with a click on a country on a digital map of the world that was color-coded to show at a glance the various levels of surveillance in each country.

Wyden, who has been a Paul Revere in Congress on these matters, repeatedly warning that surveillance is out of control, has been grateful for the growing bipartisan coalition on the issue in Congress. Now that NSA evidence was on the table, more people took seriously his warning that the country was faced with an emergency due to overreaching intelligence. In a speech after the release of the first NSA files, he said:

> We find ourselves at a truly unique time in our constitutional history. The growth of digital technology, dramatic changes in the nature of warfare and the definition of the battlefield, and novel courts that run counter to everything the Founding Fathers imagined, make for a combustible mix. . . . If we don't take this opportunity to change course now, we will all live to regret it.

Wyden's remarks were a strong echo of a warning not heeded that was made by Senator Frank Church during the 1976 Senate investigation of intelligence agencies by the committee he chaired. Church said even then that the NSA had unique invasive capacities. Fearful of what would happen if the NSA ever turned its highly charged spying powers onto Americans—as it now has—Church warned:

> The National Security Agency's capability at any time could be turned around on the American people, and no American would have any pri-

vacy left, such is the capability to monitor everything: telephone conversations, telegrams, it doesn't matter. There would be no place to hide. If a dictator ever took over, the NSA could enable it to impose total tyranny, and there would be no way to fight back.

A dictator is not in place, but a tyranny-ready technological surveillance infrastructure is in place. Started by President George W. Bush, a president who used faulty intelligence and deliberate lies as the basis for starting the war in Iraq, the NSA's high-tech tyranny-ready surveillance infrastructure has been continued and expanded by President Obama, who promised unparalleled transparency at the start of his first administration and who is the first president who has taught constitutional law. Equally anomalous, his administration also has criminally prosecuted more government whistleblowers than have all previous presidents combined.

To a large degree, the excesses that the released NSA files document are the result of the failure of two of the key reforms created by Congress in response to the investigation and recommendations made by the Church Committee. Two key innovations put in place in the 1970s to protect Americans from abuses by intelligence agencies, the FISA Court and the congressional intelligence oversight committees, since 9/11 have become rubber stamps of the intelligence agencies, enablers of the abuses they were created to guard against and of a massive abuse that didn't exist then—blanket electronic surveillance of hundreds of millions of Americans. Some became willing enablers by virtue of not caring how far the intelligence agencies went in interpreting their legal mandate. Others became enablers by virtue of assuming they could trust the agencies to interpret their mandate as it was limited by the law. Still others have simply been afraid to ask questions they knew needed to be asked. In any event, the result has been that the strong oversight envisioned in the 1970s—and that the 9/11 Commission urged in its investigation after 9/11—dissolved as the congressional intelligence committees increasingly became primarily advocates for rather than overseers of the intelligence agencies.

Operating in secrecy, as it is required to, the FISA Court by now has written a body of secret law that is not examined in the usual chain of judicial review. It functions, some analysts have said, like a parallel Supreme Court, but without any exposure of its decisions. No one except intelligence officials and the judges themselves know the substance or rationale of the court's decisions. It also lacks the presence of an adversary, a lawyer in hearings to test the government's surveillance requests to the court. The overall secrecy of all aspects of the court and the lack of an adversarial process leave the court open to questions about how it has been possible for intelligence agencies to have such an extraordinary success rate before the court: In its thirty-five-year history, the court has rejected only eleven out of more than 34,000 surveillance requests.

PEOPLE IN OTHER COUNTRIES were enraged when they learned from reports on the NSA files that the agency had conducted blanket surveillance not only of some European countries but at thirty-eight embassies and missions, describing them as "targets." These efforts were aimed not only against countries that might be expected to be U.S. adversaries, but also against the embassies of U.S. allies—France, Italy, Greece, Japan, Mexico, Brazil, South Korea, and Turkey and European Union missions and home offices.

NSA surveillance of the EU has been extensive. It took place at the union's offices in Washington, at the United Nations, and also at its offices in Brussels. In order to hear and record discussions, NSA installed bugs in EU meeting rooms at its Washington office. Its computer network was infiltrated, giving the American intelligence agency access to emails and documents generated on EU computers. Antennas were installed to collect transmissions. The same methods were used at the Brussels headquarters of the EU and were directed from the nearby headquarters of NATO.

In collaboration with Britain's GCHQ, the NSA spied on international heads of state who attended two London conferences. The spy agencies monitored the leaders and their staffs by, among other methods, setting up an ersatz Internet café for the participants. As the leaders used the café's computers, all communications executed from the computers were collected by the spies, thanks to interception software that had been installed on them by the NSA. In addition, at one of the London conferences, forty-five intelligence analysts intercepted the leaders' cell phone calls and tracked who they were calling.

Germans reacted with more outrage than any other people to the revelations that they were under NSA surveillance. According to one of the agency's files, 500 million German communication connections were monitored every month. "It is reminiscent of methods used by enemies during the Cold War," said German justice minister Sabine Leutheusser-Schnarrenberger when she learned about the NSA program.

"The spying has reached dimensions that I didn't think were possible for a democratic country," said Elmar Bok, chairman of the Foreign Affairs Committee in the European Parliament. "The U.S., once the land of the free, is suffering from a security syndrome. They have completely lost all balance. George Orwell is nothing by comparison."

German officials, including Chancellor Angela Merkel, seemed to share Germans' concerns at first. But German officials became defensive and then nearly mute on the matter after German journalists reported that the NSA surveillance of Germans was being conducted with full cooperation of the German government. High-level NSA officials and their German counterparts have been working together closely, including holding frequent joint meetings at their headquarters in both countries. Germany, in the midst of expanding its own domestic surveillance operations, has been relying on assistance from the NSA. So strong was German outrage that before it was known that intelligence collaboration took place at the highest levels of the two governments, some called for a criminal inquiry of any German complicit in the NSA efforts.

All of this—learning about the NSA spying in Germany and about Germany's collaboration with the NSA—was a source of anger and deep disappointment for many Germans. Their reaction is shaped by several factors, including the importance many of them have placed on their country's very close post–World War II relationship with the United States and also by their deep-seated antipathy for government surveillance of citizens.

Germans have absorbed profound lessons from their recent history. Their intimate experience with living under two totalitarian systems—the Nazi regime and the communist government of the former East Germany—means, wrote one German commentator, "that the consequences of state monitoring are still in living memory." Many Germans retain strong memories of the monstrous secret police, the much-hated Stasi, who, along with their army of informers, penetrated every aspect of East Germans' lives. As a result of knowing from their experience that government surveillance of citizens can breed government control of citizens, Germans are nearly as possessed by the idea that massive government surveillance must never happen again as they are by their commitment that a Holocaust must never happen again. Furthermore, they see a relationship between these two catastrophes in their tragic past—that some people become what they may not want to become but, rather, what they think their government wants them to become, when they live in fear that their leaders know everything about them.

AS NSA FILES KEPT EMERGING, intelligence officials eventually admitted that collecting massive private information from Americans' communications has led to minimal benefit regarding the discovery of terrorists' plans. Successive reports also have made it clear that the NSA, nevertheless, has made extraordinary efforts to drill deeper and deeper to gather the communications of Americans and citizens in other countries through both legal and extralegal means and by defeating the encryption methods people have been told guarantee the privacy of their records and personal communications.

One NSA document revealed the agency scoops up millions of personal digital address books. According to NSA files reported by the *Washington Post,* the NSA collects address books at a daily rate of 444,743 from Yahoo, 105,068 from Hotmail, 82,857 from Facebook, 33,697 from Gmail and 22,881 from unnamed other providers. Every day NSA collects approximately 500,000 "buddy lists" on live-chat services and from web-based email accounts. Intelligence officials confirmed that the NSA collects lists from personal address books and other personal digital lists of "millions or ten of millions" of Americans. Because this collection takes place in undersea lines and not on American soil, the NSA has concluded it does not need to seek legal authorization from the special court that must authorize surveillance of Americans by the NSA.

The agency has gone to great lengths, along with its British counterpart, the GCHQ, to ensure that it has access to personal communications throughout the world, even to those digitized records that Internet companies and companies that conduct business on the Internet guarantee are protected by encryption and, therefore, are secure—bank transactions, purchases, and medical records. These revelations about the NSA defeating encryption were made by three news organizations, the *Guardian, The New York Times,* and ProPublica, the news website, all of which had access to the same NSA files released by Snowden.

NSA's successful attack on encryption is the result of a ten-year campaign by the NSA and GCHQ to defeat all encryption methods. The attitude of the two intelligence agencies toward their citizens is evident in the name each agency gave its decryption program. They named them after major civil war battles in their respective countries—Bullrun at NSA and Edgehill at GCHQ. Contempt also is evident in how the NSA referred in a

file to the customers whose systems it violates as a result of defeating encryption: "adversaries."

From the files, it is unclear the degree to which communication companies cooperate with the NSA on opening access to information users have
been told would be inaccessible. But given the methods the NSA has used to
obtain access, the cooperation of the companies, or even whether any given
company knows NSA has access, may be a moot point.

NSA has used covert means within the communication industry to open
gates to citizens' encrypted personal data. Through "covert partnerships,"
the American and British agencies inserted secret vulnerabilities, known as
backdoors or trapdoors, into commercial encryption software. NSA also has
used supercomputers to break encryption with what the agency calls "brute
force." A key approach to destroying encryption has been the use of covert
action "to ensure NSA control over setting of international encryption standards." An NSA file revealed that the agency works covertly "to get its own
version of a draft security standard issued by the U.S. National Institute
of Standards and Technology approved for worldwide use. An NSA file
trumpets the fact that "eventually, NSA became the sole editor" of international encryption standards. Agency success in damaging, if not destroying,
encryption also has been aided, according to one NSA file by "identifying, recruiting and running covert agents in the global telecommunications
industry." In one NSA file, the agency celebrated its success at "defeating
network security and privacy."

By these actions, some security experts say, the NSA is attacking the
Internet itself and the privacy of all users. Bruce Schneider, an encryption
specialist and fellow at Harvard's Berkman Center for Internet and Society,
told the *Post*, "By deliberately undermining online security in a short-sighted
effort to eavesdrop, the NSA is undermining the very fabric of the Internet."

THAT FIRST FILE from the Media FBI office that captured public attention in 1971, a directive to agents who spied on antiwar activists, stated that
they should *enhance the paranoia . . . get the point across there is an FBI agent
behind every mailbox.*" Paranoia—or the reality it portends—exists today
throughout the world. It has been enhanced primarily by two fears—fear
that there will be more terrorist attacks, and fear of governments' use of
increasingly invasive electronic surveillance of their own citizens and the
citizens of allied countries. Now people anywhere may wonder if there is

intelligence-gathering equipment behind every email, every phone call, every Skype conversation, every Facebook message, every chat room conversation, every Internet search, every stored document—looking at or listening to every form of personal communication accessible through modern technology.

28

Questions

J. EDGAR HOOVER BECAME director of the FBI the same way he continued being director of the bureau for forty-eight years—by not being asked questions.

Questions were not asked before he was appointed despite the fact that danger signs already were present. There was evidence then that he was willing to use government power to trample rights and damage people. There was evidence of his use of deception to build and maintain his power. There were signs he already was building the other FBI—the secret FBI the Media burglars exposed for the first time almost fifty years later.

When Harlan Fiske Stone, the eminent former dean of Columbia University Law School and future chief justice of the U.S. Supreme Court, appointed J. Edgar Hoover director of the Bureau of Investigation in 1924, he guaranteed that the bureau was likely to become precisely the opposite of what he, the new attorney general, thought it should be.

It was surprising that Stone chose Hoover. His appointment as head of the bureau, which had been founded in 1908 and would be renamed the Federal Bureau of Investigation in 1935, seemed to counter what the new president, Calvin Coolidge, had asked Stone to do when he appointed him attorney general in April 1924: clean out the corrupt and disgraceful Department of Justice and Bureau of Investigation and restore honor to both.

Stone had publicly stated during a Senate investigation in 1920 that the Palmer Raids—mass arrests in 1919 of 10,000 people that are still regarded as one of the worst violations of civil liberties in the nation's history—were an "intolerable injustice" that resulted in "cruelty to individuals." Hoover, the man Stone selected to run the bureau, had, as head of the Justice Department's Radical Division, planned the raids, named for the attorney general who authorized them, A. Mitchell Palmer. Hoover also was deeply involved in their ugly aftermath—the cruel prison conditions, the denial of due process, and the push for detainees to be deported.

The raids—lauded at first but soon regarded as a national shame—involved mass roundups of people by the bureau and local police in several cities without search warrants. People were pulled out of their beds as they slept, grabbed in dance halls and meeting places, and thrown into prisons, where they were kept in filthy conditions, denied lawyers or access to family members, and in some cities tortured. Intended by Hoover as a way to rid the country of thousands of immigrants he regarded as radicals, the raids did not fulfill his purpose. Most of the people swept up were citizens and therefore not subject to being deported. In the end, 556 were deported. When Palmer was questioned two years later at a Senate hearing on the raids, at one point the disgraced attorney general, unable to answer a particular question, deferred "to Mr. Hoover, who was in charge in this matter."

How was it possible that Stone, one of the most respected legal minds in the country and appointed attorney general with a mandate to reform the corrupt Department of Justice and its Bureau of Investigation, would choose as FBI director a man who planned and executed this mass raid that was a major source of the department's shame he was appointed to clean up?

Given what Stone either knew or could have known if he had asked questions, it is difficult to understand why Stone decided Hoover was the right person to lead the nation's top law enforcement agency, a position in which he would have enormous power either to protect or damage citizens' right to dissent, a right that Stone cherished and thought the government should zealously protect. Even more difficult to answer is the question of why Stone apparently did not ask basic questions about J. Edgar Hoover before he named him, on May 10, 1924, to be the acting director of the bureau and then, in December 1924, director.

This decision by Stone, which was, as he said, the most important decision he made while he was attorney general, had many far-reaching historic impacts on the nation. He placed Hoover in a position where, unquestioned, he could carry out secret programs that were—and were intended by him to be—a threat to countless Americans' efforts to express dissent. Stone, surely unintentionally, set young Hoover on the path that produced a deep scar on the country's civil liberties for more than half a century, a scar still visible. The scar was etched over years in secrecy in the middle of a national myth in which Americans embraced Hoover as a hero—millions of little boys wore G-man badges they retrieved from cereal boxes, dreaming of becoming FBI agents as much as they dreamed of becoming cowboys, while the secret FBI engaged in serial violations of civil liberties and worse.

The nature of much of Hoover's behavior during his early years as director remained largely unknown for years, with only his version of those years available. Even the Church Committee, despite the depth of its research and scrutiny of the director and the bureau, did not discover in the mid-1970s much information about Hoover's earliest years as director. In fact, until the 1980s it was assumed that Hoover conducted little or no political spying during the first twelve years he was director and that such activities did not begin until the administration of Franklin Delano Roosevelt, in the years leading up to World War II. The truth about Hoover's earliest years as director did not emerge until a decade after the Church Committee completed its work when scholars Athan Theoharis, Kenneth O'Reilly, and David Williams, through Freedom of Information Act requests, gained access to extensive files about that era in the bureau. It was learned then that the roots of the behavior revealed by the Media burglars and by the Church Committee were planted in those early years. For instance, Hoover did not dismantle the political surveillance operations he had put in place under Palmer, despite orders from Stone to do so. The impulse to build secret files on perceived enemies was always there, and nothing—not even an order from Stone, the man he warmly recalled as his mentor when Stone died in 1946—prevented him from indulging that obsession.

Ironically, Hoover was appointed director during, and as part of, the first major effort to bring major reform to the bureau. The second such effort, much more extensive in its investigation, recommendations, and impact, was the Church Committee. Also ironically, the Church Committee investigation was needed mostly because of the most significant failure of the first reform effort—the appointment of Hoover as bureau director.

SURELY HOOVER HIMSELF was surprised that Stone appointed him, though he indicated otherwise years later. Hoover certainly knew Stone's thinking about the Palmer Raids and their impact. He was in the Senate hearing room on February 1, 1920, the day a committee staff member read the letter Stone had written in response to a request for his assessment of the raids. Stone had strongly condemned key injustices that had taken place during the Palmer Raids:

It was inevitable that any system which confers upon administrative officers power to restrain the liberty of individuals without safeguards substantially like those which exist in criminal cases, and without adequate
authority for judicial review of the actions of such administrative officers
will result in abuse of power and in intolerable injustice and cruelty to
individuals.

Hearing those words, Hoover certainly knew he was one of those
unnamed administrative officers who had planned and carried out the
actions Stone declared intolerable.

There has been speculation, but never definitive information, about
why Stone chose Hoover—about what he knew and did not know about
Hoover's prior roles and about his ideas regarding the fundamentals of law
enforcement practices and intelligence operations. *New Yorker* writer Jack
Alexander wrote in 1937 that "unable to find a man who filled the bill to
his liking, Stone resolved to look for a promising young man who could be
trained along the line of his pet theories." In other words, if young Hoover
had followed Palmer's bad orders, he could be expected to follow Stone's
good ones. This analysis suggests that Hoover's main qualification was that
he could follow orders. Later, it was clear that, instead, he was someone who,
in relation to his superiors, calculated how to appear to be following orders.

Stone may have been naïve. He is said to have believed it would have
been impossible for someone as young as Hoover to have executed policy
decisions at the time of the Palmer Raids. He openly admired Hoover's
characteristic efficiency and willingness to make decisions quickly, and indicated he thought Hoover would develop the values most essential to the job.
Stone seemed to have so little insight about Hoover that he assumed that
through the force of his personality and his position of authority he could
influence the younger man to become a strong defender of civil liberties.

At first, things seemed to go as Stone wished, at least on the surface.
Stone appointed Hoover acting director the day after he fired William J.
Burns as director. Years later, Hoover told—and required all new agents to
be told—his memory of the exchange he claimed took place between him
and Stone the day the attorney general asked him to be acting FBI director.

According to Hoover's account, he tried to make small talk about administrative matters when he arrived in Stone's office that day in response to a
request that he appear there, but the attorney general "told me brusquely to
sit down, and looked at me intently over the desk. Then he said to me, 'Young
man, I want you to be acting director of the Bureau of Investigation.'"

Given Hoover's age and what he knew about Stone's view of the Palmer Raids, it is difficult to imagine that he entered the attorney general's office that day thinking he was about to be appointed to direct the bureau. But as he tells the story, he arrived expecting the appointment and armed with a demand about the conditions under which he would accept it. Years later, when Hoover recounted what happened in that private meeting, he said that when the job was offered, he responded, "I'll take the job, Mr. Stone, but only on certain conditions."

"What are they?" Stone is supposed to have asked.

"The Bureau must be divorced from politics and not be a catch-all for political hacks. Appointments must be based on merit. Promotions will be made only on proven ability. And the bureau will be responsible only to the attorney general."

Hoover said Stone was thrilled that he had put principle first. The attorney general, he said, responded, "I wouldn't give it to you under any other conditions. That's all. Good day."

Shortly after appointing Hoover acting director, the attorney general made an unequivocal public declaration about the peril posed to democracy by illegal surveillance. It was as though he was giving his new young director a very public order:

> There is always the possibility that a secret police system may become a menace to free government and free institutions, because it carries with it the possibility of abuses of power not always quickly appreciated or understood. The enormous expansion of Federal legislation, both civil and criminal, in recent years, however, has made a Bureau of Investigation a necessary instrument of law enforcement. But it is important that its activities be strictly limited to the performance of those functions for which it was created and that its agents themselves be not above the law or beyond its reach. . . .
>
> The Bureau of Investigation is not concerned with political or other opinions of individuals. It is only concerned with their conduct and then only with such conduct as is forbidden by the laws of the United States. When a police system passes beyond these limits it is dangerous to the proper administration of justice and to human liberty, which should be our first concern to cherish. . . .

A few days after Stone made those remarks, Hoover testified before the Senate committee then investigating his recently disgraced boss, former attorney general Harry Daugherty, who had been fired by Coolidge. Hoover used the occasion to announce that he already had fired all of the political cronies of Daugherty in the bureau and was in the process of rooting out deadwood. Future qualifications to be a bureau agent, he said, would be an academic degree, some legal training. No longer, he said, would political connections lead to an FBI job in the bureau. By February 1925, the month Stone resigned as attorney general to become a justice on the U.S. Supreme Court, Hoover had announced a significant accomplishment. Now more than half the bureau's agents had legal training and most had academic degrees. He also now required that local bureau offices be inspected periodically. Reformers were pleased that Hoover seemed to be imposing discipline in the bureau Stone once called a "lawless" organization.

In line with Stone's directive, Hoover also announced that no longer was the FBI interested in people's political opinions. But that was not true. Political spying continued.

The public didn't know that. In these, his earliest days in the bureau, Hoover had started to build the "other" FBI—the secret FBI.

Roger Baldwin, a founder and the original director of the American Civil Liberties Union in 1920, assumed Hoover was telling the truth when he told him such surveillance no longer took place. Grateful for the apparent change in Hoover's values, Baldwin established a cordial relationship with the director that began shortly after Stone appointed him. He learned later that Hoover had deceived him. "They never stopped watching us," he said in 1977. In fact, the ACLU was a favorite and continuous bureau target, with some ACLU offices infiltrated by FBI agents or informers throughout Hoover's tenure. Surveillance of the ACLU included monitoring the group's lawyers as they developed legal strategy for cases they were trying.

Future Supreme Court justice Felix Frankfurter, a close adviser to Stone, thought Stone's appointment of Hoover was a terrible mistake. The close professional relationship between Stone and Frankfurter started shortly after Stone was appointed attorney general. When Stone arrived at the department in March 1924, he told friends he felt like an outsider. "I don't know whom to trust," he remarked during that early period. One of the few people he relied on for advice was Frankfurter, then a law professor at Harvard. Of the many letters Stone received right after his appointment, the one he seemed to appreciate most was a letter from Frankfurter. In that first letter to Stone, Frankfurter wrote that nothing "had been more saddening during the last few years than the betrayal of the law by its special custodians at the Department of Justice." He told Stone he was confronted in the department by a "Herculean job." Stone wrote back that he would be grateful for Frankfurter's advice. "I need all the help I can get." That was the beginning of a continuous correspondence. They wrote to each other every few days.

Frankfurter was especially concerned about the bureau. It was widely known to be corrupt. Agents commonly took bribes or demanded kickbacks from gangsters and bootleggers. Some agents had criminal records. Stone had said he wanted to turn the bureau into "an honest, professional, law-abiding force that deserved the public trust." When Stone fired Burns as head of the bureau, Frankfurter applauded him.

In one letter to Stone, Frankfurter wrote about one of the bureau issues that concerned him most: "There can hardly be two opinions about the fact that the spy system in government has been the watershed of the improprieties, illegalities and corrupting atmosphere of recent years." In public statements, it was clear that Stone agreed with the Harvard professor on this point.

Frankfurter addressed the appointment of Hoover in a letter several days after the appointment was announced. He reminded Stone of Hoover's connection with Palmer, his courtroom defense of the Palmer Raids, and his demands to the Labor Department for deportation orders. "Nevertheless, my mouth has been sealed about the Hoover appointment . . . because I feel so deeply about the ends at which you aim in reorganization of the Bureau of Investigation, that I did not want to set my judgment against yours. . . ."

But he warned Stone, "Hoover . . . might be a very effective and zealous instrument for the realization of the 'liberal ideas' which you had in mind for the investigatorial activities of the Department of Justice when his chief is a man who cares about these ideas as deeply as you do, but his effectiveness might be of a weaker coefficient with a chief less profoundly concerned about these ideas."

There is no record of Stone responding to Frankfurter's criticism of the Hoover appointment.

STONE APPARENTLY NEVER KNEW that when he ordered the dismantling of the General Intelligence Division, Hoover made it appear that he had done so, but actually he had kept the heart of the division—the files. As head of the Radical Division, what became the General Intelligence Division, Hoover had ordered bureau agents to create dossiers on bureau critics, painting them with a wide brush, wrote Kenneth D. Ackerman, as "parlor

Bolshevists and Red sympathizers." In a remarkably short period, two years, he had assembled files on 450,000 people and organizations. The dossiers were to be used as "ammunition to smear them at a moment's notice."

In violation of Stone's orders, Hoover quietly continued building secret dossiers based on people's political opinions. He already knew how to hide files, even within the bureau. He wrote and inserted in the files official memoranda saying political spying was not taking place even as he was ordering exactly that. Sometimes when agents asked for permission to conduct political surveillance he would respond that such surveillance was illegal—making that claim even as he directed other agents to conduct it.

The people and organizations he targeted then and placed in his files would remain his targets for life. Even in those earliest years in his career, members of unions, pacifist groups, anarchists, racial justice groups, and bureau critics were regarded by Hoover, with or without evidence, as subversives who should be spied on regularly and recorded in his files. Hoover assigned agents to work with, and sometimes help direct, political surveillance conducted by the police forces' Red Squads, then common in various cities. His surveillance of the National Association for the Advancement of Colored People began then and continued for decades. Editors of black newspapers were monitored because they were suspected of "exciting the negro element of this country to riot."

During the Great Depression, Hoover assigned agents to monitor protests against the economic policies of President Herbert Hoover. Political spying also was done during this time at the request of Republican Party officials and businessmen, some of whom had easy access to the director. In 1931, at the request of Joseph R. Nutt, chairman of the board of Union Trust Company and treasurer of the Republican National Committee, five bureau agents were sent to Syracuse to interview George Menhinick, editor of *Wall Street Forecast,* a financial newsletter that reported on the "dismal situation facing American banks and investors" at that time. After the interview, an agent reported that they had "thoroughly scared" Menhinick and that he was not likely to "resume the dissemination of any information concerning the banks or other financial institutions."

While Hoover was widely assumed to be following Stone's rule that prohibited political surveillance, he also developed another skill he would use throughout his years as director—manipulating the meaning of words to suit his purposes. How he justified asking the State Department to monitor Americans traveling abroad provides an example of his early linguistic elasticity. Officially, such monitoring was to be limited to Americans who were suspected of acting on behalf of a foreign government. He reasoned that the rule could be interpreted to mean that an individual "who advocates Marxist Leninism *might just as well* be working as an agent of a foreign power," and, therefore, monitoring them could be justified. Under this stretching of the rule, Frankfurter, hardly a Marxist-Leninist, was one of many Americans spied on by the FBI while traveling overseas.

FROM WHAT IS KNOWN, Stone never asked basic questions of Hoover— never conducted an internal investigation. Just months after Stone appointed Hoover, when Coolidge nominated Stone to be a Supreme Court justice, some senators openly expressed fear that Stone's Wall Street contacts would cause him to be too protective of business interests when he was on the court. Stone responded by suggesting that senators should clarify their concerns about him by questioning him at a Senate Judiciary Committee hearing. Hearings to question high-level appointees had never been held. The one held to question Stone set the precedent for what soon became required confirmation hearings for all people appointed to the federal bench. It is unfortunate that Stone did not apply the same critical standard in assessing Hoover that he suggested the Senate should apply to himself.

Basic questions about Hoover, posed to him or to others, if answered honestly, surely would have raised profound concerns in Stone's mind. Under the circumstances, some of the questions that should have been asked are: What were Hoover's responsibilities in connection with the Palmer Raids, the prison conditions of those detained, and the aggressive efforts to deport them? What were his responsibilities when he worked directly for the disgraced Palmer, Daugherty, and Burns? What records were maintained in the General Intelligence Division, formerly Radical Division, and what happened to those records when Stone closed the division? If Stone had learned about the 450,000 files that were maintained there on individuals and groups, he probably would have asked who ordered the building of those files. If he had learned that they still existed, neatly stored away for continued use and expansion, he probably would have demanded that those files be made available for his inspection.

Because questions apparently were not asked about these files, Hoover was able to keep them and develop new plans for them—make them the initial building blocks in his lifelong dedication to creating and maintaining massive files on people whose opinions he opposed. Some of them became the first entries for his Custodial Detention Index, the list of people the FBI would detain indefinitely and without due process in the event of a national emergency. It was this index that Attorney General Francis Biddle ordered Hoover to close and to destroy, but that Hoover, in secret defiance, simply renamed and expanded. He started such defiance to authority not long after Stone appointed him.

If Stone had reviewed the index cards in those files, he would have seen Hoover's notes about the Palmer Raids, including his demands for more arrests, higher bail, fewer lawyers, and more spying. He would have seen Hoover's note about the argument he made that to give the detainees access to lawyers would "defeat the ends of justice." Stone would also have found some of his friends in the files. He would have seen files on each of the twelve law professors who in May 1920 issued the "Twelve Lawyer Report," a detailed investigation of the Palmer Raids. As Hoover would all his life with critics, when the report was issued, he immediately instructed agents to secretly investigate the scholars who wrote it. He questioned Frankfurter's loyalty to the country, and claimed that the criticism written by another professor in the group, Harvard professor Zachariah Chafee, was "reckless and untrue." He secretly tried to get Harvard trustees to fire the two men. Lacking evidence, he failed in both efforts. He probably was especially upset with the twelve professors. Their detailed documentation of the crimes perpetrated by the government in connection with the Palmer Raids and their aftermath was widely credited with turning public opinion against the raids. When the professors' report became public, there was widespread concern that the government had abandoned the rule of law.

If Stone had read those files, he might have considered more carefully whether the person who created such files, and who had not destroyed them, despite Stone's order, should be the director of the nation's most powerful law enforcement agency.

It is puzzling that Stone did not ask essential questions before he appointed Hoover. Unlike Hoover's future supervisors, Stone surely was not intimidated by the twenty-nine-year-old Hoover. Surely he did not think Hoover had a file on him, a fear that in future decades kept countless members of Congress and other officials from questioning him about his operations.

THE LACK OF QUESTIONING continued, even when Hoover, in a very rare instance, revealed the nature of his suppression plans to top officials.

On another March 8—this one in 1956—Hoover spoke before a meeting of the National Security Council. Nearly all members of President Dwight Eisenhower's cabinet, as well as other high-ranking officials in his administration, were present. Hoover's presentation, entitled "The Present Menace of Communist Espionage and Subversion," exaggerated the power and size of the Communist Party in the United States at that time. The director lamented that the U.S. Supreme Court had recently eviscerated the Smith Act, thereby making it impossible to arrest people for simply advocating subversive ideas. Instead, the bureau would have to prove advocacy of actual violent acts. Hoover was furious that the court had limited the bureau's ability to arrest communists.

But Hoover had a plan to get around the limitations caused by the Supreme Court. He would secretly suppress communism through illegal means—and later other people and organizations he opposed. Instead of arresting them, now he would secretly harass and suppress them. He described his new plan to the president and all top members of his administration that day.

Hoover told the assembled officials at that National Security Council meeting that he would now use every means available to pursue and disrupt the CPUSA. As James Kirkpatrick Davis, the first writer to reveal what transpired at this meeting, wrote, "he failed to mention that many of the means he had in mind had already been in use for some time" and that the communist "menace" no longer existed.

Eisenhower asked him to explain the counterterrorism techniques he planned to use, and Hoover responded, "Sometimes it is necessary to make a surreptitious entry where on occasion we have photographed secret communist records and other data of great use to our security." Additional counterintelligence methods that he listed included safecracking, mail interception, telephone surveillance, microphone plants, trash inspection, infiltration, and IRS investigations. In short, he said, "every means available to secure information and evidence."

Without naming it, Hoover had described about-to-be-created COINTELPRO to the president and his cabinet. Apparently no official blinked as he laid out his strategy. According to minutes of the meeting and an interview years later with Attorney General Herbert Brownell, who was present, when Hoover finished reciting his litany of the illegal activities the FBI would use, the room fell silent. The president was silent, Brownell recalled, but he seemed to nod in approval.

That was the beginning of COINTELPRO, the worst of Hoover's secret operations. Inside the bureau, two months later on May 18, 1956, he gave orders for the first COINTELPRO operation, the one against the Communist Party, to begin. At first, it was focused on communists. And then it expanded. Eventually, by the mid- to late 1960s, the operations were so diversified that anyone or any organization Hoover disapproved of could become the object of these special operations.

Hoover's presentation at that National Security Council meeting is believed to be the only time he informed a president, attorney general, or any other officials of any presidential administration about the secret illegal operations he conducted. He may have taken their silence as permanent approval of such operations, just as he assumed he could bank on President Franklin Roosevelt's approval of going after subversives as permanent approval for doing so.

By well before that day, March 8, 1956, the secret FBI already was entrenched. Hoover had concluded it was all right for him to use against American dissenters tactics of espionage normally reserved for use against foreign enemies—without regard for the legality of his approach or for the legal protection of Americans' dissent required by the Constitution. The secret FBI would expand considerably with the addition of each COINTELPRO operation from 1956 through the late 1960s.

WHATEVER THE REASON for the failure to question Hoover prior to his appointment, beginning then, in 1924, the pattern was set that would persist for a half century: Very few questions were asked of J. Edgar Hoover. No questions—therefore, no oversight—became the pattern as of the day Hoover was appointed acting director of the bureau. That frightening, damaging silence—the absence of questions—continued all the way to the next important March 8 in Hoover's life, the one in 1971, when files were stolen from the Media FBI office. After a half century of no questions, finally, when evidence from those files reached the public, it became imperative that questions be asked. That was precisely what William Davidon had thought: that if evidence could be found that the FBI was suppressing dissent, the public would demand that questions be asked and the suppression stopped.

By now, more than forty years after the burglary that revealed Hoover's secret FBI, the profound impact of the fateful appointment of Hoover has been well established, thanks to the Media files, congressional investigations, and journalists and scholars who have written articles and books and made documentary films based on bureau files released in response to requests made under the Freedom of Information Act. Together these many works have created a mosaic that can be assumed to be a fairly complete account of the actions of the person who served longer in government than any other public official and who exercised enormous power.

Gradually, it was revealed that the director had had a profoundly negative impact in some of the most important parts of American life. A few key examples:

- The generations-long quest by black Americans to claim their most basic rights as citizens was delayed by an FBI director who cautioned successive presidents against supporting their efforts. He insisted that demands for equality were inspired by communists and, as such, should be ignored. He placed massive numbers of black people under surveillance for years and conducted campaigns designed to destroy black leaders.
- The range of permissible political discourse was severely narrowed by an FBI director who assumed it was his responsibility to suppress the expression of ideas and the political campaigns of candidates he opposed, especially third-party candidates, and who kept secret files on the personal lives of politicians and other prominent persons with an eye to retaining his power through the blackmail potential of those files.
- The FBI director's dominant role behind the scenes in the various anticommunist hearings and loyalty investigations that took place in Washington and throughout the country ruined the careers and often the personal lives of thousands of Americans because of accusations, often false, from FBI informers that the people who stood accused were communists or associated with communists. The accused could not defend themselves against faceless accusers. Americans' capacity to understand communism was impaired by the atmosphere he played a key role in creating—an atmosphere in which communism was perceived as an evil religion that should be hated, feared, and shunned rather than as a powerful international movement that, like other strong ideologies, should be studied and comprehended in order to understand it rather than simply fear it. Debate and true understanding of the political forces at play during those years were paralyzed.
- The competence of the FBI itself was diminished by having as its director someone who saw himself and the bureau as beyond the law. The demand for obedience inside the bureau—in regard to matters

small, important, and silly, such as prescribing precisely how agents should celebrate the director's birthday—created a stultifying atmosphere in which form mattered more than substance and independent thinking was discouraged. After his death and the investigations of the bureau, the capacity of the FBI to transform itself was hampered by the lingering impact of such leadership.

• The evolution of American culture was constrained by having as the director of the FBI a person who seldom read or traveled but who assumed the role of arbiter of ideas and values, usually from a hostile anti-intellectual stance. He showed contempt for nearly every major writer and artist by maintaining ongoing secret files based on the bureau's secret monitoring of them.

In light of everything that has become known about Hoover and about the ruthless secret FBI he created, and in light of Americans' likely strong desire never again to permit themselves to adore, tolerate, or permit a public official to exert such profound power over them, either secretly or openly, perhaps this question still needs to be explored in order not to repeat the past:

How was it possible in a democratic society for an official to deceive the American public and many of its officials and to pervert the basic principles of democracy and an open society with such egregious secret policies and actions for nearly a half century without constraints?

Stone's failure to examine young Hoover was a significant factor. So was the continued refusal of officials throughout the forty-eight years he was director to ask questions about his operations.

QUESTIONS WERE finally asked in the mid-1970s.

As Congress and the American public headed then toward an unprecedented action—a careful examination of the secret FBI, as well as other intelligence agencies, something new was taking place. Despite, or perhaps because, the country felt the turmoil of a president recently resigning in disgrace and a nasty war finally winding down, people seemed to be willing to shed something Americans had not been without for many years, if ever—fear.

Davidon, the leader of the Media burglars, thought his generation, the World War II generation, had, in addition to becoming regarded as the "Greatest Generation," moved the country toward becoming a generation of sheep, people willing to trust their leaders without question. The joint conservative/liberal empowerment of J. Edgar Hoover after World War II without any oversight seemed to be the embodiment of Davidon's point. As William W. Keller, the international security scholar, put it, a "habit of mind" persisted that was "constantly reinforced by J. Edgar Hoover and his allies." It told us that communists had infiltrated the civil rights and antiwar movements and were about to take over the country. Fear that that was true made those and other movements automatically suspect, and slowed down every movement for equality and justice. "Blind faith and trust in the integrity of the agency," said Keller, "tended to reinforce general ignorance of internal security operations." Americans didn't ask questions about such matters. They were willing to assume those leaders knew what was best for the country and to let the leaders of these agencies do whatever they wanted.

As the congressional investigation of the FBI got under way in 1975, Americans grasped that first opportunity to ask questions, to hear evidence, and to judge whether the FBI, without oversight, had done any harm to Americans, especially to their right to dissent. The answer, from diverse corners, was a resounding yes.

In practice, the FBI has moved in and out of the reforms put in place in the 1970s. On its website today it acknowledges the positive impact the Media burglary had on the bureau:

> A radical group called "Citizens' Commission to Investigate the FBI" broke into the office in Media and stole a wide array of domestic security documents that had not been properly secured. Some [author's note: actually, only one] of the documents mentioned "COINTELPRO," or Counterintelligence Programs—a series of programs aimed to disrupt some of the more radical groups of the 1950s and 1960s. The leaking of those documents to the news media and politicians and the subsequent criticism, both inside and outside the Bureau, led to a significant reevaluation of FBI domestic security policy.

James Kirkpatrick Davis, the author of two books on Hoover's FBI and the writer who assisted Hoover's successor, retired FBI director Kelley, in writing a book on his experiences in the FBI, thinks the circumstances that led to reform in the bureau were remarkable. "In a most extraordinary paradox," he wrote, the only act that stopped wrongdoing by the FBI "was an illegal act—the Media office burglary."

ANOTHER QUESTION COMES to mind—this one about the people who first opened the door to the secret FBI and made it possible for public officials, scholars, journalists—indeed, any American—to ask questions about FBI policies and operations and get answers. Despite all that's been written here about the previously unknown Media burglars and the significant impact of their historic act of resistance, a question about them still lingers:

How *was* it possible for those eight people to be willing to take such great risks in order to search for evidence of whether dissent was being destroyed by J. Edgar Hoover?

They are modest in their explanations. When the question is asked, they often make it sound simple, as though it was just something that needed to be done, like yelling "Stop!" to someone who is about to step into traffic. But actually most of them thought long and hard about this. They considered the sacrifice. Some of the parents in the group cried many nights about what the impact might be on their children if they were arrested and sentenced to prison terms. One of them lived alone and thought of the painful loneliness she might experience in the aftermath—alone and "wanted" by the FBI for exposing the FBI.

Still, they did it.

David Kairys has some insights about them. A professor at Temple University School of Law and a defense lawyer at the Camden 28 trial, he's known some of the burglars since before the burglary. In fact, two of them approached him at the time—one shortly before the break-in, the other shortly after—and asked if he would be willing to be their lawyer if they were arrested. He said yes, of course. As the weeks, months, then years went by and he never got a call, he hoped they would be safe forever.

As he kept their secret over the years, he often thought about them. He thought about what kind of people they were, and he wondered from time to time what it took to be that brave. "On the surface," he says, "they just look like everybody else and act like everybody else. But they came to such a deep commitment." He's certain that if he had been invited to participate, he would have refused. "Just too much to risk," he says more than forty years later. "I probably would have thought about it. I might have been tempted. I would have decided not to do it."

They were needed, says Kairys, thinking of the burglars and of that era.

"There are certain points in history where a society goes so wrong, and there are certain people who will say, 'I won't stand for that. . . . I will risk career, life, limb, family, freedom. . . . And I will take this risk, and I will go and do it.'

"And it certainly is not something that's over," says Kairys. People "are going to be called upon again."

Acknowledgments

I owe thanks to many people. My deepest gratitude goes to the Media burglars. In 1971, they trusted me when, as anonymous sources, they sent copies of the stolen FBI files to me at the *Washington Post*. Now, more than forty years later, they have trusted me to reveal that they were the Media burglars, a secret they had planned never to make known. I am grateful for their enduring trust and for this opportunity to tell the story of what they did and the impact of their act of resistance.

I discovered them quite accidentally. It happened over dinner one evening at the home of Bonnie and John Raines. Between meetings in Missouri and Massachusetts, I gave myself the gift of a long weekend in Philadelphia. It was the first time I had been to Philadelphia in many years. I filled the weekend visiting people I had known when I was a reporter at the *Evening Bulletin* in the late 1960s.

I spent the first evening with the Raineses. Though we were not close friends when I lived in Philadelphia, they were people I liked and respected and looked forward to seeing again. When I arrived that evening, the three of us immediately launched into telling one another about the last decade of our lives. During dinner, their youngest child, Mary, then a teenager, joined us for a few minutes. John Raines introduced me to her with words that startled me: "Mary, this is Betty Medsger. We want you to know Betty, because many years ago, when your dad and mother had information about the FBI we wanted the American people to have, we gave it to Betty."

Another glass of wine, please. I was stunned. I could tell from Mary's pleasant but unmoved expression that the comment meant nothing to her. As she talked with her parents, my mind was racing. Maybe I misunderstood. How could John and Bonnie, this lovely suburban couple with four children, a station wagon, and a big friendly black dog named Jezebel, possibly have carried out a burglary, especially *that* burglary? I wanted to shout questions, but I restrained myself.

I had thought about the burglary often. In my journalism ethics classes at San Francisco State University, where I was then teaching, my students and I discussed the ethical issues involved when a journalist receives stolen secret files. In those classes, I enjoyed gradually moving the discussion from hypothetical cases to my real case as I told them about the time I received stolen FBI files. Some students expressed surprise that the Media burglars never had been found by the FBI. Actually, I too was surprised that they had eluded the FBI. Students asked if I had any suspicions about who they were. No idea whatsoever, I honestly answered.

Nice as Mary obviously was, I could hardly wait until she left the dining room that evening. After she did, I asked, with quite a bit of incredulity, "Are you saying you were Media burglars?" With wide glowing smiles, Bonnie and John said they were. I could hardly believe what I was hearing. Later they said they did not plan to tell me their secret that night. John just happened to blurt it out to Mary. Needless to say, I am enormously grateful for that accidental comment.

We talked for hours, my questions and their answers tumbling out. They seemed to enjoy finally talking to someone about the secrets they had shared up to then only with each other, with their oldest child, Lindsley, and, at the time of the burglary, with family members they had asked to raise their children if they were arrested and imprisoned. They answered my questions with tales that brought to mind Keystone Cops one moment and brave nonviolent resistance fighters the next. They moved me to laughter and to tears as they described the night of March 8, 1971, Bonnie casing inside the office two weeks before the burglary, the close calls right after the burglary, the years of being afraid they would be caught, and then the deep joy later of knowing it had all been worthwhile.

I could not stop thinking about what they told me. A few weeks later, I wrote to the Raineses and told them I thought it was important that the full story of their historic act of resistance and its profound impact be told. I told them I wanted to write a book and asked them if they would agree to reveal themselves publicly as Media burglars and help me find the other burglars. They liked the plan. Eventually, seven of the eight burglars were found. All agreed to participate, and five agreed to be publicly identified.

As I have researched the impact of the burglary, I have been grateful for the Freedom of Information Act and the access it made possible. Thanks for that crucial tool that empowers citizens goes to Congress members John Moss, Democrat from California; William W. Moorhead, Democrat from Pennsylvania; and Frank Horton, Republican from New York. For twelve years, Moss led the campaign in Congress to pass the first FOIA in 1966. Two presidents, Eisenhower and Johnson, strongly opposed him. For his effort, he earned an FBI file from J. Edgar Hoover, who thought a law that mandated access to files was anathema. In 1974, Moorhead and Horton led the successful effort to strengthen the original FOIA.

Thanks to the FOIA, it was possible for me to receive the 33,698-page official record of the FBI's investigation of the Media burglary, provided by the bureau in response to my FOIA request. It has been an invaluable resource. Because of greater access to bureau files after the strengthening of FOIA in 1974, many articles and books based on previously unavailable FBI files have been written and now form a substantial, and still growing, record of the history of the bureau. I am particularly indebted to Sanford Ungar, whose 1975 book *FBI: An Uncensored Look Behind the Walls* stands to this day as one of the richest accounts of how the FBI operated under J. Edgar Hoover. The many books and articles by Athan Theoharis, the historian who has written most extensively about the FBI, significantly deepened my knowledge of the bureau. The discoveries and insights of Hoover biographers Curt Gentry, Richard Gid Powers, and Kenneth D. Ackerman have also been invaluable. Some of the most impressive books about COINTELPRO, Hoover's aggressive and illegal dirty tricks operations, were written by James Kirkpatrick Davis, who wrote two books on the subject and also assisted Hoover's successor, Clarence Kelley, in writing his memoir on his years as director during the years of attempted reform at the bureau. Ward Churchill and Jim Vander Wall's published collection of COINTELPRO files was a valuable resource, as was Nelson Blackstock's collection. I am grateful to other writers who have contributed substantially to the growing body of evidence on particular aspects of Hoover's impact on society, including during the Cold War and in regard to racial issues. These scholars include William W. Keller, Kenneth O'Reilly, Robert Justin Goldstein, and David J. Garrow. Thanks for advice from Mike Ravnitsky, a leading expert on the federal Freedom of Information Act. The writings of the late Frank Donner, esteemed intelligence scholar, also enlightened me. I regret not being able to tell him I discovered he was a suspect in the Media burglary and that J. Edgar Hoover twice asked agents to break into his office, and they refused to do so. He would have appreciated the ironies.

NBC television reporter Carl Stern, whose lawsuit led to a judicial decision requiring the FBI in 1973 to reveal what COINTELPRO operations were, cannot be thanked enough for his persistence when the bureau and the Department of Justice were determined in the early 1970s to keep Hoover's secret operations sealed off from the public forever. Stern has been a valuable source during my research. So has Seth Rosenfeld, author of the 2012 book *The Subversives*. Despite the FBI spending more than half a million dollars in court efforts to prevent Rosenfeld from gaining access to crucial FBI files, he persisted and in the end meticulously documented the decades-long campaign by Hoover to damage administrators, professors, students, and academic programs at the University of California, especially on the Berkeley campus.

Several FBI officials and agents have also been very helpful. Key among them is Neil Welch. Somehow Welch managed to defy Hoover and keep his job as SAC (special agent in charge) in several cities. He not only refused to let agents he supervised participate in COINTELPRO operations, but he also conducted investigations of organized crime even as Hoover refused to acknowledge that it existed. In interviews for this book, Welch provided unique insights and information about Hoover and the FBI, the nature of intelligence operations in general, and his reaction to the Media burglary.

Frank McLaughlin, an agent at the Media office at the time of the burglary, provided detailed firsthand information about the scene at the Media office the morning after the burglary. Other agents, who have chosen not to be named, provided important information that supplements what I gleaned from the official record of the investigation. Former FBI counterterrorism agent Mike German, now a senior policy counsel for the American Civil Liberties Union on national security, immigration, and privacy, provided valuable insights about the FBI in recent years.

Like most people who have written about Hoover and the FBI, I owe an enormous debt of gratitude to the late senator Frank Church, the chair of the Senate committee known as the Church Committee, and other members of that committee who, in a largely nonpartisan approach in the mid-1970s, conducted the first investigation of intelligence agencies. The substantial record of those hearings is crucial to understanding the FBI and also to understanding the enormous impact of the Media burglary. I am grateful to the Church Committee's chief counsel, Frederick A. O. Schwarz Jr., now chief counsel at the Brennan Center for Justice at New York University School of Law, for his insights about the committee's findings and recommendations.

Excellent sources on contemporary surveillance policies and practices have included the American Civil Liberties Union, the National Security Archives, the Electronic Frontier Foundation, the Project on Government Secrecy at the Federation of American Scientists, and the work of these and other journalists: Dana Priest, William Arkin, Ellen Nakashima, and Barton Gellman of the *Washington Post*; Charlie Savage, Eric Lichtblau, and James Risen of the *New York Times*; Philip Shenon, formerly of the *New York Times*; Jane Mayer of the *New Yorker*; Glenn Greenwald of the *Guardian*; and Laura Poitras, documentary filmmaker.

Interviews with Daniel Berrigan, the Jesuit poet and antiwar activist, and other participants in the Catholic peace movement have deepened my understanding of the nonviolent resistance philosophy that was at the heart of the Media burglars' activism. I am particularly grateful to Camden defendant Bob Good.

Thanks to foundations that provided support for initial research, transcription of interviews, and the purchase of the record of the FBI investigation of the burglary: the J. Roderick MacArthur Foundation, the Freedom Forum, and the Fund for Constitutional Government. Thanks to the Rockefeller Foundation for a fellowship at its Bellagio Center. Special thanks to the patient transcribers of hundreds of hours of interviews: Gary Barker, Zachary Barton, Pam McDaniel, Wes Kirkey, Valerie O'Riordan, and Karen Racanelli. Through the Center for Investigative Reporting, the late Angus Mackenzie provided helpful advice.

Countless friends, family members, and colleagues have been supportive as I wrote this book. Special thanks to Anthony Giacchino, producer-director of the documentary film *The Camden 28*; the late Derrick Bell, law professor; the late Howard Zinn, historian; the late Anthony Lewis, *New York Times* columnist; the late Arthur Hagadus, bookstore proprietor; the late James Carey, professor of journalism; Larry Gara, historian; and Victor Navasky, former editor of *The Nation* and historian of Cold War intelligence practices. I also owe deep thanks to Philadelphia lawyer David Kairys; to Daniel Ellsberg, who made the Pentagon Papers public three months after the Media burglary; and to numerous friends, especially Maya Reiner, Joerg Weber, Diana and Hisham Matar, Susan and Albert Wells, Edna Lee, Paul van Zyl, Zoia Horn, Bill and Kari Hoover, Dean Galloway, Nancy McDermid, and Raul Ramirez.

I am especially grateful to my Brooklyn connection, Max van Zyl. He is responsible for my introduction to a great editor and publisher. It was through the network of friends Max established in second grade at his Brooklyn school that I had the pleasure and good fortune of meeting and receiving wise counsel from Robert Gottlieb, editor extraordinaire. After reading a summary of *The Burglary,* he said, "I know the perfect editor for you and for this story: Vicky Wilson." He was right. Thanks, Max. Thanks, Bob. I am deeply grateful for Gottlieb's advice and for the wise editing, overall vision, and enthusiasm of Victoria Wilson, senior vice president and editor at Alfred A. Knopf. I also am grateful for the support and expert skills of other people at Knopf who contributed significantly to bringing *The Burglary* to fruition: Katherine Hourigan, vice president and managing editor; Romeo Enriquez, production manager; Victoria Pearson, production editor; Roland Ottewell, copy editor; and Ms. Wilson's assistants, Charlotte Crowe and Audrey Silverman.

A mountain of thanks to Johanna Hamilton. Johanna, Max's mother, has been a great colleague as we have worked collaboratively on our independent projects— her documentary film, *1971,* and my book—to tell the story of the Media burglary and its impact. We have had a creative, dynamic, and mutually supportive working relationship. After many years of working alone on this story, it has been wonderful to have a partner who shares my commitment to telling it in ways both of us hope will stimulate public discourse about the need for intelligence agencies to be accountable to the public and about the need for citizens to assume responsibility for their government's actions.

I am profoundly indebted to the late Katharine Graham who, as publisher of the *Washington Post,* decided to publish stories about the stolen Media files despite the company lawyer's recommendation that they not be published. It was the first of the many times she would be confronted with a demand from the Nixon administration that she suppress a story.

I also am thankful for the gift of silence I experienced as I wrote in libraries in Mystic and Stonington, Connecticut, and Stockbridge, Massachusetts. I am especially grateful for that grand and beautiful temple of silence and thinking, the Rose Reading Room at the main branch of the New York Public Library. My laptop and I have had many productive days there in that sea of hundreds of silent readers and writers. Whoever you are, reading room companions, thanks for the inspiration.

My deepest personal thanks go to the person who has been my partner in all things as I wrote this book—my wonderful husband, John T. Racanelli. He has been an enthusiastic supporter ever since I returned from that trip to Philadelphia and greeted him at the airport with "You won't believe this! I met two of the Media burglars!" The journey to completion of this project has been his, too. He has been a wise and loving companion throughout the journey. No words can adequately express my gratitude for the support he has given.

Notes

All information attributed to Media burglars, unless otherwise indicated, is from multiple interviews conducted by the writer over two decades with seven of the eight burglars.

All information about the FBI's investigation of the Media burglary, unless otherwise indicated, is based on the 33,698-page official record of the burglary by the FBI, which was requested by the author under the federal Freedom of Information Act. Known as MEDBURG, the case was closed on March 11, 1976, and has remained unsolved.

Selected reports from the Select Committee to Study Governmental Operations with Respect to Intelligence Activities, United States Senate (known as the Church Committee), April 1976, can be found at: http://www.intelligence.senate .gov/pdfs94th/94intelligence_activities_VI.pdf.

1. IN THE ABSENCE OF OVERSIGHT

3 **had resigned in 1966:** "Nicholas Katzenbach, 90, Dies; Policy Maker at '60s Turning Points," *New York Times*, May 9, 2012.
4 **"ruled the FBI":** Katzenbach, *Some of It Was Fun*, 184.
4 **"There was no man":** Ibid., 185.
4 **Katzenbach believed:** Katzenbach testimony before Church Committee, December 3, 1975.
4 **"is almost impossible":** Ibid.
6 **"How did they know":** Author interview with former FBI agent Mike German.
7 **Contrary to the official:** Ungar, *FBI*, 283.
7 **"has operated on":** Halperin, Berman, Borosage, and Marwick, *The Lawless State*, 131.
8 **Mark Felt:** Felt, *The FBI Pyramid*, 98–99. Felt and O'Connor, *A G-Man's Life*, 92.
8 **Ironically, the burglary:** Author interview with retired Media FBI agent.

8 **The writers of every:** The authors of the following books have noted the significance of
the 1971 Media burglary:

Blackstock, *COINTELPRO*, 17, 38–39.
Burnham, *Above the Law*, 250–51.
Campbell, *Senator Sam Ervin*, 272.
Churchill and Vander Wall, *The COINTELPRO Papers*, xi, 4, 332, 347.
Cowan et al., *State Secrets*, 107–217.
Cunningham, *There's Something Happening Here*, 35–36, 67, 88, 110, 181, 194, 201.
Davis, *Assault on the Left*, 8–14, 207, 215.
————, *Spying on America*, 1, 6, 14, 181.
Davis and Kelley, *Kelley*, 158, 175.
Denenberg, *The True*, 2–3, 184–85.
Donner, *The Age of Surveillance*, 108, 157–59, 167, 169, 178, 179, 181.
Feldman, *Manufacturing Hysteria*, 292–95.
Felt, *The FBI Pyramid*, 87–99.
Felt and O'Connor, *A G-Man's Life*, 84–85, 87–92.
Gentry, *J. Edgar Hoover*, 674–76, 713.
Gillers and Watters, eds., *Investigating the FBI*, 79, 196, 203, 239, 241, 242, 243–44, 245,
246, 255, 259–60, 265, 267, 268, 269, 271, 277, 279, 281, 286, 332, 344, 351, 352, 355, 356,
357, 441, 443.
Goodman, *Static*, 46–61.
Graff, *The Threat Matrix*, 62–63.
Greenberg, *The Dangers of Dissent*, 74.
Halperin et al., *The Lawless State*, 92, 130.
Holland, *Leak*, 13.
Keller, *The Liberals and J. Edgar Hoover*, 115–16, 149–53, 194–95.
Kessler, *The Bureau*, 156.
————, *The FBI*, 15.
Moynihan, *Secrecy*, 34.
Neier, *Dossier*, 146, 151, 154, 156.
Nelson and Ostrow, *The FBI and the Berrigans*, 187–88, 191, 211.
O'Reilly, *Hoover and the Un-Americans*, 217–18, 220–21, 285, 288.
————, *"Racial Matters,"* 346–47, 351.
Powers, *Broken*, 287.
————, *Secrecy and Power*, 464–67.
Price, *Threatening Anthropology*, 17.
Rosenfeld, *Subversives*, 414, 491, 492, 639n.
Saxbe, *I've Seen the Elephant*, p. 191
Stone, *Perilous Times*, 494–96.
Sullivan, *The Bureau*, 151–52.
Summers, *Official and Confidential*, 393.
Swearingen, *FBI Secrets*, i.
Theoharis, *Abuse of Power*, 141.
————, *The FBI and American Democracy*, 137.
————, *Spying on Americans*, 148–50, 273n52.
Theoharis and Cox, *The Boss*, 425n, 426.
Ungar, *FBI*, 136–40, 268, 484–92.
Weiner, *Enemies*, 293.
Welch and Marston, *Inside Hoover's FBI*, 165–66.
Wise, *The American Police State*, 281.

The FBI website provides this description of the burglary and its impact in "A
Brief History of the Philadelphia Division," http://www.fbi.gov/philadelphia/about-us
/history/history:

The Philadelphia Division faced significant challenges in the early 1970s when it had to deal with the burglary of one of its resident agencies in 1971 and the changing national political climate after the death of J. Edgar Hoover in 1972 and the emerging Watergate scandal.

The burglary of the resident agency had taken place on the night of March 8, 1971. A radical group called "Citizens' Commission to Investigate the FBI" broke into the office in Media and stole a wide array of domestic security documents that had not been properly secured. Some [writer's note: actually, only one] of the documents mentioned "COINTELPRO," or Counterintelligence Programs—a series of programs aimed to disrupt some of the more radical groups of the 1950s and 1960s. The leaking of those documents to the news media and politicians and the subsequent criticism, both inside and outside the Bureau, led to a significant reevaluation of FBI domestic security policy.

8   **"The Media documents"**: Ungar, *FBI*, 485.
8   **"In one fell swoop"**: Holland, *Leak*, 13.
9   **"Hoover's power"**: Powers, *Broken*, 287.

2. CHOOSING BURGLARY

12 **He traveled to Vietnam:** Peter Monaghan, "The Year That Started the 60s," *Chronicle of Higher Education*, November 5, 2012. In 1965, the year before Davidon went to Vietnam, the war had escalated significantly: American troop numbers had leaped from 23,000 to 184,000 and round-the-clock bombing had begun. The intensification of the war motivated Davidon to see the impact of the war firsthand.

13 **Like other reports:** R. W. Apple Jr., "Vietnamese Seize Six U.S. Pacifists and Expel Them," *New York Times*, April 21, 1966.

14 **"the most significant":** Lyons, *The People of This Generation*, 144–66.

17 **But at the Vatican:** Carroll, *An American Requiem*, 75–76. Polner and O'Grady, *Disarmed and Dangerous*, 112, 118–19, 142–43, 169.

17 **In 1963:** Polner and O'Grady, *Disarmed and Dangerous*, 136.

17 **Pope Paul VI:** Carroll, *The American Requiem*, 155–60. Polner and O'Grady, *Disarmed and Dangerous*, 137.

18 **Spellman had always:** Carroll, *The American Requiem*, 164–69.

18 **Standing before troops:** Polner and O'Grady, *Disarmed and Dangerous*, 137.

18 **Spellman's role:** Carroll, *The American Requiem*, 164.

18 **Despite the fiercely:** Polner and O'Grady, *Disarmed and Dangerous*, 107, 109, 125–26, 156, 210.

18 **As the Catholic:** Ibid., 129, 131, 172.

19 **Spellman's authoritarian:** Carroll, *An American Requiem*, 173–74. Polner and O'Grady, *Disarmed and Dangerous*, 111–41.

19 **Nine of them:** Polner and O'Grady, *Disarmed and Dangerous*, 12, 192–94, 212, 331–32.

20 **He sent the letter:** Berrigan, *America Is Hard to Find*, 92–98.

24 **In November 1969:** Henry Kamm, "Vietnamese Say G.I.'s Slew 567 in Town," *New York Times*, November 17, 1969.

25 **American officials:** William Carlsen and Mark Simon, "Hard Line Helped Him Win, Flexibility Helped Him Stay/Ability to Compromise Replaced His Tough Stance Against UC Student Protests," *San Francisco Chronicle*, June 6, 2004.

25 **Three members:** Linda Charlton, "Search Widens for 2 Women in Townhouse Blast," *New York Times*, March 30, 1970.

25 **President Nixon announced:** "Cambodian Incursion Address," April 30, 1970, http://www.americanrhetoric.com/speeches/PDFFiles/Richard%20Nixon%20-%20Cambodian%20Incursion%20Address.pdf.

25 **By the end:** Taylor Owen, "Bombs over Cambodia," taylorowen.com, September 19, 2006. Owen, research director of the Tow Center for Digital Journalism at Columbia School of Journalism, provided this analysis from Air Force data on all American bombing of Indochina between 1964 and 1975 that was declassified and released by President Bill Clinton in 2000 when he became the first U.S. president to visit Vietnam since the war ended.

25 **Two days after:** *Ohio Politics*, 80–81.

25 **A day later:** John Kifner, "4 Kent State Students Killed by Troops: 8 Hurt as Shooting Follows Reported Sniping at Rally," *New York Times*, May 4, 1970. Robert D. McFadden, "37 College Chiefs Urge Nixon Move for Prompt Peace," *New York Times*, May 5, 1970. Martin Nolan, "What the Nation Learned at Kent State in 1970," *Boston Globe*, May 3, 2000.

25 **A few days later:** Dean, *Conservatives Without Conscience*, 85.

26 **Nixon, at the urging:** Jack Rosenthal, "President's Panel Warns Split on Youth Perils U.S.; Asks Him to Foster Unity: Near–Civil War Feared Unless Division of Society Is Ended," *New York Times*, September 27, 1970.

26 **Two students:** Roy Reed, "F.B.I. Investigating Killing of 2 Negroes in Jackson," *New York Times*, May 16, 1970.

26 **The Friday after:** Homer Bigart, "War Foes Here Attacked by Construction Workers: City Hall Is Stormed," *New York Times*, May 9, 1970. "After 'Bloody Friday,' New York Wonders If Wall Street Is Becoming a Battleground," *Wall Street Journal*, May 11, 1970. Joe Guzzardi, "View from Lodi, CA: Remembering an Earlier War in America's Streets," http://www.vdare.com/guzzardi/war_in_streets.htm, April 23, 2004.

27 **Twenty-two of those:** Robert B. Semple, "Nixon Meets Heads of 2 City Unions; Hails War Support," *New York Times,* May 27, 1970. James M. Naughton, "Construction Union Chief in New York Is Chosen to Succeed Hodgson," *New York Times,* November 30, 1972.

27 **Vice President Spiro Agnew:** Fred J. Cook, "Hard-Hats: The Rampaging Patriots," *Nation*, June 15, 1970.

27 **On August 24, 1970:** Susan Rosenfeld, "The Fatal Bombing That Historians Ignore," *Chronicle of Higher Education,* August 17, 2001.

27 **That was America:** "At War with War," *Time*, May 18, 1970.

29 **Little had been written:** Ungar, *FBI*, 484–85.

30 **The first event:** Donner, *The Age of Surveillance*, 87–90. Gentry, *J. Edgar Hoover*, 664–65. Nelson and Ostrow, *The FBI and the Berrigans*, 15–20.

30 **"Only twice":** Nelson and Ostrow, *The FBI and the Berrigans*, 15–16.

31 **He stuck with:** James T. Patterson, "The Enemy Within," *Atlantic*, October 1998.

33 **It was not known:** Gentry, *J. Edgar Hoover*, 664–67. Ungar, *FBI*, 307, 483. Donner, *The Age of Surveillance*, 87–89. Nelson and Ostrow, *The FBI and the Berrigans*, 16–20. Sullivan, *The Bureau*, 154–55.

34 **Hoover probably never:** Ungar, *FBI*, 337.

34 **The second event:** Donner, *The Age of Surveillance*, 88, 107, 117. Gentry, *J. Edgar Hoover*, 665–66. Nelson and Ostrow, *The FBI and the Berrigans*, 29–30. Author interviews with Anderson.

35 **A trip Anderson made:** George C. Wilson, "S. Viet Prison Found Shocking," *Washington Post*, July 7, 1970.

37 **One of the staunchest:** Ungar, *FBI*, 364–66. Tom Wicker, "What Have They Done Since They Shot Dillinger?," *New York Times*, December 29, 1969: Rooney, as quoted by Wicker: "I have never cut his budget and I never expect to. . . . The people don't want it cut.' "

37 **It was a brutal:** Ronald Kessler, "FBI Had Files on Congress, Ex-Aides Say," *Washington Post*, January 19, 1975.

3. THE TEAM IS FORMED

38 **"John's personality":** *Camden 28* documentary film, produced by Anthony Giacchino, 2007.

45 **The downward spiral:** "Casualties—US vs NVA/VC." Note that U.S. statistics cited here are from Combat Area Casualty File and the Adjutant General's Center file, both available from the National Archives. http://www.rjsmith.com/kia_tbl.html.

47 **It was not just Harriet Tubman:** "Media History," http://visitmediapa.com/history.

4. THE BURGLARS IN THE ATTIC

50 **For the first time:** Frank Lotierzo, "Fight of the Century: 33 Years Later and Still Nothing Like It," http://www.thesweetscience.com, March 7, 2004. Michael Silver, "Where Were You on March 8, 1971?," ESPN, November 19, 2003. "The Fight of the Century," International Boxing Hall of Fame, http://www.ibhof.com. Gary Younge, "The Fighter," *Guardian*, January 18, 2002. Hauser, *Muhammad Ali*, 173, 216–25.

51 **Even Nelson Mandela:** Jack Newfield, "The Meaning of Muhammad," *Nation*, January 17, 2002.

51 **He even enlisted:** William C. Rhoden, "At His Essence, Smokin' Joe Was More Than Just a Symbol," *New York Times*, November 13, 2011. Arkush, *The Fight of the Century*, 28–29, 132–36.

51 **It was the most anticipated:** David Hornestay, "Joe Louis Knocks Out Max Schmeling: Personal Revenge and a Political Statement," http://www.suite101.com, March 24, 2010. Dean Hybl, "Two Days in June: Max Schmeling vs. Joe Louis," http://sportsthenandnow .com, June 19, 2010. "The Fight of the Century," NPR, November 25, 2006. Hauser, *Muhammad Ali*, 225–33.

53 **Shortly after:** Fred P. Graham, "Plot to Kidnap Kissinger Is Charged; Philip Berrigan and 5 Others Indicted," *New York Times,* January 13, 1971.

70 **H. H. Wilson, a professor:** H. H. Wilson, "The FBI Today: The Case for Effective Control," *Nation*, February 8, 1971.

70 **It would later be learned:** Fred J. Cook, "On Being an Enemy of the F.B.I.," *Nation*, March 27, 1986.

72 **The director fired Shaw:** Ungar, *FBI*, 265.

72 **He said the letter:** Gentry, *J. Edgar Hoover*, 671.

73 **Another unsolvable challenge:** Note: Two future Republican candidates for president, Ronald Reagan and Bob Dole, gave campaign speeches in front of this courthouse and across the street from the former Media FBI office.

5. TIME OUT FOR WHITE HOUSE MEETING

78 **The next week:** Mary McGrory, "Kissinger Meets Plotters," *Washington Star*, March 12, 1971.

79 **Kissinger later wrote:** Kissinger, *White House Years*, 1015–16.

6. WITH THANKS TO MUHAMMAD ALI AND JOE FRAZIER

86 **In New York:** William N. Wallace, "Worldwide Televising of Fight Is the Biggest Item in a $25 Million Gamble, Most Will Watch on Home Screens, but Viewing in U.S., England and Canada Is Restricted to Closed Circuit TV," *New York Times,* March 7, 1971. Jack Gould, "Broadcast of Fight Barred to Many G.I.s," *New York Times,* March 6, 1971. "Facts on Title Fight," *New York Times,* March 8, 1971. Steve Cady, "500-Man Force to Patrol Inside and Outside Arena," *New York Times,* March 8, 1971. Ian O'Connor, "The First Ali-Frazier Fight Still Electric After 35 Years," *USA Today,*

March 7, 2006. Bob Hanna, "Book Inspired Memories of 'Fight of the Century,'" *Inside Boxing*, November 27, 2007. Hauser, *Muhammad Ali*, 225–33. Arkush, *The Fight of the Century*, 148–80.

94 **By that time:** Dave Kindred, "The First Ali-Frazier Fight Was Also the Best," *Sporting News*, February 17, 1999. Arkush, *The Fight of the Century*, 181–95.

102 **As the world watched:** Dave Anderson, "Champion Floors His Rival with Left Hook in the 15th," *New York Times*, March 9, 1971. Neil Amdur, "Ali Is Silent on Way to Hospital," *New York Times*, March 9, 1971. Arthur Daley, "Epic Worth the Price," *New York Times*, March 9, 1971. Jack Gould, "Radio Gives World-Wide Fight News," *New York Times*, March 9, 1971. Hauser, *Muhammad Ali*, 233. Arkush, *The Fight of the Century*, 196–200.

103 **As Hoover retired:** "The Truth About Hoover," *Time*, December 22, 1975.

7. ESCAPE TO THE FARM

117 **In New York:** Kindred, *Sound and Fury*, 171.

8. J. EDGAR HOOVER'S WORST NIGHTMARE

118 **Frank McLaughlin:** Author interview with McLaughlin, plus his official reports.

121 **The last time:** "FBI Agents Cope with Antiquated Facilities in Covering 2 Counties," *Philadelphia Inquirer*, March 9, 1967.

124 **That morning he:** Felt, *The FBI Pyramid*, 92–99, and Felt and O'Connor, *A G-Man's Life*, 84–92. These excerpts from Felt's two books, combined with his reports in the record of the MEDBURG investigation, are records of his use of conflicting information to make the case against the agent in charge of the Media office, Tom Lewis.

127 **A retired agent:** Author confidential interview with agent who worked at Media FBI office at time of burglary.

127 **He says Lewis:** Ungar, *FBI*, 487.

128 **Hoover accepted:** "Media FBI Agent Is Suspended for 30 Days," *Philadelphia Evening Bulletin*, March 26, 1971.

128 **They organized a dinner:** "Testimonial Dinner Planned for Transferred FBI Agent," *Philadelphia Evening Bulletin*, April 9, 1971.

129 **"Hoover was enraged":** Felt, *The FBI Pyramid*, 92.

129 **when Hoover learned:** Jeremiah O'Leary, "Hoover, Angered by Theft, to Shut Small Offices," *Washington Star*, April 13, 1971.

129 **Only a very few:** Theoharis, *From the Secret Files*, 1–11. In this introduction, Theoharis provides a summary of the elaborate and complicated methods Hoover used to keep his files secret.

129 **Prior to March 1971:** Gentry, *J. Edgar Hoover*, 367–75. Ungar, *FBI*, 370. Alan Barth, "The Judith Coplon Case and the Embarrassed FBI: Bureau Lost Some Files 22 Years Ago," April 20, 1971.

130 **He even suggested:** "U.S. Says It May Drop Coplon Trial If Judge Orders 'Vital Secrets' Told," *New York Times*, June 4, 1949.

130 **When that threat:** Gentry, *J. Edgar Hoover*, 370.

131 **It is believed to be:** "FBI Head Reported to Have Resigned," *New York Times*, June 15, 1949.

131 **The prosecutor complied:** "Clark Backs FBI in Coplon Case but He 'Regrets' Use of Reports," *New York Times*, July 2, 1949.

131 **Compared to the:** "Film 'Communists' Listed in FBI file in Coplon Spy Case," *New York Times*, June 9, 1949. Cabell Phillips, "Activities of the FBI Come Under Scrutiny," *New York Times*, June 19, 1949.

131 **"dossiers being laid out":** Phillips, "Activities of the FBI."

132 **In the unanimous opinion:** *United States v. Coplon*, United States Court of Appeals Second Circuit, 185 F.2d. 629 (2d Cir. 1950).

132 **The illegalities included:** Charles Grutzner, "Coplon Wire-Taps Denied, Admitted: F.B.I. Witness First Disclaims Awareness, Then Tells of Destroying Reports," *New York Times*, December 23, 1949.

132 **Despite Hoover's humiliation:** Gentry, *J. Edgar Hoover*, 373.

132 **Finally, in an unusual:** Sidney E. Zion, "U.S. Drops Charges in Coplon Spy Case," *New York Times*, January 7, 1967.

133 **But in light of:** Gentry, *J. Edgar Hoover*, 373–75. Theoharis and Cox, *The Boss*, 257–61.

134 **When the National Lawyers Guild:** Gentry, *J. Edgar Hoover*, 370.

136 **Agents were especially interested:** Barry Wingard, "The Trial of the Flower City Conspiracy," *Harvard Crimson*, December 2, 1970. "Flower City Eight Convicted, Sentenced," *Harvard Crimson*, December 4, 1970.

141 **The FBI had helped prepare:** Richard Halloran, "Aide to Mitchell Opposes Any Curb on Surveillance," *New York Times*, March 10, 1971. "Can Government Investigate Anyone?," *Washington Post*, March 12, 1971. Spencer Rich, "Rehnquist Civil Liberties Stance Eyed," *Washington Post*, October 26, 1971. Charns, *Cloak and Gavel*, 187n7. Neier, *Dossier*, 155–56.

143 **Rehnquist's claim:** Tom Wicker, "The Goat and the Cabbage Patch," *New York Times*, March 11, 1971.

9. FBI AND BURGLARS IN A RACE

144 **Four days after:** Mary McGrory, "Kissinger Meets Plotters," *Washington Star*, March 12, 1971.

150 **The *Delaware County Daily Times*:** "Davidon Unveils Plot Against the FBI," *Delaware County Daily Times*, March 12, 1971.

159 **Reluctantly, the director:** Ungar, *FBI*, 488.

159 **This unusual security arrangement:** Author interview with Jack Ryan, former FBI agent, in Peoria, Illinois.

10. TO PUBLISH OR NOT TO PUBLISH

163 **The bureau needed:** Interview of Terry Neist, FBI agent, by Sam Green.

171 **At bureau headquarters:** Ken Clawson, "Stolen FBI Reports Sent to McGovern, Rep. Mitchell," *Washington Post*, March 23, 1971.

177 **The story was distributed:** Betty Medsger and Ken Clawson, "Stolen Documents Describe FBI Surveillance Activities," *Washington Post*, March 24, 1971.

177 **The same day:** "Mitchell Issues Plea on F.B.I. Files: Asks Press Not to Publish Date on Stolen Papers," *New York Times*, March 24, 1971.

178 **As Nelson revealed:** Nelson, *Scoop*, 156–60. Nelson died in 2009 before he finished his memoir; it was completed in 2013 by his wife, journalist Barbara Matusow.

178 **In 2011, the *Times*:** Richard A. Serrano, "An FBI Director with a Grudge," *Los Angeles Times*, November 6, 2011. In this story Serrano reports that Nelson's FBI file, received by the *Times* through an FOIA request, revealed that during 1970 and 1971 Hoover conducted a campaign to get the *Times* to fire Nelson. The director claimed he had been told Nelson was going to write a story saying the director was a homosexual. Nelson, in response to an editor's request, wrote a statement that was sent to Hoover in which he strongly denied ever suggesting Hoover was a homosexual. At that time, Hoover was angry with Nelson because of the book he and then *Charlotte Observer* journalist Jack Bass recently had written about the role of FBI agents in the Orangeburg Massacre, when three black students were killed by the gunfire of state highway patrolmen on the campus of South Carolina State College in Orangeburg. Nelson and Bass reported that

three FBI agents watched state troopers fire on black students but later denied they were present.

179 **In 2013, Graham:** Author interview with Fred Graham, April 2013.

11. APPROPRIATE FOR THE SECRET POLICE OF THE SOVIET UNION

183 **In an editorial:** "What Is the FBI Up To?," *Washington Post*, March 25, 1971. "Congress and the FBI," *Washington Post*, April 12, 1971.

185 **"are questions too fundamental":** "How Much Do We Really Know About the Work of the FBI?," *Philadelphia Inquirer*, March 28, 1971.

185 **"Little confidence":** "Policies of Paranoia," *New York Times*, March 29, 1971.

186 **Not everyone thought:** "Letters to the Editor, the Stolen FBI Documents and the Story About Them," *Washington Post*, March 31, 1971.

187 **"The quick succession":** Christopher Lydon, "Ervin Rules Out Inquiry into F.B.I. Now," *New York Times*, April 19, 1971.

188 **The most visible FISUR techniques:** Ungar, *FBI*, 489–90.

188 **They continued to look like:** Donald M. Janson, "Theft of Documents," *New York Times*, March 12, 1972.

189 **"Your FBI in Action":** Donald M. Janson, "Philadelphia Fair 'Exposes' F.B.I.: Angry Powelton Residents Satirize Agents in Area," *New York Times*, June 6, 1971. Joe Sharkey, "Powelton 'Tribute' to FBI Puts Emphasis on Exposure," *Philadelphia Inquirer*, June 6, 1971.

190 **In addition to finding:** Ungar, *FBI*, 490.

196 **It had all started:** Laurence Stern, "FBI Records Dispute Stand by Kissinger," *Washington Post*, June 12, 1974.

198 **If there was an investigation:** Gentry, *J. Edgar Hoover*, 679. Liddy, *Will*, 215.

198 **Within two hours:** "Justice Dept. Asks Hill Inquiry on FBI," *Washington Post*, April 8, 1971. Robert M. Smith, "Kleindienst Assails Boggs; Invites Inquiry into F.B.I.," *New York Times*, April 8, 1971. "Kleindienst Modifies Suggestion Congress Investigate the F.B.I.," *New York Times*, April 9, 1971.

198 **Failing to convince:** Schwarz and Huq, *Unchecked and Unbalanced*, 18.

199 **On March 25, 1971:** "CIA Domestic Activities," March 25, 1971, MORI DocID: 1451843, CIA Family Jewels, National Security Archive.

200 **When written responses:** Ibid.

200 **One official:** Thomas H. Karamessines, "Meeting with MAG Group," December 21, 1971, MORI DocID: 1451843, CIA Family Jewels, National Security Archive.

200 **Less than a month later:** Richard Halloran, "Rare Speech Discloses Some Russians Aided U.S. in Cuban Crisis," *New York Times*, April 15, 1971.

200 **Helms, in the only:** Richard Halloran, "Helms Defends the C.I.A. as Vital to a Free Society," *New York Times*, April 15, 1971. "Excerpts from Speech by Helms to Society of Newspaper Editors," *New York Times*, April 15, 1971.

200 **A few months later:** W. E. Colby, attachment to letter from "CIA Activities in the United States," April 21, 1972, MORI DocID: 1451843, CIA Family Jewels, National Security Archive.

201 **The CIA had been conducting:** Schwarz and Huq, *Unchecked and Unbalanced*, 37–43.

201 **Six months after:** "CIA Domestic Activities," November 1971, MORI DocID: 1451843, CIA Family Jewels, National Security Archive.

202 **Like Hoover's need:** Mackenzie and Weir, *Secrets*, 48.

203 **Henceforth, Colby wrote:** Ibid., 49.

203 **After years of:** Richard Helms, oral history, conducted February 2 and March 15, 1988, CIA Oral History Program, https://www.cia.gov/library/center-for-the-study-of -intelligence/csi-publications/csi-studies/studies/vol51no3/reflections-of-dci-colby-and -helms-on-the-cia2019s-201ctime-of-troubles201d.html.

12. I'M THINKING OF TURNING YOU IN

205 **"It was like":** Anthony Giacchino interview of Terry Neist, *Camden 28* documentary script, 24.

208 **However, when a new:** Donner, *The Age of Surveillance*, 90. "Indictment in a Bizarre 'Plot,'" *New York Times*, May 2, 1971.

209 **Scholarly papers:** Watters and Gillers, eds., *Investigating the FBI*. This book is a collection of the papers and discussions presented at Princeton's Conference on the FBI.

210 **One of the people:** Alan Brinkley, "Dreams of a G-Man," *New York Review of Books*, April 23, 1987.

218 **At such times:** Author interview with lawyer David Kairys. About whether people in the peace movement thought Grady was involved in Media, he said, "I agree that Grady did, often by silence and smiles, let others think he did Media. He left that impression on me." A Camden defendant, Bob Good, said in an October 2009 email exchange with the author, "I also only received a smile whenever I would try to ask any more about it. . . . I have always understood that John was the prime mover behind it, but it is honestly only my understanding. . . . I have never heard any direct accounting."

13. BEING AMERICAN WHILE BLACK AND OTHER INSIGHTS FROM MEDIA

226 **More than anything:** William Greider, "Analysis of Stolen FBI Documents Provides Glimpse of Bureau at Work," *Washington Post*, July 4, 1971.

227 **It was learned:** Nicholas M. Horrock, "N.A.A.C.P. Checked 25 Years by the F.B.I.: No Illegal Activities Found—Women's Movement Also Monitored by the Bureau," *New York Times*, April 29, 1976.

240 **The young agent:** Schott, *No Left Turns*, 36. Actually, it has been said that the director had the same antipathy to pear-shaped heads that he had to pinheads. Schott describes the dismissal of a new agent with a pinhead.

240 **Weight requirements:** Ungar, *FBI*, 266.

244 **He unpacked:** Author conversation with Don Oberdorfer. Gentry, *J. Edgar Hoover*, 663.

245 **The director could not:** Clawson, "FBI's Hoover Scores Ramsey Clark, RFK; Praises Mitchell as 'Very Human,'" *Washington Post*, November 17, 1970.

14. THE SUBTERFUGE CONTINUES

250 **The full explanation:** William Greider, "10,000 'Potential Subversives': U.S. Keeps Index for Emergency Arrests," *Washington Post*, June 13, 1971.

251 **It was later revealed:** Schwarz and Huq, *Unchecked and Unbalanced*, 33.

254 **When Attorney General:** Robert Justin Goldstein, "The FBI's Forty-Year Plot," *Nation*, July 1, 1978. Theoharis, *Spying on Americans*, 43–44.

256 **Congress achieved:** Theoharis, *Spying on Americans*, 40–64.

258 **It was during debate:** Keller, *The Liberals and J. Edgar Hoover*, 34.

259 **So great was his public:** Sullivan, *The Bureau*, 35–37.

259 **The public relations arm:** John Fischer, "Personal and Otherwise: J. Edgar Hoover and the Politicians," *Harper's*, March 1954: ". . . The FBI Legend has now become enshrined in the American Credo, along with George Washington's cherry tree and Paul Revere's horse. For many years it has been skillfully built up by one of the most sustained publicity operations on record. Millions of words annually—in TV and radio, comic books, suspense novels, films and news stories—are still being devoted to the creation of a highly idealized stereotype of the G-man . . . by the FBI's own publicity outfit, which is widely regarded as one of the best in Washington—second, indeed, only to that of the Marine Corps."

259 **Stuart Ewen:** Ewen, *PR!*, 364–65.

> In 1922, Walter Lippmann postulated that to be successful in mobilizing public opinion around a cause, it is necessary to delineate your opposition as villains and conspirators. . . . A vigorous conservative publicity machine took Lippmann's axiom to heart. From the late forties onward, it became increasingly common to characterize the New Deal's social Keynesian as nothing less than a perfidious drift toward communism. A foreign evil menaced the home front, and governmental activism in social and economic affairs was its most tangible expression. One of the nation's leading publicists in this regard was J. Edgar Hoover. . . . Following this lead, notorious congressional committees (the House Un-American Activities Committee and the Senate Internal Security Subcommittee) launched investigations of Communist infiltration in the United States, and—also marching to Hoover's drumbeat—the commercial media system increasingly presented frightful dramatizations of what would happen if the "Red Menace" was permitted to succeed.

> One item created by the bureau for children was the *Child Molester's Coloring Book*. Episodes of Disney's *Mickey Mouse Club* were filmed in Hoover's office with the Mouseketeers happily dancing by Dillinger's face mask, the director's favorite relic of the bureau's best years. Once Walt Disney unintentionally offended his friend Hoover. A chubby cat in an animated film was identified as an undercover FBI agent known as D.C. (Darn Cat). As an official FBI memo put it, the cat "happily forages in garbage cans every night." That cat, noted the memo, "seems to ridicule the FBI agent." A memo written by one of the highest officials at FBI headquarters, and not with tongue in cheek, concluded, "Every effort will be made through the Los Angeles office to protect the Bureau's interest in this proposed movie. Recommendation: The Crime Records Division will continue to follow this matter closely . . . to ensure that . . . the Bureau's interests are protected." An apologetic Disney changed the script and promised he would never again portray the bureau "other than in a favorable light due to his high esteem for the Director and the Bureau."

260 **With a few notable exceptions:** Ungar, *FBI*, 178.

261 **In the fall of 1971:** Louis Fisher, "Detention of U.S. Citizens," CRS Report for Congress, April 28, 2005 (analysis of U.S. detention policies, 1950 through post 9/11 detention of "enemy combatants").

262 **When President Nixon:** "Statement on Signing Bill Repealing the Emergency Detention Act of 1950," September 25, 1971.

267 **Immediately after:** Gentry, *J. Edgar Hoover*, 653.

269 **Hoover's secret FBI had trumped:** Theoharis, in his introduction to *A Guide to the Microfilm Edition of the J. Edgar Hoover Official and Confidential Files*, ix, describes the methods used by the director to catalog his secret files.

15. COINTELPRO HOVERS

272 **My story on the files:** Betty Medsger and Ken Clawson, "FBI Secretly Prods Colleges on New Left," *Washington Post*, April 6, 1971.

272 **But in that same memorandum:** Davis, *Assault on the Left*, 207, based on FBI Memorandum, Headquarters to Field Offices, April 8, 1971, 216n39.

273 **He took that extreme step:** Theoharis, *Spying on Americans*, 150.

275 **There was evidence:** "The File on J. Edgar Hoover," *Time*, October 25, 1971.

275 *Life* **ran a striking image:** "The 47-Year Reign of J. Edgar Hoover: Emperor of the FBI," *Life*, April 9, 1971.

275 **A month after the** *Life* **cover:** Sally Quinn, "The Night the Director Stole the Show," *Washington Post*, May 25, 1971.

275   **President Nixon defended:** Richard Nixon, Panel Interview at the Annual Convention of the American Society of Newspaper Editors, April 16, 1971. Available at website of the American Presidency Project, http://www.presidency.ucsb.edu/ws/index .php?pid=2982&st=&st1=.

276   **With 5,500 members:** William W. Turner, "Mr. Hoover's Loyal Legion," *Nation*, February 7, 1972.

277   **One of the benefits:** Ungar, *FBI*, 273.

277   **On April 17, 1971:** Nash, *Citizen Hoover*, 243–43.

278   **Hoover spoke:** Ungar, *FBI*, 257.

278   **"The great majority":** "The File on J. Edgar Hoover," *Time*, October 25, 1971.

279   **Only a few hours:** Christopher Matthew, "Nixon Personally Ordered Break-in: He's on Tape Demanding Theft at Brookings Think Tank," *San Francisco Chronicle*, 1996. Nixon Tapes, Nixon-Hoover conversation, June 30, 1971.

281   **"He should get":** Michael Wines, "Tape Shows Nixon Feared Hoover," *New York Times*, June 5, 1991.

281   **Nixon had a meeting:** Gentry, *J. Edgar Hoover*, 691, 699–703.

281   **It was G. Gordon Liddy:** Wines, "Tape Shows Nixon Feared Hoover." Liddy, *Will*, 238–50.

282   **When the president learned:** Robert M. Smith, "After Almost Half a Century, the Process of Selecting a Director of the F.B.I. Begins; Bureau Policies to Face Wide Scrutiny by the Public," *New York Times*, May 3, 1972. John P. MacKenzie, "Hoover: Monument of Power for 48 Years," *Washington Post*, May 3, 1972.

282   **Haldeman suggested:** "Nixon and the FBI: The White House Tapes," National Security Archive, http://www.gwu.edu/~nsarchiv/NSAEBB/NSAEBB156/.

282   **Hoover's remains lay:** "Lying in State," Architect of the Capitol, http://www.aoc.gov /nations-stage/lying-state.

283   **Felt also took over:** David Robb, "The Other Secret Life of Watergate's Deep Throat," *Hollywood Today*, March 9, 2008.

283   **In his eulogy:** President Richard Nixon, "Eulogy Delivered at Funeral Service for J. Edgar Hoover," May 4, 1972, http://www.presidency.ucsb.edu/ws/print.php?pid=3397. Also available on YouTube: http://www.youtube.com/watch?v=6-BbMC6bUn4.

16. VICTORY AT CAMDEN

287   **Hardy made his first:** Robert Hardy, *Camden 28* documentary script, 10.

291   **In an indication:** Ungar, *FBI*, 482–83.

295   **According to a minute-by-minute:** Sullivan, *The Bureau*, 152–53.

296   **after he was killed:** "William C. Sullivan, Ex-F.B.I. Aide, 65, Is Killed in a Hunting Accident," *New York Times*, November 10, 1977. Novak, *The Prince of Darkness*, 210.

297   **"Three guys jumped me":** Michael Doyle, *Camden 28* script, 20.

298   **Given his strong opposition:** Ibid., 3.

299   **"What do you do":** Ibid., 1.

299   **The bureau's sense of triumph:** Hoover/Mitchell press release, August 22, 1971.

299   **About the same time:** Donald B. Proctor, "Accused Camden Leader Linked to Media Raid," *Philadelphia Evening Bulletin*, August 30, 1971.

300   **He sent letters:** Kissinger, letter acknowledging J. Edgar Hoover's August 23, 1971, letter about Camden arrests, September 2, 1971.

301   **When they arrived:** Joan Reilly, *Camden 28* script, 14.

301   **It did not take long:** Mike Giocondo and Michael Doyle, *Camden 28* script, 21.

301   **Hardy reported what:** Hardy, *Camden 28* script, 26.

302   **One day Sandy Grady:** Doyle, *Camden 28* script, 27.

303   **When the Camden defendants:** Author interview with Michael Doyle.

303   **"And I remember the three of us":** Ibid.

303 **Three days later:** Ibid.
304 **After the funeral:** Ibid.

17. DEFEAT AT CAMDEN

311 **Just a month after:** Frank Donner, "A Special Supplement: The Theory and Practice of American Political Intelligence," *New York Review of Books*, April 22, 1971, 27.
314 **In a step:** Robert W. Hardy Affidavit, filed in County of Philadelphia, February 28, 1972. Donald M. Janson, "F.B.I. Is Accused of Aiding a Crime: 'Camden 28' Informer Says He Acted as 'Provocateur,'" *New York Times*, March 16, 1972. "The Law: Informers Under Fire," *Time*, April 17, 1972.
315 **"They reassured me":** Robert Hardy, *Camden 28* script, 35, 40.
317 **As the Camden trial:** Kairys, *Philadelphia Freedom*, 214.
318 **On the witness stand:** Ibid., 209–14. Donald M. Janson, "Informer Testifies F.B.I. Had Him Provoke Camden Draft File Raid," *New York Times*, April 11, 1973.
320 **When the defendants met:** Kairys, *Philadelphia Freedom*, 190–96.
321 **One by one:** Ibid., 214. Betty Medsger, "Justice in a Camden Court," *Progressive*, October 1973, 3 (reprint).
321 **Howard Zinn told:** Zinn, *Camden 28* script, 42. Kairys, *Philadelphia Freedom*, 214.
322 **Never in a courtroom:** Elizabeth (Betty) Good, *Camden 28* script, 45. Kairys, *Philadelphia Freedom*, 214.
323 **She had just assumed:** Good, *Camden 28* script, 47.
323 **Betty Good surprised:** Medsger, "Justice in a Camden Court," *Progressive*, October 1973.
324 **Kairys emphasized:** Kairys, *Philadelphia Freedom*, 218–22.
325 **"No, you will":** Doyle, *Camden 28* script, 50.
325 **On the fourth day:** Kairys, *Philadelphia Freedom*, 223. Medsger, "Justice in a Camden Court."
325 **The hum of conversations:** Trial transcript, 8792.
326 **Chief prosecutor John Barry:** Medsger, "Justice in a Camden Court."

18. THE SECRET FBI EMERGES

330 **For Kelley, those years:** Ungar, *FBI*, 466–69, 575.
330 **Occasionally, for instance:** "Still Wanted," *Time*, December 12, 1977.
331 **Representative Hale Boggs:** Donner, *The Age of Surveillance*, 117.
332 **Stern persisted:** Letters: Stern to Deputy Attorney General Kleindienst, March 20, 1972; Kleindienst to Stern, April 25, 1972; Stern to Kleindienst, June 30, 1972; Stern to Deputy Attorney General Ralph E. Erickson, August 21, 1972; Stern to Erickson, August 31, 1972; Stern to Acting FBI Director L. Patrick Gray, September 6, 1972; Gray to Stern, September 18, 1972; Stern to Erickson, September 29, 1972; Stern to Kleindienst, October 26, 1972; Stern to Erickson, January 12, 1973.
333 **At first, the department appealed:** Laurence Stern, "Hoover War on New Left Bared," *Washington Post*, December 7, 1973. In this story is a brief description of Acting Attorney General Robert Bork's decision to release the first COINTELPRO file to NBC reporter Carl Stern. Bork: "The law and the public policy expressed in the Freedom of Information Act did not warrant appealing the District Court decision." Laurence Stern, author of the article, reports that the release of the COINTELPRO file was the "first time the Justice Department released documents in a Freedom of Information Act challenge." "Mr. Hoover's Dirty Tricks," *Washington Post*, March 15, 1974.
335 **Long issued a statement:** Book II, Final Report of the Select Committee, April 26, 1976. Theoharis, *Spying on Americans*, 113. Gentry, *J. Edgar*, 587.
335 **FBI director Kelley opposed:** Ungar, *FBI*, 32–34.
336 **Four months after:** Saxbe, *I've Seen the Elephant*, 193. Hearing on FBI Counterin-

telligence Programs, November 20, 1974, House of Representatives, Civil Rights and Constitutional Rights Subcommittee of the Committee on the Judiciary.

338 **Two days before:** Ungar, *FBI*, 470. "Hoover's Closet," *Time*, December 2, 1974.

339 **The tipping point:** Seymour Hersh, "Huge CIA Operation Reported in U.S. Against Anti-War Forces, Other Dissidents in Nixon Years, Files on Citizens: Helms Reportedly Got Surveillance Data in Charter Violation," *New York Times*, December 22, 1974.

340 **The programs that:** Ungar, *FBI*, 479.

341 **"It was not uncommon":** Jim Edwards, "The Journalist and the G-Man," *Brill's Content*, November 2000.

19. CRUDE AND CRUEL

342 **Antiwar activists' oranges:** David J. Garrow, "FBI Political Harassment and FBI Historiography: Analyzing Informants and Measuring the Effects," *Public Historian* 10, no. 4 (Autumn 1988): 5–18.

342 **Agents hired prostitutes:** Theoharis, *J. Edgar Hoover, Sex, and Crime*, 100.

342 **The Media break-in changed:** Author interview with Athan Theoharis, February 2013.

343 **"an embryonic version":** Donner, *The Age of Surveillance*, 183.

343 **"The bureau constituted itself":** Ibid., 180.

343 **"highly personalized":** Ibid., 177.

343 **Files were maintained:** John M. Goshko, "Hoover's Files Focus on Sex Scandals: Voracious Collector of Rumors," *Washington Post*, November 24, 1976. Theoharis, *J. Edgar Hoover, Sex, and Crime*, 57–115.

343 **"As the director saw":** Ungar, *FBI*, 466.

344 **Frustrated by recent:** Davis, *Assault on the Left*, 4–5. Note: It was the Supreme Court's 1956 reinterpretation of the Smith Act that was particularly upsetting to Hoover. Passed in 1940, it made it a crime to advocate the overthrow of the government by violence. In 1956, as Davis summarizes the court's action, "simple advocacy alone of ideas was not, in and of itself, punishable. The government would now have to prove advocacy of actual violent actions in order to obtain convictions."

344 **The Church Committee investigation:** William M. Kunstler, "Writers of the Purple Page," *Nation*, December 30, 1978. In summarizing what emerged from the records of the Church Committee and the Socialist Workers Party trial, Kunstler notes that "it is possible for the first time to put in one place the staggering dimensions of what turns out to have been not merely a 'rough, tough, dirty business' but an everyday tool of law enforcement." Crewdson, "F.B.I. Was Not as Advertised and Won't Ever Be the Same," *Nation*, August 1, 1976.

344 **"The FBI abuses":** F. A. O. Schwarz Jr., "Intelligence Activities and the Rights of Americans," *Record of the Association of the Bar of the City of New York* 32 (January/ February 1977).

345 **On the first day:** Schwarz, testimony on first day of Church Committee investigation of FBI, "Intelligence Activities—Federal Bureau of Investigation," 30, November 18, 1975.

345 **He used his secret power:** John Kifner, "F.B.I. Sought Doom of Panther Party: Senate Study Says Plot Led to Internal Splits, 'Gang Warfare' and Killings," *New York Times*, May 9, 1976.

345 **"Never once":** Schwarz and Huq, *Unchecked and Unbalanced,* based on Church Committee, Book II, 14, 141.

346 **Schwarz has concluded:** Ibid., 6, 45.

346 **Among all of the political:** Garrow, *The FBI and Martin Luther King Jr.*, 101–50.

347 **Chicago Black Panther leader:** Jeffrey Haas, "Fred Hampton's Legacy," *Nation*, November 24, 2009. Gentry, *J. Edgar Hoover*, 620–21.

348 **People knowledgeable:** Rosenfeld, *Subversives*, 419–24, 429, 432–35, 441, 445–46. Seth Rosenfeld, "FBI Files Reveal New Details About Informant Who Armed Black Pan-

thers," *Mother Jones*, September 7, 2012, http://cironline.org/reports/fbi-files-reveal
-new-details-about-informant-who-armed-black-panthers-3833.

348 **In Memphis:** Marc Perrusquia, "FBI Admits Noted Memphis Civil Rights Photogra-
pher Ernest Withers Was Informant," *Memphis Commercial Appeal*, July 3, 2012. Perrus-
quia, "Memphis FBI Agent Led Cadre of Informants That Included Ernest Withers,"
Memphis Commercial Appeal, December 19, 2010. Perrusquia, "Withers Secretly Gave
FBI Photos of Martin Luther King's Staff, Spied on Memphis Movement," *Memphis
Commercial Appeal*, March 30, 2013.

348 **A Los Angeles agent:** Gentry, *J. Edgar Hoover*, 647. "The FBI vs. Jean Seberg, *Time*,
September 24, 1979. Ronald J. Ostrow, "FBI Probe of Actress Jean Seberg Found More
Extensive Than Reported," *Los Angeles Times*, January 9, 1980. Kevin Roderick, "Bel-
lows, Jean Seberg and the FBI," *LA Observed*, March 13, 2009. Lorraine Bennett,
"Actress Jean Seberg Found Dead in Her Auto in Paris," *Los Angeles Times*, Septem-
ber 9, 1979. "FBI Admits Spreading Lies About Jean Seberg," *Los Angeles Times*, Sep-
tember 13, 1979. Ronald J. Ostrow, "Extensive Probe of Jean Seberg Revealed: FBI File
Shows Actress Was Investigated from 1969 to '72," *Los Angeles Times*, January 6, 1980.
Allan M. Jalon, "A Faulty Tip, a Ruined Life and Hindsight," *Los Angeles Times*,
April 23, 2002.

350 **Publicly, he was the ringmaster:** Schrecker, *The Age of McCarthyism*, 27.

350 **In fact, Hoover provided:** Oshinsky, *A Conspiracy So Immense*, 257.

350 **He gave HUAC:** J. Edgar Hoover, "Speech Before the House Committee on Un-
American Activities," March 26, 1947, http://voicesofdemocracy.umd.edu/hoover
-speech-before-the-house-committee-speech-text/.

351 **The job of HUAC:** Navasky, *Naming Names*, 319.

351 **Those unverified:** O'Reilly, *Hoover and the Un-Americans*, 195.

351 **The accused had no access:** Robert Justin Goldstein, "Prelude to McCarthyism: The
Making of a Blacklist," *Prologue* (journal of the U.S. National Archives & Records
Administration) 38, no. 3 (Fall 2006), http://www.archives.gov.

352 **The large contribution:** Athan Theoharis, "The FBI and the American Legion Contact
Program, 1940–1966," *Political Science Quarterly* 100, no. 2 (Summer 1985): 271–86.

352 **In an internal memorandum:** Sullivan to DeLoach memorandum, July 19, 1966.

352 **That is illustrated:** Theoharis, *J. Edgar Hoover, Sex, and Crime*, 150–51.

353 **To name a few:** Mitgang, *Dangerous Dossiers*, 37–188. Raines, *Alien Ink*, 187–266,
319–65.

353 **Science fiction writers:** Alison Flood, "Ray Bradbury Investigated for Communist
Sympathies," *Guardian*, August 30, 2012.

353 **So were some publishers:** Mitgang, *Dangerous Dossiers*, 194–208.

353 **A wide array:** Peter Dreier, "Albert Einstein: Radical Citizen and Scientist," *Truthout*,
June 25, 2012, http://truth-out.org/news/item/9192-albert-einstein-radical-citizen-and
-scientist. Jerome, *The Einstein File*, 121, and many other pages.

353 **"The politics of alien":** Arthur Miller, "Why I Wrote *The Crucible*," *New Yorker*, October 21, 1996. Miller, "Are You Now or Were You Ever?," *Guardian*, June 17, 2000.
Ungar, *FBI*, 257.

354 **"he tangled with the FBI":** Tom Knudson, "FBI Was Out to Get Freethinking
DeVoto," *High Country News*, August 8, 1994.

355 **"We have occasional qualms":** Bernard DeVoto, "Due Notice to the FBI," *Harper's*,
October 1949.

356 **For instance, when he:** Theoharis and Cox, *The Boss*, 37.

356 **It was widely believed:** Ungar, *FBI*, 257.

356 **at least 150:** Angus Mackenzie, "Sabotaging the Dissident Press," *Columbia Journalism
Review*, March–April, 1981.

357 **Consistent with Hoover's:** Ibid., 129.

357 **To deal with professors:** Rosenfeld, *Subversives*, 29.

358 **Some universities:** Schrecker, *No Ivory Tower*, 43–47, 264. George Striker, "College

Files Open to Official Investigations," *Columbia Spectator*, April 8 1953. Lewis, *Cold War on Campus*, 19.

358 **For campuses in small towns:** David M. Oshinsky, "Cold War on Campus," *New York Times*, September 28, 1986.

358 **Entire academic disciplines:** Keen, *Stalking Sociologists*, 5, 203–7. Price, *Threatening Anthropology*, 3, 6, 346.

358 **A 1958 study:** Keen, *Stalking Sociologists*, xvii.

359 **The threatening atmosphere:** Lewis, *Cold War on Campus*, 14–15.

359 **the type of research:** Ibid., 205–6.

359 **In one of Hoover's largest:** Rosenfeld, *Subversives*. This book traces Hoover's thirty-year effort to control the University of California and, in the process, destroy the reputations of and remove administrators, faculty, and students, an effort in which Ronald Reagan joined him after becoming governor of California in 1967.

359 **The files on the Berkeley:** Ibid., 517n5.

360 **The FBI had been:** Ibid., 157–59.

360 **Savio was followed:** Ibid., 499.

360 **"I know Kerr is":** Seth Rosenfeld, "The Cautionary Tale of Clark Kerr," *Los Angeles Times*, December 4, 2003. Kerr, *The Gold and Blue*, 69. "In Memoriam—Clark Kerr," posted by the faculty senate of the University of California upon the death of Kerr, December 1, 2003, http://senate.universityofcalifornia.edu/inmemoriam/clark kerr.html. In his memoir, Kerr described Hoover's scribbled note—"I know Kerr is no good"—and wrote that "I look on this as an honorary degree."

361 **When President Johnson:** Rosenfeld, *Subversives*, 229–31.

361 **It was not the first time:** Ibid., 232–33.

361 **Against his own judgment:** Ibid., 3–5.

362 **Hoover often treated:** Gentry, *J. Edgar Hoover*, 645. Ungar, *FBI*, 475. Schwarz and Huq, *Unchecked and Unbalanced*, 18, based on Church Committee Report, Book III, 425–26.

362 **But for the sake of:** Rosenfeld, *Subversives*, 233–40, 334–36.

362 **On January 20, 1967:** Ibid., 371–74.

362 **The FBI fought strenuously:** Ibid., 505–12.

363 **Senator Dianne Feinstein:** Ibid., 508.

363 **He stated that:** Ibid., 509.

364 **Hoover's perception:** Charns, *Cloak and Gavel*, 2.

364 **In 1965:** Theoharis, ed., *From the Secret Files*, 272–73. Charns, *Cloak and Gavel*, 59.

365 **The FBI director was watching:** Alterman, *When Presidents Lie*, 198, 224, 232.

366 **Two years after:** Dallek, *Flawed Giant*, 352–53, 367, 369–70, 371.

366 **Throughout the Vietnam War:** Ungar, *FBI*, 479–80.

366 **It was difficult for:** Marchetti, *The CIA and the Cult of Intelligence*, 229–30.

367 **In response to:** "F.B.I. Files Reply to Damage Suit," *New York Times*, April 4, 1976.

367 **From 1960 to 1966:** John M. Crewdson, "F.B.I.'s Tardiness Is Facing Inquiry: Justice Department Lawyers Heard About Burglary Files Just Before Disclosure," *New York Times*, April 4, 1976. Crewdson, "Justice Department Indicates It Might Not Defend 3 F.B.I. Agents in Suit by Socialists Workers Party," *New York Times*, May 11, 1976. Crewdson, "U.S. Won't Defend 2 Agents of F.B.I.," *New York Times*, May 13, 1976.

369 **Levi ordered the FBI:** ". . . Mr. Levi Calls a Halt," *New York Times*, April 1, 1976.

369 **Remarkably:** "Enough Is Enough," *New York Times*, October 10, 1975.

370 **Their difficulties pale:** "Burton Vows FBI Probe: Claims Hoover Knew of Miscarriage of Justice," *60 Minutes*, January 25, 2002. "What's in a Name?," *Buffalo News*, June 7, 2002. Fox Butterfield, "Hoover's F.B.I. and the Mafia: Case of Bad Bedfellows Grows," *New York Times*, August 25, 2002. Robert Barnes and Paul Lewis, "FBI Must Pay $102 Million in Mob Case: Agency Knew Witness Lied in Naming Four Men, Judge Says," *Washington Post*, July 27, 2007. Pam Belluck, "U.S. Must Pay $101.8 Million for Role in False Convictions," *New York Times*, July 27, 2007. Shelley Murphy and Brian

R. Ballou, "U.S. Ordered to Pay $107.7 Million in False Murder Convictions: FBI Withheld Evidence in '65 Gangland Slaying," *Boston Globe*, July 27, 2007. Jonathan Saltzman, "U.S. Won't Appeal Verdict in Case of Four Framed by FBI," *Boston Globe*, May 1, 2010. Judge Nancy Gertner, United States District Court for the District of Massachusetts, *Peter J. Limone, et. al., Plaintiffs, v. United States of America, Defendant*, Civ. Action No. 02cv10890-NG, Memorandum and Order Re: Bench Trial, 1–223, July 26, 2007.

372 **Former FBI director Robert Mueller:** Kevin Cullen, "A Lingering Question for the FBI's Director," *Boston Globe*, July 24, 2011.

373 **Another federal judge:** Laurence H. Silberman, "Hoover's Institution," *Wall Street Journal*, July 20, 2005.

374 **He also recommended:** Robert Novak, "Removing J. Edgar Hoover's Name," *Lincoln (NE) Tribune*, December 1, 2005. Johanna Neuman, "A Chorus of Hoover Critics," *Los Angeles Times*, December 31, 2005.

374 **Considered a classic:** Aaron Latham, "Top Secrets at Top Cost," *Washington Post*, July 25, 1970. A few observations about the then under construction headquarters, which Hoover had been involved in designing for more than a decade: More space was provided for domestic intelligence than for criminal investigations; the space allocated for (predigital) intelligence files would occupy more than a half million square feet, one-third of the total floor space; the director wanted but failed to get approval for a nuclear reactor on the bottom floor; Hoover adamantly opposed having any freestanding columns because he thought they would provide ideal cover for assassins. Bryan Bender, "FBI Gives a Glimpse of Its Most Secret Layer," *Boston Globe*, March 29, 2010. The volume taken up by the "most highly sensitive" files Hoover kept separate from other files in a "special file room" became so large that in 1961 the files were moved to another building "out of fear that the Justice Department Building, where [the bureau] was housed, could not withstand the weight." That building, at 9th Street and Constitution Avenue, is a massive steel-framed structure.

20. CLOSING CASES

Unless otherwise indicated, all comments and information attributed to Neil Welch are from interviews conducted with him in person, by phone, and in correspondence.

378 **As Kelley gradually:** Tom Wicker, "What Have They Done Since They Shot Dillinger?," *New York Times*, December 28 1969: "Hoover had written and insisted throughout the fifties and sixties that there was no Mafia; and of the hundreds of bureau agents in the New York area, [Robert] Kennedy found only two assigned to organized crime."

380 **Their attitude:** Ibid.: A Justice Department official says, "If you want to screw an agent, just go to Hoover and tell him you were talking with the agent and he gave you a good idea."

382 **The committee members:** Marro, "Choice to Head F.B.I. Still Eludes Carter," *New York Times*, July 31, 1977.

382 **J. Edgar Hoover understood:** Welch and Marston, *Inside Hoover's FBI*, 280–81.

383 **As he settled into:** Ibid., 253.

384 **In the aftermath:** Ungar, *FBI*, 484–85; this false information about the burglars, provided to Ungar by an anonymous source, was the basis of descriptions used by most authors who wrote subsequently about the burglary.

387 **By 1976:** "Kelley Apologizes for F.B.I. Actions," *New York Times*, May 9, 1976.

22. UNCONDITIONALLY POSITIVE

408 **Then, in the first semester:** *Peace in Vietnam*. This report prepared by the American Friends Service Committee motivated Forsyth to become an antiwar activist.

428 **In a sign of:** Invitation to Retrospective of the Camden 28 Trial, May 4, 2002.

428 **Forsyth spoke up:** Transcript of video of Retrospective, May 4, 2002.

428 **"We *are* a nation":** Ibid.

24. BUILDING LITTLE POCKETS OF LIFE

451 **As Bonhoeffer:** Robertson, *The Shame and the Sacrifice*, 176.

25. YOU DIDN'T DO THAT

471 **Interestingly, the two primary:** E. Forrest Harris Sr., "The Black Church's Influence on Dietrich Bonhoeffer," http://www.bonhoeffer.com/art4.htm. Scott Holland,
"First We Take Manhattan, Then We Take Berlin: Bonhoeffer's New York," http://
www.crosscurrents.org/holland. David Pacchioli, "Bonhoeffer's Dilemma," http:rps
.psu.ooo5/bonhoeffer.html. Robertson, *Shame and the Sacrifice*, 54–68, 141–73.

478 **In a forceful private memo:** Laurence Stern, "Humphrey Early Critic of Viet War,"
Washington Post, May 9, 1976. Ted Van Dyk, "HHH: Insights and Memories," *Washington Post*, June 6, 1976.

26. FRAGILE REFORM

488 **At the end of its work:** Schwarz and Huq, *Unchecked and Unbalanced*, 50.

488 **The effort to turn:** Kathy Olmsted, "Lies About the Church Committee," *Chronicle of
Higher Education*, August 25, 2009.

488 **One of the first attacks:** Schwarz and Huq, *Unchecked and Unbalanced*, 52.

489 **Such attacks:** Ibid., 225n46. Mary Ferrell, "Post-Watergate Intelligence Investigations,"
http://www.maryferrell.org. Chris Mooney, "Back to Church," *American Prospect*,
December 19, 2001.

489 **In March 2005:** James Ridgeway, "The Bush Family Coup: Son Revisits the Sins of the
Father on America," *Village Voice*, December 27, 2005.

490 **Setting a ten-year limit:** Vivian S. Chu and Henry B. Hogue, "FBI Directorship:
History and Congressional Action," Congressional Research Service, June 7, 2011, 1.
Schwarz and Huq, *Unchecked and Unbalanced*, 54.

490 **In 1978:** Schwarz and Huq, *Unchecked and Unbalanced*, 53.

490 **A fierce debate:** "The F.B.I. Under Law," editorial, *Nation,* October 6, 1979. "Sympo-
sium: Chartering the F.B.I.," *Nation*, October 6, 1979. "Proposed Charter for F.B.I.
Criticized," *New York Times*, November 5, 1979. Schwarz and Huq, *Unchecked and
Unbalanced*, 51.

492 **The politics of intelligence:** Schwarz and Huq, *Unchecked and Unbalanced,* 54.

492 **With Congress's failure:** Berman, *Domestic Intelligence*, 10–12. "The Federal Bureau
of Investigation's Compliance with the Attorney General's Investigative Guidelines:
Historical Background of the Attorney General's Investigative Guidelines," Special
Report, Office of the Inspector General, September 2005.

493 **It was a sign:** Schwarz and Huq, *Unchecked and Unbalanced*, 55.

493 **For instance, Jennifer Dohrn:** Amy Goodman and Juan González, "Jennifer Dohrn:
I Was the Target of Illegal FBI Break-ins Ordered by Mark Felt aka 'Deep Throat,'"
Democracy Now!, June 2, 2005.

494 **When Reagan pardoned:** Ronald Reagan, "Statement on Granting Pardons to
W. Mark Felt and Edward S. Miller," April 15, 1981, http://www.reagan.utexas.edu
/archives/speeches/1981/41581d.htm.

494 **When Felt's history:** Ruth Marcus, "Deep Throat on Trial," *Washington Post*, December 20, 2008. Colby King, "Deep Throat's Other Legacy," *Washington Post*, June 4,
2005.

495 **After that report:** Schwarz and Huq, *Unchecked and Unbalanced*, 56.

495 **In hindsight:** Philip Shenon, "F.B.I. Papers Show Wide Surveillance of Reagan Critics," *New York Times*, January 28, 1988. "How Did the F.B.I. Go Astray?," editorial, *New York Times*, February 6, 1988. Gentry, *J. Edgar Hoover*, 758–59. Schwarz and Huq, *Unchecked and Unbalanced*, 58–59.

496 **At first, he defended:** Philip Shenon, "F.B.I.'s Chief Says Surveillance Was Justified," *New York Times*, February 3, 1988.

496 **Sessions later confessed:** Philip Shenon, "F.B.I. Reportedly Faults Its Inquiry on Foes of Latin America Policy," *New York Times*, June 4, 1988.

496 **At the White House:** Philip Shenon, "Reagan Backs F.B.I. over Surveillance," *New York Times*, February 4, 1988.

496 **It was now more difficult:** Schwarz and Huq, *Unchecked and Unbalanced*, 61.

496 **A *New York Times* editorial:** "The F.B.I. Confesses," editorial, *New York Times*, September 17, 1988. Philip Shenon, "F.B.I. Is Willing to Erase Names from Its Records," *New York Times*, September 17, 1988. Chip Berlet, "Re-framing Dissent as Criminal Subversion: Paradigm Shift and Political Repression," PublicEye.org.

498 **The single most important:** O'Reilly, *Hoover and the Un-Americans*, 289.

499 **'as bad as possible':** "Veto Battle 30 Years Ago Set Freedom of Information Norms: Scalia, Rumsfeld, Cheney Opposed Open Government Bill," November 23, 2004, Briefing Book No. 142, National Security Archive.

500 **His order to the:** National Commission on Terrorist Attacks upon the United States, *Final Report of the National Commission on Terrorist Attacks upon the United States*, July 22, 2004. Lichtblau, *Bush's Law*, 84.

500 **"I felt like":** Brian McNeill, "FBI Director and Jefferson Medal Recipient Robert Mueller '73 Reflects on Bureau's Transformation After 9/11," *UVA Lawyer*, Spring 2013, 12.

500 **Overnight, the FBI's mandate:** Lichtblau, *Bush's Law*, 81–90.

501 **It was later discovered:** Shenon, *The Commission*, 245–48, 274.

502 **By the time:** Shenon, *The Commission*, 364–69.

502 **In the years before 9/11:** Philip Shenon, "Urging Swift Action, Panel Warns Deadlier Attacks Are Likely," *New York Times*, July 22, 2004.

502 **One FBI official:** Lichtblau, *Bush's Law*, 85–86.

503 **The bureau's pre-9/11 failures:** David Johnston and Neil A. Lewis, "Traces of Terror: The Congressional Hearings: Whistle-Blower Recounts Faults Inside the F.B.I.," *New York Times*, June 7, 2002. Eric Lichtblau, "Report Details F.B.I.'s Failure on Two Hijackers," *New York Times*, June 10, 2005. Lichtblau, *Bush's Law*, 121–23. Shenon, *Commission*, 48, 241–42. Philip Shenon, "The Terrible Missed Chance," *Newsweek*, September 4, 2011.

504 **"The problem was mostly":** Shenon, *The Commission*, 270.

504 **In some parts of the country:** Priest and Arkin, *Top Secret America*, 270–73. Aaronson, *The Terror Factory*, 42. Charlie Savage, "F.B.I. Scrutinized for Amassing Data on American Communities," *New York Times*, October 20, 2011.

505 **The expanded use:** Jerome P. Bjelopera, "The Federal Bureau of Investigation and Terrorism Investigations," Congressional Research Service, April 24, 2013, 9–11. Priest and Arkin, *Top Secret America*, 134–135.

505 **Agents could target:** Berman, *Domestic Intelligence*, 21–22.

505 **Mukasey validated:** "A New Rush to Spy," editorial, *New York Times*, August 22, 2008. "Another Invitation to Abuse," editorial, *New York Times*, October 19, 2008. Charlie Savage, "Loosening of F.B.I. Rules Stirs Privacy Concerns," *New York Times*, October 29, 2009.

505 **Instead, the Obama administration:** "Backward at the FBI," editorial, *New York Times*, June 18, 2001. Ernesto Londono, "Drones Cause 'Growing Hatred of America,' Bipartisan Senate Panel Told," *Washington Post*, April 23, 2013.

506 **So were crucial:** Eric Lichtblau, "F.B.I. Said to Lag on Translating Terror Tapes," *New York Times*, September 28, 2004.

506 **In their series and book:** Dana Priest and William M. Arkin, "A Hidden World, Growing Beyond Control," from "Top Secret America" series, *Washington Post*, July 19, 2010.

507 **As large digital haystacks:** Lichtblau, *Bush's Law*, 85. Bjelopera, "The Federal Bureau of Investigation and Terrorism Investigations," 26–27.

507 **Assessing the impact:** Richard Clarke, *Frontline* interview, April 30, 2013.

507 **"More is good":** Jeff Stein, "FBI Cheating Confirmed by Justice Department," *Washington Post*, September 27, 2010. "Investigation of Allegations of Cheating on the FBI's Domestic Investigations and Operations Guide (DIOG) Exam," Inspector General, Department of Justice, September 2010.

507 **For instance, available:** Bjelopera, "The Federal Bureau of Investigation and Terrorism Investigations," 26. Marshall Curtis Erwin, "Intelligence Issues for Congress," Congressional Research Service, April 23, 2013. "A Ticking Time Bomb: Counterterrorism Lessons from the U.S. Government's Failure to Prevent the Fort Hood Attack," Special Report by Senate Committee on Homeland Security and Governmental Affairs, February 3, 2011, 7–89.

507 **In the latter case:** Scott Shane, "Wide U.S. Failures Helped Airliner Plot, Panel Says," *New York Times*, May 19, 2010.

508 **The new FBI secrecy:** Eric Schmitt and Julia Preston, "Senators Say Case Indicates That Problems Persist in Agencies' Data Sharing," *New York Times*, April 23, 2013.

27. THE NSA FILES

510 **The most startling aspect:** Glenn Greenwald, "NSA Collecting Phone Records of Millions of Verizon Customers Daily," *Guardian*, June 5, 2013.

510 **accessing all of it:** Barton Gellman and Laura Poitras, "U.S., British Intelligence Mining Data from Nine U.S. Internet Companies in Broad Secret Program," *Washington Post*, June 6, 2013. Glenn Greenwald, "XKeystone: NSA Tool Collects 'Nearly Everything a User Does on the Internet,'" *Guardian*, July 31, 2013. Scott Shane and David E. Sanger, "Job Title Key to Inner Access Held by Snowden," *New York Times*, June 30, 2013.

510 **NSA's main partner:** Eric Lichtblau and Michael S. Schmidt, "Other Agencies Clamor for Data N.S.A. Compiles," *New York Times*, August 3, 2013.

511 **released to journalists:** Mirren Gidda, "Edward Snowden and the NSA Files—Timeline," *Guardian*, July 25, 2013. Barton Gellman, Aaron Blake, and Greg Miller, "Edward Snowden Comes Forward as Source of NSA Leaks," *Washington Post*, June 9, 2013.

511 **"another capability":** Nick Hopkins, Julian Borger, and Luke Harding, "GCHQ: Inside the Top Secret World of Britain's Biggest Spy Agency," *Guardian*, August 1, 2013.

511 **denied the reports:** Declan McCullagh, "NSA Spying Flap Extends to Contents of U.S. Phone Calls," CNET News, June 15, 2013.

511 **"clearly erroneous":** Dan Roberts and Spencer Ackerman, "Clapper Under Pressure Despite Apology for 'Erroneous' Statements to Congress," *Guardian*, July 1, 2013.

512 **"They can literally watch":** Gellman and Poitras, "U.S., British Intelligence Mining."

512 **GCHQ created Tempora:** Nick Hopkins, Julian Borger, and Luke Harding, "GCHQ: Inside the Top Secret World of Britain's Biggest Spy Agency," *Guardian*, August 1, 2013.

512 **They can convey:** James Ball, Luke Harding, and Juliette Garside, "BT and Vodafone Among Telecoms Companies Passing Details to GCHQ," *Guardian*, August 2, 2013.

512 **"exploit any phone":** Hopkins, Borger, and Harding, "GCHQ."

512 **"to tap directly into":** Ibid.

514 **a bipartisan group:** "A Bipartisan Warning on Surveillance," editorial, *New York Times*, July 25, 2013.

514 **James Sensenbrenner:** Jonathan Weisman, "Momentum Builds Against N.S.A. Sur-

veillance," *New York Times*, July 28, 2013. Dan Roberts and Spencer Ackerman, "Anger Swells After NSA Phone Records Court Order Revelations," *Guardian*, June 6, 2013. Timothy B. Lee, "Here's Why 'Trust Us' Isn't Working for the NSA Any More," *Washington Post*, July 30, 2013.

514 **called Snowden a traitor:** Jillian Rayfield, "Dick Cheney Praises NSA Surveillance Program," *Salon*, July 16, 2013. "Surveillance: Snowden Doesn't Rise to Traitor," editorial, *New York Times*, June 11, 2013.

515 **if it could quantify:** Spencer Ackerman and Dan Roberts, "NSA Surveillance: Lawmakers Urge Disclosure as Obama 'Welcomes' Debate," *Guardian*, June 9, 2013.

515 **Boundless Informant:** Glenn Greenwald and Ewen MacAskill, "Boundless Informant: The NSA's Secret Tool to Track Global Surveillance Data," *Guardian*, June 11, 2013.

515 **repeatedly warning:** David A. Fahrenthold, "With NSA Revelations, Sen. Ron Wyden's Vague Warnings About Privacy Finally Become Clear," *Washington Post*, July 28, 2013.

515 **"We find ourselves":** Senator Ron Wyden, address, Center for American Progress, July 23, 2013.

515 **Church warned:** Glenn Greenwald, "Surveillance State Evils," *Salon*, April 21, 2012.

516 **become rubber stamps:** Eugene Raineson, "Edward Snowden's NSA Leaks Show We Need a Debate," *Washington Post*, June 10, 2013.

516 **parallel Supreme Court:** Eric Lichtblau, "In Secret, Court Vastly Broadens Powers of N.S.A.," *New York Times*, July 6, 2013.

517 **at thirty-eight embassies:** Laura Poitras, "NSA Spied on European Union Offices," *Der Spiegel*, June 29, 2013. Ewen MacAskill and Julian Borger, "New NSA Leaks Show How US Is Bugging Its European Allies," *Guardian*, June 30, 2013.

517 **two London conferences:** Scott Shane and Ravi Somaiya, "New Leak Indicates Britain and U.S. Tracked Diplomats," *New York Times*, June 16, 2013.

517 **Germans reacted:** Stephen Castle, "Report of U.S. Spying Angers European Allies," *New York Times*, June 30, 2013.

517 **"The spying has reached":** Claus Hecking and Stefan Schultz, "EU Official Questions Trade Negotiations," *Der Spiegel*, June 30, 2013.

518 **became defensive:** "The German Prism: Berlin Wants to Spy Too," *Der Spiegel*, June 17, 2013. "'Prolific Partner': German Intelligence Used NSA Spy Program," *Der Spiegel*, July 20, 2013.

518 **a criminal inquiry:** Michael Birnbaum, "European Anger over U.S. Spying Turns Inward," *Washington Post*, July 17, 2013.

518 **two totalitarian systems:** "Prism Spying 'Attacks Basic Civil Rights,'" *Der Spiegel*, June 11, 2013.

519 **minimal benefit:** Dan Roberts, "Patriot Act Author Prepares Bill to Put NSA Bulk Collection 'Out of Business,'" *Guardian,* October 10, 2013.

519 **digital address books:** Barton Gellman and Ashkan Soltani, "NSA Collects Millions of E-Mail Address Books Globally," *Washington Post,* October 14, 2013.

519 **protected by encryption:** James Ball, Julian Borger, and Glenn Greenwald, "Revealed: How US and UK Spy Agencies Defeat Internet Privacy and Security," *Guardian,* September 5, 2013; Nicole Perlroth, Jeff Larson, and Scott Shane, "N.S.A. Able to Foil Basic Safeguards of Privacy on Web," story published jointly by *New York Times* and *ProPublica*, September 5, 2013.

28. QUESTIONS

522 **His appointment:** Ungar, *FBI*, 48. Ackerman, *Young J. Edgar*, 1.

522 **Stone had publicly:** Ackerman, *Young J. Edgar*, 6.

522 **Hoover, the man:** Theoharis, *The FBI and American Democracy*, 24, 176. Ackerman, *Young J. Edgar*, 6.

523 **The raids—lauded:** Theoharis, *The FBI and American Democracy*, 26–27. Schwarz and Huq, *Unchecked and Unbalanced*, 15. Ackerman, *Young J. Edgar*, 380.

523 **When Palmer was:** Ackerman, *Young J. Edgar*, 354.

523 **How was it possible:** Ibid., 6–7, 372.

523 **The scar was etched:** Ibid., 5.

524 **It was learned then:** Theoharis, *Spying on Americans*, 255n8. Theoharis, *The FBI and American Democracy*, 36. O'Reilly, *Hoover and the Un-Americans*, 18–19, 21.

524 **The impulse to build:** Ackerman, *Young J. Edgar*, 379.

524 **He was in the Senate:** Ibid., 360, 372.

525 ***New Yorker* writer:** Ibid., 375.

525 **Years later, Hoover:** Ibid., 6.

526 **But as he tells:** Ibid., 3.

526 **"I'll take the job":** Ungar, *FBI*, 48.

526 **A few days after:** Ungar, *FBI*, 49. Ackerman, *Young J. Edgar*, 378. Lowenthal, *The Federal Bureau of Investigation*, 445.

527 **Reformers were pleased:** Schwarz and Huq, *Unchecked and Unbalanced*, 210n10, from Alpheus Thomas Mason, *Harlan Fiske Stone: Pillar of the Law*, 149.

527 **"They never stopped":** David Williams, "'They Never Stopped Watching Us': FBI Political Surveillance, 1924–1936," *UCLA Historical Review* 2 (1981). David Williams, "The Bureau of Investigation and Its Critics, 1919–1921: The Origins of Federal Political Surveillance," *Journal of American History* 68, no. 3 (December 1981).

527 **Surveillance of the ACLU:** O'Reilly, *Hoover and the Un-Americans*, 19–20.

527 **Future Supreme Court justice:** Ackerman, *Young J. Edgar*, 380.

527 **The close professional relationship:** Ackerman, *Young J. Edgar*, 374.

527 **"I don't know":** Ibid., 2.

528 **But he warned Stone:** Ibid., 381.

529 **In a remarkably short period:** Ibid., 7.

529 **During the Great Depression:** O'Reilly, *Hoover and the Un-Americans*, 19–20.

530 **From what is known:** Ackerman, *Young J. Edgar*, 377, 381.

530 **Stone responded by:** Biographies of the Robes: Harlan Fiske Stone, http://www.pbs.org/wnet/supremecourt/capitalism/print/robes_stone.html.

531 **If Stone had reviewed:** Schwarz and Huq, *Unchecked and Unbalanced*, 14–15.

531 **He secretly tried:** Theoharis, *The FBI and American Democracy*, 28.

531 **On another March 8:** Davis, *Assault on the Left*, 4–6. Minutes of the 279th meeting of the National Security Council, Cabinet Room of the White House, March 8, 1956.

532 **"he failed to mention":** Davis, *Assault on the Left*, 5.

534 **The generations-long quest:** Theoharis, *The FBI and American Democracy*, 123.

534 **The FBI director's dominant:** Priest and Arkin, *Top Secret America*, 132. Athan Theoharis, interview by Johanna Hamilton, February 2013. O'Reilly, *Hoover and the Un-Americans*, 288–89.

536 **"habit of mind":** Keller, *The Liberals and J. Edgar Hoover*, 112.

536 **"In a most extraordinary":** Davis, *Assault on the Left*, 214–15.

537 **David Kairys has:** From comments at 2002 reunion of Camden 28 participants and in interview.

Bibliography

BOOKS

Aaronson, Trevor. *The Terror Factory: Inside the FBI's Manufactured War on Terrorism*. Brooklyn, NY: Ig Publishing, 2013.

Ackerman, Kenneth D. *Young J. Edgar: Hoover, the Red Scare, and the Assault on Civil Liberties*. New York: Carroll & Graf, 2007.

Alterman, Eric. *When Presidents Lie: A History of Official Deception and Its Consequences*. New York: Penguin, 2004.

Arkush, Michael. *The Fight of the Century: Ali vs. Frazier, March 8, 1971*. Hoboken, NJ: John Wiley & Sons, 2008.

Baskir, Lawrence M., and William A. Strauss. *Chance and Circumstance*. New York: Alfred A. Knopf, 1978.

Berman, Emily. *Domestic Intelligence: New Powers, New Risks*. New York: Brennan Center for Justice, 2011.

Berrigan, Daniel. *America Is Hard to Find*. Garden City, NY: Doubleday, 1972.

Bonhoeffer, Dietrich. *Letters and Papers from Prison*. New York: Collier, 1967.

Campbell, Karl E. *Senator Sam Ervin, Last of the Founding Fathers*. Chapel Hill: University of North Carolina Press, 2007.

Carroll, James. *An American Requiem: God, My Father, and the War That Came Between Us*. Boston: Houghton Mifflin, 1996.

Chang, Nancy. *Silencing Political Dissent*. New York: Seven Stories Press, 2002.

Charles, Douglas M. *The FBI's Obscene File: J. Edgar Hoover and the Bureau's Crusade Against Smut*. Lawrence: University Press of Kansas, 2012.

Charns, Alexander. *Cloak and Gavel: FBI Wiretaps, Bugs, Informers, and the Supreme Court*. Chicago: University of Illinois Press, 1992.

Churchill, Ward, and Jim Vander Wall. *The COINTELPRO Papers: Documents from the FBI's Secret Wars Against Domestic Dissent*. Boston: South End Press, 1990.

Cortright, David. *Soldiers in Revolt: GI Resistance During the Vietnam War*. Chicago: Haymarket Books, 1975.

Cowan, Paul, Nick Egleson, and Nat Hentoff with Barbara Herbert and Robert Wall. *State Secrets: Police Surveillance in America*. New York: Holt, Rinehart & Winston, 1974.

Dallek, Robert. *Flawed Giant: Lyndon Johnson and His Times, 1961–1973*. New York: Oxford University Press, 1998.

Davis, James Kirkpatrick, *Assault on the Left: The FBI and the Sixties Antiwar Movement*. Westport, CT: Praeger, 1997.

———. *Spying on America: The FBI's Domestic Counterintelligence Program*. New York: Praeger, 1992.

Dean, John. *Conservatives Without Conscience*. New York: Viking, 2006.

DeBenedetti, Charles. *An American Ordeal: The Antiwar Movement of the Vietnam Era*. Syracuse, NY: Syracuse University Press, 1990.

Demaris, Ovid. *The Director: An Oral Biography of J. Edgar Hoover*. New York: Harper's Magazine Press, 1975.

Diamond, Sigmund. *Compromised Campus: The Collaboration of Universities with the Intelligence Community, 1945–1955*. New York: Oxford University Press, 1992.

Donner, Frank J. *The Age of Surveillance: The Aims and Methods of America's Political Intelligence System*. New York: Vintage, 1980.

Elliff, John T. *The Reform of FBI Intelligence Operations*. Princeton, NJ: Princeton University Press, 1979.

Ewen, Stuart. *PR! A Social History of Spin*. New York: Basic Books, 1996.

Feingold, Russ. *While America Sleeps: A Wake-up Call for the Post-9/11 Era*. New York: Crown, 2012.

Feldman, Jay. *Manufacturing Hysteria: A History of Scapegoating, Surveillance, and Secrecy in Modern America*. New York: Pantheon, 2011.

Felt, Mark. *The FBI Pyramid from the Inside*. New York: Putnam, 1979.

Felt, Mark, and John O'Connor. *A G-Man's Life: The FBI, Being "Deep Throat," and the Struggle for Honor in Washington*. New York: PublicAffairs, 2006.

Foerstel, Herbert N. *Freedom of Information and the Right to Know: The Origins and Applications of the Freedom of Information Act*. Westport, CT: Greenwood, 1999.

Garrow, David J. *The FBI and Martin Luther King Jr.: From "SOLO" to Memphis*. New York. W. W. Norton, 1981.

Gentry, Curt. *J. Edgar Hoover: The Man and the Secrets*. New York: W. W. Norton, 1991.

Glain, Stephen. *State vs. Defense: The Battle to Define America's Empire*. New York: Crown, 2011.

Goldstein, Robert Justin. *American Blacklist: The Attorney General's List of Subversive Organizations*. Lawrence: University Press of Kansas, 2008.

Gray, L. Patrick, III, with Ed Gray. *In Nixon's Web: A Year in the Crosshairs of Watergate*. New York: Times Books/Henry Holt, 2008.

Guzder, Deena. *Divine Rebels: American Christian Activists for Social Justice*. Chicago: Lawrence Hill, 2011.

Halperin, Morton H., Jerry J. Berman, Robert L. Borosage, and Christine M. Marwick. *The Lawless State: The Crimes of the U.S. Intelligence Agencies*. New York: Penguin, 1976.

Hauser, Thomas. *Muhammad Ali: His Life and Times*. New York: Simon & Schuster, 1991.

Helms, Richard, with William Hood. *A Look over My Shoulder: A Life in the Central Intelligence Agency*. New York: Ballantine, 2003.

Holland, Max. *Leak: Why Mark Felt Became Deep Throat*. Lawrence: University Press of Kansas, 2012.

Jerome, Fred. *The Einstein File: J. Edgar Hoover's Secret War Against the World's Most Famous Scientist*. New York: St. Martin's, 2002.

Johnson, Loch K. *A Season of Inquiry: Congress and Intelligence*. Chicago: Dorsey, 1976.

Kairys, David. *Philadelphia Freedom: Memoir of a Civil Rights Lawyer*. Ann Arbor: University of Michigan Press, 2008.

Katzenbach, Nicholas deB. *Some of It Was Fun: Working with RFK and LBJ*. New York: W. W. Norton, 2008.

Keen, Mike Forrest. *Stalking Sociologists: J. Edgar Hoover's FBI Surveillance of American Sociology*. New Brunswick, NJ: Transaction, 2004.

Keller, William W. *The Liberals and J. Edgar Hoover: Rise and Fall of a Domestic Intelligence State*. Princeton, NJ: Princeton University Press, 1989.

Kelly, John F., and Phillip K. Wearne. *Tainting Evidence: Inside the Scandals at the FBI Crime Lab*. New York: Free Press, 1998.

Kerr, Clark. *The Gold and the Blue: A Personal Memoir of the University of California, 1949–1967*. Berkeley: University of California Press, 2003.

Kindred, Dave. *Sound and Fury: Two Powerful Lives, One Fateful Friendship*. New York: Simon & Schuster, 2007.

Kissinger, Henry. *White House Years*. Boston: Little, Brown, 1979.

Lewis, Lionel S. *Cold War on Campus: A Study of the Politics of Organizational Control*. New York: Transaction, 1989.

Lichtblau, Eric. *Bush's Law: The Remaking of American Justice*. New York: Pantheon, 2008.

Liddy, G. Gordon. *Will: The Autobiography of G. Gordon Liddy*. New York: St. Martin's Paperbacks, 1980.

Long, Michael G. *Marshalling Justice: The Early Civil Rights Letters of Thurgood Marshall*. New York: Amistad, 2011.

Lowenthal, Max. *The Federal Bureau of Investigation*. New York: William Sloane Associates, 1950.

Lyons, Paul. *The People of This Generation: The Rise and Fall of the New Left in Philadelphia*. Philadelphia: University of Pennsylvania Press, 2003.

Mackenzie, Angus, with David Weir. *Secrets: The CIA's War at Home*. Los Angeles and London: University of California Press, 1997.

Marchetti, Victor, and John D. Marks. *The CIA and the Cult of Intelligence*. New York: Alfred A. Knopf, 1974.

McGowan, Edward. *Peace Warriors: The Story of the Camden 28*. New York: Circumstantial Productions, 2001.

Mitgang, Herbert. *Dangerous Dossiers*. New York: Primus/Donald I. Fine, 1988.

Nash, Jay Robert. *Citizen Hoover*. Chicago: Nelson-Hall, 1972.

Navasky, Victor. *Naming Names*. New York: Viking, 1980.

Neier, Aryeh. *Dossier: The Secret Files They Keep on You*. New York: Stein & Day, 1975.

Nelson, Jack. *Scoop: The Evolution of a Southern Reporter*. Edited by Barbara Matusow. Jackson: University Press of Mississippi, 2013.

Nelson, Jack, and Ronald J. Ostrow. *The FBI and the Berrigans: The Making of a Conspiracy*. New York: Coward, McCann & Geogheghan, 1972.

Novak, Robert D. *The Prince of Darkness: 50 Years Reporting in Washington*. New York: Crown, 2007.

O'Grady, Jim, and Murray Polner. *Disarmed and Dangerous: The Radical Lives and Times of Daniel and Philip Berrigan*. New York: Basic Books, 1997.

Ohio Politics. Kent, OH: Kent State University Press, 1994.

Olmsted, Kathryn S. *Challenging the Secret Government: The Post-Watergate Investigations of the CIA and FBI*. Chapel Hill: University of North Carolina Press, 1996.

O'Reilly, Kenneth. *Hoover and the Un-Americans: The FBI, HUAC, and the Red Menace*. Philadelphia: Temple University Press, 1983.

———. *"Racial Matters": The FBI's Secret File on Black America, 1960–1972*. New York: Free Press, 1989.

Oshinsky, David M. *A Conspiracy So Immense: The World of Joe McCarthy*. New York: Free Press, 1983.

Peace in Vietnam: A New Approach in Southeast Asia; A Report Prepared for the American Friends Service Committee. New York: Hill & Wang, 1966.

Polner, Murray, and Jim O'Grady. *Disarmed and Dangerous: The Radical Lives and Times of Daniel and Philip Berrigan*. New York: Basic Books, 1997.

Powers, Richard G. *Broken: The Troubled Past and Uncertain Future of the FBI*. New York: Free Press, 2004.

———. *Secrecy and Power: The Life of J. Edgar Hoover*. New York: Free Press, 1987.

Powers, Thomas. *Intelligence Wars: American Secret History from Hitler to Al-Qaeda*. New York: New York Review of Books, 2004.

Price, David H. *Threatening Anthropology: McCarthyism and the FBI's Surveillance of Activist Anthropologists.* Durham, NC: Duke University Press, 2004.

Priest, Dana, and William M. Arkin. *Top Secret America: The Rise of the New American Security State.* New York: Little, Brown, 2011.

Robertson, Edwin. *The Shame and the Sacrifice: The Life and Martyrdom of Dietrich Bonhoeffer.* New York: Collier, 1988.

Raines, Natalie. *Alien Ink: The FBI's War on Freedom of Expression.* New York: William Morrow, 1992.

Rosenfeld, Seth. *Subversives: The FBI's War on Student Radicals and Reagan's Rise to Power.* New York: Farrar, Straus & Giroux, 2012.

Saxbe, William B. *I've Seen the Elephant: An Autobiography.* Kent, OH: Kent State University Press, 2000.

Schmidt, Regin. *Red Scare: FBI and the Origins of Anticommunism in the United States, 1919–1943.* Copenhagen: Museum Tusculanum Press, 2000.

Schott, Joseph L. *No Left Turns.* New York: Ballantine, 1975.

Schrecker, Ellen. *The Age of McCarthyism: A Brief History with Documents.* Boston: St. Martin's, 1994.

———. *Many Are the Crimes: McCarthyism in America.* New York: Little, Brown, 1998.

———. *No Ivory Tower: McCarthyism and the Universities.* New York: Oxford University Press, 1986.

Schwarz, Frederick A. O., Jr., and Aziz Z. Huq. *Unchecked and Unbalanced: Presidential Power in a Time of Terror.* New York: New Press/Brennan Center for Justice, 2007.

Shenon, Philip. *The Commission: The Uncensored History of the 9/11 Investigation.* New York: Twelve, 2008.

Shipler, David K. *Rights at Risk: The Limits of Liberty in Modern America.* New York: Alfred A. Knopf, 2012.

Smist, Frank J., Jr. *Congress Oversees the United States Intelligence Community, 1947–1989.* Knoxville: University of Tennessee Press, 1990.

Stone, Geoffrey R. *Perilous Times: Free Speech in Wartime; From the Sedition Act of 1798 to the War on Terrorism.* New York: W. W. Norton, 2004.

Sullivan, William C., with Bill Brown. *The Bureau: My Thirty Years in Hoover's FBI.* New York: W. W. Norton, 1979.

Swearingen, M. Wesley. *FBI Secrets: An Agent's Exposé.* Boston: South End Press, 1995.

Theoharis, Athan G. *Abuse of Power: How Cold War Surveillance and Secrecy Policy Shaped The Response to 9/11.* Philadelphia: Temple University Press, 2011.

———. *Chasing Spies: How the FBI Failed in Counterintelligence but Promoted the Politics of McCarthyism in the Cold War Years.* Chicago: Ivan R. Dee, 2002.

———. *The FBI and American Democracy: A Brief Critical History.* Lawrence: University Press of Kansas, 2004.

———. *J. Edgar Hoover, Sex, and Crime.* Chicago: Ivan R. Dee, 1995.

———. *Spying on Americans: Political Surveillance from Hoover to the Huston Plan.* Philadelphia: Temple University Press, 1978.

———, ed. *A Culture of Secrecy: The Government Versus the People's Right to Know.* Lawrence: University Press of Kansas, 1998.

———, ed. *From the Secret Files of J. Edgar Hoover.* Chicago: Ivan R. Dee, 1991.

———, ed. *A Guide to the Microfilm Edition of the J. Edgar Hoover Official and Confidential File.* Introduction. Bethesda, MD: University Publications of America, 1990.

Theoharis, Athan G., and John Stuart Cox. *The Boss: J. Edgar Hoover and the Great American Inquisition.* Philadelphia: Temple University Press, 1988.

Thomas, Louisa. *Conscience: Two Soldiers, Two Pacifists, One Family—A Test of Will and Faith in World War I.* New York: Penguin Press, 2011.

Thompson, Nicholas. *The Hawk and the Dove: Paul Nitze, George Kennan, and the History of the Cold War.* New York: Henry Holt, 2009.

Turner, William W. *Hoover's FBI.* New York: Thunder's Mouth, 1970.

Ungar, Sanford J. *FBI*. Boston: Atlantic Monthly Press/Little, Brown, 1976.

Unger, David C. *The Emergency State: America's Pursuit of Absolute Security at All Costs*. New York: Penguin Press, 2012.

Watters, Pat, and Stephen Gillers, eds. *Investigating the FBI*. New York: Doubleday, 1973.

Weiner, Tim. *Enemies: A History of the FBI*. New York: Random House, 2012.

———. *Legacy of Ashes: The History of the CIA*. New York: Doubleday, 2007.

Welch, Neil J., and David W. Marston. *Inside Hoover's FBI: The Top Field Chief Reports*. New York: Doubleday, 1984.

Wise, David. *The American Police State: The Government Against the People*. New York: Random House, 1976.

Wise, David, and Thomas B. Ross. *The Invisible Government*. New York: Vintage, 1974.

Zegart, Amy B. *Spying Blind: The CIA, the FBI, and the Origins of 9/11*. Princeton, NJ: Princeton University Press, 2007.

Zinn, Howard. *Passionate Declarations: Essays on War and Justice*. New York: Harper Perennial, 2003.

ARTICLES, SPEECHES, REPORTS

Amdur, Neil. "Ali Is Silent on Way to Hospital," *New York Times,* March 9, 1971.

Anderson, Dave. "Champion Floors His Rival With Left Hook in the 15th," *New York Times,* March 9, 1971.

Apple Jr., R. W. "Vietnamese Seize Six U.S. Pacifists and Expel Them," *New York Times,* April 21, 1966.

Ball, James; Julian Borger; and Glenn Greenwald. "Revealed: How US and UK Spy Agencies Defeat Internet Privacy and Security," *The Guardian,* September 5, 2013

Barnes, Robert, and Paul Lewis. "FBI Must Pay $102 Million in Mob Case: Agency Knew Witness Lied in Naming Four Men, Judge Says," *Washington Post,* July 27, 2007.

Barth, Alan. "The Judith Coplon Case and the Embarrassed FBI: Bureau Lost Some Files 22 Years Ago," *Washington Post,* April 20, 1971.

Belluck, Pam. "U.S. Must Pay $101.8 Million for Role in False Convictions," *New York Times,* July 27, 2007.

Bender, Bryan. "FBI Gives Glimpse of Its Most Secret Layer," *The Boston Globe,* March 29, 2010.

Bennett, Lorraine. "Actress Jean Seberg Found Dead in Her Auto in Paris," *Los Angeles Times,* September 9, 1979.

Berlot, Chip. "Re-framing Dissent as Criminal Subversion: Paradigm Shift and Political Repression," PublicEye.org.

Berman, Emily. "Domestic Intelligence: New Powers, New Risks," Brennan Center for Justice at New York University School of Law, 2011.

Bigart, Homer. "War Foes Here Attacked by Construction Workers: City Hall Is Stormed," *New York Times,* May 9, 1970.

Bjelopera, Jerome P. "The Federal Bureau of Investigation and Terrorism Investigations," *Congressional Research Service,* April 24, 2013.

Brinkley, Alan. "Dreams of a G-Man," *The New York Review of Books,* April 23, 1987.

Butterfield, Fox. "Hoover's F.B.I. and the Mafia: Case of Bad Bedfellows Grows," *New York Times,* August 25, 2002.

Cady, Steve. "500-Man Force to Patrol Inside and Outside Arena," *The New York Times,* March 8, 1971.

Calabresi, Massimo, and Michael Crowley. "Homeland Insecurity: Do We Need to Sacrifice Privacy to Be Safer?" *Time Magazine,* May 13, 2013.

Carlsen, William, and Mark Simon. "Hard Line Helped Him Win, Flexibility Helped Him Stay/Ability to Compromise Replaced His Tough Stance Against UC Student Protests," *The San Francisco Chronicle,* June 6, 2004.

Charlton, Linda. "Search Widens for 2 Women in Townhouse Blast," *New York Times,* March 30, 1970.

Chu, Vivian S., and Henry B. Hogue. "FBI Directorship: History and Congressional Action," Congressional Research Service, June 7, 2011.

Clawson, Ken. "FBI's Hoover Scores Ramsey Clark, RFK; Praises Mitchell as 'Very Human,' " *Washington Post,* November 17, 1970.

Clawson, Ken. "Stolen FBI Reports Sent to McGovern, Rep. Mitchell," *Washington Post,* March 23, 1971.

Colby, W.E. "CIA Activities in the United States," MORI DocID: 1451843, CIA Family Jewels, National Security Archives.

Cook, Fred J. "Hard-Hats: The Rampaging Patriots," *The Nation,* June 15, 1970.

Cook, Fred J. "On Being an Enemy of the F.B.I.," *The Nation,* March 22, 1986.

Crewdson, John M. "F.B.I.'s Tardiness Is Facing Inquiry: Justice Department Lawyers Heard About Burglary Files Just Before Disclosure," *New York Times,* April 4, 1976.

Crewdson, John M. "Justice Department Indicates It Might Not Defend 3 F.B.I. Agents in Suit by Socialists Workers Party," *New York Times,* May 11, 1976.

Crewdson, John M. "U.S. Won't Defend 2 Agents of F.B.I.," *New York Times,* May 13, 1976.

Cullen, Kevin. "A Lingering Question for the FBI's Director," *The Boston Globe,* July 24, 2011.

Daley, Arthur. "Epic Worth the Price," *New York Times,* March 9, 1971.

DeVoto, Bernard. "Due Notice to the FBI," *Harper's,* October 1949.

Donner, Frank. "A Special Supplement: The Theory and Practice of American Political Intelligence," *The New York Review of Books,* April 22, 1971.

Dreier, Peter. "Albert Einstein: Radical Citizen and Scientist," *Truthout* website, June 24, 2012."

Edwards, Jim. "The Journalist and the G-Man," *Brill's Content,* November 2000.

Erwin, Marshall Curtis. "Intelligence Issues for Congress," *Congressional Research Service,* April 23, 2013.

Ferrell, Mary. "Post-Watergate Intelligence Investigations," http://maryferrell.org/wiki/index.php/Post-Watergate_intelligence_investigations

Fischer, John. "Personal & Otherwise: J. Edgar Hoover and the Politicians," *Harper's Magazine,* March 1954.

Fisher, Louis. "Detention of U.S. Citizens," Congressional Research Service Report for Congress, April 28, 2005.

Flood, Alison. "Ray Bradbury Investigated for Communist Sympathies," *The Guardian,* August 30, 2012.

Franklin, Ben A. "They've Probably Got You On the List," *New York Times,* December 27, 1970.

Gallagher, Ryan. "Judge Declares FBI Surveillance Gag Orders Unconstitutional," *Slate,* March 15, 2013.

*Garrow, David J. "Political Harassment and FBI Historiography: Analyzing Informants and Measuring the Effects," *Public Historian* Volume 10, No. 4, Autumn 1988.

Gellman, Borton, and Ashkan Soltani. "NSA Collects Millions of E-Mail Address Books Globally," *The Washington Post,* October 14, 2013.

George, Thomas. "Fight of the Century: Muhammad Ali's Legacy Grows in Defeat," www.aol.news, February 24, 2011.

Gertner, Judge Nancy. United States District Court for the District of Massachusetts, Peter J. Limone, et. al., Plaintiffs, v. United States of America, Defendant, Civ. Action No. 02cv10890-NG, Memorandum and Order Re: Bench Trial, pp. 1–223. July 26, 2007.

Giacchino, Anthony. Interview with Terry Neist, Camden 28 documentary. 265

Goldstein, Robert Justin. "Prelude to McCarthyism: The Making of a Blacklist," The U.S. National Archives & Records Administration, Fall 2006, Vol. 38. No. 3, www.archives.gov.

Goldstein, Robert Justin. "The FBI's Forty-Year Plot," *The Nation,* July 1, 1978.

Goodman, Amy, and Juan Gonzalez. "Jennifer Dohrn: I Was the Target of Illegal FBI Break-ins Ordered by Mark Felt aka 'Deep Throat,' " *Democracy Now!,* June 2, 2005.

Goshko, John M. "Hoover's Files Focus on Sex Scandals: Voracious Collector of Rumors," *Washington Post*, November 24, 1976.

Gould, Jack. "Broadcast of Fight Barred to Many G.I.s," *New York Times*, March 6, 1971.

Gould, Jack. "Radio Gives World-Wide Fight News," *New York Times*, March 9, 1971.

Greenwald, Glenn. "Are All Telephone Calls Recorded and Accessible to the US Government?" *The Guardian*, May 4, 2013.

Greider, William. "10,000 'Potential Subversives': U.S. Keeps Index for Emergency Arrests," *Washington Post*, June 13, 1971.

Greider, William. "Analysis of Stolen FBI Documents Provides Glimpse of Bureau at Work," *Washington Post*, July 5, 1971.

Greider, William. "U.S. Keeps Top Secret List of 'Subversives,' " *Washington Post*, June 21, 1971.

Grutzner, Charles. "Coplon Wire-Taps Denied, Admitted: F.B.I. Witness First Disclaims Awareness, Then Tells of Destroying Reports," *New York Times*, December 23, 1949.

Guzzardi, Joe. "View From Lodi, CA: Remembering an Earlier War in America's Streets," www.dare.com/guzzardi/war_in_streets.htm April 23, 2004.

Haas, Jeffrey. "Fred Hampton's Legacy," *The Nation*, November 24, 2009.

Haber, Joyce. "Miss A Rates as Expectant Mother," *The Los Angeles Times*, May 19, 1970.

Halloran, Richard. "Aide to Mitchell Opposes Any Curb on Surveillance," *New York Times*, March 10, 1971.

Halloran, Richard. "Rare Speech Discloses Some Russians Aided U.S. in Cuban Crisis," *New York Times*, April 15, 1971.

Hanna, Bob. "Book Inspired Memories of 'Fight of the Century,' " *Inside Boxing*, November 22, 2007.

Harris Sr., E. Forrest. "The Black Church's Influence on Dietrick Bonhoeffer, http://www .bonhoeffer.com/art4.htm.

Helms, Richard. "An Address by Richard Helms, Director of Central Intelligence Agency," American Society of Newspaper Editors, April 14, 1971. https://www.cia.gov/library/ center-for-the-study-of-intelligence/csi-publications/csi-studies/studies/vol51no3/reflec tions-of-dci-colby-and-helms-on-the-cia2019s-201ctime-of-troubles201d.html

Hersh, Seymour M. "Huge C.I.A. Operation Reported in U.S. Against Antiwar Forces, Other Dissidents in Nixon Years, Files on Citizens: Helms Reportedly Got Surveillance Data in Charter Violation," *New York Times*, December 22, 1974.

Holland, Scott. "First We Take Manhattan, Then We Take Berlin: Bonhoeffer's New York," http://www.crosscurrents.org/hollandandf20.htm

Hoover, J. Edgar. "Speech Before the House Committee on Un-American Activities," March 26, 1947. http://voicesofdemocracy.umd.edu/hoover-speech-before-the-house-committee-speech -text/

Hornestay, David. "Joe Louis Knocks Out Max Schmeling: Personal Revenge and a Political Statement," March 24, 2010, www.suite101.com

Hybl, Dean. "Two Days in June: Max Schmeling vs. Joe Louis," http://sportsthenandnow .com June 19, 2010.

Jalon, Allan M. "A Break-in to End All Break-ins," *Los Angeles Times*, March 8, 2006.

Jalon, Allan M. "A Faulty Tip, a Ruined Life and Hindsight," *Los Angeles Times*, April 23, 2002.

Janson, Donald M. "F.B.I. Is Accused of Aiding a Crime: 'Camden 28' Informer Says He Acted as 'Provocateur,' " *New York Times*, March 16, 1972.

Janson, Donald M. "Informer Testifies F.B.I. Had Him Provoke Camden Draft File Raid," *New York Times*, April 11, 1973.

Janson, Donald M. "Philadelphia Fair 'Exposes' F.B.I.: Angry Powelton Residents Satirize Agents in Area," *New York Times*, June 6, 1971.

Janson, Donald M. "Theft of Documents from F.B.I., Unsolved After a Year's Inquiry," *New York Times*, March 12, 1972.

Johnson, David, and Neil A. Lewis. "Traces of Terror: The Congressional Hearings; Whistle-Blower Recounts Faults Inside the F.B.I." *New York Times,* June 7, 2002.

Karamessines, Thomas H. "Meeting with MAG Group," December 21, 1971, MORI DocID: 1451843, CIA Family Jewels, National Security Archive.

Kifner, John. "F.B.I. Sought Doom of Panther Party: Senate Study Says Plot Led to Internal Splits, 'Gang Warfare' and Killings," *New York Times,* May 9, 1976.

Kifner, John. "4 Kent State Students Killed by Troops: 8 Hurt as Shooting Follows Reported Sniping at Rally," *New York Times,* May 4, 1970.

Kindred, Dave. "The First Ali-Frazier Fight Was Also the Best," *The Sporting News,* February 17, 1999.

King, Colby. "Deep Throat's Other Legacy," *Washington Post,* June 4, 2005.

Knudson, Tom. "FBI Was Out to Get Freethinking DeVoto," High Country News, August 8, 1994.

Latham, Aaron. "FBI: Top Secrets at Top Cost," *The Washington Post,* July 25, 1970.

Leonard, Andrew, "Obama's Wiretap America," *Salon,* May 8, 2013.

Lichtblau, Eric. "F.B.I. Said to Lag on Translating Terror Tapes," *New York Times,* September 28, 2004.

Lichtblau, Eric. "Report Details F.B.I.'s Failure on Two Hijackers," *New York Times,* June 10, 2005.

Lichtblau, Eric. "New Guidelines Would Give F.B.I. Broader Powers," *New York Times,* August 21, 2008.

Londono, Ernesto. "Drones Cause 'Growing Hatred of America,' Bipartisan Senate Panel Told," *The Washington Post,* April 23, 2013.

Lotierzo, Frank. "Fight of the Century: 33 Years Later and Still Nothing Like It," www .thesweetscience.com, March 7, 2004.

Lydon, Christopher. "Ervin Rules Out Inquiry Into F.B.I. Now," *New York Times,* April 19, 1971.

Mackenzie, Angus. "Sabotaging the Dissident Press," *Columbia Journalism Review,* March-April, 1981.

MacKenzie, John P. "Hoover: Monument of Power for 48 Years," *Washington Post,* May 3, 1971.

Marcus, Ruth. "Deep Throat on Trial," *Washington Post,* December 20, 2008.

Marro, Anthony. "Choice to Head F.B.I. Still Eludes Carter," *New York Times,* July 31, 1977.

Matthews, Christopher. "Nixon Personally Ordered Break-in: He's on Tape Demanding Theft at Brookings Theft Tank, *San Francisco Chronicle,* November 21, 1996.

McFadden, Robert D. "37 College Chiefs Urge Nixon Move for Prompt Peace," *New York Times,* May 5, 1970.

McGrory, Mary. "Kissinger Meets with Plotters," *Washington Star,* March 12, 1971.

McNeill, Brian. "FBI Director and Jefferson Medal Recipient Robert Mueller '73 Reflects on Bureau's Transformation After 9/11," *UVA Lawyer,* Spring 2013.

Medsger and Clawson. "Stolen Documents Describe FBI Surveillance Activities," *Washington Post,* March 24, 1971.

Medsger and Clawson. "FBI Secretly Prods Colleges on New Left," *Washington Post,* April 6, 1971.

Medsger. "Justice in a Camden Court, *The Progressive,* October 1973.

Miller, Arthur. "Are You Now or Were You Ever?" *The Guardian,* June 17, 2000.

Miller, Arthur. "Why I Wrote the Crucible," *The New Yorker,* October 21, 1996.

Murphy, Shelley, and Brian R. Ballou. "U.S. Ordered to Pay $107.7 Million in False Murder Convictions: FBI Withheld Evidence in '65 Gangland Slaying," *Boston Globe,* July 27, 2007.

Nakashima, Ellen. "Panel Seeks to Fine Tech Companies for Noncompliance with Wiretap Orders," *Washington Post,* April 28, 2013.

Naughton, James M. "Construction Union Chief in New York Is Chosen to Succeed Hodgson," *New York Times,* November 30, 1972.

Neuman, Johanna. "A Chorus of Hoover Critics," *The Los Angeles Times*, December 31, 2005.

Newfield, Jack. "The Meaning of Muhammad," *The Nation*, January 17, 2002.

Nixon, President Richard. "Cambodian Incursion speech," http://www.americanrhetoric .com/speeches/PDFFiles/Richard%20Nixon%20-%20Cambodian%20Incursion%20 Address.pdf

Nixon, President Richard. Eulogy Delivered at Funeral Services May 4, 1972, for J. Edgar Hoover, http://www.presidency.ucsb.edu/ws/print.php?pid=3397

Nolan, Martin. "What the Nation Learned at Kent State in 1970," *The Boston Globe*, May 3, 2000.

Novak, Robert. "Removing J. Edgar's Name," *Lincoln Tribune* (NB), December 1, 2005.

O'Connor, Ian. "The First Ali-Frazier Fight Still Electric After 35 Years," *USA Today*, March 7, 2006.

Olmstead, Kathy. "Lies About the Church Committee," *Chronicle of Higher Education*," August 25, 2009.

Oshinsky, David M. "Cold War on Campus," *New York Times*, September 26, 1986.

Osnos, Peter. "Obama and the World's Media," *The Platform*, February, 11, 2008, http://old .tcf.org/commentary/2008

Ostrow, Ronald J. "FBI Probe of Actress Jean Seberg Found More Extensive than Reported," *The Los Angeles Times*, January 9, 1980.

Owen, Taylor. "Bombs Over Cambodia," TaylorOwen.com, September 19, 2006.

Pacchioli, David. "Bonhoeffer's Dilemma," *Research Penn State*, http://www.rps.psu.edu/0005/ bonhoeffer.html

Patterson, James T. "The Enemy Within," *The Atlantic Online*, October 1998.

Perlroth, Nicole; Jeff Larson and Scott Shane. "N.S.A. Able to Foil Basic Safeguards of Privacy on Web," joint publication of *New York Times* and *ProPublica*. September 5, 2013.

Perrusquia, Marc. "Withers Secretly Gave FBI Photos of Martin Luther King's Staff, Spied on Memphis Movement," *The Commercial Appeal*, March 30, 2013.

Price, David H. "Spying on Radical Scholars," *Radical History Review* 79, 2001.

Priest, Dana, and William Arkin. "A Hidden World, Growing Beyond Control," from "Top Secret America" series, *Washington Post*, July 19, 2010.

Proctor, Donald B. "Accused Camden Leader Linked to Media Raid," *The Evening Bulletin*, August 30, 1971.

Pyle, Christopher H. "The Army Watches Civilian Politics," *Washington Monthly*, January 1970.

Quinn, Sally. "The Night the Director Stole the Show," *The Washington Post*, May 25, 1971.

Reagan, Ronald. "Statement on Granting Pardons to W. Mark Felt and Edward S. Miller," April 15, 1981. http://www.reagan.utexas.edu/archives/speeches/1981/41581d.htm

Reed, Roy. "F.B.I. Investigating Killing of 2 Negroes in Jackson," *New York Times*, May 16, 1970.

Rhoden, William C. "At His Essence, Smokin' Joe Was More than Just a Symbol," *New York Times*, November 13, 2011.

Rich, Spencer. "Rehnquist Civil Liberties Stance Eyed," *Washington Post*, October 26, 1971.

Robb, David. "Special Report: J. Edgar Hoover's Hollywood Obsessions Revealed," *Hollywood Report*, March 9, 2008.

Roberts, Dan. "Patriot Act Author Prepares Bill to Put NSA Bulk Collection 'Out of Business," *The Guardian*, October 10, 2013.

Roderick, Kevin. "Bellows, Jean Seberg and the FBI," *LA Observed*, March 13, 2009.

Rosenfeld, Seth. "FBI Files Reveal New Details About Informant Who Armed Black Panthers, *Mother Jones*, September 7, 2012 http://cironline.org/reports/fbi-files-reveal-new-details -about-informant-who-armed-black-panthers-3833.

Rosenfeld, Seth. "The Cautionary Tale of Clark Kerr," *Los Angeles Times*, December 4, 2003.

Rosenfeld, Susan. "The Fatal Bombing That Historians Ignore," *The Chronicle of Higher Education*, August 17, 2001.

Rosenthal, Jack. "President's Panel Warns Split on Youth Perils U.S.; Asks Him to Foster Unity: Near-Civil War Feared Unless Division of Society Is Ended," *New York Times,* September 27, 1970.

Saltzman, Jonathan. "U.S. Won't Appeal Verdict in Case of Four Framed by FBI," *Boston Globe,* May 1, 2010.

Savage, Charlie. "Loosening of F.B.I. Rules Stirs Privacy Concerns," *New York Times,* October 29, 2009.

Savage, Charlie. "F.B.I. Scrutinized for Amassing Data on American Communities," *New York Times,* October 20, 2011.

Savage, Charlie. "U.S. Weighs Wider Wiretap Laws to Cover Online Activity," *New York Times,* May 7, 2012.

Schmitt, Eric, and Julia Preston. "Senators Say Case Indicates That Problems Persist in Agencies' Data Sharing," *New York Times,* April 23, 2013.

Schwarz Jr., Frederick A. O. "Intelligence Activities and the Rights of Americans," *The Record of the Association of the Bar of the City of New York,* Vol. 32, Number ½, January/February 1977.

Semple, Robert B. "Nixon Meets Heads of 2 City Unions; Hails War Support," *New York Times,* May 27, 1970.

Serrano, Richard A. "An FBI Director with a Grudge," *Los Angeles Times,* November 6, 2011.

Shane, Scott. "Wide U.S. Failures Helped Airliner Plot, Panel Says," *New York Times,* May 19, 2010.

Sharkey, Joe. "Powelton 'Tribute' to FBI Puts Emphasis on Exposure," *The Philadelphia Inquirer,* June 6, 1971.

Shenon, Philip. "F.B.I. Papers Show Wide Surveillance of Reagan Critics," *New York Times,* January 28, 1988.

Shenon, Philip. "F.B.I.'s Chief Says Surveillance Was Justified," *New York Times,* February 3, 1988.

Shenon, Philip. "Reagan Backs F.B.I. Over Surveillance," *New York Times,* February 4, 1988.

Shenon, Philip. "F.B.I. Reportedly Faults Its Inquiry on Foes of Latin America Policy," *New York Times,* June 4, 1988.

Shenon, Philip. "F.B.I. Is Willing to Erase Names From Its Records," *New York Times,* September 17, 1988.

Shenon, Philip. "Urging Swift Action, Panel Warns Deadlier Attacks Are Likely," *New York Times,* July 22, 2004.

Shenon, Philip. "The Terrible Missed Mistake," *Newsweek,* September 4, 2011.

Silberman, Laurence H. "Hoover's Institution," *The Wall Street Journal,* July 20, 2005.

Silver, Michael. "Where Were You on March 8, 1971?" ESPN, November 19, 2003.

Smith, Robert M. "Kleindienst Assails Boggs; Invites Inquiry into F.B.I.," *New York Times,* April 8, 1971.

Smith, Robert M. "After Almost Half a Century, the Process of Selecting a Director of the F.B.I. Begins; Bureau Policies to Face Wide Scrutiny by the Public," May 3, 1972.

Stein, Jeff. "FBI Cheating Confirmed by Justice Department," *Washington Post,* September 27, 2010

Stern, Laurence. "FBI Records Dispute Stand by Kissinger," *Washington Post,* June 12, 1974.

Stern, Laurence. "Hoover War on New Left Bared," *Washington Post,* December 7, 1973.

Theoharis, Athan G. "A Guide to the Microfilm Edition of the J. Edgar Hoover Official and Confidential File," Introduction, University Publications of America.

Theoharis, Athan G. "The FBI and the American Legion Contact Program, 1940–1966," *Political Science Quarterly,* Vol. 100, Number 2, Summer 1985.

Underhill, Stephen. "J. Edgar Hoover, 'Speech Before the House Committee on Un-American Activities' (26 March 1947)," *Voices of Democracy* 3, 2008, pp. 139–161.

Wagenveld, Mark. "25 Years Ago, Before Watergate, a Burglary Changed History," *The Philadelphia Inquirer,* March 10, 1996.

Wallace, William N. "Worldwide Televising of Fight is the Biggest Item in a $25 Million

Gamble, Most Will Watch on Home Screens, but Viewing in U.S., England and Canada Is Restricted to Closed Circuit TV," *New York Times,* March 7, 1971.

Wicker, Tom. "The Goat and the Cabbage Patch," *New York Times,* March 11, 1971.

Wicker, Tom. "What Have They Done Since They Shot Dillinger?" *New York Times,* December 28, 1969.

Williams, David. "The Bureau of Investigation and Its Critics, 1919–1921: The Origins of Political Surveillance," *The Journal of American History,* Vol. 68. No. 3, December 1981.

Williams, David. " 'They Never Stopped Watching Us': FBI Political Surveillance, 1924–1936," *UCLA Historical Review,* 1981.

Wilson, George C. "S. Viet Prison Found Shocking," *The Washington Post,* July 7, 1970.

Wilson, H. H. "The FBI Today: The Case for Effective Control, *The Nation,* February 8, 1971.

Wines, Michael. "Tape Shows Nixon Feared Hoover," *New York Times,* June 5, 1971.

Wingard, Barry. "The Trial of the Flower City Conspiracy," *The Crimson,* December 2, 1970.

Younge, Gary. "The Fighter," *The Guardian,* January 18, 2002.

Zion, Sidney E. "U.S. Drops Charges in Coplon Spy Case," *New York Times,* January 7, 1967.

———. "A New Rush to Spy," editorial, *New York Times,* August 22, 2008.

———. "Another Invitation to Abuse," editorial, *New York Times,* October 19, 2008.

———. "A Review of the Federal Bureau of Investigation's Use of National Security Letters," Office of the Inspector General, Department of Justice, March 2007.

———. "A Ticking Time Bomb: Counterterrorism Lessons from the U.S. Government's Failure to Prevent the Fort Hood Attack," U.S. Senate Committee on Homeland Security and Governmental Affairs, February 3, 2011.

———. "After 'Bloody Friday,' New York Wonders If Wall Street Is Becoming a Battle-ground," *The Wall Street Journal,* May 11, 1970.

———. "At War with War," *Time Magazine,* May 18, 1970.

———. "Backward at the F.B.I." editorial, *New York Times,* June 18, 2011.

———. "Burton Vows FBI Probe: Claims Hoover Knew of Miscarriage of Justice," *60 Minutes,* January 25, 2002.

———. "Can Government Investigate Anyone?" *Washington Post,* March 12, 1971.

———. "CIA Domestic Activities," March 25, 1971, Management Advisory Group, CIA, MORI DocID: 1451843, CIA Family Jewels, National Security Archive.

———. "CIA Domestic Activities," November 1971, Management Advisory Group, CIA, MORI DocID: 1451843, CIA Family Jewels, National Security Archive.

———. "Clark Backs FBI in Coplon Case but He 'Regrets' Use of Reports," *New York Times,* July 2, 1949.

———. "Congress and the FBI," *Washington Post,* April 12, 1971.

———. "Davidon Unveils Plot Against FBI," *Delaware County Daily Times,* March 12, 1971.

———. "Enough Is Enough," *New York Times,* October 10, 1975.

———. "Excerpts from Speech by Helms to Society of Newspaper Editors," *New York Times,* April 15, 1971.

———. "FBI Head Reported to Have Resigned," *New York Times,* June 15, 1949.

———. "F.B.I. Kept Secret File on the Supreme Court," *New York Times,* August 21, 1988.

———. "FBI Admits Spreading Lies About Jean Seberg," *The Los Angeles Times,* September 14, 1979.

———. "FBI Documents Suggests Feds Read Emails Without a Warrant," *ACLU Report,* May 8, 2013.

———. "Film 'Communists' Listed in FBI File in Coplon Spy Case," *New York Times,* June 9, 1949.

———. "Flower City Eight Convicted, Sentenced," *The Crimson,* December 4, 1970.

———. "How Did the F.B.I. Go Astray?" editorial, *New York Times,* February 6, 1988.

———. "How Much Do We Really Know About the Work of the FBI?" *The Philadelphia Inquirer,* March 28, 1971.

———. "In Memoriam—Clark Kerr," posted by faculty senate of University of California upon death of Kerr, December 1, 2003. http://senate.universityofcalifornia.edu/inmemoriam/clarkkerr.html

———. "Investigation of Allegations of Cheating on the FBI's Domestic Investigations and Operations Guide (DIOG) Exam," Inspector General, Department of Justice, September 2010.

———. "Justice Dept. Asks Hill Inquiry on FBI," *Washington Post,* April 8, 1971.

———. "Kleindienst Modifies Suggestion Congress Investigate the F.B.I." *New York Times,* April 9, 1971.

———. "Letters to the Editor, The Stolen FBI Documents and the Story about Them," *Washington Post,* March 31, 1971.

———. "Media History," http://visitmediapa.com/history

———. "Mitchell Issues Plea on F.B.I. Files: Asks Press Not to Publish Date on Stolen Papers," *New York Times,* March 24, 1971.

———. "Mr. Hoover's Dirty Tricks," *Washington Post,* March 15, 1974.

———. "Policies of Paranoia," *New York Times,* March 29, 1971.

———. "Proposed Charter for F.B.I. Criticized," *New York Times,* November 5, 1979.

———. "Symposium: Chartering the F.B.I." *The Nation,* October 6, 1979.

———. "The Complete Collection of Political Documents Ripped-Off from the F.B.I. Office in Media, PA, March 8, 1971," *Win Magazine,* March 1972.

———. "The F.B.I. Confesses," editorial, *New York Times,* September 17, 1988.

———. "The F.B.I. Under Law," editorial, *The Nation,* October 6, 1979.

———. "The Fight of the Century," International Boxing Hall of Fame, www.ibhof.com

———. "The File on J. Edgar Hoover," *Time Magazine,* October 25, 1971.

———. "The Forty-seven-year Reign of J. Edgar Hoover: Emperor of the FBI," *Life Magazine,* April 9, 1971.

———. "The Law: Informers Under Fire," *Time Magazine,* April 17, 1972.

———. "The Truth About Hoover," *Time Magazine,* December 22, 1975.

———. "The FBI vs. Jean Seberg," *Time Magazine,* September 24, 1979.

———. "U.S. Judge Says It May Drop Coplon Trial If Judge Orders 'Vital Secrets' Told," *New York Times,* June 4, 1949.

———. "What Is the FBI Up To?" *Washington Post,* March 25, 1971.

———. "What's In a Name?" *Buffalo News,* June 7, 2002.

———. "William C. Sullivan, Ex-F.B.I. Aide, 65, Is Killed in a Hunting Accident," *New York Times,* November 10, 1977

FEDERAL FREEDOM OF INFORMATION ACT WEBSITE RESOURCES

http://nsarchive.wordpress.com/how-to-file-a-foia-request/
http://www.GetMyFBIfile.com
http://www.GetGrandpasFBIfile.com

Index

Page numbers beginning with 543 refer to notes.

Hiroshima, nuclear bombing of, 46, 390, 437, 438
Hitler, Adolf, 51, 471, 472
Hoffman, Julius, 398
Holder, Eric, 505
Holland, Max, 8, 494
Holocaust, 46, 47, 389, 430–1, 472, 518
Holy Outlaw, The (film), 150
Hook, The (Miller), 353–4
Hoover, Alex, 449
Hoover, Herbert, 529
Hoover, J. Edgar, *125*, 438
  agents' photos with, 122–3
  Anderson's criticism of, 34, 36–7
  as "apoplectic" about Media burglary, 129
  appointed FBI director, 522, 523–4, 525–6, 535
  Biddle's SI termination order defied by, 254–5, 265
  blackmail threats by, 198, 281, 334–5, 348, 373, 531
  blacks as targets of, 346–7
  black students as preoccupation of, 169–70, 231–2
  bronze bust of, in his home, 103
  budget hearing testimony of, 30–4, 152, 159
  Camden raid and, 299, 305, 315
  Catholic peace movement accusations of, 32–4, 53, 169, 208, 281, 288–9, 308
  civil rights movement and, 467–8
  Clawson's relationship with, 244–5
  COINTELPRO initiated by, 333, 344
  COINTELPRO supposedly terminated by, 273–4
  communism as obsession of, 350–2, 513, 534–5, 554
  communist label used as threat by, 4, 351, 533
  "Communist Menace" speech of, 350–1
  Congress as intimidated by, 30, 134, 334–5, 531
  Congressional Night dinner speech of, 278
  as consummate bureaucrat, 29
  Coplon trials and, 130–3, 134
  cult of personality surrounding, 108, 122–3
  death of, 282–4, 314
  as exempt from compulsory retirement, 267
  FBI critics harassed by, 4, 9, 72, 134, 178, 355–6
  image of agents as important to, 121
  intellectuals and artists as targets of, 353–7, 535
  Kent State shootings and, 25–6
  Kerr as target of, 359, 360–2
  on King, 346
  and Kissinger's request for illegal wiretaps, 196–8
  legacy of, 499–500, 504, 534–5
  McCarran Act subverted by, 258
  meaning of words manipulated by, 529–30
  MEDBURG investigation and, 135, 139, 153, 286, 307–8
  Media burglary as distressing to, 280
  Media files non-publication court order sought by, 265–6, 268–9

Nixon administration's desire for retirement of, 280–1
  Nixon blackmail threat by, 198, 281
  Nixon's relationship with, 266–7, 279–80, 281
  Non-Detention Act defied by, 263–5
  NSC presentation of, 532–3
  Palmer raids overseen by, 522–3, 530, 531
  "pear-shaped head" phobia of, 240
  power of, 3–4, 9, 28, 259, 345, 373, 535, 536
  Princeton FBI conference attacked by, 209
  public adulation of, 3, 4, 71, 135, 259–60
  resident agencies closed by, 158–9
  resignation offer of, 195–6
  in retaliation against agents' criticisms, 33, 72
  secrecy of files as first priority of, 129–31, 132–4, 248, 270–1, 498
  "secret and confidential" files of, 373
  stereotyping by, 226–7
  student activists as preoccupation of, 169–70
  Sullivan fired by, 280
  Supreme Court and, 363–4, 532, 557
  Tolson and, 31, 103
  U.S. version of Official Secrets Act desired by, 135
  Xerox statement reaction of, 192–3
Hoover, Sarah Davidon, *23, 191,* 446
  and father's antiwar activities, 449, 450–51
Hoover's FBI: The Inside Story (DeLoach), 343
House of Representatives, U.S.
  Appropriations Subcommittee of, 31, 37, 152
  Civil Rights and Constitutional Rights Subcommittee of, 336–9
  Government Reform Committee of, 372
  Judiciary Committee of, 262, 336, 373
  Un-American Activities Committee (HUAC) of, 262, 267, 350–1
  see also Congress, U.S.; Senate, U.S.
Hoyer, Steny, 514
Hruska, Roman L., 31
"Huge CIA Operation Reported in U.S. Against Anti-War Forces" (Hersh), 339–40
Humphrey, Hubert, 256, *395,* 465
  in election of 1968, 486
  Vietnam War and, 478
Huston, Tom Charles, 267
Huston plan, Hoover's blocking of, 198, 266, 267–8

In Fact, 340, 341
  writers, academics, and artists, as targets of FBI investigations, 353–63
intelligence agencies
  Congress and FISA Court as rubber stamps for, 516
  9/11 Commission report on, 502
  post-9/11 expansion of, 506–7
  public debate on role of, 8
  reform of, 488–509
  undifferentiated data collected by, 507, 509
  see also CIA; FBI; National Security Agency